The Editor-in-Chief and Editors of the *Oxford History of the British Empire*
acknowledge with gratitude support from

The Rhodes Trust

The National Endowment for Humanities, Washington, DC

St Antony's College, Oxford

The University of Texas at Austin

THE OXFORD HISTORY OF THE BRITISH EMPIRE

THE OXFORD HISTORY OF THE BRITISH EMPIRE

Volume I. *The Origins of Empire*
EDITED BY Nicholas Canny

Volume II. *The Eighteenth Century*
EDITED BY P. J. Marshall

Volume III. *The Nineteenth Century*
EDITED BY Andrew Porter

Volume IV. *The Twentieth Century*
EDITED BY Judith M. Brown and Wm. Roger Louis

Volume V. *Historiography*
EDITED BY Robin W. Winks

THE OXFORD HISTORY OF THE BRITISH EMPIRE

Wm. Roger Louis, D.Litt., FBA

*Kerr Professor of English History and Culture, University of Texas, Austin
and Honorary Fellow of St Anthony's College, Oxford*

EDITOR-IN-CHIEF

~

VOLUME II

The Eighteenth Century

~

P. J. Marshall, D.Phil., FBA

*Emeritus Professor of Imperial History, King's College, London
and Honorary Fellow of Wadham College, Oxford*

EDITOR

Alaine Low, D.Phil.

ASSISTANT EDITOR

OXFORD
UNIVERSITY PRESS

OXFORD

UNIVERSITY PRESS

Great Clarendon Street, Oxford OX2 6DP

Oxford University Press is a department of the University of Oxford.
It furthers the University's objective of excellence in research, scholarship,
and education by publishing worldwide in

Oxford New York

Auckland Cape Town Dar es Salaam Hong Kong Karachi
Kuala Lumpur Madrid Melbourne Mexico City Nairobi
New Delhi Shanghai Taipei Toronto
With offices in
Argentina Austria Brazil Chile Czech Republic France Greece
Guatemala Hungary Italy Japan South Korea Poland Portugal
Singapore Switzerland Thailand Turkey Ukraine Vietnam

Oxford is a registered trade mark of Oxford University Press
in the UK and in certain other countries

Published in the United States
by Oxford University Press Inc., New York

ISBN 978-0-19-924677-9

Printed in the United Kingdom by
Lightning Source UK Ltd., Milton Keynes

FOREWORD

From the founding of the colonies in North America and the West Indies in the seventeenth century to the reversion of Hong Kong to China at the end of the twentieth, British imperialism was a catalyst for far-reaching change. British domination of indigenous peoples in North America, Asia, and Africa can now be seen more clearly as part of the larger and dynamic interaction of European and non-western societies. Though the subject remains ideologically charged, the passions aroused by British imperialism have so lessened that we are now better placed than ever to see the course of the Empire steadily and to see it whole. At this distance in time the Empire's legacy from earlier centuries can be assessed, in ethics and economics as well as politics, with greater discrimination. At the close of the twentieth century, the interpretation of the dissolution of the Empire can benefit from evolving perspectives on, for example, the end of the cold war. In still larger sweep, the *Oxford History of the British Empire* as a comprehensive study helps us to understand the end of the Empire in relation to its beginning, the meaning of British imperialism for the ruled as well as the rulers, and the significance of the British Empire as a theme in world history.

It is nearly half a century since the last volume of the large-scale *Cambridge History of the British Empire* was completed. In the mean time the British Empire has been dismantled and only fragments such as Gibraltar and the Falklands, Bermuda and Pitcairn, remain of an Empire that once stretched over a quarter of the earth's surface. The general understanding of the British Imperial experience has been substantially widened in recent decades by the work of historians of Asia and Africa as well as Britain. Earlier histories, though by no means all, tended to trace the Empire's evolution and to concentrate on how it was governed. To many late Victorian historians the story of the Empire meant the rise of world-wide dominion and imperial rule, above all in India. Historians in the first half of the twentieth century tended to emphasize constitutional developments and the culmination of the Empire in the free association of the Commonwealth. The *Oxford History of the British Empire* takes a wide approach. It does not depict the history of the Empire as one of purposeful progress through four hundred years, nor does it concentrate narrowly on metropolitan authority and rule. It does attempt to explain how varying conditions in Britain interacted with those in many other parts of the world to create both a constantly changing territorial Empire and evershifting patterns of social and economic relations. The *Oxford History of the British Empire* thus deals with the impact of British imperialism on dependent peoples in a broader sense than was usually attempted in earlier historical writings, while it also takes into account the significance of the Empire for the Irish, the Scots, and the Welsh as well as the English.

Volume II, *The Eighteenth Century*, deals with the crucial period in the creation of the modern British Empire. It shows how migration, religion, trade, and war created an Empire in America and later in Asia, and how, though the American Revolution severely damaged the Imperial structure, the system survived and grew into an Empire that encompassed a large part of the world during the nineteenth century and for much of the twentieth. The issues dealt with in this volume therefore had clear consequences for Britain's later status as a world power and for the British domestic economy.

Among the many complex themes, there are at least three that bear on other volumes in the series. *The Eighteenth Century* raises fundamental issues concerning terminology. What was the eighteenth-century usage of the word 'Empire'? Until the middle part of the century the Empire consisted principally of Britain, Ireland, and the colonies in North America and the West Indies. Commercial expansion beyond Europe underpinned the Empire in the Atlantic, and operated with a momentum of its own in Africa and Asia. When then did the term 'British Empire' generally emerge as a coherent concept with world-wide implications? To what extent did a British 'world system' or even a British 'informal empire' come into existence during the eighteenth century?

During the eighteenth century the Empire reached one of its high points of profit and prosperity. This is the second general theme. By the end of the century Britain's economic capacity and maritime strength surpassed that of any other power. After the American Revolution the former colonies remained within the orbit of British trade and commerce. The economic system was protected by the world's most powerful navy and by military garrisons that could deploy troops throughout maritime Asia and other parts of the world.

The third theme of overarching significance is that British colonists in North America and the West Indies attached fundamental significance to their status as 'freeborn Englishmen', but in many parts of the world British rule was authoritarian. What was the meaning of British hegemony for its subjects, for communities of British origin overseas and for non-Europeans? The language of liberty informed the ideology of the American Revolution, yet plantation owners in the West Indies found no difficulty in using the same vocabulary in a slave society. In India the British ruled over vast populations and made no attempt to introduce representative institutions. Indigenous peoples in the Americas, Asia, and Africa remained a world apart from British cultural and political traditions. There were thus two sides to British dominion in the eighteenth century, the one evolving representative government, the other of 'enlightened' despotism in which can be found the origins of the idea of the 'White Man's burden'. Both traditions contributed to a British national commitment to Empire and sense of British identity in the nineteenth and twentieth centuries. It was an ambiguous legacy.

The volumes in the *Oxford History of the British Empire* do not necessarily begin or end at the same point. Historical understanding benefits from an integration and overlap of complex chronology. *The Eighteenth Century*, for example, gives comprehensive treatment to events within those hundred years, but some chapters reach back into the earlier period just as others extend to the end of the Napoleonic era. Similarly some developments that began in the late eighteenth century can best be understood in a nineteenth-century context: full treatment of territorial expansion in South-East Asia, the rise of the new Protestant missionary societies, and the campaign against the slave trade and slavery will be found in Volume III, *The Nineteenth Century*.

A special feature of the series is the Select Bibliography of key works at the end of each chapter. These are not intended to be a comprehensive bibliographical or historiographical guide (which will be found in Volume V) but rather they are lists of useful and informative works on the themes of each chapter.

The Editor-in-Chief and Editor acknowledge, with immense gratitude, support from the Rhodes Trust, the National Endowment for the Humanities in Washington, DC, St Antony's College, Oxford, and the University of Texas at Austin. We have received further specific support from the Warden of St Antony's, Lord Dahrendorf, the Dean of Liberal Arts at the University of Texas, Sheldon Ekland-Olson, and, for the preparation of maps, the University Cooperative Society. Mr Iain Sproat helped to inspire the project and provided financial assistance for the initial organizational conference. It is also a true pleasure to thank our patrons Mr and Mrs Alan Spencer of Hatfield Regis Grange, Mr and Mrs Sam Jamot Brown of Durango, Colorado, and Mr and Mrs Baine Kerr of Houston, Texas. We have benefited from the cartographic expertise of Jane Pugh and her colleagues at the London School of Economics. We are grateful to Mary Bull for her help in preparing the index. Our last word of gratitude is to Dr Alaine Low, the Assistant Editor, whose dedication to the project has been characterized by indefatigable efficiency and meticulous care.

Wm. Roger Louis

PREFACE

The importance of overseas involvement for Britain and the extent of Britain's impact on the world during the eighteenth century were at least comparable in scale to what they were to be in the nineteenth or early twentieth centuries, conventionally assumed to be the classical age of British Imperialism.

As the previous volume shows, in the second half of the seventeenth century long-distance trades were beginning to make a significant contribution to England's wealth, and the regulation of this trade and of overseas settlements was becoming a matter of concern for national governments. Late-eighteenth-century Britain was a global power, with her fleets and armies deployed all over the world. Important sections of her economy were also operating on a global scale, seeking markets and sources of commodities far beyond Europe. Increasing awareness of this great turning outwards of Britain's interests was reflected in the way in which opinion in the later eighteenth century began to envisage and to conceptualize a world-wide British Empire of rule over lands and peoples in terms that would have been alien to previous generations but were to be familiar to the British public until far into the twentieth century.

The success of the British had important consequences for others. In North America people of British origin had long competed for land and resources with French, Spanish, and Native Americans. By the end of the eighteenth century obstacles to Anglophone domination of the continent had been broken. The fate of the Native Americans would be expulsions and subjugation, while the French population had been forced to submit to British rule. The main beneficiaries of this great shift in the balance of power in North America were not, however, to be the British themselves. Over the greater part of the continent the future lay with the new republic created by successful revolt against the British Empire.

During the eighteenth century the islands and coastal regions of eastern America from the Chesapeake to Brazil saw the spectacular expansion of agriculture based on crops grown for export to Europe. Britain was at the centre of this expansion. She ran large plantation systems of her own in the West Indies, was the biggest market for all tropical produce, and was the greatest single shipper of African slaves, exporting some 3 million of them, on whom this agriculture depended.

During the eighteenth century the British ceased to be merely traders in Asia and became rulers over Indian provinces with millions of inhabitants. By 1815 it was clear that Britain would not be just one of a group of Indian powers competing against one another, but that she had become the dominant power, capable of imposing her hegemony on the whole subcontinent and beyond. After 1788, Australian Aborigines, a people hitherto with virtually no contact with Europeans, also began to feel the power of the British. The landing of the First Fleet marked the beginning of the white 'invasion' of Australia and the Pacific.

This volume draws on a rich diversity of scholarship. Britain itself is no longer taken for granted as in older traditions of Imperial history. There are chapters on the economic, political, and intellectual foundations of Empire at home. Outside Britain, the perspective is global, covering what has long been seen as an Atlantic system, whose elements, North America, the West Indies, and the slave coasts of West Africa, were closely linked, together with the very different worlds of Asia and the Pacific. The traditional themes of Imperial history 'from above', governance, the political problems posed by the American Revolution and the new empire in India, war, and economic regulation, are reinterpreted in the light of current findings. Perspectives reflecting something of the abundance of recent research 'from below' on the peoples caught up in Empire are offered in chapters on the experience of black people, of Native Americans, of the population of the East India Company's provinces, and of the British emigrants to the New World.

The book is divided into thematic chapters, dealing with the Empire as a whole, and regional ones, dealing with specific parts of it. The thematic chapters come first. In most cases, these chapters, dealing with migration, economics, religion, war, identity, and scientific knowledge, cover the whole period from the late seventeenth century to the early nineteenth century. There are, however, certain exceptions. Two parallel chapters dealing with war go up to 1793 and are followed by a separate chapter on the great conflict with Revolutionary and Napoleonic France. The thirteen North American colonies featured so largely in questions of an Imperial system of government, of the working of an Imperial economy, and of the early development of a sense of Imperial identity, that these chapters focus almost entirely on the period before the loss of America. These themes are therefore taken up again for the years after 1783 in the last chapter, which assesses the Empire without America and tries to link this volume with the one on the nineteenth century that is to follow.

The regional chapters begin with one on Ireland, which was already playing its role in later Imperial history, as part colony and part partner in Empire. Clusters of chapters follow, concerned first with North America, then with the Caribbean and the slave trade, and finally with Asia and the Pacific.

P. J. Marshall

CONTENTS

LIST OF MAPS

LIST OF FIGURES

LIST OF TABLES

ABBREVIATIONS AND LOCATION OF MANUSCRIPT SOURCES

Public Record Office, London:

BT	Board of Trade
C	Chancery
CO	Colonial Office
FO	Foreign Office
HO	Home Office
SP	State Papers
T	Treasury

PRO Documents acquired by the Public Record Office by gift, deposit, or purchase (Chatham Papers)

All other abbreviations and manuscript sources will be found in the first reference in each chapter.

LIST OF CONTRIBUTORS

THOMAS BARTLETT (Ph.D., Queen's University, Belfast) MRIA is Professor of Modern Irish History, University College, Dublin. He is the author of *The Fall and Rise of the Irish Nation* and co-editor, with Keith Jeffrey, of *The Cambridge Military History of Ireland*.

H. V. BOWEN (Ph.D., Wales) is Senior Lecturer in Economic and Social History at the University of Leicester. He is the author of *Revenue and Reform: The Indian Problem in British Politics, 1757–1773* and *Elites, Enterprise, and the Making of the British Overseas Empire, 1688–1775*.

STEPHEN CONWAY (Ph.D., London) is Reader in the Department of History at University College, London. He is the author of several articles on American revolutionary history in the *William and Mary Quarterly* and of *The American War of Independence*.

RICHARD DRAYTON (Ph.D., Yale) is a Fellow of Lincoln College, Oxford. His publications include *Nature's Government: Kew Gardens, Science, and Imperial Britain, 1772–1903*.

MICHAEL DUFFY (D.Phil., Oxford) is Senior Lecturer in History and Director of the Centre for Maritime Historical Studies at Exeter University. He is author of *The Englishman and the Foreigner*; *Soldiers, Sugar and Sea Power: The British Expeditions to the West Indies and the War against Revolutionary France*, and editor of *Parameters of British Naval Power, 1650–1850*.

JACK P. GREENE (Ph.D., Duke) is Andrew W. Mellon Professor, The Johns Hopkins University. His publications include *The Intellectual Construction of America*; *Pursuits of Happiness: The Social Development of the Early Modern British Colonies and the Formation of American Culture*, and *Peripheries and Center*.

JAMES HORN (D.Phil., Sussex) is Head of the School of Historical and Critical Studies at the University of Brighton. He is author of *Adapting to a New World: English Society in the Seventeenth-Century Chesapeake* and editor, with Ida Altman, of *'To Make America': European Emigration in the Early Modern Period*.

RICHARD R. JOHNSON (Ph.D., California at Berkeley) is Professor of History at the University of Washington, Seattle. He is the author of *Adjustment to Empire: The New England Colonies, 1675–1715* and *John Nelson, Merchant Adventurer: A Life between Empires.*

BRUCE P. LENMAN (Litt.D., Cambridge), is Professor of History at St Andrews University. He is the author of *An Economic History of Modern Scotland* (winner of the Scottish Arts Council Award), *Integration, Enlightenment, and Industrialisation: Scotland, 1746–1832, The Jacobite Clans of the Great Glen,* and *The Eclipse of Parliament.*

PETER MARSHALL (Ph.D., Yale) is former Professor of American History and Institutions at the University of Manchester. He has published numerous articles on aspects of Imperial policy in the age of the American Revolution.

P. J. MARSHALL (D.Phil., Oxford) FBA is former Rhodes Professor of Imperial History at King's College, London. He has been Editor of the *Journal of Imperial and Commonwealth History* and is Associate Editor of *The Writings and Speeches of Edmund Burke.* His books include *The Impeachment of Warren Hastings* and *Bengal: The British Bridgehead.*

PHILIP MORGAN (Ph.D., London) is Editor of the *William and Mary Quarterly* at the Omohundro Institute of Early American History and Culture and Professor at the College of William and Mary. He is author of *Slave Counterpoint: Black Culture in the Upper and Lower Souths in the Eighteenth Century,* and co-editor of *Strangers Within the Realm: Cultural Margins of the First British Empire.*

PATRICK K. O'BRIEN (D.Phil., Oxford) FBA is Director of the Institute of Historical Research and Professor of Economic History, University of London. He is author of *The Economic Effects of the American Civil War* and editor of *The Industrial Revolution in Europe,* vols. 4 and 5.

JACOB M. PRICE (Ph.D., Harvard) FBA is Professor Emeritus at the University of Michigan and past President of the Economic History Association. His books include *France and the Chesapeake, Capital and Credit in British Overseas Trade, 1700–1776,* and *Perry of London.*

RAJAT KANTA RAY (Ph.D., Cambridge) is Professor and Head of the Department of History at Presidency College, Calcutta. He edited *Entrepreneurship and Industry in India, 1800–1947* and *Mind, Body and Society: Life and Mentality in*

Colonial Bengal. His books include *Social Conflict and Political Unrest in Bengal, 1875–1927* and an award-winning Bengali work on Plassey.

DAVID RICHARDSON (MA, Manchester) is Reader in Economic History at the University of Hull and former Visiting Scholar at Harvard University. He is Editor of *Bristol, Africa, and the Eighteenth-Century Slave Trade to America,* and is the author of numerous articles on the transatlantic slave trade and its impact on Africa as well as Britain.

DANIEL K. RICHTER (Ph.D., Columbia) is Associate Professor of History at Dickinson College, Carlisle, Pennsylvania. He is author of *The Ordeal of the Longhouse: The Peoples of the Iroquois League in the Era of European Colonization* and co-editor of *Beyond the Covenant Chain: The Iroquois and their Neighbors in Indian North America, 1600–1800.*

N. A. M. RODGER (D.Phil., Oxford) has been Assistant Keeper of the Public Records and is now Anderson Fellow of the National Maritime Museum. His books include *The Wooden World: An Anatomy of the Georgian Navy* and *The Safeguard of the Sea: A Naval History of Britain, Vol. I, 660–1649.*

BOYD STANLEY SCHLENTHER (Ph.D., Edinburgh) is Reader in History at the University of Wales, Aberystwyth. His books include *The Life and Writings of Francis Makemie; Charles Thomson: A Patriot's Pursuit;* and *Queen of the Methodists. The Countess of Huntingdon and the Eighteenth-Century Crisis of Faith and Society.*

RICHARD B. SHERIDAN (Ph.D., The London School of Economics and Political Science) is Professor Emeritus, Department of Economics, University of Kansas. His books include *Sugar and Slavery* and *Doctors and Slaves.* His most recent article is 'From Chattel to Wage Slavery in Jamaica' in *Slavery and Abolition.*

JOHN SHY (Ph.D., Princeton) is Professor Emeritus, University of Michigan. His books include *The American Revolution Today* and *A People Numerous and Armed: Reflections on the Military Struggle for American Independence.*

IAN K. STEELE (Ph.D., London) is Professor of History at the University of Western Ontario. His books on the first British Empire include *Betrayals: Fort William Henry and the 'Massacre', The English Atlantic, 1675–1740: An Exploration of Communication and Community, Atlantic Merchant-Apothecary, Guerillas and Grenadiers,* and *Politics of Colonial Policy.*

J. R. WARD (D.Phil., Oxford) is Lecturer in Economic and Social History at the University of Edinburgh. His publications include *Poverty and Progress in the Caribbean, 1800–1960* and *British West Indian Slavery, 1750–1834.*

GLYNDWR WILLIAMS (Ph.D., London) is Professor of History at Queen Mary and Westfield College, London. His books include *The British Search for the Northwest Passage, The Expansion of Europe in the 18th Century: Overseas Rivalry, Discovery and Exploitation, The Great Map of Mankind* (with P. J. Marshall), and *Terra Australis to Australia* (with Alan Frost).

1

Introduction

P. J. MARSHALL

For the *The Oxford History of the British Empire*, the 'eighteenth century' has been extended at both ends. Although strict uniformity has not been imposed on all chapters, this volume is for the most part set between two dates traditionally taken as marking eras in British history: 1689, the year of the Glorious Revolution, an event seen by most English people as ensuring their liberties, and 1815, the year of Waterloo, the last battle in wars between Britain and France that had begun in 1689.

The dates 1689 and 1815 also mark a phase in British expansion overseas. The wars against France were global ones affecting all parts of the Empire. Beyond that, the period was one of striking growth in Britain's world-wide interests, if not as yet one of spectacular innovation. Patterns of trade, commercial regulation, and the government of colonies, established in the later seventeenth century, were in essentials still intact in 1815. Industrialization only began to have a significant effect on manufacturing or on the technologies of war and shipping towards the end of the period. Within an established framework, however, there was a huge growth in the scale of British activities outside Europe. Both the area and the number of people under British rule increased greatly. Far more ships took out many more British goods to colonial markets and brought back much greater quantities of mostly tropical products.

Yet for all the continuities between 1689 and 1815, there was a sharp change of tempo in the middle of the eighteenth century which divides the period into two distinct phases. The Seven Years War, formally lasting from 1756 to 1763, was the watershed between them. The war revealed that most of those who ruled Britain were investing Empire with a new significance. It was seen as vital to Britain's economic well-being, to her standing as a great power, and even to her national survival. British governments began to concern themselves with colonial issues and to commit resources to overseas war on an unprecedented scale. Spectacular conquests were made in the Seven Years War. Most of the gains made in North America quickly disappeared as a result of the American Revolution, but those made in India were absorbed into an expanding Asian empire. By 1815 Britain's global trade totally eclipsed that of her European rivals and she was the possessor of the only Empire of any consequence. Her nineteenth-century hegemony outside Europe was clearly in place.

By 1689 permanent English settlement in North America had grown from the two original nuclei: the Chesapeake colonies of Virginia and Maryland and the New England colonies. More recently the English had occupied the territory between New England and the Chesapeake, principally by the conquest of New York from the Dutch and by the founding of Pennsylvania. Settlement moved further south with the occupation of what came to be North and South Carolina. To the north, the English had long fished off the coasts of Newfoundland. Furs were obtained in the far north from posts around Hudson Bay. By the beginning of the eighteenth century the population of English North America was about 265,000.[1]

During the course of the century population grew very rapidly to some 2,300,000 by 1770.[2] The area under British rule also expanded: new colonies were established to the south: Georgia and the two Floridas; and to the north: Nova Scotia and Quebec, the former New France. This great North American Empire was shattered by rebellion and war after 1776. What had been thirteen British colonies became the independent United States of America in 1783. All that was left were the colonies of the north that in the nineteenth century were to be united as the Dominion of Canada. Some half-a-million people were living in these British North American colonies by 1815.[3]

The first English West Indian settlements had been established early in the seventeenth century on Barbados and the Leeward Islands. Jamaica was added by conquest in 1655. Of a total population of some 145,000 at the beginning of the eighteenth century, three-quarters were black slaves, largely employed in sugar cultivation.[4] Success in war brought new additions: the Windward or Ceded Islands in 1763 and Trinidad and what became British Guiana as a result of the Napoleonic War. By 1815 some 877,000 people lived in the British Caribbean, of whom 743,000 were slaves.[5] Slaves came to British America through a huge British slave trade, which exported over 3.4 million people from Africa between 1662 and 1807, when the British slave trade was abolished.[6] By comparison with the size of their trade, the permanent British presence on the African continent was restricted to a few enclaves: slave-trading posts on the Gambia or the Gold Coast, the Cape of Good Hope permanently from 1806, and a settlement at Sierra Leone from 1787.

The English presence in Asia at the end of the seventeenth century was essentially a commercial one, in the hands of the East India Company, which had held a

---

[1] See below, Table on p. 100. [2] Ibid. [3] See below, p. 386.
[4] See below, p. 400. [5] See below, p. 433. [6] See below, p. 442.

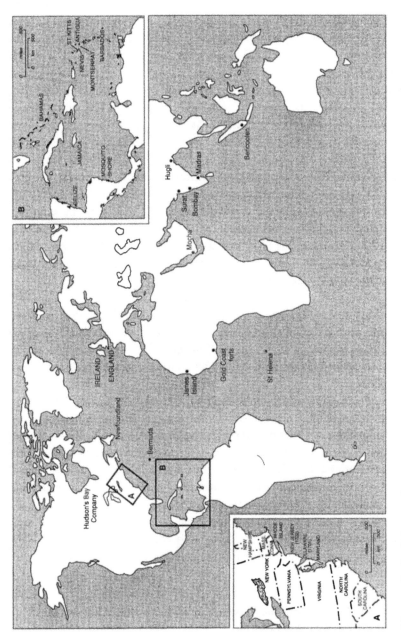

Map 1.1. England Overseas in 1689

monopoly of English trade east of the Cape of Good Hope since the beginning of the century. The most important of the Company's trading settlements were on the coast of India. It owned the island of Bombay outright, while at Madras and Calcutta Indian rulers had given the English grants of territory that included growing towns. By 1815 the British position in India had been totally transformed by a series of conquests that had brought the whole of eastern India, most of the peninsula, and a large part of the Ganges valley under direct British rule, still administered through the East India Company. A contemporary estimate was that 40 million Indian people were by then living under the Company's rule.[7] The British also occupied the coast of Ceylon, and the island of Mauritius. British influence was spreading along the Malay coast from a new settlement at Penang founded in 1786. A huge British trade was transacted through the Chinese port of Canton.

During the first half of the eighteenth century occasional British ships defied Spanish claims to a monopoly of the navigation of the Pacific. In the second half of the century voyages of exploration were despatched to the Pacific, most notably those of James Cook. The first permanent British presence in the region was established in 1788 when the First Fleet took its cargo of convicts to New South Wales. By 1811 there were some 10,000 British subjects living in New South Wales with a further 1500 in Van Diemen's Land (Tasmania).[8]

By the nineteenth century, the term 'British Empire' had a commonly accepted meaning. It was a collection of territories and peoples ruled by Britain. This usage was clearly established in the second half of the eighteenth century, but earlier generations had invested the term with different meanings that reflected a diversity of aspirations.

To describe England or Britain as an Empire, as the great lawyer Sir William Blackstone pointed out, strictly meant no more than to reiterate the claims of the Reformation Statutes of Henry VIII's reign that 'our king is equally sovereign and independent within these his dominions, as any emperor is in his empire'.[9] An empire was simply a sovereign state. From the reign of James VI and I the concept of a British Empire was used by enthusiasts for the integration of England and Scotland: together they constituted the British Empire.

During the seventeenth century claims began to be made to include the seas around Britain in any British Empire. A 1663 edition of John Selden's *Mare Clausum* told Charles II that the 'British Ocean hath been counted into the royal

---

[7] See below, p. 582.

[8] *Australians: Historical Statistics*, ed. W. Vamplew (Broadway, New South Wales, 1987), p. 25.

[9] *Commentaries on the Laws of England*, 4 vols. (1765; Oxford, 1773), I, p. 242.

patrimony of your British Empire'.[10] Claims to an empire over the seas were to be greatly extended during the wars of William III and Anne. In the early eighteenth century the poet and diplomat Matthew Prior invoked a Britain that 'rules an Empire by no Ocean bound', while the poet James Thomson wrote of Britain's 'well earned empire of the deep'.[11] Empire over the seas was extended to include English plantations across the seas. At least from 1685, maps began to delineate the extent of an 'English Empire in America',[12] which became a British one after the Union with Scotland in 1707, as in John Oldmixon's *The British Empire in America* of 1708.[13]

What terms like 'empire of the deep' meant in practice was a matter for lively debate. Some insisted that, unlike all other empires, past or present, British dominion over the seas was a peaceful enterprise. Britain's ascendancy rested on the superiority of her shipping and manufactures. Its basis was free trade, not coercion. War for trade would be self-defeating.

Most of those who gloried in Britain's 'empire of the sea', however, saw it in extremely belligerent terms. It was an empire that rested not only on commerce but on naval power exerted over Britain's European rivals. The trade of France, Spain, and the Netherlands was to be beaten off the oceans by force. Their colonies were to be sacked. Maritime wars of plunder were assured of enthusiastic support in eighteenth-century Britain. They evoked Elizabethan traditions. They were the programme of successive parliamentary Oppositions. Such wars were presumed to pay for themselves. They were fought by sailors, supposed to be the flower of English freedom, for the national objective of an expanded commerce. Continental wars, by contrast, were said to be waged for the narrow personal interests of the English monarchy, at great expense to the British taxpayer, and with standing armies, the instruments of despotism. Recent studies have clearly demonstrated the popularity of maritime war among a wide section of the population in London and in provincial English towns. A convincing case has been made that pride in Britain's maritime prowess and hatred for foreigners, above all the French and the Spanish, formed an important element in British people's sense of national identity.[14]

---

[10] Cited David R. Armitage, 'The Cromwellian Protectorate and the Languages of Empire', *Historical Journal*, XXXV (1992), p. 534.

[11] Cited Richard Koebner, *Empire* (Cambridge, 1961), p. 81.

[12] Ibid., p. 75.

[13] *The British Empire in America, containing the History of the Discovery, Settlement, Progress and Present State of all the British Colonies on the Continent and Islands of America*, 2 vols. (London, 1708).

[14] Kathleen Wilson, *The Sense of the People: Politics, Culture and Imperialism in England, 1715–1785* (Cambridge, 1995); Nicholas Rogers, *Whigs and Cities: Popular Politics in the Age of Walpole and Pitt* (Oxford, 1989).

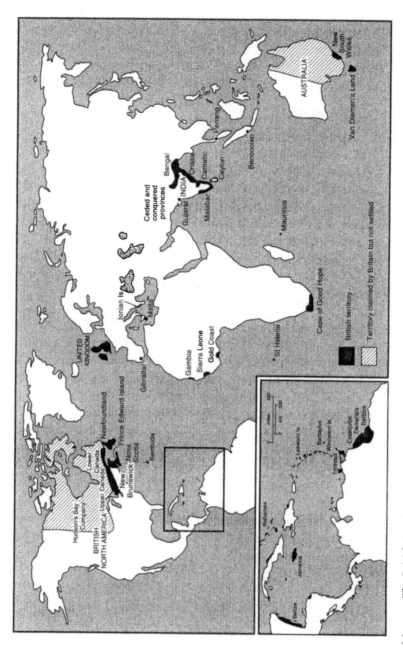

Map 1.2. The British Empire in 1815

UNITED KINGDOM

BRITISH
NORTH AMERICA
Hudson's Bay
Company
Lower
Canada
Upper Canada
New
Brunswick
Nova
Scotia
Prince Edward Island
Newfoundland
Bermuda

Gibraltar
Ionian Is
Malta

Gambia
Sierra Leone
Gold Coast

St Helena

Cape of Good Hope

Ceded and
conquered
provinces

INDIA
Gujarat
Bengal
Orissa
Carnatic
Malabar
Ceylon

Penang

Bencoolen

Mauritius

AUSTRALIA

New
South
Wales
Van Diemen's Land

British territory

Territory claimed by Britain but not settled

Bahamas
Jamaica
Belize
Leeward Is
Barbados
(Windward) Is.
Trinidad
Essequibo
Demerara
Berbice

miles   500
0   km   500

Exponents of maritime war usually insisted that Britain only acted to defend herself, be it against alleged Spanish aggression on English shipping in the Caribbean or French incursions in North America. In reality, such wars became wars of expansion. This was most marked in the thought of the elder William Pitt, the man who in the mid-eighteenth century became the embodiment of Britain's will to wage war across the world. He believed that Britain must be strong enough to give 'law to nations' and to impose its hegemony.[15] Colonial gains might accrue from successful maritime war, but it is misleading to see territorial empire as the explicit objective of such wars.[16]

Even the most belligerent exponent of an 'empire of the deep' could have serious reservations about territorial empire. The British saw themselves as a free people resisting claims to world empire by Spain and later by the France of Louis XIV, rather than as a power seeking a world empire of its own.[17] The example of the greatest of the world's territorial empires, Rome, was one that the education of the British élite had taught them to shun. The conventional wisdom was that over-expansion had ultimately destroyed Rome. The empire had become too unwieldy. Its people had lost their taste for freedom. They had been corrupted, above all by the wealth and luxury of the East. Professional armies and ambitious proconsuls had taken over. Doubts were frequently expressed about the dangers to Britain of over-expansion on the continent of America.[18] Expansion in Asia would be an unmitigated evil.

In the first half of the eighteenth century 'empire' did not necessarily mean rule over territory, but could also signify power or dominant interests outside Britain. Usage also suggests that contemporaries conceived of different 'empires' in different parts of the world, rather than of a single British Empire. References to 'the British Empire, taking all together as one body, viz. Great Britain, Ireland, the Plantations and Fishery in America, besides its Possessions in the East Indies and Africa' have, however, been found from 1743.[19] Such references become very common after the Seven Years War. From the 1760s it was conventional to speak and write of a single British Empire. Sir George Macartney—later, as Lord Macartney, an Imperial administrator in many parts of the world—wrote in 1773

---

[15] Marie Peters, 'The Myth of William Pitt, Earl of Chatham, Great Imperialist, Part I: Pitt and Imperial Expansion, 1738–1763', *Journal of Imperial and Commonwealth History*, XXI (1993), p. 55.

[16] Bob Harris, ' "American Idols": Empire, War and the Middling Ranks in Mid-Eighteenth-century Britain', *Past and Present*, CL (1996), pp. 111–41.

[17] Anthony Pagden, *Lords of All the World: Ideologies of Empire in Spain, Britain and France, c.1500 to c.1800* (New Haven, 1995).

[18] Ibid., pp. 103–06.

[19] Cited James Truslow Adams, 'On the Term British Empire', *American Historical Review*, XXVII (1922), p. 488.

of 'this vast empire on which the sun never sets and whose bounds nature has not yet ascertained'.[20] Arthur Young began his *Political Essays Concerning the Present State of the British Empire* of 1772 with the proposition that 'The British dominions consist of Great Britain, Ireland and divers colonies and settlements in all parts of the world. There appears not any just reason for considering these countries in any other light than as parts of one whole.'[21] John Campbell wrote two years later in his *Political Survey of Britain* of 'the Extent of the British Empire and the Grandeur to which it is arrived'.[22] Such surveys of the Empire established a genre with a long life, carried on, for instance, by Patrick Colquhoun's *Treatise on the Wealth, Power and Resources of the British Empire in Every Quarter of the Globe* of 1814.

Such language reflects the stark fact that the consequence of successful war had been territorial empire round the world. The Seven Years War ended in 1763 with the acquisition of Canada, the Floridas, and additional West Indian islands. Two years later, the East India Company was granted the revenues and effective rule over the province of Bengal. Success was greeted with foreboding as well as triumphalism. Radical-minded men, like Josiah Tucker, the Dean of Gloucester, saw the American Revolution as a welcome opportunity to get rid of unwanted Imperial encumbrances. The prospect of empire in India aroused anguished misgivings, often vented in attacks on the 'Nabobs', who sullied Britain's name with their cruelty, as well as threatening to introduce tendencies to despotism and an influx of luxury. Yet for the majority of British opinion there could be no going back. To surrender territorial empire would be to surrender the assets that enabled Britain to keep France at bay. Too many interests, in commerce, in the ownership of new lands, and in official posts in new colonies, were now locked into territorial empire.[23] Nor was there any widespread inclination to turn back from it. It had become part of contemporaries' sense of Britain's eminence in the world. Even the gentle William Cowper could assure the shade of Queen Boadicea that:

> Regions Caesar never knew
> Thy posterity shall sway,
> Where his eagles never flew,
> None invincible as they.[24]

In spite of the loss of America, Britain resumed world-wide territorial expansion, especially in the great wars against France that lasted with brief intervals from 1793

---

[20] See below, p. 262.

[21] (London, 1772), p. 1.

[22] 2 vols. (London, 1774), II, p. 694.

[23] P. J. Marshall, 'Empire and Opportunity in Britain, 1763–75', *Transactions of the Royal Historical Society*, Sixth Series, V (1995), pp. 111–28.

[24] 'Ode' (1782).

to 1815. An expanded and strengthened British Empire was the only victor of that 'great Imperial and naval Armageddon'.[25]

Even in the early seventeenth century, English and Scots had merged in a common 'British' venture, the 'planting' of Ulster. In the later seventeenth century 'enclaves' of Scottish and Irish settlers established themselves in predominantly English colonies in North America or the West Indies.[26] In 1695 Scottish ambitions for a separate role overseas were signalled by the creation of a 'Company of Scotland trading to Africa and the Indies'. Its main enterprise, the settlement at Darien in Central America, ended in heavy loss in 1700.[27] With the Union of 1707, creating a United Kingdom with about a million Scots and some 5 million English and Welsh, the integration of Scotland into what became beyond question a British Empire was very close. Ireland, with its population of some 2 million doubling during the course of the eighteenth century, was also heavily involved in the Empire, although the Irish did not get the full commercial access to it, granted to the Scots in 1707, until late in the century.

During the eighteenth century the volume of Irish and Scottish emigration to British America was much larger than English emigration.[28] Scots and Irish soldiers were essential to the world-wide deployment of the British army. A high proportion of the East India Company's army officers and civilian servants were Scottish. By the 1740s Scots firms based on Glasgow had won a large stake in the tobacco trade of the Chesapeake,[29] while Ireland, in spite of prohibitions before the 1780s on direct dealing in certain commodities, developed profitable colonial trades, notably in provisions and linen.[30]

Certain features of eighteenth-century Britain left their mark on the British Empire. British people believed that the power of their government was limited, being ultimately subject to the will of the people expressed by their representatives in Parliament, and that they enjoyed a greater level of personal freedom than virtually any other European people. Historians, while recognizing the potency of libertarian rhetoric and the reality of the restraints on executive authority, now tend to see the British state as an unusually strong one, especially in areas where Parliament willingly sanctioned the state's ambitions, by enabling it to raise taxes

---

[25] See below, p. 203.

[26] See Vol. I, Nicholas Canny, 'The Origins of Empire: An Introduction'.

[27] David Armitage, 'The Scottish Vision of Empire: The Intellectual Origins of the Darien Venture', in John Robertson, ed., *A Union for Empire: Political Thought and the British Union of 1707* (Cambridge, 1995), pp. 97–118.

[28] See below, p. 32.

[29] See below, pp. 92–93.

[30] See below, pp. 255–59.

and borrow money in order to fight wars of which Parliament approved.[31] The Empire reflected this apparent paradox of weakness and strength in the eighteenth-century British state. Much was left to private initiative. Pennsylvania and Maryland remained in the possession of the families that had founded them. The management of other settlements and even, in India or the Canadian north, of great tracts of territory was entrusted to trading companies. New colonial ventures, such as Georgia and Sierra Leone, began as private undertakings. Voluntary associations promoted exploration and the propagation of Christianity. Most British people overseas enjoyed extensive civil rights and managed their own affairs through representative Assemblies with little effective interference from metropolitan authority. Yet they and their trade enjoyed the protection of the most powerful navy in the world, and at the end of the century of large military garrisons and expeditionary forces.

The formal basis of Empire was the authority of the Crown. Colonies were the King's dominions or were territories acquired by private bodies acting on the authority that the Crown had vested in them. The will of the Crown was expressed through orders emanating from the King's Privy Council, one of his Secretaries of State, or some other government department. Those who held senior offices in most colonies did so by appointment from the Crown. In short, 'Monarchy was at the legal core of the Empire'.[32]

Yet the great questions of authority within the Empire, especially in the second half of the eighteenth century, concerned not so much the power of the Crown over its subjects overseas as the power of Parliament. The exercise of royal powers over colonies was rarely contentious. They operated through well-established channels and could generally be moderated or even circumvented without provoking a crisis. But with the rise of the 'elected' over 'the anointed' and 'the appointed' in Britain and throughout the Empire, Parliament's claims became the issue through which differing interpretations of the Empire were contested.[33] For most British people, an effective British Empire required obedience to Parliament's sovereignty in every part of it. But for people of British origin living overseas, their status as free-born Englishmen depended on the freedom of what were, in their eyes, bodies that were the equivalent of Parliament, that is, the Irish Parliament or the Assemblies in the West Indian and North American colonies.

In the early eighteenth century conflicts between Parliament's authority and the claims of colonial Assemblies rarely surfaced. Parliament's concern was largely with regulating colonial trade, which was an area where its jurisdiction was well

---

[31] See below, pp. 63–70.   [32] See below, p. 105.   [33] See below, pp. 115–17.

established. A series of statutes, beginning with one passed in 1660, laid down provisions binding on 'the Lands, Islands, Plantations or Territories to his Majesty belonging... in *Asia, Africa,* or *America*'.[34] These statutes were the famous Navigation Acts, which created an Imperial trading system that remained essentially in force until well into the nineteenth century. All colonial trade was to be carried in English or colonial ships. So-called enumerated products, at first tobacco, sugar, cotton, and dyestuffs, to which other commodities, such as rice and naval stores, were added, could only be exported to England and, after 1707, to Scotland, or to British colonies. Most European goods intended for the colonies had to go via Britain.

From the 1760s, however, legislation directed towards Britain's overseas interests was much more varied in its scope and Parliament asserted its authority in unequivocal terms. The Declaratory Act of 1766, aimed at recalcitrant Americans, was the strongest statement of Parliament's authority: Parliament had the power 'to bind the Colonies and People of *America,* Subjects of the Crown of *Great Britain,* in all cases whatsoever'.[35] By then Parliament had already made the most contentious of all its claims, the right to levy colonial taxes, most notoriously in the Stamp Act of 1765, to which colonial Americans took the strongest exception. In a statute enacting a constitution for Quebec in 1774, Parliament formally recognized the Catholic Church within a Protestant British Empire by guaranteeing the conquered French 'the free Exercise of the Religion of the Church of *Rome*'.[36] Parliament used its powers to modify the charters, that is, the grants of royal privileges, of colonies or trading bodies, such as Massachusetts or the East India Company. In 1807 it made illegal the long-established slave trade on which the prosperity of the West Indian colonies and many merchants and investors was thought to depend.

The ferocity of North American resistance to Parliament's claims, leading to war and breakup of the Empire, and the success of the Irish Parliament in asserting its legislative sovereignty in 1782 induced some caution in the use of parliamentary power. Taxation was renounced. Yet the supreme power over the British Empire remained that of Parliament. The British Parliament formally accepted no equals within the Empire until 1931.

Whatever Parliament might claim for itself, the strength of local legislatures, the autonomy of private bodies, the weakness of the agencies of royal government concerned with colonial administration, and the failure of the formidable British military machine ultimately to suppress British colonial subjects in a war that

---

[34] 12 Chas. II, c. 18.   [35] 6 Geo. III, c. 12.   [36] 14 Geo. III, c. 83.

lasted from 1775 to 1783, all indicated the limitations on the authority that Britain could assert over its Empire.

The Empire was, however, held together by ties that went beyond the exercise of formal authority. The eighteenth-century Empire has been described as an 'empire of goods'.[37] The commercial life of the Empire was subject to metropolitan regulations, embodied in the Navigation Acts, but these were to a considerable degree self-enforcing, due to the strength of the British economy, reflected in the size of Britain's market for what the colonies produced, the cheapness and abundance of the manufactured goods with which they could be supplied, the huge volume of British shipping, and the extensive credit available to producers and merchants in the Empire. Even in the late seventeenth century, English manufacturers met the needs of the colonies not only for basic textiles and hardware, but also for such items as parrot cages and tombstones.[38] Industrialization, which by the 1780s was transforming the production of cotton cloth and iron, strengthened Britain's competitive edge. When the North American colonies gained their independence, and with it freedom from the Navigation Acts, they still remained effectively within 'the empire of goods'.

The extent to which the peoples of the Empire consumed goods from Britain, clothes, furniture, or porcelain and earthenware, which reflected metropolitan taste and fashion, is one of many indications of the cultural ties that united the British Atlantic Empire. Such ties got stronger during the eighteenth century. Books published in Britain were shipped across the Atlantic in great quantities. English *belles-lettres* were studied as the model of polite learning. Colonial élites took English and especially London manners as their model. A sense of common identity, a 'Britishness', or more precisely an essential 'Englishness', that could be adapted to local circumstances and be combined with local patriotisms, united Scots, many Irish, and those who lived in North America and the West Indies. Central to this sense of identity were the rights of Englishmen as a free people. Irish Protestants developed a kind of 'colonial' nationalism, but this was based on 'the defence of their rights as the English-born-in-Ireland' and resentment that the English of England did not extend to them the full rights of Englishmen.[39] The process of 'Anglicization' in the North American colonies in the years up to the Revolution has been much studied. Americans measured their progress by the extent to which they were matching what England had achieved.[40] 'Secure in their British liberty... Americans were never more British than in 1763.'[41] The defence of

---

[37] T. H. Breen, 'An Empire of Goods: The Anglicization of Colonial America, 1690–1776', *Journal of British Studies*, XXV (1986), pp. 467–99.

[38] See Vol. I, chap. by Nuala Zahedieh.

[39] See below, pp. 259–61.

[40] See below, p. 298.   [41] See below, p. 308.

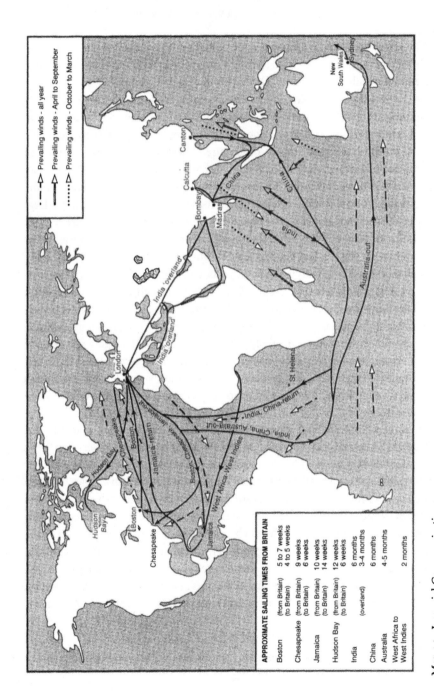

Map 1.3. Imperial Communications

APPROXIMATE SAILING TIMES FROM BRITAIN

Boston	(from Britain)	5 to 7 weeks
	(to Britain)	4 to 5 weeks
Chesapeake	(from Britain)	9 weeks
	(to Britain)	6 weeks
Jamaica	(from Britain)	10 weeks
	(to Britain)	14 weeks
Hudson Bay	(from Britain)	12 weeks
	(to Britain)	6 weeks
India		6 months
	(overland)	3-4 months
China		6 months
Australia		4-5 months
West Africa to West Indies		2 months

Prevailing winds - all year
Prevailing winds - April to September
Prevailing winds - October to March

Hudson Bay
Boston
Chesapeake
Boston
Chesapeake
Jamaica-return
Boston, Chesapeake, Jamaica-return
Jamaica
West Africa-West Indies
London
India 'overland'
India 'overland'
India, China, Australia-out
India, China-return
St Helena
Bombay
Madras
Calcutta
Canton
China
China
India
Australia-out
New South Wales
Sydney

8

the rights of Englishmen provided the ideology for resistance to Britain up to 1776. West Indian whites found no difficulty in using the language of English liberty in slave societies.

The effectiveness of any British Empire, whether it was based on the exercise of authority, on mutually beneficial trading relationships, or on the dissemination of metropolitan culture and values, depended on effective communications.

The eighteenth century was not marked by a spectacular revolution in seaborne communications. The striking improvements in navigational techniques, such as the calculation of longitude by chronometers, did not initially have a major impact on the routine communications of Empire. There were, however, significant developments in the design of ships that enabled them to be manned by smaller crews and therefore to be operated more cheaply. Above all, there were far more ships making long-distance voyages. The British merchant fleet, including a large American contribution before the Revolution, became easily the world's biggest. In 1815 the tonnage of British shipping employed in Atlantic and Asian routes was six times larger than it had been in 1686.[42] During the eighteenth century ships tended to be handled more efficiently in ports, so that they spent less time between voyages, and sailing times generally fell, especially for high-cost voyages carrying news or orders; but, in as much as enormous variations make this concept meaningful, the 'approximate' sailing times for trade or passengers (shown in a table on Map 1.3) did not alter fundamentally. The great change of the eighteenth century was the vastly increased number of sailings, which, carrying ever more people and goods together with news and information of all kinds, was to 'shrink' the British Atlantic and to bring the peoples who lived around it 'closer together as a community'.[43]

By contrast, Britain and British India remained remote from one another. Sailing times round the Cape for relatively small numbers of very big ships could vary from four months to a year, six months being a rough average. Early in the eighteenth century the East India Company despatched an average of eleven ships a year to India and China; in the first decade of the nineteenth century over a hundred Company ships would be at sea in any year. These ships ensured the flow of orders and responses through which London kept control over British India. They were also the vehicle for an expanding trade in high-value goods, such as tea, silk, or textiles. It would, however, require many more ships costing much less before Asia could challenge the Atlantic colonies as a source of bulk commodities, such as cotton or sugar. The founding and maintaining of a colony in Australia is

---

[42] See below, p. 54.

[43] Ian K. Steele, *The English Atlantic, 1675–1740: An Exploration of Communication and Community* (New York, 1986), pp. 213, 273.

the most striking evidence of all of the Imperial reach of the eighteenth-century sailing ship. When the system was in full swing, convicts could be delivered in under four months.

The British Empire of the first half of the eighteenth century was essentially an Atlantic one, peopled by inhabitants of British origin, and held together by economic and cultural ties with Britain, as much as by the exertion of authority. Yet even within colonies that prided themselves on being extensions of British society overseas, there were large elements of the population that were not British. North America attracted many German immigrants during the eighteenth century. Conquest brought French people under British rule in Canada and some Caribbean islands.

By far the largest non-British population of the Empire originated in Africa. Enslaved Africans constituted the overwhelming majority in the West Indies and an increasing proportion, amounting to approximately one-fifth, of the population of the thirteen colonies on the eve of the Revolution. The numbers of slaves and the economic importance of slavery within the British Empire progressively increased throughout the eighteenth century. In essence, a slave was a person over whom another person had rights that amounted to property. The precise status of slaves in any part of the Empire varied according to the enactments of different colonial legislatures. Slavery was not a condition recognized by English law. Even so, it was assumed that several thousand slaves were being held in Britain at any time in the eighteenth century, even after the famous judgement of Lord Chief Justice Mansfield in the case of James Somerset in 1772, which did no more than lay down that a slave might not be forcibly removed from England. There was little opposition from British opinion either to the trade in slaves or to the institution of slavery before the rise of the popular anti-slavery movement in the 1780s.[44]

The indigenous peoples of the Americas were also almost entirely beyond the pale of Britishness. Most of the original population of the British West Indies were exterminated either before or shortly after English occupation. Caribs, however, survived in some numbers in the islands of Dominica and St Vincent, acquired in 1763. British troops fought a war against the Caribs of St Vincent in 1772 and confined them to lands set aside for them. On the North American mainland such conflicts with indigenous peoples had a long history and were to continue throughout the eighteenth century. The expansion of British settlement had reduced a small number of Native Americans to subordinate communities within the boundaries of colonies, while the majority lived in varying degrees of proximity

---

[44] See below, p. 471; the anti-slavery movement is dealt with in Vol. III.

with the colonial frontiers, but were tied to the British by complex links of economic and military interdependence. The importance of Indians as trading partners of the British declined throughout the eighteenth century, but their role in war, first against the French, then against the rebellious colonies, and later still against the United States in 1812 remained a significant one. The British victory in one set of conflicts and defeat or stalemate in the others had the same consequences for the Indians, who were losers in all three.[45]

By 1815 by far the largest part of the population of the British Empire lived in the provinces conquered by the East India Company. The empire that developed in India from the 1760s was entirely different from the Atlantic one. It was an empire of rule over a vast indigenous population that provided the labour and technical and commercial expertise on which British trade depended, and which paid the taxes that sustained a system of government completely without the representative institutions that had developed in the Americas. A British Governor and a small cadre of British officials ruled without any formal consent of those over whom they ruled, although with much active participation of Indians in the machinery of government. British Collectors and Magistrates appointed to Districts supervised a taxation system and the administration of laws that were Hindu or Muslim in substance, even if European elements quickly intruded. By 1815 British government in India was supported by a great army of some 140,000 Indian soldiers and 30,000 British ones.[46]

A new ideology of rule developed for a new kind of empire. That British liberty could not be extended to India was a proposition never questioned. Indians were to be ruled by methods thought to be appropriate to them. Strong government powers would be used for what was considered to be the good of the people. Although there was no place for Indian representation, Indians would be guaranteed security for their lives and property under the law. British rule would thus be 'enlightened', if, of necessity, authoritarian. This marked a fundamental change in Imperial governance. The pattern of representative government based on the rights of Englishmen, first established around the Atlantic, would spread to Australia, New Zealand, and southern Africa in the nineteenth century; the Indian model of authoritarian government would be exported to Asia and the rest of Africa.

British institutions, values, and culture were carried across the world by the migration of British people and the establishment of British rule. The extent to which the possession of an Empire left its mark on Britain in return is, however, harder to assess.

---

[45] See below, p. 349.   [46] See below, p. 582.

Until recently, debate has focused almost exclusively on the economic consequences of Empire for Britain. Historians writing within the Marxist tradition have long seen the wealth extracted from colonial trades and the plunder of India as having had an important role in the accumulation of capital that made industrialization possible. 'The enormous contribution to Britain's industrial development' made by 'the triangular trade' between Britain, Africa, and the West Indies, that is, the slave trade, was, for instance, a major theme of Eric Williams's *Capitalism and Slavery*.[47] While great fortunes were undoubtedly made out of West Indian planting, and Indian service and colonial trades clearly enriched certain ports and their hinterlands, other historians have still argued that the overall Imperial contribution to Britain's economic development may not have been a very significant one. Two chapters in this volume offer a positive assessment of the consequences of Empire. They both point out that, while the growth of the British population and of exports to Europe were relatively slow for most of the century, the population of the colonies and their demand for manufactured goods grew rapidly. This colonial demand was to 'make necessary or at least hasten the technological transformation of several long-established branches of British industrial life'.[48] It is difficult to envisage 'an alternative blueprint for national development' to eighteenth-century Britain's commitment to 'sustained levels of investment in global commerce, naval power, and, whenever necessary, the acquisition of bases and territory overseas'.[49]

The debate about the effects of Empire have widened from the purely economic to such questions as the importance of Empire in influencing Britain's role in Europe. Did Imperial commitments come to dominate her foreign policy and defence strategies?[50] More recently, questions have been raised about the role of Empire in Britain's sense of national identity or in British culture. Some strong claims have been made. 'That the British Empire permeated Georgian English culture at a number of levels, from literature and theater to philanthropy, fashion, gardening and politics' is said to be 'beyond dispute'.[51] Propositions about an Imperial identity or culture must, however, take account of what contemporaries understood by 'Empire' and of the way in which this changed during the eighteenth century.[52] In the first half of the century, English nationalism was strongly identified with a flourishing oceanic commerce and with naval successes against European rivals. Colonies were recognized to be an important element in English

---

[47] *Capitalism and Slavery* (1944; London, 1964), p. 105.
[48] See below, p. 99.
[49] See below, pp. 76; 461–62.
[50] See below, pp. 169–71.
[51] Wilson, *The Sense of the People*, pp. 23–24.
[52] See Vol. I, chap. by David Armitage.

claims to maritime supremacy, but a sense of Britain as the centre of a world-wide Empire of rule, which included dominion over non-European peoples, came late in the century. By then many people in the British Isles had evidently begun to see the possession of a territorial Empire as a distinctive feature of British identity. 'The Establishments we have made in all Parts of the World' were said in 1774 to be an integral part of Britain's 'Fame' and 'Power', as well as being vital to her commerce.[53]

The influence of the greatly increased scale of contact with the world beyond Europe is evident in many aspects of eighteenth-century life: in patterns of consumption, both of food and clothing; in themes for poetry, novels, and theatrical spectacles; and, as a later chapter shows, in providing abundant data for what would come to be called 'science'. Whether she possessed an Empire or not, Britain, like all western European countries, would have been subject to influences from other continents. Nevertheless, specific connections can be made between the possession of Empire and, for instance, the acquisition of scientific knowledge. The extent of Britain's Imperial possessions made London the entrepôt for recorded observations as well as for tropical products, and stimulated the despatch of British expeditions of discovery and the spread across the world of British learned societies and botanical gardens. Thus British science was particularly open to the influences that ensued from world-wide trade and Empire.[54] Similarly, although what has been called the Oriental Renaissance, that is, the stimulus given to European thought and literature by increased knowledge of Asian cultures, sank its deepest roots in Germany, whose states did not possess overseas empires, Britain's Imperial involvement in India meant that the movement began with British writers, Sir William Jones, Robert Southey, and Lord Byron.

By 1689 two hundred years of European expansion since Columbus had profoundly reshaped the world. In the Americas indigenous states had been overthrown and their peoples had been decimated by disease. A new order of European empires had been created in their place. With the exception of the rich Portuguese colony of Brazil, Central and South America were dominated by a Spanish empire that remained in the eighteenth century a source of great wealth for Europe through its silver exports and its imports of manufactured goods. The British and French jostled one another for dominance over the eastern half of North America.

Direct European political control was minimal in Africa or Asia until the British began their Indian conquests in the later eighteenth century. Without having established any significant system of colonial rule, the western European nations

---

[53] See below, p. 220.   [54] See below, pp. 250–51.

competed along the West African coast for trade, above all for cargoes of slaves. The Dutch East India Company had imposed its authority with varying degrees of effectiveness over Java, the Molucca islands, and coastal Ceylon. Elsewhere in Asia, it, like its British competitor before the 1760s, traded from a network of enclaves or ports to which the Dutch had been granted access. The great Asian empires, the Ottomans, the Safavids of Persia, the Mughals in India, and the Chinese, had actually extended their domains during the first two centuries of European expansion. In the eighteenth century only the Chinese empire continued to grow. The Ottomans, the Safavids, and the Mughals all suffered serious reverses. There was also clear evidence that the military balance on land was beginning to follow the balance of force at sea, which from the sixteenth century had gone wholly in Europe's favour and was not to adjust itself until the early twentieth century. The success of British forces in India, matched by that of Austrians and Russians against the Turks, impressed perceptive observers, like Adam Ferguson, luminary of the Scottish Enlightenment. European 'Mercenary and disciplined armies' were, he wrote, now 'ready to traverse the earth'. 'Effeminate kingdoms and empires...from the Sea of Corea to the Atlantic Ocean' could no longer contain them.[55]

Further reordering of the world took place during the eighteenth century. The British were then the main beneficiaries. They lost the largest part of their North American colonies, but made spectacular gains in India at the expense of what had once been the Mughal empire. Pressure was brought to bear in various ways on other Asian empires, but neither the Turks, the Persians, nor the Chinese parted with territory. Very little was also taken from those European empires regarded by the British as potentially the most vulnerable. Portugal, Britain's ally throughout the eighteenth century, lost nothing to her. Spain lost Gibraltar and Minorca (finally recovered in 1802), the Floridas (also recovered), and Trinidad in the Napoleonic War. Otherwise, the Spanish American empire survived the onslaughts of the British, only to break up as its subjects rejected its authority in the early nineteenth century. The Dutch lost nothing to Britain until the Napoleonic War, when most of their territories were overrun. At the end of the war Britain kept three ex-Dutch colonies on the South American mainland that were later combined to form British Guiana, as well as the Cape of Good Hope and coastal Ceylon.

The European empire that lost most to the British in the eighteenth century was that of France, the power that Britain feared the most and regarded as by far her most serious rival. Britain and France were formally at war seven times from 1689 to 1815. As a result of these wars, the French surrendered virtually all their North

---

[55] *An Essay on the History of Civil Society,* Duncan Forbes, ed. (Edinburgh, 1966), p. 154.

American territory, several West Indian islands, and Mauritius in the Indian Ocean, as well as being forced to accept a limited commercial role in India. For all their apparent success, however, the eighteenth-century British viewed the power of France with grave anxiety. The French army was a huge one by comparison with Britain's. Although the building programmes that had given France the largest navy in Europe at the end of the seventeenth century were scaled down, France still maintained a powerful battle fleet, some two-thirds the size of Britain's, for instance, in 1775.[56] The French also had the capacity to ravage English seaborne trade through commerce raiding, which was especially devastating in the early wars. Underlying French military power was an economy that grew significantly, if unevenly, its overseas trade increasing faster than that of Britain for most of the century. French colonial trades, above all the sugar, coffee, and dyestuffs from immensely successful West Indian plantations, were an important part of this expansion.

What was seen to be at stake for Britain in these wars was not just wealth, but national survival. Except for the American War of 1778 to 1783, Britain and France fought one another both in Europe and overseas. A France that dominated Europe would, the British feared, be able to invade the British Isles. Colonial wars and Britain's ability to defend itself and to intervene in Europe seemed, however, to be closely linked. By the 1740s British statesmen saw their naval and military capacity as depending crucially on colonial and oceanic trades. These generated a significant portion of the wealth on which taxation and government credit depended.[57] Conversely, to destroy France's colonial trade would, it was supposed, greatly weaken her capacity to make war anywhere.

Conquests in India or made elsewhere from European rivals, together with the seizure of land from indigenous peoples in North America or Australia, greatly extended the British Empire during the eighteenth century. Britain's involvement in the world outside Europe was, however, by no means confined to her Empire, that is, to the dominions of the British Crown. Britain had long sought to gain commercial access to the empires of other European powers or to the territory of African or Asian rulers. By the end of the eighteenth century a large part of Britain's non-European trade was in fact going to areas that the British did not rule, especially to the independent United States of America, to Latin America, to the coast of West Africa, and to China. British diplomacy was actively engaged in seeking commercial concessions from the Mississippi to the Chinese coast, and Britain had a world-wide military and naval presence.

---

[56] See below, p. 185.   [57] See below, pp. 73–74.

All this evidence suggests that Britain's role in the eighteenth century can no more be assessed solely in terms of an Empire of rule than it can be in the nineteenth or the twentieth centuries. Concepts such as that of a British 'informal empire' which did not depend on actual rule, a British system of 'influence', or a British 'world-system' may well be relevant for the eighteenth century as well as for later periods.

Historians have indeed applied such concepts to the eighteenth century. The theme of Vincent Harlow's two volumes on *The Founding of the Second British Empire* is that from 1763 the British had systematically pursued projects of what Harlow called 'informal empire' in the Far East, the Pacific, and in the Americas.[58] Interpretations of the rise of western economic hegemony over the world have focused on Britain's role in the eighteenth century. Late eighteenth-century London has been described as 'the centre of the world' in the sense that it was at the centre of a European 'world-economy' that was casting 'a mighty shadow' over the rest of the world.[59] Alternatively, Britain is said to have been at the centre of the western European 'core' of the 'world-economy' that had 'incorporated' the Americas in the sixteenth century, and from about 1750 was embarking on a new phase of expansion that would end in the incorporation of India, West Africa, and the Ottoman Empire.[60]

The existence of an informal empire or the exercise of economic hegemony supposes that Britain could effectively impose its will on otherwise independent states or that it was at least able to dominate key sectors of their economies. For much of the eighteenth century, for all the strident claims to exercise an empire over the seas, Britain's capacity to do either was in fact limited: Britain was only the strongest naval power among a number of European states with powerful navies, and its manufactures faced stiff competition, for instance, from the textiles of other European countries, notably France. By the end of century, however, conditions had changed. Britain had acquired an absolute naval dominance and its cotton textile and metal industries were undergoing rapid development.

Search for an eighteenth-century informal empire begins conventionally and with good reason with Portugal and Brazil. Even in the first half of the eighteenth century, Portugal and its colonies were virtual satellites of Britain. Portugal was dependent on British military protection in war and its markets had been opened to British trade by treaty. This influence gave Britain access to Brazil, Portugal's

---

[58] Vincent T. Harlow, *The Founding of the Second British Empire, 1763–1793*, 2 vols. (London, 1952–64), I, pp. 1–3.

[59] Fernand Braudel, trans. Siân Reynolds, *Civilization and Capitalism, 15th–18th Century*, 3 vols. (London 1984), III, *The Perspective of the World*, pp. 29, 273.

[60] Immanuel Wallerstein, *The Modern World-System*, 3 vols. (New York, 1974–89).

wealthy American colony. The first half of the century was the age of Brazil's gold boom. Legally Brazilian gold had to be exported to Portugal, but in large quantities it then passed to Britain in return for huge imports of British manufactured goods, many of them destined for Brazil, or to be transhipped from Brazil into the Spanish colonies around the River Plate. Financed by gold, British exports to Portugal doubled in value from over £355,000 a year at the beginning of the century to over £1 million by 1750. At least one-third of the annual output of Brazilian gold ended up in Britain.[61]

Unlike Portugal, eighteenth-century Spain generally resisted British blandishments and tended to ally with France, Britain's inveterate enemy. Diplomacy gained a concession in 1713 in the grant to Britain of the *Asiento*, or the right to supply slaves and send an annual merchant ship to Spanish America. Settlements on the coast of Central America that later became British Honduras were sustained in the face of unremitting hostility from Spain. Otherwise the Spanish stood firm and their empire in America remained legally closed to the British. Repeated attempts were made to break in and to establish British enclaves by force, but no lasting bridgehead was ever achieved. Nevertheless, Britain traded with Spanish America throughout the eighteenth century, both legally through British shipments to Cadiz, which were then taken to America in Spanish ships, and illegally. The illegal trade involved direct transactions with Spanish America from the British colonies in the West Indies. Spanish communities round the Caribbean obtained British manufactured goods from Jamaica in return for exports of hides, dyes, cotton, or coffee, supplemented by bullion. A detailed estimate for the years 1748 to 1765 put shipments of Spanish bullion to the British colonies at £3,255,654, most of which was received in Jamaica.[62]

At the end of the eighteenth century Britain was in an unassailable position as the dominant power outside Europe. The instruments through which she was to exert world-wide influence during the nineteenth century were already coming into place. The navies of her European rivals, which had pressed Britain very hard in the War of American Independence from 1778 to 1783, were destroyed during the wars between 1793 and 1815.[63] British investment overseas was still relatively limited, but the capacity of British merchants to extend credit could not be matched by their European rivals, as they found when they tried to compete with Britain in the markets of the newly independent United States. As industrialization gathered pace, British goods became even more competitive. Supre-

---

[61] François Crouzet, 'Angleterre-Brésil, 1697–1850: un siècle et demi d'échanges commerciaux', *Histoire, Economie et Société*, II (1990), pp. 288–317.

[62] L. S. Sutherland, 'The Accounts of an Eighteenth-Century Merchant: The Portuguese Ventures of William Braund', *Economic History Review*, First Series, III (1931–32), p. 370.

[63] See below, p. 204.

macy in India by the end of the eighteenth century meant that Britain could deploy military resources all over maritime Asia on a scale that no other European power could hope to match.

In a few cases there is unmistakable evidence that late eighteenth-century Britain's economic, naval, or military muscle had been converted into effective domination beyond the bounds of Empire. Great Indian states like Hyderabad or Oudh were clamped from the 1760s into a vice from which there could be no escape. Their rulers did the will of the East India Company or they faced extinction. The British West Indian economy had expanded to take in territory nominally ruled by other powers. Colonies that were nominally Dutch or Danish were dominated by British capital and British planters.[64]

Elsewhere the extent of British domination was more debatable. When the Speaker of the House of Representatives, Henry Clay, described the United States of America in 1820 as 'independent colonies of England', 'politically free' but 'commercially slaves',[65] he was reflecting on the degree to which the American economy remained tied to Britain after independence. By the 1790s Britain was taking about half of America's exports and was supplying the United States with up to four-fifths of its imports.[66] Yet in spite of Britain's economic preponderance, the American political system lay well beyond the reach of British influence. The United States imposed embargoes on British trade and eventually fought a war against Britain.

In Brazil, by contrast, Britain was able to exercise effective political influence when the Portuguese royal family moved there under British protection in 1807. Britain's trade, already considerable since Brazil became an important source of raw cotton in the 1780s, grew spectacularly when Brazilian ports were opened to British ships in 1808. Large quantities of manufactured goods were sold on credit. Within a year, however, the boom subsided, leaving exporters with heavy debts. Extremely favourable terms were extracted from Brazil in a treaty signed in 1810, and trade revived, Brazil becoming Britain's most important commercial outlet in Latin America.

The Spanish government made no formal concessions to foreign trade with its colonies, but it lost its capacity to keep out British trade. After 1796 war virtually eliminated both Spanish and French trade, leaving only the British as

[64] Richard B. Sheridan, *Sugar and Slavery: An Economic History of the British West Indies, 1623–1775* (Barbados, 1974), pp. 442–45.

[65] Cited Drew R. McCoy, 'An Unfinished Revolution: The Quest for Economic Independence in the Early Republic', in Jack P. Greene, ed., *The American Revolution: Its Character and Limits* (New York, 1987), p. 131.

[66] Charles R. Ritcheson, *Aftermath of Revolution: British Policy toward the United States, 1783–1795* (Dallas, 1969), p. 188.

the suppliers of manufactured goods to the colonies. As individual colonies declared their independence, they, like Brazil, opened their ports to the British without restriction. A speculative boom followed, as British merchants poured in goods excluded from Europe by the Napoleonic blockade. This proved short-lived, as did another wave of speculation in the 1820s in the government funds of the new republics.

To claim that a British informal empire replaced the old colonial systems throughout the Americas is to underestimate the political and economic obstacles to effective domination. Only in Brazil did the British find pliant political collaborators in the early years after independence. In the United States Britain could exert no political influence, although there was a population long habituated to British goods and able to pay for them through large exports of primary produce, and there were credit networks which could sustain a huge volume of trade. In ex-Spanish America, on the other hand, the British faced both political and economic uncertainties and commercial expectations were only slowly fulfilled. There was a promising demand for British goods in the towns, but payment for them, except where bullion or commodities like cotton could be obtained in return, proved difficult to arrange, while credit-worthy merchants seemed to be few and far between.

The British did not develop a political role in West Africa which matched the extent of their trade on the coast until well into the nineteenth century. Where trade was conducted from permanent settlements, small garrisons at the British forts constituted no threat to African states. As shippers of about a half of all the slaves exported from Africa, that is, some 3.4 million people, the British were the largest foreign traders on the coast. Even so, they faced severe competition from other Europeans and could not 'control slave supply or, except on rare occasions, manipulate prices paid for slaves to their own advantage'. African commercial and political élites managed the trade and extracted a high level of profit.[67] The slave trade was very important to those élites and inflicted incalculable suffering to millions of people, yet the economy of western Africa as a whole remained largely self-contained.

Empire in India gave the British both the incentive and the power to play an active role in other parts of Asia. From the middle of the eighteenth century, with the conquest of Bengal, the British were able to maintain warships and regiments in India and to raise huge Indian armies. The defence of India, especially after the French invasion of Egypt in 1798, drew the British into the Middle East. Alliances were signed with the Ottoman Empire and with Persia, while troops and fleets were despatched to Egypt, the Red Sea, and the Persian Gulf. The French were kept

---

[67] See below, p. 463.

out of the Levant, but the British were unable to establish an enduring influence over either the Ottoman or the Persian governments.

Control of Indian resources also enabled the British to act forcefully in South-East Asia, an area long dominated by the Dutch East India Company. In the French Revolutionary and Napoleonic Wars, when the Netherlands allied with France, Dutch settlements, including Java, were seized throughout the Indonesian archipelago. At the end of the war, however, the Dutch were restored throughout the archipelago, leaving only the coast of Malaya as a British sphere.

British relations with China in the late eighteenth century are a clear illustration of the limits on British political or commercial influence in Asia outside India. The Chinese government was not prepared to make political concessions. The East India Company was only granted access to the single port of Canton, where the Company had no exemptions from strictly imposed regulations. Commercially, the British were only of marginal importance to the Chinese. The demand in China for British manufactures was small. While the British dominated the carrying trade of the Indian Ocean, in the China Sea British shipping was of less account than Chinese shipping. In 1796 one thousand ocean-going junks were based on the port of Amoy alone, trading between China, the Philippines, Thailand, and the Indonesian archipelago.[68] For the British, tea imported from Canton had become a national drink, consumed by the vast majority of the population down to the very poorest. Yet in Chinese terms the British tea trade was of no great significance. It generated valuable local revenue, but it is estimated that it took off less than 15 per cent of the annual tea crop, destined in the main for a vast internal market.[69]

At the end of the eighteenth century Britain was by far the most powerful European presence in Asia. But over much of Asia indigenous political systems were still largely beyond the reach of British diplomatic blandishments or even the threat of British warships and Indian troops, while intercontinental trade had little influence on most Asian economies. Concepts of informal empire are even more difficult to apply to Asia, outside the Indian subcontinent, or to Africa, than they are to the Americas.

British statesmen in the late eighteenth century were sometimes given to musing that a world-wide network of commerce was preferable to an Empire of rule over land and people.[70] Some historians have argued that a 'revulsion against

---

[68] Ng Chin Keong, 'The South Fukienese Junk Trade', in E. B. Vermeer, ed., *Development and Decline of Fukien Province in the Seventeenth and Eighteenth Centuries* (Leiden, 1990), p. 309.

[69] Susan Naquin and Evelyn S. Rawski, *Chinese Society in the Eighteenth Century* (New Haven, 1987), p. 104.

[70] Most obviously, Lord Shelburne, Harlow, *The Second British Empire*, I, p. 436.

colonisation', accentuated by the quarrel that led to the loss of most of Britain's dominions in North America and coinciding with the rise of industrialization, brought about a shift away from an empire of rule to the pursuit of trade and influence throughout the world. Trade, it has been argued, came to be preferred to dominion.[71]

By the end of the eighteenth century British economic interests were certainly becoming increasingly 'global', in the sense that they were spreading beyond the limits of the Empire. The United States, Britain's largest market and eventually the main source of cotton, her most important raw material, was outside the Empire. So too was China, source of tea. Markets in Latin America seemed to have high potential. British ministers were well aware of the significance of these areas to an economy whose needs were changing rapidly with industrialization and they energetically promoted policies for gaining access to them.

Such policies were not, however, pursued at the expense of an Empire of rule. There was no revulsion against territorial Empire. The existing Empire was to be defended and its resources were to be developed to the full. The huge deployment of British troops and warships in the West Indies in the 1790s, virtually regardless of crippling casualties from disease, demonstrated the government's sense of priorities. The defence of India also become a major British concern. In the Revolutionary and Napoleonic Wars Britain went over to the offensive outside Europe, adding greatly to its dominions in the West Indies, India, and around the Indian Ocean. Whatever else they may have been, these wars were also the last of the great eighteenth-century wars for empire from which Britain emerged with much colonial booty.[72]

The continuing pursuit of dominion reflected a deep national commitment to Empire as an integral part of Britain's power and standing in the world and of British people's sense of who they were.

[71] Ibid., I, p. 4.   [72] See below, p. 206.

Select Bibliography

BERNARD BAILYN and PHILIP D. MORGAN, eds., *Strangers within the Realm: Cultural Margins of the First British Empire* (Chapel Hill, NC, 1991).

C. A. BAYLY, *Imperial Meridian: The British Empire and the World, 1780–1830* (London, 1989).

H. V. BOWEN, *Elites, Enterprise and the Making of the British Overseas Empire, 1688–1775* (London, 1996).

JOHN BREWER, *The Sinews of Power: War, Money and the English State, 1688–1783* (London, 1989).

ANGUS CALDER, *Revolutionary Empire: The Rise of the English-Speaking Empires from the Fifteenth Century to the 1780s* (London, 1981).

RALPH DAVIS, *The Industrial Revolution and British Overseas Trade* (Leicester, 1979).

JACK P. GREENE, *Peripheries and Center: Constitutional Development in the Extended Polities of the British Empire and the United States, 1607–1788* (Athens, Ga., 1986).

VINCENT T. HARLOW, *The Founding of the Second British Empire, 1763–1793*, 2 vols. (London, 1952–64).

RICHARD KOEBNER, *Empire* (Cambridge, 1961).

FREDERICK MADDEN with DAVID FIELDHOUSE, eds., *Select Documents on the Constitutional History of the British Empire and Commonwealth*, vol. II, *The Classical Period of the First British Empire, 1689–1783. The Foundations of a Colonial System of Government*; vol. III, *Imperial Reconstruction, 1763–1840. The Evolution of Alternative Systems of Colonial Government* (Westport, Conn., 1985–7).

P. J. MARSHALL, 'The Eighteenth-Century Empire', in Jeremy Black, ed., *British Politics and Society from Walpole to Pitt, 1742–1789* (London, 1990), pp. 177–200.

PETER N. MILLER, *Defining the Common Good: Empire, Religion, and Philosophy in Eighteenth-Century Britain* (Cambridge, 1994).

ANTHONY PAGDEN, *Lords of all the World: Ideologies of Empire in Spain, Britain and France, c.1500 to c.1800* (New Haven, 1995).

D. C. M. PLATT, *Latin America and British Trade, 1806–1914* (London, 1972).

A. N. PORTER, ed., *Atlas of British Overseas Expansion* (London, 1991).

JOHN ROBERTSON, ed., *A Union for Empire: Political Thought and the British Union of 1707* (Cambridge, 1995).

IAN K. STEELE, *The English Atlantic, 1675–1740. An Exploration of Communication and Community* (New York, 1986).

LAWRENCE STONE, ed., *An Imperial State at War: Britain from 1689 to 1815* (London, 1994).

KATHLEEN WILSON, *The Sense of the People: Politics, Culture and Imperialism in England, 1715–1785* (Cambridge, 1995).

2

British Diaspora: Emigration from Britain, 1680–1815

JAMES HORN

Surveying the Empire in 1815, Patrick Colquhoun reflected on the felicity of the times. Defeat of Napoleonic France after a long and arduous struggle removed Britain's most potent colonial rival and confirmed her as the world's greatest imperial power. The vast agglomeration of territories, littorals, islands, fortified trading posts, entrepôts, and protected waters, stretching from the inhospitable shores of Van Diemen's Land to the Pacific coast of North America, embracing an enormous diversity of peoples and cultures, offered seemingly limitless opportunities for further expansion and development. Britain's dependencies would absorb her 'redundant Population' of unemployed and destitute, provide distant prisons for banished criminals, guarantee strategic interests, and, supported by a powerful marine, lay the foundations of global markets and trade for the century to come. To Colquhoun, the bounty of Empire represented wealth and resources on an incalculable scale requiring little more than judicious government and careful husbandry to reap the benefits.[1]

That Britain's overseas possessions should have spanned the globe by the early nineteenth century would have seemed improbable to all but the most enthusiastic promoters of imperial projects a century before. Despite the impressive increase of transoceanic commerce during the seventeenth century, principally with America and Asia, the extent of territory directly under the Crown remained limited compared to future conquests. The acquisition of new lands and establishment of permanent colonies were confined largely to the western hemisphere. Hence John Oldmixon's description of Empire in 1708, altogether more modest in conception than that of Colquhoun, considered only British settlements in the Caribbean and North America where the total population of whites and slaves already exceeded 400,000.[2] In contrast, English possessions in Africa, India, and

---

[1] Patrick Colquhoun, *A Treatise on the Wealth, Power, and Resources of the British Empire in Every Quarter of the World...*, 2nd edn. (London, 1815).

[2] John Oldmixon, *The British Empire in America, containing the History of the Discovery, Settlement, Progress, and Present State of all the British Colonies on the Continent and Islands of America*, 2 vols. (London, 1708); John J. McCusker and Russell R. Menard, *The Economy of British America, 1607–1789* (Chapel Hill, NC, 1985), Table 3.1, p. 54.

the Far East were largely restricted to a scattering of trading posts and factories inhabited by small European populations, located on coasts and rivers along the main shipping routes, who carried on business under the aegis of local rulers. Commercial ascendancy, not territorial expansion, was the imperative of trading companies in Africa and Asia.

But if the Empire in 1700 was a shadow of what it would become a hundred years later, developments in the first period of English overseas expansion were none the less significant. The distinction between colonies (plantations) settled permanently by British immigrants—raising staples, fishing, and farming—compared to enclaves and trading posts occupied by chartered companies, whose main intent was to secure and direct the trade of indigenous populations, became increasingly evident during the course of the century. In the Americas, European invasions and diseases decimated native populations and led to a scramble for lands on a continental scale that resulted in a chequer-board of Euro-American colonies reaching from the Arctic Circle to Tierra del Fuego. Britain, principally England, experienced a huge exodus of settlers, rich and poor, who took ship seeking their fortune 'beyond the seas' in mainland America and the Caribbean. The destinations and composition of emigrant groups varied, as did their motives for leaving, but the impetus for large-scale migration was firmly established by the 1630s as well as the means of transporting people across the ocean. Although the direction of migratory flows was not predetermined, North America would continue to attract the majority of British emigrants for the next three centuries.

Emigration and migration were a single impulse. The Atlantic colonies were not isolated fragments cut off from one another and, from the beginning, whether or not settlers opted to stay in one place or move elsewhere depended on economic cycles and changing perceptions of opportunity. Large numbers of Chesapeake immigrants eventually ended up in the Carolinas, Pennsylvania, or the lands beyond in the Ohio Valley. Thousands of settlers migrated from the Middle Colonies and New England to Canada, Nova Scotia, New Brunswick, and the Isle of St John, and numerous Georgia planters moved on to East and West Florida. Flux and mobility were vital aspects of migrant experience in the New World, and the tramp of migrants from one region to another was an enduring feature of the American social landscape. Similarly, the ebb and flow of commerce, changes in agreements with local rulers and traders, switches in government policy, and the shifting sands of foreign relations demanded a flexible response to settlement in Africa and Asia. With the development of an increasingly complex global economy in the eighteenth century, the search for fresh commercial outlets dictated highly mobile populations and, consequently, civilian and military personnel of the great trading companies travelled from place

to place as circumstances required. East and west, movement defined the early
Empire.

Magnitude and Pace

During the seventeenth century two significant features characterized emigration
from the British Isles. Of the approximately 1 million people who migrated, about
70 per cent were English, most of whom went to growing English plantations in
Ireland and America. By pre-modern standards the scale of emigration was
enormous. Although annual migration from England was higher in the nineteenth
century, rates of emigration relative to the domestic population never exceeded
those of the period between 1646 and 1670 (Fig. 2.1). Across the late sixteenth and
seventeenth centuries, England, and to a lesser extent Scotland and Ireland,
experienced the first waves of mass emigration. Second, the movement of some
400,000 English and Irish settlers to America represented the transfer of a massive
labour force, essential for the development of staple agriculture—sugar and
tobacco—in the West Indies and on the Chesapeake. In response to plantation
colonies' voracious demand for labour the great majority of white settlers
migrated as indentured servants, contracted to serve in tobacco- and sugar
fields, typically between four and seven years in return for their passage across
the Atlantic, board, and freedom dues. American staples were raised not by
indigenous peoples supervised by tiny immigrant élites, but by large numbers of
poor British men and women together with (especially in the West Indies) African
slaves. Rather than soldiers or *encomenderos*, as was the case with Spain, most

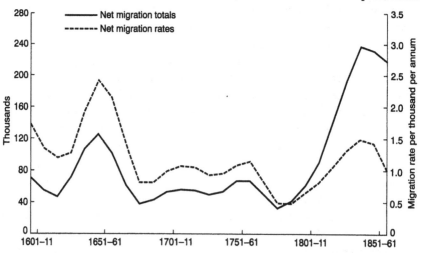

Figure 2.1. Net Migration from England, 1601–1861

TABLE 2.1. *Emigration from the British Isles to America, 1600–1780* (thousands)

	1601–1700	1701–80
England and Wales	350	80
Scotland	7	75
Lowland		60
Highland		15
Ireland	20–40	115
Ulster		70
Southern		45
TOTAL	377–97	270

Sources: Canny, ed., *Europeans on the Move* (see n. 6 below), pp. 39–75, 76–112, 113–149; Henry A. Gemery, 'European Emigration to North America, 1700–1820: Numbers and Quasi-Numbers', *Perspectives in American History*, I (1984), pp. 283–342; Galenson, *White Servitude*, Tables H3–H4, pp. 216–18; Fogelman, 'Migrations to the American Colonies', *Journal of Interdisciplinary History*, pp. 691–709.

British immigrants who made their way to the New World ended up as field-hands and small planters.[3]

Strikingly different patterns of emigration emerged in the eighteenth century. A key change was the sharp decline of English migration to North America in contrast to the rise of Scottish and Irish emigration. Settlers from England and Wales fell from 350,000 in the seventeenth century to less than 100,000 in the period down to 1780, compared to an increase in Irish emigrants from 30,000 to at least 115,000 and of Scottish settlers from 7,000 to 75,000 (Table 2.1). Even before the tide of Irish migration after the American Revolution, 70 per cent of all British settlers who arrived in America between 1700 and 1780 were from Ireland and Scotland. Whereas seventeenth-century settlement had been mainly English, eighteenth-century emigration was emphatically British.[4]

Decennial totals calculated by Fogelman indicate the rates of emigration from England and Wales, Scotland, and Ireland, 1700–75 (Table 2.2). The figures are open to question. Scottish migration totals seriously underestimate the magnitude of Lowland emigration before 1750, while the estimate for English migration (44,100) is too low when compared to 29,000 Welsh migrants. Moreover, his figures do not include immigration to the West Indies, which may have attracted up to 150,000 British immigrants and 'sojourners' during the century. None the less, the major contours of movement are broadly accurate and illustrate the slow

[3] Henry A. Gemery, 'Markets for Migrants: English Indentured Servitude and Emigration in the Seventeenth and Eighteenth Centuries', in P. C. Emmer, ed., *Colonialism and Migration. Indentured Labour Before and After Slavery* (Dordrecht, 1986), pp. 33–54; David W. Galenson, *White Servitude in Colonial America: An Economic Analysis* (Cambridge, 1981), pp. 4, 23–50, 81–96.

[4] See sources, Table 2.1.

TABLE 2.2. *Emigration from the British Isles to the thirteen colonies, 1700–1775* (decennial estimates)

Decade	England and Wales	Scotland	N. Ireland	S. Ireland	Total
1700–09	700	200	600	800	2,300
1710–19	2,200	500	1,200	1,700	5,600
1720–29	3,700	800	2,100	3,000	9,600
1730–39	8,100	2,000	4,400	7,400	21,900
1740–49	12,400	3,100	9,200	9,100	33,800
1750–59	14,600	3,700	14,200	8,100	40,600
1760–69	19,700	10,000	21,200	8,500	59,400
1770–75	11,700	15,000	13,200	3,900	43,800
TOTAL	73,100	35,300	66,100	42,500	217,000

Source: Adapted from Fogelman, 'Migrations to the American Colonies', Table 1, p. 698.

start to the century, the gathering pace of movement in the 1730s and 1740s, and the tremendous wave of emigration that washed across the British Isles from the Shetlands to Kinsale in the quarter of a century before the outbreak of the American War.[5]

No reliable statistics are available for the post-war period, but it appears that immigration rose sharply after 1783. Irish immigrants to the United States, Newfoundland, and New Brunswick (chiefly from Ulster) may well have exceeded 100,000–150,000 alone between 1780 and 1815, compared to modest levels of English, Welsh, and Scottish emigration. Growing anxiety about the haemorrhage of manpower during a time when the population was needed at home inclined the government to discourage emigration until after the French wars, favouring instead the employment of itinerants and the poor in vital industries or in the military. Most Scottish emigrants in this period were drawn from the Highlands (approximately 10,000 out of 15,000) and went to the Maritime Provinces, notably the north-east shore of Nova Scotia, Cape Breton, and Prince Edward Isle (formerly St John's), or to eastern Upper Canada where Scottish communities already existed (see Map. 17.1). They joined the surge of Loyalist emigration from the United States in which tens of thousands of civilians, former army officers and men, together with several thousand free blacks and Indians migrated to lands administered under the British Loyalist assistance scheme.[6]

---

[5] Aaron Fogelman, 'Migrations to the Thirteen British North American Colonies, 1700–1775: New Estimates', *Journal of Interdisciplinary History*, XXII (1992), Table 1, p. 698.

[6] Henry A. Gemery, 'The White Population of the Colonial United States, 1607–1790', in Michael R. Haines and Richard H. Steckel, eds., *A Population History of North America* (Cambridge, forthcoming),

War had a significant impact on the rate of emigration and development of transoceanic commerce. Britain was involved in seven large-scale conflicts between 1688 and 1815, making up sixty-two years of the period. All the major series of emigration records exhibit troughs during war years, followed by peaks in the immediate aftermath. Hostilities disrupted trade, cut off markets, and forced up shipping costs. The expansion of England's overseas trade, a marked feature of the previous fifty years, came to a halt in the late 1680s and the growth of the English mercantile marine slowed for the next half-century. During the War of the League of Augsburg (1688–97) and the War of the Spanish Succession (1702–13) freight and insurance charges on tobacco and sugar more than doubled, causing the volume of exports and quantity of shipping to fall. Post-war recessions punctuated the course of colonial trade throughout the century as colonies re-adjusted to peacetime conditions after years of disruption and conflict.

Slumps in emigration during wartime were a consequence also of the rapid expansion of the military which absorbed enormous numbers of men. British armed forces increased from around 135,000 in the early eighteenth century to approaching 200,000 during the Seven Years War and over 400,000 by 1812. Although a significant proportion recruited or pressed into the army and navy were foreigners, nevertheless the drain on the domestic male population between the ages of 18 and 55 remained considerable. Throughout the century the military was both a major competitor with the colonies for manpower and a vital stimulus of emigration. In periods of war the supply of prime indentured servants dwindled, but in the aftermath tens of thousands of ex-servicemen were thrown on to a saturated labour market and the servant trade quickly revived.[7] The Imperial struggle with France and strategic interests along the Atlantic coast of Canada encouraged the British government to become directly involved in pro-moting settlement. Using public funds, an expedition of 2,500 settlers to Nova Scotia was mounted in 1749 of whom a quarter were men recently disbanded from 'His Majesty's land and sea service'. After the end of the Seven Years War more than a dozen colonial and Highland regiments were brought to the areas around St John

---

Table 8; Kerby A. Miller, *Emigrants and Exiles: Ireland and the Irish Exodus to North America* (Oxford, 1985), p. 169; Maldwyn A. Jones, 'Ulster Emigration, 1783–1815', in E. R. R. Green, ed., *Scotch-Irish History* (New York, 1969), p. 49; T. C. Smout, N. C. Landsman, and T. M. Devine, 'Scottish Emigration in the Seventeenth and Eighteenth Centuries', in Nicholas Canny, ed., *Europeans on the Move: Studies on European Migration, 1500–1800* (Oxford, 1994), pp. 97, 102. For British North America after 1783, see below pp. 381–82.

[7] Farley Grubb and Tony Stitt, 'The Liverpool Emigrant Servant Trade and the Transition to Slave Labour in the Chesapeake, 1697–1707: Market Adjustments to War', *Explorations in Economic History*, XXI (1994), pp. 388–91; Linda Colley, *Britons: Forging the Nation, 1707–1837* (London, 1992), pp. 101, 286–87; John Brewer, *The Sinews of Power: War, Money, and the English State, 1688–1783* (London, 1989), pp. 30–32. Colquhoun, *Treatise*, p. 47.

and Fredericton, and elsewhere thousands of Scots, Scots-Irish, and Catholic Irish who had served in the campaigns of 1756–63 and 1776–83 settled in the South, western Pennsylvania, New York, on the New England frontier, and in Canada.[8]

North America and the West Indies attracted the great majority of British emigrants during the century, but conquests and the acquisition of territories in Africa, Asia, and Australia created new possibilities for those who chose (or were forced) to work overseas. The expansion of Britain's Empire in the second half of the eighteenth century extended the range of options open to prospective migrants for settlement, trade, and service. Compared to the New World, immigration to Africa and Asia was small-scale throughout the early modern period, a reflection of very different conditions encountered by Europeans in the eastern hemisphere. In the multicultural and heterogeneous trading systems of the west coast of Africa and the Indian Ocean, British merchants were not only engaged in cut-throat competition for long-distance and 'country' trade with other Europeans (notably the Portuguese, Dutch, and French), but also with African and Asian merchants who remained highly effective at least until the late eighteenth century. Not until the 1750s and 1760s did the British assume a significant territorial presence in India, and not until the nineteenth century was there a sustained effort to bring territories in the Far East and Africa under direct Crown control.

British settlements in Africa and Asia were largely the outcome of private monopolistic initiatives to establish and maintain highly profitable commerce. Botany Bay was different again. It was not settled as a trading post, despite a few grandiose paper projects, and neither did it have much strategic significance, lying too far to the south of established shipping lanes and commercial centres to exert any influence. The principal reason for the colony was to rid Britain of dangerous felons.[9] Like the tattered army of masterless men a century before, growing populations of criminals incarcerated in gaols and prison hulks were perceived as an alarming threat to public order and private property. Under the terms of the Transportation Act (4 Geo. I, c. 11), some 49,000 felons from England and Ireland were removed to the American colonies between 1718 and 1775. After the Revolution, Botany Bay replaced America as the principal destination of Britain's convicts. Nearly 12,000 men and women were transported between 1787 and 1810, at the rate of 500 to 1,500 a year, and another 17,400 were banished between 1811 and 1820. On the other side of the world, five months sailing time from London, a new kind of colony emerged, sponsored by the government and designed specifically as

---

[8] Helen I. Cowan, *British Emigration to British North America: The First Hundred Years* (Toronto, 1961 edn.), pp. 4–12; J. M. Bumsted, *The Peoples of Canada*, Vol. I, *A Pre-Confederation History* (Toronto, 1992) pp. 121–23. D. Campbell and R. A. MacLean, *Beyond the Atlantic Roar: A Study of the Nova Scotia Scots* (Toronto, 1974), pp. 38–58.

[9] See below, pp. 566–67.

a distant prison camp from which the chances of return to Britain were as remote as the place itself.

Leaving Home

Despite a decline in numbers compared to the previous century, indentured servants (including convicts) continued to make up the majority of emigrants from the British Isles to America until the Revolution. Nearly 70 per cent of migrants from England in 1773–76 were servants and it is probable that a similar proportion applies earlier in the century.[10] Contemporary opinion was generally critical, describing them variously as beggars, petty criminals, prostitutes, and riffraff swept from city slums and port towns. 'The generality of the inhabitants in this Province', William Eddis wrote from Maryland in 1770, 'conceive an opinion that the difference is merely nominal between the indented servant and the convicted felon.'[11] Occupations of male servants who emigrated from Bristol and London in the late seventeenth and eighteenth centuries, however, reveal a trend towards more respectable, if modest, social origins (Table 2.3). Across the period, the proportion of men from skilled and semi-skilled backgrounds rose steadily, while the number of servants from unskilled work or those registered without a designated occupation (an indication of low status) fell. On the eve of the American Revolution, less than a fifth of male servants were described as labourers compared to 69 per cent from artisanal and service backgrounds. According to Bernard Bailyn, there was no mass exodus of 'destitute unskilled urban slum dwellers and uprooted peasants' from either England or Scotland, rather movement was characterized by 'certain segments of the lower middle and working classes, artisans, and craftsmen with employable skills, for whom emigration would seem to have represented not so much a desperate escape as an opportunity to be reached for'.[12]

Yet, if by the end of the colonial period the social origins of servants had shifted from the lower to lower-middle classes, it is unlikely that the transition occurred much before 1760. While changes in occupations indicate a steady fall in the numbers of the unskilled, the average age of male servants (19 to 20 years, 1718–59) nevertheless suggests that most occupied a relatively humble status.[13] By the Seven Years War factors promoting migration may have shifted towards pursuit of opportunities in the New World, but there were still many for whom emigration

[10] Bernard Bailyn, *Voyagers to the West: A Passage in the Peopling of America on the Eve of the American Revolution* (New York, 1986), pp. 166, 175–76.

[11] Aubrey C. Land, ed., *Letters from America by William Eddis* (Cambridge, Mass., 1969), pp. 37–38.

[12] Bailyn, *Voyagers*, p. 160; Galenson, *White Servitude*, pp. 35, 40, 52, 57.

[13] The average age of those departing in the 1680s was 21 to 22 years and 21 to 23 between 1773–75.

TABLE 2.3. *Occupations of male servants who emigrated from Bristol and London to America, 1683–1775* (%)

Category	Bristol 1684–86 (N 369)	London 1683–84 (N 655)	London 1718–59 (N 3,013)	London 1773–75 (N 3,359)
Agriculture	4	9	11	16
Food and Drink	2	2	4	7
Metal, Wood, and Construction	7	6	18	29
Textiles and Clothing	15	8	14	19
Services	2	10	10	14
Labourer	12	5	6	15
Not Given	58	60	37	0

Source: Adapted from Galenson, *White Servitude*, Tables 3.1, 3.3, 4.1, 4.5, pp. 35, 40, 52, 57.

constituted a last hope to throw off the hardship and lack of prospects which dogged them at home. For those whose expectations of earning a living in London, Bristol, and other port towns quickly faded as they tramped the streets in a vain attempt to find work, the colonies provided a final gamble in the search for subsistence.

One such emigrant was William Roberts, an indentured servant who embarked for America in the spring of 1756. His background is obscure, but at the time of departure he was young, single, and living in London, possibly with his parents. He had evidently fallen on hard times. His coat and some other clothes had been pawned, and he described his shoes as so worn 'they will hardly keep upon my feet'. The particular reasons that prompted him to emigrate are unknown, but it appears he was out of work and had little immediate prospect of finding any. A wealthy uncle, apparently unwilling to help him at home, promised to provide support should he go to the colonies. In a letter written to his parents several years later, Roberts recalled the 'find Stores [fine stories] of what he doo for me but I have Receive non[e] nor yett a Letter'. He ended up in Maryland where, after serving his term, he spent the rest of his life working as a smallholder raising tobacco, never escaping the poverty that stigmatized his life as a young man in London.[14]

Free emigrants (unencumbered by indentures) who left for America came from an equally wide range of backgrounds as servants, but there was a clear preponderance of men from mercantile and trading occupations. A regular flow of merchants, petty traders, and factors from England's major ports made their

[14] James Horn, 'The Letters of William Roberts of All Hallows Parish, Anne Arundel County, Maryland, 1756–1769', *Maryland Historical Magazine*, LXXIV (1979), pp. 117–32.

way to the colonies from Florida to Nova Scotia to set up on their own account or represent established businesses. Of 181 men who went to Virginia between 1689 and 1815, the majority (59 per cent) described themselves as merchants and mariners, just over a fifth were professionals (ministers, surgeons, and apothecaries), and the remainder came from a miscellany of backgrounds ranging from shipwrights, cooks, and grocers to gentlemen.[15] With the increasing volume of trade and the expansion of territory, especially after 1763, growing numbers of young men from the upper and middle classes moved to the colonies to work in trade and business or to take up posts in the military and provincial government.

Emigrants came from all over the country, but London and the surrounding counties stand out as particularly important. Between 1718 and 1759, from a quarter to 41 per cent of indentured servants were from London and another 12 per cent came from the Home Counties and south-east England (Table 2.4).[16] Similarly, in the 1770s over half of all English emigrants, free and unfree, were from the city and its environs. As in the seventeenth century, the attraction of London can be attributed to the prospects it offered to thousands of hopefuls who streamed into the city every year from all parts of the British Isles to take up positions or look for work, swelling the population to around three-quarters of a million by 1775. Many poor emigrants were drawn from new arrivals who 'arrived in waggon loads' daily and who, often disoriented and friendless, were unable to find a niche for themselves in the hurly-burly of metropolitan life. In the mid-eighteenth century it was said that if newcomers 'cannot get such employment as they expected or chuse to follow, many of them will not go home to be laughed at...but enlist for soldiers, go to the plantations Etc. if they are well inclined; otherwise they probably commence thieves and pickpockets'. An enormous pool of unemployed men, women, and children, an inevitable consequence of the irregularity of work, provided a dependable source of cheap, surplus labour ripe for the picking as potential colonists.[17] By the 1770s, prospects may have improved for lower-class emigrants. As noted earlier, the majority came from skilled and semi-skilled backgrounds rather than the desperate urban poor, and there was frequently little to distinguish them from free artisans and tradesmen who left at the same time for similar reasons.

---

[15] Colonial Williamsburg Foundation, CVRP, Wills; W. G. Stanard, comp., *Some Emigrants to Virginia...*(Richmond, Va., 1915), pp. 7–94; Ian Charles Cargill Graham, *Colonists from Scotland: Emigration to North America, 1707–1783* (Ithaca, NY, 1956), pp. 117–18.

[16] John Wareing, 'Migration to London and Transatlantic Emigration of Indentured Servants, 1683–1775', *Journal of Historical Geography*, VII (1981), p. 369.

[17] Bailyn, *Voyagers*, pp. 107–10, 271–85; M. Dorothy George, *London Life in the XVIIIth Century* (London, 1925), p. 347, n. 2. Over half of transported convicts who boarded ship in England, 1718–75, were from London and neighbouring counties. A. Roger Ekirch, *Bound for America: The Transportation of British Convicts to the Colonies, 1718–75* (Oxford, 1987), pp. 23–24.

TABLE 2.4. *Regional origins of indentured servants who emigrated from London to America, 1684–1759* (%)

Region	1684–86 (N 1,114)	1718–29 (N 1,412)	1730–39 (N 1,497)	1749–59 (N 260)
London	41	35	41	27
Home Counties and South-East	11	12	12	12
Midlands	14	15	12	17
Eastern Counties	4	6	5	2
North	12	11	12	12
South West	10	13	9	15
Wales	1	2	2	2
Other	7	7	8	14

Source: Adapted from Wareing, 'Migration to London and Transatlantic Emigration', *Journal of Historical Geography*, VII (1981), Table 1, p. 369.

Outside London and the south-east, the most important source of English emigrants on the eve of the American Revolution was Yorkshire. Bailyn has argued that the character of Yorkshire emigration was significantly different from that of southern and central England and labels the two migrations as 'provincial' and 'metropolitan'. In the latter, emigrants were predominantly single young men who went to the colonies as indentured servants, most serving in Virginia and Maryland. Provincial emigrants were typically independent householders from farming backgrounds who migrated in family groups to New York, North Carolina, and Nova Scotia. Rent increases were instrumental in persuading many hard-pressed tenant farmers from the East and North Ridings of Yorkshire to leave, encouraged by the activities of entrepreneurs and land speculators who held out favourable prospects of prime land at reasonable rates in America. Letters sent back to Yorkshire by migrants urged kin and friends to join them in the colonies. In Nova Scotia clusters of Yorkshire families settled in the Cumberland Basin, on Shepody Bay, and along the Petitcodiac River, where they intermarried and established new generations, gradually mixing with Scottish, Irish, German, American, and Acadian settlers.[18]

Across much of the period, Welsh emigration can be accounted part of the broader English movement. From similar backgrounds and leaving for similar reasons, Welsh migrants who moved to London, Bristol, Liverpool, and the lesser outports went to America alongside thousands of their English contemporaries and, apart from (in some cases) distinctive surnames, are largely indistinguishable from them. An important exception was the movement of Nonconformists,

[18] Bailyn, *Voyagers*, pp. 201–07; 361–429.

notably Quakers and Baptists. Quakerism spread rapidly throughout Welsh-speaking rural areas in the second half of the seventeenth century, particularly in central and north-west Wales. Approximately 2,000 Friends left for America between 1682 and 1700, of whom the majority went to Pennsylvania, encouraged by the Quaker William Penn, where they settled west of the Schuylkill River in an area called the 'Welsh Tract'. The strengthening of transatlantic connections facilitated a steady if modest flow of Dissenters, principally to Pennsylvania, Delaware, and West Jersey, well into the eighteenth century, attracted by the prospect of economic opportunities as well as religious toleration. By 1770 there may have been as many as 300 Baptist churches in mainland America, and Welsh (or Welsh-Americans) were prominent among their leaders.

A resurgence of Dissent in the final decades of the eighteenth century, together with harvest failures and economic dislocation following the outbreak of the French wars, created the conditions for an abrupt upturn in emigration during the 1790s. In north Wales, where a new missionary crusade by Baptists and Methodists was under way, the 'talk of the whole country' was of 'the war and emigration'. George Lewis, an Independent minister of Caernarfon, wrote in the autumn of 1793 of political disabilities suffered by Dissenters, high rents, and burdensome taxes. 'Tythes for the maintenance of the established clergy are so heavy,' he complained, 'the common people find it extremely difficult to procure the necessities of life.' 'The oppressed poor', Joshua Thomas reported earlier in the year, 'are too poor to pay their Passage . . .', and could not raise the fare even if they were 'to sell all they have'. Not one in twenty, a contemporary reckoned, had 'the means of conveying himself and his family to a land of Plenty'. Rather than the desperate rural poor, it was the lower-middling and middling classes—small farmers and artisans hit hard by crop failures, famine prices, and industrial disruption, together with Nonconformist ministers seeking liberty of conscience and better livings—who emigrated. Many were spurred on by fear of financial ruin or religious persecution, but some took with them the precious dream of a new 'Cambria in the American West', where they could live and worship together in liberty, free from political oppression by the British government. In the event, the vision of a separatist Welsh-speaking homeland had no more success in the United States than it did in Britain, and quickly faded after the collapse of the utopian Welsh settlement of Beulah, Pennsylvania.[19]

---

[19] For Welsh emigration generally, see A. H. Dodd, *The Character of the Early Welsh Emigration to the United States*, 2nd edn. (Cardiff, 1957). H. M. Davies, '"Very Different Springs of Uneasiness": Emigration from Wales to the United States of America during the 1790s', *Welsh History Review*, XV (1991), pp. 370–71, 377–84, 395; Gwyn A. Williams, *The Search for Beulah Land: The Welsh and the Atlantic Revolution* (London, 1980), pp. 20–21, 130–34, 147, 163. I am grateful to Huw Bowen for his advice.

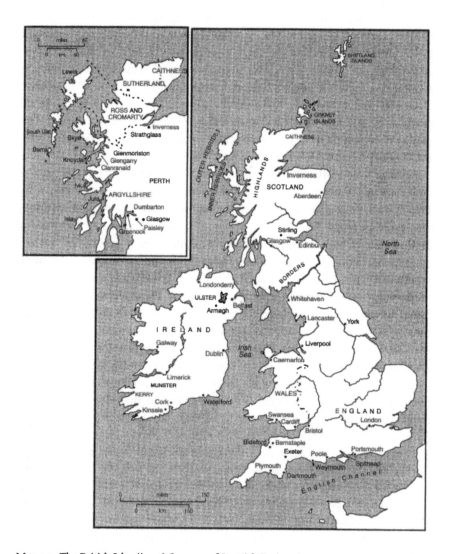

Map 2.1. The British Isles (inset) Sources of Scottish Emigration

Scottish emigration in the eighteenth and early nineteenth centuries was composed of two very different movements from the Lowlands and Highlands.
Sustained Lowland migration to America began in the 1680s and 1690s with
small-scale attempts to establish settlements in East Jersey, South Carolina, and
Darien, but not until the second quarter of the eighteenth century did traffic across

the Atlantic develop into significant proportions. Spurred on by the economic advantages that accrued in the years following the Union of Parliaments in 1707, merchants, manufacturers, and professional men quickly took advantage of partnership in one of the most extensive trading empires in the world. The growing contribution of Scotland to the metropolitan economy affected all parts of the country but was particularly noticeable in the Lowlands, where the concentration of towns, population, mineral resources, prime farming land, and capital accentuated age-old cultural differences with the Highlands. As elsewhere in Scotland and the British Isles, the pulse of emigration quickened dramatically after the end of the Seven Years War, and the Lowlands contributed about 30,000 migrants to the transatlantic stream between 1763 and 1775 alone, most of whom ended up in the American backcountry and Canada.[20]

Scottish merchants were especially prominent in the Chesapeake tobacco trade, establishing a network of stores at the head of navigable rivers and purchasing directly from planters to whom they supplied credit and goods. Glasgow firms such as Cunninghame, Speirs, Glassford, Buchanan, and Simson played a vital role in the expansion of tobacco cultivation into the piedmont (foothills) and in the development of the cargo trade. By the 1730s Clydeside tobacco merchants rivalled their English competitors in Bristol and Whitehaven, and by 1760 Glasgow had overtaken London as Britain's premier tobacco port. 'I observe', Philip Fithian wrote from Virginia in 1773, 'that all the Merchants and shopkeepers...through the Province, are young Scotch-men...' Besides merchants and storekeepers, educated Scots established themselves throughout the Carolinas, Middle Colonies, backcountry, Canada, and the West Indies, as attorneys, surgeons, teachers, and ministers. Virtually the entire colonial medical profession was Scottish-trained and more than 150 Scottish doctors emigrated to America during the century. Scottish ministers dominated the Presbyterian and Anglican churches and Scottish tutors were widespread throughout the middle and southern colonies. The emigration of the educated and skilled reflected a 'growing sense among Scotland's upper and middle classes of an emerging affinity between Scotland and America as linked provincial societies' within the Empire.[21]

---

[20] Eric Richards, 'Scotland and the Uses of the Atlantic Empire', in Bernard Bailyn and Philip D. Morgan, eds., *Strangers Within the Realm: Cultural Margins of the First British Empire* (Chapel Hill, NC, 1991), pp. 67–114.

[21] Jacob M. Price, 'The Rise of Glasgow in the Chesapeake Tobacco Trade, 1707–1775', *William and Mary Quarterly*, Third Series, XI (1954), pp. 179–99; T. M. Devine, *The Tobacco Lords: A Study of the Tobacco Merchants of Glasgow and their Trading Activities* (Edinburgh, 1975); Hunter Dickinson Farish, ed., *Journal and Letters of Philip Vickers Fithian: A Plantation Tutor of the Old Dominion, 1773–1774* (Charlottesville, Va., 1957), p. 29; W. R. Brock, *Scotus Americanus: A Survey of the Sources for Links Between Scotland and America in the Eighteenth Century* (Edinburgh, 1982), chaps. 3, 5–6; Smout, Landsman and Devine, 'Scottish Emigration', in Canny, ed., *Europeans on the Move*, pp. 90–100.

Throughout the period substantial emigration took place from the western parts of the Borders. During the seventeenth century, Galloway—the counties of Wigtown, Kirkcudbright, and Dumfries—supplied thousands of migrants to Ireland, attracted by the prospect of good, fertile land and cheap rents. Migration to America in the following century was an extension of the trend: the impulse was the same but the direction of movement had altered. Owing to the consolidation of farms, removal of subtenancies, and tighter regulations governing conditions of entry and tenancy, access to smallholdings became increasingly restrictive. Large-scale sheep farming was introduced into southern Scotland in the first quarter of the century, and one outcome, according to Revd Robert Woodrow, was 'certain great depopulations...and multitudes of familys turned out of their tacks and sent a-wandering'. As agrarian and industrial change accelerated during the second half of the century, especially after 1780, so added impetus was given to intra-regional migration and to the flow of commerce and people overseas.[22]

Migration was also significant from the industrial regions of the West Lowlands, where unemployment was a major cause of large numbers of artisans leaving textile centres such as Glasgow, Greenock, and Paisley during the 1770s. The financial crisis and failure of the Ayr Bank in 1772–73 led to a widespread and intense depression, reducing thousands of cloth workers 'to the utmost distress for want of employ', many of whom were forced to emigrate 'to prevent them from starving'. In the spring of 1774 a Glasgow gentleman wrote that the 'distress of the common people here is deeper and more general than you can imagine. There is an almost total stagnation in our manufactures, and grain is dear; many hundreds of labourers and mechanics, especially weavers in this neighbourhood, have lately indented and gone to America...' In February the *Commerce* left Greenock for New York with seventy-seven weavers and their families from Paisley and thirty-three persons of various trades from Glasgow who reported their reason for going as 'Poverty and to get Bread'. Similarly, poverty was the main reason for the departure of 147 emigrants from the Borders and Glasgow three months later. Alongside the exodus of the poor were migrants from modest backgrounds of the Clyde Valley who, affected by the slump in business following the 1772–73 crash, determined to seek their fortune in the colonies. Pooling resources, groups of tenant farmers from the shires of Renfrew, Dumbarton, and Stirling formed associations to fund their transportation and the purchase of land in

[22] T. M. Devine, 'Introduction: The Paradox of Scottish Emigration', in Devine ed., *Scottish Emigration and Scottish Society* (Edinburgh, 1992), p. 6; Devine, *The Transformation of Rural Scotland: Social Change and the Agrarian Economy, 1660–1815* (Edinburgh, 1994), pp. 165–66; Ian Adams and Meredyth Somerville, *Cargoes of Despair and Hope: Scottish Emigration to North America, 1603–1803* (Edinburgh, 1993), p. 25.

America. The Scots American Company of Farmers, known as the Inchinnan Company, took up a tract of 23,000 acres in Ryegate, New York, and sponsored the movement of settlers to the region, each paying their own costs according to their means.[23]

Emigration from the Scottish Highlands, of small proportions before mid-century, grew rapidly after the end of the Seven Years War and may have totalled 15,000–20,000 beween 1760 and 1775. On the eve of the American Revolution, approaching a fifth of all British emigrants were from the Highlands and islands off Scotland, second only to London as a source of migrants.[24] Migration was a response to the profound changes that swept the region following the Battle of Culloden in 1746, which transformed traditional society and released forces that were to have far-reaching consequences. Recent writers have emphasized the social impact of agrarian improvement and rent inflation after 1760. Higher rents were a simple and convenient method of increasing income, and lairds could claim it encouraged greater efficiency on the part of tenants by promoting productivity and reducing waste. Many landowners 'systematically subordinated their estates to the pursuit of profit', and in so doing brought about a fundamental realignment in the laird–tenant relationship, from one based on a finely graded system of reciprocal duties and loyalties to one founded on money and market rates. As the objective became to extract more income from the land, changes were introduced to make estates profitable—the expansion of sheep-walks, abolition of joint tenancy settlements, imposition of the croft system, and the commutation of rents in kind to cash—which undermined the traditional position of tacksmen, who held land directly from the chiefs and acted as their intermediaries, and of the tenantry whose military role was no longer relevant.[25]

Yet as contemporaries observed, higher rents and changes in land management did not create a dispossessed peasantry who moved to America out of sheer desperation. Josiah Tucker commented in 1773 that Highlanders who sailed from the north of Scotland and the islands 'were far from being the most indigent, or the least capable of subsisting in their own Country. No; it was not Poverty or Necessity which compelled but Ambition which enticed them to forsake their native Soil.' Touring the Inner Hebrides in the same year, Samuel Johnson noted that 'many men of considerable wealth have taken with them their train of labourers and dependants' to America. The *Scots Magazine* reported in the spring

---

[23] Bailyn, *Voyagers*, 198; Graham, *Colonists from Scotland*, pp. 25, 27–29.

[24] Bailyn, *Voyagers*, p. 111. J. M. Bumsted estimates 20,000–25,000 Scots, divided roughly equally between Lowlanders and Highlanders, emigrated to America, 1763–75, *The People's Clearance: Highland Emigration to British North America, 1770–1815* (Edinburgh, 1982), p. 9.

[25] T. M. Devine, 'Landlordism and Highland Emigration', in Devine ed., *Scottish Emigration*, pp. 93–94; Bumsted, *The People's Clearance*, pp. 2–6.

of 1771 that a 'large colony of the most wealthy and substantial people in Sky[e]' were 'making ready to follow [emigrants from Islay] in going to fertile and cheap lands on the other side of the Atlantic ocean'. It was the loss of men of substance and the rapidity with which the 'epidemick' desire of 'wandering' swept the glens in the 1770s that so alarmed commentators and which stimulated a wide-ranging public debate about the deleterious effect of emigration on Highland society and the depopulation of 'Old Caledon'.[26]

Three- or four-fold rent increases, set in the broader context of the commercialization of Highland agriculture, were undoubtedly a major stimulus to movement, but migrations from particular regions of western and northern Scotland suggest more complex reasons behind decisions to move. While the national rate of population increase between 1755 and the 1790s was relatively modest by western European standards, some regional populations did grow quickly. The population of western districts of mainland Highland shires such as Ross and Cromarty, Inverness, and Argyll, from where emigration was considerable, grew by 29 per cent between 1755 and 1801, and the population of the Western Isles increased by over 50 per cent. In the 1770s it was estimated that the land could provide work for only half the able men who lived in the Highlands. Movement to the Lowlands, cities, or military service were the usual outlets for the young, single, and landless, but from the mid-eighteenth century America became an increasingly attractive alternative. From 1749, with the establishment of Halifax, Nova Scotia, plans to settle colonies north of New England were put in place and elaborated after the conquest of French North America. North Carolina and New York remained the major destinations of migrants before 1775, but after the war Highlanders streamed into three regions already settled by their compatriots: the Isle of St John, the Pictou area of Nova Scotia, and the Glengarry district of Upper Canada.[27]

An impression of the reasons behind emigration can be found in the individual testimonies of men and women who left from a number of coastal villages in Sutherland aboard the *Bachelor* bound for North Carolina in 1774. William Gordon, a farmer of 60 years, left with his wife and six children, encouraged by two of his sons who were already in North Carolina. He complained that he was now paying sixty merks for land that had once cost eight and that he had suffered a serious loss of cattle in the harsh winter of 1771–72. He saw little hope of any immediate change for the better and had opted to leave to improve the prospects of his children. William MacKay, also a farmer, 37, from Caithness, had a brother

---

[26] Graham, *Colonists from Scotland*, pp. 39–41, 58–72; Bumsted, *The People's Clearance*, pp. 14–18.

[27] Bumsted, *The People's Clearance*, chaps. 2–3.

and sister in Carolina who had assured him that any 'sober industrious man could not fail of living comfortably, lands could be rented cheap, and ... the soil was fertile'. What finally persuaded him to go, however, were changes in the local economy: the collapse of the cattle market and a steep rise in rent. Letters received from settlers who had migrated from the region a year earlier promised a better living in America and had led to emigration becoming the 'sole topic of conversation, all over that part of Scotland'. Elizabeth Macdonald, a single woman of 29, a servant, believed quite simply that opportunities were better in Carolina and went to join her friends.[28]

As elsewhere in the British Isles, a combination of influences was responsible for the increasing rate of emigration in the early 1770s. The 'Black Winter' of 1771–72, the worst in living memory, led to cattle plague and crop failure and was followed by a wet winter the following year which produced serious food shortages. Bishop John Macdonald wrote in the spring of 1772 that there had been 'a great loss of Cattle and the prospect of great dearth of provisions everywhere in the Highlands, which will probably forward some thousands more to America'. Religious controversy was another significant influence on Highland emigration. Beginning with the Catholic migrations from the Clanranald estates of South Uist and adjacent mainland in 1772 following attempts by the local laird to enforce Presbyterianism on his tenants, over the next forty years thousands of Catholic migrants from the islands, Glengarry, Barra, and Strathglass took ship in the wake of rising rents and wholesale evictions. In May 1786 it was reported that 'Last year upward of 300 souls left Glengarry and its neighbourhood almost all Roman Catholics and settled in Canada above Mont-Real, where were already settled about 800 Highlanders...' Edward Fraser, customs collector at Inverness, commented in 1802 that 'Roman Catholics all over the West Coast are ready at a month's notice, if they can prevail on their priest to go'. By 1810 about one-third of the entire Catholic population had left the Highlands and Islands for America, 'to the irretrievable loss of Britain...'[29]

With the failure of Highland development schemes, the stepping up of clearances and further subdivision of holdings, emigration continued after the American War and surged briefly in the early years of the nineteenth century. Between 1801 and 1803, 7,000 migrants left for British North America, once again provoking government concern about the drain on population during a period of national

[28] Donald Mackay, *Scotland Farewell: The People of the Hector* (Toronto, 1980), pp. 62, 68–70; Bailyn, *Voyagers*, pp. 195–96, 508.
[29] Kathleen Toomey, 'Emigration from the Scottish Bounds, 1770–1810, and the Role of the Clergy', unpublished Ph.D. thesis, Edinburgh, 1991, pp. i, 90–94, 149, 169, 256; Adams and Somerville, *Cargoes of Despair and Hope*, pp. 63–71.

crisis. Many migrants from the shires of Perth and Argyll, like earlier settlers, complained of high rents, evictions, and 'Want of Employ'. Some were attracted to sponsored projects, such as those of the Earl of Selkirk at Baldoon, near Detroit, in 1804, and Red River, near Lake Winnipeg, which were intended to preserve Gaelic-speaking enclaves from the sort of pernicious commercial influences undermining traditional ways of life at home. For many Highlanders, emigration was not motivated primarily by considerations of material gain but was reluctantly per-ceived as a necessary, if painful, means 'to preserve in the New World that which was being destroyed in the Old'.[30]

Irish emigration shared much in common with that of Scotland and, at least in the case of Ulster, was intimately related. Three distinct trends had emerged by the time of the Treaty of Limerick: the beginnings of migrations of Protestant Dis-senters, notably Presbyterians and Quakers; a long-established trade in indentured servants, mostly Catholics; and the temporary migration of labourers and seamen to the Newfoundland fisheries.[31]

The first of the Ulster migrations took place between 1718 and 1720 when about 3,000 settlers left for the colonies, principally owing to the falling-in of generous leases granted by landowners in the 1690s to attract Scottish immigrants. Alex-ander McCulloch wrote to his landlord in September 1718 and reported that 'a great many in this cuntry ar[e] going thither [America] (having the great incour-eagment from ther freinds that ar[e] gon)'. Such were his own 'misfortouns' that he was determined to go himself. Crop failure, cattle disease, and high food prices brought people in many areas to the brink of famine and left the 'dismal marks of hunger and want' etched on their faces. A similar combination of high rents and disastrous harvests, together with a slump in the linen industy, persuaded thou-sands more to leave between 1725 and 1729. Reminiscent of Dr Johnson's Hebri-dean 'epidemick' nearly half a century later, Hugh Boulter, Archbishop of Armagh, wrote in 1728 of an infatuation with emigration. 'We have had three bad harvests together... The humour has spread like a contagious distemper, and the people will hardly hear anybody that tries to cure them of their madness.' Severe food shortages and 'dearness of provision' reduced many small farmers and labourers to destitution, encouraging thousands to take up indentures for service in America rather than starving at home. The 'richer sort', it was reported in 1729, believed 'that if they stay in Ireland their children will be slaves and that it is better for them

---

[30] Bumsted, *The People's Clearance*, pp. 188–213, 220; Smout, Landsman and Devine, 'Scottish Emigration', in Canny, ed., *Europeans on the Move*, pp. 110–11.

[31] Audrey Lockhart, *Some Aspects of Emigration from Ireland to the North American Colonies between 1660 and 1775* (New York, 1975), p. 15.

to make money of their leases while they are still worth something to inable them to transport themselves and familys to America', than be subjected to the same poverty as their under-tenants. During the 1730s the tide of migration receded, but after two wet and cold summers famine struck again in 1741, followed by epidemics of 'fluxes and malignant fevers which swept off multitudes of all sorts; whole villages laid waste by want and sickness and death in various shapes'. Possibly as many as 300,000 died in what was remembered for generations as *bliadhain an 'air*, year of slaughter, the worst natural disaster to befall the country before the Great Famine.[32]

Continued efforts by landlords to improve their land and the value of rentals, together with periodic famine and the ensuing spiralling cost of food, created the basic preconditions underlying Protestant emigration down to mid-century. In addition, slumps in the linen industry had an increasingly important effect on the lives of thousands of poor cottier-weavers who had multiplied rapidly in the province after 1720. During the climax of Ulster emigration between 1770 and 1775, a severe recession put roughly a third of weavers in the region out of work. Across the eighteenth century, the rapid commercialization of Ulster's economy caused the emiseration of large numbers of the most vulnerable sections of the working classes in town and country alike, and explains why at least half of Protestant emigrants, the displaced poor condemned by contemporaries as idle and worthless, could not raise their passage money and went to America as indentured servants or 'redemptioners' (servants given the opportunity to buy their freedom by paying the cost of their passage shortly after arrival).

Besides these negative influences a number of more positive developments emerged during the period. The growing importance of the provision trade in beef, pork, and butter, and increasing shipments of manufactured goods after mid-century, linked the region to an array of American ports and offered migrants a variety of destinations for starting out life anew. To a degree, emigration became self-sustaining. Some colonies, such as South Carolina and Georgia, offered cheap land and other inducements to immigrants willing to settle in the backcountry. Letters from migrants encouraging families, relatives, and friends to follow in their wake became more compelling in the context of commercial and territorial expansion after 1760.[33]

[32] R. J. Dickson, *Ulster Emigration to Colonial America, 1718–1775* (London, 1966), p. 33; S[cottish] R[ecord] O[ffice], GD 10 14121 1/46; Miller, *Emigrants and Exiles*, p. 153; J. L. McCracken, 'The Social Structure and Social Life, 1714–1760', in T. W. Moody and W. E. Vaughan, eds., *A New History of Ireland*, vol. IV, *Eighteenth-Century Ireland, 1691–1800* (Oxford, 1986), pp. 33–34.
[33] Marianne S. Wokeck, 'German and Irish Immigration to Colonial Philadelphia', *Proceedings of the American Philososphical Society*, CXXXIII (1989), p. 134; Miller, *Emigrants and Exiles*, chap. 4.

Accounts of migration from northern Ireland have tended to overshadow movement from other parts of the country during the century. Catholic migration was not as large as the better-known Protestant movement, but recent estimates suggest that about 45,000 emigrants left southern Ireland between 1700 and 1780, compared to 70,000 from Ulster. Some leaving from southern ports, such as Dublin, Cork, and Kinsale, were Protestant, but it is likely that Catholics made up at least 25–30 per cent of the total flow in the period. General conditions that affected Ulster migration also affected Catholic migration. Famine and weak markets led to indebtedness and poverty in the countryside until economic recovery in the 1740s. Even after the economy broke free of the cycles of depression and stagnation which had afflicted it since the 1690s, periodic slumps could have severe consequences in the short term. Major reasons given for the migration of 1753, when approximately 4,000 people left Dublin for America, were 'Want of Tillage' and the depression of the local linen industry. Agrarian discontent in the 1760s in Munster, which led the Whiteboys to strike at high tithes, rack-rents, taxes, and enclosure, took place against a background of recurrent crop failures. Viscount Weymouth, Lord Lieutenant of Ireland, reported in 1769 that 3,800 looms had fallen into disuse in Cork and its neighbourhood owing to the illegal importations of calicoes from India. Many of the unemployed and starving emigrated. Similarly, the major depression in the linen industry of 1772–73 (which also affected Scotland) caused substantial emigration from manufacturing areas in south and west Ireland.[34]

In certain respects, of course, the Catholic experience was at variance with that of Protestants. Presbyterians might believe that they were the victims of discriminatory policies of the Anglican Ascendancy just as were Catholics, but they were not subject to the same limitations with respect to inheritance of property, security of tenure, and the right to vote, introduced in the early eighteenth century to contain the Catholic presence in Irish life. Neither had they suffered from dispossession and removal from their lands which characterized the English 'conquest' of Ireland in the seventeenth century. Nevertheless, it would be misleading to represent Catholic emigration in the eighteenth century as a religious hegira from persecution and oppression, just as to contrast the localism and dependence of the Catholic peasantry with assertive and independent Presbyterian emigrants is a simplification of complex events. Throughout the period, large numbers of recruits for the colonies, Catholic and Protestant, were drawn from the lower ranks of society—labourers, small farmers, cottier-weavers, and artisans—who, to varying degrees, had little to lose by emigrating. The fortunes of Irish settlers in

---

[34] L. M. Cullen, 'The Irish Diaspora of the Seventeenth and Eighteenth Centuries', in Canny, ed., *Europeans on the Move*, pp. 113–49; Lockhart, *Some Aspects of Emigration from Ireland*, pp. 22, 50–58.

America depended in the long run less on their religious convictions than on the development of strong local economies and the health of the Atlantic commercial community.[35]

A key characteristic of the post-1760 period was the increasing numbers of skilled and independent migrants, 'exercising real choice' in opting to leave Ireland, against a background of growing prosperity and trade. As commerce flourished and channels of communication were strengthened, so the cost of passage fell and the colonies became increasingly attractive and accessible. At the very least, 69,000 settlers emigrated between 1750 and 1775 and double that number from the end of the American War to 1815. The majority who left after 1780, farmers and artisans of middling status, may well have seen possibilities in the new United States or British North America unattainable at home. But alongside migrants of 'comfortable circumstances' was a steady flow of poorer people who had fallen victim to the periodic recessions, such as those of 1801–02 and 1810–14. More ominous were growing signs in the early nineteenth century of industrial decay across a wide range of manufactures which could not compete with cheap English imports. Rapid population growth, industrial atrophy, and entrenched rural poverty in those areas where subdivision of land led to bare subsistence agriculture proved harbingers of a greater tragedy yet to come.[36]

The Lure of Empire

Swept up in the vortices of long-distance trade and inter-colonial rivalries, most emigrants who left Britain during the eighteenth century settled in New World colonies as merchants, planters, field-hands, and farmers, or served with the great mercantile company in the East. As in the previous century, merchants were responsible for the transportation of the mass of settlers, servants, and slaves to America, and provided the financial backing necessary for territorial expansion in pursuit of profit. Thousands of factors and supercargoes emigrated to set up merchant houses, country stores, and plantations, frequently in transatlantic partnerships. Alongside them from all parts of Britain was a steady flow of professional men and artisans—teachers, doctors, accountants, ministers, weavers, smiths, carpenters, and others—in continual demand as the colonies expanded and matured. They, like independent farmers and tenants, took ship in the expectation of a better life for themselves and their families or, in less happy cases, emigrated in a last gamble to escape financial ruin.

[35] R. F. Foster, 'Ascendancy and Union', in Foster, ed., *The Oxford History of Ireland* (Oxford, 1992), pp. 136–38; Miller, *Emigrants and Exiles*, pp. 140–68.

[36] Cullen, 'Irish Diaspora', in Canny, ed., *Europeans on the Move*, pp. 143–48; Miller, *Emigrants and Exiles*, chap. 5.

A large proportion of migrants, perhaps as many as a half, went to America as indentured servants and remained an important source of labour despite the large increase in slave importations during the period. Many were drawn from the middle and upper ranks of the lower classes, working men and women who could not afford the cost of passage but who believed that opportunities in the colonies were brighter than at home. At the lower end were those 'of no occupation', or 'the very meanest of People', who emigrated out of desperation during years of food shortages and industrial depression. Emigration by the poor, free and unfree, represented one response to the growing commercialization of society that affected many regions of the British Isles after 1760, but which was particularly significant in the Highlands and manufacturing districts of the western Lowlands and Ulster. Far from restraining migration by providing new employment, agri-cultural improvement and industrialization stimulated a continuing exodus of people unable to find work at home or who sought to conserve traditional ways of life in New World settings.[37]

Between 1689 and 1815, well over a million Europeans moved to mainland North America and the British West Indies, the first great surge beginning in the 1750s and the next after the American wars. Hundreds of thousands of settlers from the British Isles, the Rhineland, Swiss cantons, and other German-speaking territories of western and central Europe poured into the backcountry, pushing across the Susquehanna River into the rich lands of the Cumberland Valley, south along the Great Wagon Road to the Shenandoah Valley, the Carolinas, and Georgia, and beyond the Appalachians to the vast expanse of the Ohio River basin (see Map 13.1). The American Revolution produced its own convulsion of movement, unleashing centrifugal forces that were to have an enduring impact on the new republic and remaining British possessions in America. Tens of thousands of civilians, black and white, fled from the thirteen colonies to other parts of the Atlantic rim during the conflict, while tens of thousands more trekked further into the American interior once the war was over, to Kentucky, Tennessee, and the central plains, foreshadowing the major westward migrations of the nineteenth century. All along the expanding frontier, Irish, German, Swiss, Highland Scots, English, and Welsh settlers, together with African slaves and local Indian tribes, evolved as locally distinctive societies, where ethnic diversity and the continual movement of people in and out were taken for granted.[38]

As the Empire reached its apogee, so contrasts in the experiences of migrants became increasingly evident. 'I take the first opportunity that has been given us', wrote a female convict from Botany Bay in 1788, 'to acquaint you with our

---

[37] Devine, 'Paradox of Scottish Emigration', in Devine ed., *Scottish Emigration*, p. 6.
[38] Bailyn, *Voyagers*, pp. 24–28.

disconsolate situation in this solitary waste of the creation. Our passage...was tolerably favourable; but the inconveniences since suffered for want of shelter, bedding Etc., are not to be imagined by any stranger.' Everyone, she continued, 'is so taken up with their own misfortunes that they have no pity to bestow upon others'. On the other side of the world, fifteen years earlier, Highlanders aboard the *Hector* were appalled to find on their arrival at Pictou, Nova Scotia, not the tamed frontier of growing communities, cultivated fields, and newly laid-out roads they were expecting but a wilderness of dense forests interspersed by a few miserable clearings and log houses. After the long voyage in the hope of finding a new Scotland, some were so overwhelmed by despair they wished to return home at once. 'We've turned Indians right enough,' wrote a settler from Carolina, 'in the gloom of the forest none of us will be left alive, with wolves and beasts howling in every cranny. We're ruined since we left King George.'[39]

But if emigration represented a form of exile to men and women who saw themselves abandoned on a distant shore, for others it represented fresh opportunities and new horizons. Dr Roderick Gordon of King and Queen County, Virginia, a Scot, confided to his brother in 1734: 'pity it is that thousands of my country people should stay starving att home when they may live here in peace and plenty, as a great many who have been transported for a punishment have found pleasure, profit and ease and would rather undergo any hardship than be forced back to their own country.' James Guthrie firmly believed that Jamaica had everything 'for the comfort of man and beast', while John Rae, who settled in Georgia, wrote to a relative living near Belfast that 'nothing would give me more satisfaction than to be the means of bringing my friends to this country of Freedom...for I bless God for it I keep as plentiful a table as most gentlemen in Ireland, with good punch, wine, and beer. If any person that comes here can bring money and purchase a slave or two, they may live very easy and well.' America before the Revolution was described as a 'paradise' where newcomers 'had nought to do but pluck and eat'.[40] If not paradise, the New World, like other parts of the rapidly growing Empire, offered the prospect to hundreds of thousands of British emigrants of a better future for themselves and their families and a life-style in the colonies that would have been impossible at home.

[39] Patricia Clarke and Dale Spender, eds., *Life Lines: Australian Women's Letters and Diaries, 1788 to 1840* (London, 1992), chap. 1; Bailyn, *Voyagers*, pp. 395; Charles W. Dunn, *Highland Settler: A Portrait of the Scottish Gael in Nova Scotia* (Toronto, 1953), pp. 27–28.

[40] SRO, RH 15/1/95, GD 44 14/4/9; Harold E. Davis, *The Fledgling Province: Social and Cultural Life in Colonial Georgia, 1733–1776* (Chapel Hill, NC, 1976), pp. 23–24; Adams and Somerville, *Cargoes of Despair and Hope*, p. 197.

Select Bibliography

IAN ADAMS and MEREDYTH SOMERVILLE, *Cargoes of Despair and Hope: Scottish Emigration to North America, 1603–1803* (Edinburgh, 1993).

BERNARD BAILYN, *Voyagers to the West: A Passage in the Peopling of America on the Eve of the American Revolution* (New York, 1986).

J. M. BUMSTED, *The People's Clearance: Highland Emigration to British North America, 1770–1815* (Edinburgh, 1982).

NICHOLAS CANNY, ed., *Europeans on the Move: Studies on European Migration, 1500–1800* (Oxford, 1994).

T. M. DEVINE, ed., *Scottish Emigration and Scottish Society* (Edinburgh, 1992).

R. J. DICKSON, *Ulster Emigration to Colonial America, 1718–1775* (London, 1966).

A. ROGER EKIRCH, *Bound for America: The Transportation of British Convicts to the Colonies, 1718–1775* (Oxford, 1987).

AARON FOGELMAN, 'Migrations to the Thirteen British North American Colonies, 1700–1775: New Estimates', *Journal of Interdisciplinary History*, XXII (1992), pp. 691–709.

DAVID W. GALENSON, *White Servitude in Colonial America: An Economic Analysis* (Cambridge, 1981).

HENRY A. GEMERY, 'Markets for Migrants: English Indentured Servitude and Emigration in the Seventeenth and Eighteenth Centuries', in P. C. Emmer, ed., *Colonialism and Migration. Indentured Labour Before and After Slavery* (Dordrecht, 1986), pp. 33–54.

IAN CHARLES CARGILL GRAHAM, *Colonists from Scotland: Emigration to North America, 1707–1783* (Ithaca, NY, 1956).

ROBERT HUGHES, *The Fatal Shore: A History of the Transportation of Convicts to Australia, 1787–1868* (London, 1987).

ALAN L. KARRAS, *Sojourners in the Sun: Scottish Migrants in Jamaica and the Chesapeake, 1740–1800* (Ithaca, NY, 1992).

AUDREY LOCKHART, *Some Aspects of Emigration from Ireland to the North American Colonies Between 1660 and 1775* (New York, 1975).

ANTHONY McFARLANE, *The British in the Americas, 1480–1815* (London, 1994).

KERBY A. MILLER, *Emigrants and Exiles: Ireland and the Irish Exodus to North America* (Oxford, 1985).

T. W. MOODY and W. E. VAUGHAN, eds., *A New History of Ireland*, Vol. IV, *Eighteenth-Century Ireland, 1691–1800* (Oxford, 1986).

ERIC RICHARDS, *A History of the Highland Clearances*, 2 vols. (London, 1985).

JOHN WAREING, 'Migration to London and Transatlantic Emigration of Indentured Servants, 1683–1775', *Journal of Historical Geography*, VII (1981), pp. 356–78.

MARIANNE S. WOKECK, 'German and Irish Immigration to Colonial Philadelphia', *Proceedings of the American Philosophical Society*, CXXXIII (1989), pp. 128–43.

3

Inseparable Connections: Trade, Economy, Fiscal State, and the Expansion of Empire, 1688–1815

PATRICK K. O'BRIEN

The period between the Glorious Revolution and the final defeat of Napoleon at Waterloo was marked by vigorous growth of both the British economy and of a British Empire built on transcontinental trade. This chapter examines the connections between economic growth and Imperial expansion. It will concentrate on British domestic resources, latent and evolving, which made possible the acquisition of territory overseas and the enforcement of contracts required for long-term commercial relations with the Americas, Asia, Africa, and eventually, Australasia. It will enquire from whom, from what, and from where in the economy did the outward thrust to venture outside the realm and beyond Europe originate. It will ask what structural and political conditions sustained the momentum of the thrust through major wars and minor conflicts with European powers between 1689 and the Congress of Vienna in 1815, which marked the final defeat of Iberian, Dutch, and above all French pretensions to contain British imperialism and commerce with Asia, Africa, and the Americas.

Global Commerce and Domestic Economic Growth

Between the accession of Elizabeth I and the Restoration of Charles II, the volume of English-made goods sold abroad grew at a rate of just over 1 per cent a year. That rate accelerated between 1660 and 1700 and then fluctuated over cycles of faster, slower, and even negative growth, for instance between 1763 and 1783, around a mean annual rate of 1.5 per cent from 1697 to 1815. Commodity exports increased much more rapidly than the growth of population and faster than the growth of the national product as a whole. Something like 8 per cent of the nation's gross domestic product (goods and services) may have been sold overseas in the reign of William III. The share rose unsteadily and probably peaked at around double that proportion in the reign of George III. Since exports consisted overwhelmingly of manufactures, it is important to observe that over two long swings in industrial expansion, between 1700 and 1760 and again from 1780 to 1801, about half of the increment to manufactured output was sold overseas. Furthermore, the bulk of all extra industrial output sent abroad travelled outside traditional European markets, which had absorbed all but 10 per cent of English-made exports as late as the 1660s, to American, African, and Asian consumers, who probably purchased up to 70 per cent of exports during the years of war with Napoleon between 1803 and 1815.[1] Although the data can be disaggregated into commodities and markets, and in other illuminating ways, at the macro level the figures and contemporary commentaries validate the point that the growth of British industry from the Restoration onwards was promoted by increasing involvement with the international economy in general and with an 'Imperial' system in particular.

Participation in global commerce included much more than the simple recourse to the exchange of industrial goods made in Britain for the foodstuffs, raw materials, and high-quality manufactures imported from continents outside Europe. The capital and labour, free, indentured, and above all the slave labour, required for the cultivation of crops and the exploitation of natural resources in the Americas, Africa, Asia, and Australasia had to be transported to the coast, from port to port, and carried across oceans to the farms, plantations, mines, forests, and fishing grounds of new worlds. Transcontinental trade had to be financed, insured, and protected. It required ships and sailors. Above all, it had to be organized. From the time of the Commonwealth in the 1650s onwards, British merchants, shippers, bankers, and other intermediaries played an ever more important role in the co-ordination of global commerce. Their endeavours received strong support from the Navigation Acts, enforced by the Royal Navy, which protected them against foreign competition, particularly from Dutch middlemen.[2]

Unfortunately, the profits, wages, and interest that accrued to the national economy from 'invisibles' (i.e. from the sale of international services) cannot be added up. Some clues exist as to how they grew before 1815. For example, merchant ships registered in England and Wales rose from 340,000 tons in 1686 to 2,477,000 tons by 1815. The tonnage of ships cleared through British ports for the Caribbean, North America, and Asia over the century rose from 82,000 tons in 1686 to 182,000 tons by 1771–73 and up to 467,000 before 1815.[3]

---

[1] Growth rates for the volume of *domestic* exports and their ratios to national income can be calculated from data and sources cited by P. K. O'Brien and S. L. Engerman, 'Exports and the Growth of the British Economy from the Glorious Revolution to the Peace of Amiens', in Barbara L. Solow, ed., *Slavery and the Rise of the Atlantic System* (Cambridge, 1991), pp. 177–209, esp. pp. 179–83.

[2] Larry Sawers, 'The Navigation Acts Revisited', *Economic History Review* (hereafter *EcHR*), Second Series, XL (1992), pp. 262–84.

[3] Ralph Davis, *The Rise of the English Shipping Industry* (London, 1962), pp. 17 and 27, and John Marshall, *A Digest of All the Accounts* (London, 1833), pp. 206–07.

Revenues that accrued to Britain from servicing the evolving global economy can also be traced in figures for official values of re-exports. These figures include: tropical groceries, sugar, tea, tobacco, coffee, cocoa, and spices; Asian and European textiles, calicoes, nanqueens, silks, and linens; and raw materials, hemp, flax, dyestuffs, all of which were carried into British ports, warehoused under bond, and virtually exempted from the payment of customs duties, before being sent on to markets, mainly in Europe, but also to the Empire, Africa, and Asia. In volume terms, Imperial and foreign produce re-exported from Britain overseas multiplied some ten times between the Glorious Revolution and Waterloo.[4] Furthermore, the returns, which accrued to merchants, shippers, brokers, insurers, and bankers for managing these trades, increased even more rapidly as London and the outports took over business from rival entrepôts on the continent, Amsterdam, Hamburg, Lisbon, Cadiz, Bordeaux, La Rochelle, and Nantes, particularly in wartime when the Royal Navy closed off sea lanes to French, Dutch, and Spanish ships engaged in oceanic trade. As English shippers penetrated the Indian Ocean and China Seas, they began to displace Indian, Chinese, and Arab merchants, long established in the intra-Asian carrying trades.[5]

Invisible earnings provided revenues over and above those obtained from exporting British-made commodities on world markets and thereby covered deficits on the balance of commodity trade, which probably widened over the eighteenth century.[6] Growing engagement as Europe's main entrepôt for the storage, distribution, and finance of re-exports also provided merchants with the diversity of products required to foster commerce with the Baltic and China, where demand for British-made goods could otherwise be satisfied only at disappointingly low levels of trade. Re-exports conserved bullion, the period's 'hard currency', which operated as the reserve for the nation's system of paper credit and also as the government's war chest for the purchase of armaments and for the payment of troops deployed overseas in times of conflict. Multilateral exchanges facilitated the growth of trade as a whole and thereby expanded markets for British industry around the world.

Underlying the growing involvement in global trade, of which the expanding Empire was a conspicuous part, were structural preconditions within the home economy that encouraged private enterprise to venture overseas. They will be examined in the sections that immediately follow. Private initiatives were,

---

[4] D. A. Farnie, 'The Commercial Empire of the Atlantic, 1607–1783', EcHR, Second Series, V (1962–63), pp. 205–18. The data are cited in n. 1 above.

[5] See below, pp. 493–94.

[6] Elise S. Brezis, 'Foreign Capital Flows in the Century of Britain's Industrial Revolution: New Estimates, Controlled Conjectures', EcHR, Second Series, LXVIII (1995), pp. 46–67.

however, sustained by the indispensable support lent by the British state, and the second half of the chapter is concerned with the role of government.

The Industrialization of the Work-force

Long before 1688 abundant natural resources, including fertile land, coal, and other minerals, had moved the economy towards a range of possibilities, denied to European rivals less favourably endowed. England's foremost comparative advantage had developed, however, through a steady accumulation of skilled labour capable of manufacturing commodities that might be profitably traded on world markets for imports desired by English consumers. In the late seventeenth century, when English exports still included such primary produce as grain, coal, and other raw materials, their composition was already dominated by manufactures, particularly woollen textiles.[7] Between 1688 and 1815 elastic supplies of relatively cheap labour, both skilled and unskilled, organized by merchants who had the 'know-how' and capital required, enabled an increasingly diversified range of tradeable products, principally textiles, but also hardware, leather, and other goods, to be sold on world markets.

By the seventeenth century, the industrialization and urbanization of the work-force had proceeded further than elsewhere on the continent with the exception of the Netherlands, and a high proportion of the English population, freed from agriculture, produced goods and supplied tradeable services for sale primarily on home and European markets, but already on some scale to consumers in the Americas, Africa, and Asia.[8] England's early industrialization began with a process of occupational, regional, and local specialization, often called proto-industrialization. Internal trade had been encouraged by a politically unified home market, secure from external aggression, and a benign geography of differentiated natural resources, of traversable terrains and navigable waterways, which made the transportation of manufactures, of food, fuel, and raw materials around the coast and inland relatively easy.

In time, proto-industrialization within some regions led to higher levels of specialization and to advantages associated with the geographical concentration of manufacturing activity. This evolution, whereby diverse industries agglomerated within confined localities and interconnected one with another, was generating technological progress before the end of the eighteenth century and was moving some manufacturing processes into the steam-powered factories that became the

---

[7] Ralph Davis, 'English Foreign Trade, 1660–1700', *EcHR*, Second Series, VII (1954), pp. 150–66.
[8] A. E. Wrigley, 'Urban Growth and Agricultural Change in England and the Continent in the Early Modern Period', *Journal of Interdisciplinary History*, XV (1985), pp. 683–728.

hallmark of the first industrial revolution. Mechanization and the reorganization of industry did not take place on a significant scale, however, until the time of conflict with the North American colonies. That seems too late in the century to be closely correlated with the rise of transcontinental trade or the acquisition of territory and property rights overseas—developments that had continued unabated since the time of Cromwell. Before the industrial revolution the primary precondition for a sustained commitment to global trade was the early industrialization of a work-force capable of supporting increasing levels of trade with distant markets, and paid wages that allowed families down the social scale to consume tropical groceries carried from the Americas and Asia in ever increasing volume into British ports. This capacity expanded in the wake of the Glorious Revolution, when England's involvement with transcontinental commerce superseded that of its imperial rivals, Portugal and Spain, then France, and eventually even the Netherlands by a growing margin.

Agriculture, Land, and Coal

Behind the industrialization of the work-force stood agriculture, admired throughout Europe as the bedrock upon which Britain's expanded engagement with global commerce rested. The steady release of labour, raw materials, investible funds, and taxes from the farming sector to industry, to commerce, to the towns, and to the Empire overseas depended upon a progressive agriculture. Industrial and urban workers and their families had to be fed at prices that left them with enough purchasing power to spend on manufactured goods and imports. Organic materials, which formed the basis for a wide range of agro-industrial activity, needed to be delivered cheaply and in quantity. Surplus funds from rents and profits derived from farming financed the construction of towns, transportation networks, and port facilities. Agrarian-based taxes paid for a substantial share of the costs of the Hanoverian state's increasing commitment to the protection of trade, and of Empire.

After the Restoration, property rights to land and to sub-soil minerals became more secure and more concentrated in private hands. Farms expanded in size and the tenurial system, dominated by large-scale tenant farms, promoted production for markets and encouraged innovation. Over the next century and a half agriculture became more market-oriented and supportive for an industrializing, urbanizing, and trading economy.

Agriculture should neither be reified into the 'leading sector'; nor should much credit for its transformation be accorded to aristocratic owners of large estates. England, along with other regions of North-Western Europe, happened to be geographically endowed with the kinds of soils, elevations, and climates hospitable to best-practice techniques available to European farmers in the seventeenth and eighteenth centuries. Nitrogen-fixing crops, mixed husbandry, land-saving rotations, and improved drainage diffused easily and raised yields per acre cultivated and output per worker employed. Furthermore, the country's inegalitarian system of property rights, which had evolved since the Norman Conquest, allowed for larger enclosed farms and put pressure even on families with some limited access to land to find alternative employment outside agriculture. The 'push' on landless people, English, Scottish, and Irish, to migrate into local industry, to towns further away, and also across the Atlantic was stronger than it was elsewhere in Europe, particularly in France and Iberia but also in the Netherlands.[9]

Even before the growth of population accelerated after mid-century, domestic agriculture not only supplied most of the food and raw materials and significant shares of the investible funds required to support industrialization and trade, but exported surplus grain to feed the populations of Dutch, Portuguese, and other towns that formed part of Britain's traditional trading networks on the continent.[10] Shortly after the Seven Years War the country 'matured' into a net importer of foodstuffs. Despite the growing influx of meat and dairy produce from Ireland and the supplementing of the nation's monotonous diet with such delectable imports as tea, sugar, coffee, chocolate, spices, and exotic fruits and vegetables, basic foodstuffs from domestic agriculture continued to a large degree to feed a population which grew and became urbanized at faster rates than elsewhere in Europe. Apart from cotton fibres, raw silk, timber, indigo, and hemp, Britain's primary sector also supplied most of the inputs demanded by industries processing organic materials and raw food into 'manufactured output'.[11]

Britain's and Ireland's complementary agrarian achievements did not for a long time provide higher standards of living for the majority of the rural and urban populations, particularly during the decades of rapidly rising food prices from the 1750s to the 1820s. Yet the growth in agricultural production was sufficient to ensure that living standards did not, as was often predicted, fall to the point where a check to population growth would have inhibited migration to the towns, industrialization, and participation in overseas trade and Empire. Although the post-1750 rise in food prices reduced the purchasing power available to British families to spend on manufactured goods, that shift not only prompted indus-

[9] Patrick K. O'Brien, 'Path Dependency or Why Britain became an Industrialized, Urbanized Economy Long before France', *EcHR*, Second Series, XLVIX (1996), pp. 213–49; see also above, pp. 28–51.

[10] David Ormrod, *English Grain Exports and the Structure of Agrarian Capitalism, 1700–1760* (Hull, 1985).

[11] Mark Overton, *Agricultural Revolution in England: The Transformation of the Agrarian Economy, 1500–1850* (Cambridge, 1996).

trialists and merchants to cut costs to maintain sales on the home market but pushed them to search for compensatory markets overseas as well as in the protected markets in the Empire.[12] Fortunately, agricultural output increased enough to feed the majority of a rapidly rising population. Had eighteenth-century Britain been forced to import large quantities of food, terms for the exchange of its manufactured exports for food and raw materials could have been sharply and persistently unfavourable. A really adverse shift would have reduced the gains from trade and brought the whole outward and Imperial orientation of the nation's economic strategy into question.[13] Instead, Britain's exceptional endowments, not just of land but also of mineral ores, copper, iron, lead, tin, and salt, and above all her abundant supplies of accessible energy in the form of coal, reinforced that orientation.

Coal carried coastwise, along rivers and eventually by canals, provided a cheap and reliable source of power for a whole range of energy-intensive and taxable industries, which included brewing, dyeing, refining salt and sugar, boiling soap, making bricks and glass. Coal was also used in the smelting, forging, casting, and finishing of valuable and strategically useful metals, such as iron, copper, tin, and lead. Most coal was moved by sea and the waterborne coal trade operated as one of the kingdom's principal nurseries for seamen, pressed into the Royal Navy in wartime. As a form of energy, coal substituted for animal and manpower in agriculture, transportation, and construction. This released yet more labour for manufacturing and commercial services. Populations which could be kept warm and dry in winter, required fewer calories per unit of work. They could huddle comfortably and work more vigorously in London and in other Imperial ports such as Bristol, Liverpool, and Glasgow, where their health improved because heat protected them against the elements and hot food, cooked with this cheap fuel, was less likely to diffuse diseases among urban populations. In short, coal operated in the same way as agriculture and allowed Britain to industrialize, to urbanize, to trade, and to release to its colonies a relatively large share of its workforce well before the upswing in population that occurred after mid-century.[14]

Merchants and Commercial Credit

Landowners, some of whom also owned coal and minerals, were alive to the material gains and power that would accrue to them from commitment to a

[12] Patrick K. O'Brien, 'Agriculture and the Home Market for English Industry', *English Historical Review*, C (1985), pp. 1–18.
[13] N. F. R. Crafts, *British Economic Growth During the Industrial Revolution* (Oxford, 1985), pp. 141–52.
[14] A. E. Wrigley, *Continuity, Chance and Change. The Character of the Industrial Revolution in England* (Cambridge, 1988).

maritime Empire. It was, however, merchants who supplied most of the capital and credit and managed Britain's increasing involvement in global trade. Indeed, the role of merchants in organizing, co-ordinating, and sustaining commerce between the metropolitan centre and the ports, towns, naval bases, forts, settlements, mines, plantations, farms, and fisheries of a far-flung Empire and Britain's networks for international trade can hardly be overstated. By linking producers and consumers in Europe, Africa, Asia, and the Americas into an embryo world economy, merchants can be represented as precursors of modern multinational corporations.[15] Equally the differences between then and now are marked. With the conspicuous exception of the East India Company, but also of the South Sea, Hudson's Bay, Royal African, and Levant companies, corporate organizations based in London played little part in the management of Britain's global trade. After 1688, when Parliament became less inclined to renew trade monopolies, corporate forms of organization for the conduct of global trade faded away. Merchants operated in partnerships, kin groups, and a variety of associations, formed and reformed for particular voyages and ventures. They collected, gathered, and processed information; drew upon their talents, education, experience, and reputations; connected their partners to relatives and their religious and business networks in distant ports; all in order to operate together, and with greater chances of success, in what was an extremely uncertain environment for international business.[16]

That environment contained familiar hazards associated with traversing seas and oceans, dealing with extreme climatic conditions, and coping with new diseases. For all such risks, the sciences, medicines, and transportation technologies of the eighteenth century continued to provide palliatives but not solutions. Meanwhile, the co-ordination of markets across space, time, and cultures embodied economic and political uncertainties that even the most astute business acumen could only partially alleviate. Alien consumers with peculiar tastes, the slow diffusion of commercial intelligence, competition from fellow countrymen and enemy rivals, and the unpredictable occurrence of war, called for levels of skill, flexibility, and foresight in the management of global and Imperial trade that exceeded by a wide margin the expertise required to operate within established intra-European trades or domestic trades.

The finance and professional skills required to engage in servicing the international economy had been accumulating among communities of merchants in London, Bristol, and other port cities along the west coast well before 1688. By

[15] David Hancock, *Citizens of the World. London Merchants and the Integration of the British Atlantic Community, 1735–85* (Cambridge, 1995).

[16] Jacob. M. Price, 'What did Merchants Do? Reflections on British Overseas Trade, 1660–1760', *Journal of Economic History*, XLIX (1989), pp. 267–84.

the time of the Glorious Revolution, London's merchants, shippers, warehouse-men, and financiers more or less ran Britain's transcontinental trade. The capital's hegemony over western ports diminished over the eighteenth century as Londoners made economic space for the prosperity of Bristol and for the rise of Glasgow and Liverpool, as well as other smaller and more specialized British and Irish coastal towns involved with oceanic trade and Empire.[17]

Keen competition kept London's merchants alive to possibilities for recruiting new skills, to opportunities for investment, and wherever feasible, to the relocation of their operations outside the expensive confines of the metropolis. Throughout the period London dominated the outports by a large, if decreasing, margin. In scale and scope the capital's communities of merchants reinvigorated themselves decade after decade by absorbing Dutchmen, Huguenots, Jews, and Germans from across the North Sea and the Channel and by attracting ambitious newcomers from all over the British Isles to an already prosperous capital city with long-established success in European and Mediterranean commerce.[18]

Of all the manifold skills required for successful participation in global trade, ready access to and the management of credit were paramount. Buying and selling upon distant markets in the interiors of far-away continents; collecting cargoes, hiring crews, and fitting out ships operating away from home ports for months on end; storing inventories of crops and raw materials harvested seasonally; ware-housing stocks of manufactures gathered over dispersed locations; delivering untrained slaves for work in gangs on plantations, are all examples of tasks undertaken by merchants that required circuitous chains of credit to lubricate the flows of production, distribution, and exchange across the time spans and distances involved in transcontinental commerce.

Functionally, the production, transportation, distribution, and finance of trade are interrelated. Indeed, before the rise of specialist international banks, they were often undertaken as conjoined activities by merchants. With some, but rarely enough, liquid capital at their disposal, merchants organized and acted as guarantors for deferred systems of payments all along the line from sites of production, through networks of transportation and distribution to points of sale. In the Middle Ages Italian merchants, and in the sixteenth and seventeenth centuries their Flemish successors, developed the paper instruments, the contractual rules, and the institutions required for long-distance trade. Later on, London and Britain emulated Amsterdam and the Netherlands in increasing the amount and

---

[17] Kenneth Morgan, *Bristol and the Atlantic Trade in the Eighteenth Century* (Cambridge, 1993); P. G. E. Clemens, 'The Rise of Liverpool, 1665–1750', *EcHR*, Second Series, XXIX (1976), pp. 211–25.

[18] David Ormrod, 'The Atlantic Economy and the "Protestant Capitalist International", 1651–1775', *Historical Research*, LXVI (1993), pp. 197–208.

extending the range and sophistication of the system. As financiers, London's merchants not only augmented the volume and velocity of credit but reallocated purchasing power from those who could afford to wait, but who wished to earn interest, to those who had to be paid quickly in order to produce the commodities and capital goods and to hire the labour and transportation they required to engage in oceanic trade.[19]

With substantial capitals of their own and borrowing on the basis of their reputations, London merchants acquired the skills needed to raise the finance as well as to manage the distribution of traded goods around the world. Over time, merchants, wholesalers, warehousemen, and other middlemen who specialized in the finance of trade matured in the metropolis and other port cities into fully fledged international bankers. By the second half of the eighteenth century, London boasted a variegated system of financial intermediation, rivalled only by Amsterdam. Credit became cheaper and was available to sustain the development of established enterprises in agriculture, transportation, industry, and trade throughout the kingdom, as well as its Empire and trading networks overseas.[20]

The whole credit system evolved, moreover, without serious hindrance from central government and the courts. Punishments for those who could not meet their debts remained severe and probably deterred many would-be entrepreneurs from taking more than carefully calculated risks. Nevertheless, rules for the extension of credit could be left to the prudence and honour of businessmen. The law confined itself to the protection of creditors from fraud but recognized bills of exchange as assignable and negotiable instruments of credit, that is, as paper promises that could circulate as money. No legal restrictions were placed on the foundation and activities of city and country banks.[21]

In 1694 the embryo credit system was underpinned by the foundation of a private corporation, the Bank of England, which assumed responsibility for managing the government's debt, particularly the arrangements to cover any short-term borrowing required to meet day-to-day expenditures in anticipation of revenues from taxation or from long-term loans. The Bank's notes, issued to government paymasters, became currency and quickly matured to supplement bullion as 'reserve assets' for the nation's and the Empire's supply of money and credit. Once established, the Bank extended its responsibilities to assume a role akin to a 'lender of last resort', and granted discount facilities for top-class

[19] Jacob M. Price, 'Credit in the Slave Trade and Plantation Economies', in Solow, ed., *Slavery and the Rise of the Atlantic System*, pp. 293–339.

[20] Larry Neal, *The Rise of Financial Capitalism. International Capital Markets in the Age of Reason* (Cambridge, 1990).

[21] J. Hoppit, *Risk and Failure in English Business, 1700–1900* (Cambridge, 1987).

bills of short maturity to major London merchants and businessmen. That facility, allowed only to clients of status from the City, tended to be used sparingly. On several occasions of crisis the Bank did, however, discount bills of exchange and thereby helped to restore confidence in the pyramid of paper credit upon which government and mercantile transactions, both domestic and overseas, rested. In short, one important consequence of the financial revolution of the period from 1694 to 1713 was to create stable conditions for the extension and integration of a national and Imperial capital market centred on London.[22]

As it developed and improved in efficiency, that market supported increasing demands from government, from internal trade, and from global commerce. Fortunately, it was neither unduly trammelled by legal controls imposed on the activities of banks and other institutions supplying money and credit nor undermined by reckless behaviour on the part of the state. Financial difficulties certainly emerged, particularly during the long and expensive conflicts with France from 1689 to 1713 and again from 1797 to 1819.[23] Major crises of confidence in paper credit, rampant inflations, and unmanageable depreciations in the external value of sterling did not, however, occur. On the contrary, during most wars the security and ease of access afforded to movements of funds into and out of London attracted capital from Europe, particularly the Netherlands, into the assets of the government and supported both British and European commerce with the Americas, Africa, and Asia. Inflows of capital apparently played a significant, if alas unmeasurable, role in alleviating the potentially serious effects emanating from borrowing by the state and the disruptions to foreign trade occasioned by warfare at sea and on land among European armies fighting in the Americas, the Caribbean, Asia, and Africa.[24]

The Emergence of a Successful Fiscal State

Favourable natural endowments, proto-industrialization, an enterprising community of merchants, and the construction of responsive financial institutions enabled the expansion of trade and Empire to take place. In addition, two 'political' elements, one fiscal and the other military, promoted and sustained the outward thrust of the nation's conjoined commercial and strategic policies during the final phase of what is often termed Europe's mercantilist era.[25]

[22] Michael Collins, Money and Banking in the U. K. A History (London, 1988).

[23] Patrick K. O'Brien, 'Public Finance in the Wars with France', in H. T. Dickinson, ed., Britain and the French Revolution, 1789–1815 (London, 1989), pp. 165–87.

[24] Brezis, 'Foreign Capital Flows'.

[25] For 'mercantilism' see below, pp. 71–72.

Although Britain's public finances and military power can be connected in circuitous as well as obvious ways to the evolving strength of the domestic economy, on balance, it seems that the economy was driven forward by the state rather than the state being driven by the economy.

On the fiscal side the discontinuity in the scale of naval and military activity has been clearly measured in terms of an initial upswing in the taxes collected and money borrowed by central government between 1689 and 1713—a period of nearly continuous warfare and preparations for war against France, Spain, and their allies which followed the Glorious Revolution.[26] Just before James II fled to France, the Stuart regime appropriated roughly 3 per cent to 4 per cent of England's national income as taxes, spent £2 million on the army and navy, and carried a royal debt of about the same amount. Shortly after the accession of George I, the Hanoverian regime commanded taxes equal to 9 per cent of England's and Scotland's national income. Peacetime expenditure on the army and navy had increased by a factor of three in real terms and Parliament provided for taxes to service a national debt that had reached a nominal capital of just over £36 million. After an interregnum of peace under Sir Robert Walpole from 1722 to 1739, loans and military expenditures all climbed from plateau to plateau and reached a peak after nearly a quarter of a century of warfare against Revolutionary and Napoleonic France that would have seemed inconceivable to James II. By the 1820s, when the country's currency had been restored to the gold standard, taxes had risen by a multiplier of 14.4 compared to those of his brief reign and the nominal capital of the state's funded debt amounted to more than twice the national income—a ratio remarkable for the period and astonishing even by the standards of profligate borrowing displayed by many governments of the late twentieth century.[27]

Nearly all the money taxed and borrowed by the Orange and Hanoverian state was used to defend the realm, to subsidize allied armies, and when necessary, to wage war in Europe, to protect British trade, to acquire territory, bases, and populations overseas, and to secure access to markets and resources in Africa, Asia, and the Americas. How did the government of a small island economy raise the resources required to consolidate a regime, integrate a kingdom, and to acquire such a huge territorial and maritime Empire overseas in the space of 127 years? Nothing in the realm's turbulent fiscal history, from the reign of Henry VII through to the accession of William III, suggested that its rulers could readily tax

---

[26] M. J. Braddick, *The Nerves of State: Taxation and the Financing of the English State, 1558–1714* (Manchester, 1996).

[27] Patrick K. O'Brien, 'The Political Economy of British Taxation, 1660–1815', *EcHR*, Second Series, XLI (1988), pp. 1–32.

their subjects or borrow the huge sums of money required to support the role of a great power overseas.[28]

The Rise of a National Debt

Yet as early as 1713, the Treaty of Utrecht confirmed the emergence of Britain as the leading naval and military power in Europe and as a mercantile and industrializing economy on its way towards dominance in supplying services, shipping, credit, insurance, and distribution, as well as manufactured commodities to global markets. When they signed that treaty, Queen Anne's ministers knew that by dint of political persuasion and administrative innovation, they and William III's financial advisers before them, had managed to borrow unprecedented sums of money on the London capital market. Furthermore, under pressure from wartime necessity, Parliament had acquiesced step by step in a sharp rise in taxation in order to service a debt that was no longer simply royal but had become a national obligation in all but name.[29]

Between 1693 and 1713, ministers experimented with methods and instruments for borrowing long and medium term, developed elsewhere in Europe, particularly in the Netherlands, which included tontines, annuities for lives and shorter periods, and loans linked to lotteries. They also devised conversion operations, whereby holders of Exchequer, naval, and other bills owed money due for regular repayment by departments of state, were persuaded to exchange their claims to reimbursement, maturing in the short term, for negotiable and assignable rights to payments of interest secured on tax revenues for generations to come. To consolidate its power at home and abroad the new regime also 'squeezed' substantial loans out of the re-incorporated East India Company in 1698 and the South Sea Company in 1711, which were awarded monopoly rights to trade with Asia and Spanish America in return. In 1694, in exchange for a loan of £1.2 million, the state also accorded privileges to the newly founded Bank of England, which included a monopoly of the rights to issue banknotes in London, a franchise for the circulation of Exchequer and other bills in anticipation of taxes and the profits obtained from holding the balances of departments of state. In short compass, the Bank matured into the government's bank and its directors became a fount of advice to ministers and the Treasury in their dealings with the metropolitan money market.[30]

---

[28] John Brewer, *The Sinews of Power. War, Money and the English State, 1688–1783* (London, 1989).

[29] J. R. Jones, 'Fiscal Policies, Liberties and Representative Government during the Reigns of the Last Stuarts', in Philip T. Hoffman and Kathryn Norberg, eds., *Fiscal Crises, Liberty and Representative Government, 1450–1789* (Stanford, Calif., 1994), pp. 67–95.

[30] P. G. M. Dickson, *The Financial Revolution in England. A Study in the Development of Public Credit, 1688–1751* (1967; Ipswich, 1993), chaps. 3–10.

By the end of the first of seven major conflicts with France and her allies, a national debt, a government bank, and procedures for negotiating the flotation of long-term loans on the London capital market were in place. Alarm over the novelty and size of the debt emerged first during the brief interlude of peace from 1698 to 1702, when servicing costs absorbed just a quarter of tax revenues. Thereafter, that ratio jumped as recourse to long-term loans became the dominant mode employed by Chancellors of the day to fund nearly all military and naval expenditures occasioned by war. For example, in the War of the Spanish Succession the proportion of *incremental* expenditures, largely for the navy and army, funded by long-term loans came to 74 per cent; for the War of the Austrian Succession, 1740–48, that ratio amounted to 79 per cent; an even higher percentage of expenditure on the highly successful Seven Years War came from increases to the national debt; while 81 per cent of the unprofitable allocations to suppress the American rebellion, 1776–83, consisted of borrowed money. Loans provided more than 70 per cent of all the extra money spent by government on the warfare from 1793 to 1802 which reached stalemate at the Peace of Amiens. During the final struggle against Napoleon from 1803 to 1815 that proportion fell to around 30 per cent, largely because Pitt succeeded in introducing an income tax in 1799.[31]

Long-term borrowing provided ministers with the means to rearm, to mobilize the forces of the Crown speedily without recourse to prolonged and potentially acrimonious discussions with Parliaments about subsidies and other 'extraordinary' taxes levied for wars in previous centuries. As a market for raising money in London gradually evolved and machinery for borrowing matured, Parliaments simply sanctioned the imposition of sufficient taxes to meet the interest, amortization, and other changes attached to particular loans, raised for the most part in circumstances of war when Members of the House found it unpatriotic to refuse supply. In effect, Parliament passed forward to future generations what might have proved to be an intolerable burden of sharp and immediate rises in taxation.

Politicians, investors, and taxpayers certainly became vocally concerned in the aftermath of every war about the scale of accumulated debt and the burden of taxes required for its service. Yet ministers managed to assuage radical predictions of national bankruptcy and to allay the political envy aroused by a supposed stranglehold on power, exerted by a parvenu, 'monied interest' of dubious birth and probity. In wartime, Chancellors of the day conducted negotiations for loans with growing expertise. They managed the accumulating debt efficiently enough to avoid the crises of confidence that afflicted the public finances of the *ancien régime*

---

[31] O'Brien, 'The Political Economy of British Taxation'.

in France in the wake of the Seven Years War and more seriously after Bourbon intervention in the War of American Independence.[32]

Taxation

Success in raising loans rested ultimately upon the legal, administrative, and political skills of ministers. They had to persuade Parliament, the aristocracy, gentry, and middling sort to comply with the state's ever-increasing demands for revenues, transferred in large part as interest to holders of the debt but also allocated to fund the mounting costs of the armed forces, required to defend the realm, to conduct a European policy, and to secure a maritime Empire overseas. Over the period 1688–1815, the proportions of tax revenues allocated to service government debt increased from less than 5 per cent before the Glorious Revolution, reached 56 per cent just after the War of American Independence, and remained in the 50 per cent range for the early decades of the nineteenth century. King William's accession, and his war from 1689 to 1697, certainly altered perceptions of the fiscal capacities, responsibilities, and opportunities for the English state.[33] After Waterloo, the expensively secured victory over Napoleonic pretensions to hegemony in Europe allowed Victorian statesmen to roll back the state and to defend Britain and her vast Empire overseas on a military and naval establishment that absorbed a share of the national income no higher than in Stuart times. In between, the tax burden went up and up but, thanks to the funding system, without any of the leaps that might otherwise have led to serious opposition and to a fiscal crisis of the state.

Tax evasion occurred on a considerable scale, indeed whenever taxpayers could defraud the revenue without risk of detection. But somehow an aristocratic and unrepresentative regime, serviced by an ostensibly incompetent and corrupt administration, managed to appropriate what was, by European standards, a remarkable share of national income from a people depicted by some historians as ungovernable.[34]

Economic growth, accompanied by the diversification of consumption and the reorganization of production, helped to bring both an increased volume and a greater variety of goods and services into the net for purposes of taxation, but the

[32] Philip T. Hoffman, 'Early Modern France, 1450–1700', in Hoffman and Norberg, *Fiscal Crises, Liberty and Representative Government*, pp. 226–52.

[33] P. K. O'Brien and P. Hunt. 'Excises and the Rise of a Fiscal State in England, 1586–1688', in W. M. Ormrod, R. J. Bonney, and M. M. Bonney, eds., *Crises, Revolutions and Self-Sustained Growth. Essays in European Fiscal History, 1130–1830* (Stanford, Calif., 1997).

[34] Frank O'Gorman, 'The Recent Historiography of the Hanoverian Regime', *Historical Journal*, XXIX (1986), pp. 1005–20.

connections between the development of the economy and the state's fiscal base are complex and difficult to unravel. Recently revised conjectures about the numbers suggest that the British economy grew more slowly and steadily through time than traditional accounts of the industrial revolution have indicated. Between 1688 and 1815 tax revenues increased much more rapidly than the economy at large—by a factor of eighteen in real terms compared to a multiplier of around three for gross national output. Central government's 'take' in the form of taxes fluctuated, rising in wartime and falling back when hostilities ceased, but the state pushed it up to a ratio of nearly 20 per cent of national income in the closing years of war with Napoleon. Economic growth and structural change helped by making the tasks of tax assessment and collection easier for revenue departments to administer and more tolerable than they could have been for the citizens of more stationary, rival economies on the continent.[35] But the impressive fiscal successes of the Hanoverian regime owed as much to the supportive public consensus over the broad objectives of external policy as to the opportunities created by developments in the economy.

Ministers of the Crown and their advisers, working within the constraints of parliamentary and pressure group politics, had to find a way through major institutional and administrative constraints in order to widen and deepen the state's fiscal base for taxation. They made one huge and costly error when Parliament attempted after the Seven Years War to extend taxation to include the populations and assets of the thirteen colonies in North America and the West Indies. Within Britain, governments proceeded in an altogether pragmatic manner to tolerate rather blatant levels of underpayment by the Scots, and by the Irish, for defence and for access to English and to Imperial markets. Realistically, ministers also chose to ignore demands for reform to the anomalous valuations of land and other types of wealth assessed for taxation in different counties. Indeed, for several decades direct taxes moved more or less off the political agenda. At the same time, the possibilities for raising substantial revenues from trade became rather seriously constrained by organized smuggling, by the web of regulations enveloping economic relations between Britain and her colonies, and by tariff treaties with other European powers. In these circumstances, Chancellors of the Exchequer turned to the imposition of excises on domestic production to find effective solutions to the problem of servicing the debt and funding Britain's expanding military and naval commitments overseas.

[35] Patrick K. O'Brien, 'Central Government and the Economy, 1688–1815', in Roderick Floud and Donald McCloskey, eds., *The Economic History of Britain*, 2nd edn., 3 vols. (Cambridge, 1994), pp. 205–41.

Compassion, or perhaps a prudent anticipation of potential outbreaks of disorder, restrained Chancellors from pushing the incidence of indirect taxes too far in a blatantly inequitable direction. Taxes on salt, candles, beer, cider, soap, starch, or leather offended the ideological sensitivities of many Members of Parliament but their opposition could be placated by calibrating rates of tax to fall less onerously on necessities perceived to be consumed by the poor. Most indirect taxes, customs certainly but also many excise duties, fell upon expenditures that ministers could present as luxurious or superfluous, so that the payment of taxes on consumption was perceived to be voluntary in their eyes. Over time, taxation on expenditures became widely spread across society and less concentrated on those with property and higher incomes than had been the case in the late seventeenth century. No politician pretended that the burdens involved in paying for the defence of the realm and the acquisition of a maritime Empire could or should be levied 'progressively' upon those best able to carry the mounting costs of imperialism, and an aggressive stance in great power politics.[36] However, the incidence of taxation certainly shifted in a somewhat more equitable direction after Pitt introduced the first income tax in 1799.

As Adam Smith and the premature lobby for free trade delighted to observe, taxes restrained and distorted the overall growth of the economy. Nevertheless, accelerated and rather impressive rates of economic development continued despite taxation, perhaps because many of the more technologically progressive and expanding sectors of industry, cottons, linens, woollens, and metals, successfully resisted the imposition of excise duties. With the exception of coal, salt, and timber, industry's raw materials also remained exempt from internal duties. As it evolved, the system of indirect taxation displayed a discernible bias in favour of import substitution and export promotion. In spite of a long tradition of liberal rhetoric and anachronistic attacks on mercantilism, it now seems to historians that the fiscal policies pursued before 1846 may not have done much to restrain the evolution of the most efficient market economy in Europe, particularly when the benefits to trade and industrialization that flowed from military and naval expenditures are taken into an account of gains as well as of costs.[37]

Every social group, particularly the middling sort, who felt discriminated against, disliked the rise and diffusion of taxes on their expenditures. Nevertheless, the penumbra of such levies, dominated by excises, seem to have been selected and administered in ways that headed off any serious parliamentary or extra-parliamentary opposition to fiscal policies. Somehow the economy remained on course.

---

[36] Peter Mathias, *The Transformation of England* (London, 1979), pp. 116–30.

[37] J. V. Beckett and Michael Turner, 'Taxation and Economic Growth in Eighteenth-Century England', *EcHR*, Second Series, XLIII (1990), pp. 377–403.

Over the long run the achievement of the 'fiscal state' was to have raised enough money to carry Britain, its industry, its trade, and its Empire to the pinnacle of security from external aggression and to the hegemony in global commerce that Britain enjoyed for something like a century after 1815.

Aristocratic, Mercantile, and Popular Cultures of Compliance with Taxation and Support for Imperialism

Britain's achievement depended, moreover, on a measure of compliance with the policies of government that had not existed under the Tudor and Stuart regimes. For the period from 1689 to 1815, what appears in retrospect is a mainstream of widely diffused approval across social ranks for the state's foreign and commercial strategy; this approval persisted on balance even during the unprofitable and divisive conflict with the American colonists. Over the long eighteenth century the national identity of Britons widened to include the Scots and the nation's culture was gradually reordered to sustain a stronger imperialistic impulse, which made it easier for governments of the day to mobilize the forces of the Crown and, albeit with difficulty, to appropriate the money they required in order to confront Britain's rivals for trade and Empire.

Articulate opponents of this maritime and Imperial destiny are much harder to find than in the period after 1846, when Adam Smith's precocious ideas for free trade and an alternative economic strategy matured into an official policy and an enduring ideology. When they did emerge, enemies of the consensus over commercial-cum-imperial policies tended to come from enlightened intellectual fringes of the political nation speaking out of tune and out of time. Within an increasingly cohesive and hegemonic culture, marked by loyalty to the Crown, deference to aristocracy, and adherence to a flexible but encompassing and defining Protestant religion, dissenting voices could, moreover, be isolated for preaching Jacobite sedition earlier in the century and as subversive of property and the constitution in the wake of the American rebellion and the French Revolution later on.

Traditional religious and deferential predispositions, common to most British people, supported and in effect promoted the foreign, commercial, and Imperial policies pursued after 1688.[38] Such preconditions operated, however, to reinforce actions taken and not taken by governments, widely, and correctly, perceived to be in the interests of British trade, which furthered the accumulation of many forms of wealth. Trade also complemented investment in the navy and protected the security of the realm. Aristocrats, merchants, and industrialists came to

[38] Linda Colley, *Britons. Forging the Nation, 1707–1837* (London, 1992).

co-operate in what has been felicitiously depicted as a culture of 'gentlemanly capitalism'.[39] There would seem to have been no real or perceived economic conflicts between landed aristocrats and other propertied interests towards the sustained naval and military investment by governments, which in effect underpinned the commitment by merchants and industrialists, and by extension their workforces, to commerce on a trans-European scale.

During this period of state-building and warfare among continental powers, Britain's businessmen anticipated that markets for manufactured exports in Europe would continue to be constricted by tariffs and other political barriers to trade. Antipathy to the construction of the largest and most effective navy in Europe could hardly come from merchants, who demanded protection from enemy fleets and privateering during the years of warfare and who wanted sea lanes cleared of pirates and of competitors in breach of the Navigation Acts in times of peace.[40] There is a short list of critics, who can be recognized as old Whigs or free traders in waiting; most British merchants, however, shared the central mercantilist assumption of the day, namely, that the volume of international commerce in both commodities and services continued to grow, if at all, but slowly, and that national success depended on the sustained use of force, backed up by a skilful deployment of diplomacy in order to make and to retain economic gains at the expense of their major rivals—Spain, Portugal, and above all the Netherlands and France. Merchants pressed for safe and unimpeded access to the consumers and sources of supply of all other European powers and their colonies in the Americas, Africa, and Asia, as well as for entrée to the Mughal and Chinese empires in the East. Without any semblance of shame, they also supported the relatively more effective implementation by the Royal Navy of Britain's own colonial regulations and navigation codes, which not only discriminated strongly against other Europeans but also, less stringently and consistently, against Irish and American trade within the Empire. Free intra-Imperial trade, however, attracted growing support from merchants as time went on.[41]

Merchants rarely spoke in unison. Indeed, well-organized groups representing trades with particular colonies and foreign markets, such as the East and West Indies, or those dealing in specific commodities such as in silks or high-quality linens, often conflicted with and countervailed each other. Nevertheless, close

---

[39] P. J. Cain and A. G. Hopkins, *British Imperialism: Innovation and Expansion, 1688–1914* (London, 1993), chap. 2.

[40] Daniel A. Baugh, 'Maritime Strength and Atlantic Commerce. The Uses of "a Grand Marine Empire"', in Lawrence Stone, ed., *An Imperial State at War. Britain from 1689 to 1815* (London, 1994), pp. 185–223.

[41] Nancy Koehn, *The Power of Commerce. Economy and Governance in the First British Empire* (Ithaca, NY, 1994).

co-operation between merchants and ministers, the links between merchants and the navy, and the involvement of merchants in the extension and governance of the Empire came to be recognized as valuable and normal by the court and by aristocratic governments alike.[42] Down to 1784, on all matters, economic, diplomatic, and military affecting Britain's relations with India and other parts of Asia, merchants organized corporately in the form of the East India Company actually ruled an Asian Empire without intervention from the national government.[43]

Ministers of the Crown responsible for formulating the strategic, foreign, and Imperial policies within which the nation's commerce with the outside world operated, represented no material interest that could be plausibly separated from the concerns and aspirations of British merchants and export industries located in several regions of the kingdom. On the contrary, the further and deeper integration of a small island economy into the world economy at large could only foster the accumulation of wealth by aristocrats, landowners, and gentry, who dominated Parliaments and royal councils. Within a system of property rights which visibly concentrated the ownership of cultivable land, forests, and mineral wealth in the hands of a hereditary ruling élite, the owners of these assets and their *équipe* of lawyers, clergymen, servants, and other dependants could perceive that it would be prudent as well as paternal to find alternative employment for the growing population of poor families denied access to land and other forms of capital. Landowners could then with greater impunity reorganize their estates into larger, less labour-intensive farms, enclose commons, and evict cottars and squatters. Potential threats to the security of their assets and property rights from crime, political expropriation, disorder, and even from rates, levied to relieve poverty, could only be diminished by the creation of opportunities for employment in industry, trade, and urban services, and by emigration to the Empire.

Global trade, urbanization, and industrialization augmented demands for the food, raw materials, minerals, timber, urban sites and buildings, and transportation routes owned and controlled by aristocrats and gentry. As internal and external markets widened, their rents, particularly in towns, continued to rise. Compared to these tangible and obvious economic benefits, their antipathies to the elevation of a mercantile and a monied interest appear to be nothing more than cultural.[44] Furthermore, neither of these less-than homogeneous groups challenged their position within society, let alone within the state. Landowners avoided most of the serious risks involved in investing directly in the development

---

[42] Daniel A. Baugh, 'Great Britain's Blue Water Policy, 1689–1815', *International History Review*, X (1988), pp. 33–38.

[43] See below, pp. 530–44.

[44] For an interpretation which emphasizes cultural conflict, see Kathleen Wilson, *The Sense of the People, Politics, Culture and Imperialism in England, 1715–85* (Cambridge, 1995).

of global commerce and British industry, but they did diversify their portfolios to take advantage of new opportunities for capital gains created by trade and the growth of a market for dealing in government bonds that made up the national debt. Taxes went up, but for several decades fell relatively lightly upon their wealth. They used subsidies and tariffs to protect agriculture from foreign and even from Irish competition. Cadets, relatives, and friends from families of the gentry enjoyed much of the patronage engendered by an expanding state. Disputes that appeared from time to time between the ruling élites and other orders with a stake in the accumulating wealth of this polite society cannot be represented as serious conflicts of economic interest. Before the passage of the Corn Laws, which came on to the statute book in the wake of victory over Napoleon, no real divisions over external policy between agrarians and traders or agrarians and industrialists marked the rise of a fiscal-military state in Britain.

On the contrary, monarchs and aristocrats repeatedly extolled the virtues and the power of commerce. Few statesmen entertained doubts about the dominant consensus that the expansion of trade, of a maritime, and eventually even of a territorial Empire, could only be beneficial for the economy, good for employment, and profitable for families of noble birth. As the élite, they remained keen to maintain social distinctions and distances from merchants and others of the middling sort and to hold on to political power. Ballasted by a culture of obsequious deference to inherited rank and pushed forward by the winds of popular acclaim for imperialism, Britain's aristocracy became enthusiastic about sailing the ship of state into blue waters far from home.[45] They realized that everyone could make economic gains from high and sustained rates of public investment in naval power, which could be used for defence against invasion and for the protection of trade and a maritime Empire overseas.

Discord emerged from time to time largely because the Crown and its ministers had to think more broadly than merchants about the integration of the kingdom and the balance of power in Europe. It was fortunate for merchants that, for strategic as well as commercial reasons, aristocrats saw no good reason to separate naval support for global trade and the acquisition of a maritime Empire from Britain's strategic interests as a European power. They profitably conflated the two objectives into a combined strategy.[46] Public investment in royal dockyards, the construction of warships, and the recruitment of young sailors into the navy expanded between 1688 and 1815. At the same time, Hanoverian ministers appreciated that naval power, as the proven safeguard and deterrent against invasion from

[45] Kathleen Wilson, 'Empire of Virtue. The Imperial Project and Hanoverian Culture, c.1720–1785', in Stone, ed., *An Imperial State at War*, pp. 128–64.

[46] Sari R. Hornstein, *The Restoration Navy and English Foreign Trade, 1674–88* (Aldershot, 1991); Patrick Crowhurst, *The Defence of British Trade, 1689–1815* (Folkestone, 1977). See below, pp. 169–72.

the continent, also depended upon the accumulation and maintenance of merchant ships, skilled seamen, knowledge, and organizational capacities, built up and sustained by private investment in port facilities, shipbuilding, and in the kingdom's mercantile marine and the fishing fleets. They also knew that colonies in the Americas could supply, albeit at higher prices, some of the timber, pitch, tar, hemp, and iron required to build and maintain warships. They appreciated that strategic imports required by the Royal Navy continued, moreover, to be purchased from the Baltic, where a persistent imbalance in trade could, they observed, only be sustained through the enterprise of merchants who re-exported tropical groceries and bullion obtained from trading with the British and with the Iberian empires respectively.[47]

At the end of the day, Hanoverian strategy and diplomacy, which always included a measure of continental commitment, did preserve the realm, its capital assets, and its possessions overseas from invasion, damage, and destruction. As aristocrats with a foot in Europe, Hanoverian statesmen developed a fine-tuned diplomatic appreciation of the territory, bases, and global trades that Britain could safely retain at successive settlements from 1713 to 1815. With the costly exception of the War of American Independence, there is no evidence that their strategic policies did anything other than assist British merchants to achieve the dominant position in global commerce they occupied after Waterloo.

Conclusions

Progress towards the Vienna settlement, when Britain finally emerged as the hegemonic naval, commercial, Imperial, and industrial power, had never been linear. Narratives dealing with particular reigns, Cabinets, wars, and campaigns, will expose how unplanned, fortuitous, contingent, and even chaotic Britain's climb to hegemony had really been.[48] In taking the years between 1688 and 1815, as one period, this chapter has emphasized structural conditions that carried Britain, its economy, and its Empire forward through time. Several inseparable and favourable connections between resources and institutions allowed Britain and not Portugal, Spain, the Netherlands, or above all France to dominate global commerce. Benign natural endowments, the early industrialization of the workforce, the prior and steady accumulation of the mercantile and financial skills required to manage global commerce, strong and consistent support from an effective fiscal state, dominated by perceptive aristocrats, are among the structural

[47] Robert Greenhalgh Albion, *Forests and Sea Power. The Timber Problem of the Royal Navy, 1652–1862* (Cambridge, Mass., 1926).

[48] See below, pp. 151–67.

preconditions that emerge decade after decade, war after war, until an era of mercantilist struggles for trade and Empire virtually came to an end on the seas at Trafalgar and on land at Waterloo.

This chapter has elaborated upon the economic, fiscal, political, and cultural conditions which allowed Britain to achieve the hegemonic status it occupied in the international economic order for roughly a century after Waterloo. There is another and equally interesting debate about the costs and benefits to Britain of the mercantilist and imperialist policies pursued after the Glorious Revolution. Could Britain have industrialized without acquiring an Empire?

Taking a cue from David Hume and quotations from Adam Smith, a predominantly North American school of economic historians have used counter-factual and cliometric (quantitative) techniques to demonstrate that participation in intercontinental trade and Empire probably made only a small contribution to the rise of the first industrial nation. Indeed, their models and numbers suggest that trade and Empire emanated from domestic economic growth rather than the other way round.[49] Their provocative hypotheses rest, however, upon a foreshortened time scale for the analysis of the essentially long-term nature of Britain's transition to an industrial society. Their parsimonious models of connections between trade and growth seem under-specified. For example, and for purposes of econometric measurement, they assume full employment and insist that there were alternative, and only marginally less productive, uses for the resources actually deployed by both private enterprise and the state to acquire an Empire and a hegemonic position in global commerce between 1688 and 1815. As liberal sceptics about Empire, several economic historians have also separated the acquisition of colonies from the protection of trade. In order to measure the costs and benefits that might have arisen from a disembodied imperialism, they have resorted to an analysis based upon an altogether unrealistic counter-factual; namely, an international economic order, operating between 1688 and 1815 under competitive conditions, virtually free from governmental interference with trade and untroubled by warfare.[50]

Latterly, the chronology, assumptions, and the data upon which the modern scepticism about the role of trade and denigration of mercantilism and Empire are based have been challenged and revised.[51] Since Adam Smith, the liberal critique of

[49] The debate is critically reviewed by Joel Mokyr in 'Editor's Introduction', in Joel Mokyr, ed., *The British Industrial Revolution: An Economic Perspective* (Boulder, Colo., 1993), pp. 69–78.

[50] P. R. Coelho, 'The Profitability of Imperialism: The British Experience in the West Indies, 1768–72', *Explorations in Economic History*, X (1973), pp. 253–80.

[51] S. Smith, 'British Exports to Colonial North America and the Mercantilist Fallacy', *Business History*, XXXVII (1995), pp. 45–63 and J. C. Esteban, 'Britain's Terms of Trade and the Americas, 1772–1821', Unpublished Paper, University of Waterloo, Canada, 1994.

Hanoverian commercial and Imperial policy has occupied too much of the high ground of academic discourse. It is time to rescue the consensus and success of the period from the condescension of posterity. Very few critics of mercantilism and Imperialism writing between 1688 and 1815 developed an alternative blueprint for national development that might have carried Britain to the position within the international order that the country occupied when Castlereagh signed the Treaty of Vienna. Nearly everyone at the time perceived that economic progress, national security, and the integration of the kingdom might well come from sustained levels of investment in global commerce, naval power, and, whenever necessary, the acquisition of bases and territory overseas.

Select Bibliography

DANIEL A. BAUGH, 'Maritime Strength and Atlantic Commerce. The Uses of "a Grand Marine Empire"', in L. Stone, ed., *An Imperial State at War. Britain from 1689 to 1815* (London and New York, 1994), pp. 185–223.

C. A. BAYLY, *Imperial Meridian. The British Empire and the World, 1780–1830* (London, 1989).

JEREMY BLACK, *A System of Ambition? British Foreign Policy, 1660–1793* (London, 1991).

R. C. BLITZ, 'Mercantilist Policies and the Pattern of World Trade, 1500–1750', *Journal of Economic History*, XXVII (1967), pp. 39–55.

H. V. BOWEN, *Elites, Enterprise and the Making of the British Overseas Empire, 1688–1775* (London, 1996).

JOHN BREWER, *The Sinews of Power. War, Money and the English State, 1688–1783* (London, 1989).

P. J. CAIN and A. G. HOPKINS, *British Imperialism, Innovation and Expansion, 1688–1914* (London, 1993).

LINDA COLLEY, *Britons. Forging the Nation, 1707–1837* (London, 1992).

PATRICK CROWHURST, *The Defence of British Trade, 1689–1815* (Folkestone, 1977).

D. A. FARNIE, 'The Commercial Empire of the Atlantic, 1607–1783', *Economic History Review*, Second Series, V (1962–63), pp. 205–18.

DAVID HANCOCK, *Citizens of the World. London Merchants and the Integration of the British Atlantic Community, 1735–85* (Cambridge, 1995).

KNICK HARLEY, 'Foreign Trade, Comparative Advantage and Performance', in Roderick Floud and Donald McCloskey, eds., *The Economic History of Britain since 1700*, 2nd edn., 3 vols. (Cambridge, 1994), I, pp. 300–31.

JOEL MOKYR, 'Editor's Introduction', in Joel Mokyr, ed., *The British Industrial Revolution: An Economic Perspective* (Boulder, Colo., 1993), pp. 69–78.

KENNETH MORGAN, *Bristol and the Atlantic Trade in the Eighteenth Century* (Cambridge, 1993).

PATRICK K. O'BRIEN, 'The Political Economy of British Taxation, 1660–1815', *Economic History Review*, Second Series, XLI (1988), pp. 1–32.

JACOB M. PRICE, 'What did Merchants do? Reflections on British Overseas Trade, 1660–1790', *Journal of Economic History*, XLIX (1989), pp. 267–84.

J. D. TRACY, ed., *The Political Economy of Merchant Empires. State, Power and World Trade, 1350–1750* (Cambridge, 1991).

J. R. WARD, 'The Industrial Revolution and British Imperialism, 1750–1850', *Economic History Review*, Second Series, XLVII (1994), pp. 44–64.

KATHLEEN WILSON, *The Sense of the People. Politics, Culture and Imperialism in England, 1715–85* (Cambridge, 1995).

A. E. WRIGLEY, 'Urban Growth and Agricultural Change in England and the Continent in the Early Modern Period', *Journal of Interdisciplinary History*, XV (1985), pp. 683–728.

4

The Imperial Economy, 1700–1776

JACOB M. PRICE

Statesmen and Merchants: Introduction

An analysis of an 'imperial economy' must start with the recognition that such a concept embraces two distinct clusters of phenomena. On the one hand, there is the 'empire', a political entity with laws and the means of enforcing (or attempting to enforce) them; on the other, there are the economic activities that take place in more or less open markets. Participants in an imperial economy would tend to make decisions by quite different criteria, depending on whether they were thinking primarily of laws and orders; or of market conditions, particularly prices. Statesmen as well as merchants might find their options limited by what Harold Innis called 'the penetrative powers of the price system'.[1]

'Empire' in this chapter will mean the 'commercial Empire', that is, both lands indisputably under English or (from 1707) British sovereignty and other territories over which the Crown did not claim sovereignty, but in which the market activities of British subjects were regulated by parliamentary statutes and other emanations of power. Much of the West African coast and the 'East Indies' fall into the latter category, discussed in greater detail in other chapters. From the standpoint of the merchant and the responsible bureaucrats, the 'Empire' as an effective jurisdiction was really created by the Acts of Trade and Navigation of the mid-seventeenth century.[2] These measures treated the whole 'commercial Empire' as a coherent trading area subject in some matters to a relatively uniform system of law. Supervision was made more regular by the establishment of the Board of Trade in 1696, but relatively few significant changes were made in the character of the system thereafter until the establishment of the West Indian free ports in 1766.[3] Despite this institutional stasis, the living organism of the commercial Empire experienced

---

[1] Cf. Harold A. Innis, 'The Penetrative Powers of the Price System', *Canadian Journal of Economics and Political Science*, IV (1938), pp. 299–319.

[2] See above, pp. 10–11.

[3] The most notable exceptions were the permission granted for direct export from the American colonies to southern Europe of rice (1730) and sugar (1739). On free ports, see below pp. 423–24.

a vast increase in population and trade between 1696 and 1775, changes increasingly significant for the home country (Tables 4.1 and 4.2). With the growth of their population and income, England's (and later Britain's) trade with the dependencies around the Atlantic and Indian Oceans rose as a proportion of the country's total foreign commerce. Contemporaries who noted this development almost uniformly appeared to regard it as desirable, though different segments of the political nation based their favourable attitude on different considerations.

To many in the government, England's expanding colonial trade was but one manifestation of its emergence as a major sea power. England had a quarter of the population of France and thus, as Charles II reminded his sister, could only be 'considerable by our trade and power by sea'.[4] Trade and sea power were obviously mutually dependent. Trading vessels needed the protection of the Royal Navy in wartime, while a sea power needed a large pool of experienced, skilled, or 'prime' seamen. From the sixteenth century, the great vocational academies training such seamen were the fisheries and the long-distance trades. Competition in the carrying trades was particularly bitter. Towards the end of the seventeenth century, among European powers, the Dutch still led in tonnage employed in intra-European trade, but the English were beginning to pull ahead in shipping employed in the long-distance (mostly colonial) trades.[5] The need for shipping in these trades was a considerable stimulus to the English shipbuilding industry. The strategic importance of a large mercantile fleet with its tens of thousands of experienced seamen created a national defence interest supporting that part of the Navigation Acts designed to keep as much as possible of England's colonial trade in English-built and manned vessels. Taking the trade legislation as a whole, the encouragement of navigation (and hence of national security) was an objective even more urgent than the protection either of domestic industry or of Crown revenues.

National defence inevitably required a regular supply of all the shipbuilding materials needed by the Royal and mercantile navies. In both the seventeenth and eighteenth centuries, much of this vital material came from Norway, Russia, and the Baltic, whence supplies could be jeopardized in wartime or even in those ostensibly peaceful years in the first half of the eighteenth century when political quarrels strained British diplomatic relations with Sweden or Russia. It was therefore important for national security that statesmen take advantage of potential alternative supplies of naval stores and wood products in the North American

---

[4] Robert M. Bliss, *Revolution and Empire: English Politics and the American Colonies in the Seventeenth Century* (Manchester, 1990), p. 171.

[5] Jacob M. Price, 'The Map of Commerce', in J. S. Bromley and others, eds., *The New Cambridge Modern History*, 9 vols. (Cambridge, 1957–70), VI, pp. 871–73.

colonies. In 1705 Parliament adopted more or less successful subsidies for imports from the colonies of tar, pitch, turpentine, masts, yards, and bowsprits as well as a less successful subsidy for hemp.

In the eighteenth century, as in the seventeenth, statesmen associated the relief of rural poverty with the expansion of markets for rural manufactures—whether at home or abroad. As the expansion of most European markets for English or British products was rendered extremely difficult by hostile foreign protectionism and regulation, would-be expanders of exports came to focus their dreams and efforts on more remote areas. Both the East and West Indies eventually became attractive markets for English exports of hardware, but textiles faced great obstacles in Asia. The successive East India Companies had to export silver (originating mostly in Spanish America) because they were never able to sell enough English or British manufactures of any sort to pay for all the East India produce for which they could find markets at home—imports which embarrassingly included silks and cottons. By contrast, the new colonies in North America and the West Indies took an ever mounting total of English manufactures—woollens in particular for the more northerly. The total population of the North American and West Indian colonies increased about sevenfold between 1700 and 1775 (or nine times for North America alone).[6] By the latter date, the implications for British industrial employment were significant.

Foreign trade was not, however, undertaken by politicians or manufacturers but by merchants. For them, decisions about activity and risk-taking were ultimately determined by their calculations of likely profit and loss, usefully framed within the bookkeeping concept of the 'adventure'. If an adventure involved exchanging British products overseas for other goods to be sold at home, what, after deducting prime cost, freight, insurance, taxes, commissions, interest, and all other expenses, did one's final accounting show? Costs and prices at every stage could vary from year to year, but merchant adventurers had to start with some reasonable confidence in both the market abroad for their export cargoes and the market at home for their returns. It has been argued that the great driving force in English commercial expansion overseas in the sixteenth and seventeenth centuries was not the statesman's search for export markets but the merchant's search for imports—goods for which there was an evident demand in England, a demand demonstrated by the importation of such goods from other European entrepôts. Thus, the East India Company of London sent ships into the Indian Ocean to search for the spices, silks, and calicoes (and later tea and coffee) for which home demand was established, while private merchants in London, Bristol, and other ports undertook trade to the West Indies and North America seeking sugar,

---

[6] Table 4.1.

tobacco, dyestuffs, and later rice, coffee, and cotton, for all of which demand was equally assured at home or nearby.[7]

British Imports from the Commercial Empire

Relatively good but not perfect quantitative data are available on British imports from the colonies and other commercially dependent areas in America, Africa, and Asia. Customs officials compiled detailed annual accounts of English foreign trade from 1696. For Scotland, summary data are available from 1740 and full data from 1755. Equivalent data for the North American colonies are available only for 1768–72, but for earlier years some scattered figures survive on individual colonies or commodities. The purely commercial records of the East India Company were for the most part destroyed when after the Mutiny the Company was wound up in 1858, but summary or broken data survive. Thus measurements of commodity flows, and the like, within the trading Empire can be precise on some topics and not on others.[8]

By value the most important colonial import was West Indian sugar. By the mid-eighteenth century sugar had passed linen to become the most valuable British import—a rank it held till passed by raw cotton c.1825.[9] English and British sugar imports rose steadily from 8,176 tons in 1663 to over 25,000 tons by 1710 and over 97,000 tons in 1775.[10] This growth was increasingly based on the home market. As late as 1699–1701, re-exports to foreign markets had accounted for 38.2 per cent of imports, but by 1733–37 this had dropped to 10.1 per cent.[11] Consumption of sugar in Britain and Ireland rose from about four pounds per head p.a. in 1700–09 to eleven pounds in 1770–79. By contrast, French consumption then was only

---

[7] Cf. Robert Brenner, *Merchants and Revolution, Commercial Change, Political Conflict, and London's Overseas Trade, 1550–1653* (Princeton, 1993), pp. 39–45.

[8] Cf. Sir George [N.] Clark, *Guide to English Commercial Statistics, 1696–1782* (London, 1938), pp. 1–44; Jacob M. Price, 'New Time Series for Scotland's and Britain's Trade with the Thirteen Colonies and States, 1740 to 1791', *William and Mary Quarterly* (hereafter *WMQ*), Third Series, XXXII (1975), pp. 307–25. Summary data including breakdowns by colonies can be found in John J. McCusker and Russell R. Menard, *The Economy of British America, 1607–1789* (Chapel Hill, NC, 1985). A detailed analysis of the North American data can be found in James F. Shepherd and Gary M. Walton, *Shipping, Maritime Trade and the Economic Development of Colonial North America* (Cambridge, 1972).

[9] Ralph Davis, 'English Foreign Trade, 1660–1700', *The Economic History Review* (hereafter *EcHR*), Second Series, VII (1954), pp. 164–65, and 'English Foreign Trade, 1700–1774', *EcHR*, Second Series, XV (1962), pp. 300–01; and *The Industrial Revolution and British Overseas Trade* (Leicester, 1979), pp. 118–19.

[10] Richard B. Sheridan, *Sugar and Slavery: An Economic History of the British West Indies, 1623–1775* (Barbados, 1974), p. 489; Richard S. Dunn, *Sugar and Slaves: The Rise of the Planter Class in the English West Indies, 1624–1713* (Chapel Hill, NC, 1972), p. 203.

[11] Sheridan, *Sugar and Slavery*, pp. 493–95.

slightly over two pounds per head.[12] This meant that from the great expansion of their West Indian production, the French could create a substantial re-export trade, particularly to the Netherlands, while British West Indian production was almost totally absorbed by consumption in the British Isles and British North America.

Quite similar to sugar in its orientation to British home demand was the trade in colonial dyestuffs. Since the production of woollens was easily the most important English industrial activity, and since linens were an important manufacture deliberately encouraged in politically sensitive Scotland and Ireland, those industries' need for assured supplies of dyestuffs could not be neglected by government. Since those that could be grown in Britain itself did not usually produce colours of the first quality, the British textile industry required substantial imports from more appropriate climes: English dyestuff imports alone rose in value from £226,000 p.a. in 1699–1701 to £506,000 in 1772–74.[13] Some (logwood, brazilwood, and cochineal) could not be produced in the British colonies and had to be purchased from foreigners. It was thus in the national interest to encourage the cultivation of those, including braziletto and indigo, which could be grown in British territories. Unfortunately for British industrial security, in the second quarter of the eighteenth century the cultivation of the latter product in the British West Indies declined as planters found sugar more profitable. The share of England's dyestuff imports coming directly from the Americas declined from 48 per cent in 1722–24 to 25 per cent in 1752–54. Thus British drysalters had to obtain their needed supplies of indigo from France, whose West Indian colonies had continued production. Such dependence became dangerous when a new cycle of war between Britain and France started in 1744. Fortunately, it had become apparent by that time that indigo could also be grown in North America. Planters in South Carolina had learned by experiment that indigo might thrive on the higher, dryer soils inland. In 1748 this cultivation was encouraged by a parliamentary bounty of sixpence per pound. This subsidy stimulated production sufficiently so that, by the time of the next war in 1756–63, substantial quantities of Carolina indigo began to reach Britain. Despite reservations on quality, in the next generation indigo was—after rice—the second most valuable product exported from the southernmost continental colonies.

A more valuable commodity whose importation responded most amazingly to growing home demand was tea from China. Its importation, monopolized by the

---

[12] Noel Deerr, *The History of Sugar*, 2 vols. (London, 1949–50), II, p. 532; John J. McCusker, *Rum and the American Revolution*, 2 vols. (New York, 1989), I, p. 310; John R. MacCulloch, *A Dictionary of Commerce and Commercial Navigation*, 2nd edn., 2 vols. (London, 1834), II, p. 1088.

[13] Davis, 'Foreign Trade, 1700–1774', p. 300.

East India Company, increased one hundredfold in value from about £8,000 in 1699–1701 to £848,000 in 1772–74. Almost all was consumed in Britain, Ireland, and the British colonies in America and helped sustain the growing demand for sugar.

A further group of products whose importation was sustained by growing demand within Britain consisted of the products of the North American forests and seas, raw materials for British industries: whale-oil, skins and furs, and shipbuilding supplies. The beaver skins of North America were an important raw material for English felt and hatmakers. From the forests of the continent came also substantial quantities of masts, deals, pitch, and tar so needed by shipbuilders, as well as staves needed by barrelmakers, and potash and pearl ash used in soapmaking and glassmaking and in fulling and bleaching textiles. Most of the colonies also had their own shipbuilding industries constructing ocean-going vessels as well as smaller craft for river and coastal trades. As almost all the raw materials for shipbuilding were plentiful and inexpensive in North America, colonial-built ships could be and were sold advantageously in Britain itself from the late seventeenth century. Orders were also sent out by merchants in England and Scotland for vessels to be built to their specifications. On the eve of the American Revolution about one-third of the British-registered tonnage known to the underwriters at Lloyd's had been built in the North American colonies, which earned about £140,000 p.a. from such sales.[14]

Another strategic product, iron, was equally dependent on forests, if not necessarily those of North America. England was relatively well endowed with iron, copper, lead, and tin and had significant metallurgical industries from at least the sixteenth century. Charcoal, the fuel used in the furnace to convert English iron ore into pig iron and, at the forge, to convert pig iron into more usable bar iron, was made from wood grown locally in specially planted coppices. New coppices could be and were planted but took twenty years to reach the desired growth. Thus, even before 1600, part of England's iron needs was met by imports from the Baltic. The fraction imported rose steadily through the seventeenth and eighteenth centuries, provoking a crisis in 1717–18 when deteriorating diplomatic relations led to a suspension of bar iron imports from Sweden. The crisis revealed a marked difference of interest between the iron-making trades (furnaces and forges) and the iron-fabricating trades. The iron users, allied with the Virginia merchants, tried in 1718–20 to persuade Parliament to encourage iron production in the American colonies by removing import duties on iron produced there. (The Virginia merchants were particularly interested because iron made ideal ballast on

[14] Jacob M. Price, 'A Note on the Value of Colonial Exports of Shipping', *Journal of Economic History* (hereafter *JEH*) XXXVI (1976), pp. 704–24.

vessels laden with relatively light tobacco.) In this effort, the advocates of the American source were defeated by the greater political weight of the ironmasters and their landlord allies. Nevertheless, serious beginnings were being made in iron production in the North American colonies, particularly Pennsylvania, Maryland, and Virginia. A new deterioration of British–Swedish relations in the 1740s ultimately led to acts of 1750 and 1757 removing import duties on American colonial pig- and bar iron. Since the former duties had not been very high, their removal had only a modest effect on iron imports from the colonies which doubled between the 1730s and 1770s, but remained only a small fraction of total imports.[15]

English demand for raw cotton grew steadily in the first three quarters of the eighteenth century. In 1772–74 cotton imports, worth then about £137,000 p.a., came mostly from the West Indies (64 per cent) and the Levant and southern Europe (28 per cent). During the American Revolutionary War the explosion in the English cotton industry began, raising imports of raw cotton by 1794–96 to about six times those of 1772–74, with the West Indies still the leading source. However, by 1804–06 the United States had become Britain's primary cotton supplier, a rank which it held until the Civil War. Thus only in the crucial early decades of the cotton industry's growth was the Imperial supply from the West Indies essential.[16]

Thus far, we have been considering a group of commodities imported into Britain from the colonies and Asia primarily to satisfy demand in Britain and dependent areas. There were, however, other important British colonial imports from the 'commercial Empire'—particularly tobacco, rice, and coffee—whose volume far exceeded domestic requirements, thus making the prosperity of those trades dependent on demand in wider sections of Europe. By the later seventeenth century the British Chesapeake colonies had become the most important suppliers of American tobacco to western Europe. The very rapid growth in colonial shipments slowed down in the last decades of the century, by which time re-exports already accounted for two-thirds of England's imports. Difficulties in expanding the labour force help account for an ensuing stagnation in tobacco exports during the first quarter of the eighteenth century. Growth resumed thereafter, so that British imports of 1771–75 were three times those of

---

[15] On iron imports, see Thomas Southcliff Ashton, *Iron and Steel in the Industrial Revolution* (Manchester, 1951), chap. 5; G. Hammersley, 'The Charcoal Iron Industry and Its Fuel, 1540–1750', *EcHR*, Second Series, XXVI (1973), pp. 593–613; and Sven-Erik Åström, *From Stockholm to St. Petersburg: Commercial Factors in the Political Relations between England and Sweden, 1675–1700* (Helsinki, 1962), pp. 14, 110, 113, 138–39, 143.

[16] For cotton imports, see Alfred P. Wadsworth and Julia de Lacy Mann, *The Cotton Trade and Industrial Lancashire, 1600–1780* (Manchester, 1931), p. 521; R. Davis, *Industrial Revolution*, p. 41.

1721–25. The stagnation in cultivation meant higher prices, particularly during 1713–25, which gave the more substantial planters the wherewithal to import African slaves instead of English indentured servants.[17] The black population in the Chesapeake—unlike that in the West Indies—grew naturally as did the white population, the increases in both supporting the resumed growth of production. The British government helped in 1723 by conceding the total refund or drawback of import duties on the re-export of British colonial tobacco. This made it politically acceptable for foreign tobacco monopolies—particularly the French—to make major regular purchases of British tobacco. By the eve of the American Revolution about 85 per cent of Britain's tobacco imports were re-exported, with 25 per cent of the total export crop going to France alone. (Because of its value to the French *fisc*, this trade was permitted to continue in war as in peace.)[18]

Rice was a less controversial commodity but equally dependent on the re-export market in Europe. Its serious commercial cultivation in South Carolina began in the 1690s with the introduction of a superior larger-grained variety from Madagascar. Unlike tobacco, which required little in the way of investment beyond a few simple field tools, a press, and a drying shed, rice required substantial investment in irrigation and thus from the beginning was associated with fairly large establishments. In this its cultivation was socially closer to that of sugar than to that of tobacco. Production in South Carolina and Georgia reached 5.8 million pounds p.a. in 1715–24, 29.5 million pounds in 1735–44, and 72 million pounds in 1765–74. During 1768–72 about 65 per cent of colonial rice exports went to Britain, 18.3 per cent to the West Indies, and 16.7 per cent to southern Europe. The large fraction sent to the mother country was much more than could be consumed there. The necessary re-exports ranged from 87 per cent of English rice imports in 1718–23 to 89 per cent in 1753–62 and 95 per cent for Scottish imports in 1756–62.[19] Starting in 1730, a series of parliamentary acts provided that rice could be exported directly from South Carolina (and later from other colonies) to points in Europe south of Cape Finisterre (at the north-west corner of Spain) provided that a licence was obtained in London and a minimal duty paid there. The impressive growth of rice

---

[17] Jacob M. Price and Paul G. E. Clemens, 'A Revolution of Scale in Overseas Trade: British Firms in the Chesapeake Trade, 1675–1775', *JEH*, XLVII (1987), p. 5 and works cited there.

[18] Jacob M. Price, *France and the Chesapeake: A History of the French Tobacco Monopoly, 1674–79 . . .*, 2 vols. (Ann Arbor, 1973), I, pp. 563–85, II, p. 849; US Bureau of the Census, *Historical Statistics of the United States . . . to 1970* (Washington, 1975), II, pp. 1189–91.

[19] McCusker and Menard, *Economy of British America*, p. 174; *Historical Statistics of the United States* (Washington, 1975) II, p. 1192; Board of Trade commercial accounts in C[olonial] O[ffice] 390/5, f. 119, 121 and CO 390/9, ff. 4, 56; Treasury accounts: Scotland in T[reasury] 36/13, ff. 258, 289. See also Kenneth Morgan, 'The Organization of the Colonial American Rice Trade', *WMQ*, Third Series, LII (1995), pp. 433–52.

re-exports suggests that these concessions in the navigation and revenue regulations were productive.

Coffee was the third major re-export commodity. In the 1690s the English and Dutch already had factories at Mocha on the Red Sea to purchase coffee for shipment to India, whence it was forwarded to Europe. By about 1710 the English, Dutch, and French were cutting costs by sending whole shiploads of coffee from Mocha directly to Europe around the Cape of Good Hope without trans-shipment in India. The trade proving profitable, the enhanced demand for coffee led in the 1720s and 1730s to its introduction into the Americas. By 1772–74 when England's coffee imports were sixteen times as heavy as at the beginning of the century, the West Indies were providing about twenty times as much coffee as Asia. This was, however, a commercial boom rather than a consumer revolution. During 1756–75 almost 94 per cent of the coffee imported into England was re-exported, primarily to the Low Countries, Germany, and northern Europe.[20]

The willingness of the British government to encourage such re-export business through the total or near total drawback (repayment) of import duties is all the more remarkable when one remembers that import duties were very often committed to guarantee the payment of interest or annuities on different sections of the national debt. Thus, when Parliament conceded total or near total drawback of duties on most re-exported commodities, it was making a major concession, placing the encouragement of colonial commerce (via the re-export trades) above the narrow fiscal interest of the state.[21] The re-export trades also had a further, if indirect, strategic benefit. It is easy enough to assume that commodities such as tobacco, rice, and coffee (and rum in certain decades), over 80 per cent of which were re-exported, might have enhanced the incomes of merchants, shipowners, and mariners but were of little importance to the national economy. It should be remembered, however, that the ports to which these goods were re-exported lay in areas with which Britain otherwise would have had a very unfavourable balance of trade. Thus, to a significant degree the re-export of colonial products, particularly tobacco, rice, and coffee, helped pay for the imports of all those useful raw materials from northern Europe—especially iron, flax, hemp, masts, deals, pitch, and tar—that kept thousands of sailors and tens of thousands of workers busy in Britain.[22]

[20] Elizabeth B. Schumpeter, *English Overseas Trade Statistics, 1697–1808* (Oxford, 1960), p. 60; Kristof Glamann, *Dutch–Asiatic Trade, 1620–1740* (Copenhagen, 1958), chap. 10.

[21] See above, pp. 67–70.

[22] J. M. Price, 'Multilateralism and/or Bilateralism: The Settling of British Trade Balances with the North, ca. 1700', *EcHR*, Second Series, XIV (1961), pp. 254–74.

Exports

The resources which colonial populations earned selling goods to Britain were for the most part used to purchase slaves, goods, or services in their area or to make purchases in Britain itself. Even when specific trading decisions were made by export merchants in Britain, the basis of such decisions had to be overseas demand for particular goods in specific markets. With the growth of population, white and black, in the American colonies, the share of English or British exports going thither increased impressively. In 1700–01 North America, the West Indies, the East Indies, and Africa bought £656,000 worth of English-made goods or 14.7 per cent of English domestic exports. By 1772–73 the share of British domestic exports going to these markets had risen to 50.9 per cent. Within the American–African sphere, North America was the most important destination of exports for both England and Britain (Table 4.4).

The broad class of textiles constituted an impressive 49.8 per cent of British exports to the commercial Empire in 1772–74 or 53.4 per cent of exports to America and Africa (Table 4.5). Woollens, as the most important British manufacture, were understandably the most important textile export, both to the world and to the commercial Empire, particularly to the thirteen North American colonies (constituting 30.7 per cent of all exports thither in 1772).[23] Since 45–50 per cent of English woollen and worsted production was thought to be exported then, the 27.4 per cent of such exports that went to America and Africa in the 1770s had national significance.[24]

The next most important textile export to the Empire was linens, still five times as important as cottons on the eve of the American Revolution. For these light fabrics, the major export markets were the warmer climates of the West Indies, the southern continental colonies, and Africa. Because their labour costs tended to be higher than those prevailing elsewhere in Europe, English linen manufacturers had difficulty competing in price with imports of cheaper continental products. Scotland and Ireland were, however, lands with lower labour costs, where linen could be produced more advantageously than in England. There was, therefore, tension between Scots and Irish political interests and those substantial London

---

[23] For English exports to the colonies, see Table 4.5, and James Bischoff, *A Comprehensive History of the Woollen and Worsted Manufactures*, 2 vols. (London, 1842), I, p. 176. For the place of woollens in total English exports, cf. A. H. John, 'English Agricultural Improvement and Grain Exports, 1660-1765', in D. C. Coleman and A. H. John, eds., *Trade, Government and Economy in Pre-Industrial England: Essays Presented to F. J. Fisher* (London, 1976), p. 52.

[24] Bischoff, *Woollen and Worsted Industry*, I, p. 189; Phyllis Deane, 'The Output of the British Woollen Industry in the Eighteenth Century', *JEH*, XVII (1957), p. 214; Davis, 'English Foreign Trade, 1700–1774', p. 303.

merchants, supported by the woollen interest, who exported woollen cloth to northern Europe and brought back continental linens, a rising proportion of which was re-exported to the American colonies.

In 1705 the English Parliament gave a modest encouragement to the Irish linen industry by an act permitting Irish linens to be exported directly to the American colonies without going through England. In 1743 a small subsidy was conceded on the export to the colonies of the less expensive British and Irish linens. Under this bounty system, the trade was significantly reoriented. The re-exports of European (continental and Irish) linens primarily to America had increased from £157,000 p.a. in 1699–1701 to £301,000 in 1751–54, but stagnated thereafter (Table 4.5). Somewhat more dynamic were the direct exports from Ireland to America. The most dynamic sector, however, was that of British (English and Scottish) linens whose exports to America and Africa surged in value from nothing at the beginning of the century to £681,000 in 1772–74.[25]

Just as did linen in Scotland and Ireland, so in the English Midlands hardware directed the attention of traders towards America's growing markets. Metalware exports to the Empire increased over tenfold between 1699–1701 and 1772–74, by which time they constituted the most substantial export to the East Indies and were second only to woollens in exports to America (Table 4.5).

One ought not, however, to think of Britain's export trading relations with its overseas dependencies entirely in terms of a relatively few staple commodities. If one looks at the London directories (available from 1736), one notes the impressive number of wholesale dealers in specialized products: stationers, booksellers, mathematical instrument makers, watchmakers, jewellers, silversmiths, pewterers, coachmakers, grocers, haberdashers, milliners, lacemakers, and, at the other extreme, warehouses for ready-made shoes, saddles, bridles, and slops or workclothes. Surviving invoices of goods shipped from British firms to their American correspondents give some idea of the wide range of products that British merchants were sending to their correspondents in North America and the West Indies. It is such goods that help explain the mounting importance of the 'miscellaneous' category in Table 4.5.

The Interdependency of Colonies: The Lateral or Peripheral Trades

In addition to the well-known staple trades between the mother country and its outlying dependencies, there were other exchanges that may be termed the lateral

---

[25] For Scottish linens, see Alastair J. Durie, *The Scottish Linen Industry in the Eighteenth Century* (Edinburgh, 1979); for the Irish, see Thomas M. Truxes, *Irish–American Trade, 1660–1783* (Cambridge, 1988), chap. 9.

or peripheral trades, that is, trades between outlying sections of the commercial empire that did not go through the British entrepôt and usually were not controlled by British entrepreneurs. In the Indian Ocean, there was the vast 'country trade'.[26] Where any of this trade was carried on by British merchants resident in India but not employees of the East India Company, it is more than possible that persons resident in Britain were interested in their ventures.[27]

Of more immediate relevance are the trades linking the colonies in North America and the West Indies. In the earliest days of Massachusetts Bay, it was realized that nothing the colonists were then likely to produce could be sold in England, though they could return the furs obtained by trade with the indigenous Indians. In the beginning, therefore, only two major trading outlets were open to them: the export of fish to Iberia and the Wine Islands of Madeira and the Canaries; and the export of victuals, livestock, and forest products to the new English colonies in the West Indies. Later, as other colonies emerged along the Atlantic coast, a variety of exchanges developed between them. Some, notably Pennsylvania, Maryland, and Virginia, had cereal surpluses which they could exchange with Massachusetts and New Hampshire which usually needed to import wheat. Some colonies, particularly Pennsylvania and Maryland, were more successful in iron-smelting and developed a small trade exporting pig- and bar iron and some hardware to other colonies. The total networks of intercolonial trade were complex, though the totals for any one particular trade were rarely impressive. Some of these intercolonial exchanges went by land, for instance, along the Great Wagon Road from Philadelphia to Lancaster and York and thence across Maryland to the Valley of Virginia and the way southward. Goods that moved by these inland roads generally escaped the cognizance of customs officers and thus have left us only the most general idea of the volume and variety of their traffic. By contrast, by the 1690s the British colonies in America had, at least on paper, a comprehensive system of maritime controls, with both customs officers employed to enforce fiscal legislation and naval officers (inspectors of navigation) charged with enforcement of the acts of trade. When a separate American Board of Customs Commissioners was set up in 1767 at Boston, their establishment included an Inspector-General of imports and exports, a record-keeping officer. Thus, the clearest picture of intercolonial seaborne trade dates only from the last years of the old Empire.

---

[26] See below, pp. 493–95; K. N. Chaudhuri, *The Trading World of Asia and the English East India Company, 1660–1760* (Cambridge, 1978), esp. chap. 9; Ashin Das Gupta and M. N. Pearson, eds., *India and the Indian Ocean, 1500–1800* (Calcutta, 1987).

[27] On examples of such connections in the diamond trade, see Gedalia Yogev, *Diamonds and Coral: Anglo-Dutch Jews and Eighteenth-Century Trade* (Leicester, 1978).

During the five years, 1768–72, for which we have the fullest data, the pattern of trade between the British West Indies and British North America is quite clear and not unexpected. As it dominated exports from the islands to Britain, so did the sugar-molasses-rum group account for no less than 91.8 per cent of shipments from the British West Indies to British North America. Of the 1770 total of £762,053 sterling, rum accounted for 42.2 per cent, molasses for 26.5 per cent, and sugar for 23.1 per cent.[28] The £848,934 worth of goods sent from North America to the islands in 1770 consisted mainly of basic subsistence commodities: bread and flour (30.4 per cent); dried fish (13.8 per cent); rice (10.8 per cent); wood products (9.7 per cent), particularly pine boards and the barrel staves and headings needed by the rum-sugar-molasses producers; horses and cattle (8.8 per cent); beef and pork (7.6 per cent); and Indian corn (3.6 per cent).[29]

Much more restricted by law were the peripheral trades between the Atlantic colonies and southern Europe and Ireland. As already noted, at a quite early date in their commercial histories the more northerly colonies found that they could sell both their fish and their surplus cereals in Spain, Portugal, and the Mediterranean. Subsequent legislation permitted the shipment of rice (from 1730) and sugar (from 1739) to places in Europe south of Cape Finisterre. Although relatively little sugar was in fact shipped along these newly opened routes, the continental colonies had by 1768 developed a substantial trade with southern Europe, almost as valuable as their trade with the West Indies. In 1768–72 southern Europe took almost 80 per cent of the continental colonies' exports of wheat, which mostly came from the Middle Colonies and the Chesapeake, 35 per cent of their exports of flour and bread, and 28 per cent of exports of maize. Southern Europe also took 38 per cent of New England's exports of fish in these years and 86 per cent of those of Quebec, Nova Scotia, and Newfoundland.[30] In return, the continental colonies received wine and salt from southern Europe (including the Wine Islands)—all that was allowed under the Acts of Trade.[31] Ireland was permitted from 1664 to send the colonies victuals, primarily butter and salt beef to the West Indies, and linens from 1705. A subsequent British act of 1731 permitted the return to Ireland of non-enumerated goods from the colonies. Whenever there were poor harvests in

---

[28] Shepherd and Walton, *Shipping and Economic Development*, pp. 229–30.

[29] Ibid., p. 232.

[30] Max Schumacher, 'The Northern Farmer and his Markets during the Late Colonial Period', unpublished Ph.D. dissertation, California, Berkeley, 1948, p. 124; McCusker and Menard, *Economy of British America*, pp. 108, 115. See also Shepherd and Walton, *Shipping and Economic Development*, p. 96.

[31] Shepherd and Walton, *Shipping and Economic Development*, p. 233. For colonial imports permitted from southern Europe, see Lawrence A. Harper, *The English Navigation Laws* (New York, 1939), p. 401.

the British Isles and the price of cereals rose, Ireland was likely to receive significant quantities of North American wheat and flour. Two significant trades do not appear in the contemporary compilations by the Inspectors-General of imports and exports. One was the slave trade, to be discussed elsewhere. The other was the trade in shipping.[32]

By ordinary arithmetic, none of these trades was balanced (Table 4.6). The North American colonies imported far more from Britain than they exported thither. But these same colonies had a very favourable balance of trade with the West Indies, southern Europe, and Ireland. The West Indies in turn had a large trade surplus with Britain, part of which was used to pay for slave imports, part for paying for the islands' imports from North America. Similarly, the continental colonies' surpluses with southern Europe and Ireland could be used to cover the shortfall in direct trade with Britain. This may appear complicated but could be readily handled by bills of exchange. That is, the produce of North America could be sold in the West Indies, Iberia, or Ireland for bills of exchange on London and the surpluses and deficiencies in different branches of trade balanced on the books of London merchants. The important point is that one is not dealing with a series of bilateral exchanges but with a complex, multilateral trading system, the various parts of which have to be viewed in the context of the whole.

The Organization and Financing of Trade

The interdependence and interrelatedness of the various parts of the British commercial Empire suggest the importance of the commercial and financial institutions that animated the complex networks of trade linking them all together. The trade between Britain and the Indian Ocean and China was mono- polized after 1709 by the monolithic United East India Company.[33] The Atlantic trades, by contrast, were carried on by numerous private firms, before 1707 domiciled primarily in England. After the Union of England and Scotland in that year, Scots merchants (particularly those of Glasgow) entered these trades enthusiastically but did not assume a weighty position in the market until after 1740. There were of course active resident merchants in all of the American colonies. Their knowledge of local conditions gave them some advantages in buying and selling and ordering goods, but they often were hindered by a shortage of local capital and insurance facilities and unfamiliarity with the British whole- salers from whom they had to order manufactures. Thus, for credit, insurance, and

---

[32] Price, 'Value of Colonial Exports of Shipping', pp. 704–23.
[33] See below pp. 488–91; 547–49.

information on markets and goods, they were to a considerable degree dependent on their 'correspondents', merchants in Britain.

The local geography of the principal colonial productions is relatively well known. At the British end, the local geography of the colonial trades is more complex. During 1699–1701 about 78 per cent of England's trade with the North American and West Indian colonies was carried on by London.[34] The capital's share had, it would appear, been significantly smaller in the later seventeenth century, when numerous outports, headed by Bristol, accounted for a significant share in colonial trade. They included Whitehaven, Lancaster, Liverpool, Barnstaple, Bideford, Plymouth, Dartmouth, Weymouth, Poole, and Exeter (see Map 2.1). A great challenge to the trade of the southern and south-western outports came from the conflicts of 1689–1713. In wartime, the cargo-laden ships returning from North America and the West Indies normally came in convoys, with ships for the southern ports leaving convoy only when near their home haven. It was thus feasible to get American goods home relatively safely, but the re-export trade of these southern ports was too often left unprotected.

War had different impacts on the sugar and tobacco trades. Almost all (85 per cent in 1775) of England's imports of sugar were consumed at home, and most of the re-exported fraction went to Ireland; thus convoys to carry outward-bound re-export goods were not vital to the sugar trade. By contrast, about two-thirds of England's imports of tobacco were re-exported at the end of the seventeenth century, and about 85 per cent on the eve of the American Revolution. Thus, re-export convoys were imperative for the wartime tobacco trade. These were more regularly available at London than at the western ports.[35] Merchants in the north-western ports, however, often avoided eastbound delays by instructing their ship captains not to wait in America for convoy but to come home north about Ireland, a route with far fewer enemy corsairs, thus saving considerable time and expense. Re-exports from the north-western ports could also be made by the safer route to the north of Scotland. Despite their setbacks in the wars of 1689–1713, some of the larger south-western ports—particularly Bristol, Bideford-Barnstaple, Plymouth, and Exeter—were with the peace able to re-establish themselves in the tobacco trade, only to be struck down by the next war. By the end of the 1740s the tobacco trade at Plymouth and Exeter had disappeared while that at Bideford and Barnstaple was fading fast. By then, the commerce in that commodity had in effect been concentrated in five ports: London, Glasgow, Whitehaven, Liverpool, and

[34] Davis, 'English Foreign Trade, 1660–1700', pp. 163–65. See also McCusker, *Rum*, II, pp. 891–93.

[35] On Chesapeake convoys, see Arthur P. Middleton, *Tobacco Coast: A Maritime History of Chesapeake Bay in the Colonial Era* (Newport News, Va, 1953), pp. 289–309. For the West Indies, see Richard Pares, *War and Trade in the West Indies, 1739–1763* (Oxford, 1936), pp. 303–11, 497–98.

Bristol.[36] The sugar trade of the smaller southern ports was also adversely affected by enemy privateering, and, in the later eighteenth century, British sugar imports were substantially concentrated in the same five ports.[37] If Glasgow in some years exceeded London in the tobacco trade, the capital's lead in the sugar trade was unchallenged.

In this concentration of the American trades in a few ports, more was involved than the dangers of war. The eighteenth century also saw the concentration of both sugar and tobacco imports among fewer and larger firms. In the absence of privileged monopoly companies, at least since 1624, commerce with the English colonies in North America and the West Indies was generally open to all subjects of the Crown resident in England or the colonies. In addition to merchants large and small, hundreds of smaller men, including retailers and mariners, ventured in these trades. To reduce individual risks, trading vessels were commonly owned by several investors in shares as small as one thirty-second. Exporters too would divide their shipments among a number of vessels and several traders might be interested in a single overseas adventure. A vessel might carry the speculations of several different groups, each entrusted for sale to the captain, a supercargo, or a factor temporarily resident in the colony. These arrangements often involved long stays in the country for vessels so charged and proved costly in shipping time. Demurrage and other shipping expenses might be saved if each adventure were entrusted for sale to a factor resident in the colony who could assemble return cargoes in advance of the arrival of his employers' later ships. Such arrangements were characteristic of the larger and more efficient English firms by the later seventeenth century and of their Scots competitors in the mid-eighteenth century.

Other considerations besides the employment of resident factors gave an advantage to larger firms. In 1685 a new and heavy impost was adopted for sugar and tobacco. The impost, like other duties on these products, could be bonded but only affluent merchants could get substantial people to countersign their bonds. The impost on sugar was allowed to lapse in 1693 but the persistence of that on tobacco clearly gave the larger firms in that trade an advantage. The development of marine insurance in the late seventeenth and early eighteenth centuries also made it less necessary to divide one's shipping business among many vessels. This made it less risky for larger firms to own or charter whole vessels whose movements could be co-ordinated with factors and correspondents in America to reduce shipping time and expenses. During the wars of 1689–1713 the gap widened

[36] Jacob M. Price and Paul G. E. Clemens, 'A Revolution of Scale in Overseas Trade', pp. 39–40.
[37] Kenneth Morgan, *Bristol and the Atlantic Trade in the Eighteenth Century* (Cambridge, 1993), p. 190. Table 4.6 suggests much about the ability of war to redirect trades away from the more exposed southern routes.

between falling prices in America and scarcity-heightened prices in Europe, inducing some of the larger planters to follow the examples of local merchants and consign their tobacco or sugar to commission merchants in England. Such consignments usually went to the larger English firms with good credit and established reputations. Finally, one must keep in mind that the proportion of tobacco imports re-exported rose from about 66 per cent at the end of the seventeenth century to 85 per cent in the early 1770s. Small importers did not have very much market strength in dealing with large foreign buyers, particularly the French and other monopolists, who of necessity preferred buying from the larger British houses that could make bargains for the major supplies needed. Sugar did not face equivalent re-export problems, but the relatively small number of large sugar refiners in each port probably exerted pressures that worked to the advantage of the larger importers. Thus, in both commodities, few buyers (oligopsony) stimulated the emergence of fewer, larger sellers (oligopoly).

All these changing circumstances worked together to increase the size of the average firm importing sugar or tobacco and to decrease the number of names in the trades. At London, the number of names importing tobacco declined from 573 in 1676 to 56 in 1775, while the importation of the average firm increased fortyfold. At Bristol, the number of similar importers decreased from 467 in 1672 to seventeen in 1789, while the importation of the average firm increased twenty-eight times. Liverpool and Glasgow were not very active in tobacco before the impost was adopted in 1685 and thus did not have the host of small importers characteristic of London and Bristol in the time of Charles II. However, both ports show a trend in 1700–75 towards fewer and larger firms importing tobacco. At Glasgow, the imports of the average firm increased elevenfold between 1722 and 1775. Equivalent data are not available for sugar except at Bristol where the number of importers declined from 402 in 1672 to 106 in 1789 while the importation of the average firm rose twenty-sixfold.[38]

There were essentially three predominant institutional forms in the trade between America and Britain: (1) direct trade in America through the employees (on salaries) or agents (on commission) of the British firms; (2) correspondence between merchants in Britain and merchants in America; and (3) consignments from planters in America to commission merchants in Britain. Before 1689 most of the London and Bristol trade with America was direct trade through employees or agents, though there were a few merchants and large planters in the colonies who corresponded with houses in England. During the wars of 1689–1713 the normal gap between Chesapeake prices and English prices widened and more of the bigger

---

[38] Price and Clemens, 'A Revolution of Scale', pp. 1–43; Morgan, *Bristol and the Atlantic Trade*, pp. 158–59, 191–92.

planters tried to improve their lot by consigning part of their production to commission merchants in England to be sold on their account, just as local merchants did with the tobacco that came to them in trade. The planter consignment system was probably at its peak during 1713–40, but even then it was less important than direct trade. As the Scottish stores in the interior attracted more and more of local production, the share of direct trade rose again after 1740. On the eve of the American Revolution tobacco shipments to Britain can be divided among the following major trading modes used in the important Upper District of James River (with *estimates* for the whole Chesapeake in parentheses):[39]

Scots factors to employers in Scotland	55.1 (43.4) per cent
English factors to employers in England	16.0 (20.3) per cent
Virginia merchants to correspondents in England	19.9 (25.3) per cent
Virginia planters, etc. to merchants in England	8.3 (10.5) per cent

All these trading modes were also known in the West Indies, though the Scottish presence there before 1776 was much less evident than the English. Although no exact measurement is now possible, it seems highly probable that the planter consignment system was more important in the Caribbean than in the Chesapeake.[40] The author of an English tract published c.1732 noted that the English sugar merchants were no longer as domineering *vis-à-vis* the planters as they had been in the earlier years of settlement when they supplied the planters with all necessities upon credit and sent ships for their sugar. In later years, 'as the Planters grew rich, they sent us the Produce of their Plantations upon their own Accounts, and with the Proceeds thereof furnished themselves with what they wanted; so that for many Years that Trade has been for the greatest Part manag'd by themselves, and our Merchants get little by them more than their Commission, and a low Freight'.[41] Direct trade did not, however, disappear completely in the West Indies and very likely recovered somewhat after 1750.

The likelihood that large planters were relatively more numerous in the West Indies than in the Chesapeake may help explain another observable phenomenon. Absentee proprietors were quite rare in the Chesapeake. There were a few, of

[39] Upper James River District Manifest Book, 1773–75, in Virginia State Library, Auditor of Public Accounts no. 301. The percentages given are for the year 1 June 1773–31 May 1774. Although the percentage going to Scotland from this district then was over 55% of total shipments to Britain, British customs records show that Scottish tobacco imports in 1773–74 were only 43.4% of total British imports. The estimates compensate for this discrepancy.

[40] K. G. Davies, 'The Origins of the Commission System in the West India Trade', *Transactions of the Royal Historical Society*, Fifth Series, II (1952), pp. 88–107.

[41] *The Dispute between the Northern Colonies, and the Sugar Islands, set in a Clear View* (London, c.1731–32), p. 1.

course, usually merchants who had done well in the Chesapeake and had acquired some land there which they retained when they returned to England. The phenomenon is reported much more frequently in the Caribbean where successful planters also chose to return to England, leaving the supervision of their estates to substantial local figures to whom they gave powers of attorney.

The establishment and expansion of each and every branch of the colonial market economies required land, labour, and capital. Unimproved land was almost valueless in the early days of any particular colony, and the migration of entirely free labour generally quite limited in scope. Capital could, however, be used to purchase slave- and indentured labour as well as the equipment needed for agricultural productions—ranging from the spade and hoe sufficient for tobacco to the boilers and related equipment needed to extract sugar in a cane mill. As few of the pioneer entrepreneurial agriculturalists had brought much wealth with them, credit from the first was perceived to be the key to rapid colonial development. But what could be the basis of such credit? Unimproved land had little value in the first years of settlement, but after a colony had been settled a generation or more, improved land in desirable locations acquired some market value and could be the basis for mortgage-backed credit. Until that stage was reached, prudent credit had to be fairly short term, based largely on the seller's personal evaluation of the credit-worthiness of the buyer, and the seller-lender's expectation of the support of the local community. Strains and ill-will were inevitable. Colonial legislatures in both North America and the islands were under continuing pressure to protect the planter or farmer from his creditors, but there was also a creditor interest in the legislatures able to restrain this pressure significantly; where such restraints failed, royal disallowance of colonial debt legislation occurred frequently. The entire matter was finally settled—at least in a legal sense—by the Colonial Debts Act of 1732 which made real estate liable for book debts and for obligations secured by bond. Mortgages and bonds thereafter made longer-term credit more feasible, though book debts had still too frequently to be taken into the local courts. In the plantation colonies, credit was particularly valued for the purchase of slaves. The big slave traders were, however, increasingly unwilling to grant such credit, passing the responsibility on to the local merchant-factors who sold slaves for them and dealt with the planter buyers. Such factors had to find affluent persons as sureties for the valuable slaves they received on consignment from the slave traders. Thus, complex networks of credit and credit guarantees criss-crossing the ocean were necessary to supply the fields with the slaves desired.[42]

---

[42] Jacob M. Price, 'Credit in the Slave Trade and Plantation Economies', in Barbara L. Solow, ed., *Slavery and the Rise of the Atlantic System* (Cambridge, 1991), chap. 12.

Implications for the Mother Country

The colonial trades had somewhat different significance for statesmen and merchants. To Charles II, a major consideration was the contribution of long-distance trades to England's sea might. The American and West Indian trades were the great employers of English shipping, One estimate shows their required tonnage going up from 70,000 tons in 1686 to 153,000 tons in 1771–73,[43] while all British foreign trade in the latter years needed only 375,000 tons of shipping, though that the actual total of English owned shipping during the latter years was about 581,000 tons. Both estimates are probably too conservative, for *Lloyd's Register* of 1775 lists vessels totalling 979,263 tons.[44] It is clear, though, that colonial trade contributed significantly to the growth of the British merchant fleet, both on the supply (shipbuilding) side and the demand (freight carrying) side. Moreover, by the 1770s the tonnage reported was probably being utilized much more efficiently. Improvements in postal service and the growing density of British merchants' agents and correspondents in the colonies meant that cargoes could be provided in advance and vessels turned around much more quickly.[45]

However much statesmen may have been pleased by the increase in men and tonnage employed in colonial and other overseas trade, for merchants shipping was simply a means towards an end. Their primary goal was the purchase and return of commodities in demand in Britain and northern Europe. Thus the British and continental consumers were the ultimate creators and controllers of the market forces expanding the total volume of British colonial trade. Certain products were returned primarily for the British and Irish markets: sugar, dye-stuffs, tea, naval stores, and ship timbers. Other commodities were brought back in quantities that far exceeded internal demand and had for the most part to be re-exported to Europe: tobacco, rice, and coffee. The government clearly understood the difference between the two groups. Importers of commodities usually re-exported could give bond for most of the duties instead of paying in cash and received total or fairly generous 'drawbacks' of duties at re-exportation. The commodities needed by the internal economy were helped by subsidies for naval stores, masts, hemp, and indigo, and customs concessions for iron. In so far as all

---

[43] Davis, *English Shipping Industry*, p. 17.

[44] George Chalmers, *Opinions on Interesting Subjects... Arising from American Independence* (London, 1784), p. 99.

[45] Shepherd and Walton, *Shipping and Economic Development*, chap. 5; Morgan, *Bristol and the Atlantic Trade*, pp. 45–54; Richard Dell, 'The Operational Record of the Clyde Tobacco Fleet, 1747–1775', *Scottish Economic and Social History*, II (1982), pp. 1–17.

these trades were expanding down to the American Revolution, the policies can be described as generally successful in their own terms.

A final question that looms very large in some discussions is the impact of expanding colonial commerce on British society and economy. From the time of Defoe onwards, Englishmen and Scotsmen had no doubt that there was a noticeable effect. They could see, in particular, the new docks at Liverpool and the newly built areas of the major port towns. The better-informed knew of the leading role played by merchants in establishing not just firms trading overseas but insurance enterprises and private banks as well. But can one be more quantitatively precise? The most basic fact about eighteenth-century Britain was that population grew very slowly, usually less than 0.5 per cent p.a., in England down to c.1770. This meant that the total English population increased only by a third between 1700 and 1776. During this same period, total exports of English goods increased by about 122 per cent or 137 per cent for manufactures alone. In 1772–74 about 55 per cent of manufactured exports went to the American colonies and the East Indies.[46] The impact of such proportions on domestic industry depends, of course, on the proportion of the output of any particular manufacture exported. Nicholas Crafts estimated that exports' share of 'gross industrial output' rose from 24 per cent in 1700 to 35 per cent in 1760.[47] His figures fit well with other scattered estimates of the export share of industrial production: 20–25 per cent for British linens and cottons c.1770–74, but 45–50 per cent for woollens and worsteds, 42 per cent for bar and wrought iron, and 40 per cent for the copper-brass group. In the exceptional cases of the Birmingham and Wolverhampton hardware trades and the West Riding woollen and worsted manufacture, c.1760–75, contemporaries estimated that exports took over 70 per cent of production.[48]

With a relatively static population and exports pushing up aggregate demand, there were bound to be awkward pressures in the market. The market itself could, of course, alleviate some of these pressure, by exploiting new sources of supply or by importing semi-processed products that would mitigate tightness in domestic supplies. Only when these market adjustments proved insufficient to eliminate bottlenecks and the attendant price-rises did pressure for technological change become effective. The charcoal needed in English iron-making furnaces and forges came from specially planted coppices that took about twenty years to mature. More coppices could be planted but in the short-run a noticeable rise in demand for iron would result in charcoal shortages and higher prices. By the end of the

---

[46] Davis, 'English Foreign Trade, 1700–1774', pp. 302–03.

[47] N. F. R. Crafts, *British Economic Growth during the Industrial Revolution* (Oxford, 1985), pp. 132–33.

[48] Jacob M. Price, 'What Did Merchants Do? Reflections on British Overseas Trade, 1660–1790', *JEH*, XLIX (1989), pp. 267–84.

seventeenth century, iron imports equalled or exceeded domestic production.[49] In the new century, the growth of the American colonies greatly increased the demand for nails and hardware. Between 1699–1701 and 1772–74 there was a tenfold increase in English exports of metalware, three-quarters of which went to the American colonies and the East Indies.[50] Thus, English iron fabricators needed increased supplies of both pig iron from North America and bar iron from Sweden and Russia. Although many English furnace owners knew of Abraham Darby's successful use of coke early in the eighteenth century, they were not inclined to try the new process as long as the price of charcoal remained tolerable in England. Only when charcoal became too expensive during and after the Seven Years War did many turn to coke.[51]

Textile exports did not grow as rapidly as hardware, c.1700–75, mostly because woollens, the leading item, was already England's leading manufacture and export in 1700. The manufacture and export of the lesser textiles did grow, however, and bottlenecks not surprisingly appeared. The most noticeable was in spinning, characteristically done on the putting-out system by the wives and daughters of rural labourers and small farmers. Expanding such a labour force was very difficult in the short run. But, the market for a time alleviated the pressure by bringing in foreign semi-processed inputs, for example, woollen yarn from Ireland and linen yarn from the Baltic. This option was not, however, available for cotton, imported mainly from the West Indies by the mid-eighteenth century.[52] Thus, even though the cotton manufacture in the third quarter of the eighteenth century was not as important as that of woollens or linens, it was in cotton that rising demand, domestic as well as export, created bottlenecks serious enough to stimulate the first experiments with spinning machinery.

In short, demand arising from the commercial Empire must be viewed as an important part, but only a part, of the aggregate demand experienced by British manufacturers. It was the indisputable rise in total demand in the course of the eighteenth century that created the 'bottlenecks' or problems in manufacture that encouraged the well-known experiments in new methods in both metallurgy and spinning. Just as British market demand helped create the plantation economies of the West Indies and the more southerly parts of North America, so did overseas demand make necessary or at least hasten the technological transformation of several long-established branches of British industrial life.

[49] G. Hammersley, 'The Charcoal Iron Industry', pp. 602–03.
[50] Davis, 'English Foreign Trade, 1700–1774', pp. 302–03.
[51] Charles K. Hyde, *Technological Change and the British Iron Industry, 1700–1870* (Princeton, 1977), chap. 4.
[52] Davis, 'English Foreign Trade, 1700–1774', pp. 300–01.

TABLE 4.1. *Estimated population of the British Isles and the British Colonies in the western hemisphere, 1650–1772 (thousands)*

	England	Scotland	Ireland	N. America	West Indies
1650/51	5,228			55	59
1671	4,983				
1686/87	4,865		2,167		
1700/01	5,058			265	147
1711/12	5,230		2,791		
1726	5,450		3,031		
1750/51	5,772			1,206	330
1754/55		1,265	3,191		
1756	5,993				
1770/71	6,448			2,283	479
1772			3,584		

Sources: (England): E. A. Wrigley and R. S. Schofield, *The Population History of England 1541–1871* (Cambridge, Mass., 1981), p. 208–09; (Scotland and Ireland): B. R. Mitchell and Phyllis Deane, *Abstract of British Historical Statistics* (Cambridge, 1962), p. 5; (America): McCusker and Menard, *The Economy of British America*, p. 54.

TABLE 4.2. *England's commodity imports from Asia, Africa, and America, 1700–1773* (annual averages in thousands of pounds sterling, official values)

	1699–1701	1722–24	1752–54	1772–74
Comestibles				
Spirits (rum, etc.)	0 (10)	6 (23)	70 (88)	163 (205)
Sugar	630 (630)	928 (928)	1,302 (1,302)	2,362 (2,364)
Tobacco	249 (249)	263 (263)	560 (560)	518 (519)
Drugs	20 (53)	30 (60)	100 (179)	95 (203)
Pepper	103 (103)	17 (17)	31 (31)	33 (33)
Tea	8 (8)	116 (116)	334 (334)	848 (848)
Coffee	9 (27)	123 (127)	53 (53)	436 (436)
Rice	0 (5)	52 (52)	167 (167)	340 (340)
Raw Materials				
Silk	42 (346)	50 (693)	94 (671)	156 (751)
Cotton	24 (44)	45 (49)	56 (104)	88 (137)
Dyestuffs	93 (226)	155 (318)	98 (386)	170 (506)
Timber	14 (138)	13 (157)	90 (237)	114 (319)
Oil (whale, etc.)	19 (141)	26 (122)	43 (130)	93 (162)
Skins and hides	23 (57)	34 (66)	46 (72)	111 (164)
Corn	0	0	0	51 (398)
Manufactures				
Calicoes	367 (367)	437 (437)	401 (401)	697 (697)
Silks and mixed	107 (208)	146 (208)	96 (112)	76 (82)

Note: The figures in parentheses represent total imports.

Source: R. Davis, 'English Foreign Trade', pp. 300–01.

TABLE 4.3. *Geographical distribution of English/British imports from Asia, Africa, and America* (annual averages in thousands of pounds sterling)

a. *England and Wales only*

	1700–1701	1730–1731	1750–1751	1772–1773
North America	372	655	877	1,442
The Fisheries	0	6	7	21
West Indies	785	1,586	1,484	3,080
Africa	24	43	43	80
East Indies	775	943	1,101	2,203
World	5,819	7,386	7,855	12,432

b. *England and Scotland*

	1772–1773	1780–1781	1789–1790	1797–1798
North America	1,997	219	1,351	1,696
The Fisheries	27	42	188	248
West Indies	3,222	2,322	4,045	5,982
Africa	80	29	87	62
East Indies	2,203	1,749	3,256	5,785
World	13,595	11,189	18,476	23,903

Source: Phyllis Deane and W. A. Cole, *British Economic Growth 1688–1959* (Cambridge, 1962), p. 87.

TABLE 4.4. *Geographical distribution of English/British exports to America, Asia, and Africa* (annual averages in thousands of pounds sterling)

	England 1700–01	England 1750–51	England 1772–73	Britain 1772–73	Britain 1789–90
a. Home produce and manufactures					
North America	256	971	2,460	2,649	3,295
West Indies	205	449	1,168	1,226	1,690
East India	114	585	824	824	2,096
Africa	81	89	492	492	517
TOTAL (above)	656	2,094	4,944	5,191	7,598
World	4,461	9,125	9,739	10,196	14,350
b. Re-exports					
North America	106	384	522	605	468
West Indies	131	140	169	176	202
East India	11	68	69	69	77
Africa	64	99	285	285	282
TOTAL (above)	312	691	1,045	1,135	1,029
World	2,136	3,428	5,800	6,930	5,380

Source: Deane and Cole, *British Economic Growth*, p. 87.

TABLE 4.5. Exports and re-exports from England/Britain to America, Asia, and Africa, 1699–1774 (annual averages in thousands of pounds sterling; official values)

From:	1699–1701 England		1751–54 England		1772–74 England		1784–86 Britain		1794–96 Britain	
To:	America & Africa	East India	America & Africa	East India	America & Africa	East India	America & Africa	East India	America & Africa	East India
Exports										
Woollens	185	89	374	230	1,148	189	1,013	160	2,597	582
Linens	0	0	189	2	681	6	619	5	799	8
Cottons, etc.	16	0	78	0	176	0	456	0	2,630	1
Silks	36	0	60	1	133	3	264	5	497	4
Metalware*	73	10	331	84	755	148	892	278	1,941	1,128
Hats, etc.*	24	2	59	20	93	10	249	35	696	60
Miscellaneous	141	10	480	301	995	334	1,583	1,287	2,459	1,504
Total manufactures	475	111	1,571	638	3,981	690	5,076	1,770	11,619	3,287
Total exports	539	122	1,707	667	4,176	717	5,465	1,813	12,628	3,539
Re-exports										
Calicoes/cottons†	45	0	32	0	85	0	126	0	257	0
Silks, etc.	14	0	76	0	210	0	173	1	431	0
Linens	157	0	301	0	285	0	44	0	34	0
Total manufactures	252	3	432	2	596	7	356	1	724	0
Tea	0	0	113	0	82	0	60	0	31	0
Total comestibles	34	9	148	38	273	32	319	38	510	31
Total raw materials	26	2	47	41	103	24	53	30	56	56
Total re-exports	312	14	627	81	972	63	728	69	1,290	87
Total exports and re-exports	851	136	2,334	748	5,148	780	6,193	1,882	13,918	3,626

Notes: * Includes hats only to 1774, but hats, garments, and haberdashery in 1784–96.
† 'Calicoes' in re-exports to 1774; 'cottons', 1784–96.

Sources: R. Davis, 'English Foreign Trade, 1700–1774', pp. 302–03; Industrial Revolution and British Overseas Trade, pp. 94–95, 102–03.

TABLE 4.6. *Summary of the trade of the commercial Empire, 1699-1791* (annual average, in thousands of pounds sterling; official values)

a. *British data on trade with the Thirteen Colonies and States and the West Indies*

	English imports	English exports	Scottish imports	Scottish exports	British imports	British exports
With the Thirteen Colonies and States						
1699–1701	302	364	—	—	—	—
1740–43	793	832	90	100	883	932
1744–48W	632	698	121	149	753	847
1749–55	891	1,238	185	136	1,076	1,374
1756–62W	705	1,811	275	147	980	1,959
1763–69	1,117	1,861	392	230	1,510	2,090
1770–74	1,271	2,762	524	299	1,796	3,061
1784–87	750	2,181	95	235	845	2,416
1788–91	958	2,822	157	187	1,115	3,009
With the West Indies						
1688–1701	742	359	—	—		
1740–43	1,304	831	28	14	1,331	845
1744–48W	1,183	670	24	31	1,207	701
1749–55	1,596	693	35	43	1,630	736
1756–62W	2,105	1,030	55	73	2,160	1,103
1763–69	2,744	1,109	150	72	2,896	1,180
1770–75	3,124	1,341	160	68	3,284	1,409
1776–82W	2,577	1,238	170	174	2,701	1,318
1783–87	3,346	1,336	229	158	3,576	1,494
1788–91	3,526	1,742	368	299	3,894	2,041

b. *Some other trades of the American Colonies*

	North American exports to British West Indies	North American imports from British West Indies	North American exports to Southern Europe	North American imports from Southern Europe
1768	534	498	380	77
1769	641	723	597	81
1770	745	762	551	75
1771	745	599	552	66
1772	883	837	586	84

Note: W = war years.

Sources: J. M. Price, 'New Time Series for Scotland's and Britain's Trade with the Thirteen Colonies and States, 1740 to 1791', *William and Mary Quarterly*, Third Series, XXXII (1975), pp. 318–25; *Historical Statistics of the United States*, II, pp. 1176–78; Shepherd and Walton, *Shipping and Economic Development*, pp. 222–30; Sheridan, *Sugar and Slavery*, pp. 500–01; House of Lords Record Office, 20 Nov. 1775; B[oard] [of] T[rade] 6/185 ff. 183–206.

Select Bibliography

K. G. DAVIES, *The Royal African Company* (London, 1957).

RALPH DAVIS, 'English Foreign Trade, 1700–1774', *Economic History Review*, Second Series, XV (1962), pp. 285–303.

THOMAS M. DEVINE, *The Tobacco Lords: A Study of the Tobacco Merchants of Glasgow and their Trading Activities* (Edinburgh, 1975).

RICHARD S. DUNN, *Sugar and Slaves: The Rise of the Planter Class in the English West Indies, 1624–1713* (Chapel Hill, NC, 1972).

JOSEPH A. ERNST, *Money and Politics in America, 1755–1775: A Study of the Currency Act of 1764 and the Political Economy of Revolution* (Chapel Hill, NC, 1973).

DAVID W. GALENSON, *White Servitude in Colonial America: An Economic Analysis* (Cambridge, 1981).

LAWRENCE A. HARPER, *The English Navigation Laws* (New York, 1939).

JOHN J. MCCUSKER, *Rum and the American Revolution* (New York, 1989).

—— and RUSSELL R. MENARD, *The Economy of British America, 1607–1789* (Chapel Hill, NC, 1985).

JOSEPH J. MALONE, *Pine Trees and Politics: The Naval Stores and Forest Policy in Colonial New England, 1691–1775* (London, 1964).

KENNETH MORGAN, *Bristol and the Atlantic Trade in the Eighteenth Century* (Cambridge, 1993).

RICHARD PARES, *Yankees and Creoles: The Trade Between North America and the West Indies Before the American Revolution* (New York, 1956).

JACOB M. PRICE, *Capital and Credit in British Overseas Trade* (Cambridge, Mass., 1980).

—— *The Atlantic Frontier of the Thirteen Colonies and States* (Aldershot, 1996).

DAVID RICHARDSON, 'The Eighteenth Century British Slave Trade: Estimates of its Volume and Coastal Distribution in Africa', *Research in Economic History*, XII (1989), pp. 151–95.

JAMES F. SHEPHERD and GARY M. WALTON, *Shipping, Maritime Trade, and the Economic Development of North America* (Cambridge, 1972).

RICHARD B. SHERIDAN, *Sugar and Slavery: An Economic History of the British West Indies, 1623–1775* (Barbados, 1974).

BARBARA L. SOLOW, ed., *Slavery and the Rise of the Atlantic System* (Cambridge, 1991).

IAN K. STEELE, *The English Atlantic, 1675–1740: An Exploration of Communication and Community* (New York, 1986).

THOMAS M. TRUXES, *Irish–American Trade, 1660–1783* (Cambridge, 1988).

5

The Anointed, the Appointed, and the Elected: Governance of the British Empire, 1689–1784

IAN K. STEELE

Whether through benign Whiggery or the tyranny of entrenched élites, govern-ance of the disparate kingdoms, companies, and colonies of the British Empire was not seriously challenged during the three generations after 1689. This stability contrasted with earlier Stuart convulsions and with the subsequent American Revolution. Elaboration of some royal political, administrative, and judicial institutions contributed to this stability, as did war with France, but until 1760 effective administrative power remained diffuse, flexible, and limited. Few Imper-ial, corporate, or colonial directives could be enforced by fleets and regiments, or by courts. Most decisions were negotiated, moderated, appropriated, evaded, or even resisted through layers of governance. Even though the administrative structure remained founded upon the Crown, the increasing political legitimacy of the elected over the anointed and appointed was a major trend of the century after 1689. The rise of the colonial Assemblies was one manifestation of this change; the increasing power of the British Parliament, especially the King-in-Parliament under George III, was another. The consolidation of these two power bases eventually destroyed the flexibility of Imperial government, affecting and reflecting the broader crisis of the American Revolution. In sum-marizing these developments, it is useful to sketch the operation of Imperial and colonial governance in the generation after 1689, then to consider major changes in each of the next three generations.

1689–1714

Monarchy was at the legal core of the Empire, presuming, inviting, or demanding the allegiance of the English, Irish, Scots, and naturalized foreigners, whether in royal kingdoms, royally chartered trading companies, or royal or chartered colon-ies. William III's 1688 invasion made him effective head of state, Commander-in-Chief, and Governor of the Church of England. However, a cautious Parliament presumed to alter the royal succession and abolish royal life revenues in favour of more restrictive annual financial grants. Although Whig opponents of Stuart royal power had been vindicated by revolution and now held many royal offices, Whig notions of natural rights and contract theories of government would be corrosive to traditional royal authority.

Challenges from the Scottish and Irish kingdoms had completely disabled English royal power at various times during the seventeenth century, and these challenges persisted after 1689. Scots would show spasmodic resistance to the alien Hanoverians, and to aspects of 'British' integration that had begun with the accession of James VI to the English throne and accelerated with the 1707 Act of Union. This created the single kingdom and Parliament of Great Britain that included forty-five Scottish Members of Parliament. The Jacobite risings of 1715 and 1745 challenged Protestant Scots as well as Hanoverians, though ultimately strengthening both. Thorough integration of Scotland's dominant political culture defined Britain as a unitary, not a federal, state. This close integration of England and Scotland would have Imperial constitutional repercussions, and not only because Scots were prominent among later British Imperial administrators.[1]

The Williamite reconquest of Ireland, and consequent stringent Penal Laws against the Roman Catholic majority, left Ireland's small Protestant élite vulnerable to the British power that guaranteed their position. Admittedly, the Irish Parliament met regularly after 1692, and its management involved Irish political 'undertakers' who controlled considerable patronage power in return. However, appointed Englishmen dominated high political and ecclesiastical offices, controlled legislation through Poynings' Law, and kept an army of 12,000 regulars in Ireland at Irish expense. The English tendency to regard Ireland as a colony rather than a kingdom became more prevalent after the Scottish union with England, and the British Parliament asserted unconditional authority to legislate for Ireland with the Declaratory Act of 1720. Ironically, Imperial authoritarianism in Ireland was initially challenged less than was the negotiated political integration of Scotland into Britain.[2]

Royal chartered companies were more independent than some royal kingdoms, enjoying expansive privileges that became legal authority to raise money, conduct courts, negotiate trading concessions, develop colonies, and initiate wars. Stuart kings had awarded monopolies to the Hudson's Bay Company, the Royal African Company, and the East India Company, all trading beyond the more familiar

[1] See John Robertson, ed., *A Union for Empire: Political Thought and the Union of 1707* (Cambridge, 1995); Richard Sher and Jeffrey Smitten, eds., *Scotland and America in the Age of the Enlightenment* (Edinburgh, 1990); Linda Colley, *Britons: Forging the Nation, 1707–1837* (London, 1992); Daniel Szechi and David Hayton, 'John Bull's Other Kingdoms: The Government of Scotland and Ireland', in Clyve Jones, ed., *Britain in the First Age of Party* (London, 1987), pp. 241–80.

[2] See below, pp. 259–64.

North Atlantic basin. Whig opposition to royal monopolies ensured that English interlopers into those trades were not prosecuted during the War of the League of Augsburg, and the companies themselves were challenged soon thereafter. In 1698 Parliament permanently destroyed the Royal African Company's trading monopoly, did not grant the troubled Hudson's Bay Company the parliamentary charter it sought,[3] and chartered a New East India Company that would not be combined with the old until 1709.

Although war had postponed Whig attacks on chartered monopoly trading companies, it prompted intrusion into governance of some American proprietary colonies. William Penn, Quaker proprietor of Pennsylvania, and Cecilius Calvert, second Lord Baltimore and Catholic proprietor of Maryland, were both deemed unsuitable to command colonies at war with France. When a new charter was granted to Massachusetts in 1691, a royal Governor was imposed permanently, together with royal review of legislation. A more systematic administrative attack was mounted on all chartered colonies after the Peace of Ryswick, reviving a centralizing policy pursued in the 1680s. Meeting effective proprietary lobbying and parliamentary reluctance to invade landed property rights, these attacks accomplished only the negotiated surrender of the charters of East and West New Jersey.

Imperial authority over royal colonies in America and the West Indies was exercised directly in the name of the monarchs. This included royal approval of relevant parliamentary legislation, royal proclamations, appointment and instruction of royal Governors, review of acts passed by colonial legislatures, and the hearing of colonial legal appeals by the King-in-Council. The Privy Council issued royal proclamations, reviewed laws passed by colonial Assemblies, and heard colonial petitions and legal appeals. Until 1696, most of the Privy Council's Imperial business was conducted through its Lords of the Committee of Trade and Plantations, complete with a knowledgeable clerical staff and a considerable records office.

To forestall parliamentary intrusion into royal authority in 1696, William III's ministers created the durable Lords Commissioners of Trade and Plantations, commonly known as the Board of Trade. This office inherited most of the functions and records of its predecessor, but not its powers. The Board of Trade was an advisory body that reported to the Privy Council through the Secretary of State for the Southern Department, and to Parliament upon request. The Board of Trade drafted the commissions and instructions for royal Governors, corresponded with them, and gathered information from royal officials, colonial Councils and Assemblies, and from Imperial, colonial, and chartered company petitioners and

---

[3] E. E. Rich, *Hudson's Bay Company, 1670–1870*, 3 vols. (Toronto, 1958–60), I, pp. 355–67.

lobbyists. The only patronage power which the Board initially exercised was the recommendation of members of colonial Councils, chosen from nominations by Governors. In its energetic first years, this clearing-house of Imperial business developed a system of colonial vice-admiralty courts and encouraged colonial governments to appoint regular agents to expedite decision-making in Whitehall. In the interval of peace between 1697 and 1702, the Board co-ordinated one major attack on piracy and another on colonial proprietary and chartered governments. In wartime, defence of colonies and trade eclipsed most administrative and constitutional issues and the limited successes of the Board of Trade were achieved by convincing Parliament that some of its own substantial customs revenues from colonial imports, channelled by the Navigation Acts, needed additional legal protection.

The royally appointed Secretaries of State for the Southern Department were central to the policies, politics, and patronage of the eighteenth-century Empire. In addition to wide-ranging European diplomatic and military responsibilities, the Secretary of State for the Southern Department was the royal executive officer who reported on colonial matters to the ministerial 'cabinet' and to the Privy Council, and who distributed resulting orders in the monarch's name. There were ten different Secretaries of State for the Southern Department in the twenty-five years after 1689, a pace of change that enhanced the role of the Board of Trade in routine colonial matters. However, Secretaries of State like Daniel Finch, second Earl of Nottingham, and Henry St John, Viscount Bolingbroke, supervised Imperial policy and patronage closely. Gubernatorial appointments were strongly politicized by some Secretaries of State, making Governors vulnerable to politically inspired displacement. In a time when short-lived ministries ranged from the Junto group of Whigs to High-Flying Tory, the Secretaries of State and the Board of Trade seldom pursued co-ordinated policy initiatives for long, and those anxious to abort them usually found opportunities.

The Treasury was the royal department that influenced Imperial policy-making most, and often dominated its execution. The Treasury collected English and colonial customs duties, excise taxes, postal revenues, and a variety of royal dues. Its Board of Customs Commissioners oversaw collectors and comptrollers of customs in both English and colonial ports, as well as the misnamed 'colonial naval officers', who were bonded recorders of ship movements through colonial ports. Although the Treasury eventually had more than ninety Imperial patronage appointments, its greatest power was withholding payment, which could veto or delay projects already approved by the entire government.

The Admiralty provided convoys for colonial and company trades, and a few royal navy 'guardships' to protect favoured colonies from maritime enemies. Colonial vice-admiralty courts, operating without juries, were established throughout the colonies by 1700 and the High Court of Admiralty in London was the final court of appeal in maritime cases. The Admiralty also authorized letters of marque to privateers and provided passes to protect merchantmen from Barbary corsairs. Through its subsidiary Navy Board, the Admiralty encouraged production of colonial pitch, tar, and turpentine to curb prices from regular Baltic suppliers. Colonists were much less enthusiastic about Admiralty attempts to reserve American timber suitable for masts and to 'impress' merchant sailors.

Although the English army was used successfully to defend the new monarchs against Scottish and Irish supporters of James II in 1689 and 1690, and expanded more than tenfold during the next generation, the army could not escape its association with Cromwellian and Stuart tyranny, and remained politically suspect throughout the eighteenth century. A civilian Board of Ordnance provided a serious check on the army by supervising artillery officers, engineers, and all forts and barracks in Britain, as well as the supply of muskets and cannon for English, Scottish, and East India Company troops. Parliament exercised more direct control by debating army estimates, by requiring the annual renewal of the Mutiny Act, and by controlling the size of the divided peacetime forces for England and Scotland (8,000), Ireland (12,000), and America (c.2,400).

Parliament's place in Imperial government, versus that of the colonial Assemblies, eventually became the administrative, political, and constitutional issue that destroyed the first British Empire. However, Parliament's history to 1689 was a route map that colonial Assemblies followed to curb royal and administrative ambition, and Parliament remained the exemplar and sometimes the patron of colonials trying to limit the power of royal departments and officers. Parliament's role in determining the succession in 1689 proved, in retrospect, to be stronger in constitutional theory than it had been in immediate political practice. While most later apologists for colonial constitutional autonomy emphasized early Stuart precedents, it was the exercise of Parliament's power during the generation after 1689 that better indicated the working assumptions about the 'Imperial constitution' of the Georgian Empire.[4]

Despite its own continuing challenges to the Crown, Parliament usually reinforced royal Imperial power in the generation to 1714. Although Parliament threatened to establish its own Board of Trade, it passed numerous laws to strengthen the Crown in the colonies. These included an act to settle the Newfoundland trade (1699), an act against piracy (1700), an act to regulate privateers in America (1708), and an act to establish the value of specific foreign coins in the

---

[4] H. T. Dickinson, 'The Eighteenth-Century Debate on the Sovereignty of Parliament', *Transactions of the Royal Historical Society*, Fifth Series, XXVI (1976), pp. 189–210; I. K. Steele, 'The British Parliament and the Atlantic Colonies to 1760: New Approaches to Enduring Questions', *Parliamentary History*, XIV (1995), pp. 29–46.

colonies (1708). On two occasions Parliament came close to passing comprehensive bills to resume all proprietary and charter governments to the Crown (1701, 1702). The 1696 Navigation Act strengthened enforcement of Imperial trade regulations dating back to 1650 and authorized new prerogative vice-admiralty courts in the colonies. Most of this legislation illustrates that Parliament did not balk at strengthening royal Imperial authority when that protected customs revenues.

Governance in the kingdoms, companies, and colonies of the English Empire varied enormously in 1690 but ultimately derived legal legitimacy from the Crown. Admittedly, the Crown had no direct representative at all in the forts of the Hudson's Bay Company, Royal African Company, or East India Company, and none but customs officers in the chartered colonies of Rhode Island, Connecticut, or the Carolinas. The new Massachusetts Charter of 1691, however, imposed a royal Governor with nearly as much power as those of the unchartered royal colonies of New Hampshire, Virginia, the Leeward Islands, and Barbados, and those of the 'conquered colonies' of Jamaica and New York. Extension of direct royal government to New Jersey, Nova Scotia, and the Carolinas, indicated a trend away from chartered colonial governments in favour of more direct royal control.

A royally appointed Governor or Lieutenant-Governor exercised executive, judicial, and legislative authority in each royal colony. The Governors represented a monarchical power that was supposedly stronger in the colonies than in England; the Governor not only exercised most of the functions of the Crown, but also some delegated functions of the Secretaries of State and the Treasury, as well as serving as vice-admiral and military Commander-in-Chief. In Barbados, the Leeward Islands, and Virginia, the Crown had the permanent customs revenue it had lost in England in 1689, and Governors in other royal colonies were repeatedly urged to seek similar resources. Governors called and dissolved the elected colonial Assemblies and retained a veto over their legislation. The Governor also nominated members for the colonial Council, a group of a dozen prominent men who served as a legislative upper house, as the highest colonial court of appeal, and as an executive advisory group to the Governor. The Governor could suspend Council members, and make temporary appointments to fill vacancies. The Governor appointed or confirmed other colonial office-holders, including the colonial secretary, the attorney-general, the colonial naval officer, the customs collector, and county justices.

Gubernatorial power was seldom all that it seemed, even during this generation of war with France that gave opportunities for leadership by the local Commander-in-Chief. Governors arrived with elaborate, and mostly secret, royal instructions prepared by the Board of Trade, detailing Imperial objectives and how Governors were to respond in a wide variety of circumstances. Most Governors had few or no royal troops to command. The Governors of the Bahamas, Bermuda, Jamaica, New York, and South Carolina controlled the independent companies stationed there, but the full regiments of regulars in Acadia and the Leeward Islands were not directly controlled. Governor Daniel Parke of the Leeward Islands was unique in overruling the colonel of a regular regiment and ordering it, on his own authority, to use its bayonets to disrupt the Antigua Assembly in 1710; he became the only royal Governor assassinated in the first British Empire, and no culprits were ever identified.[5] A Governor's admiralty powers proved solely judicial, though it took numerous disputes to establish, by the 1730s, that he had no authority over naval captains commanding vessels in colonial waters. Formal powers were also subject to political encroachment from London. Although most royal Governors had military experience, and William III and Marlborough exercised some direct influence in these appointments, Governors were also political appointees of specific English administrations. Governors were thus vulnerable to changes in English politics and to pressure from English mercantile and religious lobbies pursuing their own interests and those of their colonial allies.

Upon arrival, the powers that a royal Governor carried from London were further compromised by the need to negotiate power with colonial leaders. By the 1690s, the royally appointed colonial Council had judicial, legislative, and executive powers intended to assist, but also to check, the exercise of gubernatorial power. Councillors were usually selected by the Board of Trade from prominent and 'well disposed' colonials nominated by previous Governors. Councillors, appointed for life, were unpaid but likely to acquire the best administrative and judicial offices that were in the gift of the Governor. The Council's only function independent of the Governor was as a legislative upper house, and the Governor's exclusion from the Council during such business was not uniformly adhered to until the 1730s. When a colony was without a Governor or Lieutenant-Governor, the senior councillor became acting Governor. A Governor's powers to appoint judges, grant lands, try serious cases, hear legal appeals, or issue public monies, were all to be exercised jointly with the colonial Council.

After 1689, Imperial authorities accepted elected colonial Assemblies as necessary for legislation and local taxation in all established colonies. Some colonial Assemblies, like those of Jamaica and Barbados, had already established substantial powers and privileges. Other Assemblies, like those in South Carolina, Georgia, and Nova Scotia, would still be fighting similar battles with mixed success seventy years later. Appealing to charter rights, rights of Englishmen, and usage, colonial Assemblies gradually expanded their powers over public accounts and

---

[5] *Calendar of State Papers, Colonial Series, America and the West Indies*, W. N. Sainsbury and others, eds., 43 vols. (London, 1860–1963) [hereafter *CSPC*], *1710–1711*, nos. 125, 674, 677, 683, 783.

expenditures, the issue of paper money, and the salaries and fees of royal officials. Assemblies also eroded gubernatorial powers to nominate or appoint revenue officials, colonial agents, public printers, and judges, and to manage the Indian trade, military affairs, and local courts. Assemblies met more often in the generation of war that ended in 1714, especially in those West Indian and North American colonies facing serious threats from Spanish or French neighbours, and were able to exploit fiscal necessities to expand their authority. The Imperial government never formally altered its position that colonial Assemblies were privileges granted by the monarch rather than the inherent rights of the colonial peoples. This assumption was one reason why some royal instructions to Governors became increasingly unrealistic.

The unequal struggle between Governors and Assemblies prompted Imperial recourse to another power, the review of colonial legislation by the English government. The laws of all colonies except Connecticut and Rhode Island were subject to royal disallowance. The power to disallow those colonial laws found contrary to English statutes curbed some colonial legislative ambitions and taught Assemblies to use due process and conventional legal language, to avoid contradicting existing laws, and to impose reasonable punishments. One initial flaw in the process was that colonial Assemblies could pass temporary laws that expired before there was time for Imperial review.

Governors were reminded of long-standing instructions not to approve temporary laws.[6] From 1706, most colonial laws were allowed to 'lye by' unconfirmed in London though operative in the colonies. Should objections arise, the Board of Trade reviewed the law for royal confirmation or disallowance. Even more significant was an order to all Governors specifying that acts affecting royal prerogative or the private property of subjects were to include suspending clauses that postponed their operation until confirmed in London. Although Governors sometimes omitted suspending clauses in error or in return for local political concessions, this device became ubiquitous and effective enough to become a significant colonial grievance.[7]

Imperial legal power reached inside the colonies, where it was both applied and appropriated. Colonial courts were anxious to elicit obedience and impose order on new, rapidly changing, and socially disparate communities. English common law arrived with the English settlers, as a shared vehicle to protect persons and property and eventually as a shared legal culture. Colonial courts nurtured deference to English law as a necessary part of asserting their own power. The

---

[6] L. W. Labaree, ed., *Royal Instructions to British Colonial Governors, 1670–1776*, 2 vols. (New York, 1935), I, pp. 127–29.

[7] *CSPC, 1706–1708*, nos. 502, 529, 582–83, 632; Labaree, *Royal Instructions*, I, pp. 142–43.

royally appointed Governor and Council constituted the highest civil and criminal court in those colonies directly under the Crown, and decisions in major civil cases could also be appealed from any colony to the royal Privy Council. Royal or gubernatorial appointees served as attorneys-general, and as judges and officers of the vice-admiralty courts that tried prize cases, maritime wage disputes, and some violations of the Acts of Trade, in addition to supervising marine insurance appraisals. In Virginia, the oldest and largest English colony in the Americas, Governors appointed the judges, sheriffs, coroners, clerks, and even the overseers of the highways who assisted the county court judges. Virginia's justices of the peace were 'His Majesties Justices' who sat beneath the royal coat of arms in county court-houses that displayed royal portraits, and heard court pronouncements that ended with 'God Save the King'.

Royal symbols of majesty may have helped enforce English common law and colonial statute law, but they were also used to bolster, not challenge or mock, the authority of relatively new local élites determined to collect debts, to enforce tax collection, and to extract deference. Royal legal authority was readily appropriated and English common law nursed anti-authoritarian views. English common law rested upon community values, and was remembered and applied variously in Puritan, Quaker, and Anglican colonies. Its seventeenth-century English champions had made the rights of Englishmen into a bulwark against royal power that proved more enduring in the colonies than in England. However hegemonic the legal system may have been in structure, it functioned primarily as a local vehicle of negotiated dispute settlement.[8]

The relative importance of county, parish, and town institutions varied considerably between the colonies. The southern mainland and West Indian colonies were similar to Virginia, but mid-Atlantic America had a more varied inheritance, ranging from the centralized Quaker Pennsylvania county system to the intense localism of factionalized New York. In New England, the elected overwhelmed the appointed in local government as thoroughly as the Congregational marginalized the Anglican. New England town government was an amalgam of several English forms, built upon a broadly based town meeting that annually elected selectmen as well as the constables, clerks, tax gatherers, and the surveyors of highways and of fences. However, the royal Governors and Councils of Massachusetts and New Hampshire appointed justices of the peace, as did the elected Governors, Councils, and Assemblies of Connecticut and Rhode Island. Although New England justices of the peace were almost exclusively judicial officers, they still brought royal

[8] A. G. Roeber, *Faithful Magistrates and Republican Lawyers: Creators of Virginia Legal Culture, 1680–1810* (Chapel Hill, NC, 1981); Bruce H. Mann, *Neighbors and Strangers: Law and Community in Early Connecticut* (Chapel Hill, NC, 1987); 'Explaining the Law in Early American History—A Symposium', *William and Mary Quarterly* (hereafter *WMQ*), Third Series, L (1993), pp. 1–50.

symbols into the localities.[9] Throughout the colonies, the more substantial planters, farmers, and merchants supported their own political and social claims by
appropriating and sharing executive and judicial power that was ultimately royal.

During the generation before 1714, the expanding system of British Imperial
governance, reinforced by the need to fight wars against France, retained a unity
symbolized by the Crown. Although most Imperial administrators favoured close
supervision of colonies, lobbyists intent upon subverting Imperial initiatives had
numerous opportunities to exploit conflicting institutional and departmental
priorities, all subject to the unprecedented demands of European war and English
political convulsions. In leaving colonial defence to the colonies, the Imperial
government was forced to compromise on the involvement of the Assembly in
military appointments, strategy, public credit, and spending. The consolidation of
the power of colonial Assemblies is one theme that has come to be well understood. Less is known about concurrent extensions of Assembly power at the
expense of parish, town, and county, justified by wartime need to support frontiers, by intercolonial economic rivalries and boundary disputes, and by claiming
to defend local rights against Imperial initiatives.[10]

1714–1748

Many American revolutionaries, and modern historians, looked back favourably
to the British Empire as it existed between 1714 and 1748. It was generally a time of
peace and prosperity, of social and economic integration of the Atlantic Empire of
interdependent economies, of shared tastes for British consumer goods, and of a
sense of Imperial community sustained by newspapers, books, and travellers.
However, nostalgia for this period centred primarily upon the perceived wisdom
of Hanoverian Whig governance, dominated by patronage politics and labelled
'salutary neglect'.

Limited by their foreign language and interests, the first Hanoverian kings
watched the advance of Cabinet government in Britain, and the gradual transformation of the rhetoric of British and Imperial politics. 'Britons' and 'Britannia'
emerged as symbols of a patriotism less focused on the monarch than earlier.
Opposition politicians talked less of royal tyranny and more of ministerial corruption. The colonial language of rights and liberties also separated the symbolically

---

[9] Bruce C. Daniels, ed., *Town and County: Essays on the Structure of Local Government in the
American Colonies* (Middletown, Conn., 1978); A.G. Roeber, 'Authority, Law, and Custom: The Rituals
of Court Day in Tidewater Virginia, 1720 to 1750', *WMQ*, Third Series, XXXVII (1980), pp. 29–52; Alan
Tully, *Forming American Politics: Ideals, Interests, and Institutions in Colonial New York and Pennsylvania*
(Baltimore, 1994), pp. 330–40.
[10] David Grayson Allen, *In English Ways* (Chapel Hill, NC, 1981), pp. 223–42.

useful monarch from Imperial ministers and Governors, whose every resistance to colonial ambitions could be dubbed corruption.

The British Empire was not neglected and government preoccupations were not always salutary during the long ministry of Robert Walpole (1721–42) and Thomas Pelham-Holles, Duke of Newcastle, as Secretary of State for the Southern Department (1724–48) and director of Imperial appointments. Walpole and Newcastle cared deeply about all appointments and used them to sustain a majority in the British House of Commons by rewarding individuals and electoral interest groups. This preoccupation with the rewards of office had noticeable effects on the governing of the Empire. In London, appointees to the Board of Trade, the Admiralty, or the Customs service accepted these offices more as political rewards than as tasks requiring competence and diligence. Appointees were not to embarrass their patrons by showing incompetence or by taking politically disruptive policy initiatives. Discouragement of administrative initiative by office-holders went further. A government uncommonly preoccupied with electoral considerations gave exceptional access and attention to interest groups, be they mercantile, religious, or ethnic.

The Board of Trade became a negotiator between interests, rather than a policy-making body. Its massive 1721 report on the state of the colonies, countering French expansion in the Mississippi Valley and seeking sweeping changes to colonial government, was the last major policy statement for a generation. Resumption of charter colonies was a traditional nostrum, as was the insistence that royal officers in the colonies serve in person rather than by deputy. Appointment of a Captain-General or Lord-Lieutenant for all the North American colonies was a bold suggestion, modelled on the governments of the Leeward Islands and Ireland. The Board of Trade called for Cabinet rank for its own leader, concentration of Imperial business in its own office, and elimination of delays and confusion caused by having three competing executive channels for Imperial matters: the Secretary of State, the Privy Council, and the Board of Trade. The report summarized concerns of the previous generation; failure to act on most of the recommendations represented the new generation's preference for patronage over policy.[11]

The British Parliament became more visibly the ultimate arbiter of Imperial affairs. Its triumphal Declaratory Act asserting its authority over the Irish Parliament in 1720 resurrected a parliamentary supremacy unlike anything legislated since the aberrant Rump Parliament of 1649. Imperial administrators presumed such a power extended to the colonies, and Parliament passed twenty-nine acts concerning colonial trade, customs, and piracy between 1714 and 1739. These laws

---

[11] C[olonical] O[ffice] 324/10, pp. 396–431.

had run a gauntlet of intense British and colonial lobbying, and did so without any constitutional challenge.[12]

Even Parliament's Imperial trade legislation could become hostage to patronage politics; nearly half of the new trade laws were passed during the Excise Crisis of 1727–33. Walpole's uncharacteristically bold plan to convert the British import duties on wine and tobacco into more efficiently collected excise taxes prompted powerful public and parliamentary opposition. To recover political support, Walpole placated numerous interest groups with legislative concessions, a number of which affected the Empire. The Irish lobby gained direct importation of some colonial products after 1731 and the East India Company, generally well protected by its phalanx of MPs and its role as a major government creditor, gained further monopoly protection with its charter renewal in 1733. English hatters won a 1732 law prohibiting the colonial export of hats, and a well-organized philanthropic lobby gained a charter for Georgia, including unprecedented annual parliamentary grants.

More significant was the lobbying by West Indian sugar interests to restrict trade between neighbouring French islands and British North America. Inexpensive French colonial molasses had become central to the burgeoning American rum industry, as well as being widely used as a sweetener. The West Indians, including absentee planters serving as Members of Parliament, won a clear political victory with the passing of the Molasses Act of 1733. This allowed British colonies to import French West Indian sugar and molasses, but levied higher duties than on products of the British islands. This differential duty was a new approach to channelling Imperial trade; complete prohibitions had previously been customary. Failure to enforce the law illustrates another aspect of intense patronage politics; a law could be passed to placate one interest group, and remain unenforced to placate another.

Although buried in the midst of the calm of early Georgian 'political stability', the Excise Crisis indicated several changes in governing the Empire. Walpole ran his government as First Lord of the Treasury, the post that was usually prime-ministerial thereafter. Understandably, his Whig and Tory opponents continued to rail against the corruption and abuse of parliamentary power, providing a vocabulary for later American resistance, while also provoking clearer assertions of parliamentary supremacy in Britain.[13] English merchants and tradesmen used urban politics more confrontationally, both in and out of Parliament, particularly

---

[12] 6 Geo. I, c. 5; Labaree, *Royal Instructions*, II, pp. 754–56.

[13] Isaac Kramnick, 'Augustan Politics and English Historiography: The Debate on the English Past, 1730–35', *History and Theory*, VI (1967), pp. 33–56; Dickinson, 'The Eighteenth-Century Debate', pp. 189–210; Richard R. Johnson, '"Parliamentary Egotisms": The Clash of Legislatures in the Making of the American Revolution', *Journal of American History*, LXXIV (1987), pp. 337–62.

to press for aggression against the Bourbons.[14] This new political culture was quickly shared by the colonies. Passage of the Molasses Act clearly demonstrated that well-prepared American lobbies had failed to overcome their more powerful West Indian rivals. The Molasses Act was not primarily a revenue measure but it was, none the less, a parliamentary law that levied a tax on imports into the colonies. Imperial centralizers would later regard this as precedent-setting; American patriots would look back on the law as West Indian corruption and Imperial disregard for America, and would consider the resulting widespread smuggling as the beginning of resistance that eventually undermined Imperial control.[15]

Preoccupation with patronage in Walpole's government affected the colonial Empire in other ways. Governors with powerful patrons and political ability could enjoy extended careers, like those of William Gooch in Virginia (1727–49), Robert Hunter in New York and Jamaica (1710–19, 1728–34), Edward Trelawny in Jamaica (1738–52), and William Shirley in Massachusetts (1741–56). Assumptions and techniques comparable to those of the British ministry were used in the colonies, minimizing debate over principles, and compromising to placate competing interests. Francis Nicholson, a veteran Governor who had made many enemies in his stormy thirty-four-year career, was now instructed: 'One would not Strain any Point where it can be of no Service to our King and Country, and will Create Enemys to ones Self.'[16]

Erosion of gubernatorial power was also accelerated by London interference in the few patronage appointments not already appropriated by colonial Assemblies. Walpole's management of the British House of Commons could extend to appointments by royal patent of colonial naval officers, customs collectors, and attorneys-general. By 1747 the Duke of Newcastle directly controlled ninety-two colonial 'patent offices'.[17] Patent officers could not be removed by Governors, became magnets for political intrigue against Governors, and often sought the financial rewards of office without regard for royal policy. Those patent officers who chose to remain in England, while a local deputy carried out their duties, were even less likely to put policy before profit.

The rise of colonial Assemblies may have been encouraged by wartime defence, but the process continued unchallenged during the long Peace of Utrecht. Rapid

[14] Nicholas Rogers, *Whigs and Cities: Popular Politics in the Age of Walpole and Pitt* (Oxford, 1989), pp. 13–129, 404.

[15] Jacob M. Price, 'The Excise Affair Revisited: The Administrative and Colonial Dimensions of a Parliamentary Crisis', in Stephen B. Baxter, ed., *Britain's Rise to Greatness, 1660–1763* (Berkeley, 1983), pp. 257–321; Paul Langford, *The Excise Crisis: Society and Politics in the Age of Walpole* (Oxford, 1975).

[16] Charles Delafaye to Nicholson, 26 Jan. 1722, printed in Jack P. Greene, ed., *Settlements to Society, 1584–1763* (New York, 1966), pp. 231–32.

[17] L. W. Labaree, *Royal Government in America* (New Haven, 1930), p. 102 n.

colonial population growth fuelled increasing production of export staples as well as consumption of British manufactures. In increasingly complex and stratified colonial societies, political leadership became more specialized and even professional. Major elected and appointed offices became the near-monopoly of an increasingly endogamous 'better sort' and, despite comparatively broad franchises, fewer voted and more incumbents enjoyed re-election. Colonial Assemblies became the centres of power and effective Governors became political managers more than vice-regal executives. Although the Governor of Jamaica finally won a half-century fight for a permanent revenue in 1728, the Massachusetts House of Representatives won a more characteristic victory when its prolonged fight against a permanent revenue act ended in 1735.[18] The rise of the legal profession in the colonies and in their Assemblies reflected and accelerated the complexity of political and legal cultures, while reducing intercolonial differences and drawing all towards British procedures.

Colonial politics were relatively stable after the Peace of Utrecht, and any colonial disorder was directed more against colonial than Imperial governments. The expanding colonial economies and populations prompted slave rebellions and conflicts with invaded Amerindian communities. Rapid expansion of the Carolinas provoked war with the Tuscarora (1711–13) and the Yamasee (1715–18). Failure of the provincial government and proprietors of South Carolina in the latter war prompted a local coup through which the colony offered itself directly to the Crown. Africans became the largest racial group in South Carolina and, like Amerindians, were victims of South Carolina's expanding staple economy. The Stono slave rebellion late in 1739 sent shock waves through the continental colonies. Anglo-Spanish hostility, which contributed to that rebellion, had intensified in the Caribbean and along the Florida–Carolina frontier in the 1730s, and the British government proved surprisingly ready to increase its involvement. The first British naval base in America was developed at English Harbour, Antigua after 1729, the same year North and South Carolina became royal colonies by parliamentary purchase. The new colony of Georgia appropriated Spanish lands with British government help, which included a charter, an annual parliamentary subsidy, and a regiment of regular troops. Imperial government was welcomed on frontiers where aggressive British colonists had provoked slave rebellion, Indian war, or foreign hostility.

Outbreak of the popular and predatory British war against Spain illustrates the impact Imperial excitement could have on British politics. Walpole had maintained peace with France and Spain as a prerequisite for his political system. One

---

[18] Richard L. Bushman, *King and People in Provincial Massachusetts* (Chapel Hill, NC, 1985), pp. 118–20.

of his bellicose parliamentary critics, Admiral Edward Vernon, led a tiny squadron that captured the strategic Spanish Caribbean port of Porto Bello in 1739, fanning British and colonial enthusiasm for the still undeclared War of Jenkins' Ear. Vernon became a popular political hero, symbolizing aggressive virtues and denouncing Walpole as corrupt and effeminate.[19] This mood, caught in James Thomson's popular song 'Rule Britannia' (1740), allowed colonial Governors to be selective in granting military commissions and contracts, and in screening recruits eager to join the 1741 siege of Cartagena. The British government paid, armed, and supplied the 3,600 North American volunteers involved in this disaster, heralding commitments to come.

New Englanders, who loyally contributed to the Cartagena campaign, also expanded northward seeking the lands of the Abenaki and the illicit trade of Acadia and Louisbourg. The military weaknesses of Louisbourg in the 1740s invited even greater ambitions. Governor William Shirley of Massachusetts displayed superb political skills in exploiting Imperial connections, local ambitions and fears, as well as considerable military patronage, to manage the Massachusetts legislature in the royal interest. Once the War of the Austrian Succession brought Anglo-French hostilities to North America, Shirley initiated the Pepperrell–Warren expedition that took Louisbourg. The massive response, a seventy-six-vessel French fleet sent to retake Louisbourg the following year, was ominous. Although never reaching its destination, it prompted naval assistance for Massachusetts and unwelcome intrusions into local government. Tensions erupted in a three-day impressment riot in November 1747 that went far beyond earlier incidents and was marked by hostage-taking, widespread looting, and the refusal of the Boston militia to restore order. The price of expansion was rising beyond New England's resources, as it had done long before in the West Indies.

1748–1763

Although the third Anglo-French war ended in stalemate like the others, the governance of the Empire did not revert to the untroubled politics of peacetime patronage. The Pelham–Newcastle ministry was forced to bolster its parliamentary support in 1748 by making John Russell, Duke of Bedford, the Secretary of State for the Southern Department. Bedford soon had his efficient and ambitious friend George Dunk, Earl of Halifax, appointed as President of the Board of Trade. Halifax was determined to support royal Governors against the power of the colonial Assemblies and to resist French 'encroachments' in North America. His

[19] Kathleen Wilson, 'Empire, Trade, and Popular Politics in Mid-Hanoverian Britain: The Case of Admiral Vernon', *Past and Present*, CXXI (1988), pp. 74–109.

Board of Trade won control of most major colonial appointments during the decade after 1751 and held Governors to rewritten instructions. He favoured strong measures against France and Spain in America, gaining immediate support from Bedford, from the royal Duke of Cumberland, and from numerous other politicians and bureaucrats. The government now gave charters to companies speculating in Ohio Valley lands, established the settlement and naval base at Halifax, Nova Scotia, and extended direct royal government to Georgia. Defence considerations, and the discontent of Iroquois allies, led the Board of Trade to encourage ambitious plans for intercolonial co-operation, most evident in the Albany Conference of 1754. The revitalization of the Board of Trade had refocused Imperial authority, but war postponed the application of the new administrative rigour.

The outbreak of war in 1754 again aborted most efforts to curb the relentless rise of the colonial Assemblies, though Parliament did chastise the Jamaica Assembly in 1757 for encroachment on the prerogative.[20] The first three British commanders in North America, Edward Braddock, William Shirley, and the Earl of Loudoun, were unable to win support from colonial Assemblies or victories from French armies. The Assemblies effectively raised and supplied their own armies, free of serious gubernatorial or British army control, and imposed limits on strategies by enlistment conditions and defensive priorities. Earlier Imperial attempts to control colonial public credit, most recently through the Paper Money Act of 1751, lapsed as Assemblies expanded paper debt to pay war costs.

The most fateful changes in the governance of the Georgian Empire followed from the urgent British need to win what had been, until 1757, a disastrous war. Appointment of the eloquent and industrious, if arrogant, William Pitt as Secretary of State for the Southern Department and effectively Prime Minister, charmed the heavily taxed British public and reassured government suppliers and debtholders. Charismatic Imperial patriotism in the 'national interest' was in power, prepared to spend whatever was necessary to win the war. Pitt cut the powers of the Commanders-in-Chief in America, assumed management of an enlarged war effort, and negotiated directly and generously with colonial Assemblies. British military spending in America expanded rapidly, and co-operation blossomed once Pitt's 'subsidy plan' promised full reimbursement of most colonial expenses beyond levy money and pay for colonial troops. One result of Pitt's approach was a flush of military successes from Montreal to Martinique and Manila. Victory demonstrated that effective Imperial co-operation was possible, at a price, though British fleets, regulars, and money could not always overcome colonial political

[20] Jack P. Greene, 'The Jamaica Privilege Controversy, 1764–66: An Episode in the Process of Constitutional Definition in the Early Modern British Empire', *Journal of Imperial and Commonwealth History* [hereafter *JICH*], XXII (1994), pp. 16–53.

suspicions, military jealousies, or even persistent colonial trade with the enemy. A second result was prompt British payment of approximately half the total colonial war expenses, putting most colonial governments into a comparatively strong fiscal position. A third, and most dangerous, consequence was that, over the next three decades, successive British ministries and Parliaments would scramble unavailingly to solve debt problems derived, first of all, from the Seven Years War and then from the later American war, provoked in part by unsuccessful attempts to solve these problems.[21]

1763–1784

Governance of the British Empire lost much of its flexibility in the wake of the accession of English-born King George III and the decisive victory over France in America and India. George III was determined to rule as 'King-in-Parliament', combining the anointed with the elected in a government he intended to manage personally. For colonial Assemblies, agents, and lobbies, this automatically meant more extensive, and expensive, parliamentary lobbying against greater odds. George III proved unable to establish a stable ministry in the first decade of his reign, and rapid changes in political leadership meant more initiative for senior departmental bureaucrats, many of whom supported tighter Imperial control. Political change and instability also brought new patterns to interest-group politics, with attendant administrative implications. By 1760, customs and excise taxes together represented 68 per cent of government revenues, increasing ministerial concern for those British exports that provided wages for British workers, who consumed heavily taxed imports like sugar, tobacco, and tea. New commercial and industrial interests gained political influence, especially as policy advisers. Changing political culture 'out of doors' in England and America stimulated popular petitions, protests, embargoes, and riots, as well as clubs and fund-raising dinners in support of dissidents such as John Wilkes and John Horne Tooke. Understandably, those in power showed a growing preoccupation with maintaining order.

New additions to the British Empire in India, Africa, and America in the 1763 Peace of Paris increased administrative and defence costs while encouraging more authoritarian experiments, particularly because none of these acquisitions were Anglophone.

---

[21] Richard Middleton, *The Bells of Victory: The Pitt–Newcastle Ministry and the Conduct of the Seven Years' War, 1757–1762* (Cambridge, 1985), pp. 55, 88; Marie Peters, 'The Myth of William Pitt, Earl of Chatham, Great Imperialist. Part I: Pitt and Imperial Expansion, 1738–1763', *JICH*, XXI (1993), pp. 31–74; Julian Gwyn, 'British Government Spending and the North American Colonies', *JICH*, VIII (1980), pp. 74–84.

As with America, British ministries became entangled in fiscal solutions involving the East India Company, especially after it acquired the lucrative but overvalued *diwani*, or the right to collect the revenue of Bengal. In 1767, the year of the Townshend duties on the American colonies, the British government claimed all Indian territory from which the Company collected taxes, then settled for an annual company payment of £400,000 to the British government. In 1772 the same credit crisis that shook the rest of the Empire brought the over-extended East India Company near bankruptcy. To restore confidence and discipline, and protect its own fiscal and political interests, North's ministry passed both the Tea Act and the Regulating Act the following year. The first would precipitate the final crisis in North America, and the second allowed Warren Hastings to undertake his controversial defence of British interests in India during the American Revolution.[22] Because a sovereign King-in-Parliament could not be a vassal to anyone, and because Indian or French objections to formal British expansion in the East could generate costly conflicts, the new Indian Empire was governed from behind two legal veils, which masked the reality that the provinces were now British possessions. Authority remained with the private and transnational East India Company, which governed in the name of the Mughal Emperor, to whom the Company was ostensibly a vassal.

In the new West African colony of Senegambia, the British government attempted an unsuccessful prototype for Crown Colony government. Legislative power was given to the Governor and appointed Council. Justices, sheriffs, and constables were nominated and the Anglican church was supported. Here the British government paid the costs of government, reviewed legislation, and heard judicial appeals.[23] As in India, this was government without an elected Assembly.

British intentions for newly acquired territories in America were different, at least as stated in the famous Royal Proclamation of 7 October 1763. Confirming recent diplomacy, and ignoring intruding colonial settlers, the proclamation declared the Ohio–Mississippi watershed as Crown land for Amerindian use, with regulated trade and no white settlement. To encourage development of the other new colonies, the boundaries of Nova Scotia and Georgia were expanded, and legislative Assemblies were promised to replace military governments in East and West Florida, the Windward Islands, and Quebec. East and West Florida, from which most of the Spanish population emigrated, were promptly granted full royal government by Governor, appointed Council, and elected Assembly. The Windward Islands of St Vincent, Tobago, Dominica, and Grenada were treated similarly, despite the presence of some 3,500 French Catholic

---

[22] See below, pp. 539–40.   [23] 5 Geo. III, c. 44.

inhabitants on Grenada, who were given the franchise and soon won the right to hold office.

Quebec was another matter. Acquisition of Catholic Quebec represented both a tenuous conquest and a significant challenge to the dominance of Protestants throughout the British Empire in Ireland, Scotland, and the Americas. Prerogative government was customary in New France, and survived after 1763 because paternalism suited British gubernatorial prejudices and fears. Although Quebec's 70,000 French inhabitants were assured religious toleration, they were given neither the representation nor the taxation that the Proclamation had promised. An appointed Governor, Council, and judiciary cautiously applied British criminal law and French civil law. This approach was confirmed in the Quebec Act of 1774, by which time the British government was even less inclined to add Quebec to its roster of unmanageable American Assemblies.

Although British control of Canada survived invasion and British defeat in the American Revolution, the Quebec Act was superseded. American Loyalist refugees migrated north to Nova Scotia and Quebec, prompting the creation of the separate colonies of New Brunswick, Prince Edward Island, and Cape Breton, and the creation of Upper (Ontario) and Lower (Quebec) Canada in 1791.[24] Elected Assemblies, accepted by the British government since 1689 as prerequisite to local taxation, were granted everywhere except underpopulated Cape Breton. However, in the wake of the American Revolution the new Governor and Lieutenant-Governor in the Canadas had broader patronage and fiscal powers, support from an established church aided by 'clergy reserves' of Crown land, and had not only the traditional appointed executive Councils but new appointed legislative Councils that became oligarchic upper houses. Appointed power was reinforced, and could enlist considerable support in reaction to recent experience.

After 1763 war debts and new colonial administrative and military costs drove successive British ministries to seek an American revenue, and to do so with strong parliamentary support. George III's first ministry, headed by John Stuart, Earl of Bute, agreed to leave an army of 10,000 men to guard the new acquisitions in America and the West Indies, optimistically presuming that the costs would be borne by the colonies, as had long been the practice with the British army in Ireland. The Sugar Act of 1764, the Stamp Act of 1765, and the Townshend duties of 1767 demonstrated ministerial use of parliamentary power for revenue purposes, and increased colonial use of effective 'out of doors' protest. The fiscal preoccupation of senior colonial administrators was also evident from the increased use of the Royal Navy for customs enforcement, the establishment of an American Board of Customs Commissioners based in Boston (1767), and the reinforcement of the

---

[24] See below, pp. 375–86.

Vice-Admiralty Courts (1768).[25] Ironically, the Tea Act of 1773 was a tax reduction to expand markets for the nearly bankrupt East India Company rather than an American revenue measure, but the strong colonial reaction indicated that the contest was developing beyond a dispute about parliamentary right to tax the colonies. British administrative initiative now shifted to the recently established American Department, where Lord Dartmouth was Secretary of State for the American Colonies, but the real authority rested with his under-secretaries, John Pownall and William Knox. Pownall, Secretary of the Board of Trade under Halifax and under-secretary in the American Department from its inception in 1768, was instrumental in the stern response to the Boston Tea Party. The British Empire in North America took twelve years to unravel after 1764; royal power had collapsed in as many days in 1689. Imperial government had developed a great deal of legitimacy in the intervening seventy-five years.[26]

Although the revolutionary crisis was the culmination of the contest between colonial Assemblies and British Parliaments, it is noteworthy that revolution initially disrupted the Assemblies' leadership. Having built power and reputation by claiming to defend colonists from Imperial impositions, the Assemblies could only protest to London against the new Imperial taxes; the published assembly 'resolves' exhorted colonials to do what the Assemblies could not. The successful non-importation agreements and extra-legal riots had been the work of others, including the Sons of Liberty, the Stamp Act Congress, and the Boston Committee of Correspondence. Although royal Governors had lost power, they prevented Assemblies from meeting legally, moderated their protests, and could veto legislation that was revolutionary. It was self-appointed revolutionary town and county committees that initiated the civil war, that forced county courts to close, took over local government functions, and closed the unrevolutionary General Assembly of Pennsylvania. The first Continental Congress of 1774 created a Continental Association to endorse the local committees that already enforced embargoes and harassed the uncommitted. By the following summer a few Assemblies were bypassed completely, but the rest were transformed into broadly elected new state congresses, monopolizing power while drafting the state constitutions. The colonial élites had recovered from a momentary loss of power. Unitary Imperial government was replaced with a confederacy of almighty Assemblies; the US Congress would have enduring difficulty attempting to recover powers formerly exercised by the King-in-Parliament.

The Imperial government made significant concessions to the West Indian colonies and to Ireland, in contrast to the authoritarian regimes in newly acquired

---

[25] See below, pp. 331–33.
[26] John M. Murrin, 'Political Development', in Jack P. Greene and J. R. Pole, eds., *Colonial British America* (Baltimore, 1984), pp. 408–56.

colonies and the confrontation with American Assemblies. In the West Indies, where seventeenth-century Assemblies had pioneered protests against prerogative authority, there was considerable planter sympathy for the American revolutionaries. This was checked by the attacks of American privateers, and by a 1776 Jamaican slave revolt in the 'spirit of Dear Liberty'. West Indian Assemblies saw the North American revolt as a warning and an opportunity to exploit the implications of Lord Mansfield's judgement in *Campbell* v. *Hall* (1774), that the monarch alone could neither tax nor legislate for colonists who had been promised a legislature. Besieged West Indian royal Governors lost additional authority, especially in fiscal and military affairs. The Irish Protestant establishment tempered its sympathies for Americans with fear of the French, but exploited the opportunity created by the radical Irish Volunteers, who built a sizeable following using American parallels. British moves to liberalize Irish trade laws, soften the penal code, alter the ancient Poynings' Law, and to repeal the hated Irish Declaratory Act of 1720, were all concessions extracted from an Imperial administration openly recruiting Irish Catholics for the British army, and nervous about Irish loyalty.

The impact of the American Revolution on British Imperial governance was extensive. The administration of Lord North had reliable royal and parliamentary support, but there were two years of severe political convulsions thereafter. Empire intruded on British politics again, as it had in 1739–40 and 1757–60, this time destroying the North ministry in 1782 and bringing down Charles James Fox's coalition ministry and his India Bill in the general election of the next year. The abolition of the Board of Trade and the Secretary of State for America in 1782 at once assigned blame, saved money, and presumed a reduction in Imperial business that did not prove justified.

The Empire had worked, despite claims made when the Board of Trade was abolished in 1782. For a century British and colonial merchant fleets had followed Imperial laws requiring them to deliver those increasingly popular exotic commodites that enticed the English to pay taxes. British Protestant communities had used Imperial identities and justifications, and occasional Imperial assistance, against Amerindian, Indian, and European rivals, as well as Scottish Jacobites, Irish Catholics, Acadian neutrals, and West Indian and North American slave communities. When Imperial assistance was minimal, these threats prompted decentralization of political power. When Imperial assistance was substantial, as during the Seven Years War, external threats could draw the Empire closer together, though the governing machinery of the Empire had not been designed for efficient marshalling of Imperial resources for war. Complete Imperial victory over external rivals, on the other hand, encouraged Imperial administrators to expect more integration, and colonial communities to tolerate less. Where victory over external rivals and subject peoples was not possible, as was the case with the West Indian planters or the English-speakers of Quebec, both of whom remained loyal in 1776, rebellion and secession from the Empire was not possible either.

Governance of the Empire had primarily concerned political, economic, and social control within the British communities of the Atlantic Empire. Non-hereditary colonial leaders had appropriated royal legitimacy to establish and preserve their position within new anglophone communities. It was usually easy enough to 'stack' compatible loyalties to town, county, colony, and Empire, even if colonial leaders took up Whiggish notions in defence of local interests against real and pretended Imperial intrusion. The structure of colonial government after 1689, by Governor, Council, and Assembly, had been both appointed and elected, both traditional and adaptable. In a political culture progressively empowering the elected over the appointed, the rise of the colonial Assemblies proved to be as relentless as the growing power of a Parliament into which the royal prerogative had been folded. Polarization of elected colonial and Imperial political power, as well as stimulating the flow of alienating political posturings to and fro across the Atlantic, weakened those interpretive 'shock absorbers' of the Empire, the Governors, the colonial agents, and the merchant lobbies.

Changes in British executive and legislative power had preserved the twinned royal and elective legitimacies, then welded them together as King-in-Parliament. Discontented Americans could not divide these two. What began as a traditional resistance against perceived corruption, with some vocal support in London, was forced to become a civil war about secession and republicanism. The reluctance and divisions among the revolutionaries was a significant tribute to a British Imperial administrative system that had acquired legitimacy and had proved adaptable. Those colonies, companies, and kingdoms that remained loyal gave continuing legitimacy and renewed strength to the governance system. The power of the appointed would be refurbished in new colonies, and spread as Crown Colony government even to the oldest West Indian colonies. A Parliament that was now indisputably supreme would once again both instruct and obstruct elected colonial legislatures; together they would help sustain several more generations of Imperial governance.

Select Bibliography

ARTHUR HERBERT BASYE, *The Lords Commissioners of Trade and Plantations Commonly Known as the Board of Trade, 1748–1782* (New Haven, 1925).

H. V. BOWEN, *Revenue and Reform: The Indian Problem in British Politics, 1757–1773* (Cambridge, 1991).

DORA MAE CLARK, *The Rise of the British Treasury: Colonial Administration of the Eighteenth Century* (New Haven, 1960).

RICHARD S. DUNN, *Sugar and Slaves: The Rise of the Planter Class in the English West Indies, 1624–1713* (Chapel Hill, NC, 1972).

JACK P. GREENE, *The Quest for Power: The Lower Houses of Assembly in the Southern Royal Colonies, 1689–1776* (Chapel Hill, NC, 1963).

—— *Peripheries and Center: Constitutional Development in the Extended Polities of the British Empire and the United States, 1607–1788* (Athens, Ga., 1986).

—— *Negotiated Authorities: Essays in Colonial Political and Constitutional History* (Charlottesville, Va., 1994).

JAMES A. HENRETTA, *'Salutary Neglect': Colonial Administration under the Duke of Newcastle* (Princeton, 1972).

RICHARD R. JOHNSON, *Adjustment to Empire: The New England Colonies, 1675–1715* (New Brunswick, NJ, 1981).

NANCY F. KOEHN, *The Power of Commerce: Economy and Governance in the First British Empire* (Ithaca, NY, 1994).

L. W. LABAREE, *Royal Government in America* (New Haven, 1930).

PHILIP LAWSON, ed., *Parliament and the Atlantic Empire* (Edinburgh, 1995).

ALISON GILBERT OLSON, *Making the Empire Work: London and American Interest Groups, 1690–1790* (Cambridge, Mass., 1992).

E. B. RUSSELL, *The Review of American Colonial Legislation by the King in Council* (New York, 1915), pp. 54–58, 88–89.

JOSEPH HENRY SMITH, *Appeals to the Privy Council from the American Plantations* (New York, 1950).

IAN K. STEELE, *Politics of Colonial Policy: The Role of the Board of Trade in Colonial Administration, 1696–1720* (Oxford, 1968).

L. S. SUTHERLAND, *The East India Company in Eighteenth-Century Politics* (Oxford, 1952).

AGNES M. WHITSON, *The Constitutional Development of Jamaica, 1660 to 1729* (Manchester, 1929).

6

Religious Faith and Commercial Empire

BOYD STANLEY SCHLENTHER

Religion in the developing eighteenth-century British Empire was directly affected by a burgeoning commercial culture. Strenuous efforts by the Church of England to co-ordinate its activities in the Atlantic world were seriously undercut. Growing colonial impulses intent on celebrating the blessings of free trade in goods were accompanied by equally potent forces expounding free trade in religious ideas and practices. By the second half of the century this had swamped any hope of a religiously unified Empire and had firmly established religious competition throughout the New World marketplace.

By the beginning of the eighteenth century, religion in England's Atlantic outposts of Empire formed a variegated patchwork. The New England colonies of Massachusetts, Connecticut, and New Hampshire, although not theocracies, had Puritan establishments rooted deep in Congregationalist soil, where church and state were mutually supportive. Each had clearly defined parish systems served by tax-supported ministers. Tiny Rhode Island, huddled amongst its New England neighbours as a nervous vanguard of religious liberty, was peopled mainly by Quakers and Baptists.

To the south, in the Chesapeake colonies of Virginia and Maryland, it was the Church of England that was established by law. Anglicanism had this position from Virginia's early years, and it was secured in Maryland in the aftermath of the Glorious Revolution. Following the turn of the century, establishments were achieved in North and South Carolina. In each of these plantation colonies clearly defined Anglican parishes served as administrative units of government. The absence of a colonial bishop meant that in practice ecclesiastical affairs, including the employment of parish clergymen, rested in the hands of laymen: the local planter élite and the Crown-appointed Governors. In spite of the 1689 English Act of Toleration, in all these colonies with religious establishments, whether Congregationalist or Anglican, freedom of religious expression was constrained. In fact, at the beginning of the eighteenth century non-Anglicans in England generally had greater religious choice than those who dissented from the colonial church establishments.[1]

Between New England and the southern plantation provinces lay the Middle Colonies of New York, New Jersey, and Pennsylvania. Originally a Dutch settlement, after the English take-over in 1664 attempts were made to establish the Anglican church in New York. Yet the diversity of the population thwarted such efforts, and in spite of pretensions to the contrary, the Church of England never secured an unequivocal establishment. The same was true in New Jersey, with its substantial numbers of Presbyterians and Quakers. The colony most open to diversity was the last founded during the seventeenth century. Pennsylvania was the child of William Penn, who saw it not only as a haven for his fellow Quakers but also as a 'Holy Experiment' in religious freedom. Therefore, numerous churches and sects, combined with various new ethnic strands, produced during the eighteenth century a mixed multitude in Pennsylvania where Quakers became a decided numerical minority in their own colony.

Thus, into the eighteenth century the mainland colonies were clearly mapped-out religiously by a Congregationalist establishment in New England (apart from Rhode Island), an Anglican establishment in the southern plantation colonies (although secure only in Virginia and Maryland), and a lack of any legal religious establishment in the colonies which lay between. The century saw the establishing of further colonies to the far north, when Acadia (later Nova Scotia), Hudson Bay, and Newfoundland were ceded to Great Britain by the Treaty of Utrecht (1713), and these gains were further extended by the Treaty of Paris (1763) to include Cape Breton, the St Lawrence islands, and Quebec. In all these 'Canadian' territories the Church of England became the officially established religious order, at least notionally.

In the West Indian islands of the Atlantic rim the Anglicanism of the white settlers had taken root in a predominantly slave culture increasingly devoted to the production of sugar cane. By the late seventeenth century all of Barbados's eleven parishes were served by Anglican clergymen; with the most fully developed parish system in any of the islands, it probably also had the best-educated clerics, who formed an important element of the planter élite.[2] During the same period Jamaica had fifteen parishes, but only six had churches, and only four of

---

[1] John M. Murrin, 'Religion and Politics in America from the First Settlements to the Civil War', in Mark A. Noll, ed., *Religion and American Politics from the Colonial Period to the 1980s* (New York, 1990), pp. 19–43, esp. 21.

[2] Michael Craton, 'Reluctant Creoles. The Planters' World in the British West Indies', in Bernard Bailyn and Philip D. Morgan, eds., *Strangers Within the Realm. Cultural Margins of the First British Empire* (Chapel Hill, NC, 1991), pp. 314–63, esp. 360; Hilary McD. Beckles, *A History of Barbados. From Amerindian Settlement to Nation-state* (Cambridge, 1989), p. 46.

these had clergymen. Of the Leeward Islands, only St Kitts (with six) and Nevis (with four) had churches. Apparently the general pattern was for ministers to be supported not by parish tithes but by legislatively granted stipends. As in Virginia, wealthy planters controlled local government, including ecclesiastical affairs. In lieu of a bishop, an island's Governor acted as the effective head of the church, holding the right to license, appoint, and dismiss all clergymen. The amount of toleration fluctuated, but into the eighteenth century the inhabitants in all the islands were increasingly given substantial religious liberty.[3]

These scattered West Indian islands had begun to coalesce into a broader Imperial economy, modelled on the sugar success of Barbados and bound to Britain and the mainland colonies by interlocking circuits of intercolonial and transatlantic trade. To the north of these Caribbean colonies were the other British islands of Bermuda and the Bahamas, which had not developed staple crop economies, but ones centred on shipbuilding, fishing, and other commercial activities related to the sea. Here the Anglican church was more successful. After the first quarter of the eighteenth century, for example, nearly 90 per cent of the population of Bermuda adhered to the Church of England.[4]

From the outset of the eighteenth century the religious life of the mainland colonies was marked by the aggressiveness of a reinvigorated Anglicanism, especially where it was not by law established. The cutting-edge of this activity was in the New England and Middle Colonies, where there was most lost ground to be recovered. London's concern for a co-ordinated Empire seemed to invite an effort to draw back into the Anglican fold those sheep whose seventeenth-century forebears had escaped the Church of England in order to seek their own New World ecclesiastical pastures. From the non-Anglican perspective it must have seemed as if what their forefathers had fled now threatened them in their American haven. Before 1680 the story of the Anglican church in America is confined almost totally to the Chesapeake colonies of Virginia and Maryland. Yet in 1698 the Society for Promoting Christian Knowledge (SPCK) was established, commencing a programme of dispersing Bibles and other Christian literature in the North American mainland and island colonies. With such a view in mind, the founder of the SPCK, Dr Thomas Bray, spent several months in Maryland during 1700,

---

[3] Edward Long, *The History of Jamaica* (London, 1774), pp. 234–40; Anthony McFarlane, *The British in the Americas, 1480–1815* (London, 1994), p. 75. See also David Watts, *The West Indies: Patterns of Development, Culture and Environmental Change since 1492* (Cambridge, 1987), p. 209; Richard S. Dunn, *Sugar and Slaves. The Rise of the Planter Class in the English West Indies, 1624–1713* (Chapel Hill, NC, 1972), pp. 103, 104, 128–29, 157, 184.

[4] Jack P. Greene, *Pursuits of Happiness. The Social Development of Early Modern British Colonies and the Formation of American Culture* (Chapel Hill, NC, 1988), p. 154.

returning to England to publish that year in London his *A Memorial Representing the Present State of Religion on the Continent of North America.*

A direct result was the formation in 1701 of the prime instrument for energetic Imperial Anglicanism: the Society for the Propagation of the Gospel in Foreign Parts (SPG). Up to the War of Independence the SPCK and SPG sent thousands of pamphlets and other religious publications for distribution to the American public, with the SPCK in addition sending whole collections of books to form parish libraries. The SPG sent men. Between 1701 and 1783 it despatched more than 600 clergymen to the colonies, who founded about 300 churches outside of Virginia and Maryland.[5] This was a body of 'good Soldiers of Jesus Christ', whom Thomas Jefferson would later less favourably dub 'Anglican Jesuits'.[6] Thomas Bray's approach had been gentle, focusing on the un-churched, yet those who followed him viewed themselves more as storm-troopers, the ecclesiastical arm of eighteenth-century imperialism. While Crown officials regulated trade and military forces carried the sword against French and Spanish papists, SPG missionaries would bear what they trusted would be a cross of triumph. Thus, the SPG saw that a significant part of its mission was to act as a handmaid to Empire in the context of renewed rivalry with Roman Catholic France and Spain. This note was struck frequently and with force. The Bishop of Chester in 1709 called upon the Society to remember its responsibility for saving 'Infidels from being made a Prey to the church of Rome, that most unsound and corrupt part of the Christian Church, and which, so industriously compasseth Land and Sea to make Proselytes to it'.[7]

In mounting missions among non-whites, those SPG efforts that focused on native Indians showed very limited return.[8] Much more was accomplished amongst black slaves. No other agency throughout the Imperial eighteenth century worked as assiduously to convert and secure humane treatment for the victims of slavery. This activity was most pronounced where it was most needed: in the plantation colonies of the mainland south and on the islands. In Charles Town (Charleston), South Carolina, the SPG established a school for sixty black boys and girls, but in Barbados the planters were more recalcitrant. When Christopher Codrington left substantial portions of his estate to the SPG for a college

---

[5] John Calam, *Parsons and Pedagogues: The S.P.G. Adventure in American Education* (New York, 1971), pp. 62–102; Jon Butler, *Awash in a Sea of Faith: Christianizing the American People* (Cambridge, Mass., 1990), p. 127.

[6] White Kennett, *An Account of the Society for Propagating the Gospel in Foreign Parts* (London, 1706), p. 8; John Frederick Woolverton, *Colonial Anglicanism in North America* (Detroit, 1984), p. 89.

[7] William Dawes, *A Sermon Preach'd before the Society for the Propagation of the Gospel in Foreign Parts* (London, 1709), p. 21.

[8] Woolverton, *Colonial Anglicanism*, pp. 99–104; Peter Michael Doll, 'Imperial Anglicanism in North America, 1745–1795', unpublished D.Phil. thesis, Oxford, 1989, pp. 48–53.

(which came to bear his name), he stipulated one purpose to be the provision of Christian education for slaves. However, the planter-dominated island government refused, and not until late in the century did it provide for Anglican ministers to offer such instruction.[9] It is clear that, left to their own devices and desires, plantation owners were generally happy for their slaves to remain unchristianized. Such efforts as there were required the Imperial thrust of a missionary society directed from the centre.

In practice, the SPG's main targets were non-Anglican Protestants. Such men as George Keith, whose ecclesiastical somersault had followed an arc from Presbyterian to Quaker until he landed on Anglican feet, with the convert's zeal returned to Pennsylvania armed with Church of England ordination to mount frontal attacks on his former Quaker co-religionists. Now he claimed that being separated from the Church of England 'is very hainous'.[10] It was the arrival at Congregationalist Connecticut's Yale College in 1718 of a substantial shipment of books from the SPCK that precipitated the most dramatic single Anglican advance during the colonial period. This library of books, including a wide collection of writings by seventeenth-century Anglican divines, had a decided impact. Four years later the head of Yale, two of its tutors, and four neighbouring Congregationalist ministers publicly announced that they had joined the Church of England. Two of them immediately travelled to England for episcopal ordination and returned home as missionaries of the SPG. These Anglican converts had such an influence upon the growth of their new church in New England that Yale came to contribute more ministers to the colonial Church of England than did the Anglican College of William and Mary, founded in Virginia in 1693.[11] The Church of England had established a bridgehead in New England, offering a decided alternative to Puritanism's previous near monopoly. Of the ninety-two Anglican clergymen who served in Connecticut from 1702 to 1785, sixty were New England-born converts from Congregationalism.[12] The Anglican advance was substantial enough to force Massachusetts and Connecticut to allow Church of England supporters in certain circumstances to divert financial support from the established Puritan parish ministers to their own clerics. In lieu of the presence of bishops, the oversight of

[9] Beckles, *History of Barbados*, pp. 88–89.

[10] George Keith, *The Notes of the True Church With the Application of them to the Church of England, and the Great Sin of Separation from Her* (New York, 1704), p. 4; Gerald J. Goodwin, 'The Anglican Middle Way in Early Eighteenth-Century America: Anglican Religious Thought in the American Colonies, 1702–1750', unpublished Ph.D. dissertation, Wisconsin, 1965, chap. 1.

[11] Goodwin, 'Anglican Middle Way', chap. 3; Richard Warch, *School of the Prophets: Yale College, 1701–1740* (New Haven, 1973), pp. 96–121.

[12] Frederick V. Mills, *Bishops by Ballot: An Eighteenth-Century Ecclesiastical Revolution* (New York, 1978), p. 7.

the Church of England in the colonies had by the beginning of the century been lodged with the Bishop of London. It is hardly surprising that such an arrangement proved inadequate for the development of Imperial Anglicanism. One Bishop of London was to lament that the care of the colonial church 'is improperly lodged, for a Bishop to live at one end of the world, and his Church at the other, must make the office very uncomfortable to the Bishop, and in a great measure useless to the people'.[13] The lack of resident episcopal oversight led Bishops of London to create the post of commissary. The holders of this office were ordained clergymen vested with authority to visit local colonial parishes, gather conventions of Anglican ministers, and in general attempt to supervise on the ground the coordination and advance of the Church of England in its Imperial settings. What a commissary could not do was to ordain clergymen, confirm communicants, or consecrate churches and burial grounds. Nowhere in colonial America would there be 'holy ground'. Commissaries were employed extensively during the eighteenth century, with widely varying degrees of usefulness, the most remarkable of their number being James Blair, who held the post in Virginia for fifty-three years. As commissary, local parish minister, and head of the Church of England's first colonial college, William and Mary (established with large gifts of money from the Archbishop of Canterbury and the Crown), Blair consolidated his many positions for the furtherance of the Church of England in America.

An additional piece in the patchwork of Anglican authority in the colonies was the role of royal Governors, who assumed responsibility for assigning ministers to parishes. A man like Francis Nicholson was well positioned to further the work of the SPG, of which he was a charter member. From 1690 to 1728, as Lieutenant-Governor or Governor in turn of Virginia, Maryland, Nova Scotia, and South Carolina, Nicholson pulled numerous ecclesiastical strings to strengthen the Anglican cause. But in practice Governors' strings became constantly tangled with those of the activities of the SPG and the Bishop of London's commissaries. These overlapping efforts show the near impossibility of any co-ordinated plan for Anglican hegemony in the eighteenth-century Empire.

Such Anglican advance as there was did not go unanswered. The creation of the SPG in 1701 in its turn stimulated the competitive organizational consolidations of other mainland colonial denominations. In 1708 Connecticut moved a step from localized Congregationalism to a Presbyterian polity by adopting consociations to supervise church life and practice. The preceding year Pennsylvania Baptists organized their Philadelphia Association, and during the same period Quakers

---

[13] Bishop of London to Philip Doddridge, 11 May 1751, in William Stevens Perry, ed., *Historical Collections Relating to the American Colonial Church*, 5 vols. (Hartford, Conn., 1870–78), I, p. 373.

in Pennsylvania defensively turned their attention to tightening internal discipline. Yet these actions were limited to particular colonies.

The most important ecclesiastical response to an aggressive Anglicanism was the formation in 1706 of the first American presbytery. Presbyterianism had been slow to develop in the Atlantic Empire, with only a handful of congregations at the turn of the century. This new organization—the first intercolonial body of any kind—drew these churches into an authoritative church judicature across colonial boundaries. Spearheading its organization was the Ulster-born graduate of the University of Glasgow, Francis Makemie, ordained by an Ulster presbytery in the early 1680s, perhaps specifically for service in America.[14] The new American presbytery assumed full responsibility for ordaining ministers and establishing and controlling congregations. Its challenge to the Anglican enterprise was immediately recognized by the SPG:

[The Church of England in New Castle, Delaware, has] a very worthy Man Mr. Ross, but the Place is very unhappy in being divided. The Greatest part are Presbyterians and the Division is much greater than ever by the late coming of one MacKenney [i.e. Makemie] a great Pillar of that Sect who travels thro' all the main like a Bishop having his Pupills to attend him and where he comes Ordains Ministers and executes all the Powers of a Bishop ... Those that ought to Contribute to his [i.e. Ross's] Support are joyned with the presbyterians, so that he hath but very little to support him.[15]

In the immediate aftermath of the formation of the presbytery, Makemie became embroiled in fierce conflict with the royal Governor of New York and New Jersey, Edward Hyde, Lord Cornbury. In his role as Governor, Cornbury had been assiduous in attempting to proceed on the pretence of an Anglican establishment. He had previously taken action against Presbyterian and Dutch Reformed ministers, especially on Long Island, by imposing new SPG clerics on parishes that already maintained settled Presbyterian ministers.[16] By refusing to allow the Presbyterian Makemie to preach in New York and securing Makemie's imprisonment when he did, Cornbury fanned the flames of local resentment against the new Anglican aggressiveness. When at the ensuing trial Makemie was declared innocent, a significant blow was struck against imperial Anglican attempts to force ecclesiastical establishment, especially in a colony like New York with its mixed ethnic and religious make-up.[17] Subsequent Church of England growth in the

---

[14] Boyd Stanley Schlenther, ed., *The Life and Writings of Francis Makemie* (Philadelphia, 1971), pp. 13–14.

[15] Robert Quary to Bishop of London, 20 Jan. 1708, Lambeth Palace Library, SPG Letterbooks, Series A, vol. 4, no. 36.

[16] Robert Hastings Nichols, *Presbyterianism in New York State* (Philadelphia, 1963), pp. 19–25; Randall H. Balmer, *A Perfect Babel of Confusion. Dutch Religion and English Culture in the Middle Colonies* (New York, 1989), pp. 83–88.

[17] Schlenther, *Francis Makemie*, pp. 21–25, 155–244, 263–65.

colony had to focus far more on wooing than wrestling non-Anglicans into submission.

Throughout the Imperial period in America religious groups such as the Church of England, the Dutch Reformed Church, and the Quakers were hamstrung by having their ultimate sources of ecclesiastical control in the Old World. Groups such as the Baptists, the Congregationalists in New England, and most spectacularly, the Presbyterians centred in the Middle Colonies, surged ahead largely owing to the religious reins they held in their own hands. The original presbytery by the eve of American Independence had subdivided and multiplied into eleven presbyteries, with over 150 ministers serving more than 300 churches spread from New York to South Carolina and even the West Indies. Throughout the period up to the Revolution the 'Americanized' churches all had established control of their own organizations. None the less, the activities of the SPG paid dividends. From just under 300 in 1750, Anglican congregations had grown to 400 by 1770.[18]

Religious competition, sparked by an aggressive Anglicanism, marked the early years of the eighteenth century in the mainland colonies. In spite of the advances made, organized Anglicanism had arrived in America too late to flower extensively outside Virginia and Maryland: the roots of religious pluralism were too deep. Moreover, the diverse—the divisive—nature of mainland colonial politics and geography confronted Anglican missionaries with a map that defied unification. By mid-century, mainland American religious pluralism was distinctive within the western world. Most distinctive was Pennsylvania, with its extensive religious freedom: 'We find there Lutherans, Reformed, Catholics, Quakers, Mennonists or Anabaptists, Herrnhuters or Moravian Brethren, Pietists, Seventh Day Baptists, Dunkers, Presbyterians, Newborn, Freemasons, Separatists, Freethinkers, Jews, Mohammedans, Pagans.'[19]

At the heart of this diversity beat something more than religion. From the outset of seventeenth-century settlement in the Atlantic world following the end of war with Spain in 1604, religious groups had been both spurred and facilitated by England's commercial expansion. Even the most religiously self-conscious settlements in Puritan New England could not have been established without the concomitant questing for overseas trade. Into the eighteenth century a commer-

---

[18] Minutes of the Synod of New York and Philadelphia, 1775, *Records of the Presbyterian Church in the United States of America* (Philadelphia, n.d.), p. 461; *Aitkin's General American Register* (Philadelphia, 1774), pp. 182–91; Edwin Scott Gaustad, *Historical Atlas of Religion in America* (New York, 1962), p. 9.

[19] Gottlieb Mittelberger, *Journey to Pennsylvania in the Year 1750 and Return to Germany in the Year 1754*, in Louis B. Wright and Elaine W. Fowler, eds., *English Colonization of North America* (London, 1968), pp. 102–03.

cial and trade revolution greatly enhanced the spread of new religious activity.[20]
The seventeenth-century colonies had been formed haphazardly for the most part,
with religion an important spearhead for various sects and denominations. In the
eighteenth century religious settlement was largely trade-driven, and this was true
not only of newcomers but for the increasing internal migrations within colonial
America. Church groups were directly influenced, and changed, by the need to
participate in the new market-place economy. An imperially minded church was
able to use the SPG to capitalize on this expansion. With the opening of new trade
networks, not only could missionaries and printed matter be sent into the
Chesapeake Bay but now also up the various rivers, from New England to South
Carolina. The new political stability in England, linked with the expansion of trade
in a newly reorganized Empire based upon earlier trade regulations, meant that
Anglican buildings could be built and fitted-out as befitted a true English church.
This was facilitated in Virginia by a new political and economic maturation
centred in the planter élite. The number of Virginian Anglican church buildings
nearly doubled from thirty-five in 1680 to sixty-one in 1724, and as they increased
in number so they did in imported English trappings.[21] Elsewhere, the goods
imported in the expanding Empire provided the opportunity for refinement that
led a number of colonials to convert to the Church of England, finding in it a
history, stability, order, and liturgy that denoted their own increased prosperity
and position in society. As Anglicans built churches of some style and refinement
in all the major coastal towns during the early decades of the century, other
religious bodies were stimulated to erect structures of competing stature. Transatlantic trade also produced the opening of channels of new thought and experience through travel and imported books.[22] On the other hand, it could produce
decidedly negative results. The SPG emerged during the period of large-scale trade
in black slaves. Even those religious leaders who questioned slavery could not
recommend hindering the increase, since 'we are a People who live and maintain
our selves by *Trade*; and ... if *Trade* be lost, or overmuch discouraged, we are a
ruined Nation.'[23]

[20] Neil McKendrick and others, *The Birth of a Consumer Society: The Commercialization of
Eighteenth-Century England* (Bloomington, Ind., 1982), pp. 117–40, 146–94; T. H. Breen, '"Baubles of
Britain": the American and Consumer Revolutions of the Eighteenth Century', *Past and Present*, CXIX
(1988), pp. 73–104; Breen, 'An Empire of Goods: the Anglicization of Colonial America, 1690–1776',
Journal of British Studies, XXV (1986), pp. 467–99.

[21] Butler, *Awash in a Sea of Faith*, p. 100; Dell Upton, *Holy Things and Profane. Anglican Parish
Churches in Colonial Virginia* (New York, 1986), pp. 101–62.

[22] Richard L. Bushman, *The Refinement of America: Persons, Houses, Cities* (New York, 1992),
pp. 169–80.

[23] William Fleetwood, *A Sermon Preached before the Society for the Propagation of the Gospel in
Foreign Parts* (London, 1711), p. 17.

Within the context of trade, London non-Anglican merchants helped their co-religionists to migrate throughout the North Atlantic world. Huguenots and Jews, among others, established trading networks which linked the English provinces to London and overseas. In the highly competitive new colonial religious era, those groups not undergirt by a tax-supported local establishment drew heavily on the resources of their British co-religionists. By the middle of the eighteenth century there were Jewish synagogues in Newport, Rhode Island; New York City; and Charles Town, South Carolina. Yet the Society of Friends probably had a greater proportion of merchants than other denominations, and the Quaker commercial caste came close to monopolizing Philadelphia's trade in the early years of the century. In turn, this Quaker-dominated merchant élite, together with the Congregationalist merchants who held economic sway in New England, now became challenged by trade-led Anglicans, encouraged by the activities of the SPG. Colonial Congregationalists had no similar support group to protect their interests. When Governor Joseph Dudley of Massachusetts converted from Congregationalism to Anglicanism, his identification with a group of wealthy merchants added fuel to the engines of competition. Among these were Huguenots, French Protestants, who had already found religious refuge in England. Those who went on to America were typically young and materially minded, who in the main affiliated with the rising Anglican merchant class. When Dudley secured tax money to assist them to build a new church in Boston, he was praised by the London Huguenot Threadneedle Street Church, from 'Gentlemen concerned in providing Masts', lauding him for assisting in developing the mast trade. Huguenots in the colonies were virtually dependent upon this London congregation for financial support.[24]

Enterprise and opportunity also became intertwined with the Imperial expansion of another denomination, one that sprang from non-English soil. The New World activities of Presbyterianism's Francis Makemie offer a striking confirmation of the commercial dimension of the new religious migrations. After his arrival in America he immediately set about reconnoitring the coasts of Maryland, Virginia, North Carolina, and Barbados. Makemie saw himself as a scout both religious and commercial on behalf of his fellow Ulster Presbyterians.[25] By 1687 he had established a legal residence on Virginia's eastern shore, as a base from which to carry out trade and missionary work with Barbados. His trading interests in Barbados led him to remain on the island during most of this period. From there,

[24] Alison Gilbert Olson, *Making the Empire Work. London and American Interest Groups, 1690–1790* (Cambridge, Mass., 1992), pp. 7–8, 73, 74, 82, 83, 84 (quotation). See also, Jon Butler, *The Huguenots in America* (Cambridge, Mass., 1983), pp. 53–54, 57–60, 85–86, 200–02.

[25] Francis Makemie to Increase Mather, 22 July 1684, in Schlenther, *Francis Makemie*, p. 249.

in the spirit of what he saw as a new religious epoch for the Empire in the heady aftermath of the Glorious Revolution, Makemie wrote *Truths in a True Light*, a pamphlet urging Protestants to sink their differences in the face of the Church of Rome. Well before his crossing of swords with Lord Cornbury, Makemie pleaded the ecclesiastical equality of Presbyterianism and Anglicanism by the astute argument that in Scotland Presbyterianism was the established form of the church and that, therefore, those of the Anglican persuasion in that country were Dissenters.[26]

Makemie returned to Virginia in 1698; with over 5,000 acres of land, he was the second largest landowner in his county, and during the next few years devoted much of his time to plantation and commercial ventures. When visiting Philadelphia in the early 1690s, he had gathered a small group of Presbyterians in 'The Storehouse', which was used during weekdays in trade with Barbados; and for a number of years Philadelphia's Presbyterians continued to worship there amidst the stored indigo, cotton, wool, tobacco, and ginger. This whiff of trade remained in Makemie's nostrils, and on a 1705 visit to London he published *A Plain and Friendly Perswasive to the Inhabitants of Virginia and Maryland, For Promoting Towns and Cohabitation*. Like some leading Virginians and a number of officials in England, Makemie was deeply worried by the lack of commercial centres in the Chesapeake colonies and their resulting total dependence upon plantation crops. It was towns in South Carolina, Barbados, Pennsylvania, New York, and New England that were the engines for those colonies' advancing commerce. In contrast, Virginia and Maryland were being outstripped. These other colonies were carrying from the Chesapeake

the little scattered Coin we have among us, they buy up our old Iron, Brass, Copper, Pewter, Hides and Tallow, which we often want, and might use our selves: They carry away our Wheat; and return it again to us in Bread and Flower [*sic*], and make us pay for transporting, grinding, boulting and baking... All which Disadvantages, with many more, we could effectually prevent by Towns and Cohabitation.

Moreover, churches and schools flourished only in 'Christian Towns and Cities', and Makemie even used his appeal to encourage the activities of the SPG (once again, he was writing before the clash with Cornbury). Thus establishing towns in a hitherto plantation-dominated economy would lead to a much-needed diversity. It would encourage the settlement of tradesmen and craftsmen, in addition to a 'Confluence of people' who would stream to the west to produce not tobacco, but commodities such as timber and foodstuffs that could be fed into the

---

[26] *Truths in a True Light. Or, a Pastoral Letter, to the Reformed Protestants in Barbadoes* (Edinburgh, 1699), printed in Schlenther, *Francis Makemie*, pp. 109–34. For Makemie in Barbados, see pp. 15–16.

manufacturing processes of the new urban centres he desired.[27] Makemie remained a tobacco planter and slave-owner, and his commercial appeal was not a negation of his economic self-interest;[28] none the less, towns would provide a 'publick market' which would offer noble competition, both commercial and religious.[29] Makemie's recipe for economic, social, and religious diversification and competition was not to the taste of the Crown. Keeping colonies such as Virginia and Maryland as producers of primary goods upon which duties could be collected served much better.

Francis Makemie formed the first American presbytery in 1706. As ministers and lay elders representing congregations across colonial boundaries met in regular session, their conversation turned on more than purely religious affairs. This pan-colonial organization was put in place on the eve of the substantial emigration of his fellow-Presbyterians from Scotland and Ulster. The 1707 union of the Scottish and English Parliaments in effect transformed the English into the British Empire. Forbidden by the Navigation Acts from trading with the English colonies prior to 1707, any Scot interested in colonial service or trade supported the new Union as an expansive opportunity; and the newly organized Presbyterian church in the colonies gained from the free movement of energetic Scots, together with money and men provided by the Church of Scotland.

After 1707 Lowland Scots staged an invasion of the colonies, seeking the financial rewards of a now British Empire. Large numbers settled in the commercial void of the Chesapeake, assuming the role of the merchants, bankers, and traders that Virginia and Maryland wanted through their lack of towns. The Scottish Presbyterian commercial class became the 'money-changers in the temple of American liberty', and many also prospered in the Caribbean.[30]

However, the greatest influx into eighteenth-century American Presbyterianism was from Ulster. Scores of thousands of Ulster Scot Presbyterians followed Makemie's footsteps. The overwhelming majority of the Ulster settlers were Presbyterians, who more than any other source added to the numerical resources

---

[27] Makemie, *A Plain and Friendly Perswasive* (London, 1705), in Schlenther, *Francis Makemie*, pp. 146, 148; Char Miller, 'Francis Makemie: Social Development of the Colonial Chesapeake', *American Presbyterians. Journal of Presbyterian History*, LXIII (1985), pp. 333–40.

[28] A Petition of Francis Makemie and Others to the Governor of Virginia, Regarding Custom Duties on Tobacco Trade Between Virginia and Maryland, 2 Nov. 1705, in Schlenther, *Francis Makemie*, pp. 262–63.

[29] Makemie, *Plain and Friendly Perswasive*, in ibid., p. 146.

[30] Ian Graham, *Colonists From Scotland* (Ithaca, NY, 1956), p. 163 (quotation); J. M. Price, 'The Rise of Glasgow in the Chesapeake Tobacco Trade, 1707–1775', *William and Mary Quarterly* (hereafter *WMQ*), Third Series, XI (1954), pp. 179–99; Alan L. Karras, *Sojourners in the Sun. Scottish Migrants in Jamaica and the Chesapeake, 1740–1800* (Ithaca, NY, 1992).

of the new American denomination. They were driven not by religious oppression; their harrassment at Anglican hands in Ulster had largely come to an end
with the accession of George I in 1714. Just as they consolidated their religious
liberties in the north of Ireland they commenced a mass migration to America,
settling primarily in Pennsylvania, with large numbers slipping by mid-century
into western Maryland, Virginia, the Carolinas, and Georgia. In Ulster, spurred
by the investment of newly arrived Huguenots at the turn of the century,[31] they
had engaged extensively in linen-weaving as well as in agriculture. It seems that
most Ulster emigrants in colonial America were farmer-weavers, basing their
work on a combination of flax production and the spinning and weaving of fine
linen cloth. Moreover, European emigration to America always tended to follow
the paths of transatlantic commerce, and during the eighteenth century most
of the vessels leaving Belfast and Londonderry for America were engaged in the
flax-seed trade, of which Philadelphia was the leading colonial centre. Everything converged to make Pennsylvania the area which came most to bear
Ulster's imprint. Yet even though it was economic opportunity rather than
religious persecution that drove them thither, Presbyterianism was a badge of
identity, providing the ethnic-religious context in which their industry flourished.[32]

At the end of the colonial period Presbyterianism produced another leading
minister who, like Makemie, wedded faith to economic expansion. John Witherspoon arrived in 1768 to assume the headship of the Presbyterians' one colonial
college, the College of New Jersey, at Princeton. From the time of his arrival he was
actively involved in land speculation on the north shore of Nova Scotia, joined
with a number of Presbyterian merchants in the Middle Colonies who had
been instrumental in securing his emigration. He went on to become involved
in further large-scale land speculation in northern New York. The religious-
economic encouragement given by Presbyterians like Witherspoon contributed
to a mighty upsurge in land-hungry arrivals from Scotland during the decade
before the outbreak of the War of Independence, especially in the frontier areas of
Nova Scotia, New York, and North Carolina. In Scotland, Witherspoon had served
as minister in Paisley, a highly economically unstable textile centre, and this
induced a large number from that area to follow his emigrating lead.[33] Advertising
for settlers in Scottish newspapers and weaving commercial themes into the fabric

[31] Charles Wilson, *England's Apprenticeship, 1603–1763* (London, 1965), pp. 197–98.

[32] See above, pp. 46–47. Maldwyn A. Jones, 'The Scotch-Irish in British America', in Bailyn and Morgan, *Strangers Within the Realm*, pp. 284–313, esp. 287, 292, 293, 298–302.

[33] See above, pp. 42–43. Bernard Bailyn, *Voyagers to the West. Emigration from Britain to America on the Eve of the Revolution* (London, 1987), pp. 26–27, 198, 287, 390–97, 610–37; Varnum Lansing Collins, *President Witherspoon*, 2 vols. (Princeton, 1925), I, pp. 148–55.

of his preaching, he displayed a striking ability to reconcile language, commercial and religious, appealing to settlers by a presentation of prosperity and piety. A revival of trade denoted, he said, a revival of religious dedication. It was in this vein that Witherspoon appealed to the Presbyterian commercial and artisan groups in the west of Scotland to emigrate.[34]

It was the 'Great Awakening' that most decisively hammered religion into the Imperial framework of commerce. The Awakening was a series of revivals throughout the colonies which countered what revivalists perceived to be supine formal practice and a belief in salvation through leading a moral life. These revivals were at their height in New England and the Middle Colonies during the early 1740s and in the southern colonies during the following decade and beyond.

This evangelical revival movement was given intercolonial luxuriance and coherence by the far-flung preaching of the Englishman, George Whitefield. Ordained an Anglican priest in 1739, he made seven preaching journeys to America, encompassing over nine years, until his death in 1770. Referring to himself as 'an amphibious itinerant',[35] Whitefield was steeped in the commercial ethos of Empire. A 'Pedlar in Divinity', he adopted and adapted market language and techniques to his transatlantic missions in new and unparalled ways. 'The devotion and business of a Methodist go hand in hand', he wrote,[36] initiating his first American mission by hawking a shipload of manufactured goods he had brought with him from England. Most important, he was himself deliberately and carefully marketed, especially in a colonial press just at the point of massive expansion, with printers increasingly publishing not for principle but for profit. To those like Benjamin Franklin, Whitefield offered the prospect of rich returns, since evangelists commanded an enormous market.[37] The amount of colonial newspaper coverage of Whitefield's preaching tours was staggering. During the height of the Great Awakening in the early 1740s, Great Britain's war with Spain was the only other event that matched the coverage of his activities. Moreover, each year from 1739 to 1745 American publishers released more works by Whitefield than by any other person. Not only his public preaching

---

[34] Ned C. Landsman, 'Witherspoon and the Problem of Provincial Identity in Scottish Evangelical Culture', in Richard B. Sher and Jeffrey R. Smitten, eds., *Scotland and America in the Age of the Enlightenment* (Edinburgh, 1990), pp. 29–45, esp. 38–42.

[35] George Whitefield to Charles Wesley, 17 March 1763, Methodist Archives, John Rylands University Library of Manchester, PLP 113.1.20.

[36] George Whitefield, *Sermons on Important Subjects* (London, 1825), p. 654.

[37] Frank Lambert, 'Subscribing for Profits and Piety: the Friendship of Benjamin Franklin and George Whitefield', *WMQ*, Third Series, L (1993), pp. 529–48, esp. 535, 542.

but his utilization of the press made the Awakening a truly intercolonial phenomenon.

The evangelical revivals staged by Whitefield and his associates were both a confirmation and an acceleration of the consumer revolution and free market mentality as it bore upon religion. The Awakeners borrowed from the world of commerce new techniques (such as aggressive advertising) and terminology (such as representing salvation as a market transaction) to reach vastly expanded audiences. Whether for older settlers or newer arrivals, the freedom to pick and choose from among a widening variety of religious expressions provided a heady prospect.[38] These commercial and religious choices combined potently, producing a rapidly increasing breakdown in the former patterns of settlement, with a shift from communal to personal interests. Notably, the traditional unified New England village was seriously undermined. This not only splintered many Congregationalist parishes but also gave opportunity for groups like Baptists to make inroads, as they and Presbyterians likewise did in Anglican Virginia.[39] These new choices led men to plunge into market-place priorities, claiming their 'consumer' rights as individuals as well as contributing to a 'democratization' of American Christianity.[40] The Great Awakening and its resulting measurable manifestations in subsequent decades[41] best illustrates the interlocking nature of religious and economic change—or, more precisely, how new religious and economic opportunities supported one another.

In vastly broadening people's choices, the revival movement was, literally, a spirited step forward given spring by the rapidly expanding commercial market. The irony was that although George Whitefield was an Anglican clergyman, in practice he was a godsend to colonial non-Anglicans. At this time he was facing increasing opposition from bishops regarding his English activities. Turning the tables on these ecclesiastical authorities in England, Whitefield attacked colonial Anglicans and cut his clerical cloth to suit the predominant Dissenting ethos in America,[42] directing much of his activity against the SPG. Although a number of American Dissenters turned to cling to the Anglican church as their 'only ark

[38] Frank Lambert, 'Pedlar in Divinity': George Whitefield and the Transatlantic Revivals, 1737–1770 (Princeton, 1994), p. 196; Harry S. Stout, The Divine Dramatist: George Whitefield and the Rise of Modern Evangelicalism (Grand Rapids, Mich., 1991), pp. xvi–xviii, 35–36.

[39] Gregory H. Nobles, Divisions Throughout the Whole. Politics and Society in Hampshire County, Massachusetts, 1740–1775 (Cambridge, 1983), pp. 47–49, and chaps. 4 and 5; Timothy D. Hall, Contested Boundaries. Itinerancy and the Reshaping of the Colonial American Religious World (Durham, NC, 1994), pp. 116–29.

[40] See Nathan O. Hatch, The Democratization of American Christianity (New Haven, 1989).

[41] Hall, Contested Boundaries, esp. chap. 4; John L. Brooke, The Heart of the Commonwealth. Society and Political Culture in Worcester County, Massachusetts, 1713–1861 (Cambridge, Mass., 1989), chap. 3.

[42] Goodwin, 'Anglican Middle Way', pp. 234–75.

of safety' during the floods of the Awakening's 'monstrous enthusiasm',[43] it was an unequal exchange. Colonial Anglicanism found itself swimming against an over-powering current of evangelical Protestantism which was to be, even more than in the past, the most distinguishing feature of American religious life and practice. By vigorously opposing the revivals and the fertile Dissenting earth from which they sprang, colonial Anglicanism made itself all the more 'foreign'.

Itinerants like Whitefield were mobile metaphors for change and potential disorder, to the extent that their itinerancy stands as a model for the fast-developing transatlantic mercantile world. In this context, the Anglican church in the mainland colonies, together with non-revivalist New England Congrega-tionalists, was placed at a decided disadvantage through adhering to the parish system. A parish not only represented a stable European civilization in the New World; it also fostered the ties of tradition. Where the parish system was linked to a legally established church, such as in Puritan New England or the Anglican south, the exuberant new religious groups thrown up by the Great Awakening viewed the parish as a symbol of oppression to be destroyed. Moreover, demographic pres-sures had pushed children of seventeenth-century settlers to eastern port towns or to the frontiers to seek prosperity.[44] These uprooted were now prime targets for religious revival. As Whitefield exploited market-place and mobility for religious ends, he and his fellow travelling revivalists seriously undercut the economic monopolies hitherto operated by a wealthy colonial élite, thereby greatly encour-aging competitive entrepreneurs on the rise. All this consumer activity con-tributed to the breaking-down of old structures of deference in society, which had been a hallmark of parish stability. To the economically mobile and energe-tically evangelical, a firmly defined parish bespoke a feudal past rather than a productive future.

As long as Anglicanism was associated with landed stability, the rising market-place would keep it at best on the defensive: witness the vulnerability of Virginian planters to the economic incursions of the Lowland Scot managers of the tobacco trade. Yet owing to the Chesapeake's lack of urban centres, it was far more difficult for market-place Christianity and its stimulating of various new religious groups to flourish, except in newly established self-selecting communities. In Virginia, for example, Whitefield quickly reached the conclusion that his 'greatest probability of doing good' was among Ulster Presbyterians, 'who have lately settled in the mountainous parts of that province. They raise little or no tobacco, but things that

---

[43] Samuel Johnson to Archbishop of Canterbury, 20 March 1759, in E. B. O'Callaghan and Berthold Fernow, eds., *Documents Relative to the Colonial History of the State of New York*, 15 vols. (Albany, NY, 1853–87), VII, p. 372.

[44] Hall, *Contested Boundaries*, pp. 4, 14, 19, 110–11.

are useful for common life.'[45] Largely protected by Imperial acts of religious toleration, for those who, like Whitefield, saw the Empire as their parish, the Empire was also their market-place.

The Great Awakening revivals in America must be seen in the context of similar developments in Britain and Europe.[46] During the 1740s a group of 'awakened' ministers in Scotland commenced an ongoing programme of prayer, with the purpose of reviving vital faith throughout Christendom, or, more precisely, the Empire. Utilizing the print trade, they despatched to the colonies several hundred copies of their 'Memorial' to this effect. The New England revival leader Jonathan Edwards promoted it in print and in extensive correspondence. This 'concert for prayer' offered a means for Christians throughout the Empire to unite in a common mission. The project continued to involve colonial evangelicals for many years, in the process heightening the force of millenarianism that was increasingly a mark of the revival-minded in the colonies. Once in full flow, it was argued, this millennial revival flood would spread beyond the Empire: 'The *Pope* in the *West*, and *Mahomet* in the *East*, with their Powers will be utterly ruined.'[47]

The Imperial commercial links, most especially those of printing and bookselling, were vital for the intercolonial and transatlantic nature of the revivals. The ocean-street was two-way. Not only did writings from England fuel the American Awakening, but at least as important was the influence of the colonial revivals upon English and Scottish evangelicals, detailed through the writings of Americans such as Jonathan Edwards. For example, Whitefield's work in England was quickly known in America through the activities of commercial printers and influenced Edwards's revivals, which in turn became a deliberate model for evangelicals in Scotland. Whitefield's career is a parable of this transatlantic context. Soliciting funds in Great Britain for his American ventures, he received the support of those like the Countess of Huntingdon, who at his death assumed responsibility for his Bethesda Orphanage in Georgia. Yet the sharpening edge of religious choice and Imperial crisis leading to the War of Independence meant that Americans were increasingly unwilling to see religious interests and institutions controlled from afar. Enterprises such as Bethesda would be in American hands or

---

[45] *George Whitefield's Journals* (Edinburgh, 1960), p. 389 (9 Jan. 1740).

[46] See W. R. Ward, *The Protestant Evangelical Awakening* (Cambridge, 1992); Susan [Durden] O'Brien, 'A Transatlantic Community of Saints: The Great Awakening and the First Evangelical Network, 1735–1755', *American Historical Review*, XCI (1986), pp. 811–32.

[47] Hall, *Contested Boundaries*, pp. 105–09; Ruth H. Bloch, *Visionary Republic; Millennial Themes in American Thought, 1756–1800* (Cambridge, 1985), pp. 10–50; Samuel Buell, *A Faithful Narrative of the Remarkable Revival of Religion in the Congregation of East-Hampton on Long-Island, in the Year of our Lord 1764* (New York, 1766), p. 24 (quotation).

none.[48] The Empire-facilitated Awakening had ironically made a significant contribution to the demand for 'American' rather than Imperial religious structures. The end of Empire, of course, placed a decided financial pinch on the new American foot. In 1783 John Witherspoon naïvely set out for Great Britain in an attempt to solicit funds for the Presbyterians' College of New Jersey. The mission was a disaster. After a year he returned to America having netted for the college £5. 14s. 0d.[49]

The burgeoning Empire provided the framework for the American settlement of a number of new religious bodies. Overwhelmingly, these were not only non-Anglican but non-English, in the process greatly adding to the mainland colonies' Dissenting majority and market mentality.[50] The vigorous church expansion into the Atlantic rim of Presbyterians from Ulster and Scotland is a noted example, but these were British subjects. During the eighteenth century it became official government policy, based on practical considerations, to offer refuge and British nationality to various persecuted European religious groups. Georgia, established during the 1730s with a combination of philanthropic, commercial, and defence motives, provided a haven for a number of such people, especially from Germany. A key group was the Salzburger settlement at Ebenezer, under the sponsorship of the SPCK, which gave some sorely needed ballast to the shaky ship of Georgia's economy, as well as providing new opportunities for German commercial interests. Also notable were the Moravians, who later moved into Pennsylvania and other colonies. Though never numerous, they viewed themselves as a missionary enterprise and eagerly seized their opportunity in Empire to facilitate missions among the American Indians, as well as in the Caribbean and Newfoundland.[51] The pragmatic British policy of religious toleration enabled the eighteenth-century Empire to act as a recruiting ground for new economically productive subjects. Whether by plan or by practice, a religiously open door was a prime reason that the British Empire far outstripped rival nations in the ability to attract settlers.

Imperial authorities in London were now far more interested in an expanding commercial Empire than in any notion of imposing Anglicanism. Government officials set their face against the increasingly vocal appeals from Anglican leaders

---

[48] Boyd Stanley Schlenther, '"To Convert the Poor People in America": The Bethesda Orphanage and the Thwarted Zeal of the Countess of Huntingdon', *Georgia Historical Quarterly*, LXXVII (1994), pp. 225–56.

[49] Collins, *President Witherspoon*, II, pp. 140–45.

[50] John J. McCusker and Russell R. Menard, *The Economy of British America 1607–1789* (Chapel Hill, NC, 1985), chap. 9; Greene, *Pursuits of Happiness*, pp. 47–50.

[51] Renate Wilson, 'Continental Protestant Refugees and their Proctectors in Germany and London: Commercial and Charitable Networks', *Pietismus und Neuzeit*, LX (1994), pp. 107–24; Benjamin Latrobe, *A Succinct View of the Missions Established* (London, 1771), pp. 8–13, 15–19, 23–27.

for the establishing of colonial bishops: a colonial episcopate would have run counter to more overriding Imperial motives. Anglican attempts to claw their way into new favoured positions were thwarted by the government's refusal to sanction such appointments.

> We are a Rope of Sand; there is no union, no authority among us; we cannot even summon a Convention for united Counsell and advice, while the Dissenting Ministers have their Monthly, Quarterly, and Annual Associations, Conventions... to advise, assist, and support each other.[52]

Since in England bishops were not only ecclesiastical leaders but officials of the state, non-Anglicans in America considered that they had good reasons for blocking efforts to introduce an episcopate: they feared for not only their religious but their political liberties. This contest continued, with ministers of the SPG bombarding London with appeals for colonial bishops, which came to grief on the rock of Imperial reality. The introduction of bishops might have assisted the Church of England in America, but, it was reasoned, it would only incense the overwhelmingly non-Anglican population.[53] London sought to avoid anything that might tear the sinews of the commercial system, and by rejecting the pleas for bishops believed that it was securing colonial allegiance to Empire. While less than 10 per cent of the English population in 1776 were Dissenters from the Church of England, more than 75 per cent of Americans were.[54]

The divisions among certain American denominations during the period between the Awakening and the Revolution were rooted in more than religious belief and practice. In Philadelphia, at the time of the Revolution, religious scores were paid in the coin of bitter commercial competition. Although its ethics condemned unrestrained capitalism, in practice Quakerism had provided strong support for financial enterprise. Mercantile ties throughout the Atlantic world gave Quaker merchants significant advantages during the eighteenth century, and in thriving Philadelphia, the 'Mart of Nations', they formed a greater proportion of merchants than any other religious group and were at the apex of the city's life.[55] They tended to be the older, more established elements among the merchant

---

[52] Henry Caner to Archbishop of Canterbury, 7 Jan. 1763, Perry, *Historical Collections*, III, p. 490.

[53] Doll, 'Imperial Anglicanism', p. 176.

[54] Patricia Bonomi, 'Religious Dissent and the Case for American Exceptionalism', in Ronald Hoffman and Peter J. Albert, eds., *Religion in the Revolutionary Age* (Charlottesville, Va., 1994), pp. 31–51, esp. 33. For the pre-Revolutionary struggle over the question of colonial bishops, see Doll, 'Imperial Anglicanism', chap. 5; Carl Bridenbaugh, *Mitre and Sceptre. Transatlantic Faiths, Ideas, Personalities, and Politics, 1689–1775* (New York, 1962).

[55] *Virginia Gazette*, 5 March 1752 (quotation); Frederick B. Tolles, *Meeting House and Counting House* (1948; New York, 1963), chaps. 5 and 6; David Hackett Fischer, *Albion's Seed. Four British Folkways in America* (New York, 1989), pp. 558–60.

fraternity, and together with leading Anglican merchants largely opposed any radical measures in the growing American patriot conflict with the commercial Empire. Their pacifism as Quakers and profit as merchants made them particularly odious to merchants with new wealth, who were mainly Presbyterians, and in the coming struggle leading commercial Quakers were particularly targeted for harassment.[56]

The American war for independence struck a heavy blow not only on Britain's Imperial structure but on the colonial Church of England. Two-thirds of Anglican clergymen, especially those directly in the employ of the SPG, departed. Therefore, the vast majority of the parishes which had been laboriously constructed during the previous fifty years were left leaderless, and of all colonial denominations Anglicanism suffered most severely by the Revolution. For some Americans the Anglican church, through word and ritual, had maintained the 'rhythm' of Imperial life. When the revolution came, that rhythm was broken. Even if Anglicanism had fully succeeded in achieving its goals in eighteenth-century America, it would have been to replicate the English parish system, based on the broad coherence of all Christians living within a given geographical unit. That was hardly the pattern to commend itself to a questing and factious people who sought in unfettered competition to gain constant advantage over others in their new free market society. Those Anglican ministers who remained saw the only way forward was for their new American church to be one denomination amongst others, one that adopted a polity expressly dismantling the Imperial pretensions of the office of bishop. The role of its new bishops was 'Americanized' by making them directly responsible to diocesan conventions in which the laity and lower clergy were powerfully represented by voice and vote.[57]

As the pieces of Great Britain's North American Empire were reshuffled during the concluding years of the century, the 'Canadian' provinces acted as a bolt-hole for a substantial number of Loyalists. What had not proved possible for Anglicans in the now-revolted thirteen colonies to the south had a far better chance of being put into action. The introduction of bishops was the most visible sign of this new ecclesiastical opportunity, and Charles Inglis, formerly an Anglican clergyman in New York, became the first Bishop of Nova Scotia in 1787. The former Governor of New Hampshire, John Wentworth, became the Governor of Nova Scotia, now able to fulfil his Anglican colonial vision. However, Anglicanism was clearly outnumbered in what was to become Canada. Roman Catholics were overwhelmingly in

[56] Jack D. Marietta, *The Reformation of American Quakerism, 1748–1783* (Philadelphia, 1984), chap. 10; Thomas Doerflinger, 'Philadelphia Merchants and the Logic of Moderation', *WMQ*, Third Series, XL (1983), pp. 197–226, esp. 214–17; Boyd Stanley Schlenther, *Charles Thomson. A Patriot's Pursuit* (Newark, Del., 1990), pp. 88, 98–106, 130, 137, 157–58.

[57] Woolverton, *Colonial Anglicanism*, pp. 228–38; Mills, *Bishops by Ballot*, pp. 282–307.

the majority in Quebec (Lower Canada), with 150,000 in contrast with a total Protestant population of 1,200; Quebec had not a single place of worship dedicated to the use of Anglicans as late as 1794, even after a Church of England bishop had been consecrated for the province the preceding year.[58] Catholics formed a majority in Newfoundland and around Hudson Bay and constituted the largest religious group in Cape Breton and Prince Edward Island by the end of the eighteenth century. In fact, by the 1780s Imperial authorities had in practice turned their backs on attempting to enforce proscriptions against Catholics in the various 'Canadian' provinces. Following the capture of Quebec from the French, Roman Catholics there had been given the right to have a bishop, under British supervision. In addition, by the Quebec Act of 1774 Parliament had given Quebec's Catholic church legal rights to its lands, and members of that faith were granted full civil rights as subjects of an officially Protestant Empire. This pragmatic toleration may have helped to secure Quebec's loyalty to the Empire during the American Revolution. The horrified reaction to the Quebec Act by Protestant Dissenters in the about-to-revolt colonies made it clear that Roman Catholics would have fared far differently under American control.[59]

Following American Independence, a Methodist Conference was organized in the Maritime Provinces in 1788, made possible by a significant emigration of economically distressed tradesmen, craftsmen, farmers, and labouring poor Wesleyan Methodists, especially from the Yorkshire Dales.[60] From New England, several thousand settlers had been recruited for Nova Scotia shortly before the War of Independence. Children of the Great Awakening, they, together with substantial numbers of Scots Presbyterians, added a further strong non-Anglican presence to the emerging Canada.[61]

The aftermath of the American Revolution had little impact on the ecclesiastical life of the West Indies. There, it was the status of the slaves which constituted the continuing challenge to the churches. In the face of a generally quiescent Anglican establishment that was loath to undermine the plantation economy, it was the activities of evangelical Christians that would contribute to change. The Moravians, taking full advantage of their freedom of movement and action within the British Empire, had established a mission to slaves on Jamaica in the 1750s. Now,

[58] Doll, 'Imperial Anglicanism', pp. 206, 237, 264–75, and chap. 7.

[59] See John S. Moir, *The Church in the British Era: From the British Conquest to Confederation* (Toronto, 1972); George A. Rawlyk, *Revolution Rejected, 1775–1776* (Scarborough, Ontario, 1968); J. M. Bumsted, 'The Cultural Landscape of Early Canada', in Bailyn and Morgan, *Strangers Within the Realm*, pp. 363–92, esp. 377–78, 388; Judith Fingard, *The Anglican Design in Loyalist Nova Scotia, 1783–1816* (London, 1972), chap. 2.

[60] Bailyn, *Voyagers to the West*, pp. 373–87, 420–26.

[61] Fingard, *Anglican Design*, chap. 6.

thirty years later, Wesleyan Methodists, led by Thomas Coke, commenced similar activities throughout the West Indies. These religious impulses, together with the implications of radical political ideals emphasizing human freedom, coalesced with the economic arguments of men such as Adam Smith—which challenged slavery as a negation of free trade and commerce—to contribute to the abolition of the slave trade and, ultimately, to slavery itself in the West Indies.[62]

Great Britain's eighteenth-century Empire was driven by market-place rather than meeting-house. If the choice was between ecclesiastical purity and extended commercial success, the latter held sway. Following American independence, an Anglicanism now disestablished in all the new United States found its only way forward to be a full acceptance of the implications of the unrestrained trade wrought by the revolt from Empire. Now 'Episcopalians', they were forced, with all others, to compete in a market-place rigged no longer to any faith's advantage or disadvantage. Ironically, an increasingly 'planned' interdependent Imperial economy had provided the context for a striking freedom of economic opportunities in which the rising forces of entrepreneurial market capitalism were given space to grow apace. This free market competition had direct implications for the breakup of Empire. In the end, religious, commercial, and political streams merged. The Great Awakening had taught men to make new choices in open market terms and had greatly increased the sense of individual destiny in America. As they revolted against an Empire based on commercial control to claim free trade and open access to new lands, the new Americans at the same time laid claim to an unhindered religious life. To survive, all churches were forced to engage in a competitive scramble for souls. Free trade in commerce, and faith, was the new world order.

---

[62] Mary Turner, *Slaves and Missionaries. The Disintegration of Jamaican Slave Society, 1787–1834* (Urbana, Ill., 1982), chap. 1.

Select Bibliography

BERNARD BAILYN and PHILIP D. MORGAN, eds., *Strangers Within the Realm. Cultural Margins of the First British Empire* (Chapel Hill, NC, 1991).

PATRICIA U. BONOMI, *Under the Cope of Heaven: Religion, Society, and Politics in Colonial America* (New York, 1986).

CARL BRIDENBAUGH, *Mitre and Sceptre: Transatlantic Faiths, Ideas, Personalities, and Politics, 1689–1775* (New York, 1962).

JON BUTLER, *Awash in a Sea of Faith: Christianizing the American People* (Cambridge, Mass., 1990).

PETER MICHAEL DOLL, 'Imperial Anglicanism in North America, 1745–1795', unpublished D. Phil. thesis, Oxford, 1989.

EDWIN SCOTT GAUSTAD, *Historical Atlas of Religion in America* (New York, 1962).

GERALD J. GOODWIN, 'The Anglican Middle Way in Early Eighteenth-Century America: Anglican Religious Thought in the American Colonies, 1702-1750', unpublished Ph. D. dissertation, Wisconsin, 1965.

TIMOTHY D. HALL, *Contested Boundaries: Itinerancy and the Reshaping of the Colonial American Religious World* (Durham, NC, 1994).

RONALD HOFFMAN and PETER J. ALBERT, eds., *Religion in the Revolutionary Age* (Charlottesville, Va., 1994).

FRANK LAMBERT, '*Pedlar in Divinity*': *George Whitefield and the Transatlantic Revivals, 1737–1770* (Princeton, 1994).

JOHN S. MOIR, *The Church in the British Era: From the British Conquest to Confederation* (Toronto, 1972).

ALISON GILBERT OLSON, *Making the Empire Work: London and American Interest Groups, 1690–1790* (Cambridge, Mass., 1992).

FREDERICK B. TOLLES, *Meeting House and Counting House* (1948; New York, 1963).

W. R. WARD, *The Protestant Evangelical Awakening* (Cambridge, 1992).

JOHN FREDERICK WOOLVERTON, *Colonial Anglicanism in North America* (Detroit, 1984).

7

Colonial Wars and Imperial Instability, 1688–1793

BRUCE P. LENMAN

There is a long tradition that sees empire-building as the manifest destiny of eighteenth-century Britain. The winning of gains overseas has been assumed to have been the objective which all right-minded British leaders made their absolute priority. They were rewarded by a succession of victories on land and sea, which marked eighteenth-century Britain's unstoppable ascent to Imperial greatness.

Some historians still see an inexorable growth in Britain's Imperial power throughout the eighteenth century, rooted in the steady rise of British commercial supremacy and of the British mercantile marine.[1] To others, the story is more complex. They argue that for much of the eighteenth century Imperial objectives were not the main considerations dominating British policy and that Britain did not have the capacity to make conquests at will all over the world. In his chapter on the role of the navy, Nicholas Rodger points out that 'Eighteenth-century Britain was a European power...threatened by powerful neighbours', and that the first priority of the Royal Navy was to protect Britain from invasion, not to conquer an overseas Empire. Naval forces were generally concentrated in European waters with only limited detachments overseas.[2]

This chapter deals with the use of force overseas. The priorities of the eighteenth-century British army were at home or in Europe. It was only slowly turned into an instrument for protecting Britain's colonies or subjugating those of other powers. Colonial wars were at first limited ones largely waged by colonial forces, British Americans and such Indian allies as they could secure, or the troops of the East India Company. From mid-century there was a marked increase in the deployment of the British army overseas. Results were, however, uneven: victories in the Seven Years War were followed by defeat in the American War. It was only after the wars that began in 1793 that the British army and the new Indian army

---

[1] Daniel A. Baugh, 'Maritime Strength and Atlantic Commerce: The Uses of "a Grand Marine Empire"', Lawrence Stone, ed., *An Imperial State at War: Britain from 1689 to 1815* (London, 1994), pp. 185–223. See chap. by Patrick K. O'Brien.

[2] See below, pp. 169–72.

were able effectively to join with the navy in imposing 'an extra-European *Pax Britannica*'[3]

The Unintended Consequences of the Glorious Revolution

To patriotic Englishmen of the eighteenth century and to many since, liberty, Protestantism, and Imperial expansion seemed to be inextricably connected. The Glorious Revolution, which was deemed to have secured the constitution and the Protestant succession, was therefore seen as a crucial pre-condition for the eighteenth-century drive for Empire, freeing England from the continental preoccupations of the Stuarts to enable it to fulfil its destiny overseas.

The reality was different. The Stuart Kings, Charles II and James II, had been interested and active beyond Europe. James II had encouraged the East India Company to embroil itself in 1688 in ultimately unsuccessful wars against the Mughal empire in India and the kingdom of Siam. Substantial royal naval and military forces had not been committed in America, but James II had created the Dominion of New England to control the northern colonies, justifying the exercise partly by the need for unity in the face of the French in Canada. William III, by contrast, had intervened in England in 1688 for reasons almost exclusively connected with the balance of power in continental Europe and he neglected colonial interests in the subsequent war. The peoples of the English colonies in America were enthusiastic supporters of the Glorious Revolution, but it was to involve them in over twenty years of war between 1689 and 1713. These wars were fought not for Imperial aggrandizement, but to protect English colonies from French attacks.

The principal military developments produced by the Revolution were a British commitment to the alliance formed to resist the European ambitions of Louis XIV of France, and the creation of the first truly British army. It was of massive proportions compared with any previous expeditionary forces, as it had to carry weight in the murderous infantry battles in its main theatre of operations, Flanders. To divert English resources from the continent, the French applied pressure on the English North American colonies from Canada. Following the formal declaration of war in 1689, the new Governor of Canada, the Comte de Frontenac, dispersed his 1,500 regulars and 2,000 Canadian militia in raids against New York and New England frontier communities, bringing home through their horrors the implications for colonial Englishmen of being at war with a great military monarchy.[4] Thus the new King, William III, had generated an Imperial

---

[3] See below, pp. 205–06.
[4] W. J. Eccles, *The Canadian Frontier, 1534–1760*, revised edn. (Albuquerque, N. Mex., 1983), chap. 6.

dimension to the War of the League of Augsburg between 1689 and 1697, without himself having a serious interest in that dimension.

Apart from skirmishes with Spaniards on their southern frontier in the mid-1680s, English American colonists had not waged war against a European foe since the early seventeenth century. King William's War (as the war in America came to be known) taught self-help. William III's indifference to colonial issues, obsession with Flanders, and relative neglect of commerce-protection because of his recklessly aggressive use of the Royal and the Dutch navies, both in the eastern Atlantic and the Mediterranean, deprived English America of protection against French raiders and privateers.[5] New York and New England had to look to themselves and their sister colonies. Minuscule garrisons of royal troops had to be augmented by mobilizing the militias within the colonies and by raising provincial regiments for offensive operations. Massachusetts sent its Governor, Sir William Phipps, to capture the principal settlement in French Acadia, Port Royal, a privateer base on the Bay of Fundy, in 1690. In the same year, at an intercolonial conference at New York, New York, Massachusetts, New Plymouth, and Connecticut planned the conquest of Canada by a dual attack up through Lake George and down the St Lawrence. Weather and lack of co-ordination led to failure.

Indian allies were crucial. After 1689 'the North American conflict' between Indians and between Indians and Europeans 'melted into the Anglo-French imperial struggle'.[6] The French tried to overrun the north-east frontier of New England by means of the Abenaki Indians, who had a long history of warfare with the English colonies. Twice the Abenaki were forced into truces. On the New York frontier the English had forged what was to be a long-lasting alliance with the Iroquois people. During the war, New York's poverty and Whitehall's failure to provide meaningful military support meant that the Iroquois did nearly all the fighting against the French and their Indian allies.[7] By 1694, however, the Iroquois were negotiating a truce with Frontenac, after a despairing appeal to the Governor of New York, who could offer little. Frontenac's successor concluded in 1701 a general peace in which the Iroquois promised neutrality in future Anglo-French wars. For New York, this was a disaster.

It was just as well for the English that Louis XIV never responded to Frontenac's repeated pleas for military and naval forces adequate to expand the scope of his original orders, to destroy not just New York, but Boston also, deporting their surviving heretical inhabitants. Even so, when the war ended without boundary changes in America in 1697, the French were in a very strong position. Under

---

[5] D. W. Jones, *War and Economy in the Age of William III and Marlborough* (Oxford, 1987).
[6] See above, p. 354.
[7] Ibid.

Pierre Le Moyne d'Iberville they had ravaged the inadequately fortified Hudson's Bay Company forts and remained in the ascendant in the Hudson Bay area. Their privateers, when not scouring the New England coast, had played a key role in devastating attacks on English fishing settlements in Newfoundland, where a strong naval force had to be sent in 1697 to recover and refortify St Johns.

The regular forces of the Crown had not even been deployed on a large scale in the West Indies, for all their economic importance. English settlers in the Caribbean experienced lethal violence, but received little metropolitan aid. Such expeditions as the London government despatched to the West Indies between 1689 and 1697 tended to be inadequate and were frustrated by disease and French fortifications. Jamaica fought off a French invasion attempt with a combination of buccaneers and militia. Yet, in spite of neglect from home, experience of this war dampened any ideas in the West Indies as elsewhere that autonomy was a practical colonial option in a predatory world.

Though the European East India companies sensibly kept a pact of neutrality in Asian waters from 1689 to 1697, the English Company was severely affected by the war. Its ships were vulnerable to French action as soon as they entered the South Atlantic, and all the western approaches to England were hazardous. Yet the Company was the main source of saltpetre, an essential ingredient in gunpowder. By its charter the Company was obliged to furnish the 2,000–3,000 tons needed in a war year at a fixed price.[8] The Dutch example showed that heavy investment in forts and conquest in Asia undermined profitability, but so did lack of adequate naval protection in the Atlantic, as demonstrated by the loss of five returning East Indiamen reputedly worth £1 million.

The Rising Importance of Colonial Theatres of War

Between 1689 and 1697 the English monarchy had committed few resources outside Europe. During the War of the Spanish Succession, which broke out in 1702, much more strategic emphasis was to be placed on overseas Empire, even though the Central European and Mediterranean theatres, which yielded great victories such as that at Blenheim, were always of greater significance until the last years of the war. The importance of the New World was much enhanced, since there was now a danger that the French would not only place a Bourbon prince on the Spanish throne, but would be able to dominate and colonize the Spanish Indies from within, using their wealth to tip the European balance irreversibly in favour of France. Genuine French worries about the capacity of Spanish arms in a period

---

[8] Historical Manuscripts Commission, *House of Lords Manuscripts*, New Series, I, *1693–1695* (London, 1900), pp. 370–71, no. 821; II, *1695–1697* (London, 1903), p. 34, no. 955.

of revolts and economic crisis in Spanish America had provoked increasing French intervention in the Spanish empire. The French Guinea Company was granted the *Asiento* for importing slaves in 1702, and for eleven years France not only dominated the legal trade with Spanish America from Cadiz, but also provided warships to guard it.[9]

British and French fleets were immediately despatched to the West Indies on the outbreak of hostilities. Neither fleet was able decisively to take the offensive. Neither Jamaica nor Barbados was attacked, but fighting in the Leeward Islands was at times fierce. A successful raid by the French on Nevis in 1706 was said to have led to losses that amounted to £1 million. In the Bahamas, Spanish raids destroyed the principal settlement of New Providence, the Lords Proprietors of the islands failing to send out arms, ammunition, and stores. Though the London government did intermittently send naval forces to other more valuable Caribbean colonies, it never sent enough to crush the depredations of French privateers.

It was, however, primarily in terms of naval dispositions that the London authorities showed a more responsible attitude towards English overseas interests after 1702. An East Indiaman which had sailed for the Coromandel Coast and the Ganges in 1700 was met at St Helena on the way back 'with 6 sail of man a war which conducted us home'.[10] A squadron had been sent to St Helena to convoy the ships of the East India Company from that watering and provision port of call.

In North America the English government at first did far less. Strategically, Queen Anne's War, as it is better known in America, was fought on a radically different basis from its predecessor because of a shift in policy adopted in 1700–01 by Louis XIV and his ministers. They decided not only to sustain the new French settlement, Louisiana, which Iberville had established in 1698 at the mouth of the Mississippi, despite its worthlessness as a fur-producing area, but also to link it up with Canada as a barrier against the Anglo-Americans. This was a dog-in-the-manger policy, for it involved the religious manipulation of Indians with a view to confining the British colonists to the east of the Alleghenies. It would tie up British resources but, as the French minister Colbert had seen long before, it would provoke a mortal struggle.[11]

Tactically, the war followed the pattern of the previous conflict. The northern front was essentially a Massachusetts affair. In 1702 the Abenaki made a successful attack on the settlement at Deerfield. But a string of stockaded towns provided an effective screen, so that no Massachusetts town had to be abandoned during the

[9] Murdo J. Macleod, 'Spain and America: The Atlantic Trade, 1492–1720', Leslie Bethell, ed., *Cambridge History of Latin America*, 11 vols. (Cambridge, 1984–95), I, pp. 383, 385.

[10] Henry Clerk to Sir John Clerk, 25 Sept. 1702, Scottish Record Office, Clerk of Penecuik Papers, GD 5218/52.

[11] W. J. Eccles, *Canada under Louis XIV, 1663–1701* (London, 1964), pp. 247–49.

war. The Massachusetts economy surged, helped by the protection for its West Indian trade provided by the Royal Navy. The relatively dense pattern of settlement and the immediate nature of the French threat created a degree of military cohesion in Massachusetts which matched its maritime vigour and enabled it to force a stand-off in its conflict with the much more militarized society of French Canada, with its far more abundant regular troops.[12]

There was stalemate in the south. A Franco-Spanish attack in 1706 on Charleston, South Carolina, failed, as did the Governor of Carolina's attempts to destroy Spanish Florida. His frontier raids failed to capture the northernmost Spanish stronghold of St Augustine but did succeed in wrecking its network of allied Indian communities. Though the French in Louisiana held their ground, their influence over the local Indians declined.

If the War of the Spanish Succession in North America generally followed the pattern of the previous war, one episode prefigured a new kind of imperial warfare. A Scotsman, Samuel Vetch, a recent immigrant into New York, talked the Board of Trade in London into offering a major British contribution to a two-pronged attack on New France via the St Lawrence and Hudson River–Lake Champlain corridor. Despite widespread enthusiasm and real commitment in New York as well as Massachusetts, attempts to implement the scheme failed. In 1710 Royal Navy warships and marines as well as New England regiments captured Acadia and left Vetch to preside over a conquered province renamed Nova Scotia. An expedition for New France which left England in sixty-four ships with 5,000 troops aboard in May 1711 came to grief, partly due to delay in integrating colonial supplies and troops, but mainly because of poor navigation in the St Lawrence, which cost eight ships in bad late-August weather. This débâcle has led to a persistent tendency to underestimate this first massive deployment of metropolitan troops in North America by the British government.

Peace negotiations began in Europe in 1711. On 11 April 1713 the Treaty of Utrecht concluded the war. Despite the impressive military performance of New France and the failure of the British expedition of 1711, British ministers insisted upon and obtained a series of renunciations by France in the New World. At the cost of abandoning their continental allies, the British brought off 'one of the most sensational coups in the history of the British Empire'.[13] The slave *Asiento* for Spanish America, the French half of the island of St Kitts, Newfoundland, Nova Scotia, and the Hudson Bay territories all passed to Britain. The war may have been fought for the most part in Europe, but Britain took its gains on a world-wide scale.

[12] John W. Shy, 'A New Look at the Colonial Militia', *William and Mary Quarterly*, Third Series, XX (1963), pp. 175–85.
[13] See Vol. I, chap. by Jonathan I. Israel.

An Imperial War and its Frustrations

Although European priorities soon asserted themselves, the next round of wars in which Britain was involved began in 1739 for specifically commercial objectives outside Europe. By then Britain's main concern was with the Spanish in America.

During the years of peace between 1713 and 1739, the French colonies ceased to be the focus of metropolitan British fears and ambitions. On the other hand, a Board of Trade report of 1721 emphasized the potential for Anglo-Spanish conflict in the south, stressing that South Carolina was vulnerable to Indian incursions and to pressure from Spanish Florida, as well as to a possible French thrust east from Louisiana down the Altamaha River.[14] The establishment of the colony of Georgia in 1732 was originally sponsored by humanitarian and commercial groups, but it had strategic implications. To Spain it represented aggression against Spanish claims north of Florida, and worsened Anglo-Spanish relations, already under strain because of the problems of distinguishing between legitimate and illegitimate British trade with Spanish colonies in the Caribbean. Attempts to adjust differences by the Treaty of Seville in 1729 and the Convention of Pardo in 1739 failed in the face of a mounting campaign by the political opponents of Sir Robert Walpole to drive him into a war. Those who pushed for war held out the prospect of spectacular British gains at the expense of Spain. Yet should they succeed in dominating the vast Spanish empire in the Americas, the British would pose an unacceptable threat to the European balance. Critics of so dangerous a policy were not lacking in Britain. The Prime Minister was one. Trade with peninsular Spain was valuable. Walpole's supporters asserted that only men of straw backed a policy which threatened an important commerce for hypothetical American gains. In reality, the business community seems to have been divided.[15] Yet Britain was by October 1739 involved in the War of Jenkins' Ear against Spain. It was the first British war to be fought, at least ostensibly, over colonial issues.

The course of the war belied the hopes of those who had promised spectacular gains at the expense of Spain in America. Admiral Edward Vernon, who opened the Caribbean campaign with a swift seizure of Porto Bello in November 1739, was a supporter of the parliamentary Opposition, who blamed his naval colleagues and Walpole for his subsequent failure against Cartagena. Attempts to conquer Cuba and Panama proved expensive failures. General James Oglethorpe, the founder of Georgia, failed in 1740 to capture St Augustine, the northern garrison post of Spanish Florida, but he successfully repulsed a Spanish invasion of Georgia

---

[14] Trevor Richard Reese, *Colonial Georgia: A Study in British Imperial Policy in the Eighteenth Century* (Athens, Ga., 1963), p. 13.

[15] Paul Langford, *A Polite and Commercial People: England, 1727–1783* (Oxford, 1989), pp. 51–53.

in 1742. The circumnavigation of the world by Commodore George Anson, and his capture in the Pacific of the fabulous Manila galleon in 1743, were by-products of an unsuccessful war.[16]

France would not allow Britain to take the Spanish empire apart, as an early mobilization of the French navy showed. The formal outbreak of war between Britain and France came in March 1744, but the conflict was then fought in the context of the War of the Austrian Succession, which involved a massive diversion of French forces to Germany and the Netherlands. British troops were also deployed on the continent. Colonial warfare thus once again became a subordinate issue in a European conflict. To crush the Jacobite rebellion of 1745–46 Britain even had to withdraw troops from Europe, allowing the French to overrun the Austrian Netherlands.

The war overseas was left, as before, largely to colonial troops. British arms at first fared badly. The French built a series of forts to protect Canada from invasion, while most Iroquois were anxious to uphold a neutral position between the French and the British.[17] Success came to the British in 1745 when the forces of New England combined with the Royal Navy to capture Louisbourg, the French stronghold on Cape Breton Island, dominating the St Lawrence. However, subsequent operations against Quebec were failures, and by late 1745 and throughout 1746 the frontier settlements of the northern British colonies reeled under repeated raids by the French and their Indian allies.

It was the hope of both the British and the French East India companies that a neutrality could be maintained in India in spite of the outbreak of the European war in 1744. Negotiations were, however, broken off on the orders of the British government. Neutrality had favoured France, the weaker naval power. Paradoxically, the early assertion of British naval ascendancy in the Bay of Bengal galvanized Jean-François Dupleix, the Governor-General at Pondicherry, to try to recover his personal losses and those of the Company by military means. The arrival of a squadron from the French base at Mauritius destroyed British local naval superiority. The French launched a successful amphibious attack in 1746 on Madras, the main British settlement. A powerful British fleet arrived in mid-1748 but failed to turn the tables before the news of peace came from Europe.

The Peace of Aix-la-Chapelle of 1748 was based on the *status quo ante bellum*. Louisbourg and Madras were returned to their former owners. British hopes for easy pickings in Spanish America had proved delusive. Yet by the end of the war, British naval supremacy was pushing Dupleix on to the defensive in India, threatening the loyalty of France's American Indian allies by depriving Canada

---

[16] See below, p. 554.   [17] See below, p. 358.

of trade goods, and undermining the finances of Louis XV by interdicting French trade.

William Pitt, speaking for the opposition to Walpole, had argued in 1739 that Britain with more ships in its harbours than all the navies of Europe could muster, and an overwhelming concentration of white colonists in its American provinces, could impose its will on imperial Spain. This was not true. The great Spanish viceroyalties in the Americas were largely self-sufficient units of enormous extent whose political and economic centres were often deep in the interior and at a high elevation. English colonial populations were remote from these Spanish-American heartlands, and could only mount amphibious attacks, which were at best peripheral pin-pricks rather than lethal blows. For the British West Indian merchants, whose ambition and greed had been a major influence for belligerence, war had proved a counter-productive policy. Instead of increasing their potentially lucrative trade with Spanish America, the British West Indies were forced back on sugar monoculture.[18]

Dangerous Triumph: The Seven Years War

The war that lasted from 1739 to 1748 had begun as an Imperial one, but its main theatre had soon shifted to Europe, even for a time to the British Isles, and few gains were achieved overseas. For the next round of wars, beginning in 1754 and ending in 1763, Britain's principal commitments throughout the period were to be outside Europe, where spectacular gains were made. The Seven Years War was truly an Imperial war for Britain in a way that no previous war had been.

Britain's main victim was to be France, not Spain. Imperial France was much more vulnerable to Pitt's calculations than imperial Spain. French America consisted of sugar islands open to attack or of unprofitable continental settlements, vitally dependent on imported subsidies, reinforcements, or trade goods for Indian allies, which could be cut off by British naval superiority. Nevertheless, in the early 1750s Britain appeared to be on the defensive against an aggressive France which was testing the limits of the peace of 1748.

In India Franco-British rivalry entered into an acute phase with the outbreak of succession disputes in both the Carnatic and in Hyderabad. Skirmishing in the Carnatic in the aftermath of the French capture of Madras in 1746 had revealed the startling superiority of modern European infantry to sub-Mughal cavalry. Indian sepoy infantry could be created in the European mould at a fraction of the cost of European soldiers. By 1750 Dupleix had placed French nominees backed by French

---

[18] Richard Pares, *War and Trade in the West Indies, 1739–1763* (1936; London, 1963), pp. 63–64 and chap. 3.

troops in possession of both disputed successions, but at the cost of forcing the British East India Company into adopting similar methods.[19] Robert Clive emerged as a Company soldier and political opportunist of genius. Dupleix's wars and his own and his associates' corruption virtually bankrupted the French Company, which ordered his supersession and the opening of peace negotiations with the British. Agreements reached in India were never ratified at home and the two Companies were drawn into renewed hostilities as part of the general European war.

In North America, when a flood of superior, cheaper trade goods threatened their grip on the western Indian peoples, the French decided to use force to assert their sovereignty over the Ohio valley. When Céloron de Blainville led a powerful military force through the upper Ohio valley in the summer of 1749, expelling traders and laying the foundations of future French sovereignty, he was bound to trigger a reaction from British colonial élites. A 'frontier' culture as a thing apart did not exist: territorial ambition ran deep into the heart of still-fluid colonial societies. The first shots of the backwoods war were fired by Colonel George Washington's Virginia militia as they tried in vain to challenge the French expulsion of the Virginian-sponsored Ohio Company from the forks of the Ohio in April 1754.

The British reply was an ambitious series of counter-attacks spearheaded by the despatch early in 1755 of General Edward Braddock with a force of two regular regiments to challenge the new French presence on the Ohio. This was an exercise in deterrence by the administration of the Duke of Newcastle. It might have worked, but for the neglect to send out the usual flanking troops on the very last stage of his march on Fort Duquesne on the Ohio, which led to Braddock's total defeat and death at the hands of Indian allies of the French. A French and Indian war was now unavoidable, even though London did not at this point want to embark on what was to prove its most successful ever Imperial conflict. War wrecked Newcastle's hopes for reduced government expenditure, lower interest rates, and lower taxation. He was, however, locked into a set of naval and military responses which led to the Anglo-French war declared in May 1756. Newcastle vacillated between paralysis and the hope that a revival of the concept of 'local belligerency' would confine combat to America.[20] After Vice-Admiral Edward Boscawen had failed to prevent the landing of French reinforcements at Louisbourg in 1755, this was a recipe for disaster. Britain's strategic position was, however, greatly enhanced when France joined a European coalition to attack Britain's new ally, Prussia. French resources became committed primarily to the

---

[19] See below, p. 501.
[20] Reed Browning, *The Duke of Newcastle* (New Haven, 1975), pp. 206–18.

European theatre, where Britain supported Prussia with subsidies and an army operating in Germany.

The offensives launched against the French in North America in 1755 only won complete success in Nova Scotia. There British and New England troops drove out the French forces. The remaining French population, the Acadians, ended up crushed between the ideological ruthlessness of their priests, for whom the French and the Catholic cause were one, and the Acadians a tool, and the military ruthlessness of the British, who in 1755 rounded up and expelled them as a likely fifth column. Brutal but effective, the expulsion doomed French hopes of recovering the lost province. Elsewhere, professional troops, together with the Canadian militia and extensive alliances with Indians, enabled the French to dominate the wilderness war and inflict further defeats on the British regular and colonial forces, culminating in the capture in 1757 of Fort William Henry at the foot of Lake George.

Defeat stimulated the Anglo-Americans into unprecedented unity and effort. Great sums of money were laid out during the course of the war. The British Treasury spent nearly £5.5 million on the army in America, nearly £1 million on the navy, and over £1 million to reimburse the colonies for their troops.[21] Colonial contributions to the war have been put at £2.5 million.[22] A huge army was assembled: 45,000 British regulars and American provincials were available for the campaign of 1758 under Jeffrey Amherst. Weight of numbers enabled the British to achieve the objective which they set themselves late in the war of not merely containing Canada by establishing a satisfactory military frontier, but of conquering it and completely removing the French presence from North America.

The British suffered a last defeat when 3,800 French beat off 15,000 attackers at Fort Ticonderoga in 1758. But elsewhere the French were driven back into New France, whose citadel, Quebec, was assaulted from the St Lawrence by Major-General James Wolfe. Wolfe's victory in death on the Heights of Abraham in September 1759 was a battle which Montcalm, the French commander, should not have fought. Later, reinforced, and arriving from the flank, Montcalm would probably have won.[23] As it was, the French counter-offensive of 1760 nearly recaptured Quebec. In 1760, however, Montreal, the last major French position in Canada was captured and New France surrendered.

[21] Julian Gwyn, 'British Government Spending and the North American Colonies, 1740–1775', in Peter Marshall and Glyn Williams, eds., *The British Atlantic Empire Before the American Revolution* (London, 1980), p. 77.

[22] Jack. P. Greene, 'The Seven Years' War and the American Revolution: The Causal Relationship Reconsidered', ibid., p. 98.

[23] W. J. Eccles, 'The Battle of Quebec: A Reappraisal', *Essays on New France* (Toronto, 1987), pp. 125–33.

In the years after 1758 the British launched amphibious operations in the Caribbean, capturing the important sugar islands of Guadeloupe and Martinique, as well as Grenada, Dominica, Tobago, and St Vincent. The taking of Senegal and Goree in West Africa gave Britain the largest of France's slave-trading bases.

A naval squadron together with a force of regular troops under Robert Clive was sent to India in 1754. They joined the Company's troops fighting the French in the Carnatic and Hyderabad. In 1756 news that Siraj-ud-Daula, the young Nawab of Bengal, had seized the East India Company settlement at Calcutta offered the Company servants in Madras the chance to open a new frontier of manipulation and plunder which, they had learnt, paid better than trade.[24] The East India Company itself was not interested in doing more than repulse French attacks. It rightly saw involvement in purely Indian wars as ruinous. It could not, however, control its servants, who now had powerful forces under command. They not only recovered Calcutta and took the French Bengal settlement at Chandernagore, but they deposed Siraj-ud-Daula in favour of a rival who had extravagantly bribed Clive and other East India Company servants to make him Nawab. This was achieved in 1757 after the encounter at Plassey, more a violent intrigue than a battle. Since 1720 a major section of the Bengal economy had passed into European hands. After Plassey the British had power commensurate with their economic stake. They raised sepoy forces to defend the new regime from Dutch, Maratha, and Mughal attacks. In 1760 the East India Company began to demand the cession of revenue-yielding districts to pay its troops and another Nawab was deposed. Bengal was becoming a British province (see Map 23.1).

William Pitt had been in effective control of the British war effort since 1757. To most contemporaries he was the architect of victory and a great Imperial states-men, even if historians now question the originality of his ideas or the scope of his strategic vision. While there may have been a consensus in British government circles about the overwhelming importance of the war overseas, Pitt had a ruthless will to win that war regardless of cost.[25] In October 1761 he resigned because the Cabinet would not back a pre-emptive strike against a Spain known to be on the verge of entering the war on the French side. Particularly after the accession of George III in 1760, the political nation's war-weariness was real, its fear of soaring war debt acute. When war was eventually declared on Spain in January 1762, further victories confirmed the inability of the Bourbon powers to resist Hano-verian Britain in the Imperial arena. Manila in the Philippines fell, as did the great

---

[24] J. D. Nichol, 'The British in India, 1740–1763', unpublished Ph.D. thesis, Cambridge, 1976.

[25] For recent interpretations, see Richard Middleton, *The Bells of Victory: The Pitt–Newcastle Ministry and the Conduct of the Seven Years' War, 1757–1762* (Cambridge, 1985); Marie Peters, 'The Myth of William Pitt, Earl of Chatham, Great Imperialist, Part I: Pitt and Imperial Expansion 1738–1763', *Journal of Imperial and Commonwealth History*, XXI (1993), pp. 31–74.

fortified port of Havana in Cuba, where the Spaniards had thoughtfully concentrated huge amounts of bullion. The Seven Years War ended with spectacular
British gains in India and a total British triumph in North America.

Over-Extension, Failure, and Recovery

The British Empire after the triumphant Peace of Paris of 1763 was both vulnerable
and unstable. France, rid of the strategic liability of New France, was preparing for
the next war, as was Spain, determined to recover Florida, another British gain.
British victories in India and in North America had been won by unstable
coalitions. In India victory had been won by a combination of military and
naval units provided by the Crown and of armies raised by the Company, which
had funded the joint forces by taxes collected from its Indian client states in Bengal
and the Carnatic. This alliance held. The Company co-operated with the national
government in peacetime as in war and it turned the richest of its client states,
Bengal, into a directly ruled province, over which it was able to maintain a firm
control. In America, where the British army had depended on Indian allies, vital
for scouting, and on provincial regiments supplied by the colonies, the wartime
alliance did not hold. First the Indians and then the Americans refused to accept
the new terms for co-operation, unilaterally imposed by Britain. In particular,
colonial Americans refused to pay part of the cost of a permanent British garrison.

   In North America the Indians of the Great Lakes region resented the complete-
ness of the British victory. No longer able to balance between two European
powers, they rapidly grasped that the British Commander-in-Chief regarded
their claims to be independent peoples with scorn. The upshot was the widespread
Indian assault on British forts in the region in 1763–64, often oversimplified into
Pontiac's Rising. Fought to a deadlock, the conflict led to more conciliatory
policies put into effect by Amherst's successor and by Sir William Johnson,
Superintendent of the Northern Indian district.[26]

   The deployment of British troops in America during the Seven Years War had
been on a quite unprecedented scale. Even before the end of the war, the decision
was taken to break further with precedent and to maintain a large peacetime
garrison, initially fixed at 10,000 men, in the colonies. Defence was no longer to be
left largely to colonial forces. Britain would assume direct responsibility. To
American opinion, this large peacetime British military presence was in itself
evidence that long-established colonial autonomies were under threat, the more
so since the army was involved in some of the most contentious new exertions of

---

[26] See below, p. 364; Richard White, *The Middle Ground: Indians, Empires and Republics in the Great
Lakes Region, 1650–1815* (Cambridge, 1991), chaps. 7, 8.

British authority, such as the fixing of a line to limit western settlement after 1763. Above all, it was ostensibly to pay part of the costs of the new garrison that British parliamentary taxes were imposed on the colonies after 1764. Thus a triumphant war in America had created problems of Imperial defence whose solutions became an important element in the slide towards open American resistance. Far from preserving the Empire, the British army in America after 1763 helped materially to provoke the crisis which lost it.

The war between Britain and the American colonies that broke out in 1775 is fully dealt with elsewhere in this volume.[27] The war was protracted and its outcome was for long uncertain. At the outset, General Gage, Governor of Massachusetts and British Commander-in-Chief, reckoned that he needed 20,000 men to begin to reconquer the region, but he had only 3,500 with him in a besieged Boston. That up to 56,000 men eventually served in America shows how seriously the possible loss of the colonies was taken, but 56,000 were still far too few. In the early years of the war there was no limit to the withdrawals George Washington was prepared to make to keep the American Continental Army in being, while its capacity for sudden counter-offensives, as at Trenton on Christmas Day 1776, forced the British to keep their field army concentrated and so deprived them of their ability to protect Loyalists from vicious intimidation by Patriots. The same pattern repeated itself when the main military effort shifted to the southern colonies at the end of 1779. Troops of the Continental Army were badly beaten in the south in 1780, but swarms of militia-based Patriot guerrillas made it impossible to hold more than Georgia and lowland South Carolina. It is doubtful whether the London government could ever have suppressed revolts in societies 3,000 miles away in which all adult white males were normally armed, indeed, were obligated to have arms for militia duty. They could never have afforded the forces necessary to occupy a vast area with some 3 million inhabitants.

Foreign intervention brought about the final British defeat in North America, when a temporary loss of naval control to a French squadron under Admiral de Grasse led to the surrender in October 1781 at Yorktown on the Chesapeake of the army that had been operating in the south under Lord Cornwallis. This defeat destroyed the British will to fight on for the subjugation of America.

For some years after 1763, a French or Spanish counter-stroke to avenge the humiliations of the Seven Years War had been kept in check by a policy of aggressive naval deterrence. This had worked in the Falkland Islands crisis of 1770–71. When the Spanish evicted a small British presence on the islands, the British mobilized warships for retaliatory action. France was unwilling to support

---

[27] See chaps. by John Shy and Stephen Conway.

Spain in the event of war and Spain had to come to terms.[28] By 1778, however, when France entered the American War, the French had achieved a rough naval equality with Britain and the entry of Spain into the war the following year gave the Bourbons a superiority.[29] In 1780 the Dutch also joined in against Britain.

The international war was fought in the West Indies and India, as well as in North America. After abandoning an American military effort, which by 1782 would have become unsustainable due to shipping shortages,[30] the British eventually fought France to a standstill. A string of islands was lost in the West Indies, but Admiral Sir George Rodney's victory over Admiral de Grasse at the Battle of the Saintes in April 1782 thwarted the Franco-Spanish plan for a combined assault on Jamaica as a corollary to Yorktown. Dutch intervention in the war eventually damaged Dutch commerce and colonies much more than Britain's. Spanish involvement failed to realize its prime objective of recovering Gibraltar.

A débâcle on the American scale could have occurred in Asia. Instead of reaping the harvest of its great gains in the period of the Seven Years War, the East India Company encountered severe financial difficulties, which brought it to bankruptcy in Britain in 1772.[31] The main cause of its difficulties in Britain was the great cost of the wars that were being waged by its servants in India. The Company had become a territorial power drawn into conflict with other Indian powers, in particular with the Marathas in western India and with Mysore in the south. A great Indian coalition was formed against the British.[32] These wars drained the resources being raised in Bengal after the grant in 1765 of the *diwani* or revenue administration of the province. Money had to be spent on ever larger sepoy armies rather than being passed to Britain through increased cargoes of Asian commodities. Wars against Indian powers, like war between the British and their American subjects, presented opportunities for French intervention. In 1782 a French naval squadron landed troops to support Haidar Ali of Mysore, the most formidable of the Indian states. The Governor-General of Bengal, Warren Hastings, was, however, able to sustain the British position against both the French and the Indian coalition. The large armies raised by the Company reinforced by British troops and warships ensured its survival. The cost of survival in terms of Indian taxation and resources extracted from its Indian allies was, however, very great.

Robert Clive had died in 1774, convinced that he lived in a disintegrating Empire. There was much to be said for this opinion by 1783. Britain had been

---

[28] Nicholas Tracy, *Navies, Deterrence and American Independence: Britain and Sea-power in the 1760s and 1770s* (Vancouver, 1988).

[29] See below, p. 185.

[30] David Syrett, *Shipping and the American War, 1775–83* (London, 1970).

[31] See below, pp. 537–38.

[32] See below, pp. 519–20.

forced to recognize the independence of the thirteen colonies, even if successes at the end of the war had limited Britain's losses to her European enemies in the Peace of Versailles to the island of Tobago and some West African trading bases to France as well as the cession of Florida to Spain. Moreover, the Irish Volunteer movement of some 60,000 at its peak had given Irish public opinion a focus through which to demand redress of grievances with the implication that force would be used were redress refused.[33] With America largely lost; British India wasted by war, famine, and corruption; Ireland restive; and the British West Indies in economic difficulties, it looked in 1783 as if the British Empire faced an uncertain future.

In fact, Britain was still a formidable Imperial power, even if the American Revolution and the subsequent war had exposed the constraints on that power, temporarily masked by the triumphs of the Seven Years War. Britain had no absolute naval supremacy; other powers were building ships in the 1780s at an alarming rate from Britain's point of view.[34] Britain's world-wide power depended on European allies and on being able to divide and distract her potential European enemies; on maintaining the support of partners within the Empire, especially the colonial American and Irish élites; and on securing at least the acquiescence of some of the major Indian states.

Within these constraints Britain showed that she could still act effectively after 1783. Supported by a coalition of Indian allies, Lord Cornwallis, Governor-General since 1786, was able in 1792 to defeat Mysore, whose troops had in the past defied those of the Company. In 1790 the threat of naval mobilization could again be used to coerce Spain. This time the episode was about access to the Pacific coast of North America. Spain seized British ships at Nootka Sound, but with no prospect of French support, the Spanish had to make restitution.[35]

From the 1790s the constraints that had limited the exercise of Britain's world-wide power for so long finally began to dissolve.[36] During the great wars against Revolutionary and Napoleonic France, Britain took the opportunity of destroying not only the French navy but those of Spain and the Netherlands as well; by 1815 the Royal Navy had as many ships as the rest of the world's navies combined. During the wars Britain's territorial possessions had grown greatly and her hold over her Empire had become much stronger. Ireland was now incorporated into the Union. Indian states that could contest British supremacy had been subjugated, so that the East India Company no longer had to seek allies in order to maintain a balance of power in India. Potentially disobedient colonial élites had been tied much more closely to Britain by a new sense of British nationalism based

---

[33] See below, pp. 265–66.
[34] See below, pp. 185–86.
[35] See below, pp. 571–72.
[36] See discussion by Michael Duffy, below, pp. 203–06.

on fear of the radicalism of the French Revolution.[37] While the British grew stronger, other European empires were disintegrating. Rich pickings were taken from them by the British. France lost Saint-Domingue, the most valuable of all its possessions, to slave insurrection and Spain was losing nearly all its American dominions to rebellious creoles.

Britain's apparent world-wide supremacy after the Seven Years War had been vulnerable and insecure; her supremacy in 1815 was unshakeable. From such a position of strength, it is hardly surprising that world-wide supremacy came to seem in retrospect to have been Britain's inevitable destiny. This is not, however, how most contemporaries saw the matter in the eighteenth century. Unaware of Britain's destiny, their use of military power to create an Empire was often faltering and uncertain. Failure was for long as frequent as success.

[37] C. A. Bayly, *Imperial Meridian: The British Empire and the World, 1780–1830* (London, 1989), chaps. 4, 5.

Select Bibliography

SEEMA ALAVI, *The Sepoys and the Company: Tradition and Transition in Northern India 1770–1830* (Delhi, 1995).

JEREMY BLACK and PHILIP WOODFINE, eds., *The British Navy and the Uses of Naval Power in the Eighteenth Century* (Leicester, 1988).

STEPHEN CONWAY, *The War of American Independence* (London, 1995).

W. J. ECCLES, *The Canadian Frontier 1534–1760*, revised edn. (Albuquerque, N. Mex., 1983).

RICHARD HARDING, *Amphibious Warfare in the Eighteenth Century: The British Expeditions to the West Indies 1740–42* (Woodbridge, 1991).

D. W. JONES, *War and Economy in the Age of William III and Marlborough* (Oxford, 1987).

JAMES P. LAWFORD, *Britain's Army in India from its Origins to the Conquest of Bengal* (London, 1978).

DOUGLAS E. LEACH, *The Northern Colonial Frontier, 1607–1763* (New York, 1966).

—— *Arms for Empire: A Military History of the British Colonies in North America, 1607–1763* (New York, 1973).

PIERS MACKESY, *The War for America, 1775–1783* (London, 1964).

RICHARD MELVOIN, *The New England Outpost: War and Society in Colonial Deerfield* (New York, 1989).

RICHARD MIDDLETON, *The Bells of Victory: The Pitt–Newcastle Ministry and the Conduct of the Seven Years' War, 1757–1762* (Cambridge, 1985).

RICHARD PARES, *War and Trade in the West Indies, 1739–1763* (Oxford, 1936).

GEOFFREY PARKER, *The Military Revolution: Military Innovation and the Rise of the West, 1500–1800*, 2nd edn. (Cambridge, 1996).

HOWARD H. PECKHAM, *The Colonial Wars, 1689–1762* (Chicago, 1964).

JOHN SHY, *A People Numerous and Armed: Reflections on the Military Struggle for American Independence*, revised edn. (Ann Arbor, 1990).

DAVID SYRETT, *The Royal Navy in American Waters, 1775–1783* (Aldershot, 1989).

JAMES TITUS, *The Old Dominion at War: Society, Politics and Warfare in Late Colonial Virginia* (Columbia, SC, 1991).

STEPHEN SAUNDERS WEBB, *The Governors General: The English Army and the Definition of Empire* (Chapel Hill, NC, 1979).

———, *Lord Churchill's Coup: The Anglo-American Empire and the Glorious Revolution Reconsidered* (New York, 1995).

8

Sea-Power and Empire, 1688–1793

N. A. M. RODGER

Eighteenth-century Britain was a European power, closely interested in the balance of power on the continent, not only or principally because she was ruled by a Dutch or Hanoverian sovereign, but because she felt herself threatened by powerful neighbours. It has been easy for later historians to underestimate the instability and insecurity of eighteenth-century Britain. No doubt foreigners, contemplating the ceaseless flux of parliamentary government from the reassuring solidity of absolute monarchy, exaggerated Britain's real weakness. They did not need to exaggerate the fears of people living a day's sail from the largest army in Christendom, to say nothing of a legitimate pretender to the throne and the horrors of Catholicism. The motives which first created a dominant English navy in the 1650s, and which kept the British fleet the largest in Europe, were overwhelmingly defensive. The navy's primary function was to guard against invasion, for which purpose the bulk of the fleet was almost always kept in home waters. Its essential duty remained in 1815 what it had been for at least 400 years: to guard the Narrow Seas.

The threat of invasion had to be taken seriously in wartime, and the navy was Britain's only credible defence against it. The ease with which the French could pin down large naval forces merely by assembling a body of troops on the Channel coast was one of the real weaknesses of the British navy in the eighteenth century. Lacking, or at least believing themselves to lack, an effective army, successive British governments tied down a large part of the fleet in the Channel in moments of crisis, while the French were able to devote all their available naval strength to the offensive, and often to seize the initiative from a numerically stronger enemy.[1] Even without the threat of invasion, the British army had sometimes to be used as a substitute for a navy which was not strong enough to meet all the demands upon it. The celebrated raids on the coast of France organized by the elder William Pitt

---

[1] J. R. Jones, 'Limitations of British Sea Power in the French Wars, 1689–1815', and Jeremy Black, 'Naval Power and British Foreign Policy in the Age of Pitt the Elder', in Jeremy Black and Philip Woodfine, eds., *The British Navy and the Use of Naval Power in the Eighteenth Century* (Leicester, 1988), pp. 33–49; 97–99. Jeremy Black, 'British Naval Power and International Commitments: Political and Strategic Problems, 1688–1770', in Michael Duffy, ed., *Parameters of British Naval Power, 1650–1850* (Exeter, 1992), pp. 39–59.

during the Seven Years War, so often treated on their own strategic merits or demerits, were offered as an inadequate substitute for the fleet in the Baltic demanded by Britain's ally Frederick II of Prussia, which could not be provided for want of ships.[2]

The primacy of home defence has tended, however, to be obscured by the approach traditional among naval historians. The founders of scholarly naval history in the late nineteenth century, who defined their subject in terms which are still widely accepted, were naturally interested in the connection between seapower and Empire. For them it was important to show how the navy had made the Empire, for it was self-evidently the Empire which defined and established Britain's greatness. Moreover, writers such as Sir John Laughton and Sir Julian Corbett were not simply studying naval history in a spirit of disinterested enquiry; they were engaged in a movement to reform the Royal Navy of their day in which historical research played an essential part. Naval history was a practical tool with which to open various neglected subjects, among them the defence of trade. They therefore stressed the navy's role in the creation and defence of the Empire.[3] Moreover, trade and Imperial defence long continued to be the principal justifications argued for the size and structure of the Royal Navy, both abroad (for example at the inter-war naval disarmament conferences) and at home. Only in recent years, with the British Empire largely dismantled and the British merchant fleet greatly reduced, has it become possible to study British naval history with less distraction from current policy.

This historiographical tradition has tended to give non-specialist historians the impression that the navy always existed primarily to support overseas expansion and defend overseas trade. It is often assumed or implied that Britain had a long-term naval strategy of 'blue-water' expansion, enforced by the blockade of enemy naval ports, but steadily directed towards Imperial ends. So long as Europe remained weak and divided, this naval policy sufficed to gain Britain access to a

[2] P. F. Doran, *Andrew Mitchell and Anglo-Prussian Diplomatic Relations during the Seven Years War* (New York, 1986), pp. 144–47. Black, 'Naval Power and British Foreign Policy', p. 102. Richard Middleton, *The Bells of Victory: The Pitt–Newcastle Ministry and the Conduct of the Seven Years' War, 1757–1762* (Cambridge, 1985), p. 26. John B. Hattendorf and others, eds., *British Naval Documents, 1204–1960*, (Navy Records Society, CXXXI, 1993), pp. 329–31.

[3] Donald M. Schurman, *The Education of a Navy: The Development of British Naval Strategic Thought, 1867–1914* (London, 1965), and *Julian S. Corbett, 1854–1922: Historian of British Maritime Policy from Drake to Jellicoe* (London, 1981). James Goldrick and John B. Hattendorf, eds., *Mahan is not Enough: The Proceedings of a Conference on the Works of Sir Julian Corbett and Admiral Sir Herbert Richmond* (Newport, RI, 1993). Eric Grove, 'La Pensée naval britannique depuis Colomb', in Hervé Coutau-Bégarie, ed., *L'Évolution de la pensée navale*, 5 vols. (Paris, 1990–95), II, pp. 115–33. Barry D. Hunt, 'The Strategic Thought of Sir Julian S. Corbett', in John B. Hattendorf and Robert S. Jordan, eds., *Maritime Strategy and the Balance of Power: Britain and America in the Twentieth Century* (London, 1989), pp. 110–35.

rising share of the wealth of the world at an economical price. Only with the rise of the continental military powers in the late nineteenth century, it is argued, did the unified industrial empires of the railway age outclass the dispersed economic structures of the older maritime imperial systems. The change is always symbolized by the appointment of Sir John Fisher as First Sea Lord in 1904, the calling home of the bulk of the Royal Navy to face the German threat in the North Sea, the conclusion of an alliance with Japan, and the adoption of a 'Continental Commitment' to France; all ushering in an age in which the Empire, and by implication the navy, were increasingly an inescapable burden rather than a source of strength.[4]

This view of the place of the Royal Navy in British history is still widely accepted, but it has been undermined at virtually every point. In the first place, it is necessary to stress that all discussion of British naval strategy in the eighteenth century is anachronistic, in that there was then nothing which could accurately be described as naval strategy. The word 'strategy' only entered the English language around 1800, as a borrowing from French, then used chiefly in its Greek sense to refer to the art of the general.[5] When Corbett published his great study of 'maritime strategy' in 1911, he was consciously borrowing the word from the German military theorist Clausewitz and applying it in a context in which it was still not customary.[6] Eighteenth-century British statesmen and admirals knew neither the phrase nor the thing. Navies and fleets existed, and they had of necessity some ideas about how to use them, but those ideas tended to be pragmatic, often detailed, not based explicitly on any developed theory of naval strategy as a whole. For contemporaries, British policy towards the outside world was a single, large subject with many aspects.[7] In part it was a matter of traditional diplomacy, especially in dealings with other countries in Europe. In this context eighteenth-century Englishmen thought first of the survival of the 'Revolution Settlement' of 1689 (by which Parliament legitimized the seizure of the throne by the Protestant Dutch Prince William III from his father-in-law, the Catholic James II) and of the 'Protestant Succession' of 1714 (when James's son was again excluded from the throne by the succession of the Elector of Hanover as King George I). The threat was always Bourbon absolutism and Catholic reaction, both promoting a Stuart restoration.[8] This directed attention towards the continent so effectively that, at least up to the mid-century, the advocates of oceanic warfare felt themselves to be a

---

[4] Paul M. Kennedy, *The Rise and Fall of British Naval Mastery* (London, 1976).

[5] The first citation in the *Oxford English Dictionary*, 2nd edn., is 1810.

[6] *Some Principles of Maritime Strategy* (London, 1911); see the Introduction.

[7] Jeremy Black, *British Foreign Policy in the Age of Walpole* (Edinburgh, 1985). H. M. Scott, *British Foreign Policy in the Age of the American Revolution* (Oxford, 1990).

[8] Jeremy Black, *Natural and Necessary Enemies: Anglo-French Relations in the Eighteenth Century* (London, 1986).

neglected minority. 'I have sometimes wondered', complained Swift in 1711 in his celebrated pamphlet *The Conduct of the Allies,*

how it came to pass, that the Style of *Maritime Powers*, by which our Allies, in a sort of contemptuous manner, usually couple us with the *Dutch*, did never put us in mind of the Sea; and while some Politicians were shewing us the way to *Spain* by *Flanders*, others by *Savoy* or *Naples*, that the *West-Indies* should never come into their Heads.[9]

It would be going too far to say that the West Indies never came into ministers' heads, but they did so primarily as a source of trade, and commerce itself was often thought of as the essential support of an effective naval defence. 'The undoubted Interest of England is Trade,' declared a pamphleteer in 1672, 'since it is that alone which can make us either *Rich* or *Safe*, for without a powerful Navy, we should be a Prey to our Neighbours, and without Trade, we could have neither sea-men or Ships.'[10] The trades to the East and West Indies carried much weight, but they could not be, and were not, considered in isolation from Europe. Relations with European maritime powers (mainly France, Spain, and the Netherlands) heavily affected trade overseas, and many colonial imports were re-exported in refined or manufactured form to the continent. The finance of government, particularly but not only in wartime, was closely connected with the profitable foreign trades which generated so much liquid capital, and made possible the debt finance essential to modern war. Diplomacy, commerce, and finance all had their impact on the House of Commons, the great theatre in which every aspect of national policy was expressed in political—and very often ideological—terms. Each of these aspects of national policy had naval implications, and could be seen to influence the employment of British fleets and squadrons. What contemporaries were not in the habit of doing was isolating the naval implications of policy. Their approach helped them to form foreign policy as a coherent whole, but it did not encourage them to consider in any detail how it might be worked out at sea.

The navy itself was in no condition to supply the want of any specifically naval policy-making. Modern navies apply much of their effort to planning for war in every forseeable situation, and justify their existence largely in terms of their readiness for war. Eighteenth-century navies were not blind to the need to be ready for war, but for many reasons advance planning was both more difficult and less urgent for them.[11] First among the difficulties was the entire absence of any naval staff. The 'retinue' of an eighteenth-century British admiral consisted largely

[9] Quoted by Nicholas Tracy, *Attack on Maritime Trade* (London, 1991), p. 29.

[10] Ibid., p. 41.

[11] N. A. M. Rodger, 'The West Indies in Eighteenth-Century British Naval Strategy', in Paul Butel and Bernard Lavallé, eds., *L'Espace Caraïbe: théâtre et enjeu des luttes impériales, XVIe–XIXe siècle* (Bordeaux, 1996), pp. 38–60, and 'La Mobilisation navale au XVIIIème siècle', in Martine Acerra and others, eds., *État, marine et société: Hommage à Jean Meyer* (Paris, 1995), pp. 365–74.

of domestics and young gentlemen hoping to rise on his patronage to become officers. His 'staff', in the modern sense, consisted of his secretary, who handled the administrative business of the squadron with the assistance of one or two clerks. In addition he might (but did not usually) have a First Captain (in addition to the flag-captain) to assist him in handling his fleet, and he might entrust intelligence or diplomatic correspondence to the flagship's chaplain.[12] Otherwise he was on his own.

The Admiralty which stood at the head of British naval administration was no better placed to help. Its tiny staff consisted almost entirely of civilian clerks engaged in routine administrative business.[13] The only sea officers present were the naval members of the Board of Admiralty. It was common, though not invariable, for the Board to include at least one senior officer of weight and experience, and this senior officer might or might not be the same person as the First Lord who presided over the Admiralty Board and represented the navy in Cabinet. The junior members of the Board, who were essentially political placemen with no important functions, might include one or two officers, often elderly and long retired, but there was for long periods no more than one active sea officer on the Board. It was perfectly possible to have an Admiralty headed by a civilian virtually without professional assistance. For much of the War of American Independence Lord Sandwich, the First Lord, had only one professional colleague, Lord Mulgrave, who was absent at sea and able to advise only by letter. The First Lord might and did settle grand strategy with his Cabinet colleagues, but it could only be worked out in detail by the Navy and Victualling Boards, on the administrative side, and the Commander-in-Chief, on the operational side.[14]

Nor was there any forum for the discussion of strategy, or indeed of any other aspect of the naval profession. There were no institutions of higher study for the profession of arms, and no idea of encouraging officers to study it. Intelligent admirals hoped their officers would read history and other books, but there was no professional literature they could suggest that dealt with strategy. There were numerous manuals on navigation, gunnery, naval architecture, and other technical subjects; and a growing interest in tactics and signalling;[15] but the literature on naval warfare in general consisted of a handful of works translated out of French, none of which dealt with strategy in any coherent fashion.[16]

[12] N. A. M. Rodger, *The Wooden World: An Anatomy of the Georgian Navy* (London, 1986), pp. 17–18.

[13] G. F. James, 'The Admiralty Establishment, 1759', *Bulletin of the Institute of Historical Research*, XVI (1938–39), p. 24.

[14] N. A. M. Rodger, *The Admiralty* (Lavenham, Suffolk, 1979), pp. 53–89.

[15] Thomas R. Adams and David W. Waters, eds., *English Maritime Books Printed Before 1801* (Providence, RI, 1995).

[16] Paul Hoste, *Naval Evolutions: Or, a System of Sea-Discipline* (London, 1762), trans. C. O'Bryen from *L'Art des armées navales* (Lyons, 1697). Sebastien François Bigot de Morogues, *Naval Tactics, or a*

So the functions of the navy were conceived of within the context of national policy rather than professional doctrine. Foreign policy was, if not the prisoner of ideology, at least a hostage to ideological language. The Act of Settlement of 1701, which regulated the Protestant succession to the throne, attempted to forbid any foreign monarch (meaning the Electors of Hanover), from allowing the interests of his continental possessions to deflect his British policy. This made it easy for opponents of government to present any continental involvement, especially (after 1714) an involvement with Hanover, as the poisoned fruit of needless continental entanglements. Overseas expeditions, on the other hand, were (as Swift implied) the English way of warfare; patriotic and profitable. Hence, for example, the public excitement surrounding Admiral Edward Vernon's capture of the Spanish Caribbean port of Porto Bello in 1739.[17] Sir Robert Walpole's ministry had chosen both the strategy and the admiral, in spite of his energetic opposition politics: 'He is certainly much properer than any officer we have to send, being very well acquainted in all that part of the West Indies, and is a very good sea officer, whatever he may be, or has been, in the House of Commons.'[18] They might reasonably have hoped to be given credit for his initial success, but the associations of this politician, and this sort of campaign, soon transformed it for the Opposition into 'our honest Admiral's triumph over Sir Robert and Spain'—in that order.[19] So what purported to be a strategic debate was in many cases a disguised form of ideological contest, where foreign policy acted as the surrogate of domestic politics.[20]

The most important development of the eighteenth century in strategic thinking (if we may apply the term anachronistically) was the establishment in the 1740s of the Western Squadron. The idea of guarding the English Channel by keeping the main fleet not in the Channel itself but out to windward in the Western Approaches was not a new one—something like it had been adopted in 1588 on the advice of Sir Francis Drake—but it was first articulated and thoroughly developed during this war. The principle was simple. For most of the year the

Treatise of Evolutions and Signals (London, 1767), trans. from *Tactique navale...* (Paris, 1763). Jacques Bourdé de Villehuet, *The Manoeuverer, or Skilful Seaman...* (London, 1788), trans. from *Le Manoeuvrier* ... (Paris, 1765). Jacques Raymond, vicomte de Grenier, *The Art of War at Sea...* (London, 1788), trans. from *L'Art de la guerre sur mer...* (Paris, 1787). On these writers see Hubert Granier, 'La Pensée navale française au XVIIIᵉ siècle' in Coutau-Bégarie, ed., *L'Évolution de la pensée navale*, III, pp. 33–56.

[17] Kathleen Wilson, 'Empire, Trade and Popular Politics in Mid-Hanoverian Britain: The Case of Admiral Vernon', *Past and Present*, CXXI, (1988), pp. 74–109.

[18] Daniel A. Baugh, ed., *Naval Administration, 1715–1750*, (Navy Records Society, CXX, 1977), p. 15.

[19] Quoted by Stanley Ayling, *The Elder Pitt* (London, 1976), p. 66.

[20] N. A. M. Rodger, 'The Continental Commitment in the Eighteenth Century', in Lawrence Freedman, Paul Hayes, and Robert O'Neill, eds., *War, Strategy and International Politics: Essays in Honour of Sir Michael Howard* (Oxford, 1992), pp. 39–55.

prevailing winds blow from the south-west, up the Channel. Neither France nor Spain had a naval base in the Channel, so any enemy fleet had to come from the westward. An invasion force might sail from the ports of Normandy and Britanny, but it would sail without naval escort unless a fleet came up the Channel to cover it. Most of Britain's foreign trade (the Baltic trade excepted) came up and down the Channel. If the main fleet cruised to the westward off the mouth of the Channel it was well placed to cover convoys outward and homeward bound, to watch the main French naval base at Brest and intercept fleets coming and going from it, to guard against any attempt to invade Ireland, and to block, or at least pursue an enemy fleet entering the Channel. One single fleet, held within easy reach of home where it could be effectually controlled and maintained, was able to satisfy all the most essential British strategic requirements at once. In developing this principle Vernon was one of the most important theorists, and Admiral George Anson, as Commander-in-Chief of the Western Squadron for most of 1746 and 1747, the most influential practitioner.[21]

The principle of a Western Squadron in one form or another formed the core of Britain's naval strategy for a century and more. The practical application of the policy, however, always aroused disagreement. The cruising grounds of the squadron covered an area of tens of thousands of square miles from Cape Clear to Finisterre, only a tiny part of which could possibly be watched at any one time. If the squadron stayed at sea together for as long as possible, it increased its chances of fighting a decisive action if it met an enemy fleet, but it increased the wear and tear on the ships, especially if it stayed out in the autumn, the season of the equinoctial gales, but also of the rich convoys coming home from the West and East Indies. An autumn cruise might protect the trade at the cost of crippling the squadron for months. If the ships were dispersed in small groups on cruising stations trade might be better protected, but there was a risk of defeat in detail. If the squadron lay in port it kept in the best condition to meet the enemy, but the worst position to do so. The choice of port was also controversial: Spithead or St Helen's (off Portsmouth) were convenient but too far up Channel; Torbay was dangerously exposed either to enemy attack or to a south-easterly wind; Cawsand Bay at the mouth of Plymouth Sound was a cramped and even more exposed anchorage, while the Hamoaze off Plymouth Dockyard itself took far too long to get in and out of. If the Western Squadron attempted a blockade of Brest, where should it take station? To lie off Brest itself in south-westerly winds was very dangerous, and arguably unnecessary when the French could only sail on an east

[21] Michael Duffy, 'The Establishment of the Western Squadron as the Linchpin of British Naval Strategy', in Duffy, ed., *Parameters of British Naval Power*, pp. 60–81. H. W. Richmond, *The Navy in the War of 1739–48*, 3 vols. (Cambridge, 1920), III, pp. 6–8, 20–23, 82–84, 226–29. B. McL. Ranft, ed., *The Vernon Papers* (Navy Records Society, XCIX, 1958), pp. 436–37, 441, 451–52, 459.

wind; but to lie, say, in Torbay until the wind veered might give the enemy 200 miles' start.

These questions continued to be debated as long as warships were driven by the wind and Britain and France regarded one another as potential enemies. There were no absolute right or wrong answers to them, and in different circumstances different admirals and Admiralties adopted different approaches.[22] In the 1740s Vernon argued for keeping the main Western Squadron at sea 'in Soundings' (meaning the Western Approaches), with a force of smaller ships to guard the Narrow Seas against invasion:

I have always looked upon squadrons in Port, as neither a Defence for the Kingdom, nor a security for our Commerce; and that the surest means for the preservation of Both, was Keeping a strong Squadron in Soundings, which may answer both these Purposes, as covering both Chanels and Ireland, at the same time it secures our Commerce.[23]

Anson agreed, but rather favoured keeping the main force in port until the enemy were known to be preparing to put to sea, and not risking dispersal until he had been met and defeated—for which he was attacked by commercial interests for neglecting their trade.[24] 'The French can never be so much annoy'd,' he wrote, 'nor this Kingdom so well secured, as by keeping a strong Squadron at home, sufficient to make detachments, whenever we have good intelligence that the French are sending ships either to the East or West Indies.'[25] Lord Sandwich, already at the Admiralty though not yet First Lord, argued strongly that concentrating either at sea or in port threw away the opportunity to damage the enemy by intercepting his trade, that detachments could be made while still leaving a sufficient force together for any emergency, and that it was not necessary to allow the threat of invasion to paralyze all offensive measures. 'By immediately recalling them [cruisers], we shall fall into the same trap which has, during the whole war, been so successfully laid for us, of giving way to every sudden alarm, and by that means have missed every opportunity fortune would have thrown in our way.'[26] In other words, he argued for running greater risks than Anson, but arguably put a lower priority on winning a decisive victory. In practice it was Anson's opinion which was dominant, and his policy which led to the two naval victories of 1747.[27]

---

[22] There is an excellent discussion in A. N. Ryan, 'The Royal Navy and the Blockade of Brest, 1689–1805: Theory and Practice', in Martine Acerra, José Merino, and Jean Meyer, eds., *Les Marines de guerre européennes, XVII–XVIIIe siècles* (Paris, 1985), pp. 175–93.

[23] Quoted in N. A. M. Rodger, *The Insatiable Earl: A Life of John Montagu, Fourth Earl of Sandwich, 1718–1792* (London, 1993), p. 36. Cf. Ranft, ed., *Vernon Papers*, pp. 446, 451.

[24] Richard Pares, *War and Trade in the West Indies, 1739–1763* (Oxford, 1936), p. 299.

[25] Rodger, *Insatiable Earl*, p. 37.

[26] Sir John Barrow, *The Life of George Lord Anson* (London, 1839), p. 155.

[27] See the discussion in Richmond, *Navy in the War of 1739–48*, III, pp. 21–23.

Two things will be noted from the views of those responsible for establishing the Western Squadron: they were thinking largely of home waters, and they did not mention blockade. Close blockade, so often referred to as a 'traditional' British practice, was in fact an unusual and exceptionally difficult approach, requiring a large superiority of force, and neither possible nor useful in many circumstances. It was in practice applied only for fairly short periods.[28] What was traditional, or became so from the 1740s, was the policy of dominating home waters, and especially the Western Approaches, as the best method of guarding against the risk of invasion, protecting British trade, and interfering with the trade and naval operations of the enemy.[29]

The principle of the Western Squadron rested on the intelligent exploitation of geography, but geography had left it one serious weakness. The fact that France's two main naval ports were on different coasts was a continual problem for the French, making it difficult to unite their fleets into a single main force. But the remoteness of Toulon from the cruising grounds of the Western Squadron made it impossible to cover except by making a detachment to the Mediterranean, or at least as far as Gibraltar. The British were faced with the disagreeable choice, either of dividing their forces in the face of the enemy and running the risk of defeat in detail, or of leaving the Toulon squadron unwatched, a strategic 'wild card' which might be played without warning anywhere in the world. If the naval war went well, the British could usually build up enough strength to cover the Mediterranean, but this luxury was seldom available in the opening phases of a war. In the initial months of three successive wars, in 1744, 1756, and 1778, the Toulon squadron seriously embarrassed the British.

One of the advantages of the Western Squadron was that it could be treated as a strategic reserve of ships, already operational and 'worked up' to efficiency, from which detachments could be made, if necessary to distant waters. Its chief contribution to naval operations in the colonies, however, was the opportunity it gave to defeat the enemy at home. Dominance of the Western Approaches made it increasingly difficult for France, and to a lesser extent Spain, to send ships and squadrons to and from the West or East Indies. If dominance could be extended to the Mediterranean it would become almost impossible. Both trade convoys and squadrons of warships were liable to interception and defeat in detail, and a series of such defeats could progressively establish a level of control of European waters which cut off French or Spanish colonies from their mother countries. This in turn

---

[28] Ryan, 'Blockade of Brest'; also 'William III and the Brest Fleet in the Nine Years' War', in Ragnhild Hatton and John S. Bromley, eds., *William III and Louis XIV: Essays 1680–1720 by and for Mark A. Thomson* (Liverpool, 1968).

[29] Daniel A. Baugh, 'Great Britain's "Blue-Water" Policy, 1689–1815', *International History Review*, X (1988), pp. 33–58.

allowed small British forces in distant waters to undertake operations without fear of interference. The most remarkable example of this was the expedition which in 1762 captured Manila, in the Philippines: a small, ramshackle force improvised from the resources available in the Bay of Bengal sufficed (with a good measure of luck and daring) to take one of the largest and richest Spanish cities in the world.[30] It would have been inconceivable to risk so small a force on so great an under-taking if British naval superiority in European waters had not provided an absolute guarantee against the possibility of Spanish reinforcements. The same principle applied generally in the West Indies, though in these less distant waters it was not usually possible to offer so certain a protection against interference, and expeditions had to be more heavily escorted.

Like the Spaniards, but unlike the French, the British habitually kept standing overseas squadrons to protect colonies and trade, but they were not the key to success in imperial naval warfare. Indeed, with the partial exception of the East Indies squadron, they were not primarily designed or disposed for naval warfare against European enemies. It was to protect both legal trade and smuggling into Spanish colonies, against the linked threats of pirates, coastguards, and privateers, that British overseas squadrons were established in the Americas in the late seventeenth and early eighteenth centuries, and they remained too small, too scattered, and by no means rightly disposed to resist powerful squadrons from Europe.[31] In the Caribbean the British had two squadrons, those of the Leeward Islands and Jamaica. Both were small, consisting of a handful of frigates and smaller craft, supported by small careening yards at Port Royal, Jamaica, and English Harbour, Antigua. There were no docks, and the frigates had to be replaced every two or three years to save them from the shipworm. The stations were essentially arranged for peacetime purposes, and reflected the patterns of trade. From the point of view of naval strategy, it was a grave error to establish the bigger squadron at Jamaica, far to leeward of almost all the British colonies and unable to support them at all. It was equally unfortunate to fix a naval yard at the leeward end of the Leeward Islands, for though English Harbour was a good (if small) harbour and convenient for homebound convoys, it was very badly placed for any offensive operations against the French islands to windward. In practice, even in wartime the West Indian squadrons remained largely cruiser forces devoted to the protection of trade, reinforced from time to time to undertake specific offensive operations. If major forces came out from home, it was usually

[30] Nicholas Tracy, *Manila Ransomed: The British Assault on Manila in the Seven Years War* (Exeter, 1995).

[31] I. R. Mather, 'The Royal Navy in America and the West Indies, 1660–1720', unpublished D.Phil. thesis, Oxford, 1996.

necessary to establish temporary bases convenient for the intended operations; the permanent naval yards were quite unsuitable.[32]

In all the wars of the eighteenth century except one, it was superiority in European waters which made possible successful operations overseas, and the bulk of the navy was held at home. Early in the Seven Years War, in 1757, for example, 71 per cent of the ships and 67 per cent of the men were serving in home waters, and another 12 per cent of the ships and 18 per cent of the men in the Mediterranean.[33] Between 1757 and 1762, 64 per cent of the 'ship-days' of the navy were served in home waters or the Mediterranean.[34] In this, the most successful war of colonial conquest Britain ever fought, the bulk of the navy stayed at home—and by doing so, it made those conquests possible. It was the command of the Western Approaches won in 1759 at the Battles of Lagos (on the coast of Portugal) and Quiberon Bay (on the coast of France) which made possible the subsequent expeditions to Cape Breton, Canada, Havana, Manila, and elsewhere.

The importance of controlling the Western Approaches is much clearer to the twentieth-century historian, with Corbett's strategic analysis available, than it was to the men of the mid-eighteenth century. It seemed to them that the Seven Years War had fundamentally changed their situation, and invalidated the policies of the past. Their attention was increasingly turning overseas, indeed, it has been argued that the process of detachment from the continental system had begun in the late 1740s,[35] and it was certainly accelerated by the acquisitions of this war, and the accession of George III in 1760, a sovereign less interested in Hanover than his German-born grandfather and great-grandfather had been. By 1763 it was difficult for the British to convince themselves, and impossible for them to convince anyone else, that the ambitions of France were still the great and permanent threat to the liberties of Europe. In the years following the war, they were unable to reconstruct a continental alliance against France, an 'Old System' such as had been the foundation of British foreign policy for most of the past seventy-five years.[36] It was now more plausible for the Duc de Choiseul, minister from 1758 to 1770, to present France as the defender of Europe's commercial freedom against the

[32] Daniel A. Baugh, *British Naval Administration in the Age of Walpole* (Princeton, 1965), pp. 341–72. Pares, *War and Trade in the West Indies*.

[33] Hattendorf, ed., *British Naval Documents*, pp. 381–82.

[34] Rodger, *Wooden World*, App. II.

[35] This is the theme of Manfred Mimler, *Der Einfluss kolonialer Interessen in Nordamerika auf die Strategie und Diplomatie Grossbritanniens während des Österreichischen Erbfolgekrieges, 1744–1748* (Hildesheim, 1983); see esp. pp. 198–204. Other authorities, such as Gottfried Niedhart, *Handel und Krieg in der Britischen Weltpolitik, 1738–1763* (Munich, 1979), put the change rather later.

[36] H. M. Scott, '"The True Principles of the Revolution": The Duke of Newcastle and the Idea of the Old System', in Jeremy Black, ed., *Knights Errant and True Englishmen: British Foreign Policy, 1660–1800* (Edinburgh, 1989), pp. 55–91. Rodger, *Insatiable Earl*, pp. 105–07.

arrogance of British sea-power.[37] In the circumstances the idea of reconstructing the 'Old System' was increasingly implausible and irrelevant, and less attractive to the British themselves as their own policies increasingly looked across the oceans to a future founded on overseas trade and a colonial Empire.[38]

It was not clear, however, whether this new direction of policy implied a new way of employing the navy. In the past the priorities had been defensive and the threats near at hand. If the traditional threat had been substantially reduced, if Britain's hopes and ambitions now lay overseas, what was the implication for the disposition of the fleets? There was no intellectual tradition or mechanism for planning which could have helped to answer this question. When France entered the American War in 1778, the British had to face what seemed to be an unprecedented strategic situation, without the help of any developed ideas of strategy. The bulk of opinion in the Cabinet, led by Lord George Germain, the Colonial Secretary, argued that America was the issue of the war, and there the bulk of the navy should be concentrated. Lord Sandwich, the First Lord of the Admiralty, and Admiral Augustus Keppel, commanding the main fleet in the Channel, seem to have believed in the traditional principle of concentrating in home waters to achieve decisive victory, before dispersing to exploit the resulting command of the sea in distant waters. It is hardly possible to doubt that they were fundamentally right, even if they were much less than clear in their expression. The British situation was worse than it had ever been at the outbreak of a major war. Lord North's ministry's misguided attempts to appease France by delaying mobilization (against Sandwich's urgent pleas) had given France a rough equality in strength, with the grave risk that Spain would enter the war and confer overwhelming superiority (as she did in 1779).[39] The bulk of the British army and much of its naval manpower was in America, a hostage to the fortunes of war in European waters. In this very dangerous situation it was doubly necessary to concentrate on the essential point, and the French decision to send the Toulon squadron across the Atlantic in the spring of 1778 gave the British an opportunity to make up for delayed mobilization and achieve an early superiority. They threw it away by making an equivalent detachment to America from Keppel's fleet.[40]

---

[37] Frank Spencer, ed., *The Fourth Earl of Sandwich: Diplomatic Correspondence 1763–1765* (Manchester, 1961), p. 8. H. M. Scott, 'The Importance of Bourbon Naval Reconstruction to the Strategy of Choiseul after the Seven Years' War', *International History Review*, I (1979), pp. 20–35.

[38] Daniel A. Baugh, 'Maritime Strength and Atlantic Commerce: The Uses of a "Grand Marine Empire"', in Lawrence Stone, ed., *An Imperial State at War: Britain from 1689 to 1815* (London, 1994), pp. 185–223.

[39] Daniel A. Baugh, 'Why did Britain lose Command of the Sea during the War for America?', in Black and Woodfine, eds., *The British Navy and the Use of Naval Power*, pp. 149–69; and 'The Politics of British Naval Failure, 1775–1777', *American Neptune*, LII (1992), pp. 221–46.

[40] Rodger, *Insatiable Earl*, pp. 243–44; 275–79. David Syrett, 'Home Waters or America? The Dilemma of British Naval Strategy in 1778', *Mariner's Mirror*, LXXVII (1991), pp. 365–77.

Thus a war started in which the British repeatedly dispersed their strength in remote parts of the world. Eighteenth-century communications did not allow fleets on the other side of the Atlantic to be controlled in any effective manner, either locally or from home, and the result was a series of undirected random cruises in which British and French squadrons blundered aimlessly around the New World, occasionally encountering one another in strength and circumstances which were completely unpredictable. Sandwich, alone among the Cabinet ministers, seems to have had some sound strategic instincts, but there is no evidence that he ever gave them coherent expression, and he certainly did not convince his colleagues. As the war developed, and Britain's peril from French and Spanish invasion fleets in the Channel grew greater, they took more and more of the ships and scattered them further and further away from the only waters where their presence might have won the war, and their absence nearly lost it. By 1782 Sandwich and his naval advisers were seriously planning to disband the Western Squadron altogether and send the bulk of the fleet to the West Indies.[41] They were prevented by the fall of the North ministry, brought about in part by defeats which were directly caused by the absence of a coherent strategy. It was true that Rear-Admiral Thomas Graves was unlucky to meet the French fleet under Comte de Grasse off the Virginia Capes in 1781, the battle which led indirectly to the surrender of Lord Cornwallis's army, the fall of Lord North, and the independence of the United States—but it was entirely the fault of North's administration that everything depended on luck, when it might have rested on the intelligent application of effort at the critical point. They did not deserve the good fortune which brought about Sir George Rodney's victory in the West Indies at the Battle of the Saintes next year (which saved Jamaica from invasion and propelled the French towards peace negotiations), for they had done equally little to make it certain.

The British never made the same mistake again. Empire undoubtedly rested on sea-power, but after the American War that sea-power was only dispersed into distant waters in a limited and subsidiary form. The first and chiefest duty of the Royal Navy was always the defence of Britain against invasion, followed by the protection of trade, with colonies a poor third in the order of priority—but because her European enemies were also her Imperial rivals, because they needed naval success either to invade Britain, or for maritime war in distant waters, it was possible for the same fleets to cover operations all over the world while remaining concentrated in European waters. The one war in which this principle was forgotten and the squadrons were allowed to disperse into colonial waters, was the war in which the colonies were lost, and the mother country might very well

---

[41] Rodger, *Insatiable Earl*, pp. 293–94.

have been, but for the incompetence of Britain's enemies. The Battle of the Saintes in 1782 was the first and last major action ever fought by the principal British fleet outside European waters. The principal British fleet did not leave European waters again until 1944 (though Sir John Fisher seriously planned the abandonment of battleship building and the dispersal of the main fleets around the world, and might have repeated the strategy of the 1770s had he been allowed to).[42] When war again broke out in 1793, the British had been cured of their obsession with colonies. Once again they recognized that the real peril lay close at hand, and once again they concentrated their fleets in European waters to face it. Great expeditions sailed for distant waters to attack and conquer enemy colonies—but the main fleets did not go with them. They remained in the Western Approaches, where the dockyards were at hand to maintain them, where they could be effectively controlled on the basis of recent intelligence. Here they could dominate the only enemies that mattered; from the command of these waters, the command of the world derived.

[42] Nicholas A. Lambert, 'Admiral Sir John Fisher and the Concept of Flotilla Defence, 1904–1909', *Journal of Military History*, LIX (1995), pp. 639–60; and 'British Naval Policy, 1913–1914: Financial Limitation and Strategic Revolution', *Journal of Modern History*, LXVII (1995), pp. 595–626.

Select Bibliography

DANIEL A. BAUGH, 'Great Britain's "Blue-Water" Policy, 1689–1815', *International History Review*, X (1988), pp. 33–58.

—— 'Maritime Strength and Atlantic Commerce: The Uses of a "Grand Marine Empire"', in Lawrence Stone, ed., *An Imperial State at War: Britain from 1689 to 1815* (London, 1994), pp. 185–223.

—— 'Why did Britain Lose Command of the Sea during the War for America?', in Jeremy Black and Philip Woodfine, eds., *The British Navy and the Use of Naval Power* (Leicester, 1988), pp. 149–169.

JEREMY BLACK, 'British Naval Power and International Commitments: Political and Strategic Problems, 1688–1770', in Michael Duffy, ed., *Parameters of British Naval Power, 1650–1850* (Exeter, 1992), pp. 39–59.

—— 'Naval Power and British Foreign Policy in the Age of Pitt the Elder', in Jeremy Black and Philip Woodfine, eds., *The British Navy and the Use of Naval Power in the Eighteenth Century* (Leicester, 1988), pp. 91–107.

JULIAN S. CORBETT, *Some Principles of Maritime Strategy* (London, 1911).

MICHAEL DUFFY, 'The Establishment of the Western Squadron as the Linchpin of British Naval Strategy', in Duffy, ed., *Parameters of British Naval Power, 1650–1850* (Exeter, 1992) pp. 66–81.

AZAR GAT, *The Development of Military Thought: The Nineteenth Century* (Oxford, 1992).

JAMES GOLDRICK and JOHN B. HATTENDORF, eds., *Mahan is not Enough: The Proceedings of a Conference on the Works of Sir Julian Corbett and Admiral Sir Herbert Richmond* (Newport, RI, 1993).

ERIC GROVE, 'La Pensée naval britannique depuis Colomb', in Hervé Coutau-Bégarie, ed., *L'Évolution de la pensée navale*, 5 vols. (Paris, 1990–95), II, pp. 115–33

BARRY D. HUNT, 'The Strategic Thought of Sir Julian S. Corbett', in John B. Hattendorf and Robert S. Jordan, eds., *Maritime Strategy and the Balance of Power: Britain and America in the Twentieth Century* (London, 1989), pp. 110–35.

J. R. JONES, 'Limitations of British Sea Power in the French Wars, 1689–1815', in Jeremy Black and Philip Woodfine, eds., *The British Navy and the Use of Naval Power in the Eighteenth Century* (Leicester, 1988), pp. 33–49.

RICHARD MIDDLETON, *The Bells of Victory: The Pitt–Newcastle Ministry and the Conduct of the Seven Years' War, 1757–1762* (Cambridge, 1985).

BRYAN RANFT, 'The Protection of British Seaborne Trade and the Development of Systematic Planning for War, 1860–1906', in Ranft, ed., *Technical Change and British Naval Policy, 1860–1939* (London, 1977), pp. 1–22.

N. A. M. RODGER, 'La Mobilisation navale au XVIIIème siècle', in Martine Acerra, Jean-Pierre Poussou, Michel Vergé-Franceschi, and André Zysberg, eds., *État, marine et société: Hommage à Jean Meyer* (Paris, 1995), pp. 365–74.

—— 'The Continental Commitment in the Eighteenth Century', in Lawrence Freedman, Paul Hayes, and Robert O'Neill, eds., *War, Strategy and International Politics: Essays in Honour of Sir Michael Howard* (Oxford, 1992), pp. 39–55.

A. N. RYAN, 'The Royal Navy and the Blockade of Brest, 1689–1805: Theory and Practice', in Martine Acerra, José Merino, and Jean Meyer, eds., *Les Marines de guerre européennes, XVII–XVIIIe siècles* (Paris, 1985).

DONALD M. SCHURMAN, *Julian S. Corbett, 1854–1922: Historian of British Maritime Policy from Drake to Jellicoe* (London, 1981).

—— *The Education of a Navy: The Development of British Naval Strategic Thought, 1867–1914* (London, 1965).

9

World-Wide War and British Expansion, 1793–1815

MICHAEL DUFFY

Britain's long wars against Revolutionary France and against Napoleon (1793–1802, 1803–14, 1815) resulted in the most complete triumph in the great age of European imperial warfare and left her as the predominant maritime and imperial power. This eventuality may have been hoped for in 1793, but the totality of its fulfilment was unexpected. Few of the new acquisitions in 1815 had been aimed at in 1793: indeed, many had belonged to powers which had been allied to Britain at the start of these wars. As these powers were pulled into the French orbit the British occupied their colonies to prevent their strategic use by France. The enlarged British Empire of 1815 was not the triumphant fulfilment of any detailed master-plan. Events in Europe became the main preoccupation, while Imperial strategic planning chiefly looked westward: initially to acquire an enlarged Empire in the Caribbean; thereafter to acquire an Empire of trade and trading bases on the American mainland, particularly in Latin America. Yet in the event by far the biggest expansion of Empire was not in the West but in the East, and these wars indeed mark the real, unplanned, and unintentional, 'swing to the East' of British Imperial development.

Britain embarked on the most successful Imperial wars in her history looking back rather than forward, and to considerations that were fundamentally defensive, financial, and naval rather than aggressively Imperial and territorial: the strategy was dominated by memory of the alarms and humiliations of the War of American Independence, in which the old Empire had come closer to annihilation and Britain closer to major invasion than ever before in the century. This traumatic experience left the British convinced that security ultimately depended on their ability to establish beyond future hazard financial and naval superiority over their rivals. That searing memory proved remarkably enduring: even in the climactic year of the Battle of Trafalgar a pamphleteer still felt the need to point out that 'if we want to make a comparison between the naval power of England and that of France and Spain, we must not compare it with the strength of their navies in the year 1780, when they bid us defiance at Plymouth, but take things actually as they are at this present time'.[1]

In fact, Britain's strategic problems had increased rather than receded in the decade following the end the American War. The naval arms race, in which Britain pushed her rivals to make peace by outbuilding them,[2] continued thereafter and extended to the arsenals of all the maritime states of Europe from the Baltic to the Black Sea. Between 1775 and 1790 the warship tonnage of the European powers increased by 46.4 per cent, reaching unprecedented levels which threatened to tie down and exhaust British financial and naval strength, jeopardizing alike her trade, Empire, and home defence in future wars (see Table 9.1).

In 1787–88 the Younger Pitt succeeded in winning back a predominant influence over the Dutch from France. This helped to alleviate the problem by bringing the Dutch navy on to the British side of the naval equation and increased the security of Britain's eastern Empire by removing the threat from the Dutch bases at the Cape, Ceylon, and Java. The first fruits of this new alliance were seen in Dutch naval support during the Nootka crisis with Spain in 1790. That crisis also highlighted the parlous state of the French navy and the disorder in the French colonies

TABLE 9.1. *The strengths of the European navies, 1775–1790* (tonnage of sailing vessels above 500 tons in 000 displacement tons)

	1775	1780	1785	1790
Britain	327.3	351.6	433.2	458.9
France	190.1	260.8	259.6	314.3
Spain	188.8	185.0	198.4	242.2
Russia (incl. Black Sea)	77.9	76.3	127.3	181.7
Netherlands	67.5	70.0	85.0	117.4
Denmark/Norway	80.9	83.7	84.4	86.0
Sweden	50.0	50.0	66.4	44.8
Portugal	39.3	35.7	33.7	40.6
Naples	4.4	3.0	7.6	21.2
Venice	17.4	17.6	20.4	20.6

Source: J. Glete, *Navies and Nations. Warships, Navies and State Building in Europe and America, 1500–1860*, 2 vols. (Stockholm, 1993), II, App. 2, pp. 553–695 (figures to 1790 adapted to a common 500 tons baseline with Table 9.3 below).

[1] William Playfair, *Causes of the Decline and Fall of Nations* (London, 1805), p. 9. The invasion scare was actually in 1779.

[2] See Daniel A. Baugh, 'Why did Britain Lose Command of the Sea During the War for America?', in Jeremy Black and Philip Woodfine, eds., *The British Navy and the Use of Naval Power in the Eighteenth Century* (Leicester, 1988), pp. 149–69.

engendered by the Revolution which prevented France from supporting its Spanish ally. British ministers preferred, however, to concentrate on building up Britain's long-term financial resources against any future struggle rather than going for quick conquests.[3] Only in India was advantage taken of the French plight when, in the Third Mysore War (1790–92), Governor-General Cornwallis exploited the withdrawal of the French garrison from Pondicherry to defeat the most Francophile of the independent Indian rulers, Tipu Sultan, and strip him of half of his territories, thus greatly reducing the biggest obstacle to British influence over southern India.

It was not the opportunity to strip the French empire that induced Pitt to go to war in 1793, though this was considered a likely advantage.[4] Rather, the British government responded to the French threat to overturn Pitt's triumph of 1787 and wrest back control over the Dutch, their navy, and their overseas bases. When the French would neither renounce their threats to the United Provinces nor evacuate the adjacent Austrian Netherlands, ministers took the firm stand that led to the French declaration of war on 1 February 1793. It was at this point that Pitt's war minister, the Home Secretary (from 1794 Secretary of State for War) Henry Dundas, sought a permanent eradication of the French naval menace that had wrecked the American War as he remembered only too well, having been a member of Lord North's government. Besides the government's European aim of ensuring its control over the Dutch by strengthening the Austrian Netherlands as a barrier to French aggression, Dundas now looked to destroy French naval power and France's long-term means of rebuilding it while proportionately expanding British power.[5] The opportunity was available, since the self-confident French Revolutionaries had managed to alienate their former ally Spain with its powerful navy and hence stood isolated in the struggle, while the revolutionary strife in the French colonies produced requests from dissident planters for British assistance.

The Imperial war strategy of Dundas and Pitt was primarily directed at the conquest of France's rich West Indian colonies, with secondary targets in France's trading posts in India and its Indian Ocean bases on the Île de France and Île de Bourbon (Mauritius and Réunion). Sir Charles Grey would sail with 17,000 men to the West Indies in the autumn of 1793, to conquer both Martinique and Saint-Domingue (the richest single colony in all the European empires) and be able to

---

[3] Grenville to Orde, 6 Oct., 16 Dec. 1790, 6 April 1791, C[olonial] O[ffice] 72/4; Historical Manuscripts Commission, *Manuscripts of J. B. Fortescue, Esq., Preserved at Dropmore*, II (London, 1894), pp. 176, 181.

[4] 3rd Earl of Malmesbury, ed., *Diaries and Correspondence of James Harris, First Earl of Malmesbury*, 4 vols. (London, 1844), II, pp. 501–02.

[5] Dundas to Richmond, 8 July 1793, B[ritish] L[ibrary], Bathurst Papers, Loan 57/107.

return to join in attacks on the French naval arsenals at Toulon and Brest in 1794. In the meantime, it was hoped that the fleet might strike a decisive blow against the French navy. Dundas told Sir Gilbert Elliot 'that after such a blow to the French naval power the capture of the West Indian islands will prevent their restoring it, and this he states as the principal object proposed by the war in favour of Great Britain in compensation for our charge in it'. Dundas asserted that 'if these great blows can be struck...this country...may probably long rest in quiet'.[6]

The strategy was enthusiastically endorsed by many in Britain, but at its heart was less the direct object of expanding the British Empire than of destroying French naval and commercial power. '[W]hether France or England has the Islands it must give a superiority of a fleet to the possessor', noted another minister, Lord Amherst.[7] French Saint-Domingue in particular had boomed dramatically in the 1780s (its foreign trade was bigger than that of the entire United States). France's Caribbean colonies were responsible for two-fifths of its total foreign trade, two-thirds of its ocean-going shipping tonnage, and a third of its registered seamen if dependent coastal trade was added. It was believed that the loss of its colonial trade would be a major blow to France's finances, and together with the loss of the trained seamen nurtured by that commerce would deprive France of the financial and skilled manpower resources to sustain a large navy. With a collateral increase in British commercial power through the new conquests, Britain would become dominant in both naval power and overseas trade for many years to come.[8]

For the first two years of the war the policy seemed on the point of success. The most exposed French overseas possessions were quickly overrun by adjacent British garrisons: the islands of St Pierre and Miquelon off Newfoundland (a threat to the British fisheries); the French bases in India (Pondicherry, Chander-nagore, Mahé, and their factories at Calicut, Surat, and Masulipatam); the former British Caribbean colony of Tobago. The limits achievable in this way were reached in June 1793 when an attempt on Martinique with internal royalist support failed: any further gains required expeditions from Britain. Here, however, Dundas found himself short of the means to implement his ambitious plans. The difficulties

---

[6] Journal entry, 8–9 Sept. 1793, reprinted in Paul Kelly, 'Strategy and Counter Revolution: The Journal of Sir Gilbert Elliot, 1–22 September 1793', *English Historical Review* (hereafter *EHR*), XCVIII (1983), p. 340 (p. 346 further sketches the anticipated British gains from the war, including a footing in Corsica to watch Toulon); 'Hints suggested by the perusal of Lord Mulgrave's letter', 27 Aug. 1793, H[ome] O[ffice] 50/455.

[7] Diary entry 10 Dec. 1793, Kent Record Office, Amherst Papers, U1350, 099/2.

[8] *The Times*, 8 Feb. 1793, 28 April, 19, 21 July 1794. See Michael Duffy, *Soldiers, Sugar and Seapower. The British Expeditions to the West Indies and the War Against Revolutionary France* (Oxford, 1987), chap. 1, for a full exposition of this theme.

of mobilizing both a sufficient army and navy at the start of a war forced the abandonment of the proposed expedition to seize Mauritius, while the needs of the European war where troops were required to prop up the Flanders front, help the insurgent Vendean royalists, and occupy the unexpectedly surrendered Toulon in late 1793 led to Grey's expedition departing for the Caribbean with only half of its intended force. Grey's small army was still sufficient to capture Martinique (March 1794), St Lucia (April), Guadeloupe (May), and Port-au-Prince, the capital and main commercial port of Saint-Domingue (June). In April 1794 Pitt could talk confidently to the Committee of West India Planters and Merchants of his intention 'at any price' to retain all the West India Islands after the war, and plans for their provisional administration were designed to ensure their smooth assimilation into the Imperial government (see Map 19.1).[9]

While France's long-term naval power was being undermined, powerful blows were also struck against its existing strength. The French naval challenge never fully recovered from the capture or destruction of thirty-two ships of the line (as against sixteen launched) in the first thirty months of the war.[10] Although Britain was unable to hold Toulon, resultant damage to ships and naval stores permanently weakened France's Mediterranean fleet, while Britain secured and held for three years a valuable strategic base on the adjacent French island of Corsica.

However, by mid-1795 the Imperial war began to go seriously wrong as France found other means to put the British Empire in mortal danger. Despite complaints by anti-revolutionaries like Burke, by Britain's allies, and by subsequent historians, the needs of the European war had a greater effect in taking British troops from the Imperial war than vice-versa. Grey had insufficient men to complete his conquest of the French islands, and his overstretched and exhausted troops rapidly fell victim to disease. The failure to send reinforcements because of the deteriorating continental campaign saw the offensive wither away with the interior of Saint-Domingue and the northern ports of Cape François and Port de Paix still in enemy hands. Grey was unable to stop a small French expedition from recovering Guadeloupe (June–December 1794). With their ability to succour their colonies by traditional means now limited, the French resorted to revolutionary means instead. They emancipated and armed their slaves and exploited discontented Francophone and native inhabitants on the British islands to encourage revolt in

[9] David Geggus, 'The British Government and the Saint-Domingue Slave Revolt, 1791–1793', EHR, XCVI (1981), p. 304; Hawkesbury to Grey 23 May, to Williamson 9 Sept. 1794, BL Add MSS 38310, ff. 108 and 114–15.

[10] Martine Acerra and Jean Meyer, Marines et révolution (Rennes, 1988), pp. 152–184; Jonathan R. Dull, 'Why Did the French Revolutionary Navy Fail?', Proceedings of the Consortium on Revolutionary Europe (1989), II, pp. 121–37.

Grenada and St Vincent in March 1795. With British defences stretched to the limit, the French recovered St Lucia in June, and although a landing to raise revolt in Dominica failed, their counter-offensive achieved an unexpected bonus in August when a British show of force designed to intimidate the free, half-African, half-Carib Maroon population of Jamaica into quietude misfired and the largest Maroon community at Trelawny Town rose in revolt. The summer of 1795 saw the very real danger of Britain's Caribbean colonies, her principal overseas capital investment,[11] following the example of their North American neighbours in successful, French-assisted revolt against British rule. The attempt to seize all the French Caribbean colonies had rebounded into the threatened loss of those of Britain.

The second way that the French sought to overcome their disadvantages in the maritime and imperial war was to coerce other continental naval powers into adding their fleets and colonial bases to the French war effort. This danger first materialized when the French overran the United Provinces in January 1795, following the collapse of the Flanders front, and captured the ice-bound Dutch fleet. The very danger that the war had been intended to prevent, French dominance over the Dutch, thus became reality. Dundas was forced to react quickly and forces were hastily scraped together and diverted to take into British 'protection' the strategic Dutch bases now menacing India and Britain's Far Eastern trade. Three thousand men were sent to the Cape of Good Hope, which surrendered in September 1795 (a Dutch relief expedition was surrounded and forced to surrender at Saldanha Bay in the following August); two expeditions from Madras took the key strategic bases of Trincomalee in Ceylon and Malacca in the Straits of Sumatra in August 1795. The last Dutch stronghold in Ceylon, Colombo, finally fell in February 1796. However, as one menace was contained, so another erupted, when French pressure induced the entry of Spain into the war on France's side in October 1796, forcing the overstretched Royal Navy to evacuate Corsica and withdraw from the Mediterranean.

The third French threat to the British Empire was through encouraging rebellion in Ireland. The first French agent reached Dublin in May 1793, a second in April 1794. The disorganized state of Irish disaffection and suspicion of French Revolutionary irreligion and confiscation of property, however, meant that not until early 1796 was there a determined Irish approach for French assistance. Only bad weather prevented a French expedition landing in Bantry Bay in December 1796, but the effort temporarily shattered the French fleet, while defeats to the

---

[11] A 1789 Privy Council estimate put British West Indian investment at £37 millions; the West Indian planter and historian Bryan Edwards in 1790 claimed £70 millions compared with £18 millions in the East India trade, Duffy, *Soldiers, Sugar and Seapower*, p. 17.

Spanish fleet in February and the Dutch in October 1797 further postponed aid to Irish rebels.[12]

These delays enabled Pitt and Dundas to mount a massive effort to settle the Caribbean crisis. In the autumn of 1795 the biggest single British overseas expedition yet attempted—27,000 men—assembled at Portsmouth and Cork. British financial and commercial investment in the Caribbean was such that in both the War of American Independence and in this war it was recognized that the loss of the West Indian colonies, particularly Britain's richest single colony Jamaica, would precipitate a financial collapse that would destroy British ability to continue fighting. Dundas, who only a year before had told the Prime Minister that 'all wars are a contention of purse', was particularly sensitive to this danger.[13] Half of the line infantry regiments of the British army would be sent to suppress the revolts and conquer all the remaining French possessions in a single season, thus eliminating possible recurrence of the danger and counterbalancing French successes in Europe. However, the immense logistical problems such an expedition created (it required 100,000 tons of shipping—about one-eighth of all British oceanic tonnage—to transport it) delayed its departure, and an extremely stormy autumn drove it back twice. Eventually ministers managed to despatch 35,000 men to the Caribbean between August 1795 and May 1796. The Trelawny Maroons were induced to surrender in Jamaica (December–January), the Dutch South American colonies of Demerara, Essequibo, and Berbice were occupied (April), St Lucia recaptured (May), and the revolts in Grenada and St Vincent suppressed (June 1796). Unfortunately, the bulk of the expedition arrived too late to evict the French from Guadeloupe or their remaining strongholds in Saint-Domingue, and when it was consequently forced to remain in garrison it was slaughtered by yellow fever and malaria in the ensuing summer 'sickly season'. Britain's financial ability to continue the war was secured, but at the heavy cost of 14,000 troops who died in the Caribbean in the course of 1796.[14]

After all the bright hopes of 1793–94, the collapse of the war in Europe, where one by one Britain's allies made peace between 1795 and 1797, and the new naval and revolutionary threats forced Dundas to reappraise his expectations of the maritime and Imperial war. It now had a twofold purpose: first, to ensure that Britain would have the resources to continue fighting for as long as was necessary,

---

[12] Marianne Elliot, *Partners in Revolution. The United Irishmen and France* (New Haven, 1982); Michael Duffy, 'War, Revolution and the Crisis of the British Empire', in Mark Philp, ed., *The French Revolution and British Popular Politics* (Cambridge, 1991), pp. 118–45.

[13] Dundas to Pitt, 9 July 1794, PRO 30/8/157 f. 176; Julian S. Corbett and Herbert W. Richmond, eds., *The Private Papers of George, 2nd Earl Spencer, 1794–1801*, 4 vols. (London, 1913-24), I, p. 318; Sir John Fortescue, ed., *The Correspondence of King George the Third*, 6 vols. (London, 1927–28), IV, p. 483.

[14] Duffy, *Soldiers, Sugar and Seapower*, pp. 159–257.

and secondly to strengthen Britain's bargaining position at the conference table. In 1799 Dundas declared it his rooted and unalterable opinion that

Great Britain can at no time propose to maintain an extensive and complicated war but by destroying the colonial resources of our enemies and adding proportionately to our own commercial resources, which are, and must ever be, the sole basis of our maritime strength. By our commerce and our fleet, we have been enabled to perform those prodigies of exertion which have placed us in the proud state of pre-eminence we now hold.[15]

In practice this became the fall-back defensive strategy for successive British governments in these wars. Repeatedly they sought to encourage the great military powers of central and eastern Europe to take up arms to drive France back into its old frontiers and if possible overturn the Revolution and Napoleon. Repeatedly this offensive European strategy collapsed through French battlefield supremacy: a second coalition in 1799 saw the retirement of Russia (1800) and Austria (1801); a third coalition in 1805 saw the defeat of Austria (1805), Prussia (1806), and Russia (1807); Austria tried and failed again in 1809, and Russia did not come forward again until 1812. Apart from a temporary peace of exhaustion in 1802–03, Britain kept fighting, turning to her defensive strategy when offensive opportunities failed. As a necessarily long-term mode, however, this set limits to expensive offensive operations overseas. It was necessary to conserve resources for survival and to build up reserves to support any renewed efforts of the European powers. The need to economize marked the end of the era of large and exhausting overseas expeditions (the transport costs of the massive 1795–96 Caribbean expedition alone came to over £1 million). It signified the end of Dundas's great Caribbean offensive, which was fast draining the small British army of its available manpower, and where the costs of large expeditions no longer seemed commensurate with the returns likely to accrue from them. Dundas made one last effort with a 4,500-strong expedition against the more weakly held Spanish Caribbean islands in 1796–97. This achieved quick success in the capture of Trinidad in February 1797, but in May the assault force was repulsed at Puerto Rico, and it became clear that major targets would only be gained by bigger expeditions than ministers could afford to deploy in this disease-ridden theatre. When Dundas floated a proposal for a 20,000 strong expedition against Cuba in August 1800 he met with a cold reception from his colleagues and the King.

Instead, a new strategy was devised for the Caribbean. British commitments were cut back to what was manageable with more limited resources. In 1798 a non-aggression pact was concluded with Toussaint l'Ouverture, black leader of the

[15] Edward Ingram, ed., *Two Views of British India* (Bath, 1970), p. 206. See also Dundas's defence of his war policy in March 1801 in William Cobbett, *The Parliamentary History of England . . . from 1066 to the Year 1803*, 36 vols. (London, 1806–20), XXXV, cols. 1072–73.

ex-slave French army in Saint-Domingue, in return for British withdrawal from that colony. Thenceforth major reinforcements would only be sent if a French attack threatened: in 1805 5,000 men were assembled at Cork in case successive raids by the French Rochefort and Toulon squadrons developed into something more serious. Otherwise, any further acquisitions would be windfall gains won and defended by local garrisons from their existing strength or with minor reinforcement. Dutch Surinam (1799) and Curaçao (1800), French St Martin's (1801), and Swedish St Bartholomew and Danish St Thomas and St Croix (during the British effort to break the Baltic Armed Neutrality in 1801) were occupied in this way during the French Revolutionary War, and so, when war was renewed in 1803, were French Tobago and St Lucia and the Dutch Guiana colonies of Demerara, Essequibo, and Berbice (1803), Surinam (1804), Curaçao and the Danish islands (1807), and French Cayenne (1809). Not until 1809 were major forces brought in from other American garrisons in Nova Scotia and Bermuda to help reconquer Martinique, on the understanding that they were not to be exposed to high casualties and would be sent back before the start of the sickly season. This was repeated with Guadeloupe in 1810. A final significant innovation was to form regular black West Indian regiments, originally by buying slaves, though they were collectively emancipated in 1807. The 8,000 men so recruited composed one-third of the Caribbean garrison strength, the idea was to avoid the high casualties among European troops by using others more suited to the climate.[16]

British Caribbean strategy thus turned from major offensives to consolidation and *ad hoc* accumulation. It was enough to provide Britain with a solid commercial base from which to continue the wars. Free from the competition of devastated Saint-Domingue, the British colonies witnessed a boom in production supplemented by Caribbean conquests and by the Dutch Guiana colonies in particular, which reportedly attracted £18 millions of British investment during their occupation between 1796 and 1802 and which by 1805, following their recapture in 1803, were producing more cotton for the British textile mills than all the British West Indies combined.

The needs of a long-term war of attrition, however, required ever larger supplies and markets to counteract the ever expanding French power in Europe, and it was generally believed that where this might most advantageously be secured without the human and financial cost of Caribbean warfare was in mainland Latin America. Britain had long been looking to break into the Spanish American market, the commercial potential of which was believed to be immense and which was the main world source for bullion, urgently needed for hard specie to finance the

---

[16] Duffy, *Soldiers, Sugar and Seapower*, pp. 362–67; Roger N. Buckley, *Slaves in Red Coats; The British West India Regiments, 1795–1815* (New Haven, 1979).

British war effort. The creole population was known to be disaffected towards Spanish imperial government. The British Caribbean islands and captured Spanish Trinidad provided the necessary advanced bases for an assault on the adjacent mainland, while the occupation of the Dutch Cape of Good Hope in 1795 and again in 1806 provided a similar base for an assault on the southern part of the continent. Between 1797 and 1808 plans were repeatedly considered for taking control of strategic points of the Spanish American empire.[17]

In 1796 Dundas planned an expedition from the Cape to La Plata and Chile; in 1800 he urged expeditions to Buenos Aires and New Orleans. In 1801 the new Addington ministry planned a landing in Venezuela, and in 1804 when Spain re-entered the war Dundas considered a similar project. In 1806, on the independent initiative of the naval commander at the Cape, Sir Home Popham, an attack was finally launched which captured Buenos Aires, and which was expanded into a major operation against La Plata and Chile when the European war collapsed. Plans were also renewed for operations against Venezuela and Mexico, the latter supported by an expedition from India against its Pacific coast, and these schemes were revived again by the Portland ministry when Napoleon took over Spain in 1808.

How far did such designs amount to a project to establish a new British continental Empire in the Americas at Spanish expense? At the very least, conquests could become bargaining counters to trade at a peace conference in return for opening the continent to British commerce. The main military object of the expeditions was to occupy strategic points from which to establish commerce with Spanish America—Trinidad, Buenos Aires, New Orleans—and it seems to have been intended to retain some of these if possible: in this way British influence could be established without requiring the burdens of direct rule over the whole continent. There was always a dichotomy, however, between what was achievable by British conquest or by encouraging liberation movements within Spanish America. Given the small British forces available, it was tempting to play the French game of stirring revolt. Ever since the Nootka crisis with Spain in 1790, the Venezuelan Francisco Miranda had been urging British support for his plans to liberate his homeland. At this, however, ministers hesitated. Once begun there was no certainty where revolt would go, and no commercial benefit was worth precipitating a French-style democratic revolution. On the other hand, Dundas's fear that the United States would try to break into this market without concern for the revolutionary consequences led him to contemplate intervention 'to direct and

[17] John Lynch, 'British Policy and Spanish America, 1783–1808', *Journal of Latin American History,* I (1969), pp. 1–30; William W. Kaufmann, *British Policy and the Independence of Latin America, 1804–1828* (New Haven, 1951), chaps. 1–3.

regulate the transition of South America from under the yoke of Spain into some other form of regular and legitimate government'.[18]

The fact that there was so little practical achievement from so many Latin American projects shows how far Imperial ambitions were actually subordinated to European considerations in these wars. Dundas's 1796 projects were speedily shelved in view of crisis in Europe and peace discussions. Those in 1800 and 1801 were subordinated to European needs and peace negotiations, as well as to the urgent need to get the French out of Egypt. In 1804–05 Pitt deferred his Spanish American projects so as not to offend the Russians, with whom he hoped to ally and who were alarmed about growing British Imperial and commercial ascendancy as well as hoping to induce Spain to forsake the French connection. When the troops landed by Popham were overwhelmed by a rising in Buenos Aires in August 1806, over 11,000 men were deployed in La Plata in the second biggest expedition sent overseas between 1796 and 1814. Montevideo was captured in February 1807, but the attempt to regain Buenos Aires ended in catastrophic defeat, with the death or capture of half the attacking force (5 July 1807). Its commander, General John Whitlocke, extricated the survivors by agreeing to evacuate the entire region. The disaster showed the impossibility of the conquest mode and convinced all that only co-operation with liberation movements would achieve results.[19] That too, however, had to be set aside when Napoleon's take-over of Spain led to revolt in 1808. With an opportunity to revive the war in Europe, Sir Arthur Wellesley's intended Central American expedition was diverted to the Peninsula, and ministers sought to avoid upsetting their new Spanish ally. When revolt developed in Spanish America in 1810, ministers tried to keep rebel emissaries at arms length, but their efforts to bring about a compromise peace (including trade concessions) and to induce Spain to concentrate on the war in the Peninsula alienated the Spanish, who saw British merchants already exploiting the commercial opportunities of the rebellion.[20] Already the evacuation of the Portuguese royal family under British 'protection' to Brazil in 1807 had resulted in the opening up of Brazilian trade and provided an indirect trade route into the La Plata area. The loosened Spanish hold over their American colonies now provided the trade that British manufacturers and merchants wanted without military occupation.

[18] Ingram, ed., *Two Views of British India*, pp. 188–89; Marquess of Londonderry, ed., *Correspondence, Despatches and Other Papers of Viscount Castlereagh*, 12 vols. (London, 1848–53), VII, pp. 284–85.

[19] Confirming Castlereagh's conclusions, 'Memorandum for the Cabinet, 1 May 1807', *Correspondence of Castlereagh*, VII, pp. 314–24.

[20] Charles Esdaile, 'Contradictions in the Implementation of British Grand Strategy, 1808–1814', *Consortium on Revolutionary Europe* (1989), pp. 544–49; C. K. Webster, ed., *Britain and the Independence of Latin America, 1812–1830*, 2 vols. (Oxford, 1938), II, pp. 309–16.

There still remained the aim of opening up trade with the North American continent. The revival of Dundas's 1800 proposal to seize New Orleans was thwarted by its cession to France and subsequent sale to the United States in 1803. However, in 1812 the Americans declared war on Britain after finally losing patience with British regulation of neutral shipping and continued British assistance to Indians within the United States. When the initial American attempts to conquer Canada were repulsed and the fall of Napoleon released troops for deployment in North America, this war opened new opportunities for containing American expansion and gaining control of trade outlets. Plans were made to rectify the Canadian border and to take New Orleans. A 6,000-strong expedition was assembled for its capture whose commander was instructed that, depending on the course of the war, New Orleans might be returned to improve peace terms or retained as the price of peace. The prospect was, however, fleeting. A raiding force that captured and burned Washington was repulsed from Baltimore, while an invasion of New York was defeated at Plattsburg (11 September 1814). Together with problems over the European settlement, these setbacks hastened a compromise peace re-establishing the territorial *status quo* (the Treaty of Ghent, 24 December 1814), though news of it did not arrive before the British assault on New Orleans was crushingly repulsed and its commander killed on 8 January 1815.[21]

Ultimately, Britain did emerge from the Imperial war in the Americas with more territory. In the Caribbean, Tobago, lost in 1783 and returned to France in 1802, was finally retained, and Britain kept St Lucia to watch the French base at Martinique. Britain's principal gains, however, were on the northern coast of South America and in fact from its allies at the start of these wars: Trinidad, as an entrepôt to Spanish America, and the commercial colonies of former Dutch, now British, Guiana. Other continental hopes were set aside. In so far as Britain began these wars with a vision of creating a new Empire, it had looked to do so in the Americas, and it was to that end that most Imperial war planning was directed. Bloody defeats on Saint-Domingue in 1798, at Buenos Aires in 1807, and at New Orleans in 1815 wrecked such dreams, though the collapsing state of the Spanish and Portuguese empires opened prospects for an informal empire of trade that had not existed before. The reason for the relative lack of success in the Americas was clear: Britain's small army, debilitated further by disease and European distractions, was unable to inflict decisive demoralizing defeat on larger hostile local populations.

Instead of a new territorial Empire in the West, Britain unexpectedly ended the wars with a new Empire in the East. A turning-point for the British Empire occurred around 1798 when three events led the course of Empire in new directions.

---

[21] David R. Hickey, *The War of 1812* (Urbana, Ill., 1989), esp. pp. 204–13, 294–96.

First, the long-feared Irish rebellion broke out. A variety of factors limited internal support and the Royal Navy efficiently shut off major French help, so that the rebellion was quickly suppressed, but it gave Pitt the chance to press his aim of a more consolidated home *imperium* by effecting the Union of Great Britain and Ireland on 1 January 1801. Secondly, the British withdrawal from Saint-Domingue terminated the attempt to establish a major new Empire in the West Indies. And thirdly, two ambitious men arrived in the East in 1798: Napoleon invaded Egypt, and Richard Wellesley reached India as the new British Governor-General.

Dundas feared that Bonaparte's Egyptian expedition was ultimately destined for India. In fact the French were pursuing Levantine interests and had developed no immediate plans to go further,[22] but the move touched British nerves. Dundas at once took steps to bolt the door to India by sending a naval squadron to the Red Sea and 5,000 reinforcements to India. He desperately sought to have the French evicted from Egypt before peace came under discussion—eventually persuading a reluctant Cabinet and King to send there the biggest expedition after 1796, 15,000 men from the Mediterranean and 6,000 from India via the Red Sea, who expelled the French in 1801.[23] Fear that France would gain control of the Levant route to India also produced far greater involvement with Turkey. Co-operation from 1798 to 1801 was followed by conflict in 1807 when the Turks seemed to have succumbed to French influence. A squadron under Admiral Duckworth was sent to threaten Constantinople in an attempt to force the Turks into renouncing their pro-French stance, and 6,000 men occupied Alexandria to prevent a new French invasion of Egypt. When the Turks armed the Dardanelles, however, Duckworth was forced into a hasty withdrawal, while the Alexandria garrison was eventually evacuated after being hemmed in when two successive forays were slaughtered. Their humiliating failure showed the limits to the power Britain could exert if the Levant was hostile.[24]

Hence, one major consequence of the Egyptian expedition was the development of a new British Imperial policy for the Mediterranean. Hitherto ministers had focused attention on the need for a new western Mediterranean base to replace Minorca (lost in 1782) for preventing any westward naval excursions from Toulon or Cartagena. Corsica proved an unstable, troublesome substitute after it offered itself for annexation, and few regretted its evacuation in 1796.[25] When the Royal

---

[22] Siba P. Sen, *The French in India, 1763–1816* (New Delhi, 1971), pp. 555–59.

[23] See Piers Mackesy, *British Victory in Egypt 1801: The End of Napoleon's Conquest* (London, 1995); Edward Ingram, 'The Geopolitics of the British Expedition to Egypt' (four parts), *Middle Eastern Studies*, vols. XXX–XXXI (1994, 1995).

[24] Piers Mackesy, *The War in the Mediterranean, 1803–10* (London, 1957), pp. 154–99.

[25] Elliot's journal, 20 Sept. 1793, *EHR*, XCVIII (1983), p. 346; Elisa A. Carrillo, 'The Corsican Kingdom of George III', *Journal of Modern History*, XXXIV (1962), pp. 254–74; Desmond Gregory, *The Ungovern-*

Navy returned to the Mediterranean in 1798 it captured and held Minorca until 1802. The French conquest of Malta *en route* for Egypt however, pointed to the need for a base in the eastern Mediterranean. Pitt's government had contemplated negotiating for the acquisition of Malta from the Knights of St John in 1793, and its capture from French occupation in 1800 led to its retention, illegally in 1802–03 on the pretext of French non-performance of the peace treaty.[26] Malta was soon found useful as a support-base for operations in southern Italy and a smuggling-base to evade Napoleon's Continental System in southern Europe. However, the French occupation of the Italian peninsula in 1806 then necessitated British occupation of Sicily (which fed Malta) from 1806 to 1814. Moreover, as the French extended their dominion to the Adriatic, controlling Venice, Dalmatia, and occupying Corfu (1807), Malta was insufficient to guard the way east. This led to British occupation of the Ionian Islands and to the capture and retention of Corfu at the end of the war. The peace settlement left Britain with an island empire of bases in the central Mediterranean.[27]

The events of 1798 had more momentous repercussions for India itself (see Map 23.1). The new Governor-General, Wellesley, arrived with strong personal motives to relaunch a flagging political career, but whether he brought any deliberate plan of Imperial expansion is debatable.[28] It has been suggested that the alarms he raised of French intrigue or invasion stimulating Indian revolt were simply a pretext for a nakedly expansionist policy,[29] but recent events in the Caribbean and Ireland had shown the frightening reality of such dangers and he looked to eliminate them while he still had the opportunity. His initial objects were fundamentally defensive: to eradicate French influence before any French military expedition arrived to encourage rebellion against British power. His solution, planned at the Cape on the way out, was to expel the foreign mercenaries (who included many Frenchmen) employed by the Indian princes to officer European-style corps in their armies, disband those corps, and replace them with East India Company sepoys subsidized by the princes. In return for the Company providing disciplined troops and guaranteeing their possessions, the princes would pay for

able Rock. *A History of the Anglo-Corsican Kingdom and its Role in British Mediterranean Strategy During the Revolutionary War (1793–1797)* (London, 1995).

[26] Elliot's journal, 20 Sept. 1793, *EHR*, XCVIII (1983), p. 346; Edward Ingram, 'The British Annexation of Malta, 1800–1807', *Consortium on Revolutionary Europe* (1989), pp. 923–30; Desmond Gregory, *Malta, Britain and the European Powers, 1793–1815* (London, 1996).

[27] Mackesy, *War in the Mediterranean*, pp. 7–17, 105–13, 351–58.

[28] For recent debate on this issue see Edward Ingram, *Commitment to Empire; Prophecies of the Great Game in Asia, 1797–1800* (Oxford, 1981), pp. 117–24; Iris Butler, *The Eldest Brother. The Marquess Wellesley* (London, 1973), pp. 79–81, 117.

[29] Notably by Edward Ingram, 'The Defence of British India. I: The Invasion Scare of 1798', *Journal of Indian History*, XLVIII (1970), pp. 581–82.

the troops, have no relations with foreign powers without British consent, and allow British intervention in their governments if they failed to maintain payment. Wellesley soon came to the view that the economical policy operated by the East India Company of maintaining its influence by means of a balance of power among the independent princes of India was too precarious and should be replaced by a policy of British predominance at whatever cost.[30]

On his arrival Wellesley quickly succeeded in pressurizing the Nizam of Hyderabad to replace his notoriously republican French officers and their corps with Company troops. His most crucial early move, however, was a pre-emptive strike against Tipu Sultan. The ruler of Mysore was as much a victim of the French as of the British: deceived by French adventurers into secretly applying for assistance to Mauritius where there was none to give, and betrayed when a public proclamation by the French governor revealed his overture.[31] The news of Tipu's embassy, followed soon after by that of Bonaparte's arrival in Egypt, provided a powerful lever to persuade Dundas and the reluctant East India Company into sanctioning an extension of British rule to remove the danger of a revival of French influence. A whirlwind campaign in early 1799 took the British forces and their allies to his fortress capital of Seringapatam, where Tipu was killed in the breach and his *imperium* dissolved. The former Hindu ruler was restored in return for a subsidiary alliance, while the Company was given sovereignty of the Malabar coast of south-western India, depriving the French of a possible future landing point. Extensions of the subsidiary policy followed rapidly under the pretext of the continuing French threat. The original Hyderabad treaty was re-negotiated to include the cession of territory to pay the cost of maintaining the troops, while the rulers of Tanjore and Arcot were persuaded into treaties which turned the Carnatic into British-run protectorates.

In northern India an alternative French ally, Zeman Shah of Afghanistan, was paraded as the apparent danger to be guarded against in the hope of bringing the adjacent Maratha confederacy into the subsidiary system and extending it in Oudh. The ploy was successful with the Nawab-Wazir of Oudh, who disbanded his own army and took on a larger Company contingent paid for by cessions of frontier territory.[32] The Marathas, however, were the strongest independent native power in India and proved resistant to Wellesley's diplomatic guile. It was only a fortunate twist in the perennial internal strife within the Confederacy that gave

[30] Ingram, *Commitment to Empire*, chaps 4, 5, and 7.
[31] Sen, *French in India*, pp. 549–55.
[32] This was the culmination of a longer-term process: see P. J. Marshall, 'Economic and Political Expansion: The Case of Oudh', *Modern Asian Studies*, IX (1974), pp. 465–82.

Wellesley his chance to break their power. When its titular head, the Peshwa of Poona, was overthrown by one of his chieftains, he agreed to a subsidiary treaty placing himself under British protection.

The Marathas had Europeanized their armies, possessing an artillery vastly superior to that of British or Company forces, a well-disciplined infantry trained by European (mostly royalist French) officers, and a large cavalry skilled at irregular warfare. News of Anglo-French peace negotiations, however, determined Wellesley that he must force the issue before the French were restored to their posts in India and could combine with the opponents of the Peshwa's alliance.[33] He had advantages of his own: a larger British army, a larger, better-quality Company sepoy army, and far more cavalry than ever before in India; the magnificent herd of nearly 250,000 draught cattle captured from Tipu Sultan, which improved the mobility of his field forces; the immeasurably superior financial backing the Company received from Indian bankers to sustain its war effort.[34] Contacts had already been made which secured the defection of many of the Marathas' European officers at crucial points in the ensuing war, thus demoralizing their troops and depriving them of leadership. The continued divisions within Maratha ranks meant that their most powerful chieftain was supported by only one other when he took up arms against the British in 1803, a third coming forward in 1804 only after these had been defeated. Even so, the victories won by Wellesley's brother Arthur (the future Duke of Wellington) at Assaye and Argaum, and Gerard Lake's more significant victories at Delhi and Laswari, were the hardest yet won in India.[35] Lake's capture of Delhi took the protectorate of the Mughal Emperor from the hands of the Marathas into those of the Company.

Two hard-fought campaigns in 1803-04 effectively destroyed much of the power and residuary cohesion of the Confederacy. Although Lake's quadruple repulse from the walls of Bharatpur in early 1805 deprived Wellesley of complete victory, the last major independent rivals to British power and influence in the subcontinent were largely subdued and brought within the subsidiary system. Coupled with the acquisition of coastal Ceylon, retained at the Peace of Amiens in 1802, Britain at last gained a political dominance over India secure from all European rivals. Ruthlessly pursued by Wellesley, British expansion in India had parallels with Napoleon's advance in Europe which did not escape some onlookers.

---

[33] Robert R. Pearce, ed., *Memoirs and Correspondence of the Most Noble Richard Marquess Wellesley*, 3 vols. (London, 1846), II, p. 313; A. S. Bennell, 'The Anglo-Maratha Confrontation of June and July 1803', *Journal of the Royal Asiatic Society* (1962), II, pp. 107-31.

[34] See below, pp. 517-18.

[35] John Pemble, 'Resources and Techniques in the Second Maratha War', *The Historical Journal*, XIX (1976), pp. 375-404; Randolf G. S. Cooper, 'Wellington and the Marathas in 1803', *International History Review*, XI (1989), pp. 31-38.

Admiral Sir Edward Pellew, arriving to command the East Indies squadron in 1805, confided to a friend that 'I fear we are aggrandising in this Country full as much as your friend Bony at home'.[36]

The East India Company's more secure position in India and the escalating size of its army provided opportunities to project British power beyond the Indian subcontinent and capture the remaining eastern bases of France and its allies. Wellesley's own wish was to use the Indian army in expeditions against Java or Mauritius, but these were postponed when Dundas asserted the priority of removing the French from Egypt, where the intended Mauritius expedition was despatched in 1800. Peace in 1802 did not remove Wellesley's concern to eliminate French influence; indeed, he still had not restored the former French trading bases when war was resumed a year later. But his forward policies more than doubled the size of the Company's debts and aroused mounting opposition at home. His expansive spendthrift course was finally halted by his recall in 1805. For some years the shattered state of the Company's finances brought a halt to the forward momentum given by Wellesley. However, the example of how to exploit British power in the East had been set for any future adventurous Governor-General.

The renewed European war began badly, and hopes of rapid victory collapsed with the defeat of the Third Coalition against Napoleon. Consequently the need to defend India as a major resource in a war of attrition saw Britain seeking to extend her influence throughout the southern and eastern world. The need to block the sea route to India revived interest in the Cape of Good Hope, despite the disillusioningly expensive experience of holding the barren colony which had led to its return to the Dutch in 1802. The break-out of the French Rochefort and Toulon squadrons in 1805 raised fears that they might be going to the East rather than the West Indies, and led to the reoccupation of the Cape by a 6,000 strong expedition in 1806.[37] This time the Cape was turned into one of the major strategic linchpins of the British Empire, housing a garrison large enough to act as a strategic reserve for the whole southern hemisphere, available for defensive or offensive use in theatres as far apart as India and South America. The need to prevent France gaining allies on the overland route to India led to the establishment of an Indian Board of Control Residency with the Governor of Baghdad from 1798, three Indian government missions to Persia in 1798, 1800, and 1808, and the creation of a full embassy at Tehran from 1807, besides missions to Sind and an abortive one to Afghanistan in 1808.[38] The danger of French, Dutch, or Spanish raids on the China

---

[36] C. Northcote Parkinson, *Edward Pellew, Viscount Exmouth* (London, 1934), p. 328.

[37] L. F. C. Turner, 'The Cape of Good Hope and the Anglo-French Conflict, 1797–1806', *Historical Studies Australia and New Zealand*, IX (1961), pp. 368–78.

[38] Edward Ingram, *In Defence of British India: Great Britain and the Middle East, 1775–1842* (London, 1984), chaps. 6, 8–11; G. J. Alder, 'Britain and the Defence of India—The Origins of the Problem

trade saw the Royal Navy from 1797 repeatedly escorting convoys to the Portuguese trading base at Macao, and the French invasion of Portugal in 1807 saw an attempt to take Macao under British protection (September–December 1808), aborted in the face of Chinese opposition.[39] It is likely that only the Spanish revolt against France in 1808 prevented the often proposed assault on Manila and the Philippines. Instead, two successful expeditions, one 2 thousand miles to the west, the other 2 thousand miles to the east of India showed the striking-range of the newly enhanced eastern British power, when a more expansive Governor-General, Lord Minto, despatched expeditions which captured Mauritius in 1810 and Java in 1811, eliminating all enemy bases in eastern waters.[40]

Why was this 'swing to the East' so successful? First, the sheer distance of India from Britain made it impossible to control or monitor an expansive Governor-General such as Wellesley. Secondly, there was the military force now available. The threat to India suggested by Napoleon's invasion of Egypt led to an increased British regular army establishment in India, from 10,700 in 1796 to over 26,000 in 1801 and, inclusive of the garrison of Ceylon, it remained above 20,000 thereafter.[41] The King's regiments formed the core of strike forces now greatly supplemented by the vast growth of the East India Company's sepoy army through the expansion of the subsidiary alliance system (Table 9.2). Wellesley used subsidiary alliances to extend British power further still by demanding territory rather than money, as formerly, to sustain the sepoy units.

This force was by far the biggest European-type army in the eastern world. Admittedly it had many weaknesses in its internal organization, particularly in its officer corps which produced a major mutiny of the Company's European soldiers at Masulipatam in 1809, while Madras army sepoys mutinied at Vellore in 1806 over the introduction of a European-style head-dress. Such weakness limited the use of the Indian army outside of India.[42] Nevertheless, the Bengal army in particular, recruited after 1765 from the traditional high warrior castes of eastern Oudh and Benares, now provided a formidable strike force.[43] The major

1798–1815', *Journal of Asian History*, VI (1972), pp. 14–44; M. E. Yapp, *Strategies of British India: Britain, Iran and Afghanistan, 1798–1850* (Oxford 1980), chaps. 1–2, 5.

[39] C. Northcote Parkinson, *War in the Eastern Seas, 1793–1815* (London, 1954), pp. 137, 315–33.

[40] Ibid., pp. 113–19, 375–417. Christopher D. Hall, *British Strategy in the Napoleonic Wars, 1803–15* (Manchester, 1992), pp. 145, 147.

[41] J. W. Fortescue, *A History of the British Army*, 13 vols. (London, 1899–1930), IV, pp. 719–20, 938–39; *Correspondence of Castlereagh*, VIII, pp. 110, 243.

[42] Edward Ingram, 'The Role of the Indian Army at the End of the Eighteenth Century', *Military History Journal*, II (1973), pp. 216–22; Douglas M. Peers, 'Between Mars and Mammon: The East India Company and Efforts to Reform its Army, 1796–1832', *Historical Journal*, XXXIII (1990), pp. 385–401; Fortescue, *History of the British Army*, VI, pp. 40–47; VII, pp. 578–96.

[43] C. A. Bayly, *The New Cambridge History of India*, II. 1, *Indian Society and the Making of the British Empire* (Cambridge, 1988), pp. 84–85.

TABLE 9.2. *The expansion of the East India Company army, 1793–1815*

	1793	1798	1805	1815
Bengal army				
European	5,440	7,389	7,811	12,617
Native	29,482	40,105	81,257	116,925
Madras army				
European	9,981	11,283	12,990*	13,903
Native	29,914	36,501	68,842*	57,741
Bombay army				
European	3,347	3,494	4,090	5,031
Native	10,265	14,541	17,575	23,906
Total				
European	18,768	22,166	24,891	31,611
Native	69,661	91,147	167,674	195,572
Grand total	88,429	113,313	192,565	227,183

Note: * includes detachments seconded from the Bombay army
Source: *Parliamentary Papers* (1831/32), Vol. XIII [p. 289]: Report from the Select
Committee on the Affairs of the East India Company, p. 195.

development in these wars was the use of Company sepoys for overseas expeditions which so much extended British military power in the eastern world. Hitherto their deployment outside India had been obstructed by the antipathy of high-caste sepoys to making long sea voyages, but Cornwallis made the breakthrough by the consummate care taken over sensitivities in persuading a battalion to volunteer to deal with a local alarm at a trading settlement at Bencoolen on Sumatra in 1789.[44] Thereafter they were employed alongside British units to seize the Moluccas (1795); in the Red Sea assault on Egypt (1800–1); at Macao as the intended garrison in 1808; and in 1810–11 for the massive expeditions to Mauritius (8,000) and to Java (12,000). The pattern was set for the use of Indian troops as one of the essential linchpins of British authority East of Suez for the next 130 years.

Thirdly, there was deployment of the Royal Navy on a scale never before seen over such a prolonged period and in areas never before attempted, so that it dominated the eastern seas. The seizure of the Dutch spice islands of Amboina and Banda (February–March 1796) on the initiative of the naval commander in the East Indies, Commodore Peter Rainier, established the first British footing inside the Indonesian archipelago since the seventeenth century.[45] The blockade of Java and of Mauritius provided information on seas from which British ships had

[44] Charles Ross, ed., *Correspondence of Charles, First Marquis Cornwallis*, 3 vols. (London 1859), I, p. 468.
[45] Parkinson, *War in the Eastern Seas*, pp. 91–95.

largely been excluded, and extended the viable theatre of operations. Even the annihilation of an entire frigate squadron at Grand Port in 1810 (the worst naval disaster of the whole war) failed to overturn the naval ascendancy which ensured the successful assault on Mauritius. Naval control was greatly assisted by the acquisition of Ceylon, which controlled movement between the two coasts of India, and by the capture of the Cape of Good Hope. Thereafter the capture of Mauritius and Java made control absolutely secure. All these bases, except Java, were retained at the peace in 1814–15, Java being returned to the Dutch who were regarded as a British satellite.[46] This enhanced naval presence and greatly expanded knowledge of the navigation of the eastern seas was a further essential basis of British power in the East for another 150 years.

What effect did these wars have on the British Empire? They accelerated the centralization of a ramshackle conglomerate of dependencies acquired at various times, in various ways, and variously administered. The Union of Britain and Ireland and the development of the Crown Colony government system were significant results of this war (the former the consequence of the Irish revolt, the latter initially devised for the government of Martinique in 1794 by Lord Hawkesbury to avoid giving alien colonies British-type legislatures which so disrupted internal relations and precipitated revolt in Grenada[47]). The wars precipitated a major increase in the participation of non-Europeans as the military manpower sustaining that Empire, which did induce some alteration in British attitudes to subject races. The growing Indian sepoy army became the major unifying body in India, the development and good conduct of the West India slave regiments were useful weapons in the armoury of the abolitionists in the overthrow of the slave trade in 1807, while their mass emancipation in 1807 was the first significant practical step towards wider emancipation in 1833.[48]

Above all, the wars between 1793 and 1815 constituted a great Imperial and naval Armageddon. The final British victory was so complete as to bring a decisive end to an era of 250 years of European maritime imperial rivalry. Dundas's desire to destroy the existing naval power of Britain's enemies while depriving them of the imperial trade by which they could rebuild it was largely fulfilled, not only with France but also with Spain, Holland, and lesser powers too. One by one the navies of Europe were smashed or confiscated in the course of the war. British victories over the French, Spanish, and Dutch; French destruction of smaller fleets (Venice,

---

[46] Nicholas Tarling, *Anglo-Dutch Rivalry in the Malay World, 1780–1824* (Cambridge, 1962), pp. 71–74.

[47] BL Add MSS 38351, f. 202.

[48] See Michael Duffy, 'The Impact of the French Revolution on British Attitudes to the West Indian Colonies', in David B. Gaspar and David P. Geggus, eds., *A Turbulent Time: The Greater Caribbean in the Age of the French and Haitian Revolutions* (Bloomington, Ind., 1997) pp. 88–89.

Naples) and British removal of others (Danish, Portuguese, a Russian squadron in Lisbon); plus the deterioration of existing fleets without the financial and material means to maintain or replace them, led to a situation in 1815 in which British naval strength had increased since 1790 by 32.8 per cent, whereas all others totalled 38.3 per cent *less* than in 1790 and the Royal Navy was virtually equal to all other navies combined (Table 9.3). For the foreseeable future the Royal Navy's ability simultaneously to defend both Britain and her Empire and also to dominate those of her rivals would not be called into question.

Much of this came about in an unplanned, pragmatic, and circumstantial way in the course of these wars: not within any clear overall scheme of extending Empire, but in which empire was the greatest beneficiary. Indeed, after the West Indian expeditions of 1795–97, the needs of war in Europe invariably took precedence over the war overseas with only the brief exception of the Talents Ministry in 1807. After 1796 the only significant British expeditions to sail overseas from European waters were to Egypt (1800–01), the Cape (1805–06), South America (1806–07), Egypt again in 1807, and to North America after the European war had ended in 1814 (the last three expeditions all failed). The large and successful expeditions against Guadeloupe and Martinique in 1808–09 and Mauritius and Java in 1810–11 were assembled from garrisons in neighbouring theatres. Indeed, the Imperial war was as much played out in Europe as overseas. Napoleon's plans to rebuild French power in India were postponed by the renewal of war in 1803; their revival in 1805 was overtaken by the formation of the Third Coalition; their reformulation in 1807–08 as a land and sea assault was overtaken by crisis in Spain; and they finally collapsed in 1812 with the retreat from Moscow. Just as the Elder

TABLE 9.3. *The strengths of the European navies and that of the United States, 1790–1815* (tonnage of sailing vessels above 500 tons in 000 displacement tons)

	1790	1795	1800	1805	1810	1815
Britain	458.9	511.5	545.5	571.5	673.1	609.3
France	314.3	284.4	203.6	182.2	194.3	228.3
Russia	181.7	181.7	191.9	131.9	134.1	167.3
Netherlands	117.4	76.4	40.1	43.5	40.0	71.4
Spain	242.2	264.0	226.6	138.7	100.3	59.9
Portugal	40.6	49.8	56.8	54.1	46.0	44.4
Sweden	44.8	38.9	39.8	36.7	36.7	36.5
United States	—	—	21.4	16.7	16.5	28.5
Naples	21.2	27.6	15.0	12.5	11.8	14.9
Denmark/Norway	86.0	83.6	76.5	63.2	4.2	7.8
Venice	20.6	20.9	—	—	—	—

Source: as for Table 9.1.

Pitt had claimed that America was won in Germany, so British ministers could now declare that the Empire was protected by the Peninsular War, which tied down so many French resources.[49]

By the end of 1811 every colonial possession of France and her dependants was in British hands—the most complete ascendancy ever achieved in 250 years of imperial warfare—and yet arguably the most significant capture for ensuring Britain's naval supremacy and the security of her Empire was achieved at the very end of the wars and it was in Europe. British ministers became increasingly alarmed by Napoleon's development of a major naval base and fleet at Antwerp. This threatened to overthrow Britain's well-proven strategy for home and Imperial defence of maintaining a large 'Western Squadron' off the main French naval base at Brest which fulfilled both purposes, economizing on naval resources and leaving sufficient ships to maintain squadrons throughout the Empire. The growth of the threat from Antwerp pulled major naval resources into the North Sea where they could not act as a simultaneous protection for the Empire, and absorbed ships which could not then be sent overseas (this was one of the reasons for the ministerial sanctioning of the attacks on the surviving major enemy colonial strongholds in 1808–11 so as to release the naval forces tied to watching them). So menacing did the Cabinet consider this development that in 1809, while Napoleon was occupied fighting the Austrians on the Danube, it launched a massive, 44,000-strong expedition to seize Antwerp, but this bogged down on the sickly island of Walcheren and had to be evacuated. In 1813–14 ministers were prepared if necessary to surrender most of Britain's colonial conquests to get Napoleon out of Antwerp. This was not, however, a barter which interested either Napoleon or the princes of Europe, who were anxious to preserve a sufficient French naval power to prevent British sovereignty of the seas. Fortunately for Britain, Napoleon refused to make the alternative continental sacrifices the European powers required for peace. They had to keep fighting, and Antwerp fell with Napoleon's overthrow.[50]

The final victory over Napoleon left Britain with the absolute maritime supremacy the continental powers had dreaded and the ability to dictate rather than barter for the colonial peace settlement. It has been argued that the later eighteenth century saw a switch in British preference towards an Empire of trade rather than dominion. That was not the object of Pitt and Dundas in 1793, nor was it the result in the peace settlement of 1814–15, in which Britain looked both to extend the

---

[49] Sen, *French in India*, pp. 561–86; Hall, *British Strategy in the Napoleonic War*, pp. 91–92.

[50] Richard Glover, 'The French Fleet, 1807–1814; Britain's Problem, and Madison's Opportunity', *Journal of Modern History*, XXXIX (1967), pp. 244–47; Harrowby to Bathurst, 16 Jan. 1814, BL Bathurst Papers, Loan 57/7, f. 731; Michael Duffy, 'British Diplomacy and the French Wars 1789–1815', in H. T. Dickinson, ed., *Britain and the French Revolution, 1789–1815* (London, 1989), pp. 137–44.

territorial Empire and to protect it by the control of strategic naval bases. The twenty-six British colonies of 1792 had grown to forty-three by 1816 (see Map 1.2).[51] Many of these were small strategic islands, but others were more substantial: Ceylon, the Cape, the Dutch mainland South American colonies (these last retained on the demand of British merchants and manufacturers for their cotton production, which was not outpaced by the United States until after the end of the War of 1812[52]). In addition there were the territorial gains in India, which are often overlooked since they were East India Company accessions and formed no part of the treaty. While allowing France back into its former trading posts, now disarmed, Britain retained the territorial gains of the Wellesley era. This enhanced Empire was defended by the new naval bases: St Lucia in the West Indies, the Cape of Good Hope, Trincomalee in Ceylon, Malta, and Corfu.

Meanwhile, as the British Empire expanded, those of its rivals disintegrated. Twenty-three years of British control of the seas prevented them sending sufficient reinforcements to sustain their authority. Britain could afford to return Martinique and Guadeloupe to give respectability to the restored Bourbons in France because the old core of the French empire, Saint-Domingue, was permanently lost to its former slaves. The Spanish colonies were in revolt, and the Dutch hold on the Indonesian islands so weakened as to make it reliant on British support. While the United States indeed remained a formidable extra-European rival, the independent power of Mysore and the Marathas in India had been destroyed. Britain was now in a position to impose an extra-European *Pax Britannica*. This was a position acquired by accident in that it was unplanned and accrued as a result of *ad hoc* war measures, but it was secured by the deliberate intent to procure British safety through the destruction of as much rival naval power as the Royal Navy, with the aid of the British and Indian armies, was able to achieve.

---

[51] J. Holland Rose 'The Struggle with Napoleon', J. Holland Rose and others, eds., *The Cambridge History of the British Empire*, 9 vols. (Cambridge, 1929–59), II, *The Growth of the New Empire, 1783–1870*. p. 128.

[52] Ralph Davis, *The Industrial Revolution and British Overseas Trade* (Leicester, 1977), pp. 112–17.

Select Bibliography

C. A. BAYLY, *Imperial Meridian, The British Empire and the World, 1780–1830* (London, 1989).

ROGER N. BUCKLEY, *Slaves in Red Coats, The British West India Regiments, 1795–1815* (New Haven, 1979).

IRIS BUTLER, *The Eldest Brother: The Marquess Wellesley* (London, 1973).

MICHAEL DUFFY, *Soldiers, Sugar and Seapower. The British Expeditions to the West Indies and the War against Revolutionary France* (Oxford, 1987).

—— 'War, Revolution and the Crisis of the British Empire', in Mark Philp, ed., *The French Revolution and British Popular Politics* (Cambridge, 1991), pp. 118–45.

CHRISTOPHER D. HALL, *British Strategy in the Napoleonic War, 1803–15* (Manchester, 1992).

DAVID R. HICKEY, *The War of 1812* (Urbana, Ill., 1989).

EDWARD INGRAM, ed., *Two Views of British India, The Private Correspondence of Mr Dundas and Lord Wellesley: 1798–1802* (Bath, 1970).

—— *Commitment to Empire: Prophecies of the Great Game in Asia, 1797–1800* (Oxford, 1981).

—— *In Defence of British India. Great Britain and the Middle East, 1775–1842* (London, 1984).

WILLIAM W. KAUFMANN, *British Policy and the Independence of Latin America, 1804–1828* (New Haven, 1951).

JOHN LYNCH, 'British Policy and Spanish America', 1783–1815', *Journal of Latin American History*, I (1969), pp. 1–30.

PIERS MACKESY, *The War in the Mediterranean, 1803–10* (London, 1957).

C. NORTHCOTE PARKINSON, *War in the Eastern Seas, 1793–1815* (London, 1954).

SIBA P. SEN, *The French in India, 1763–1816* (New Delhi, 1971).

NICHOLAS TARLING, *Anglo-Dutch Rivalry in the Malay World, 1780–1824* (Cambridge, 1962).

L. F. C. TURNER, 'The Cape of Good Hope and Anglo-French Conflict, 1797–1806', *Historical Studies Australia and New Zealand*, IX (1961), pp. 368–78.

M. E. YAPP, *Strategies of British India, Britain, Iran and Afghanistan, 1798–1850* (Oxford, 1980).

10

Empire and Identity from the Glorious Revolution to the American Revolution

JACK P. GREENE

How the development of a vast transoceanic empire during the early modern era affected the collective identity of the British people who dominated and defined that identity is the subject of this chapter. The earliest stages of English overseas expansion occurred during the Elizabethan and Jacobean eras, the very period when leaders of English opinion were elaborating an identity for the emerging English nation.[1] While Protestantism, social openness, intellectual and scientific achievement, and a prosperity based upon trade were all important components of that identity, liberty, under an English system of law and government, composed its principal foundation, and while, between the Elizabethan era and the American Revolution, the acquisition of colonies and other outposts would become increasingly significant in defining what it meant to be English or (after the union with Scotland in 1707) British, liberty was also the single most important element in defining a larger Imperial identity for Britain and the British Empire.

As used in this chapter, the concept of *national* or *Imperial identity* refers to the intellectual constructs by which leaders of opinion seek to identify the attributes that distinguish the people of one nation or empire from another. Invariably self-serving for the groups whose representatives articulate them, these constructs tend to be highly positive exercises in the assertion of national superiority; homogenizing; reinforcive of existing social, political, gender, ethnic, and racial hierarchies; insensitive to contradictions between them and the structure and operation of the political society they allegedly describe; and inattentive to alternative readings of the national peculiarity. Although this chapter gives some attention to some of those alternative readings, limitations of space dictate that it be principally an exercise in the recovery of the dominant discourse of English and British national and Imperial identity.

As early as the late fifteenth century, many contemporary observers, both English and foreign, agreed that the English people's unique system of law and

[1] See Liah Greenfeld, *Nationalism: Five Roads to Modernity* (Cambridge, Mass., 1992), pp. 27–87, and Richard Helgerson, *Forms of Nationhood: The Elizabethan Writing of England* (Chicago, 1992).

liberty was what principally distinguished them from all other people on the face of the globe. The proud boast of the English was that through a variety of conquests and upheavals they, unlike most other Europeans, had retained their identity as a free people by safeguarding their liberty through their laws. This boast found sophisticated expression in the English tradition of political discourse which emphasized the role of law as a restraint upon the Crown. By law, the articulators of this jurisprudential tradition meant not only statutory law as formulated by Parliament but, more particularly, the common law, that complex bundle of customs and judicial decisions which was the result of centuries of the working of the English legal system. Presumably embodying the collective wisdom of the ages, the common law, in their view, was the chief guarantor of the Englishman's celebrated right to security of life, liberty, and property through such devices as trial by jury, habeas corpus, due process of law, and representative government. Rooted in such older writings as Sir John Fortescue, *De Laudibus Legum Angliae* (written about 1470 and familiar to the English law community, though not published until 1616), this view was fully elaborated during the early seventeenth century in a series of works by several of the prominent judges and legal thinkers of the era, the most influential of whom was Chief Justice Sir Edward Coke.

Writing in an age when every other major European state, except for the Netherlands, was slipping into absolutism and when England's own Stuart kings were trying to extend the prerogatives of the Crown at the expense of Parliament, these early-seventeenth-century legal writers were anxious to erect legal and constitutional restraints against arbitrary extensions of royal power. Accordingly, they invented the tradition of an 'ancient' English constitution, antecedent to and finding expression through the common law, which could justify an expanded governmental role by Parliament, acting to protect the people against the Crown.[2] Though frequently ignored or violated since the Norman Conquest, this ancient constitution, Coke and his colleagues contended, provided the context for *legal* government in England. Composed of a variety of maxims, precedents, and principles which they traced back through Magna Carta to the ancient Saxon era, it at once served as the foundation for all governmental authority in England; confined the scope of Crown discretion, or 'will', within the limits of fundamental, natural law; and, in particular, prevented the Crown from governing without Parliament.

The early-modern jurisprudential tradition rested on a distinction, long since elaborated by Fortescue, between two kinds of monarchy, *regal* and *political*. Whereas in a regal monarchy like France, '*What pleased the prince*' had '*the force*

---

[2] J. G. A. Pocock, *The Ancient Constitution and the Feudal Law*, 2nd edn. (Cambridge, 1987).

of law', in a political monarchy like England, wrote Fortescue, 'the regal power' was 'restrained by political law'. Bound by their coronation oaths, English kings could neither 'change laws at their pleasure, make new ones, inflict punishments, and impose burdens on their subjects, also determine suits of parties at their own will and when they wish', nor keep standing armies 'without the assent of their 'subjects'. Rather, they were 'obliged to protect the law, the subjects, and their bodies and goods'. In a political monarchy, 'the will of the people' effectively became 'the source of life'; the law constituted the '"ligando" by which the community... sustained' itself; and the people who composed that community 'preserve[d] their rights through the law'.[3] The happy result of this system, according to Fortescue, was that English people, in contrast to their neighbours, were 'ruled by laws they themselves desire[d]' and were assured that 'the laws of England [would] favour liberty in every case'.[4]

For early-modern Englishmen, this unique system of law and liberty, arising from what the poet Samuel Daniel referred to in 1603 as 'the wonderful architecture of this state',[5] was the very essence of their national identity, what has been called 'the distinguishing characteristic of Englishness'. More than its Protestantism, which many other European polities shared, England's status, in John Milton's phrase, as 'the mansion house of liberty', whose people had been 'ever famous, and foremost in the achievements of liberty', had by the middle of the seventeenth century come to be identified as the core of 'England's peculiarity'.[6] English writers such as Henry Care, the popularizer of Whig theories, spelled out the conditions that rendered England a land of liberty. In most 'other Nations', including Turkey, France, and Spain, Care declared in 1682, 'the meer Will of the Prince is Law; his Word takes off any Man's Head, imposes Taxes, seizes any Man's Estate, when, how, and as often as he lists; and if one be accused, or but so much as suspected of any Crime, he may either presently execute him, or banish, or imprison him at pleasure'. Only in England were 'the Lives and Fortunes' of the people not subject to the 'Wills (or rather Lusts)' of 'Arbitrary' tyrants. The 'Constitution of our *English* Government' was 'the best in the World'.[7] The Glorious Revolution further underlined this equation of Englishness with liberty.

Throughout the eighteenth century, political polemicists engaged in a running debate over the vigour and security of British liberty. Panegyrists of the Whig regime insisted that liberty had never been 'so largely and so equally diffused

---

[3] Sir John Fortescue, *De Laudibus Legum Angliae*, ed. S. B. Chrimes (Cambridge, 1942), pp. 25, 27, 31, 33, 79, 81.

[4] Ibid., pp. 25, 87, 105, 115, 139.

[5] Samuel Daniel, *Defense of Rime* (1603), as quoted by Helgerson, *Nationhood*, pp. 36–37.

[6] Greenfeld, *Nationalism*, p. 77.

[7] Henry Care, *English Liberties*, 5th edn. (Boston, 1721), pp. 1–3.

amongst all Orders of men, in any Country as "tis here, and now".[8] A simple comparison of 'present times with the past', or 'our own condition with that of other countries', the novelist Henry Fielding declared in 1749, revealed that Britons' 'present happy condition' as a 'free people' was far superior: Britons now enjoyed 'our lives, our persons, and our properties in security', were the 'free masters of ourselves and our possessions, as far as the known laws of our country will admit', and were 'liable to no punishment, no confinement, no loss, but what those laws subject us to'.[9] Even those who emphasized the threat of contemporary political or social corruption to British liberty and were anxious about the health of the constitution tended to agree with the moralist John Brown that 'the Spirit of Liberty' had 'produced more full and compleat effects in our own Country, than in any known Nation that ever was upon Earth'.[10]

Notwithstanding the fact that critics of the Whig regime, beginning in the middle decades of the eighteenth century, increasingly pointed out the social limits of British liberty,[11] this libertarian interpretation of Britain's constitutional situation remained dominant. In terms reminiscent of Fortescue and Care, its exponents continued to assert that Britain exceeded all other countries in perfection of constitution and enjoyment of liberty and to ponder, with Fortescue, 'why this law of England, so worthy and so excellent', was 'not common to all the world'. Fortescue attributed 'this superiority' to the high fertility of England's soil, producing large crop yields which in turn fostered the extensive social independence, the spirit of intellectual inquiry, and the law-mindedness necessary to sustain a free government.[12] Eighteenth-century panegyrists expanded upon this theme, insisting that the conditions emphasized by Fortescue affected the personality and behaviour of all English people down even to the commonality, who, as Fielding wrote, 'by degrees, shook off their vassalage, and became more and more independent of their superiors' until, 'in the process of time', even 'servants ... acquired a state of freedom and independency, unknown to this rank in any other nation'.[13] By this process, in the words of the radical Whigs, John Trenchard and Thomas Gordon, 'all Men' in England became ambitious 'to live agreeably to their

---

[8] William Arnall, *Opposition no Proof of Patriotism* (London, 1735), p. 20, as quoted by Hugh Cunningham, 'The Language of Patriotism', in Raphael Samuel, ed., *Patriotism: The Making and Unmaking of British National Identity*, 3 vols. (London, 1989), I, p. 59.

[9] Henry Fielding, *A Charge Delivered to the Grand Jury* (London, 1749), in William Ernest Henley, ed., *The Complete Works of Henry Fielding, Esq.*, 16 vols. (London, 1903), XIII, pp. 209–10.

[10] John Brown, *An Estimate of the Manners and Principles of the Times* (London, 1758), p. 13.

[11] Kathleen Wilson, *The Sense of the People: Politics, Culture and Imperialism in England, 1715–1785* (Cambridge, 1995), pp. 137–236.

[12] Fortescue, *De Laudibus*, pp. 67, 69, 71, 73.

[13] Henry Fielding, *An Enquiry into the Causes of the Increase in Robbers* (London, 1751), in Henley, ed., *Complete Works of Fielding*, XIII, pp. 13–14.

own Humours and Discretion' as 'sole Lord and Arbiter of' their 'own private Actions and Property'. This passion for independence in turn encouraged Englishmen both to acquire property and to try to secure that property 'by the Laws of Liberty', which were made by 'Consent', and could not be repealed without consent.[14] Whereas in other countries liberty had sometimes and imperfectly 'been ingrafted by the Acts of Policy', observed Brown, in England it thus seemed to have been 'laid in Nature', shooting up 'from its natural Climate, Stock, and Soil'.[15] To its exponents, the truth of this line of argument seemed to be confirmed by England's economic abundance and large population, which they interpreted as both the foundations for and the effects of that island's 'inestimable Blessing of Liberty'.[16]

Why, as Montesquieu wrote, Britain was 'the only nation in the world, where political and civil liberty' was 'the direct end of its constitution', apologists for the existing order told the public over and over again, as Sir William Blackstone put it, that the 'idea and practice [of... political and civil liberty flourish[ed] in their highest vigour in' Britain, where they had been 'so deeply implanted in our constitution, and rooted in our very soil' that they could 'only be lost or destroyed by the folly or demerits of their owner'.[17] Against those who were producing mounting evidence to the contrary, some writers, such as Fielding, even argued that Britain was 'a nation so jealous of her liberties, that from the slightest cause, and often without any cause at all' they were 'always murmuring at our superiors'.[18] This was an old complaint. Before the Union of 1707 Daniel Defoe, in *The True-Born Englishman*, had trenchantly satirized the English on similar grounds.[19]

Whether they had taken its cultivation to excess or not yet taken it far enough, liberty, as Britons pointed out throughout the eighteenth century, not only remained the 'hallmark of Englishness' but rapidly became the emblem of Britishness. If Scots had their own legal system differing significantly from the English, they none the less, as Linda Colley has noted, shared with the English and Welsh the 'cult of Parliament'.[20] Moreover, the increasing use of the term 'Free-born Briton' in the decades after the Union of 1707 encouraged the emergence of 'a British imperial identity, one in which Caledonians and Americans, as well as the English, could participate'. This identity in which Protestant Irish could be

---

[14] John Trenchard and Thomas Gordon, *Cato's Letters*, in David L. Jacobson, ed., *The English Libertarian Heritage* (Indianapolis, 1965), no. 62, pp. 127–28; no. 68, pp. 177–78.

[15] Brown, *Estimate of the Manners*, pp. 13–14.

[16] *Cato's Letters*, no. 25, pp. 68, 70.

[17] Sir William Blackstone, *Commentaries on the Laws of England*, 4 vols. (1765; Philadelphia, 1771), I, pp. 126–29, 145.

[18] Fielding, *Enquiry into the Causes*, p. 20.

[19] Daniel Defoe, *The True-Born Englishman* (London, 1700), ll. 618–23.

[20] Linda Colley, *Britons: Forging the Nation, 1707–1837* (London, 1992), pp. 50, 52, 111.

included emphasized the benefits of the British 'constitution and the much-vaunted liberties it guaranteed'.[21] Especially as the Union became ever more secure in the wake of the last Jacobite uprising in 1745, writers identified all Britons with liberty and celebrated the fact that the sons, not just of Englishmen, but of all 'Britons' were 'born to Liberty'.[22]

If possession of this unique system of law and liberty was the most significant marker of the English identity during the early modern period and the British identity thereafter, Protestantism was also important to it. England was a Protestant nation, and the English were a Protestant people. In his vivid *Acts and Monuments*, first published in 1554 and republished in enlarged editions six times before 1600, John Foxe chronicled the sufferings of English martyrs at the hands of the Catholic church and heralded England as the chief bulwark against papal aggression. Citing England's prosperity, the seemingly miraculous defeat of the Armada, and the remarkable political stability enjoyed during Elizabeth I's long reign as evidence of God's favour, Foxe and other English Protestant leaders developed the idea that theirs was a nation under covenant with God.[23] Early in the seventeenth century Thomas Brightman and other Puritans took this characterization a step further to argue that England had been a nation elected by God to spearhead the Reformation and 'play a singular role in sacred, providential history'. Although their failure to persuade Elizabeth I or James I to reform the Church of England led many Puritans, including Brightman, to identify England with Laodicea, the lukewarm church of the Apocalypse, and in the 1630s stirred thousands of them to emigrate to New England, others, including John Milton, gloried in the Puritan triumphs of the 1640s as evidence that England retained her status as an elect nation.[24]

During the Elizabethan and Jacobean eras, exponents of English expansion, including the two Richard Hakluyts and Sir Walter Ralegh, had repeatedly justified aggressive action against Spain as a means to extend the domain of the true religion. Within the emerging English Empire, almost all the native Irish remained Roman Catholic. But Ireland's new English and Scottish settlers and the overwhelming majority of English and Scottish colonists who went to America were Protestant, and the English overseas Empire, from the beginning, defined itself in opposition to the Catholic empire of Spain. Yet, if the English Empire was largely

---

[21] Kathleen Wilson, 'Empire, Trade and Popular Politics in Mid-Hanoverian Britain: The Case of Admiral Vernon', *Past and Present*, CXXI (1988), pp. 94, 104.

[22] Jonas Hanway, *Letter to the Encouragers of Practical Public-Love* (London, 1758), p. 57, as quoted by Colley, *Britons*, p. 97.

[23] Greenfeld, *Nationalism*, pp. 60–66.

[24] See Avihu Zakai, *Exile and Kingdom: History and the Apocalypse in the Puritan Migration to America* (Cambridge, 1992), pp. 46–60, and *Theocracy in Massachusetts: Reformation and Separation in Early Puritan New England* (Lewiston, NY, 1994).

Protestant, the Protestantism it represented was less and less unitary. From the end of the sixteenth century, alternative theologies turned to the word of God to champion forms of church polity, modes of worship, and religious beliefs that challenged the hierarchical order of the established Church of England. Thereafter, differences between Anglicanism and Dissent were to be an enduring element in English life and the life of English communities overseas.

Indeed, after Gustavus Adolphus, rather than England, saved Protestantism in Germany during the Thirty Years War, England effectively 'ceased to be the leader of Protestant Europe',[25] and during the last half of the seventeenth century the classical persona of Britannia (which first appeared on coins of the realm in 1665) rapidly became the chief symbol of English pride, replacing the idea of England as an elect nation with the broader and more secular conception of England as the home of constitutional and religious liberty, intellectual and commercial achievement, sea-power, and emerging Imperial greatness.[26] By the eighteenth century 'the belief that the English were an elect nation... may have been of relatively minor importance' in the structure of English national identity.[27]

Yet, as Colley has argued in her magisterial effort to explain how the diverse peoples of the British Isles constructed a national identity as Britons during roughly the century and a quarter following the union between Scotland and England and Wales in 1707, the wars of 1689 to 1815 powerfully revived the conception of England or, after the Union, Great Britain as the principal champion of Protestantism. During these years, Great Britain was at war more than half of the time; Catholic France was the main antagonist, replaced between 1739 and 1744 by Catholic Spain, and the fighting stretched from Europe east to India, south to Africa, and west to the Americas. The new British nation that arose from the Union, Colley emphasizes, 'was an invention above all forged by war', with a national culture that 'largely defined itself through fighting'. But, she contends, war 'could never have been so influential without the impact of religion'. 'Protestant Britons believed they were in God's special care' and that Britain was the 'Protestant bastion against Roman ambitions'. Britons were 'Protestants struggling for survival against the world's foremost Catholic power', France.[28]

For Colley, the importance of religion in this nation-building, identity-constructing process was fundamental. 'Protestantism', she writes, 'was the foundation that made the invention of Britain possible', the 'common commitment' by which the English, Welsh, and Scots 'could be drawn together—and made to feel separate from the rest of Europe'. 'More than anything else', she argues, 'this shared

[25] Christopher Hill, 'The English Revolution and Patriotism', in Samuel, ed., Patriotism, I, p. 160.
[26] Peter Furtado, 'National Pride in Seventeenth-Century England', in ibid., p. 49.
[27] Cunningham, 'Language of Patriotism', in ibid., p. 58.
[28] Colley, Britons, pp. 5, 9, 23, 29, 367–68.

religious allegiance combined with recurrent wars ... permitted a sense of British national identity to emerge alongside of and not necessarily in competition with, older, more organic attachments to England, Wales or Scotland, or to county or village.'[29]

Colley does not explicity consider the extent to which the many colonies of settlement and other outposts in the far peripheries of the Empire shared this equation of Britishness with Protestantism. Whether this association enjoyed quite so decisive a role in the shaping of colonial identities outside New England, a region always anomalous in colonial British America, and beyond circles of religious Dissent, is doubtful. Certainly, the recurrent struggles against the Catholic powers reinforced the colonials' already strong awareness that, whatever their distance from the home islands, British peoples were overwhelmingly Protestant peoples. Especially during the Seven Years War, colonials endorsed the metropolitan view of the conflict with France as a struggle between Protestantism and Catholicism and heralded Britain's ultimate success as a victory for the Protestant Succession and an example of God's special favour toward the enlarged British Empire.[30]

But contemporaries also associated other characteristics with the emerging national identity: social openness,[31] a penchant for scientific and intellectual achievement,[32] and, most significantly, prosperity and trade. The widespread stress upon the superiority of English food ('roast beef and plum pudding') and clothing ('no "wooden shoes"') over those of other Europeans, traceable at least as far back as Fortescue, expressed pride in England's prosperity.[33] The vaunted productivity of its agriculture seemed to distinguish Britain from its continental neighbours. But pride in the relative abundance of British economic achievements rested even more firmly on commerce. This, too, was a development of long standing. Already by the late sixteenth century, the travel writer and empire promoter Richard Hakluyt praised England as an 'aggressive commercial entity' whose wealth and national importance depended 'above all on overseas trade' and

[29] Ibid., pp. 18, 54, 369.

[30] See Nathan O. Hatch, *The Sacred Cause of Liberty: Republican Thought and the Millenium in Revolutionary New England* (New Haven, 1977), pp. 36–51; Ruth Bloch, *Visionary Republic: Millenial Themes in American Thought, 1756–1800* (Cambridge, 1985), pp. 33–50. The extent to which ordinary New Englanders conceived of British war successes as evidence of Divine Providence may be followed in Fred Anderson, *A People's Army: Massachusetts Soldiers and Society in the Seven Years' War* (Chapel Hill, NC, 1984), pp. 196–223.

[31] Greenfeld, *Nationalism*, pp. 30, 47–50, 74, 86; Brown, *Estimate of the Manners*, p. 15; Defoe, *True-Born Englishman*, p. 405; Fielding, *Enquiry into the Causes*, pp. 13–14; Michael J. Hawkins, 'Ethnicity, Nationalism and the History of the British Isles', in Ladislaus Löb, István Petrovics, György E. Szöeds, eds., *Forms of Identity: Definitions and Changes* (Szeged, Hungary, 1994), p. 30.

[32] Greenfeld, *Nationalism*, pp. 79–83.

[33] Cunningham, 'Language of Patriotism', pp. 59–60.

naval power.[34] By 'vigorously' pushing 'the Increase of our Navigation and Commerce', declared the political writer John Campbell in 1774, the Tudors had so far 'excited a Multitude of bold, active, and enterprizing Persons to Hazard their Lives and Fortunes in such Undertakings'.[35] By 1600, Adam Smith noted in *The Wealth of Nations*, England was already 'a great trading country' with a 'mercantile capital [that] was very great'.[36] It had become a country that defined itself against Spain not just in terms of religion and liberty but also in terms of its peaceful 'pursuit of trade' in Europe and America, which, 'rather than conquest', stood as 'a sign of England's virtuous difference' from 'Spanish tyranny, Spanish cruelty, and Spanish ambition'.[37] After another century of commercial development, it became a cliché, as the historian John Oldmixon noted in 1708, that Britons had 'no ways of making ourselves considerable in the World, but by our Fleets; and of supporting them, but by our Trade, which breeds Seamen; and brings in Wealth to maintain them'.[38] In terms of 'the vastness and extensiveness of our trade', proudly said an anonymous British writer in 1718, 'we are the most considerable of any nation in the world'.[39]

During the eighteenth century, a 'cult of commerce became an increasingly important part of being British'.[40] Both 'the situation of our island, and the genius of our people', announced a member of the House of Lords in 1738, depended heavily upon 'the extent and security' of British navigation and trade.[41] British superiority in 'commercial arts and advantage', said a Member of Parliament on the eve of the American Revolution, was the principal reason why Britain had been 'raised ... so high among the modern nations'. Very largely 'the creature of commerce', the great 'influx of wealth', he noted, 'solely constitutes our envied power and rank in the present world'.[42] Commerce, said the Glasgow merchant Adam Anderson, 'will ever be *our* great Palladium'.[43]

---

[34] Helgerson, *Nationhood*, p. 171.

[35] John Campbell, *A Political Survey of Britain: Being a Series of Reflections on the Situation, Lands, Inhabitants, Revenues, Colonies, and Commerce of this Island*, 2 vols. (London, 1774), II, pp. 563–64.

[36] Adam Smith, *An Inquiry into the Nature and Causes of the Wealth of Nations* (1776), ed. R. H. Campbell and A. S. Skinner, 2 vols. (Oxford, 1976), II, p. 597.

[37] Helgerson, *Nationhood*, p. 185.

[38] John Oldmixon, *The British Empire in America*, 2 vols. (London, 1708), I, p. xxi.

[39] *Magnae Britanniae Notitia: Or, the Present State of Great Britain* (London, 1718), p. 33, as cited by Colley, *Britons*, p. 59.

[40] Colley, *Britons*, pp. 56, 59–60.

[41] Earl of Cholmondeley, speech, 2 May 1738, in Leo F. Stock, ed., *Proceedings and Debates of the British Parliaments Respecting North America*, 5 vols. (Washington, 1924–41), IV, p. 531.

[42] Richard Glover, speech, 16 March 1775, in R. C. Simmons and P. D. G. Thomas, eds., *Proceedings and Debates of the British Parliament Respecting North America*, 6 vols. to date (Millwood, NY, 1982–89), V, pp. 568–69.

[43] Adam Anderson, *An Historical and Chronological Deduction of the Origins of Commerce from the Earliest Accounts to the Present Time*, 2 vols. (London, 1764), II, p. 137.

Contemporary social theory, as represented by the four-stage theory of cultural development propounded by Scottish Enlightenment thinkers, saw commerce as the highest stage of social development.[44] Those who celebrated Britain's expanding commercial activity argued that commerce was principally responsible for effecting a revolution in the 'manners, customs, and habits' of the British people.[45] Specifically, they suggested that, in combination with the traditional British spirit of liberty, commerce had softened the manners of the people, made them more polite and civil, and reinforced the 'Spirit of Humanity' by which Britain had 'always been distinguished'. As evidence that this spirit was 'natural to our Nation', Brown pointed to the 'many noble Foundations for the Relief of the Miserable and Friendless; the large annual Supplies from voluntary Charities to these Foundations'; the 'Limits of our Laws in capital Cases; our Compassion for convicted Criminals; even the general Humanity of our Highwaymen and Robbers, compared with those of other Countries'.[46]

Superior humaneness, moreover, was only one of the many social traits through which, as the classical scholar Conyers Middleton wrote in his *Life of Cicero*, Britain, 'anciently the jest and contempt of *the polite Romans*', had 'become the happy seat of liberty, plenty and letters' and was now 'flourishing in all the arts and refinements of civil life'.[47] Contemporary analysts also suggested that it had changed the structure of British society in ways that contributed to a social deepening of the appreciation of the virtues of the existing constitution. 'Being more equally dispersed', wealth 'acquired by Traffic', Campbell believed, made 'more people happy' and over time so lessened social inequalities that Britons were 'no longer divided into great Lords and mean Vassals'.[48] 'The Spirit of Commerce', Brown wrote, begot 'a kind of regulated Selfishness ... which tends at once to the Increase and Preservation of Property'.[49] These developments, according to Campbell, seemed to have fostered a psychology of 'Independency' and spread a 'Consciousness' that the industry that produced wealth and independence was 'the Result of [the] Freedom' that 'derived from and' was dependent 'upon our Constitution'.[50] This widespread identification of commerce with liberty gave rise to the further conviction that, as a newspaper-writer put it in 1770, 'riches, trade and commerce' were 'nowhere to be found

---

[44] Ronald L. Meek, *Social Science and the Ignoble Savage* (Cambridge, 1983).

[45] Fielding, *Enquiry into the Causes*, pp. 13–14.

[46] Brown, *Estimate of the Manners*, pp. 14–15.

[47] Conyers Middleton, *History of the Life of Marcus Tullius Cicero* (London, 1741), as quoted by Fielding, *Enquiry into the Causes*, p. 17.

[48] Ibid.

[49] Brown, *Estimate of the Manners*, p. 15.

[50] Campbell, *Political Survey*, II, p. 705.

but in the regions of freedom', such as Britain or, to a lesser degree, the Nether-lands.[51]

Colonies were an important adjunct of commerce, and trade with the colonies constituted an expanding sector of British overseas commerce. As early as 1707, some observers thought that the colonies had been responsible for a substantial part of 'Britain's great Increase in Wealth' over the previous half-century.[52] Six or seven decades later, contemporaries disagreed about the precise extent of the colonies' contribution to Britain's overseas trade, but few doubted that that contribution was both substantial and critical. In his general *History of Commerce*, published in 1764 just after Britain's great triumph in the Seven Years War, Anderson claimed that the American plantations had been exclusively responsible for 'the change in our national circumstances' which brought the 'Britannic Empire' into being.[53] Campbell in 1774 praised the colonies as a great national resource that had 'contributed greatly to increase our Industry, and of course our Riches, to extend our Commerce, to augment our Naval Power, and consequently to maintain the Grandeur and support the Prosperity of the Mother Country'. 'What comparison can be drawn between the riches of Britain now and in the time of Queen Elizabeth?' asked the agricultural improver Arthur Young; 'yet if we come to examine the matter, we shall find the superiority of the latter times to the former, to be chiefly owing to the discovery of America' and British success in colonizing.[54] For any nation, Campbell was persuaded from the British experi-ence, the benefits 'of fixing Settlements in distant Countries for the Sake of Commerce' were 'self-evident'.[55]

For many Britons, however, colonies were not merely an economic but a civilizing project. They had already had considerable experience with peoples close to home, Gaelic Irish and Highland Scots, who, living primarily as graziers or hunters and fishermen, seemed to have no settled agriculture or permanent homes and appeared to be 'of a different and inferior race, violent, treacherous, poverty stricken, and backward'.[56] With regard to such peoples in the peripheries of the British Isles, the role of the core societies, as Sir Thomas Smith noted in 1565, was to educate them 'in virtuous labor and in justice, and to teach them English laws and civility and to leave [off] robbing and stealing and killing one

[51] *The Whisperer*, 17 March 1770, as cited by Linda Colley, 'Radical Patriotism in Eighteenth-Century England', in Samuel, ed., *Patriotism*, I, p. 172.

[52] Oldmixon, *British Empire*, I, p. xxxi.

[53] Cited in Richard Koebner, *Empire* (Cambridge, 1961), pp. 121–22.

[54] Arthur Young, *Political Essays Concerning the Present State of the British Empire* (London, 1772), p. 466.

[55] Campbell, *Political Survey*, II, pp. 561, 567.

[56] Colley, *Britons*, p. 15.

another'.[57] Thus, in the sixteenth century, exponents of English colonization of Ireland justified it as a device by which the English might foster Irish 'appreciation for civility so that they might likewise move toward freedom', Protestantism, and refinement.[58]

The encounter of British people with America, Africa, and Asia brought them face to face with peoples far more alien, against whom they defined themselves as yet more superior. Living in chiefdoms and bands, North American Amerindians occupied an extensive country which, from a European perspective, they left a waste and uncultivated wilderness. Africans and Asians lived in more complex societies, some of which had evidently once supported 'civilizations... of considerable achievement', but these societies seemed to be largely despotisms, and the African and Asian legal systems, social mores, living standards, religions, and war-making capacities, like those of the Amerindian, seemed vastly inferior to those of Britain.[59]

Regarding it as their duty and 'Birthright', as one cleric asserted in 1759, 'to carry, not only Good Manners, but the purest Light of the Gospel, where Barbarism and Ignorance totally prevailed',[60] advocates of Imperial expansion presented these 'barbarous nations' as a wide field of action for Britons to act as civilizing agents. In Africa and Asia, where the inhabitants were numerous and sedentary, they had managed by the last quarter of the eighteenth century, as Adam Smith observed, to secure their hegemony over 'many considerable settlements', but they had not yet established 'in either of those countries such numerous and thriving colonies as those in the islands and continent of America',[61] where, 'in less than Three hundred Years', wrote Campbell approvingly, they had succeeded in turning 'a great Part of the Wilds and Wastes of America' into 'rich and well cultivated Countries, settled and improved, as well as possessed by Multitudes of British Subjects'.[62]

Glossing over 'the brutal, exploitative and violent processes of "trade" and colonization (including the immensely profitable trade in slaves)', this commercial vision of the Empire thus treated colonies as 'emblem[s] of English superiority and benevolence' and justified 'British imperial ascendancy as a salvation to the

---

[57] Sir Thomas Smith, *De Republica Anglorum* (London, 1656), as quoted by Robert A. Williams, Jr., *The American Indian in Western Legal Thought: The Discourse of Conquest* (New York, 1990), p. 142.

[58] Williams, Jr., *The American Indian in Western Legal Thought*, p. 142. See also Nicholas P. Canny, 'The Ideology of English Colonization: From Ireland to America', *William and Mary Quarterly*, Third Series, XXX (1973), pp. 575–98.

[59] P. J. Marshall and Glyndwr Williams, *The Great Map of Mankind* (London, 1982), p. 3; Linda Colley, 'Britishness and Otherness: An Argument', *Journal of British Studies*, XXXI (1992), pp. 324–25.

[60] Richard Brewster, *A Sermon Preach'd on Thanksgiving Day* (Newcastle, 1759), as cited by Kathleen Wilson, 'Empire of Virtue: The Imperial Project and Hanoverian Culture c.1720–1785', in Lawrence Stone, ed., *An Imperial State at War: Britain from 1689 to 1815* (London, 1994) p. 128.

[61] Smith, *Wealth of Nations*, II, p. 634.

[62] Campbell, *Political Survey*, II, p. 634.

world'. In this way, they ensured that Britain's 'nascent imperialist sensibility'
would powerfully reinforce British national identity.[63] In contrast to those of
other European powers, the British Empire, wrote the poet James Thomson, was
obviously 'well-earned'.[64] 'There is nothing can more fully or more sensibly evince
the Truth of our Assertions in respect to the commodious Situation of this Island,
the superior Genius of its Inhabitants, and the Excellance of our Constitution,
than ... the Establishments we have made in all Parts of the World', wrote Campbell in 1774, 'for these must be considered as so many distinguishing Testimonies,
so many shining Trophies of our maritime Skill and naval Strength', trophies that
'extend[ed] the Fame, display[ed] the Power and support[ed] the Commerce of
Great Britain'.[65]

If having thriving colonies contributed so substantially to Britons' positive
sense of self during the eighteenth century, and if by the middle of the eighteenth
century Empire was 'as much a part of the national identity as the liberties and
constitutional traditions for which Britain was celebrated the world over',[66] to
what extent were the colonists themselves, including the Anglo-Irish, included in
this emerging Imperial identity? If, 'in terms of culture, religion and colour',
British people found it easy to define the 'manifestly alien' Amerindians, African
natives, or Asians of India as patently inferior peoples, the settler societies of
America with their European populations, cultures, and institutions presented a
different problem altogether.[67] With their 'ever-growing numbers and increasing
local rootedness with each succeeding generation', American creoles, of European
descent but born in America, posed 'a historically unique problem. For the first
time the metropolis had to deal with ... vast numbers of "fellow Europeans" ... far
outside Europe. If the indigenes were conquerable by arms and disease, and
controllable by the mysteries of Christianity and a completely alien political
culture ... the same was not true of creoles, who had virtually the same relationship to arms, disease, Christianity, and European culture as the metropolitans'.[68]

Moreover, European immigrants carried with them explicit and deeply held
claims to the cultures of Europe and the identities implicit in them. In extreme
climates, under primitive conditions, and with limited resources in people and
money, they endeavoured to reorder existing physical and cultural landscapes
along European lines, implanting upon them European patterns of land occupa-

---

[63] Wilson, Sense of the People, pp. 157, 282, 'Empire of Virtue', pp. 155, and 'Empire, Trade, and
Popular Politics', p. 109.

[64] James Thomson, Britannia: A Poem (London, 1729), l. 167.

[65] Campbell, Political Survey, II, p. 567 n.

[66] Wilson, 'Empire of Virtue', pp. 154–55.

[67] Colley, 'Britishness and Otherness', pp. 324–25.

[68] Benedict Anderson, Imagined Communities: Reflections on the Origin and Spread of Nationalism
(New York, 1991), pp. 58–59.

tion, economic and social organization, cultural practices, and religious, political, and legal systems, and making European languages the languages of authority. Their great physical distances from their metropolises; the social and cultural contrasts, especially during their earlier decades, between the simple and crude societies they were building and the complex and infinitely more polite societies from which they came; their situation on the outermost edges of European civilization, in the midst of populations who appeared to them to be pagan, barbarous, and savage; the presence, if not the preponderance, in their societies of aliens, in the form of Amerindians, Africans, or Asians; their frequent reliance upon new institutions, such as plantations and chattel, race-based slavery; and the metropolitan reluctance to acknowledge their Europeanness—all these were conditions that both rendered settler claims to the status of Europeans problematic and enhanced the urgency of such claims among immigrants and their creole descendants.

In the immigrants' efforts to put a European stamp upon colonial landscapes, the legal systems by which they defined the new social spaces they were creating were critical. During the second wave of European imperialism, in the nineteenth and early twentieth centuries, European law frequently served the conquerors as an instrument of domination and control. In this phase of European expansion, what was usually a relatively small group of colonizers, acting as agents of European states and as the self-appointed bearers of European cultures, sought with varying degrees of success to subject the colonized, an often vast population with ancient and complex legal systems of their own, to European legal traditions and institutions.[69] By contrast, among the many settler societies established by Europeans, first in America beginning in the sixteenth century and then in other sections of the globe starting in the nineteenth century, law functioned as the principal instrument of cultural transplantation. Intending to create offshoots of the Old World in the New, the large number of emigrants to the colonies insisted upon taking their law with them and making it the primary foundation for the new societies they sought to establish. For these societies, European law was not so much 'a tool of imperialism', a device to dominate whatever indigenous populations remained in their midst, as 'a concomitant of emigration. It was not imposed upon settlers but claimed by them.' To live under European law 'was a privilege, usually not to be granted to the indigenous people', a vivid and symbolically powerful signifier of the emigrants' deepest aspirations to retain in their new places of abode their identities as members of the European societies to which they were attached, identities that, in their eyes, both established their superiority over

[69] See W. J. Mommsen and J. A. De Moor, eds., *European Expansion and Law: The Encounter of European and Indigenous Law in 19th- and 20th-Century Africa and Asia* (Oxford, 1992).

and sharply distinguished them from the seemingly rude and uncivilized peoples they were seeking to dispossess.[70]

For English people migrating overseas to establish new communities of settlement, the capacity to enjoy—to possess—the English system of law and liberty was thus crucial to their ability to maintain their identity as English people and to continue to think of themselves and to be thought of by those who remained in England as English. For that reason, as well as because they regarded English legal arrangements as the best way to preserve the properties they hoped to acquire, it is scarcely surprising that among English colonists all over America 'the attempt to establish English law and the "rights and liberties of Englishmen" was constantly pursued from the first settlements to the [American] Revolution'.[71] The same can be said of Ireland. However, in contrast to the colonists' endeavours to incorporate English economic, social, cultural, and religious practices and institutions into the fabric of colonial life, their efforts to secure English law and liberties were, throughout the seventeenth and eighteenth centuries, contested by metropolitan authorities, who remained sceptical about not whether, but to what extent English colonists were entitled to English law and liberties.[72]

The colonial position in this contest implied a conception of colonies as extensions of Britain overseas and of colonists as Britons living 'abroad and consequently the brethren of those at home', virtual 'mirror images' of those who still resided in Britain.[73] This, as Benedict Anderson has pointed out, implied that the colonies were societies '*parallel and comparable* to those in' Britain and that, in their lives, colonists were 'proceeding along the same trajectory' as those who remained in the British Isles.[74] From this perspective, held by many people in Britain, the British Empire was 'a free and virtuous empire, founded in consent and nurtured in liberty and trade',[75] and colonists were 'fellow- subjects'[76] who, though 'living in different parts of the world', together with those who resided in Britain formed, as Young remarked in 1772, 'one nation, united under one sovereign, speaking the same language and enjoying the same liberty'.[77]

---

[70] Jörg Fisch, 'Law as a Means and as an End: Some Remarks on the Function of European and Non-European Law in the Process of European Expansion', in ibid., p. 21.

[71] George Dargo, *Roots of the Republic: A New Perspective on Early American Constitutionalism* (New York, 1974), p. 74.

[72] Jack P. Greene, *Peripheries and Center: Constitutional Development in the Extended Polities of the British Empire and the United States, 1607–1788* (Athens, Ga., 1986), pp. 7–76.

[73] Colley, *Britons*, pp. 105, 135.

[74] Anderson, *Imagined Communities*, pp. 188, 192.

[75] Wilson, *Sense of the People*, p. 277.

[76] Lord Baltimore, speech, 26 Nov. 1739, in Stock, ed., *Proceedings and Debates of the British Parliament*, V. p. 5.

[77] Young, *Political Essays*, p. 1.

For those who viewed the Empire in this expansive way, the transfer of English liberties to the colonies was precisely the characteristic that distinguished the British Empire from others. Just as Britain was the home of liberty in Europe, so also was the British Empire in America. 'Without freedom', Edmund Burke remarked in 1766, the Empire 'would not be the British Empire'.[78] In America, said Young, 'Spain, Portugal and France, have planted despotisms; only Britain liberty'.[79] 'Look, Sir, into the history of the provinces of other states, of the Roman provinces in ancient time; of the French, Spanish, Dutch and Turkish provinces of more modern date,' George Dempster advised the House of Commons in 1775, 'and you will find every page stained with acts of oppressive violence, of cruelty, injustice and peculation.'[80]

As those of similar persuasion thought more deeply about the nature of the Empire, they began to suggest that liberty not only 'distinguish[ed]' the 'British colonists...from the colonists of other nations', but was responsible for the Empire's extraordinary success.[81] In their two-volume *Account of the European Settlements in America*, Edmund and William Burke expressed their confidence that colonial commerce had flourished as it had because 'of the freedom every man has of pursuing it according to his own ideas, and directing his life according to his own fashion'.[82] As they surveyed the extraordinary growth and development of the British colonies, analysts such as John Campbell and Adam Smith concluded that, as Campbell wrote, 'in their very Nature Colonies require Ease and Freedom', and that colonization was 'not very compatible with the Maxims that prevail in despotic Governments'.[83] To Smith, the experience of the British colonies seemed conclusive proof that, along with plenty of good land, extensive liberty, permitting wide latitude in self-direction, was one of 'the two great causes of the prosperity of new colonies'.[84]

If 'notions of consent and liberty' were indeed 'central' to one contemporary conceptualization of the Empire, there was an alternative and, in Britain, more pervasive view of colonies and colonists. This competing view saw the colonies less as societies of Britons overseas 'populated with free white British subjects' than as

---

[78] Edmund Burke, Speech on the Declaratory Act, 3 Feb. 1766, in *The Writings of Edmund Burke*, Vol. II, *Party, Parliament, and the American Crisis, 1766–1774*, ed. Paul Langford (Oxford, 1981), p. 47.

[79] Young, *Political Essays*, p. 20.

[80] George Dempster, speech, 27 Oct. 1775, in Simmons and Thomas, eds., *Proceedings and Debates in the British Parliament*, VI, p. 140.

[81] Edmund Burke, *Observations on a Late State of the Nation* (London, 1769), in *Writings of Burke*, II, p. 194.

[82] Edmund and William Burke, *An Account of the European Settlements in America*, 2 vols. (London, 1757), II, pp. 75–76.

[83] Campbell, *Political Survey*, II, p. 562 n.

[84] Smith, *Wealth of Nations*, II, p. 572.

outposts of British economic or strategic power.[85] In this restrictive conception, explicit in the Navigation Acts and other Restoration colonial measures, the colonies were, principally, workshops or, in the later words of the former Governor of Massachusetts Thomas Pownall, '*mere plantations*, tracts of foreign country, employed in raising certain specified and enumerated commodities, solely for the use of the trade and manufactures of the mother-country'.[86] Increasingly after 1740, and especially during and after the Seven Years War, this view gave way to a complementary emphasis upon the colonies as instruments of British national or Imperial power. Between 1745 and 1763, intensifying rivalries with France and Spain and the growing populations and wealth of the colonies produced, for the first time among metropolitan analysts, an intensive discussion about the nature and workings of the Empire.[87]

Most of the contributors to this discussion started from the assumption that the very 'word "colony"', as Charles Townshend subsequently declared, implied not equality, but 'subordination'.[88] Contending that the colonies had been initiated, established, and subsequently succoured by the metropolitan state for the purpose of furthering state policy, they argued that the colonies always had to be considered in terms of 'power and dominion, as well as trade'.[89] In this view, the original purpose of colonization was to 'add Strength to the State by extending its Dominions', and emigrants to the colonies had always been 'subject to, and under the power and Dominion, of the Kingdom' whence they came. So far, then, from being in any sense equal to the parent state, colonies were nothing more than 'Provincial Governments . . . subordinate to the Chief State'.[90]

Such conceptions of the colonies suggested that colonists were something less than full Britons; not, as Benjamin Franklin put it in 1768, 'fellow subjects, but subjects of subjects'.[91] They also reinforced long-standing metropolitan views of colonists as people of 'vulgar descent' and unfortunate histories, the miserable

---

[85] Wilson, *Sense of the People*, p. 24.

[86] Thomas Pownall, *The Administration of the Colonies* (London, 1768), p. 282.

[87] Peter N. Miller, *Defining the Common Good: Empire, Religion and Philosophy in Eighteenth-Century Britain* (Cambridge, 1994), pp. 195–213.

[88] Charles Townshend, speech, 6 Feb. 1765, in Simmons and Thomas, eds., *Proceedings of the British Parliament*, II, p. 13.

[89] Jack P. Greene, Charles F. Mullett, and Edward C. Papenfuse, Jr., eds., *Magna Charta for America: James Abercromby's 'An Examination of the Acts of Parliament Relative to the Trade and Government of Our American Colonies' (1752) and 'De Jure et Gubernatione Coloniarum, or An Inquiry into the Nature, and the Rights of Colonies, Ancient and Modern'* (1774) (Philadelphia, 1986), p. 45; John Mitchell, *The Contest in America between Great Britain and France* (London, 1757), p. xvii, as cited in Miller, *Defining the Common Good*, p. 170.

[90] Greene, Mullett, and Papenfuse, eds., *Magna Charta for America*, p. 26.

[91] Benjamin Franklin to the *Gentleman's Magazine*, Jan. 1768, in Verner W. Crane, ed., *Benjamin Franklin's Letters to the Press* (Chapel Hill, NC, 1950), p. 111.

outcasts of Britain and Europe.[92] During the Stamp Act crisis of 1765–66, Franklin, who throughout much of the period from the mid-1750s to the mid-1770s resided in London and acted as a self-appointed cultural broker for the colonies, was dismayed to see metropolitan newspaper-writers dismiss the colonists with the 'gentle terms of *republican race, mixed rabble of Scotch, Irish and foreign vagabonds, descendents of convicts, ungrateful rebels & c.*', language that, he objected, conveyed only the most violent 'contempt, and abuse'.[93] Franklin protested that by 'lumping all the Americans under the general Character of "House-breakers and Felons"' and by 'raving' against them 'as "diggers of pits for this country", "lunaticks", "sworn enemies", "false", and "ungrateful"... "cut-throats"', British opinion in the decade after 1765 repeatedly branded the colonists as a people who, though 'descended from British Ancestors', had 'degenerated to such a Degree' as to become the 'lowest of Mankind, and almost of a different Species from the English of Britain'.[94] They were a people who were 'unworthy the name of Englishmen, and fit only to be snubb'd, curb'd, shackled and plundered'.[95] Such language identified colonists as a category of others, 'foreigners' who, however much they might aspire to be English, could never actually achieve those aspirations, and who on the scale of civilization were only slightly above the native Amerindian.[96]

The expansion of British activities in India and the massive employment of enslaved Africans and their descendants throughout the British American colonies strongly reinforced the image of colonial degeneracy in Britain. The more Britons learned about India, the more convinced they became that, as Dempster remarked in Parliament, the 'eastern species of government' and society was replete with 'rapines and cruelties'.[97] Beginning in the late 1750s, the transactions of Robert Clive and others persuaded many Britons that, in their rapacious efforts to line their own pockets, their countrymen in India had themselves often turned plunderers and been guilty of 'Crimes scarce inferior to the Conquerors of *Mexico* and *Peru*'.[98] Already by the late 1760s, the term 'nabob', initially an Indian title of rank, had become, as a contemporary complained, 'a general term of reproach, indiscriminately applied to every individual who has served the East India Company in

---

[92] Oldmixon, *British Empire*, I, p. iv.

[93] Franklin to *Gazeteer and New Daily Advertiser*, 28 Dec. 1765, in Leonard W. Labaree and others., *The Papers of Benjamin Franklin*, 27 vols. to date (New Haven, 1959—), XII, p. 414.

[94] Franklin to *Public Advertiser*, 2 Jan. 1766, ibid., XIII, p. 5; Franklin to *Gazeteér and New Daily Advertiser*, 6 Jan. 1768, ibid., XV, p. 13; Franklin to *Public Advertiser*, 5 April 1774, ibid., XXI, p. 185.; Franklin to William Franklin, 22 March 1775, in ibid., XXI, p. 598.

[95] Franklin, 'Fragments of a Pamphlet on the Stamp Act', Jan. 1766, in ibid., XIII, p. 81.

[96] Franklin, 'Examination', 1766, ibid., XIII, p. 150.

[97] Dempster, speech, 27 Oct. 1775, in Simmons and Thomas, eds., *Proceedings and Debates in the British Parliament*, VI, p. 140.

[98] *The Nabob: or Asiatic Plunderers. A Satirical Poem* (London, 1773), p. iii.

Asia' and 'implying, that the persons to whom it is applied, have obtained their fortunes by grievously oppressing the natives of India'.[99] Published in 1768, the dramatist Samuel Foote's *The Nabob* was only the most prominent of many works that presented a 'scathing indictment of the moral corrosiveness of empire in India'.[100]

Throughout the latter half of the eighteenth century, the rapidly growing anti-slavery movement more and more focused attention on the association of racial slavery with the colonies, and fostered the conviction in Britain that 'no People upon Earth' were such 'Enemies to Liberty, such absolute Tyrants', as the American colonists. With 'so little Dislike of Despotism and Tyranny, that they do not scruple to exercise them with unbounded Rigour over their miserable Slaves', colonists were obviously 'unworthy' of claims to a British identity or to the liberty that was central to that identity.[101] No less than the image of the nabob, that of the dissolute 'creolean planter'—a despot schooled by slavery in 'ferocity, cruelty, and brutal barbarity',[102] whose 'head-long Violence' was wholly unlike the 'national' temperament of the 'native genuine English'[103]—shaped contemporary metropolitan conceptions of colonists through dramatic works such as Richard Cumberland's *The West Indian* in 1772, or George Colman Jr.'s *Inkle and Yarico* in 1787.[104]

The images presented in these works and in the anti-slavery literature suggested that no people who consorted with the corrupt and despotic regimes of the East or held slaves in the American colonies could be true-born Britons who, above all, loved liberty. To reassure themselves that Britain actually was the land of freedom, metropolitan Britons had to distance themselves from such people and Britain from such places. 'In *Asia's* realms let slavery be bound', demanded one anonymous poet in 1773,

> Let not her foot defile this sacred ground,
> Where Freedom, Science, Valour fix'd their seat,
> And taught all Nations how they should be great.[105]

---

[99] *The Saddle put on the Right Horse: or, an Enquiry into the Reason Why Certain Persons have been Denominated Nabobs* (London, 1783), p. 1.

[100] Wilson, 'Empire of Virtue', p. 153; Philip Lawson and Jim Phillips, ' "Our Execrable Banditti": Perceptions of Nabobs in Mid-Eighteenth Century Britain', *Albion*, XVI (1984), pp. 225–41.

[101] Franklin, 'A Conversation between an Englishman, a Scotchman, and an American, on the Subject of Slavery', *Public Advertiser*, 30 Jan., 1770, in Crane, ed., *Benjamin Franklin's Letters to the Press*, p. 187.

[102] James Otis, *The Rights of the British Colonies Asserted and Proved* (Boston, 1764), in Bernard Bailyn, ed., *Pamphlets of the American Revolution* (Cambridge, Mass., 1965), pp. 439–40.

[103] 'Mnemon' [Edmund Burke] to *Public Advertiser*, 23 Feb. 1768, in Langford, ed., *Writings of Burke*, II, p. 76.

[104] Wilson, 'Empire of Virtue', p. 143.

[105] *Nabob: or Asiatic Plunders*, p. 38.

In the same spirit, some polemical writers called for measures to 'preserve the race of Britons from [the] stain and contamination' of American settler despotism.[106]

The long debate that preceded the American Revolution provided colonists and their advocates in Britain with an opportunity to combat this negative image. In protesting that the extensive free colonial populations were mostly 'descendents of Englishmen'[107] or Britons, and in trying to define of what their 'ancestral Englishness'[108] consisted, colonial protagonists penetrated to the essence of Englishness and Britishness as contemporaries understood it. What distinguished them from the colonists of other nations—and identified them with Britons at home—was not principally, they insisted, their Protestantism or their economic and social success, but their political and legal inheritance. '*Modern* colonists', in James Otis's view, were

the noble discoverers and settlers of a new world, from whence as from an endless source, wealth and plenty, the means of power, grandeur, and glory, in a degree unknown to the hungry chiefs of former ages, have been pouring in to Europe for 300 years past; in return for which those colonists have received from the several states of Europe, except from Great Britain only since the Revolution, nothing but ill-usage, slavery, and chains, as fast as the riches of their own earning could furnish the means of forging them.

Not just the Catholic and despotic Spanish, Portuguese, and French had been so guilty, but even the Protestant and free Dutch, who shamelessly admitted that 'the liberty of Dutchmen' was 'confined to Holland' and was 'never intended for provincials in America or anywhere else'. If 'British America' had previously been 'distinguished from the slavish colonies around about it as the fortunate Britons have been from most of their neighbours on the continent of Europe', colonial advocates argued powerfully, Britain's 'colonies should be ever thus distinguished'.[109]

To colonial protagonists in the 1760s and 1770s, the colonists' claims to share in this central component of British identity seemed unassailable. 'To the infinite advantage and emolument of the mother state', the colonists, as the Providence merchant Stephen Hopkins announced in 1764, had 'left the delights of their native country, parted from their homes and all their conveniences [, and] ...searched out...and subdued a foreign country with the most amazing travail and fortitude.' They had undertaken these Herculean tasks on the assumption

---

[106] 'A West Indian' [Samuel Estwick], *Considerations on the Negroe Cause Commonly so Called* (London, 1772), pp. 29, 43.

[107] Edmund Burke, *Observations on a Late State of the Nation*, in Langford, ed., *Writings of Burke*, II, p. 194.

[108] Anderson, *Imagined Communities*, p. 145.

[109] Otis, *Rights of the British Colonies*, in Bailyn, *Pamphlets*, pp. 436, 447, 478.

'that they and their successors forever should be free, should be partakers and sharers in all the privileges and advantages of the then English, now British constitution', and should enjoy 'all the rights and privileges of freeborn Englishmen'. Exulting in their identity as Britons, colonists took pride in having come 'out from a kingdom renowned for liberty[,] from a constitution founded on compact, from a people of all the sons of men the most tenacious of freedom'.[110] In phrases that echoed Fortescue and Coke, whom they frequently cited, they expressed their happiness that, unlike the inhabitants of most other polities, they were not 'governed at the will of another, or of others', and that they were not 'in the miserable condition of slaves' whose property could 'be taken from them by taxes or otherwise without their own consent and against their will'. Rather, they militantly asserted, they lived, like Britons in the home islands, under a 'beneficent compact' by which, as British subjects, they could 'be governed only agreeable to laws to which themselves [they] have some way consented, and are not to be compelled to part with their property but as it is called for by the authority of such laws'.[111]

The insistence with which colonial protagonists adumbrated these themes persuasively testifies to the fact that at the time of the American Revolution Britons, in the far peripheries as well as at the centre of the British Empire, still regarded liberty as the essence of Britishness. Once the actions of the metropolitan government seemed aggressively to contest their claims to a British identity, colonists made every effort to articulate and secure metropolitan acknowledgement of those claims, to make clear, as Burke said, that they were 'not only devoted to liberty, but to liberty according to English ideas and on English principles'.[112] If we can assume that the core of an Imperial identity consists of those conceptions that are most deeply felt or internalized in the far reaches as well as at the centre of an Empire, then, at least up until the American Revolution, liberty, as it had been from the beginnings of English overseas expansion, was the single most important ingredient of an Imperial identity in Britain and the British Empire. At the heart of the first British Empire had always been 'the idea of a political system co-ordinating Great Britain in lasting solidarity with communities beyond her borders whose constitutions conformed to her standards', whose political and legal institutions incorporated ancient traditions of British liberty.[113]

---

[110] Stephen Hopkins, *The Rights of the Colonies Examined* (Providence, RI, 1764), in Charles S. Hyneman and Donald S. Lutz, eds., *American Political Writing during the Founding Era, 1760–1805*, 2 vols. (Indianapolis, 1983), I, pp. 46, 49.

[111] Hopkins, *Rights of the Colonies*, in ibid., I, p. 46.

[112] Edmund Burke, Speech on Conciliation, 22 March 1775, in Thomas H. D. Mahoney, ed., *Selected Writings and Speeches on America* (Indianapolis, 1964), p. 132.

[113] Koebner, *Empire*, p. 296.

Indeed, contemporary opinion throughout the Empire fails to support recent suggestions that Britain was 'a land of liberty because founded on Protestantism and commerce'.[114] Rather, the predominant view among eighteenth-century Britons, including colonists, seems to have been that Britain was Protestant and commercial principally because founded on liberty. The break with Rome and the active cultivation of commerce were widely thought to have been a function of the intellectual and political independence of the free-born Englishman, not vice versa. Protestantism, as Burke succinctly declared, was a religion 'not only favorable to liberty, but built upon it'.[115] The expansion of commerce and Empire provided, in Campbell's words, 'the clearest Demonstration of the Excellence of this Constitution'.[116]

Established mostly by English people, the American colonies were the most prominent parts of the first British Empire. The Imperial identity constructed to include them and the Anglo-Irish emphasized liberty and its attendant benefits—Protestantism, extensive and thriving commerce, and national naval and military strength—as conditions not just of the metropolis but of the whole Empire. This identity placed its emphasis upon the dominant settler populations—the merchants, planters, farmers, professionals, and artisans in Ireland, the American colonies, the West Indies, and India—through which it was necessarily mediated. In the process, that identity tended, before the emergence of the anti-slavery movement, to conceal 'the exploitative relations upon which the empire was based',[117] the extensive use of bound labour and racial slavery in America, the discrimination against and the exploitation of Catholics through the Penal Laws in Ireland, the systematic expropriation of native lands in both America and Ireland, and the subjection of parts of India to British rule.

By fostering a dissociation of Britishness and colonialness to a degree impossible in the almost wholly settler Empire of the seventeenth and eighteenth centuries, the second British Empire, with its wide array of subject peoples and its development of 'new institutions of control, coercion and audit and of the philosophical and aristocratic identity of social or metropolitan superiority' that informed those institutions,[118] may, in combination with the emergence of full-blown 'scientific racism', have produced something of a de-emphasis upon the idea of liberty in the British Imperial identity. Yet, by simultaneously taking the lead in the anti-slavery movement and by being the first Europeans to abolish

---

[114] Colley, *Britons*, p. 103.

[115] Burke, Speech on Conciliation, 22 March 1775, in Mahoney, ed., *Selected Writings*, p. 133.

[116] Campbell, *Political Survey*, II, p. 694.

[117] Wilson, 'Empire of Virtue', pp. 149–50.

[118] C. A. Bayly, *Imperial Meridian: The British Empire and the World, 1780–1830* (London, 1989), p. 108.

slavery in their colonies, Britons also reaffirmed their conception of themselves as a nation and an Empire that stood high for liberty.[119]

[119] Phillip Buckner, 'Whatever Happened to the British Empire?', *Journal of the Canadian Historical Association* (1993), pp. 27–28.

Select Bibliography

BENEDICT ANDERSON, *Imagined Communities: Reflections on the Origin and Spread of Nationalism* (New York, 1991).

LINDA COLLEY, *Britons: The Forging of a Nation, 1707–1837* (London, 1992).

LIAH GREENFELD, *Nationalism: Five Roads to Modernity* (Cambridge, Mass., 1992).

RICHARD HELGERSON, *Forms of Nationhood: The Elizabethan Writing of England* (Chicago, 1992).

RICHARD KOEBNER, *Empire* (Cambridge, 1961).

KATHLEEN WILSON, *The Sense of the People: Politics, Culture, and Imperialism in England, 1715–1785* (Cambridge, 1995).

11

Knowledge and Empire

RICHARD DRAYTON

In the *Novum Organum* (1620), Francis Bacon prophesied that both the 'thorough passage of the world' and the advancement of learning were 'destined ... by Divine Providence' to arrive in the same age.[1] Few of his contemporaries would have shared his confidence that the newly joined kingdoms of England and Scotland had a key role to play in both processes. Neither in learning nor trade was either then a great power. They possessed great universities and distinguished scholars, but still turned to Padua and Montpellier for medicine, to Prague and Paris for mathematics and philosophy. Yet in the next two centuries Britain's intellectual pre-eminence was challenged only by France. In Isaac Newton and William Herschel, John Locke and Adam Smith, Robert Boyle and Joseph Priestley, John Ray and Robert Brown, Hans Sloane and Joseph Banks, the British Isles enjoyed philosophers, astronomers, political economists, and students of matter and life of the first rank. This unfolding of the Scientific Revolution and the Enlightenment in Britain coincided directly with the making of her Empire.

This coincidence stemmed, in part, from the cultural and political consequences of the Reformation. The Protestant assertion of the sacred prerogatives of the English *regnum* prompted the cultivation of vernacular learning, and ultimately maritime expansion. Besides the English Bible and Foxe's martyrology, the Englishing of Homer by Arthur Hall (1581) and George Chapman (1611 and 1614), and of Euclid by John Dee (1571), can be placed the *Herball* (1551), which William Turner offered 'to the proper profit of [my] naturall countre ... unto the English, my countrymen, an English herbal', or *A Geometrical Practise, named Pantometria* (1571), in which Leonard Digges declared to Bacon's father his commitment to 'storing our native tongue with mathematicall demonstrations'.[2] The patriotic energies which urged Turner or William Camden to study things English equally sparked interest in the world beyond the Pillars of Hercules. For while Dee, Walter Ralegh, or the two Richard Hakluyts were responding in part to European

---

[1] James Spedding, R. L. Ellis, and D. D. Heath, eds., *The Works of Francis Bacon*, 14 vols. (London, 1857–74), IV, p. 92.

[2] William Turner, *Herball* (London, 1551), Preface; Leonard Digges, *A Geometrical Practise, named Pantometria* (London, 1571), sig. A1ᵛ.

intellectual influence, their interest in America or Asia was quickened by the fact that ultramarine wealth allowed Philip II of Spain to equip armadas and to fund wars of religion. In defence of England's political and religious liberty, English learning and commerce began to comprehend the world.

Knowledge was Power, by which Bacon meant the survival and future prosperity of James I's two kingdoms. Astronomy and cartography were vital to navigation, while geometry had immediate ballistic implications. The title-page of *Pantometria*, for example, explicitly showed an image of a ship's position triangulated from a fortress. The law of property depended also on measurement, and while Ralegh despatched Thomas Hariot, mathematician, to map the American wilderness, William Folkingham, in *Feudigraphia* (1610), declared his epitome of surveying was 'no less remarkable for all undertakers in the Plantations of Ireland or Virginia, for all Travellers for Discoveries of Foreigne Countries'.[3] Knowledge of the rocks, plants, and animals specific to new countries was similarly precious, for it would provide both remedies to endemic diseases, by Hippocratic doctrine, and commodities for exploitation. Exotic expertise was also to be recruited, and while Hakluyt in 1579 sent a spy to discover Persian methods of dyeing, Samuel Purchas in *His Pilgrimes* (1625) reported English merchants in 1610 buying local pigments in Agra. Science would also aid agriculture and husbandry: Thomas Sprat, for example, urged his colleagues in the new Royal Society (founded in 1660) to experiment with the 'transplanting the Eastern spices and other useful Vegetables, into our Western Plantations', and with raising hemp and silkworms in the climates of Ireland and Virginia.

If knowledge was known to give practical advantages, trade and colonies, on the other hand, were recognized to offer philosophical opportunity. While Saloman's House in Bacon's *New Atlantis* (1627) housed in pacific splendour every kind of experiment, the perfection of its learning depended on the 'merchants of light' which it despatched to survey the world. Those who, after 1660, realized Bacon's utopia in the Royal Society affirmed, similarly, that commerce was the key to the improvement of natural knowledge. England's destiny, Thomas Sprat wrote in 1667, was not only to be 'mistress of the Ocean, but the most proper seat for the advancement of knowledge', for London commanded 'a large intercourse with all the Earth'.[4] Contemporaries understood that the practical demands of war and navigation had contributed much to England's scientific development.[5] A clergyman commenting on an expedition to Hudson Bay had joked in 1633, 'I suppose

---

[3] William Folkingham, *Feudigraphia [The Synopsis or Epitome of Surveying]* (London, 1610).

[4] Thomas Sprat, *The History of the Royal Society of London for the Improvement of Natural Knowledge* (1667; London, 1734), pp. 86–87.

[5] J. A. Bennett, 'The Mechanics' Philosophy and the Mechanical Philosophy', *History of Science*, XXIV (1986), pp. 1–28.

the Philosophers Stone is in the North-West Passage. For that theres so much Philosophy in the way to it.'[6] The Royal Society endeavoured in the immediate aftermath of the Navigation Acts formally to harness national trade to the chariot of English science. For how many of Europe's inconveniences might yet be solved by overseas discovery? As Robert Boyle speculated in 1663, 'How many new concretes, rich in medicinal virtues, does the new world present the inquisitive Physicians of the Old?'[7] Thus Boyle gave detailed instructions 'for the use of travellers and navigators' on the collection of specimens and the observation of natural phenomena in the first volume of the *Transactions of the Royal Society* (1666), while his colleagues issued lists of questions to mariners bound for particular countries, interrogating them on their return.[8]

This alliance between philosophy and Empire was not merely a meeting of utility and opportunity. Christian providentialism, the ideological taproot of British Imperialism, shaped both the quest for knowledge and the push for trade and colonies. The Book of Genesis sustained both Natural Theology, the idea that God should be worshipped through research in the Book of Nature, and the belief that the sons of Adam had the right and duty to study and enclose the pagan wilderness. This was most clear during the Civil War, when those who sought the Godly perfection of science were often the most fervent advocates of colonial expansion.[9] The intellectual disciples of Bacon, in particular Benjamin Worsley, later appointed by Cromwell as Surgeon-General to the army in Ireland, were framers and supporters of the Navigation Act of 1651. In Massachusetts, John Winthrop applied alchemy to agriculture, and used its techniques in iron foundries at Saugus and Lynn. The Commonwealth's philosophers arrived in Ireland behind its pikes, and made public fame and, as in the case of William Petty, private wealth, through their schemes for the study and improvement of the country. They proposed that the sale of expropriated Irish property might indeed pay for the 'Advancement of Universal Learning' in the form of an Office of Address, a projected institute of national science which we might take as the middle point

---

[6] Quoted in ibid., p. 21

[7] Robert Boyle, *The Usefulness of Experimental Natural Philosophy* (1663; Oxford, 1664), p. 44.

[8] Robert Boyle, 'General Heads for the Natural History of a Country, Great or Small; Drawn out for the Uses of Travellers and Navigators', *Transactions of the Royal Society*, I (1666), pp. 186–89, 315–16, 330–43. These were reprinted in his *General Heads for the Natural History of a Country* (London, 1692) and enlarged in [John Woodward], *Brief Instructions for Making Observations in All Parts of the World* (London, 1696).

[9] See Charles Webster, *The Great Instauration: Science, Medicine, and Reform, 1626–1660* (London, 1975), esp. pp. 34–47 and 74–75; T. C. Barnard, *Cromwellian Ireland: English Government and Reform in Ireland* (Oxford, 1975); Karen Ordahl Kupperman, 'Errand to the Indies. Puritan Colonization from Providence Island through the Western Design', *William and Mary Quarterly*, (hereafter *WMQ*), Third Series, XII (1988), pp. 70–99. See also, for Puritan hesitations, David Armitage, 'The Cromwellian Protectorate and the Languages of Empire', *The Historical Journal*, XXXV (1992), pp. 531–55.

between Bacon's imagined House of Salomon and the realized Royal Society. This was no mere opportunism; its projectors imagined it fair reward for the services universal learning imminently would render Ireland, and indeed all territory it touched. Samuel Hartlib, the Protestant intellectual, dedicating Gerard Boate's *Ireland's Naturall History* (1652) to Cromwell, promised that this was the age in which Man would regain those powers which Adam lost when an angry Creator had closed 'the conduit pipes of Natural Knowledge'; soon the 'Intellectual Cabinets of Nature [would be] opened... [and] Spiritual and Natural Sanctified Knowledge' liberated.[10] Boate explained how science would guide the redemption of this fallen land, yielding mines of iron, lead, and silver, and saving farm-land from the bog into which the native barbarians had let it decline. In Ireland, as in New England, the expansion of the empire of reason was a responsibility connected to the colonial reclamation of Eden.

If science and Empire drew utopian inspiration from Christianity, knowing the world also became important to the culture of the Anglican church. The future Bishop Sprat in his *History of the Royal Society* (1667) argued that, in alliance with scripture, science was the strongest bulwark against the threat of Enthusiasm and Superstition. Sprat and Boyle, with the later help of Newton and John Ray, domesticated science within the national church. Natural Theology, given formal expression by the devout astronomer William Derham, became equally the most important organizing idea in British science, shaping a tradition of missionary and vicarage naturalism which stretches into the Victorian era.[11] No work was more important in its propagation than Ray's *Wisdom of God Manifested in the Creation* (1691), which went through some fourteen editions in the next century. This began with quoting Psalm 104: 'How manifold are thy works, O Lord! In wisdom hast thou made them all', and proceeded to explore the Plenitude of Creation. That in America, Ray argued, there was 'as great a variety of species as with us, and yet but few common to Europe, or perhaps Africk and Asia' proved 'the Power and Wisdom of him who form'd them all'. The imperial survey of the world thus became a confirmed means of worshipping the Creator.

By the late seventeenth century, therefore, the pursuit of knowledge, commerce and colonies, religious piety, and a nascent patriotism were tightly bound together. The new natural philosophy made its own potent ideological contribution to the making of an Imperial Britain. The Scientific Revolution provided a vision of Nature ordered by laws, and subject in turn to those who discovered these rules. The simple formulae with which Robert Hooke and Robert Boyle were able to link

[10] Samuel Hartlib, 'Epistle Dedicatory', in Gerard Boate, *Ireland's Naturall History* (London, 1652), sig. A4ᵛ & ʳ.
[11] William Derham, *Physico-Theology* (London, 1713) and *Astro-Theology* (London, 1715).

force and extension, pressure and volume, the descriptions by William Harvey and Stephen Hales of the circuit of blood in mammals and of sap in plants, Edmond Halley's demonstration that comets, once tokens of divine displeasure, migrated to and away from the Earth in regular rhythms, and the laws with which Newton explained the movement of cannon-balls on earth and the most distant stars, suggested that Britain, at the dawn of the eighteenth century, enjoyed a regular, rather than miraculous, commerce with Providential truth. Where the British intervened beyond their original islands, they did so now with new confidence in their own efficiency as agents of a benevolent Providence. The same tools of measurement, calculation, and comparison used for the natural world now constructed human society as governed by process and mechanism.[12] William Petty, Charles Davenant, and Gregory King proceeded, in the late seventeenth century, to survey the human and material wealth of the kingdom, confident that they might elucidate the principles which regulated its development.[13] The apparently irresistible logic of statistics affected domestic debates about expansion. For 'Political arithmetic' encouraged Britain to take the Dutch Republic as its model, to continue its reach for Atlantic and Asian trade, and to reorganize taxation around this international exchange. Science, inherently expansive in its universal appetites, thus helped to commit Britain to this 'blue water' destiny: expansion and Empire were made into the facts of a rational Providence.

By the age of Newton, Britain's intellectual successes helped to sustain a vision of her imperial prerogatives and responsibilities. Ephraim Chambers in his *Cyclopaedia* (1728) proclaimed that the Arts and Sciences 'make the difference between your Majesty's Subjects and the Savages of Canada, or the Cape of Good Hope'.[14] For William Petty, more bluntly, the subjugation of the Irish was justified by their lack, among the other attributes of civility, of 'Geometry, Astronomy, Anatomy, Architecture, Engineering...'[15] It is worth noting that while eighteenth-century Britain envied the Chinese their ceramic skills and aesthetics, and assorted aborigines their medicines and savage nobility, it harboured no doubts as to its own pre-eminence in natural knowledge.[16] By the same token, the British now began to

---

[12] See I. B. Cohen, *Interactions: Some Contacts Between the Natural Sciences and the Social Sciences* (London, 1994).

[13] P. H. Buck, 'People who Counted: Political Arithmetic in the Eighteenth Century', *Isis*, LXXIII (1982), pp. 28–45; L. G. Sharp, 'Sir William Petty and Some Aspects of Seventeenth-Century Natural Philosophy', unpublished D. Phil. thesis, Oxford, 1977; Keith Thomas, 'Numeracy in Early Modern England', *Transactions of the Royal Historical Society*, Fifth Series, XXXVII (1987), pp. 103–32.

[14] Ephraim Chambers, *Cyclopaedia, or an Universal Dictionary of Arts and Sciences*, 2 vols. (London, 1728), I, 'Preface'.

[15] William Petty, *The Political Anatomy of Ireland* (London, 1691), p. 21.

[16] For British views of the Chinese and others, see P. J. Marshall and Glyndwr Williams, *The Great Map of Mankind: British Perceptions of the World in the Age of Enlightenment* (London, 1982).

justify conquest as the task of converting those left behind on the ladder of cultural progress to a rational economy and society. Petty, in his *Political Anatomy of Ireland* (1691), for example, presented colonial rule as political alchemy, the work of '*transmuting* one people into another'.[17] He priced the base metal of the Irish at the going rates for African slaves, £25 for men, £15 for women, and £5 for children, and suggested that England, by improving Ireland's economy, would make its inhabitants worth £70, the golden value of Englishmen. Empire was thus made into a natural and benevolent duty. The origins of the later developmental imperialism of the 'Enlightenment' lie in this tangle of scientific and national hubris. The British were learning to trust in their power to multiply the happiness of barbarians, with or without the latter's consent.

Knowledge, linked in complex ways to religion, politics, identity, to the solution of practical difficulties and the pursuit of Mammon and power, was thus a fundamental aspect of British Imperial expansion. This, however, is not to say that there were not a number of counter-currents and hesitations.[18] The political writing and fiction of Jonathan Swift, for example, are an Irish Tory's satire of the projects of Bacon and Petty. The Academy of Lagado in *Gulliver's Travels* (1726) mocked the vanity of the House of Salomon, while *A Modest Proposal* (1729) exposed the inhuman madness which the mechanical rationalism of 'Political Arithmetic' could be employed to support. Some divines might complain, with Richard Mather, the New England Congregationalist, that natural knowledge was 'not sufficient for salvation', while after the French Revolution some feared that secular learning might tend to atheism and subversion.[19] But the alliance of religion with naturalism, which survived from the age of Newton to that of Darwin, meant that very few saw science as intrinsically idolatrous. Indeed, intellectual pursuits were the complement to piety. Knowledge, associated by Christians with revelation, had absorbed a moral aura, which it bestowed in turn on those who, by education and avocation, became its servants in any corner of the globe.

The civilization at the centre of the Empire, like the settlements in the islands of the West Indies and along the mouths of North America's rivers, profited from the influence of this complex of values. Both science and empire could depend in Britain on private initiative. This helps, perhaps, to explain both Britain's cultural achievements and its ultimate mastery of France in Asia and the Americas. In

[17] Petty, *Political Anatomy*, p. 21 (my emphasis). See also Nicholas Canny, *Kingdom and Colony: Ireland in the Atlantic World, 1560–1800* (Baltimore, 1988), p. 112.

[18] See the exploration of the Civic Humanist distrust of territorial empire in David Armitage, 'The British Empire and the Civic Tradition', unpublished Ph.D. thesis, Cambridge, 1992.

[19] J. B. Morrell, 'Professors Robinson and Playfair, and the *Theophobia Gallica*: Natural Philosophy, Religion and Politics in Edinburgh', *Notes and Records of the Royal Society*, XXVI (1971), pp. 43–63.

France the Académie des Sciences and the scientific survey of the colonies were, like the Compagnies de Colonisation, actively managed by the Crown.[20] In certain periods, such as after the Seven Years War, this direction was committed and enlightened, and government and science in French colonies were examples to the world.[21] But when the Ministère de la Marine et Colonies lacked vision or courage all foundered. While, on the other hand, both British science and its commercial and colonial expansion came to benefit from alliances with the state, neither depended as fastly on the fickle patronage of kings or ministers. They were propelled instead by the speculative chaos of the coffee-houses of London. Curiosity, moral certainty, greed, and patriotism, fused into the restless enthusiasm of the volunteer.

An informal empire of gentlemanly amateurs emerged to span Britain's eighteenth-century world. Observations, information, specimens, and argument, journeyed from physicians in Edinburgh to absentee planters in London, parsons in New England, and merchants at Calcutta and Canton.

In the accumulation of learning, as in that of wealth, the 'volunteer' was often the exploiter of others' labour and expertise. 'High' science depended on the skills of craftsmen and instrument-makers, and on the insight of lesser amateurs. Élite natural history might be seen as an enterprise for the integration of the knowledge of those indigenous to particular places into central categories and collections. What is important to grasp is that this process was at work within Britain as well as overseas: the same intellectual, medical, and patriotic motives manifest in research on the exotic also inspired Robert Plot's *Natural History of Oxfordshire* (1676) and the surveys of English counties during the Napoleonic wars. Those who studied the immensity of nature turned to local people for help. The young Joseph Banks famously learned botany as much from the 'cunning women' of the Lincolnshire countryside as from Gerard's *Herbal* (1597). In the vast spaces of the earth untouched by European natural history, the traveller was even more dependent on local informants. All collectors hired assistants who helped them to discover and explain plants, animals, or minerals. Moreover, on every continent there were sophisticated native natural-historical and geographical traditions which were quietly privatized into the cultural property of Western science and of individual savants. Thus, in volume two of the *Historia Plantarum* (1688), John Ray marvelled at the immense diversity uncovered by Dutch research in the tropics: 'Who could believe that in the one province of Malabar, hardly a vast place, that there would be

---

[20] James E. McClellan, III, *Colonialism and Science: Saint-Domingue in the Old Regime* (Baltimore, 1992).

[21] See below, pp. 244–47.

three hundred unique indigenous species of trees and fruit?'[22] But the natural histories he admired—William Piso's and George Marcgrave's *De medicina Brasiliense* and *Historia rerum naturalium Brasiliae* (1648), Adrian van Rheede tot Drakenstein's *Hortus Indicus Malabaricus* and Rumpf's *Herbarium Amboinense*—were essentially digests of the botanical and medical knowledge of Brazilians and South Asians.[23] Michel Adanson's later challenge to the Linnaean system depended equally on Senegalese scientific expertise. Similarly, in the Pacific and the Arctic, geographical knowledge acquired over centuries of exploration was converted into the maps and glory of British explorers.[24] The story of such appropriations will remain a large and rich subject, not least because so many cultures were destroyed by the civilizations to which they gave their knowledge. With learning, as with sugar or any other commodity, those merchants who were its most recent owners are better rewarded than the hands which brought it out of the earth.

London sat at the centre of this system of intellectual accumulation. But if one argues that everyone in the eighteenth-century Empire lived in 'London's provinces', one must equally concede that modern London was itself constructed within these new global arrangements.[25] The cultural life of that city, and by extension of England at large, should be recognized as inseparable from the facts of commerce and colonies. This connection remains visible today in the libraries of All Souls College, Oxford, and Eton College, both built with wealth which derived principally from African slavery and West Indian sugar. The intellectual life of the learned institutions of London—the Royal Society, the Chelsea Physic Garden (1673), the Society for the Encouragement of Arts, Manufactures, and Commerce (1754), and the Linnean Society (1788)—by the same token, was nourished by East and West Indian fortunes, and often absorbed in problems of overseas administration and exploitation.[26]

Religious and scientific impulses encouraged the exotic collections of individuals such as Bishop Henry Compton, who bought and bartered his way to the finest collection of plants in Augustan England. But shells, insects, or minerals, were gathered as much for the aesthetic and possessive satisfaction they gave, as

---

[22] John Ray, *Historia Plantarum*, 3 vols. (London, 1686–1704), II (1688), sig. A3ᵛ ('Quis crederet in una provincia Malabara...inveniri').

[23] K. S. Manild, ed., *Botany and History of Hortus Malabaricus* (Rotterdam, 1980); Richard Grove, 'The Transfer of Botanical Knowledge between Asia and Europe, 1498–1800', *Journal of the Japan–Netherlands Institute*, III (1991), pp. 160–76.

[24] See below, pp. 552, 564; Michael Bravo, 'Science and Discovery in the Admiralty Voyages to the Arctic Regions in Search of a North-West Passage', unpublished Ph.D. thesis, Cambridge, 1992.

[25] I. K. Steele, 'The Empire and Provincial Elites: An Interpretation of Some Recent Writings on the English Atlantic, 1675–1740', *Journal of Imperial and Commonwealth History*, VIII (1980), p. 3.

[26] James E. McClellan III, *Science Reorganized: Scientific Societies in the Eighteenth Century* (New York, 1985); D. G. C. Allan, *William Shipley, Founder of the Royal Society of Arts* (London, 1979).

out of any pious or erudite desire to scan the *scala naturae*. Virtuosi such as Hans Sloane, William Sherard, Ashton Lever, and Joseph Banks created enormous treasuries of natural and artificial objects of all kinds.[27] Private clubs linked such gentlemen with lesser amateurs who provided them with specimens and intelligence, and direct connections with mariners and colonists. One in the Temple Coffee House, for example, joined Sloane to James Petiver, a London apothecary, praised by John Ray as 'the best skilled in Oriental & indeed all exotick plants of any man I knew... and a man of the greatest correspondence of any in England as to these matters'.[28] Agents of virtuosi and speculators in rarities, such as Petiver, cultivated contacts on the waterfront, and on vessels bound for strange lands. Thus missions against the Barbary pirates, and slavers bound for 'Ye coasts of Guinea', came to supply London with 'divers animals, shells, insects, [and] plants'.[29] Naval and army officers, planters, diplomats, and East India traders bound abroad were persuaded to harvest foreign novelties.

London was, however, only the climax of a wider pattern of activity: the countryside was as colonized by the Empire as the capital. The leading lights of the metropolis practised a kind of cultural transhumance, carrying their exotic concerns between city and countryside. Sir James Edward Smith, the Unitarian merchant, for example, transported the world, embodied in the Linnaean collections, seasonally between the city and his Norwich residence. Figures such as Smith, Sir Joseph Banks (Lincolnshire magnate and President of the Royal Society, 1778–1820), or Dawson Turner (the Yarmouth banker, antiquary, and botanist) were nuclei around which coalesced the provincial intellectual life of parsons and landed gentlemen. Many titled amateurs, such as the fifth Duke of Bedford, kept valuable collections of scientific instruments, and strange plants and animals at their country houses. The amateur astronomy and botany of George III and Charlotte in the grounds of the royal palace of Kew may be assimilated to this pattern. But such curiosity about nature and the exotic was more generally part of the fabric of the public sphere of eighteenth-century Britain.[30] Peter Collinson, the naturalist and antiquary, wrote to Linnaeus in 1747, 'We are very fond of all branches of Natural History; they sell the best of any books in England.' Interest in

---

[27] Arthur Macgregor, ed., *Sir Hans Sloane: Collector, Scientist, Antiquary, Founding Father of the British Museum* (London, 1994); John Gascoigne, *Joseph Banks and the English Enlightenment: Useful Knowledge and Polite Culture* (Cambridge, 1994).

[28] Ray to Petiver, 25 [n.d.] 1702, B[ritish] L[ibrary], Sloane MSS, 4063, f. 187. See also R. B. Stearns, 'J. Petiver Promoter of Natural Science', *Proceedings of the American Antiquarian Society*, LXII (1953), pp. 243–365.

[29] BL, Sloane MSS, 1968, p. 166 and Archives of the Royal Society, Cl. P X(i), 31.

[30] Marshall and Williams, *The Great Map of Mankind*; Paul Langford, *A Polite and Commercial People: England, 1727–83* (Oxford, 1989); Kathleen Wilson, 'Empire of Virtue: The Imperial Project and Hanoverian Culture c. 1720–1785', in Lawrence Stone, ed., *An Imperial State at War: Britain from 1689 to 1815* (London, 1994), pp. 128–64.

strange lands and people was alive in the polite culture of the age, and was
regularly attended to by popular publications such as the *Gentleman's Magazine*.

Scotland was similarly involved in the new facts of British power. It was itself
directly connected, particularly through Glasgow, with Atlantic and Asian trade
and colonies. Its intellectual life reflected this engagement. Scotland's cultural
vitality can in part be explained by local influences, in particular the renaissance in
the universities. Edinburgh, Glasgow, and Aberdeen offered instruction in natural
philosophy and nurtured scientific research a century before Oxford or Cambridge.[31] Scottish learning was also unashamed in taking a practical concern with
material improvement. The Society for Improvers in the Knowledge of Agriculture (1734) exemplified the concerns which encouraged study of natural history
and chemistry in mid-century and the great statistical surveys of the 1780s and
1790s. But if scientific activity was stimulated by agricultural enterprise, that in
turn was driven by the growth in towns and manufactures, and ultimately by the
pull, via Glasgow in the west and Edinburgh in the east, of a wider world. In these
cities, medical schools directly linked Scotland with more-distant British provinces. James Sutherland, who directed the Physic Garden in Edinburgh, for
example, received specimens from the apothecaries he trained 'as surgeons in
ships to the East and West Indies', and also from those who accompanied the
Scottish imperial adventure in Darien.[32] John Hope, instructor in *materia medica*
at Edinburgh from 1761, who founded in 1763 a Society for the Importation of
Foreign Plants and Seeds, and later John Walker, professor from 1779 to 1803,
transmitted a practical natural history to America and India via several generations of Scottish physicians. That 'civil history' and political economy which was
Scotland's principal gift to the Enlightenment must equally be understood as a
consequence of the country's new imperial situation. A Scotland which had been
pulled to the centre of the world was capable of cosmopolitan sympathies which it
could not have fostered a century before.

The evolution of Ireland's intellectual life may equally be related to its ambiguous place within the British Empire. Ireland had, of course, made its own
contribution to England: many distinguished Restoration natural philosophers—such as Robert Boyle, William Brouncker (the first President of the
Royal Society), and William Petty—were in fact either Irish or derived their wealth

[31] See, for example, Colin MacLaurin, *A Defence of the Letter Published in the Philosophical Transactions for March and April 1729 Concerning the Impossible Roots of Equations* (Edinburgh, 1730). More
generally, see Richard B. Sher, *Church and University in the Scottish Enlightenment: The Moderate
Literati of Edinburgh* (Princeton, 1985), and P. Wood, 'Science and the Aberdeen Enlightenment', in
Peter Jones, ed., *Philosophy and Science in the Scottish Enlightenment* (Edinburgh, 1988), pp. 39–64.
[32] Sutherland to Petiver, 25 March 1700, BL, Sloane MSS, 4063, ff. 9–10. On Edinburgh, see James
Sutherland, *Hortus Medicus Edinburgensis* (Edinburgh, 1683); H. R. Fletcher and W. H. Brown, *The
Royal Botanic Garden Edinburgh, 1670–1920* (Edinburgh, 1920).

or title from that island. Similarly, Protestant Ireland, particularly through Trinity College, Dublin, was fully a participant in contemporary scientific enthusiasms. William Molyneux, one of its alumni, assisted by Petty, founded the Dublin Philosophical Society in 1683 which sheltered, until 1708, mathematical, antiquarian, and natural historical research, including that of the young George Berkeley.[33] From the presses of Dublin came many treatises on geometry, mechanics, optics, and natural philosophy.[34] These books were mainly read within the university community. But there is much evidence to suggest that science had a wider appeal in eighteenth-century Ireland: William Starrat's *The Doctrine of Projectiles* (1733), for example, attracted over a hundred Irish subscribers, while in the 1730s at least one man earned his living in Dublin as a vendor of mathematical books and instruments.[35] Indeed, as in Scotland, antiquarian and scientific interests became associated, as in William Molyneux's *The Case of Ireland* (1698), with an emerging Protestant Irish patriotism. The Dublin Society for Improving Husbandry, Manufactures, and other Useful Arts of 1731 sought to put science at the disposal of Irish agriculture and industry. The brief experiment in Irish legislative independence after 1782 led directly to new intellectual initiatives: the Royal Irish Academy and the Dunsink Observatory in Dublin (both 1785); while in Armagh, Archbishop Robinson founded another Observatory (1790), in the hope that it might be the seed for a new Irish university which would 'conciliate and soften down the minds of our various sectaries in the north of Ireland, and bind them to the common interests of the empire'.[36]

Across the Atlantic, the 'pure' and practical varieties of learning also attracted the propertied mind. Religious, scientific, and economic motives inspired the natural historical survey of the resources of new territory. Colonial savants, many of whom were corresponding fellows of the Royal Society and the Society of Arts, initially directed their attentions to supplying Britain with local observations and specimens.[37] Newton's *Principia* depended, in part, on American astronomy, while the younger John Winthrop returned objects to the Royal Society from Massachusetts in the 1660s, as did Governor Sir Thomas Lynch and Hans Sloane from

---

[33] K. T. Hoppen, *The Common Scientist in the Seventeenth Century: A Study of the Dublin Philosophical Society, 1683–1708* (London, 1970).

[34] *Inter alia* Robert Steell, *A Treatise of Conic Sections* (Dublin, 1723); William Hales, *Sonorum Doctrina Rationalis et Experimentalis* (Dublin, 1728); John Stack, *A Short System of Optics* (Dublin, 1787).

[35] See Samuel Fuller, *Practical Astronomy* (Dublin, 1732).

[36] J. A. Bennett, *Church, State and Astronomy in Ireland: 200 Years of the Armagh Observatory* (Belfast, 1990), p. 5.

[37] Raymond Phineas Stearns, 'Colonial Fellow of the Royal Society of London, 1661–1788', *WMQ*, Third Series, III (1946), pp. 208–68; D. J. Struik, *Yankee Science in the Making* (New York, 1962); 'Papers and Draughts of the Reverend Mr. Banister in Virginia', BL, Sloane MSS, 4002.

Jamaica in the 1670s and 1680s.[38] But, at the same time, Winthrop and others began to study America for their own sake. The short-lived Boston Philosophical Society, founded by Increase Mather (an alumnus of Trinity College, Dublin) in 1683, committed itself, for example, to the 'rarities' of New England.[39] Natural histories of Barbados by Richard Ligon, of New England by John Josselyn, and of Carolina by John Lawson, were similarly directed as much to colonists as to a metropolitan public.[40] In the North American colonies there were high rates of literacy, active networks for communication, and with seven universities (against England's two, Scotland's four, and Ireland's one), many sources for an indigenous intelligensia.[41] Boston, New York, and in particular Philadelphia were centres of intellectual life, in exchange with each other, with Britain, and the continent of Europe.[42] Patriotism led, as in Scotland and Ireland, to the formation of learned societies, such as the American Philosophical Society (1743, refounded in 1766), and to such analogues of the Society of Arts as the Society for Promoting Arts, Agriculture, and Oeconomy of New York (1764), the Society for the Encouragement of Natural History and of Useful Arts of Barbados (1784), and the Physico-Medical Society of Grenada (1791).[43] By mid-century American natural philosophers, such as James Logan and Benjamin Franklin, made fundamental contributions to astronomy, optics, plant physiology, and the study of electricity. America, at the same time, was rediscovered through creole eyes in Thomas Jefferson's *Notes on the State of Virginia* (1781) and in the *History Civil and Commercial of the British Colonies in the West Indies* (1793) of Bryan Edwards. Unnameable Africans, whose labour made possible the philosophical leisure of Jefferson and Edwards, also explored the New World environment, but their discoveries survive only in the interstices of the folk medicine of the Antilles and the American South.

---

[38] Royal Society Archives, Cl. P X (i): 3, 4, 13, 20 and 28.

[39] Otho T. Beall, 'Cotton Mather's Early "Curiosa Americana" and the Boston Philosophical Society of 1683', *WMQ*, Third Series, XVIII (1961), pp. 360–62.

[40] Among these Richard Ligon, *A True and Exact history of the Island of Barbados* (London, 1657); John Josselyn, *New-England's Rarities Discovered: in Birds, Beasts, Fishes, Serpents And Plants Of That Country* (London, 1672); Hans Sloane, *A Voyage to the Islands Madera, Barbados, Nieves, S. Christophers and Jamaica*, 2 vols. (London, 1707–25); John Lawson, *A New Voyage to Carolina, containing the Exact Description and Natural History of that Country* (London, 1709).

[41] Richard D. Brown, *Knowledge is Power. The Diffusion of Information in Early America, 1700–1865* (Oxford, 1989).

[42] Donald Fleming, *Science and Technology in Providence, 1760–1914* (Providence, RI, 1952); F. J. Kilgrew, 'The Rise of Scientific Activity in Colonial New England', *Yale Journal of Biology and Medicine*, XXII (1949), p. 135.

[43] For North America, see Brooke Hindle, *The Pursuit of Science in Revolutionary America, 1735–1789* (Chapel Hill, NC, 1956). For Barbados and Grenada see Joshua Steele to Joseph Banks, 14 July 1781, BL, Add. MSS, 33977: f. 135; J. Steele to the Society of Arts, 14 July 1784, Society of Arts Archives, A11/45; and [?] to Sir Joseph Banks, 9 March 1791, Sutro Library, Sir Joseph Banks Correspondence, reel 20.

Outside the major areas of settlement, the outposts of British commerce also extended the scale and character of Britain's intellectual life. From the Canadian wastes, the Hudson's Bay Company, for example, supplied curiosities 'natural and artificial'.[44] After 1763 Britain's vastly augmented power and responsibility similarly encouraged new study of the culture and landscape of Asia. Warren Hastings, Governor-General of Bengal, actively promoted study of the indigenous languages of law and public life, in particular Persian and Bengali, and of the Hindu tradition.[45] Collections of strange plants and animals, arts and antiquities were returned to London. By the 1780s British India began to sustain its own centres of intellectual life. William Jones founded the Asiatick Society of Bengal in 1784, to encourage enquiry into 'the History, Civil, and Natural, the Antiquities, Arts, Sciences, and Literature of Asia'.[46] It quickly became the most important learned society in the British colonies. In his third discourse to the Society, in 1786, Jones proposed that Sanskrit was related to, and possibly the ancestor of, Greek and Latin, the 'Gothic' and 'Celtic' languages, thus laying the foundation for comparative philology.[47] Jones was only the most distinguished example of the 'cultivated talents' which established themselves in the military, medical, and civil services of the East India Company. The reports they returned on the South Asian past and present were to have enormous influence on European culture and civilization.[48]

This pattern of intellectual life, in which amateur enthusiasm drove learning and culture, survived into the next century. Those who controlled the purse-strings at Westminister preferred to leave scholarship, like charity, to the church or the volunteer. Much depended on the abilities and curiosity of such independent gentlemen as Kames, Franklin, or Jones. In this context, wealthy individuals could rise to great heights through their purchase of materials for research and others' labour and knowledge. The distinction of Sir Joseph Banks, for example, depended in part on the research institute he maintained at Soho Square where, with such distinguished naturalists as Daniel Solander and Robert Brown at his

---

[44] Royal Society Archives, Journal Book 27, pp. 199–200.

[45] P. J. Marshall, 'Warren Hastings as Scholar and Patron', in A. Whiteman, J. S. Bromley, and P. G. M. Dickson, eds., *Statesmen, Scholars and Merchants: Essays in Eighteenth-Century History Presented to Dame Lucy Sutherland* (Oxford, 1973), pp. 242–62.

[46] S. N. Mukherjee, *Sir William Jones: A Study in Eighteenth-Century British Attitudes to India*, 2nd edn. (London, 1987); O. P. Kejariwal, *The Asiatic Society of Bengal and the Discovery of India's Past, 1784–1838* (Delhi, 1988).

[47] [William Jones, ed.,] *Asiatick Researches* (London, 1788), I, pp. 415–31; P. J. Marshall, ed., *British Discovery of Hinduism in the Eighteenth Century* (Cambridge, 1970), pp. 246–61.

[48] Raymond Schwab, *La Renaissance orientale* (Paris, 1950); David Kopf, *British Orientalism and the Bengal Renaissance* (London, 1969).

disposal, he presided over collections returned from every corner of British power. Since opportunities to make a living by one's skills were very limited, the support of Banks or other patrons was vital to poor men with intellectual interests. Yet, from the middle of the eighteenth century we may see the outlines of a new regime in which the British state, very gradually, came to patronize the arts and sciences, and learning began to depend on public support. From the late eighteenth and early nineteenth centuries, the Admiralty, the War Office, East India Company, Home Office, the Board of Trade, and scientists such as Banks began to co-operate, in unprecedented ways, in projects for the systematic survey and inventory of natural phenomena, and for the management of colonial economies. This kernel of a formal empire of professional knowledge coalesced within the galaxy of amateurs.

France was central to this process. The threat of Bourbon world hegemony, and the example of French innovation, shaped Britain's encounter with the Enlightenment in the eighteenth century, in the same way that Spanish power had once catalyzed England's response to the Renaissance. By 1763 Britain had clear extra-European supremacy, but France remained dangerous, retaining powerful resources and a capacity to intervene on any ocean. The Anglo-French antagonism placed new resources behind the encyclopaedic impulses of the Enlightenment. Voyages of discovery, with their implications for commerce and naval warfare, represented a principal area of cultural competition. The French Crown, and in particular the Ministère de la Marine et Colonies, came to launch a number of elaborate and well-funded missions of exploration in mid-century, including the Paris Académie's survey of astronomy, natural history, and the Earth's curvature in Peru, Ecuador, and Lapland in the 1740s, and Nicholas Le Caille's journey to observe the Transit of Mercury from the Cape in 1751. Where France pursued advantages, Britain had to follow. In the 1760s, when the Transit of Venus was twice expected, French projects for its observation in the Pacific stimulated both the dispatch of Peter Pallas by Catherine II to Siberia and the great *Endeavour* expedition of the Admiralty under James Cook, with Joseph Banks on board, to the South Seas.[49]

British exploration in the age of Cook owed much to the example France provided of the integration of maritime and scientific aims and expertise. Before mid-century, the Admiralty had given very slender support to science, and had certainly never carried such savants as Banks or Solander as supernumeries.[50] The precedent for Cook's scientific party was French: their expedition to survey the

[49] Harry Woolf, *The Transits of Venus: A Study of Eighteenth-Century Science* (London, 1959).
[50] Glyndwr Williams, '"To Make Discoveries of Countries Unknown": The Admiralty and Pacific Exploration in the Eighteenth Century', The Caird Lecture, National Maritime Museum, Greenwich, 24 May 1995, p. 8.

Transit of Venus, which set out under Louis Antoine de Bougainville in November 1766, carried a naturalist and an astronomer. In the same way, La Perouse in *L'Astrolabe* and *La Boussole* (1785), with their remarkable company of leading scientists—two botanists, an engineer, a geographer, an astronomer, two draughtsmen, and J-A. Mongès, physicist and chaplain—set the standard which the Admiralty attempted to match in missions such as that of the *Investigator* (1801).[51] Just as the *Endeavour* expedition followed hot on the heels of Bougainville's *Boudeuse*, La Perouse left on 1 August 1785, thirty days before the British expedition in the *King George* and *Queen Charlotte* left also to the North Pacific; similarly, Matthew Flinders sailed with his team of scientists to survey the Australian coast in the *Investigator* in July 1801 behind Nicholas Baudin who had left in October 1800, for the same waters, with the *Géographe* and the *Naturaliste*. On land and sea, in West Africa and the Arctic, as in the Pacific, imperial rivalry similarly quickened British exploration. It was not merely for nostalgic reasons that, in 1771, the vessels bound on Cook's second voyage to the Pacific were initially named the *Drake* and the *Raleigh*.[52]

In the application of science to government, as well as to navigation, France spurred British emulation. The Ministère de la Marine et Colonies had applied science to the development of France's tropical possessions, despatching botanists to survey the resources of colonies, such as Michel Adanson, sent to Guyane in 1763, creating botanic gardens so that new economic crops could be introduced from the East to the West Indies, and founding forest reserves to protect the supply of rain. The success of these schemes was apparent by the 1780s, when the plantation economies of the Antilles, and in particular Saint-Domingue, were responsible for up to a half of French trade. What was significant was not merely the scale and co-ordination of these efforts, linking French colonies and trading outposts on three oceans, but their philosophical foundation. For these initiatives in the service of natural history, economic inventory, strategic intelligence, and anthropological interests, were associated with a new ideal of Enlightened administration. Britain would first attempt to match French efforts, but ultimately came under the influence of the underlying ideology.

The Scientific Revolution had persuaded many people across Europe to believe that Nature was subject to rational laws which might be discovered and applied to human purposes. The idea that Knowledge might be the basis of more efficient statecraft, already implicit in Bacon and Petty, found corresponding encourage-

[51] J. J. H. Labillardière, *Relation du voyage à la recherche de La Pérouse, pendant les années 1791–1792*, 2 vols. (Paris, 1799); John Dunmore, *Pacific Explorer: The Life of Jean-François de La Perouse, 1741–1788* (Sydney, 1985). See David Mackay, *In the Wake of Cook: Exploration, Science and Empire, 1700–1801* (London, 1985), p. 1, for a discussion of the *Investigator* as the paradigm of British scientific exploration.

[52] *Gentleman's Magazine*, XLI (1771), p. 565.

ment. Cameralists, Physiocrats, and their Scottish correspondents sought to apply
Newtonian scientific rationality to the government of economies.[53] Statesmen
around Europe became enthusiastic users of information.[54] People had to be
counted, if taxation and conscription were to be planned rationally. Land had to
be mapped and measured, and its natural resources inventoried, to allow its best
defence and exploitation. At the same, the faith that information was necessary for
efficient government produced 'knowledge panics', in which statesmen, moved by
fear more than by the rational needs of the state, anxiously sought expert advice
and organized public investigations.[55]

This enthusiasm for informed policy spread to Britain in mid-century. Careful
projects for geodesy, mapping, and ultimately census, often in response to anticipated military needs, characterized this period, with surveys of Scotland (1745–61),
Quebec (1760–61), eastern North America (1764–70), Ireland (1778–90), and
ultimately the Ordnance Survey of England itself in the 1790s.[56] If the Ordnance
Survey followed clearly on the post-1783 Cassini mappings in France, other
colonial projects equally followed French example. The activity of the French
state after 1763 to promote colonial development was admired and envied at every
frontier of British power. Johann Reinhold Forster, in his preface of 1772 to
Bougainville's *Voyage au Tour du Monde*, wrote that 'every true patriot' would
wish that the East India Company would imitate the French and despatch 'men
properly acquainted with mathematics, natural history, [and] physic' to discover
new branches of trade and commerce. The keeper of the jail in Antigua complained that: 'The French have certainly supply'd all the plants which grow in the
English islands . . . they have several Plants of the Clove tree and black pepper from
Cayenne at Guadeloupe . . . they have got two Cinnamon plants from India. The
Intendant is a man of letters a great promoter of every branch of science . . .'[57] In
1788 the keeper of the then new botanic garden in Calcutta pointed to its French
colonial predecessors and regretted 'the shame of being 20 years behind our

[53] F. Etner, 'L'Ancien Régime et le calcul économique', *Economy and Society*, XVIII (1984); A. S.
Hetherington, 'Isaac Newton's Influence on Adam Smith's Natural Laws in Economics', *Journal of the
History of Ideas*, XLIV (1983), pp. 497–505; T. W. Hutchinson, *Before Adam Smith: The Emergence of
Political Economy, 1662–1776* (Oxford, 1988); Keith Tribe, *Governing Economy: The Reformation of
German Economic Discourse, 1750–1840* (Cambridge, 1988).

[54] Torc Frängsmyr, J. L. Heilbron, and Robin E. Rider, eds., *The Quantifying Spirit in the Eighteenth
Century* (Oxford, 1990).

[55] I owe this category of 'knowledge panics' to C. A. Bayly, 'Knowing the Country: Empire and
Information in India', *Modern Asian Studies*, XXVII (1993), p. 38.

[56] Mathew Edney, 'Mapping and Empire: British Trigonometrical Surveys in India and the
European Concept of Systematic Survey, 1799–1843', unpublished Ph.D. dissertation, Wisconsin, 1990,
p. 56.

[57] H. de Ponthieu to Banks, 27 Sept. 1785, A[rchives of the] R[oyal] B[otanic] G[ardens] Kew,
B[anks] C[orrespondence], I (2), 205.

neighbours in everything of this kind'.[58] Such French experiments directly preceded and inspired the missions entrusted to William Bligh for the transfer of
breadfruit from the Pacific (1787–89 and 1793), and all of the colonial botanic
gardens, forest conservancies, schemes for plant transfer, or projects for the
scientific survey of resources, which emerged in the British Empire in the last
two decades of the century.

Something more than piecemeal imitation of policies was at work. Indeed, we
may identify a British idiom of Enlightened statecraft emerging from the 1780s,
parallel to the Bourbon, Jacobin, and Napoleonic regimes in France, within which
knowledge and expertise had new political moment.[59] After 1783 Pitt the Younger's
ministry faced a heavy burden of debt, and Whig criticism that, in alliance with the
Crown, they squandered revenue and corrupted Parliament. The ideal of progressive administration complemented limited economical and parliamentary reform,
and provided a justification for the power concentrated in the hands of the King's
favourite minister. More than ever, there was the need both to govern efficiently
and to be seen to be so doing. Many came under the direct or indirect influence of
Physiocratic and Cameralist visions of the state, aided by reason, as the pioneer of
public progress. At home and in the colonial sphere, British politicians came to
experiment with *dirigiste* policies, which often depended on the pursuit and
application of scientific knowledge. 'There is but one all-powerful cause which
instigates mankind,' the political economist Arthur Young thundered, 'and that is
GOVERNMENT.'[60] The British state increasingly turned to figures such as Jeremy
Bentham for advice on prison reform, or Richard Price for the Sinking Fund.
Henry Dundas (as Minister for India, 1793–1801, Home Secretary, 1791–94, and
Secretary of War, 1794–1801), Robert Banks Jenkinson (later Prime Minister, as
Lord Liverpool), and others of Pitt's circle recruited Sir Joseph Banks, then
President of the Royal Society, to advise on all aspects of colonial administration
and exploration, on whaling, naval stores, and the work of the Board of Trade, the
Privy Council, and the Mint. The voluntary intellectual activity of propertied
gentlemen began to be annexed to, if not absorbed within, the life of the state.
Where in mid-century, for example, the initiative of the Society of Arts had led to
the foundation of a botanic garden in St Vincent, from the 1780s the War Office
undertook its management, while, in other colonies, Governors founded

---

[58] R. Kyd, 'Remarks on the President of the Royal Society's Propositions for the Introduction of the
Tea Plant into the Company's Provinces' (1788), ARBG, Kew, Bound MSS.

[59] Here I enlarge the suggestion of C. A. Bayly, *Imperial Meridian. The British Empire and the World,
1780–1830* (London, 1989).

[60] Arthur Young, *Travels during the Years 1787, 1788, and 1789 Undertaken More Particularly With A
View To Ascertaining the Cultivation, Wealth, Resources, and National Prosperity, of the Kingdom of
France* (London, 1792), p. 29.

equivalent collections.[61] The state, for practical and ideological reasons, now intervened in the place of private enterprise in the acclimatizing of economic crops within the British Empire. Captain Bligh's voyages were only one consequence of new visions of government's prerogatives and responsibilities.

The East India Company in the 1780s similarly turned new resources to the patronage of learning. Partly it sought practical advantages. It appointed Alexander Dalrymple its 'hydrographer', and conducted important surveys of the coast of Coromandel and of routes which led to China, and in 1801 presented £1,200 in *batta* or table money to the officers of the *Investigator* voyage, in order 'to Encourage the men of Science to discover such things as will be useful to the Commerce of India to find new passages'.[62] Since the Company's wealth depended on its power to make war and raise taxes, it was anxious to have accurate maps of the country and some measure of the human and natural resources under its control.

Through cultivating literature and science, however, the Directors and servants of the Company also sought to show at home and in India that its authority was virtuous. To those who wished to impeach him in 1787 Hastings asked, in defence: 'Whether I have shown a disregard to science; or whether I have not, on the contrary, by public endowments, by personal attentions, and by the selection of men for appointments suited to their talents, given effectual encouragement to it.'[63] Encourager of Jones, and patron of natural history and the study of Indian languages and antiquities, he indeed had every reason to feel his administration had been enlightened. Such efforts were positively encouraged from Britain: when Lord Cornwallis sailed to assume his appointment as Governor-General in 1786, he was instructed to send home a Botanical Despatch in addition to the standard Political, Civil, and Military Despatches.[64] Cornwallis, and later the Marquess Wellesley (1798–1805), followed and expanded on Hastings's example. From the 1780s, astronomical surveys were planted at Madras, Calcutta, Bombay, and St Helena, and a Great Trigonometrical survey was organized.[65] The Company founded new botanic gardens while revitalizing Mughal collections, so Calcutta, Madras, and Saharanpur became centres for the study of Indian plants and for the introduction of valuable exotics.[66] Wellesley despatched Francis Buchanan,

[61] Society of Arts Archives: Minutes of Committee, 1760–62 (3): 166; 1763–64 (6): 22.

[62] Quoted in Mackay, *In the Wake of Cook*, p. 5.

[63] Marshall, 'Warren Hastings as Scholar and Patron', p. 255.

[64] G. Yonge to Banks, 8 April 1787, ARBG, Kew, B C, I (2), 263.

[65] See Edney, 'Mapping and Empire'.

[66] See D. Kumar, 'The Evolution of Colonial Science in India: Natural History and the East India Company', in John M. MacKenzie, ed., *Imperialism and the Natural World* (Manchester, 1990), pp. 51–67; S. K. Sen, 'The Character of the Introduction of Western Science in India during the Eighteenth and Nineteenth Centuries', *Indian Journal of the History of Science*, I (1966), pp. 112–22.

Nathaniel Wallich, and others on ambitious missions to collect natural and artificial curiosities and to describe the landscape and culture of Mysore, Bengal, Madras, Nepal, Ceylon, and the Malay coast.[67] In his minute of 1804, Wellesley expressed the assumption of his age: 'To facilitate and promote all enquiries which may be calculated to enlarge the boundaries of general science is a duty imposed on the British Government in India by its present exalted situation.'[68] Service to the cause of Knowledge lent dignity to an enterprise which might have appeared otherwise as mere plunder and rapine.

The Admiralty, at the end of the century, began to recruit scientific expertise, and with Banks's encouragement, to contribute to the progress of British science. In a sense this was building on older foundations: from 1714 Parliament had constituted the Board of Longitude from members of the Admiralty, mathematicians, and astronomers in order to encourage the application of science to navigation. Individual officers, such as Cook, had reached enthusiastically for new tools and methods. But the business of the navy was war, and its attitude to science often reflected some feeling that gentlemanly pursuits were unwanted distractions. Only in 1795 did the Admiralty create a Hydrographic Department and woo Dalrymple away from the East India Company.[69] But from the 1790s, and particularly early in the next century, the Admiralty and the Navy Board took a systematic interest in hydrology and exploration. The navy was also recruited to serve the Royal Society—as in the projects for plant transfer between the Pacific, Asia, and the Caribbean encouraged by Sir Joseph Banks—and for high-latitude missions to discover 'natural' standards for weights and measures.[70] The programme of hydrological surveys initiated in this period conveyed British naturalists, from Robert Brown on the *Investigator* to Charles Darwin on the *Beagle*, to more of the world than any of their European competitors. At the same time, Free Trade Imperialism could float on the fact that by the mid-Victorian era, Britain's fleets of war and trade possessed accurate charts, sextants, and chronometers. The interaction of science and sea power ultimately exceeded the most sanguine predictions of Bacon.

The more intimate involvement of knowledge and British power after 1750 created important opportunities for scientific professionals. It was at the Empire's

[67] Marika Vicziany, 'Imperialism, Botany and Statistics in Early Nineteenth–Century India: The Surveys of Francis Buchanan (1762–1829)', *Modern Asian Studies*, XX (1986), pp. 625–61.

[68] Mildred Archer, 'India and Natural History: The Role of the East India Company, 1785–1858', *History Today*, IX (Nov. 1959), pp. 736–43.

[69] Archibald Day, *The Admiralty Hydrographic Service (1795–1919)* (London, 1967); G. S. Ritchie, *The Admiralty Chart: British Naval Hydrography in the Nineteenth Century* (London, 1967); Howard T. Fry, *Alexander Dalrymple (1737–1808) and the Expansion of British Trade* (London, 1970); Christopher Lloyd, *Mr. Barrow of the Admiralty: A Life of Sir John Barrow, 1764–1848* (London, 1970).

[70] See Bravo, 'Science and Discovery', chap. 1.

frontier, rather than in London or at Oxford, that the state first became a significant employer of expertise. In an age of the gentleman amateur, missions of exploration and collection, the East India Company and the Admiralty, colonial botanical gardens and medical services provided that salaried employment through which Robert Brown, Nathaniel Wallich, William and John Herschel, and many others were enabled to pursue their avocations. Even a gentleman like Banks might be catapulted to political influence and international distinction through attaching himself to overseas adventure.

The Enlightenment encouraged official Britain to support the study of plants, minerals, and stars around the world. It also contributed a fundamental element to the ideology which sustained the Second British Empire: the faith that Empire might be an instrument of cosmopolitan progress, and could benefit the imperialized as well as the imperializers. The liberal imperialism of the nineteenth and twentieth centuries may be seen as driven by this secular species of evangelical fervour. Its secret idols were rational economy and rational administration. The gospel passed from Adam Smith and Jeremy Bentham to the nineteenth century is given particularly clear expression in *On Liberty*, where John Stuart Mill declared that 'Despotism is a legitimate mode of government in dealing with barbarians, provided the end be their improvement'.[71]

How significantly did Imperial expansion shape Britain's domestic intellectual life? Clearly the trades in sugar, slaves, and Indian cottons supported the sophisticated cultural life of the age, but might learning, particularly in the natural sciences, have prospered of its own accord? Was it perhaps true, as C. P. Lucas pronounced in the first volume of the *Cambridge History of the British Empire*, that 'the Empire has reacted more on Great Britain and its inhabitants by increasing its size than by changing its character'? Such a question is, in part, the kind of idle counter-factual with which economic historians amuse themselves. What is certain is that the British Isles were actively engaged with the wider world for two centuries before England and Scotland became Britain, and that union led to dramatically new involvement in the affairs of America, Asia, and Africa. To imagine that such intercourse had no consequences is to invest Britain's 'character' with implausible precocity and inertia. Faith in an unchanging Britain appears itself a relic of tribal arrogance, not unlike the stools on which barbarian kings persuaded themselves they sat at the Earth's still centre. The world changed Britain, it seems likely, as much as she embraced the world. But even if that experience is acknowledged as fundamental, can its influence on different branches of learning be distinguished?

---

[71] John Stuart Mill, *On Liberty* (1859; London, 1982), p. 69.

The direct impact of expansion is clear on some branches of knowledge. Information and samples from a wider world allowed John Ray, for example, to form a system by the 1680s infinitely richer than that of Turner or Gerard. By 1781 Thomas Pennant, the naturalist and antiquary, could, in turn, excuse Ray's zoology its imperfections on the ground that he lived in an age in which 'our contracted commerce deprived him of many lights we now enjoy'.[72] An older historiography might have limited such impact to the sciences of life. But the distinction between 'hard' and 'soft' sciences is not useful here. A better division would turn on the degree of dependence of disciplines on knowledge specific to particular places. On the one hand, pure mathematics, or even Hales's plant physiology, might be thought to be rediscoverable anywhere, even if context would shape the terms of rediscovery. Phenomena which are stable or regularly periodic, ubiquitous, divisible or of moderate size, and limited in formal variation, may be investigated in any isolated community. The contribution of Empire to such investigations might be assumed to be indirect. Other disciplines, on the other hand, need the world as a whole to make sense. They study things which are irregular and highly variant, and their categories depend on observation, within particular contexts, of phenomena which change too slowly to admit repeatable experiments. They thus require extensive survey, description, the formation of collections of objects or data for comparative research. The history of British botany, zoology, geology, astronomy, geophysics, anthropology or political economy, would, for example, be imponderable outside of the context of the British Empire.

It remains possible to construct Britain's intellectual relations with its eighteenth-century Empire as the story of 'expansion'. We might then reduce Jones in Bengal, Banks in Tahiti, or Jefferson in Virginia to the satellites of metropolitan learning. The cultural history of Empire, if turned into a narrative of diffusion, may still flatter a kind of racial vanity. But it would be more accurate to recognize that the 'mother country' was also a child of the same processes which made its colonies. Britain's learning, like its wealth, resulted from a system of international exchange, which depended on war and slavery. But with this violence came the transculturation of human knowledge and identity. In empires, as Gibbon understood, it is difficult to say who conquers whom. With Jones or Banks or Jefferson, we may see crucibles within which new kinds of cosmopolitan insight precipitated. Unexpected gifts of knowledge and sensibility came from the periphery in the eighteenth century, bundled with tobacco and calicoes. News of their receipt has, however, perhaps only recently arrived at the Imperial centre.

---

[72] Thomas Pennant, *History of Quadrupeds* (London, 1781), p. i.

Select Bibliography

C. A. BAYLY, *Empire and Information: Intelligence Gathering and Social Communication in India, 1780–1870* (Cambridge, 1996).

RICHARD D. BROWN, *Knowledge is Power. The Diffusion of Information in America, 1700–1865* (New York, 1989).

ARCHIBALD DAY, *The Admiralty Hydrographic Service (1795–1919)* (London, 1967).

RICHARD DRAYTON, *Nature's Government. Kew Gardens, Science, and Imperial Britain* (London, forthcoming).

MATTHEW EDNEY, *Mapping an Empire: The Geographical Construction of British India, 1765–1843* (Chicago, 1997).

HOWARD T. FRY, *Alexander Dalrymple (1737–1808), and the Expansion of British Trade* (London, 1970).

JOHN GASCOIGNE, *Joseph Banks and the English Enlightenment: Useful Knowledge and Polite Culture* (Cambridge, 1994).

RICHARD GROVE, *Green Imperialism: Colonial Expansion, Tropical Island Edens and the Origins of Environmentalism, 1600–1860* (Cambridge, 1995).

O. P. KEJARIWAL, *The Asiatic Society of Bengal and the Discovery of India's Past, 1784–1838* (Delhi, 1988).

ARTHUR MACGREGOR, ed., *Sir Hans Sloane: Collector, Scientist, Antiquary, Founding Father of the British Museum* (London, 1994).

DAVID MACKAY, *In the Wake of Cook. Exploration, Science, and Empire, 1780–1801* (London, 1985).

P. J. MARSHALL, ed., *British Discovery of Hinduism in the Eighteenth Century* (Cambridge, 1970).

—— and GLYNDWR WILLIAMS, *The Great Map of Mankind. British Perceptions of the World in the Age of Enlightenment* (London, 1982).

JAMES E. MCCLELLAN, *Science Reorganized: Scientific Societies in the Eighteenth Century* (New York, 1985).

—— *Colonialism and Science: Saint-Domingue in the Old Regime* (Baltimore, 1992).

DAVID PHILIP MILLER and PETER HANNS REILL, eds., *Visions of Empire: Voyages, Botany, and Representations of Nature* (Cambridge, 1996).

RAYMOND SCHWAB, *La Renaissance orientale* (Paris, 1950).

D. J. STRUIK, *Yankee Science in the Making* (New York, 1962).

CHARLES WEBSTER, *The Great Instauration. Science, Medicine, and Reform, 1626–1660* (London, 1975).

HARRY WOOLF, *The Transits of Venus: A Study of Eighteenth-Century Science* (London, 1959).

12

'This famous island set in a Virginian sea': Ireland in the British Empire, 1690–1801

THOMAS BARTLETT

'Ireland is too great to be unconnected with us and too near to be dependent on a foreign state and too little to be independent': C. T. Grenville's aphorism of 1784 encapsulated the inherent difficulties in the Anglo-Irish relationship. Ireland's position within the eighteenth-century Empire was even more problematic. The country was, admittedly, 'England's oldest colony', but she had been held rather than wholly governed since the twelfth century. Moreover, since 1541 Ireland had also constituted a kingdom in her own right. This regal status, along with the (albeit fitful) existence of a Parliament of undeniable medieval origins consisting of a House of Commons and House of Lords, seemed to mark Ireland off decisively from every colony subsequently acquired by England, which could only boast of assorted Assemblies, Councils, and courts. Furthermore, as an island lying closely off a larger island, itself located just off continental Europe, Ireland's geographical position meant that the eighteenth-century colonial stereotypes (extreme temperatures, exotic produce, curious animals, slavery, distance from the mother country) were conspicuously lacking there. In fact, the country grew nothing that could not be had at allegedly better quality in England. True, there was fertile land in abundance: and this was an undoubted attraction. But even if Ireland had been barren rock, her proximity to both continental Europe and to England meant that she constituted in English eyes an all-too-convenient base for foreign enemies and a likely haven for domestic rebels and malcontents. Ireland was simply 'too near', as Grenville remarked, to be left alone by England or other European powers: but proximity and colonial status seemed at odds with one another. Was there a place for a colony on the doorstep of the mother country?[1] And if Ireland was not a colony, could two kingdoms, adjacent to one another, and under the one King, coexist in the one Empire?

There was a further complication. Unlike the populations of other colonies in the Atlantic world, the population of Ireland by the late-seventeenth century

[1] See Vincent T. Harlow, *The Founding of the Second British Empire, 1763–93*, Vol. I, *Discovery and Revolution* (London, 1952), p. 505.

resolutely resisted simple categorization into colonized and colonizer. Religion, not national origins or even date of arrival, was to be the great divide: but this is not to say that Protestant–Catholic hostility is the key to understanding Irish history in this period. In the early eighteenth century Protestant Ireland was riven by rivalry between the members of the Presbyterian church and the adherents of the Established Church. The latter, called by historians the Anglo-Irish, were not at all disposed to share the fruits of the victories at the Boyne (1690) and Aughrim (1691) over the Catholic Irish with the largely Scottish, anti-episcopal, and socially inferior Dissenters. Accordingly, while the Anglican governing élite in the 1690s brought in Penal Laws against Catholics, it also legislated against Presbyterians. It did so because the Catholic threat had been seen off, because the Presbyterians seemed to be a new rival for power, and because the Anglo-Irish were confident of English goodwill and support. At an early date, however, it was made clear to the Anglo-Irish that English ministers were by no means disposed to view them as partners in the 'Glorious Revolution': certainly, there was no question of automatic access for Irish goods into the trade network of the British Empire. In this respect at least, Ireland, though at the centre of the Empire, was still irredeemably peripheral.

By the late seventeenth century, then, Ireland, 'this famous island set in a Virginian sea,'[2] resembled not so much a model colony, a *terra Florida* near home, drawn up in conformity with an official blueprint, but rather an unruly palimpsest, on which, though much rewritten and scored out, could be discerned in an untidy jumble 'kingdom', 'colony', 'dependency', and, faintly, 'nation'. The ambiguities within such designations, and the attempt to resolve the contradictions between them, are fundamental to any assessment of Ireland's developing position within the British Empire during the eighteenth century.

In 1672 Sir William Petty had forecast a splendid future for Ireland in the expanding commerce of the Atlantic world: the island, he noted, 'lieth Commodiously for the Trade of the new American world: which we see every day to Grow and Flourish'.[3] In the event, just as Ireland's strategic position athwart the main Atlantic trade routes afforded her advantages in the competition for commerce with the West Indies and with British North America, so too her apparently favourable situation could not fail to excite the resentment of competing English interests. 'Forraigne trade', considered to be the primary source of a nation's wealth, had to be jealously protected and zealously policed: colonial trade should

---

[2] Fynes Moryson, quoted in Nicholas P. Canny, *Kingdom and Colony: Ireland in the Atlantic World, 1560–1800* (Baltimore, 1988), p. 131.

[3] Quoted in Thomas M. Truxes, *Irish–American Trade, 1660–1783* (Cambridge, 1988), p. 7.

uniquely be the preserve of the mother country; Ireland, whether viewed as a dependent kingdom, domestic colony, or foreign country, fell awkwardly outside the accepted categories for full participation in the trade of the 'English Empire'.[4] Ireland, fatally, was viewed by important English vested interests as a competitor: indeed, as one pamphleteer noted, 'among the many Rivals to our Trade and Navigation, I have often thought Ireland to be the most Dangerous'.[5] These jealousies and resentments voiced by various English vested interests were given shape from the 1660s on by increasingly restrictive legislative pronouncements, usually denominated the Laws of Trade and Navigation.

By an act of 1696 no goods of any kind could be landed in Ireland from the American plantations. This remained the legal position until 1731 when a new act, the result of a successful lobbying campaign by West Indian and Irish interests in London, permitted Ireland to import non-enumerated goods from the colonies, a position unchanged until the American Revolution. So far as Asian trade was concerned, Irish merchants were also disadvantaged, though they were no worse off than their English counterparts. The East India Company had the sole monopoly and no Irish merchants as of right could take part in Indian trade. It was only in the 1790s that this monopoly was breached by Ireland.

An earlier generation of historians had been certain that the Navigation Acts 'had the effect of completely ruining the Irish Plantation trade', but it is now clear from more recent work that Ireland, so far from being excluded from colonial trade throughout the eighteenth century, actually took an active role in it. The evidence for this, both qualitative and quantitative, is decisive.[6] Yet colonial trade was always a minor segment of Irish overseas trade throughout the eighteenth century. Irish trade in this period meant in fact Anglo-Irish trade; England took over 45 per cent of the value of Irish exports in 1700, rising to 85 per cent in 1800, while some 54 per cent of Irish imports derived from England in 1700, rising to near 79 per cent in 1800.[7] A large proportion of these imports, between 50 and 60 per cent, were in fact re-exports of colonial products—especially sugar and tobacco—which by law had to be landed first in Britain before going on to their final destination. Direct Irish colonial trade was substantial enough, running at between 9 and 12 per cent of the value of Irish exports, though rarely reaching 8 per cent of imports in the period 1731–75.[8]

---

[4] Joshua Gee, *The Navigation of Great Britain Considered* (London, 1730), p. 65.

[5] Quoted Truxes, *Irish–American Trade*, p. 12.

[6] R. C. Nash, 'Irish Atlantic Trade in the Seventeenth and Eighteenth Centuries', *William and Mary Quarterly*, Third Series, XLIII (1985), pp. 329–56.

[7] L. M. Cullen, *Anglo-Irish Trade in the Eighteenth Century* (Manchester, 1968), p. 44.

[8] Truxes, *Irish–American Trade*, p. 37.

Irish exports to the West Indies and to the British colonies in North America centred on three items:[9] provisions (salted beef, pork, and butter), linen (usually the cheaper, coarser cloth), and people (passengers, convicts, and indentured servants). Especially in the early eighteenth century, Irish barrels of salted beef, butter, pork, and cheese found a ready market in the West Indies where the planter population retained the diet of the mother country. As the eighteenth century wore on, however, and as the white population of the islands decreased while competition in foodstuffs from North America grew, Irish provisions exports to the Caribbean declined. The growth in exports of salted fish from Ireland to feed the slaves in the West Indies compensated for this downturn, but in any case demand for Irish salted provisions remained buoyant in the mainland colonies. By the 1760s Irish beef, pork, and butter accounted for well over 50 per cent of all direct Irish exports to the British colonies in North America. And during the War of American Independence, Irish provisions fed both the British and the Continental army.

The balance of Irish exports to the colonies was largely made up by linen. Although this article could legally (since 1705) be exported direct from Ireland, in fact, because of the provision of a bounty on its re-export instituted in the early 1740s, the vast bulk of linen (perhaps 90 per cent) destined for North America went through England. After Britain, America was Ireland's largest customer for linen and constituted the most important market for the coarser linens that clothed the slaves (among others) and were soon known in the trade simply as 'Irish'.[10]

In a separate category of 'export' lay the direct trade in Irish emigrants. A thriving and lucrative colonial trade with Ireland was superimposed on the mechanisms by which large numbers of Irish people were transferred to the West Indies or to the mainland colonies. For this reason, then, emigration—voluntary or otherwise—should be treated as a branch of commerce. And just as statistics of trade are relatively imprecise, so too the numbers of those moving from Ireland to the West Indies and the mainland colonies must always remain problematic: voluntary emigrants may have been in the region of 65,000. To this number should be added the generally accepted figure of 10,000 convicts from Ireland, along with the figure of around 40,000 emigrants (mostly indentured servants) who went to the West Indies, though most of these came in the late seventeenth and early eighteenth centuries. In total, the net migration from Ireland to British North America, including the West Indies, for the period 1630–1775

[9] My discussion of Ireland's trade with the British colonies in North America is based on Truxes, *Irish–American Trade*.

[10] For the wider ramifications of the Irish linen trade in the Imperial economy see below, pp. 87–88.

was around 165,000, with anything up to 100,000 making the journey between 1700 and 1775, and perhaps as many more in the period up to 1800.[11]

Convicts cost around £5 per head to transport, but their work contracts were scheduled to last between seven and fourteen years and could be sold for anything up to £20. Similarly, indentured servants—those who entered voluntarily into an agreement to work in return for passage to the New World—were a valuable commodity even though their service would typically only last for four years. These servants were indeed 'bound for America' but, as has been said, 'for the ambitious and energetic poor, [indentured service] was the only practical means of removing to the colonies'.[12]

What did Ireland take from the colonies in return for these exports? Inevitably, sugar and tobacco, landed first in England or Scotland and then re-shipped for Ireland, were by far the most valuable imports from the West Indies and from the mainland colonies: at no time in the eighteenth century did Ireland's import of non-enumerated goods match the import of sugar and tobacco from Britain. Direct imports from North America were dominated by flax-seed which was paid for by Irish exports of cheap linen and by salted provisions: some 85 per cent of Irish flax-seed originated in North America. Rum distilled in the West Indies but shipped to Ireland both from the islands and from the mainland colonies was an important component in Ireland's list of colonial imports. Other direct imports were timber and lumber products, potash (enumerated in 1764 but 'non-enumerated' in 1770), and wheat and flour which supplemented imports from Britain in years of scarcity.

Any final assessment of Ireland's overall trading position within the Atlantic Empire is rendered difficult not only by the relative weight to be accorded direct and indirect exports and imports but also by the existence of two largely distinct markets, the West Indies and the mainland colonies. In her composite (direct and indirect combined) trade with the mainland American colonies up to the 1760s, Ireland enjoyed a healthy surplus. After enjoying a modestly favourable balance of payments in her composite trade with the West Indies in the middle decades of the century, as imports of sugar and rum grew, Ireland moved decisively into the red on this account. Between 1736 and 1776, the value of composite imports from the British plantations in America totalled around £12,185,000 while composite exports came in at just over £12,612,000, thus allowing a very modest trade surplus in Ireland's favour of about £500,000 over these forty years.[13] These figures prove that Ireland was never 'excluded' from colonial trade and that as often as not she

---

[11] See above pp. 46–49.
[12] Truxes, *Irish–American Trade*, p. 128.
[13] Totals from ibid., App. II, pp. 260–61, 282–83.

enjoyed a surplus in her dealings with 'our plantations in America' (as the Irish customs officials termed them). Operating under the protective carapace of Imperial regulations, Ireland did rather well in the eighteenth-century commercial Empire. Yet these conclusions in their turn, so far from resolving the question of Ireland's trading position within the Empire once and for all, must prompt a rather larger question: given that Ireland had access to an expanding colonial trade, that she enjoyed overall a modest surplus in this trade, and that Irish producers and manufacturers—and the Irish economy—benefited from this commerce, how then was it that the prosperity associated with these trades proved so brittle and ephemeral?

A brief comparison with Scotland may be instructive here.[14] Both Ireland and Scotland had an undistinguished economic base in the later seventeenth century, though on balance Ireland appeared to offer the better prospects for the future. At any rate, tens of thousands of Scots thought so, for they flocked to Ireland in the late seventeenth and early eighteenth centuries. However, by the later eighteenth century Scotland had moved decisively ahead, and throughout the nineteenth century she left Ireland behind both in manufacturing industry and agricultural output. The sources of this Scottish success story may be debated, but of prime importance was the Anglo-Scottish Act of Union of 1707 which allowed Scotland unrestricted access to the trade of the Empire. Ireland was not on nearly so favourable a footing, and hence while Scottish merchants revelled in the opportunities offered by the expanding re-export trade in tobacco and, to a lesser extent, in sugar, Irish merchants were firmly excluded. Tobacco profits partly funded the expansion of Scottish linen and underpinned improvements in Scottish agriculture. Moreover, a substantial re-export trade in tobacco centred on Glasgow promoted the growth of sophisticated financial services and institutions: lacking any re-export trade, Ireland signally failed to develop a similar infrastructure in the eighteenth century. The bounty on linen meant that the vast bulk of Irish linen was exported through England, and the Irish provisions trade was largely managed by the London sugar interest. While individual Irish merchants, and small houses, were to be found throughout the chief trading ports of the Empire, the Irish colonial trade was dominated by English merchant houses, English intermediaries, and English capital. If Ireland had had unrestricted access to the trade of the colonies, could she have profited from it? Glasgow's success with tobacco re-exports may have had much to do with a large presence of Scottish merchants in the southern mainland colonies who were able to direct the trade to that city. Certainly, when Ireland gained full access to the trade of the American colonies

---

[14] See L. M. Cullen and T. C. Smout, eds., *Comparative Aspects of Scottish and Irish Economic and Social History, 1600–1900* (Edinburgh, 1977).

after 1780, the pattern of her colonial trade did not significantly change, though perhaps the trade networks were by that date too entrenched to be easily altered.

Without doubt, Ireland benefited from the Imperial connection in the eighteenth century. Irish linen could never have found such a lucrative market outside the protected walls of the British Empire, and the Munster provisions industry centred on Cork city (the 'Kansas City of the Old Empire') took full advantage of ready access to Imperial markets. Where else could the region's agricultural surplus have gone but to the British North American colonies? Yet Irish gains from transatlantic trade did not enter deep enough into the Irish economy to foster self-sustaining development. What is not clear, however, is whether unrestricted access to all colonial trade throughout the eighteenth century would have produced that happy result: Ireland's poor economic performance in the nineteenth century may more legitimately be attributed to those insidious colonial legacies of cultural conflict, religious disharmony, and political division than to the effects of the Laws of Trade and Navigation.

Throughout the eighteenth century restrictions on Irish colonial commerce were regularly denounced as evidence both of England's resolve to keep 'poor Ireland poor' and of her determination to do down a prospective rival. Imperial trade regulations found few defenders in Ireland, while the insensitive action of the English Parliament in restricting Irish trade, colonial or foreign, wounded Irish pride. Instead of being welcomed as partners in the Glorious Revolution (and ushered to a seat at the table of Empire), Irish Protestants were dismayed to find themselves cast as colonists, with their Parliament derided as a subaltern assembly.

Ireland, a sister kingdom to England in their eyes, was contemptuously dismissed by English politicians as variously a dependent kingdom, a foreign country, or a child-colony: in no case was equality, much less joint sovereignty, on offer. In self-defence, Irish Protestants formulated a defence of their rights as the English-born-in-Ireland which they pitted against metropolitan condescension, its oppressive agents, and their colonial theory. English Imperialism was combated by 'Protestant' or 'colonial' nationalism.

This proprietary nationalism of the Protestant governing élite had diverse origins.[15] Like colonial élites everywhere, Irish Protestants slowly developed a deep affection for their adopted land and a keen appreciation of its distinctive beauties. Joined to this local affection was a profound consciousness of the historic Protestant mission in Ireland. In particular, a collective historical experience deriving from the terrifying ebbs and flows of seventeenth-century Irish history

---

[15] Thomas Bartlett, ' "A People Made rather for Copies than Originals": The Anglo-Irish 1760–1800', *International History Review*, XII (1990), pp. 11–25.

had moulded the Protestant nation of eighteenth-century Ireland in the most emphatic way. A providential reading of the rebellion of 1641, the advent of Cromwell, the threat offered by James II and the deliverance vouchsafed by William of Orange, led inescapably to the conclusion that the Protestants of Ireland were under God's special protection, that they were His chosen people in Ireland.

Protestant confidence that they constituted the 'Whole People of Ireland' (Jonathan Swift's term) was closely allied to Protestant resentment that they were 'never thanked for venturing our lives and fortunes at the Revolution; for making so brave a stand at Londonderry and Iniskilling'.[16] Denied the fruits of a victory so dearly bought by them, Irish Protestants had further cause for resentment at the curbs on Irish colonial trade. Moreover, Irish Protestants soon felt that there was a settled policy of discrimination against them where the more prestigious appointments in the Irish law, armed forces, and the Established Church were concerned. Further outrage was provoked by the flagrant abuse of the Irish pension list to pay off English jobs, and by the humiliating way that Irish peerages were bestowed on Englishmen or others who had no connection with Ireland.

Paradoxically, Protestant confidence and Protestant resentment were accompanied by residual Protestant anxiety. Irish Catholics remained a large majority on the island, maintaining close connections with the Jacobite court in France. Could the Penal Laws bring about that reconfiguration of the confessional landscape of Ireland without which Irish Protestants could not know permanent security? Irish Presbyterians, already numerically greater and expanding rapidly, caused huge concern: fiercely anti-Catholic, they were equally aggressively anti-episcopal and showed no regard for the sensitivities of churchmen. Could the Penal Laws against them curb their pretensions and restrain their ambitions? Lastly, Irish Protestants had assumed the permanence of English goodwill in the aftermath of the Glorious Revolution. This assumption had proved groundless: to their dismay, Irish Protestants found themselves regarded more as a subject people than as fellow subjects after 1690.

This 'nationalism' of Irish Protestants, a potent mixture of triumphalism, anxiety, and wounded *amour-propre*, despite what English opinion might fear, never constituted a plea for Irish secession, nor was it suspicious of Empire. Rather, those who, like William Molyneux, argued Ireland's 'Case', sought an Irish partnership in the *imperium*, demanded access to Imperial trade, and maintained that in the great wheel of Empire Ireland's natural position should be at the hub not on the rim. In seeking recognition for their achievements and sacrifices,

---

[16] Anon., *Some Remarks on the Parliament of England as Far as it Relates to the Woollen Manufacture* (Dublin, 1731), pp. 12–13.

and in attempting to discharge their Providential burden, Irish Protestants served notice on English ministers that they would not allow them to define unilaterally the Anglo-Irish relationship as simply Irish colonial subordination to Imperial England. In particular, Irish Protestants vigorously resisted the notion that Ireland was on the same footing as one of England's 'colonies of outcasts in America'.[17] Ireland's 'Case', wrote William Molyneux in his celebrated pamphlet of 1698, had to be separated from the other colonies in the Atlantic world. Ireland, he argued, was not a colony at all: she was a sister kingdom.

Molyneux's arguments were grounded on 500 years of Irish history and the whole was painstakingly researched. His critics' scornful and abusive replies fully revealed the chasm that lay between the English and Irish perceptions of the Imperial connection. To the English, Ireland was a troublesome child-colony to whom mother-England owed protection but whose primary purpose was to benefit that country. English writers professed to disbelieve that anyone could think otherwise.[18]

Given these opposing viewpoints, occasions of conflict were in fact surprisingly limited in the years up to 1750. Apart from the Wood's Halfpence dispute of the 1720s, in which Swift memorably opposed Wood's patent to coin halfpennies, relations between London and Dublin ran quite smoothly. The consolidation of the Hanover dynasty and the absence of political upheaval in England after 1714 were partly responsible for this relative calm in Ireland. Equally, the firm political control maintained by the Irish political magnates, the so-called 'Undertakers', allied to a general desire to avoid provocation, left Irish politics in a relatively somnolent state. Although the Declaratory Act of 1720 had expressly confirmed the Irish Parliament's subordinate status by maintaining that the British Parliament could pass laws to bind Ireland, no attempt was made to implement this claim. In the end, the importance of this undoubtedly contentious act remained largely exemplary.

The enactment of the Declaratory Act, the persistent restrictions on Irish legislation imposed by Poynings' Law (1494) and the informal control exercised by the London-appointed Irish government, could all be taken as proof that the Irish Parliament, notwithstanding its hereditary House of Lords, its relative antiquity, and its mimetic pageantry, was merely just another colonial Assembly in the Atlantic world. Certainly, British ministers appreciated the worth of Poynings' Law and on occasion toyed with the idea of extending it to other colonial Assemblies; and when a ringing assertion of British legislative supremacy was

---

[17] Jonathan Swift, quoted by F. G. James, *Ireland in the Empire* (Cambridge, Mass., 1973), p. 140.

[18] Thomas Bartlett, *The Fall and Rise of the Irish Nation: The Catholic Question, 1690–1830* (Dublin, 1992) p. 36.

required at the time of the repeal of the Stamp Act (1766), it was the Irish enactment of 1720 that was dusted down and adapted to fit the new circumstances. Furthermore, instructive comparisons have been found between the Irish Parliament and other local legislatures, especially in the mainland colonies of North America. In some respects the Irish Parliament was less powerful than most colonial Assemblies, but in the years up to 1750, like colonial legislatures everywhere, it assumed increasing control over finances. The Irish legislature and the other colonial Assemblies together raised that 'question of ultimate sovereignty' which was to be the rock on which the first British Empire foundered.[19] Jack P. Greene has described the Irish contribution to an emerging 'Imperial constitution', separate from the British one and yet distinct from the written charters of the various colonies. Increasingly, the British Parliament, whose own Imperial responsibilities were not so much defined as assumed, found itself struggling against the growing assertiveness of hitherto subordinate legislative bodies within the Empire, including Ireland.[20]

Ireland and the Irish Parliament fitted fitfully and uneasily into the Imperial paradigm of mother and child, metropolitan legislature and local Assembly, Imperial core and colonial periphery. Indeed, so impressive is Ireland's awkwardness in these matters that some historians have discarded the entire colonial nexus as a way of understanding eighteenth-century Ireland.[21] S. J. Connolly has argued that Ireland can be best viewed as a typical *ancien régime* society rather than as a colony; and that the Irish Parliament has more in common with, say, the Parlement of Bordeaux than the Virginia House of Burgesses. However, 'colonial' society and *ancien régime* facets could co-exist within the same polity, and the period chosen by Connolly within which to situate his thesis is peculiarly apposite for his purposes. After the Seven Years War (1756–63) the colonial dimension to Irish history reasserted itself in an unmistakable way, and Ireland, until the end of the century, was engulfed in the crisis of Empire.

Before the Seven Years War, Empire meant above all trade: after 1763 it signified dominion as well. However, the acquisition of a new Empire—'this vast empire on which the sun never sets and whose bounds nature has not yet ascertained'[22]— brought with it knotty problems of defence, finance, and administration. Follow-

---

[19] James, *Ireland in the Empire*, p. 252.

[20] Jack P. Greene, *Peripheries and Centers: Constitutional Development in the Extended Polities of the British Empire and the United States, 1607–1788* (Athens, Ga., 1987), chap. 6.

[21] S. J. Connolly, *Religion, Law and Power: The Making of Protestant Ireland, 1660–1760* (Oxford, 1992) pp. 2–3.

[22] Sir George Macartney, *An Account of Ireland in 1773 by a Late Chief Secretary of that Kingdom* (London, 1773), p. 55.

ing the war, British ministers and Imperial administrators agreed that the legislative supremacy of the British Parliament had to be made explicit, that the bonds of Empire had to be tightened up, and that the colonies had to pay their way. The case of Ireland would not be excluded from this reappraisal of the purpose of Empire.

During the Townshend viceroyalty (1767–72), the parliamentary control of the Irish political magnates—the 'Undertakers'—was broken: Lords-Lieutenant for the future would reside constantly in Ireland; Poynings' Law received a ringing endorsement; and a significant attempt was made to increase the King's hereditary revenue in Ireland so as to diminish the executive's dependence on the biannual supply voted by the Irish Parliament.[23] These initiatives were all taken at the prompting of Townshend rather than of the London government; but they should be viewed in an Imperial context, for Townshend, like his younger brother, Charles, was firmly in favour of asserting Imperial authority. 'Ireland', he wrote, 'hath not yet caught the American or English distemper', but there could be no room for complacency, and preventive measures were needed.

On coming to Ireland in 1767, Townshend's primary objective had been to obtain the Irish Parliament's agreement to augment the number of troops paid for by Ireland from 12,000 to 15,325.[24] Though sometimes seen as 'the Irish counterpart to the Stamp Act',[25] it was in fact the administrative demands of the new regimental rotation system that lay behind the proposed augmentation of the army. Since 1763 Irish regiments had been reduced in size compared to British regiments (c.280 officers and men in an Irish regiment, c.500 in a British one) and as these regiments, by the new rules, were henceforth to rotate throughout the Empire, it was necessary to have regiments everywhere of a similar strength.

That said, the proposal to augment the army in Ireland had a clear Imperial dimension. Since 1763 the problems of garrisoning a far-flung Empire had exercised the minds of British ministers. Ireland's share of the Imperial defence burden had hitherto been largely limited to supplying soldiers; and in 1767 an increase in recruits was now sought by British ministers. The difficulties that Townshend encountered in his efforts to win the Irish Parliament's agreement to this proposal persuaded him that indirect rule through Irish 'Undertakers' had to be abandoned and replaced by a new system of direct rule by a resident Chief Governor supported in the Irish Parliament by a 'Castle party' of 'Lord Lieutenant's friends'. In this respect, the new system of regimental rotation, in itself devised in response to

---

[23] Thomas Bartlett, 'The Townshend Viceroyalty', in Thomas Bartlett and D. H. Hayton, eds., *Penal Era and Golden Age: Essays in Irish History, 1690–1800* (Belfast, 1979), pp. 88–112.

[24] Thomas Bartlett, 'The Augmentation of the Army in Ireland, 1769–72', *English Historical Review*, XCVI (1981), pp. 540–59.

[25] R. G. Coupland, *The American Revolution and the British Empire* (1930; New York, 1965), pp. 97, 100–01.

vastly increased military responsibilities after 1763, ultimately triggered a profound change in the method of governing Ireland.

The unfolding of events during the Townshend viceroyalty clearly showed how Imperial defence issues could disturb Irish domestic politics; and such military questions—notably that concerning the recruitment of Irish Catholic recruits—continued to have an impact long after Townshend's departure.[26] By law, only Protestants could serve either as officers or in the ranks of the armed forces of the Crown, but the expansion of Empire, the provision of more garrisons (and the greater size of armies generally) meant that more and more soldiers were needed for Imperial service. The military reservoir of Irish Protestants, however, soon ran low, and British politicians and generals began to gaze longingly at that 'weapon of war yet untried'—the Irish Catholic. Already by the 1770s covert enlistment of Irish Catholics was under way and soon large numbers were being taken into the Marines and especially into the East India Company's army. When war broke out in the late 1770s with the American colonists and then with the French and Spanish, the government of Lord North, desperate for more soldiers, supported a policy of concessions to Irish Catholics in return for Irish Catholic recruits. By then, however, war in America had reopened more than the Catholic Question, for the whole constitutional relationship between Ireland and England was now publicly disputed.

The worsening relations between Britain and her colonies in America had not gone unnoticed in Ireland. Tens of thousands of emigrants had left Ireland during the eighteenth century. Disproportionately Presbyterian, they maintained close personal and commercial links with the home country. Irish Presbyterians in the New World may not have been united in their support for the colonial cause, but in Ireland Dissent aligned itself firmly in opposition to 'the unnatural, impolitic and unprincipled war in America'.[27]

Colonial leaders such as Benjamin Franklin were well aware of Irish sympathies and took steps to detach Ireland from England in the contest. During the Stamp Act controversy of the mid-1760s, Irish goods were specifically excluded from the colonial non-importation agreements, and there was a similar exemption for Ireland in the colonial resistance to the Townshend duties of the late 1760s. However, as the troubles deepened between mother country and colonies in the early 1770s, attitudes in the colonies hardened and Ireland was no longer so favoured. When a trade war broke out following the passing of the 'Coercive

---

[26] Bartlett, *Fall and Rise*, pp. 82–86.

[27] Quoted R. B. McDowell, *Ireland in the Age of Imperialism and Revolution, 1760–1800* (Oxford, 1979), p. 244.

Acts' in 1774, Ireland found herself, despite the best efforts of Franklin, denied the privilege of shipping her linens and provisions direct to the colonies. Irish anger at this turn of events, however, was directed more at British ineptness than at the resistance of the colonists; and that indignation was further fuelled in February 1776 by Dublin Castle's imposition of a total embargo on the export of Irish provisions to the colonies.[28] This wartime embargo aroused a storm of protest partly because it was blamed—unreasonably—for bringing on an economic recession, but especially because it confirmed the thoughtless way Irish commercial interests were handled by Britain. The latent Irish resentment against British restrictions on Irish trade was thus reawakened.

Moreover, these restrictions were viewed as an inevitable product of Ireland's constitutional subordination to Britain. A potent fusion of commercial with constitutional grievances was effected. Constitutional issues were in the air, for the war between mother country and colonies had been accompanied by furious debate on the respective obligations of each to the other, on the rights of the Imperial Parliament over the colonies, and on the location of sovereignty in the Empire.[29] These issues were argued in a veritable torrent of pamphlets, letters, and printed speeches, which overflowed into Ireland: not surprisingly, appropriate lessons were drawn. It was claimed that if the British government succeeded in taxing the colonists without their consent, then Ireland would surely be next on the list for such oppressive treatment. Evidently the cause of America, as Franklin and others never ceased to point out, was ultimately the cause of Ireland. Finally, Irish opinion quickly recognized that what the colonists were struggling to defend—essentially the right to legislate for themselves—Ireland did not even possess.

The British defeat at Saratoga in October 1777, followed by the entry of France into the war in early 1778, ushered in a period of near continual crisis in Anglo-Irish relations that only ended with the signing of the Peace of Paris in 1783. By the war's end, Irish patriot politicians had taken the opportunity afforded them by the Imperial crisis to win 'A Free Trade' and to adjust the constitutional relationship between Ireland and Britain.

Central to the great changes in these years was the formation of the Volunteers, a defence force which at its peak numbered around 60,000. These part-time soldiers were independent of Dublin Castle and had sprung up ostensibly to defend Ireland from French incursion or from raids by American privateers such as John Paul Jones. However, the Volunteers, predominantly Presbyterian in Ulster where they were strongest, but with significant Anglican support both there and

---

[28] Truxes, *Irish–American Trade*, pp. 235–45.
[29] See Greene, *Peripheries and Center*.

elsewhere, and with some tacit Catholic approval, soon realized that there was little danger of a French invasion. They quickly turned their attention to Ireland's grievances and demanded redress. Irish public opinion, hitherto inchoate, had now found a focus.

The Volunteers first addressed the restrictions on Irish overseas' commerce and demanded 'A Free Trade'. Throughout 1778 and 1779 pressure mounted on North's government to yield to Irish demands. Reports from Dublin spoke of civilian and paramilitary demonstrations, an Irish House of Commons out of control, and the widespread defection of erstwhile supporters. In November 1779 Lord North, faced with failure in America and opposition in Britain, chose to avoid confrontation in Ireland and announced sweeping concessions. Save for that portion controlled by the East India Company, Ireland was to be allowed direct access to colonial trade, 'upon equal conditions with Great Britain'. It was further promised that all the securities, allowances, and restrictions by which Anglo-Irish trade would be regularized 'should, so far as they respect Ireland, be imposed by the Irish parliament'. Last, Irish subjects were to be admitted into the Turkey Company and Irish ports were to be opened to the trade of the Levant.[30]

North presumably thought that these concessions would solve the Irish Question; he was to be speedily undeceived. Behind the merits or otherwise of Britain's restrictions on Irish trade there had always lain, as Buckinghamshire, the Lord-Lieutenant, put it, 'the constitutional question of the legislative power of Great Britain to restrain the commerce of Ireland', and indeed the power generally of the British Parliament to pass laws to bind Ireland.[31] It was naïve to expect these issues to fade away with the announcement of the trade concessions. By the end of February 1780 the future of Poynings' Law, the absence of an Irish Habeas Corpus Act, the tenure of Irish judges, and the need for an Irish Mutiny Act—all humiliating badges of Ireland's resented colonial status—had been raised in the Irish House of Commons, and it was evident that there would be further discussion of these issues in the months to come.

Events in America ultimately broke the deadlock in Ireland. The war there had taken a more favourable turn from Britain's point of view in 1780 and 1781, but in November 1781 came news of Cornwallis's surrender at Yorktown. North's government was mortally wounded, and by March 1782 his parliamentary majority had crumbled. His ministry was succeeded by that headed by Lord Rockingham and the Earl of Shelburne, a change taken by the Opposition in Ireland to herald concessions for Ireland. When the Irish Parliament reconvened

---

[30] Heron to Shannon, 15 Jan. 1780, P[ublic] R[ecord] O[ffice of] N[orthern] I[reland], Shannon MSS, D2707/A2/2/66.

[31] Buckinghamshire to Hillsborough, 14 Dec. 1779, S[tate] P[apers] 63/467, pp. 247–49.

following the Easter recess on 16 April 1782, Henry Grattan's motion calling for Irish legislative independence met with little resistance; the new Lord-Lieutenant and Chief-Secretary, the Duke of Portland and Richard Fitzpatrick respectively, considered 'the question as carried', and saw no point in further opposition.

On 18 May 1782 Shelburne informed Portland that the British Parliament had decided 'to meet the wishes of the Irish people'. The Declaratory Act was to be repealed by the British Parliament, an Irish biennial Mutiny Act allowed, and severe modifications to Poynings' Law conceded. From now on, formally rather than, as heretofore, informally, the Irish Parliament would have the initiative where legislation was concerned. In addition, Irish judges were to hold office with the same terms of tenure as their English brother judges and the appellate jurisdiction of the Irish House of Lords was restored. For the first time in the Empire, the constitution of a colony would approximate that of the mother country. By the 'Constitution of 1782' Ireland had been accorded something akin to 'Dominion status': she had, it seemed, achieved legislative independence, and she had done so within the Empire and without recourse to war. Not altogether mischievously, the American Peace Commissioner, Henry Laurens, challenged the chief British negotiator, Lord Shelburne, with having made those timely concessions to Ireland that had been peremptorily denied the American colonies—and which if granted might have prevented them seceding from the Empire.[32]

The winning of the 'Constitution of 1782' was undoubtedly the high point of Protestant Nationalism in Ireland; but amidst the euphoric celebration, and reverential invocations of the shades of Molyneux and Swift, there were those who sounded a note of caution. The opportunistic manner in which the gains had been achieved and the paramilitary agency by which they had been won gave cause for concern. The sudden eruption of the Volunteers on to the political scene, claiming the right to speak for the 'people' and threatening violence if their demands were not met, was hardly reassuring—especially as this extra-parliamentary armed body, its victory gained, showed no disposition to retire gracefully from the political arena. The Volunteers had successfully imported the gun into Irish politics; it might prove difficult to remove it. Moreover, Ireland had clearly taken advantage of England's difficulties in America to win those important concessions of 1782 (and 1779) and such opportunism held an obvious corollary for the future. An Irish crisis might provide the opportunity for the Empire to strike back; Ireland's difficulty could yet be England's opportunity. Lastly, it was

[32] A. P. W. Malcomson, 'The Treaty of Paris and Ireland', in Prosser Gifford, ed., *The Treaty of Paris (1783) in a Changing States System* (Lanham, Md., 1985), p. 75.

ominous for the future that British ministers were uneasy at what had been yielded to Ireland. Irish legislative independence was considered a threat to Imperial unity, for the constitutional concessions had starkly revealed Ireland's awkward role in the Empire. Accordingly, at the end of 1782 Shelburne called for 'the fixing by a sort of treaty, a commercial system between the two countries and a proportionable contribution to be paid by Ireland for the general protection of the Empire'.[33] Few doubted that 'a final adjustment' was needed or that it would come in time. 'It seems to me,' Edmund Burke noted, 'that this affair [the Constitution of 1782] so far from ended, is but just begun. A new order of things is commencing. The old link is snapped asunder. What Ireland will substitute in the place of it to keep us together, I know not.'[34]

In the event, nothing was done, for the times were unpropitious. Grattan denounced in advance any attempt to make Ireland pay for her independence, and suggested to those British politicians anxious that 'some solid and permanent connection should be established' that they should rather rely for future harmony on 'the ties of common interest, equal trade and equal liberty'. Having just lost a humiliating war, shed a valuable portion of Empire, and now confronting a hostile world, British ministers were understandably reluctant to put too much weight on those 'dear ties of mutual love and mutual affection' which Irish patriots offered as a substitute for Poynings' Law and the Declaratory Act.[35] Such 'dear ties' had snapped recently, and the so-called 'Renunciation crisis' of 1783, when British ministers were forced to yield yet another constitutional point to Ireland, revealed these sentiments to be altogether absent. Nor were they evident in 1785, when a calculated attempt to define precisely Ireland's position in the Empire foundered in the face of Irish pride and British insensitivity. The rejection of the Anglo-Irish commerce-defence pact of that year meant that the relationship between Britain and Ireland would remain unreformed, that the much sought-after 'final adjustment' would prove elusive, and that Ireland's position within the Empire would continue to be ambiguous. True, the King still had a veto over Irish legislation, but ministers were well aware that this blunt weapon was unlikely to forge Imperial unity: and the lofty link of a shared monarch hardly seemed to affect day-to-day policy. In fact, the frailty of this bond of a shared monarch was revealed in 1788 during the Regency crisis provoked by George III's madness. Unilateral action by the Irish Parliament raised the question: could there be a King of Ireland who was not King of England?

[33] See James Kelly, *Prelude to Union, Anglo-Irish Politics in the 1780s* (Cork, 1992), chap. 2 for a full discussion.

[34] Burke to Duke of Portland, 25 May 1782, in Thomas W. Copeland and others, eds., *The Correspondence of Edmund Burke*, 10 vols. (Cambridge, 1958–70), IV, p. 455.

[35] Kelly, *Prelude to Union*, p. 38.

Finally, the legislative independence won by Ireland in 1782 was not the sole problem for the future, nor was it the vague nature of the post-1782 Imperial connection that caused difficulties. The 'Constitution of 1782' was merely of symbolic importance and Ireland's role in the Empire had ever been indistinct and contested: what exacerbated matters was the departure of thirteen colonies from the Empire and, with them, thirteen legislatures of varying origins, nomenclature, power, and prestige. So long as the old empire had existed with its crazy-paving of legislatures, the anomalous position of the Irish Parliament had not been unique (nor of course was it unique after 1783, for there were still representative institutions in the West Indies and in the Maritime Provinces of British Canada); but there had undoubtedly been a safety-in-numbers, a comforting shared ambiguity within the pre-revolutionary Empire that had offered the Irish Parliament some protection. Shorn of its sheltering sister-institutions in the American colonies, the Irish Parliament's anomalous position after 1783 was laid bare and—despite all its new powers and enhanced prestige—a huge question-mark had been placed against its future. Viewed in this light, is it so surprising that the quest for that 'final adjustment' to the 'Constitution of 1782' should have concluded with the legislative Union of 1801?

During the 1790s, a decade of war and revolution, Ireland's hitherto abstract position as the weak link of the Empire was all too clearly revealed. The outbreak of war with revolutionary France in 1793 set the stage for yet another assault on the integrity of the British Empire, similar to that which had proved successful in the War of American Independence. Just as the American rebels had sought independence with the aid of the French, so too disaffected groups in Ireland planned secession with French help. Moreover, as in America, Dissent provided the backbone of the independence movement in Ireland, for the Presbyterians of the north of Ireland, who had begun the Society of United Irishmen in 1791, saw their opportunity to break free of Anglican rule. Irish Catholics too had no reason to love the Established Church and many were prepared to play a role in the revolutionary movement of the 1790s. Dissident elements within (or just outside) the Protestant governing élite—Arthur O'Connor, Lord Edward Fitzgerald, Theobald Wolfe Tone—were prepared to help and take a lead. Admittedly, the movement for independence in America had been made possible by the removal of the Catholic—or French—threat in 1763; and the drive to secede from the Empire had been fuelled by colonial fears that the British government ever since had sought to re-institute the French Catholic menace in Canada, and elsewhere.

The comparison with Ireland breaks down at that point: Irish Catholics indisputably remained a large majority in Ireland, and if anything Catholic assertiveness had increased in the 1790s. Given the religious furies—a legacy of the seventeenth century—that lurked just below the still surface of Irish life, surely disaffected Irish Presbyterians and their dissident Anglican colleagues ought to have trodden cautiously in the tumultuous 1790s rather than seeking to emulate their American cousins? In fact, both Presbyterian and Anglican subversives were confident that they could control the coming revolution in Ireland. Presbyterians drew encouragement from the civic virtue exhibited by those French Catholics who had deposed their king and bade defiance to the Pope: perhaps Irish Catholics were not wholly lost to the cause of liberty? Disaffected members of the Protestant Ascendancy firmly believed that they would maintain their position as the natural leaders of the country after the revolution. In any case, for both Presbyterian and Anglican radicals, the presence of a substantial French military force in Ireland would provide further reassurance that their Catholic allies would be kept under a firm military discipline.

The 1798 rebellion bore some comparison to the War of American Independence. Both were Dissent-led secessionist movements within the Empire; both faced ferocious opposition from loyalists; and both relied for ultimate success on French intervention. In the American case, French involvement tilted the balance in favour of the colonists. With hindsight, the Irish failure can be attributed to the failure of the French to invade in force. If the 20,000 soldiers commanded by Hoche had effected a landing at Bantry Bay in December 1796, they might have proved as decisive to the outcome of the Irish struggle as the military and naval forces led by Lafayette and Rochambeau had been in the American War. Certainly, the 1,000-odd French soldiers under the command of Humbert that waded ashore in Sligo in September 1798 created alarm out of all proportion to their numbers; and even though Cornwallis's army outnumbered Humbert's men many times over, he treated them with consummate caution. Having once been out-manœuvred by the French at Yorktown (with a consequent loss of the American colonies), Cornwallis was determined that a similar fate should not befall him in Ireland.

In the end, the Irish and American contests, for all their superficial similarities, were really quite distinct. The Americans went to war and then drew in the French: the United Irishmen sought to take advantage of a war already begun. There was nothing comparable in Ireland to the Continental Congress, and there was no unified rebel military command. Almost certainly, loyalism was much stronger in Ireland than in the American colonies. The decisive difference, however, lay in the fact that Ireland was perceived as vital to Britain in a way that the American colonies were not. When the French had intervened on the American side, Britain's primary concern had been for the safety of the Sugar Islands, not the mainland colonies: hence the despatch of the British fleet to the Caribbean which in turn cleared the way for the French navy to trap Cornwallis at Yorktown. With

Ireland, however, it was all radically different. The French threat to Ireland in the late 1790s forced Britain to embark on a swift military build-up on the island: by 1798 there were nearly 100,000 soldiers of various descriptions there and, as an added precaution, British naval squadrons were stationed off the Irish coasts. Ireland would never be given up to an enemy nor, unlike the American colonies, could she be allowed to go her own way. Indeed, as a result of the departure of the American colonies, Ireland may have become even more strategically important to Britain. Certainly, she was central to British plans for an assault on the French West Indies in the 1790s.

In the event, immediately on learning of the Irish rebellion, Pitt had determined that the moment had now arrived to put through a legislative union, and that trusted Imperial trouble-shooter, Cornwallis, was chosen to go to Ireland to carry out this policy. Given Cornwallis's previous experience in America and India the choice was entirely appropriate, for the proposed Union was designed to consolidate the Empire and to scotch once and for all secessionist tendencies in Ireland.

In the Union debates in the British and Irish Parliaments between 1799 and 1800 many arguments—religious, political, economic—were adduced in support of Union, and a similar plethora of points in favour can be found in the voluminous pamphlet literature that the Union proposal prompted. Most striking, however, is the frequency with which Pro-Unionists mentioned the Empire and the stress that was placed by them on Ireland's current and future role in it. Emphatically, this was to be a Union for Empire: after Union, the voice of Irishmen 'would be heard not only in Europe, but in Asia, Africa and America'.[36]

Edmund Burke would surely have approved this concentration on Empire. For him the only true union between Ireland and England was an Imperial one, and throughout his career he had looked to an Empire governed upon 'a prudent and enlarged policy'. By the time of his death in 1797, however, he had despaired of seeing this. Protestant Ascendancy in Ireland, 'Indianism' in Asia, and Jacobinism in Europe—the three great evils of the 1790s in his view—were in effect cut from the same cloth. Their thrust was to persuade 'the many' that they had no connection with 'the few', so to sever the bonds of civil society, and ultimately usher in bloody chaos. As an Irish-born English statesman of Catholic descent, Burke was uniquely placed to contemplate the blighted promise of the Old Empire, and surely he would have applauded the fresh start that Union offered.[37]

---

[36] *Substance of the Speech of the Rt Hon Henry Dundas... Thursday, February 7, 1799* (London, 1799), p. 17.

[37] Edmund Burke to Sir Hercules Langrishe, 26 May 1795, in Copeland, ed., *Correspondence of Edmund Burke*, VIII p. 254; Conor Cruise O'Brien, *The Great Melody: A Thematic Biography of Edmund Burke* (London, 1992); Terry Eagleton, *Heathcliff and the Great Hunger: Studies in Irish Culture* (London, 1995), pp. 35–53.

The emphasis on Empire revealed in the Union debates would have been unthinkable fifty years earlier, for at that time the word had meant little beyond trade, emigrants, and convicts.[38] Certainly, a few Irishmen—Arthur Dobbs, Governor of North Carolina,[39] Sir George Macartney, Imperial proconsul,[40] and Edmund Burke, scourge of Warren Hastings—had seen wider possibilities than these; indeed, some Irishmen—Sir Robert Cowan, Thomas Maunsell, General Eyre Coote, and James Alexander—had already embraced the commercial and military opportunities that India offered to make large fortunes for themselves;[41] and Irish merchants had developed a thriving colonial trade, particularly in provisions. But the Empire in general was viewed as a British or even English possession and, unlike the Scots, Irishmen were not welcomed as partners nor were they encouraged to regard it as a source of careers: they were seen as rivals and competitors. Very little Irish money was invested in the East India Company, and though there was a substantial Irish recruitment into the Company's army from the 1760s on, the number of Irish compared to Scots in the administrative branch of the Company in the eighteenth century was negligible.[42] And yet Irishmen were by no means uninterested in either colonies or Empire: Theobald Wolfe Tone, Irish separatist and republican, had urged Lord Grenville to oust the Spanish garrisons from the Sandwich Islands and to set up military colonies in their place; and in some of his writings, he complained that Ireland had no colonies of her own.[43]

Even the critics of Union were forced to recognize that it offered a gateway to Empire, and therefore they had to base their opposition to it on Imperial grounds. Thus the leading anti-Unionist, John Foster, opposed Union as a Protestant. He believed too that the financial and commercial terms were unfavourable. But he also claimed that Union would destroy the British Constitution and ultimately lead to the destruction of the Empire. Others who thought like him maintained that Union would inevitably lead to Irish secession from the Empire, with consequences fatal for Ireland, Britain, and the Empire.

In the eyes of the British government Union was an Imperial necessity. Irish legislative independence—a 'childish measure', according to Pitt—had been

---

[38] Lord Hillsborough's 1751 pamphlet calling for a legislative union, *A Proposal for Uniting the Kingdoms of Great Britain and Ireland* (Dublin, 1751), made no mention of the word 'Empire'.

[39] D. H. Rankin and E. C. Nelson, eds., *Curious in Everything: The Career of Arthur Dobbs of Carrickfergus, 1689–1765* (Carrickfergus, 1990).

[40] On whom see Peter Roebuck, ed., *Macartney of Lissanoure: Essays in Biography* (Belfast, 1983).

[41] R. B. McDowell, 'Ireland in the Eighteenth-Century British Empire', in *Historical Studies*, IX (London, 1974), pp. 49–63; PRONI, *The British Empire* (Catalogue of an Exhibition), June 1975.

[42] McDowell, 'Ireland', pp. 55–56.

[43] Marianne Elliott, *Wolfe Tone: Prophet of Irish Independence* (New Haven, 1989), pp. 55–59; Theobald Wolfe Tone, *Spanish War!* (Dublin, 1789) reprinted in W. T. W. Tone, ed., *Life of Theobald Wolfe Tone*, 2 vols. (Washington, 1826), I, pp. 327–40.

clearly revealed to be a threat to Empire, and a Union would, in the words of Castlereagh, Cornwallis's Chief Secretary, 'consolidate the strength and glory of the empire'.[44] Only in a 'General Imperial Legislature' could Ireland's many problems be viewed dispassionately and resolved without acrimony.[45] The most important of these problems was that of Catholic Emancipation, and here the message was clear: only in a 'Protestant Empire'—that is, an Empire in which Protestants were a majority, at least at the metropolitan centre—could Catholic emancipation be contemplated with equanimity. For the most part, Irish Catholics supported Union, expecting emancipation to follow, and so too did the Catholic hierarchy, possibly anticipating through access to the Empire new areas for missionary endeavour.[46]

Amongst 'the evils proposed to be cured by an Union... [were]... religious divisions, the defective nature of the Imperial connections and commercial inequalities': Pitt, for his part, had forecast an impartial legislature presiding over a vibrant economy and a country in which religious harmony reigned: but in the event, Union delivered few of the 'cures' which enthusiasts had predicted.[47] Catholic emancipation proved infinitely more difficult to put through a United Parliament than it would have been in the old Irish Parliament; contrary to predictions, Ireland did not prosper as Scotland had in the century following her Union in 1707; and religious conflicts intensified throughout the nineteenth century, and beyond.

In one vital respect, however, Union did fulfill the expectations of its promoters, for it did offer Ireland her Imperial opportunity. After 1800, the Irish of all descriptions entered enthusiastically into the business of Empire. Whether as settlers in Australia and New Zealand, missionaries in Africa and India, or soldiers, administrators, engineers, merchants, and doctors throughout the Empire, the Irish took full advantage of the Imperial opportunities opened up by Union. Irish Protestants, abandoning their experiment with nationalism, eagerly assumed an Imperial identity; but Irish Catholics, too, were by and large enthusiastic imperialists, and they took pride in the feats of Catholic Irish soldiers and the achievements of Catholic Irish missionaries ('Ireland's Spiritual Empire' abroad was roughly coterminous with the British Empire). Throughout the nineteenth

---

[44] W. Cobbett, ed., *The Parliamentary History of England...from 1066 to the Year 1803*, 36 vols. (London, 1806-20), XXXIV, cols 251–52; *A Report of Two Speeches Delivered by the Rt. Hon. Lord Viscount Castereagh in the Debates on the Regency Bill on April 11, 1799* (Dublin, 1799).

[45] *The Speech of the Rt. Hon. William Pitt in the British House of Commons on Thursday, January 31, 1799* (Dublin, 1799), p. 27.

[46] Bartlett, *Fall and Rise of the Irish Nation*, pp. 244–67.

[47] Castlereagh to Portland, 28 Jan. 1799 in Marquess of Londonderry, ed., *Correspondence, Despatches, and Other Papers of Viscount Castlereagh, Second Marquess of Londonderry*, 12 vols. (London, 1848-53), II, p. 139.

century, the Empire offered career opportunities—clerical and lay, male and female—that were simply not available in Ireland.[48] Indeed, from the 1830s on there is evidence that 'the colonial patronage' was deliberately used by the British government in order to meet the career aspirations of the Irish Catholic middle class, clamouring for tangible benefits from Emancipation.[49] The Empire was greatly admired and highly prized in nineteenth-century Ireland. The Catholic Irish nation certainly had its difficulties with the Protestant British state in the decades after Union, but the value of the Empire to Ireland meant that, in general, Irish protests were circumspect. The Repeal and Home Rule campaigns were always careful to disavow any intention of disrupting the Empire; and republican separatism was never more than a fringe movement. Throughout the nineteenth century the bond of Empire was at all times stronger than that of Union.

[48] See E. M. Hogan, *The Irish Missionary Movement: A Historical Survey, 1830–1980* (Dublin 1990); David Hempton and Myrtle Hill, *Evangelical Protestantism in Ulster Society, 1740–1890* (London, 1992), p. 52.

[49] A. T. Singleton (Private Secretary to Lord Anglesey, Lord-Lieutenant of Ireland) to Maurice Fitzgerald, 13 April 1830 (PRONI, Fitzgerald MSS, T3075/13/47); S. B. Cook, ' "The Irish Raj": Social Origins and Careers of Irishmen in the Indian Civil Service, 1855–1914', *Journal of Social History*, XX (1987), pp. 507–29.

Select Bibliography

THOMAS BARTLETT, ' "A People Made rather for Copies than Originals": the Anglo-Irish 1760–1800', *International History Review*, XII (1990), pp. 11–25.

—— 'The Augmentation of the Army in Ireland, 1769–72', *English Historical Review*, XCVI (1981), pp. 540–59.

—— *The Fall and Rise of the Irish Nation: The Catholic Question, 1690–1830* (Dublin, 1992).

NICHOLAS P. CANNY, *Kingdom and Colony: Ireland in the Atlantic World, 1560–1800* (Baltimore, 1988).

S. J. CONNOLLY, *Religion, Law and Power. The Making of Protestant Ireland, 1660–1760* (Oxford, 1992).

R. G. COUPLAND, *The American Revolution and the British Empire* (1930; New York, 1965).

L. M. CULLEN, *Anglo-Irish Trade in the Eighteenth Century* (Manchester, 1968).

—— and T. C. SMOUT, eds., *Comparative Aspects of Scottish and Irish Economic and Social History, 1600–1900* (Edinburgh, 1977).

DAVID DICKSON, *New Foundations: Ireland, 1660–1800* (Dublin, 1987).

MARRIANNE ELLIOTT, *Wolfe Tone: Prophet of Irish Independence* (New Haven, 1989).

JACK P. GREENE, *Peripheries and Centres: Constitutional Development in the Extended Polities of the British Empire and the United States, 1607–1788* (Athens, Ga., 1987).

VINCENT T. HARLOW, *The Founding of the Second British Empire, 1763–93*, Vol. I *Discovery and Revolution* (London, 1952).

F. G. JAMES, *Ireland in the Empire* (Cambridge, Mass., 1973).

JAMES KELLY, *Prelude to Union. Anglo-Irish Politics in the 1780s* (Cork, 1992).

R. B. McDowell, *Ireland in the Age of Imperialism and Revolution, 1760–1800* (Oxford, 1979).

Kerby A. Miller, *Emigrants and Exiles: Ireland and the Irish Exodus to North America* (Oxford, 1985).

T. W. Moody and W. E. Vaughan, *A New History of Ireland*, Vol. IV, *Eighteenth-Century Ireland, 1690–1801* (Oxford, 1985).

R. C. Nash, 'Irish Atlantic Trade in the Seventeenth and Eighteenth Centuries', *William and Mary Quarterly*, Third Series, XLIII (1985), pp. 329–56.

Peter Roebuck, ed., *Macartney of Lissanoure: Essays in Biography* (Belfast, 1983).

Thomas M. Truxes, *Irish–American Trade, 1660–1783* (Cambridge, 1988).

13

Growth and Mastery: British North America, 1690–1748

RICHARD R. JOHNSON

In the summer of 1690, in the aftermath of the wave of uprisings that had marked the Glorious Revolution in British North America, Colonel Cuthbert Potter rode north from Virginia as an emissary of the Jamestown government with instructions 'to ascertain the truth of matters in New England and New York'. Potter's journal recorded troubled times—attacks by hostile Indians and French pirates, widespread challenges to royal authority, and his own arrest and the forcible search of his possessions by suspicious officials in Massachusetts. Several years later Sarah Kemble Knight, a Boston businesswoman travelling to New York, added some pungent comments on the state of New England's countryside—its primitive roads, 'tottering' or non-existent bridges, 'intolerable' lodgings, and uncouth inhabitants.[1]

Half-a-century after Potter's journey, during the summer of 1744, the Scots-born Dr Alexander Hamilton painted a different picture as he travelled for the benefit of his health from Maryland to Maine and back again. No domestic wars or arrests marred his journey: instead, Hamilton recorded the hospitality he received from fellow gentry, the civic architecture of such burgeoning towns as Philadelphia and New York, and the fine points of his nightly debates on matters of politics and religion with a great diversity of travellers—Quakers, Baptists, Jews, Catholics, and representatives of almost every European nationality. Such Indians as he encountered were peaceful travellers, oyster fishermen, fellow churchgoers, or, in Rhode Island, a sachem of the Narragansetts who, living 'after the English mode', joined with his silk-gowned consort in offering his visitor 'a glass of good wine'.[2]

Hamilton's pen could be as acid as Madam Knight's in detecting flaws in colonial manners and morals. But the contrasts between the worlds each portrayed

---

[1] 'Cuthbert Potter's Journal', in Newton D. Mereness, ed., *Travels in the American Colonies, 1690–1783* (New York, 1916), pp. 3–11; 'The Journal of Madam Knight', in Wendy Martin, ed., *Colonial American Travel Narratives* (New York, 1994), pp. 52–75.

[2] Carl Bridenbaugh, ed., *Gentleman's Progress: The Itinerarium of Dr. Alexander Hamilton, 1744* (Chapel Hill, NC, 1948), p. 98.

point to the pace and character of the changes overtaking British North America in the six decades following 1690. Lacking the high drama of political revolt or domestic rebellion, the period has seemed at once diffuse and bland—more precursor than precipitant to the stirring events surrounding 1776. Factional political dispute, though vigorous, was contained within the bounds of a sustained institutional stability. Yet much was at work beneath the surface historians once characterized as 'glacial'. Recent scholarship has uncovered the period's role in launching the sustained physical and socio-economic growth that would become the hallmark of North American history for two centuries to follow. And through this growth, configuring its character and outcome, run themes that embody what may be termed the colonists' growing sense of mastery—over their environment, over others, and thus, concomitantly, over themselves. At one level this is evident in their accelerated capacity to survey and exploit the resources of land and ocean. At a second, we find more conscious efforts to comprehend and categorize the world around them, weaving more complex and considered webs of communication and exchange. At a third, and in the patriarchal and authoritarian sense of mastery, these years defined and solidified patterns of social differentiation—within families, within what had been a predominantly English settler group now diversified by waves of migration from elsewhere in Europe, and—even more formatively for America's subsequent history—within the dramatic expansion and institutional hardening of a labour system centred on the importation and enslavement of Africans. Together, by the mid-eighteenth century, these developments fostered societies that, while looking more than ever towards England for models of social and political conduct, were showing a heightened confidence in their capacity to match and even surpass the mother country.

Fundamental to this growth and mastery were the stimuli that British North America received from its ties with Europe's needs, distresses, and—especially— its conflicts. Of our period's sixty-year span, itself defined by two European events, from the Glorious Revolution to the Peace of Aix-la-Chapelle in 1748, thirty were years of transatlantic wars—of the League of Augsburg (1689–97), of the Spanish Succession (1702–13), and of the Austrian Succession (1740–48)—struggles only later Americanized in a republican spirit of ascribing unwelcome events to British monarchs as, respectively, King William's, Queen Anne's, and King George's War. These conflicts were costly to the colonies. In 1704 Governor Joseph Dudley of Massachusetts reported that he had 1,900 troops under arms defending the frontier from the French and their Indian allies, as much as one-sixth of the province's able-bodied men. Expeditions from the northern colonies aimed at capturing Quebec and French Canada in 1690 and 1711 were expensive failures, and two more were needed to achieve the conquest of the French outpost of Port Royal in 1710. Colonial regiments sent to the Caribbean to attack Spanish Cartagena in

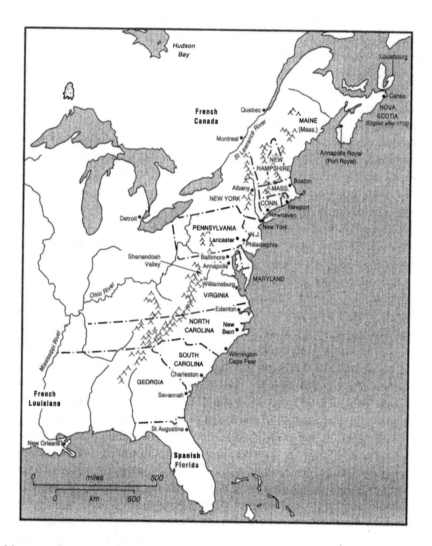

Map 13.1.   Eastern North America, 1690–1748

1741 lost as many as four-fifths of their men from warfare and disease.[3] Even during periods of formal European peace, border skirmishes plagued the frontier

---

[3] Dudley to Board of Trade, 13 July 1704, James Phinney Baxter, ed., *Documentary History of the State of Maine*, 24 vols. (Portland, 1869–1916), IX p. 19; Douglas E. Leach, *Arms for Empire: A Military History of the British Colonies in North America, 1607–1763* (New York, 1973), pp. 217–18; and, generally, Ian K. Steele, *Warpaths: Invasions of North America* (New York, 1994), chaps. 7–8.

areas of New England, the Carolinas, and the Caribbean closest to French and Spanish settlements. On the New England frontier alone, French and Indian raiders took captive more than 500 colonists for the purposes of ransom or adoption.[4] At sea, transatlantic trade and migration were significantly disrupted by privateering and piracy between 1690 and 1713 and again in the 1740s. Despite these losses, however, the colonial heartland—a band of settlement some fifty miles deep along the coastline between Boston and the Chesapeake—suffered less from warfare than did many parts of Europe. Its exports of such products as fish, grain, timber, and tobacco rose steadily, perhaps tripling in value during these years. No American colony experienced events as dramatic as the expulsion of Huguenot Protestants from France, the ravaging of the German Palatinate, and the cycle of famine and economic dislocation in Ireland. Rather, each of these European events in turn contributed to the period's most enduring legacy to British North America, the swelling of a tide of non-English immigration.

The most visible evidence of British North America's relative immunity from the insecurities of war was its dramatic demographic growth. Contemporary and subsequent estimates show the population, black and white together, growing from some 210,000 in 1690 to 445,000 by 1720 and 1,200,000 by 1750, with the decades of sharpest growth (ranging between 35 and 45 per cent per decade) matching the thirty years of relative peace between 1711 and 1740. Regionally, the rate of increase was highest in the Carolinas and Georgia and in the middle colonies of Pennsylvania, Delaware, New York, and New Jersey. Only in one region and decade, war-battered New England in the 1690s, did decennial rates of population increase fall below 24 per cent, to under 7 per cent. In the period as a whole, the absolute increase of British North America's non-Indian population was proportionately twenty-four times greater than that of England and Wales.[5]

At least two-thirds, and possibly three-quarters, of this growth were due to natural increase. A somewhat lower age of marriage than in England, a significantly lower rate of infant mortality, and a relative freedom from the intermittent harvest failures and consequent famines common in Europe all made for families that doubled in numbers each generation. Regionally, too, the seventeenth-century imbalance between the New England and Chesapeake regions, whereby the population of the first had grown largely through natural increase and the second through immigration, was now redressed in the Chesapeake by healthier conditions in newly settled regions and a more equal sex ratio. Whereas

    [4] Alden Vaughan and Daniel Richter, 'Crossing the Cultural Divide: Indians and New Englanders, 1607–1763', American Antiquarian Society, *Proceedings*, XC (1980), pp. 23–99.

    [5] John J. McCusker and Russell R. Menard, *The Economy of British America, 1607–1789* (Chapel Hill, NC, 1985), pp. 136, 172, 203, 103, 54.

in 1668 only 19 per cent of the Chesapeake's white population had been born in the region, this had risen to 55 per cent by 1700 and over 90 per cent by 1750.[6] Levels of fertility for a group of women in early eighteenth-century Prince George's County, Maryland, were more than a third above those recorded for England in the same period, with families by a first husband alone amounting to ten or eleven children. More of these children now came to maturity with both parents still living, consolidating the structure of family life already established in healthier colonies to the north. By the 1740s the same trends can be found among the black population, fostering the formation of African-American family life in ways that would make the slave societies of British North America significantly different from those of the Caribbean and South America.[7]

Supplementing this growth through natural increase, and more visibly remarkable to contemporaries, was a surge in the tide of forced and voluntary migration across the Atlantic. Recounted in greater detail elsewhere in this volume, it deserves mention here because of its major impact upon the character of British colonial settlement in North America.[8] Estimates are still—and are likely to remain—very approximate, but it seems likely that some 250,000 people came over or were brought to the English continental colonies between 1690 and 1750. Of these, well over half, perhaps 140,000, were Africans brought as slaves, either directly from the regions between Senegambia and Angola or from servitude in the plantations of the Caribbean. Of the remainder, all of European descent, at least 25,000 were convicts sentenced to transportation from Great Britain to America, with the great majority entering Virginia and Maryland, there to serve labour sentences of between seven and fourteen years.[9] Among the first commodities sold door-to-door in America were human beings, black and white, offered to prospective masters from the gangs driven inland, often in chains, from their point of disembarkation.

Many others, perhaps half the rest, also came under some form of obligation, as indentured labourers driven by economic necessity. Especially noteworthy to contemporaries was their ethnic variety. Hitherto, the European-descended population of the seaboard colonies between Maine and Carolina had been overwhelmingly English in origin save for the Dutch and Swedes settled around the Hudson and Delaware Rivers. But, beginning with the arrival of several thousand French

---

[6] Darrett B. and Anita H. Rutman, *A Place in Time*, Vol. I: *Middlesex County, Virginia, 1650–1750* (New York, 1984), p. 98; also Paul G. E. Clemens, *The Atlantic Economy and Colonial Maryland's Eastern Shore: From Tobacco to Grain* (Ithaca, NY, 1980), pp. 63–69.

[7] Allan Kulikoff, *Tobacco and Slaves: The Development of Southern Cultures in the Chesapeake, 1680–1800* (Chapel Hill, NC, 1986), pp. 70–72; see below, pp. 473–74.

[8] See chaps. by James Horn and David Richardson.

[9] Roger A. Ekirch, *Bound for America: The Transportation of British Convicts to the Colonies, 1718–1775* (Oxford, 1987), pp. 17–27.

Huguenots in the 1690s, among them such famous names as Faneuil, Bowdoin, and Laurens, successive migrations of Germans, Scots, Scots-Irish, and southern Irish reached English North America. The Germans, perhaps 35,000 in number by 1750, settled mostly in Pennsylvania and Delaware, but with substantial pockets of settlement further south. The majority came through Philadelphia, often pledging their labour or that of family members for passage money in a form of indenturing known as redemptioning. The Scots and Irish, numbering as many as 50,000 in the same years, and with the oft-neglected element of southern Irish composing at least a third of these numbers, spread out more broadly, beginning in northern New England but coming to predominate in the backcountry from Pennsylvania to South Carolina.

Some of the long-term effects of this migration were political and cultural—one observer noted that South Carolina had become 'more like a negro country' than a country settled by white people, and there was talk in Pennsylvania of banning non-English speakers from political office.[10] More immediately, however, the main impact of the combined migration and natural increase was geographical, in the form of the physical expansion of settlement. In 1690 the English mainland colonies were little more than a string of coast-bound enclaves scattered from Maine to South Carolina, with only a handful of settlements extending into the interior up such rivers as the Connecticut, Hudson, and James. For some years, under the pressure of the quarter-century of French and Indian attacks that began in 1688, the northern and eastern frontiers of New England and New York contracted rather than advanced. But the peace secured by the 1713 Treaty of Utrecht provided a more stable setting for territorial expansion fuelled by internal growth and a burst of immigration. To the north, the treaty secured English title to the disputed areas of Acadia (now English Nova Scotia centring on Annapolis Royal), Newfoundland, and Hudson Bay, confirming access to the valuable trade in fish and furs and extending British North America's territorial claims north-west to the Rocky Mountains. New England's borders were still troubled by friction with the Abenaki Indians, especially in the 1720s, but thereafter town settlement spread steadily along the eastern seaboard and up the Connecticut and Merrimack rivers, founding such communities as Waldoboro and Charlestown and Concord, New Hampshire, by the 1740s. York, Maine, sacked in 1692 with its minister shot down on his own doorstep, was well within the line of English settlement by the time of Hamilton's visit in 1744. On the Hudson, settlement moved west from Albany along the Mohawk River, threatening French Canada's lifeline down the St Lawrence River with the building of Fort Oswego on Lake Ontario in 1727.

---

[10] Peter Wood, *Black Majority: Negroes in Colonial South Carolina from 1670 Through the Stono Rebellion* (New York, 1974), p. 132.

The most dramatic growth, however, was in the southern and middle colonies, swinging the momentum of social and economic development away from New England. South of the Carolinas, Georgia was settled in the 1730s as a frontier colony. Part of the impetus for its founding came from South Carolina's desire to protect its southern flank from Spanish and Indian attacks. But the immediate initiative came from England. In a scheme reminiscent of the plans of the Virginia Company a century before, a group of pious philanthropists led by an army officer, now a Member of Parliament, General James Oglethorpe, secured a charter in June 1732 to found a colony named after King George II. Its purpose was to aid England's 'worthy poor' by providing them with limited amounts of land and the opportunity to redeem themselves and—it was hoped—the neighbouring Indians by hard work and Christian example. Unlike the Virginia Company, however, the project was to be run by trustees who were not themselves allowed to profit from the colony and whose control would give way to royal government after a period of twenty-one years. Parliament gave aid eventually totalling over £130,000 and more was collected by public subscription. In the decade after 1733, when the first group of 114 settlers, led by Oglethorpe, reached the mouth of the Savannah River, some 2,500 people migrated to the colony. Mostly English, they were soon joined by parties of Moravians and by several hundred Ashkenazic and Sephardic Jews who settled in the little port of Savannah. From the first, however, the settlers chafed at the trustees' moral programme, especially its limitation on the size and full ownership of land grants and prohibitions against importing hard liquor and black slaves. Through the 1740s Georgians gradually secured the repeal of these restrictions, concluding with the legal admission of slaves in 1750. A year later the disillusioned trustees voted to turn over their control to the Crown even before required to do so by the charter. From its utopian beginnings, Georgia became a plantation society similar to its South Carolina neighbour, with small inland farms, coastal plantations growing rice with slave labour, and an extensive trade with the Indians in skins.

Further north, by the 1720s, settlement had spread up the Schuylkill and Susquehanna Rivers in Pennsylvania. In the next decade German immigrants entered Virginia's Shenandoah Valley. The Valley became a highway—the Great Wagon Road—for successive waves of mostly German and Scots-Irish migrants moving south-west from Pennsylvania, creating a band of settlement paralleling the ocean but 200 miles inland, and reaching the northern border of South Carolina by mid-century.[11] By then, the bulk of the lands between the coast and the foothills of the Appalachians had been surveyed and bounded and much of the cultivable

[11] Robert D. Mitchell, *Commercialism and Frontier: Perspectives on the Early Shenandoah Valley* (Charlottesville, Va., 1977), pp. 15–55.

land settled. Fifteen years later the Reverend Charles Woodmason, an itinerant minister travelling in this backcountry, would express his wonder that 'this Country contains ten times the Number of Persons beyond my Apprehension'.[12]

Settlement by a new population brought dispossession for another, and the great exception to this chronicle of demographic expansion was the continued decline of the power and numbers of the Indian population within what was becoming a continuous band of European and African settlement. For some the decline was abrupt and violent. The Yamasee people living on the coast south of Charleston, for example, first allied with the arriving English against the Spanish in Florida. In 1712 and again in 1713, their warriors accompanied South Carolinian expeditions that decimated the Tuscarora Indians. By 1715, however, disputes over the trade in deerskins and Indian slaves, coupled with white territorial encroachment, prompted the Yamasees to join with the neighbouring Creeks in attacks that killed over 400 white settlers. The survivors responded with their own coalition, raising a corps of armed slaves and buying the aid of the inland Cherokee confederacy. Within two years, South Carolina's counter-attacks killed or enslaved the bulk of the Yamasee people.[13]

Further north, the Catawbas of the North Carolina piedmont emerged as a distinct confederation through the more cautious strategy of sheltering refugees from other fragmented tribes and seeking harmonious relationships with arriving settlers. By mid-century, however, they too found their lands, numbers, and autonomy steadily eroded by treaty cessions, smallpox epidemics, and a dependence on European goods.[14] Within New England, Indian resistance was already fragmented by the wars of the 1670s. The survivors gathered in reservations or scattered through white society as indentured servants, whale fishermen, and Anglicized leaders of the kind encountered by Dr Hamilton in Rhode Island. Their numbers, wrote one observer in 1714, 'are at present so thin'd as to become like two or three berries in the top of the uppermost bough'. The peoples who best sustained their power and culture were such confederacies as the Cherokees of the southern Appalachian hill-country and the Iroquois south of Lake Ontario, who deployed their position between encroaching spheres of European influence to their diplomatic and commercial advantage.[15]

[12] Richard J. Hooker, ed., *The Carolina Backcountry on the Eve of the Revolution: The Journal and Other Writings of Charles Woodmason, Anglican Itinerant* (Chapel Hill, NC, 1953), p. 56.

[13] See below, pp. 351–52.

[14] James H. Merrell, *The Indians' New World: Catawbas and their Neighbors from European Contact to the Era of Removal* (Chapel Hill, NC, 1989), chaps. 3–5. For a fuller treatment of Indian relations with the British colonies see chap. by Daniel K. Richter.

[15] Samuel Sewall to Jonathan Law, 3 May 1714, Massachusetts Historical Society, *Collections*, Sixth Series, V (1892), p. 292; Daniel Richter, *The Ordeal of the Longhouse: The Peoples of the Iroquois League in the Era of European Colonization* (Chapel Hill, NC, 1992); James H. Merrell, '"The Customs of Our

The overall demographic picture, however, is one of steady growth. Migration and the expansion of trade swelled the population of port towns: Boston's numbers rose from 7,000 to 15,000 inhabitants between 1690 and 1750, New York's and Philadelphia's from less than 5,000 to over 12,000, each with a substantial African-American population. Other smaller communities, Charleston, Newport, Salem, and Marblehead, ranged from 6,000 to 2,000 inhabitants by mid-century. Urban growth, however, fell far short of the fivefold increase of the population at large, and eighteenth-century British America remained an overwhelmingly rural landscape.

It becomes the more important, therefore, to trace this landscape's general patterns. Land grants became larger and dependent on political connections. Robert Temple, the English son-in-law of Boston merchant John Nelson, brought families from Ulster to settle large tracts in Maine claimed from Nelson's family holdings. Robert Livingston, an immigrant Scot who married into the influential Dutch Schuyler family, used his seat on the New York royal Council and some creative surveying to carve out a huge domain extending east from the Hudson River. In the northern neck of Virginia, Thomas, sixth Lord Fairfax, won legal title in 1745 to his family's claim to a proprietorship of more than five-and-a-quarter million acres. Within this principality, Robert Carter and his descendants, acting as agents for the Fairfaxes, secured 300,000 acres of their own. On Virginia's Southside, the two William Byrds, father and son, amassed 180,000 acres to which they recruited French Huguenot and then German and Swiss immigrants, founding Richmond as their base of operations.

These were among the most spectacular projects. But throughout British North America the hunger for land created a boom in its claiming and distribution, to war veterans and their heirs, to members of the Governors' Councils who oversaw the land grant process, and to younger sons escaping the effects of a legal system that, save in New England, conveyed the bulk of an estate to the eldest male heir. In new frontier communities such as Kent, Connecticut, the majority of settlers themselves speculated in land, producing disparities in wealth and status even greater than those of older settlements, and preparing the way for organized land companies such as Virginia's Ohio Company, organized in 1747 to claim trans-Appalachian lands, and the Susquehanna Company of 1753 that pressed Connecticut's title to much of the Wyoming Valley of northern Pennsylvania. George Washington's rise from obscurity as a younger son by a second marriage contained some of the classic components for success: a valuable social connection (to the Fairfax family), an alliance with a wealthy widow, and a training as a land surveyor.

Countrey": Indian and Colonist in Early America', in Bernard Bailyn and Philip D. Morgan, eds., *Strangers within the Realm: Cultural Margins of the First British Empire* (Chapel Hill, NC, 1991), pp. 117–56.

Bounding and exploiting the land, coupled with the dramatic expansion of the labour force in the middle and southern colonies, gave a powerful impetus to colonial production, especially those commodities raised for sale to Europe. Of these, the most valuable, still comprising almost half of the British mainland colonies' exports by mid-century in terms of market value, was tobacco. Long the foundation for the growth of Virginia and Maryland—the colonies 'founded on smoke'—its exports more than doubled to some 70 million pounds a year by 1750. New markets were found by re-export from England and Scotland to continental Europe. But stagnant and, after the 1720s, fluctuating prices—ranging from twopence to less than a penny per pound—prevented the growth in value of the crop from keeping pace with the rise in population. More fortunate were the rice planters of South Carolina, who found a growing market with stable prices for their product in southern Europe. Moving from an early reliance on the raising of cattle and the export of deerskins, South Carolinians increased their annual shipments of rice from 1½ million to 27 million pounds between 1710 and 1750, by which year they had also developed a second profitable crop, indigo, used in dyeing cloth. By then, too, the value of their exports per white inhabitant was four times those of their Chesapeake counterparts. South Carolina's planters emerged as the wealthiest colonists north of their brethren in the Caribbean, investing their profits in new cargoes of slaves and in the elegant mansions they built in Charleston, safely distant from the fetid, malarial swamps in which their slaves grew rice.

Further north, in North Carolina and then from Pennsylvania to New England, settlers continued to raise the hogs, corn, cattle, fruit, barley, and rye needed for their families' subsistence, with some of these affording a surplus saleable in urban markets. By mid-century, farmers tilling the lands around the navigable river valleys of the middle colonies, such as the Delaware and Hudson, had adopted the more productive tools of metal-sheathed ploughs and the cradle scythe in place of the sickle. Their produce generated a flourishing export trade through Philadelphia and New York to Europe and the Caribbean in foodstuffs, especially wheat, presaging the spectacular growth of the region later in the century. New Englanders shared in this trade, but more often as middlemen than producers. Their most important export income came from ploughing not land but sea— through cod and whale fishing, and maritime trade of the kind that brought West Indian molasses to Boston's sugar refineries and rum distilleries, and British goods for sale locally and in other colonies. One domestic product that New England could produce in abundance was timber fashioned into barrel staves, shingles (wooden tiles), boards, and naval stores, together with locally built vessels in such numbers as to compose one-third of Britain's merchant marine by mid-century. Naval stores, including pitch and turpentine, were also an important item of trade for North Carolina's 'tarheels'.

Some measure of the income generated by this economic expansion can be gauged from the growth of the mainland colonists' imports from England and Wales—the rising tide of manufactures, cloth, hardware, glass, books, firearms, and the host of items eventually listed by weary customs officials simply as 'Goods of several sorts'. The value of these imports rose steadily, accelerating in the 1740s and more than tripling to over 1 million pounds sterling a year in the half-century before 1750. Through these years, also, the value of this trade as a proportion of Great Britain's total foreign trade doubled, to nearly 10 per cent, a trend whose political implications would emerge in the 1760s as the colonists adopted the weapon of non-importation of British goods in protest against Imperial policies. The burgeoning capacity of the southern colonies—and especially South Carolina—to buy is the more striking in light of the region's simultaneous capital investment totalling more than £2 million sterling in slaves alone between 1700 and 1740.[16]

To demographic differentiation, therefore, was added one of regions, both along a north–south axis and between the ports and plantations of the tidewater and the subsistence farms of the interior. Coastal trade expanded to link these regions and to tranship products to the major ports for export to Europe and the Caribbean; roads seasonally able to sustain wagons were cut where rivers would not serve, leading into such regional centres as Boston, Philadelphia, and Fredericksburg. Word of Europe's affairs and the variety of its available products were circulated by British America's first newspapers, beginning in 1704 with the *Boston News-Letter*, and twelve in number by mid-century, including four printed in Boston and three in Pennsylvania, one a German-language paper. Postal services already running across the Atlantic began to link the larger colonial towns.[17]

With the differentiation of society came a more deliberate ordering and regulation of its components. In its strictest form, this was evident in the regulation of British America's most volatile resource and principal means of production, its labour force. White indentured servants and apprenticed children remained the core of the colonists' labour system, especially in the Middle Colonies, and contemporary court records and newspaper advertisements detail the disciplinings these relationships required—with runaways sought, abuses protested against,

---

[16] John J. McCusker, 'The Current Value of English Exports, 1697 to 1800', *William and Mary Quarterly*, (hereafter *WMQ*), Third Series, XXVIII (1971), pp. 623–27. The figure for the capital investment in slaves joins estimates of 90,000 Africans brought into South Carolina and the Chesapeake to an average price of £25 sterling per head.

[17] Edward C. Latham, *Chronological Tables of American Newspapers, 1690–1820* (Worcester, Mass., 1972), p. 4; and, generally, Charles E. Clark, *The Public Prints: The Newspaper in Anglo-American Culture, 1665–1740* (New York, 1994), and Ian K. Steele, *The English Atlantic, 1675–1740: An Exploration of Communication and Community* (New York, 1986).

labour terms extended, and insubordinations punished. William Fisher of Pennsylvania's Chester County paid for his flight with six-and-a-half years extra servitude; Margaret Chester's delivery of two bastard children on her master's time brought two further years, with the children, too, bound into the master's service.[18]

Bound servants could hope to live beyond their term of service, and a child's apprenticeship to such a trade as printing, as in the case of young Benjamin Franklin, might eventually bring a mastery of one's own. Each, in its way, was a stage in the education and socialization that might lead, life-span and gender permitting, to financial and civic independence. No comparable opportunity was open to the slave. The last decades of the seventeenth century were decisive in turning the British mainland colonies toward a full adoption of the labour system already dominant in the sugar plantations of the Caribbean. New England's, and then South Carolina's, Indian wars briefly made Indian slaves a significant proportion of their population—as much as 15 per cent of South Carolina's in 1720. But these proportions soon diminished with the influx of forced African migration. With subsequent natural increase, the black population of the lower south swelled thirtyfold, from 2,000 to 60,000 between 1690 and 1750; twentyfold, from 7,000 to 150,000 in the Chesapeake; and nearly tenfold, to over 30,000 (just above half living in New York and New Jersey) in the colonies north of Maryland. In these same decisive years, slaves as a proportion of British North America's total population rose from 7 to 20 per cent, surpassing the 10–15 per cent living as white indentured servants.[19]

To control and structure this massive influx, each colony developed a body of law and practice making slavery for blacks—but never whites—a hereditary, lifelong, colour-defined status visited on all children of a slave mother. Such legal servitude pressed hardest upon the more-than 85 per cent of African-Americans who lived south of Pennsylvania's border with Maryland, the line soon immortalized by the names of its mid-century surveyors, Charles Mason and Jeremiah Dixon. Of this population, a very few, in coastal communities or on the frontier, maintained a precarious legal or unofficial freedom. For the remainder, there were only differing patterns of lifelong labour. Thus recent scholarship has found a contrast between the closely supervised sun-up to sun-down gang labour of the Chesapeake's tobacco plantations and the 'tasking' system employed in Carolina rice fields, with the latter balancing unhealthier conditions of labour

---

[18] Sharon Salinger, 'To Serve Well and Faithfully': Labor and Indentured Servitude in Pennsylvania, 1682–1800 (New York, 1987), pp. 108, 109.

[19] Recent overviews of this crucial transition include Russell Menard, 'From Servants to Slaves: The Transformation of the Chesapeake Labor System', Southern Studies, XVI (1977), pp. 355–90, and David Galenson, White Servitude in Colonial America: An Economic Analysis (Cambridge, 1981), pp. 150–57.

against the practice of allowing slaves some freedom to grow their own food and develop separate communities once the day's prescribed tasks were completed. Coupled with the continued heavy importation of African-born slaves into the lower South, this meant that African names, languages, and customs remained much more widespread there than elsewhere in British America.[20]

Only scattered voices, as of Boston magistrate Samuel Sewall and from among the Quaker communities of Pennsylvania and New Jersey, spoke out to challenge the morality of slavery. A few echoed planter William Byrd and the trustees of Georgia in their more pragmatic concern that black slavery's spread eroded white work habits by its association of manual labour with servile status. But Byrd's own depiction of himself in biblical terms to an English correspondent as 'one of the patriarchs' surrounded by 'my flocks and herds, bond-men and bond-women', was the stronger image in linking the sanction of religion and history to the special difficulties in building civilized life in America. 'To live in Virginia without slaves', concluded Anglican minister Peter Fontaine, 'is morally impossible.'[21]

Where white voices were still or complacent, however, black bodies were in motion. Slave resistance ranged from feigned laziness or illness to arson, poisoning, and flight, both individually and in groups. Communities of runaway slaves formed in Virginia's Dismal Swamp region and further west, in the Blue Ridge Mountains. Open insurrection was often suspected but rare in practice—its most dramatic instance during these years came in South Carolina with the Stono Rebellion of 1739, when a gathering of some 100 slaves, mostly Africans from Angola, killed more than twenty whites before being dispersed and brutally suppressed. Much publicized, the uprising prompted a tightening of the network of militia patrols, scout boats, and slave-catchers authorized to take up and punish slaves found abroad without permission, measures that militarized the heartlands of southern society even as its borders became more peaceful. Individual masters sold recalcitrant slaves to the Caribbean or resorted to physical abuse of a kind almost never suffered by white servants—floggings of the sort reported as an 'unfortunate chance' by the Reverend Samuel Gray of Virginia's Middlesex County when he supervised the beating to death of his runaway mulatto servant, or the official licence extended by the Lancaster County court to its greatest local planter, Robert 'King' Carter, in 1708, to cut off the toes of two

---

[20] Philip Morgan, 'Work and Culture: The Task System and the World of Lowcountry Blacks, 1700 to 1880', WMQ, Third Series, XXXIX (1982), pp. 563–99; Wood, Black Majority, pp. 170–91.

[21] William Byrd to Charles Boyle, Earl of Orrery, 5 July 1726; to John Perceval, Earl of Egmont, 12 July 1736, in Marion Tinling, ed., The Correspondence of the Three William Byrds of Westover, Virginia, 2 vols. (Charlottesville, Va., 1977), I, p. 355; II, p. 488; Ann Maury, Memoirs of a Huguenot Family (New York, 1853), pp. 351–52.

'Incorrigible negroes'.[22] Nor was such repression confined to areas where black majorities aroused special fears. The town of New York, where slaves composed a fifth of the population, experienced one slave uprising in 1712 and a second, more suspected than actual, in 1741, in the wake of the wave of rumours that swept up the colonial seaboard following the Stono Rebellion. Months of trials and forced confessions in 1714 produced sentences showing the evolution of legal structures now shaped as much by considerations of race as of social status: of 154 blacks charged, 70 were transported, 18 hanged, and 13 burnt at the stake.[23]

Such outbursts reveal the harsh coercion underlying Byrd's patriarchal image, the moments when, as he acknowledged, 'foul means must do, when fair will not'.[24] Yet they validated rather than diminished patriarchalism's power, and the same image can be seen in softer and more subtly moulding form in the unfolding patterns of family life. Through these years, as before, the family remained the basic societal unit by which authority was channelled and exercised, labour and resources generated and allocated, and status within the larger social world defined. But some shifts of form and practice took shape. The varied circumstances of seventeenth-century settlement had fostered a marked diversity of domestic structures, ranging from New England's large and closely supervised Puritan families to the complex but curtailed relationships of a Chesapeake society riven by high mortality and a scarcity of women. A healthier demographic climate in the south, together with a transition to more geographically mobile and internally governed family units further north, now brought a greater uniformity of family structures, and ones within which longer-lived heads of households might exercise more fully the masculine authority enshrined by law. To men as husbands, their wives continued to surrender their legal identity and virtually all effective control over their affairs upon marriage; and as fathers, men's testamentary practices gave ever greater favour to sons over daughters in allocating the increasing resources in land and labour generated by British North America's spectacular economic growth.

The fruits of prosperity, however, could modify as well as reinforce the character of patriarchal authority. Economic expansion and Atlantic trade brought wealth to an upper stratum of merchants and planters, not on the scale of Europe's aristocracies, but allowing a life-style far more comfortable and even ostentatious than that of their seventeenth-century predecessors. Such families moved from rudely furnished one- or two-room houses to town-houses and plantation

[22] Rutman and Rutman, *Place in Time*, I, p. 171; Edmund S. Morgan, *American Slavery, American Freedom: The Ordeal of Colonial Virginia* (New York, 1975), p. 313.

[23] Daniel Horsmanden, *The New York Conspiracy*, ed., Thomas J. Davis (Boston, 1971), pp. 467–73.

[24] Byrd to John Perceval, Earl of Egmont, 12 July 1736, in Tinling, ed., *Byrd Correspondence*, II, p. 488.

mansions—Boston's Foster-Hutchinson and Hancock houses, Byrd's Westover, and Thomas Lee's Stratford Hall, among many examples—equipped with imported furniture and silver emblazoned with no less freshly acquired family heraldry. Chairs and china replaced stools and wooden bowls, three-pronged forks joined knives at table, and wardrobes of wigs, gowns, and brocaded waistcoats displayed—both in person and in the numerous portraits commissioned from travelling artists—their owners' aspirations to be recognized as emancipated from hard-scrabbling toil and attired as properly fledged members of an Atlantic community of gentry.[25] Symbolic of these genteel aspirations and their shaping by Old World connections was the new social ceremony of taking tea. Well established in town and plantation drawing-rooms by the 1720s, it soon infused both down and across the social order. Dr Hamilton sceptically recorded a boorish fellow traveller's claim to gentility by his donning of linen nightcaps and his boasting that 'his little woman att home drank tea twice a day,' and in 1750 two Moravian missionaries invited to breakfast with a Seneca chief on the upper Susquehanna River were surprised to be greeted by a tea table, at which their host 'prepared very good tea to which he added Indian bread'.[26]

Wifely rituals in the drawing-room and in the supervision of servants and households, set alongside masculine gatherings in pursuit of leisure or business at race-courses, fox-hunts, coffee-houses, and taverns—all indicate a separation of gender roles at upper levels of colonial society that was much slower to emerge among the many more numerous families tied to subsistence agriculture. Pulpit homilies gave a new emphasis to expounding the duties of wives and mothers, while among the young George Washington's first literary exercises was his copying of an English manual's 'Rules of Civility and Decent Behavior', that set out a gentleman's behaviour in company on matters ranging from deference to superiors to refraining from killing lice in public or spitting into the fire.[27] Elevated upon the plinths of their Georgian-style mansions and the shoulders of their servants and slaves, colonial élites were at leisure to assume the duty of commencing the refinement of America.

---

[25] Richard L. Bushman, *The Refinement of America: Persons, Houses, Cities* (New York, 1992), chaps. 2–5; Lois Green Carr and Lorena S. Walsh, 'Changing Lifestyles and Consumer Behavior in the Colonial Chesapeake', in Cary Carson, Ronald Hoffman, and Peter J. Albert, eds., *Of Consuming Interests: The Style of Life in the Eighteenth Century* (Charlottesville, Va., 1994), pp. 59–166. Carr and Walsh find a doubling of mean estate values in five Maryland counties between 1690 and 1750, with a concomitant increase in the acquisition of consumer items.

[26] Bridenbaugh, ed., *Gentleman's Progress*, p. 14; William M. Beauchamp, comp., *Moravian Journals Relating to Central New York, 1745–1766* (Syracuse, NY, 1916), pp. 64–65.

[27] Laurel Thatcher Ulrich, 'Vertuous Women Found: New England Ministerial Literature, 1688–1735', *American Quarterly*, XXVIII (1976), pp. 19–40; W. B. Allen, ed., *George Washington: A Collection* (Indianapolis, 1988), pp. 6–13.

The more deliberate ordering of society's ranks stretched and sometimes split the social fabric even as it sought to stiffen and legitimate it with more formal codes of behaviour. A different set of stresses and their attendant fault lines, though ones that likewise show renewed Old World influences at work, can be seen in the development of religious practice and belief.[28] Throughout these years particular regions still showed the imprint of the deeply felt religious purposes of their founding generations, with New England (save in heterodox Rhode Island) maintaining a legally established Congregationalism, the southern colonies predominantly but less formally upholding the Anglican Church, and the Middle Colonies, more open to religious diversity from their later foundation, according pre-eminence to their first settlers' Quaker and Dutch Reformed beliefs. These loyalties, together with their cherished institutional underpinnings, remained a point of pride and provincial identity: the emerging group of self-consciously 'American' historians, such as Cotton Mather and Thomas Prince of Massachusetts and Robert Beverley, Hugh Jones, and William Stith of Virginia, took pains to recover and embellish the distinctive traits derived from their regions' separate foundings.

But, as Cotton Mather acknowledged, New England was also 'a part of the English Nation', and both these histories and the path taken by colonial religion responded to the new context formed by the events of 1688. William of Orange's conquest of England, forcing the abdication of his Catholic father-in-law, James II, restored his new kingdom to a leadership of the international Protestant cause it had not held since the days of Elizabeth and Cromwell. In America, where fears of 'Popery and Arbitrary Government' had precipitated the armed overthrow of James's governments in New England, New York, and Maryland, William and Mary's accession allowed the colonists to represent their rebellions as acts of loyalty to an England once more worthy of their allegiance. With King William set 'as an Hook in the Nostrils of that French Leviathan', Louis XIV, Protestants could now stand together against Catholic plans for world domination—'war with none but Hell and *Rome*'.[29]

British America's Catholics, in consequence, though few in number save in Maryland, Montserrat, and Nova Scotia, remained excluded from political life and liable to summary expulsion and punitive taxation. For colonial Protestants, by contrast, England's leadership encouraged a broader comprehension within the

---

[28] For a fuller treatment of colonial religious life, see chap. by Boyd Stanley Schlenther.

[29] Address from Massachusetts, 6 June 1689, C[olonial] O[ffice] 5/855, no. 12; Cotton Mather, *A Pillar of Gratitude* (Boston, 1700), p. 33, *The Wonderful Works of God* (Boston, 1690), p. 40, and *Things for a Distress'd People to Think Upon* (Boston, 1696), p. 73. For similar fervour in later years, see Nathan O. Hatch, *The Sacred Cause of Liberty: Republican Thought and the Millennium in Revolutionary New England* (New Haven, 1977), pp. 36–44.

bounds of an established religion, one formalized by Parliament in the Act of Toleration passed in 1689. Less expansive than the liberty of conscience already permitted in Rhode Island, Pennsylvania, and New Jersey, it none the less impelled such historically more intolerant colonies as Virginia and Massachusetts (the latter through an explicit provision in its new charter of 1691) towards a grudging acceptance of the legitimacy of Protestant dissent from an established church. Subsequent Crown instructions and judgements steadily favoured colonial Dissenters seeking relief from orthodox religious regulation.

Widening this relaxation of the hitherto close ties between particular churches and states in British America was a further legacy of 1688 and its attendant quarter-century of warfare: the stream of continental European Protestant sects—Huguenots, Mennonites, Lutherans, Moravians, Schwenkfelders, and many others—who looked to England and her colonies for refuge, joining the tide from within Britain of Presbyterian Scots and Irish. Such groups might establish their own small communities—the Moravians in Bethlehem and French Huguenots in New Bordeaux—but, overall, they intermingled far more than had seventeenth-century Protestant migrants to America. The old assumption of one community, one congregation steadily eroded: by mid-century, for example, the small settlement of Germantown near Philadelphia had at least five different religious assemblies. A modern count has estimated that, between 1690 and 1750, the number of known churches and meeting houses rose more than fivefold, to nearly 1,700, outstripping the growth in the white population, save in the less churched southern colonies. Equally remarkable was the geographical spread of leading sects, planting numerous Anglican, Baptist, and Presbyterian churches in Congregational New England and Presbyterian ones in Anglican Virginia where few or none had existed in 1690.[30]

This does not suggest a time of religious lack of interest or decline, as once was thought, and contemporary statements taken to suggest this by their criticisms of their own or neighbouring denominations more plausibly point to the opposite conclusion, to zealous churchmen eager to reform their own congregations or to recruit followers by denigrating competitors in a lively religious market-place. The great majority of colonists remained committed church-goers. The famous events in Salem Village, Massachusetts, in 1692, where accusations of witchcraft spread to neighbouring towns, sending more than a hundred people to prison and nineteen to execution, document a continued popular interest in folk magic and the occult. But its treatment in court and commentary shows how thoroughly such scattered

---

[30] Edwin Scott Gaustad, *Historical Atlas of Religion in America* (New York, 1962; revised edn., 1976), pp. 5, 167, 175; Patricia U. Bonomi and Peter E. Eisenstadt, 'Church Adherence in the Eighteenth-Century British American Colonies', *WMQ*, Third Series, XXXIX (1982), pp. 268–76.

practices were encapsulated and understood within the dominant framework of Christian beliefs.

Inside this overarching Protestantism, certain patterns of development appear. Gradually replacing state coercion with voluntarism, these changes led by different roads towards more active individual participation and self-assumed responsibility in religious matters. Even the Salem trials show a willingness to find explanations for misfortune in the malice of neighbours rather than in the inscrutable ways of providence. And as the writings of such European Enlightenment figures as John Locke, Isaac Newton, and the Anglican divine John Tillotson reached a colonial readership, they heightened perceptions of humankind as beings not so much incapacitated by innate depravity as endowed with God-given reason by which they could comprehend and help shape the world about them. Boston's Cotton Mather, seeking new ways to uphold manners and morality now that royal Governors and liberty of conscience held sway in Massachusetts, appealed for privately organized moral reform societies to promote personal piety and the voluntary assumption of the duties of good citizenship. One listener, the young Benjamin Franklin, would turn this message to more secular account in his best-selling *Poor Richard's Almanac* (published annually from 1732), a collection of adages that extolled the personal virtue and material gain to be derived from self-improvement.

Every major denomination showed the influence of this more 'reasonable' and socially decorous Christianity. For some colonists, it heightened the appeal of a resurgent Anglicanism in America. But others still yearned for a faith that would set salvation above citizenship and renew the passionate individual experience of receiving God's saving grace. During the 1720s and 1730s a number of European-born clergy—among them Theodore Frelinghuysen of the Dutch Reformed church, and Presbyterians William and Gilbert Tennent—brought word to the middle colonies of the Protestant evangelistic revival then sweeping Europe.[31] Their stirring, emotional preaching, with that of Congregationalist Jonathan Edwards in upcountry Massachusetts, touched off a series of local revivals that led many to declare their ecstatic 'new birth'. Edwards spread the news of these conversions in his 1737 *Faithful Narrative of the Surprising Work of God*. Soon afterwards, the arrival in October 1739 of the famed young English evangelist George Whitefield fanned the embers of these revivals into a conflagration known to history as the Great Awakening. Whitefield, though an ordained Anglican minister, overrode sectarian differences by his willingness to carry his simple message of salvation by faith into any proffered pulpit or backcountry field. A preacher of enormous power and 'almost angelical presence', he skilfully

[31] W. R. Ward, *The Protestant Evangelical Awakening* (Cambridge, 1992).

promoted his work through advance advertising and daily publication of his journals.

Whitefield's year-long travels, with a longer visit between 1744 and 1748, stirred the colonies to a degree unprecedented since the news of the Glorious Revolution. 'My hearing him preach gave me a heart wound,' reported Connecticut farmer Nathan Cole, 'my old Foundation was broken up and I saw that my righteousness would not save me.'[32] Thousands felt the same shock, and churches everywhere reaped a harvest of conversions. But critics soon began to question both the revival's methods and its message, calling its physical exuberance mere animal passion and emotional hysteria, and charging that its arousal of young people, women, servants, and slaves posed a threat to the social order. Conservative ministers in their turn found themselves damned as 'Pharisees'—'dead dogs that can't bark'—by upstart laymen turned travelling preachers who gloried in their unlettered enthusiasm.[33] Many congregations split; and lasting schisms formed between supporters and opponents of revivalism, New versus Old Lights in Congregationalism, New against Old Side in Presbyterianism. What had begun in unity begat further division.

Scholars still debate the Awakening's larger significance. It plainly accelerated British North America's pioneering acceptance of religious voluntarism and denominational pluralism. Its revelation of the methods and efficacy of mass revivalism would add a recurring motif to American religious life. The Awakening further weakened church–state ties and challenged clerical authority and professionalism. The sharp increase in the number of Separatist and Baptist congregations testified to the many Christians who followed Nathan Cole in pursuing their spiritual convictions beyond the bounds of formally organized religion. Broader consequences followed. The catharsis of spiritual rebirth offered a new path to many who felt mired in worldliness, and fostered an inner confidence and self-definition that could override the deference traditionally accorded to a social and political élite. If the revivalists did not challenge law and authority, it has been noted, they now denied them sanctifying power.[34] Many of the divisions racking American society later in the century would be charged and legitimized by the colonists' profound and disparate religiosity.

Religion, the ordering of society, the channelling of economic growth, and the allocation of resources—all these issues resounded within the political arena, and the final element of this survey looks to the structure and workings of provincial

[32] Richard Bushman, *The Great Awakening: Documents on the Revival of Religion, 1740–1745* (Chapel Hill, NC, 1969), pp. 67–68.

[33] Ibid., p. 91.

[34] Richard Bushman, *From Puritan to Yankee: Character and Social Order in Connecticut, 1690–1765* (Cambridge, Mass., 1967), p. 193.

politics, the domestic counterpart of the pattern of Imperial governance described elsewhere in this volume.[35] In institutional terms the trend lay, for once in this period, towards a greater uniformity. The Glorious Revolution in America disrupted Stuart plans for a consolidation of colonial governments under direct royal rule. Henceforward, while individual Governors sometimes ruled more than a single colony (as when New Jersey was governed in tandem with New York between 1702 and 1736), individual governmental units were left unaltered. But what emerged in the 1690s, if more by happenstance than design, was a synthesis that combined preservation of most of the institutions of semi-autonomous and highly localized government that the colonists had developed in their founding years with an acceptance of a large measure of royal control as expressed through the Crown's appointment of Governors and other executive-branch officials. Connecticut and Rhode Island retained their charter-given rights to choose their own Governors; and the restoration, in 1693 and 1715, of the Penn and Calvert families to their proprietorships of Pennsylvania and Maryland allowed each to nominate those particular colonies' executives. In every other American colony, however, including South and North Carolina after 1720 and 1729, and Georgia after 1752, a royally commissioned Governor now ruled, assisted by Crown-appointed Councils (elected in Massachusetts) and, save in the military outposts of Nova Scotia and Newfoundland, by locally elected representative Assemblies. In political terms, and by comparison with the previous century, these were the years of the forming of a coherent, London-directed British Empire in America.

Within these royal colonies, the similarity of political structure encouraged common patterns of political behaviour. The royal Governors, usually British by birth and often military men by training, strove to deploy their powers of appointing local officials—militia officers, sheriffs, and justices of the peace—to win allies in the Assemblies and compensation for themselves. Leading colonists competed for appointment to the Council seats that conferred both social prestige and a hand in the distribution of vacant lands. Assemblymen sought legislation benefiting their constituencies and their hold on local affairs. Ideologically, closer ties of power and sympathy with the mother country fostered the colonists' more explicit self-perception of themselves as English—in the wake of 1688, several colonies passed (and the Crown disallowed) laws rehearsing Magna Carta and their entitlement to the liberties of Englishmen. Assemblies adopted privileges and procedures appropriate to their equation of themselves with England's House of Commons, and several colonies replaced their unicameral legislatures with the more parliamentary bicameral form.

[35] See chap. by Ian K. Steele.

These governments, John Dickinson would later observe, were not only '*mixt,* but *dependent*', and the tensions inherent in this description were expressed in political antagonisms.[36] Colonial legislators saw their authority as locally derived, from an electorate generally limited to white, male, Protestant freeholders but broad and empowering by contemporary standards. Royal Governors, by contrast, drew their legitimacy from a Crown across the ocean. A long-standing division within the English constitution took on a geographical dimension, one heightened by London's expressed doubts that the colonists possessed rights—or Assemblies—independent of the grace and favour of the Crown. Across the royal colonies a common scenario emerged. As a Governor sought to exercise his powers to shape policy, appoint officials, and veto legislation, the Assembly responded with the rhetoric of protecting local interests and by using its control of the granting of taxes for the support of government in ways that compelled acceptance of a larger legislative role in day-to-day administration. Though still powerful figures, the Governors were increasingly placed on the defensive, both in practice and by a lively journal and pamphlet literature critical of imported prerogative power.

How these antagonisms played out in detail, however, was shaped by local divisions and circumstances. In New York, the 1691 trial and execution of Jacob Leisler, its leader in the Glorious Revolution, plunged the colony's politics into a twenty-year blood feud that pitted English against Dutch settlers, Anglicans against other sects, and city merchants against Hudson Valley traders and landlords. A reconciliation engineered by Governor Robert Hunter in the 1710s proved only temporary. Pennsylvania was torn by contention between a Quaker élite and a faction supporting the Penn family proprietorship, each vying for the support of arriving Germans and Scots-Irish. North and South Carolina experienced prolonged and sometimes violent disputes with proprietorial officials and between the rival migrant groups, from Britain, Barbados, and Virginia, dominant in different areas of the two colonies. In every colony the pressures of war finance forced a resort to paper money, pioneered by Massachusetts in 1690, with consequent divisions between commercial creditor and rural debtor interests, especially as some colonies allowed their notes to depreciate—to a ratio of £12 to £1 sterling in Massachusetts by 1748. A second kind of paper currency, involving state-issued loans secured by mortgages on land, proved more stable but disrupted Massachusetts politics in 1740 when the Crown struck down schemes for a privately organized 'land bank'.

Yet factionalism stopped short of insurrection; and by the early 1730s politics in most colonies became visibly more stable and even cohesive. A number of capable

[36] John Dickinson, *Letters from a Farmer in Pennsylvania to the Inhabitants of the British Colonies* (Philadelphia, 1768), p. 58.

Governors, such as James Glen in South Carolina, William Gooch in Virginia, and Jonathan Belcher and William Shirley in Massachusetts, contributed to this through their skills of conciliation and management. Local leaders, for their part, had learned how to turn Whitehall's decisions and appointments in their favour by means of agents and lobbying. Calls to guard against external foes (and, in southern colonies, against the threat of slave insurrection) also helped to quiet rivalries at home. By then, too, memories of the bitter struggles of 1688–89 had given way to the mythologization of a Revolution deemed so gloriously complete as to render any further revolution and constitutional change unnecessary.

Perhaps most crucial to this greater stability, however, as Jack P. Greene has noted, was the emergence of political élites conditioned by the Revolution's constitutional heritage and willing to exercise their rivalries within the framework of mutually accepted institutions and behaviour.[37] Indicative of this more settled political climate was a heightened continuity and concentration of leadership: turnover in legislative membership declined, fewer elections were contested, and many offices, especially seats on the royal Councils, became the preserve of an interrelated cousinage of leading families.[38] The pattern was uneven, as colonies such as New York, New Jersey, and Massachusetts remained more contentious than the gentry-dominated governments of Virginia and South Carolina. By mid-century, however, colonial politics as a whole shared many of the characteristics of the differentiation and reordering visible in society at large. And this was not accidental, for both embodied the close interplay between wealth and power inevitable in permeable but hardening societies, where access to the allocation of resources from a richly endowed environment was the high road to status and success. Small though colonial governments remained in terms of offices created and taxes levied, they still exercised an exceptional range of functions at a variety of levels, and political participation, with or without formal compensation, still offered significant reward.

The six decades that followed the Glorious Revolution in British North America were a time of dramatic, indeed unprecedented, growth sustained within the bounds of a remarkable institutional stability. Settlement patterns, labour systems, and ethnicities all changed in ways that would have enduring effects upon American society. To predominantly subsistence modes of life were added others more specialized and interdependent. The colonies, even to their western edges, were drawn within an Atlantic market of staple products and European consumer goods: for Delaware Indians far up the Susquehanna River, Schachameki, 'the

---

[37] These paragraphs owe much to the essays recently republished in Jack P. Greene, *Negotiated Authorities: Essays in Colonial Political and Constitutional History* (Charlottesville, Va., 1994), esp. chaps. 6–9.

[38] Leonard W. Labaree, *Conservatism in Early American History* (New York, 1948), pp. 1–31.

place of eels', was now Schachenaméndi, 'where we get our gun barrels made straight, when they were bent'.[39]

Colonists such as Benjamin Franklin hailed this growth as progress, and rejoiced in its extent. With Franklin, too, an active solicitor of London's patronage and approval, they continued to gauge British America's advance by its correspondence to England's achievements. There were signs that in some respects—economic opportunity, political virtue, a full expression of the rights of Englishmen, and the possession of a profitable labour force—they saw themselves as already surpassing the mother country. The unexpected conquest in 1745 of the French fortress of Louisbourg by an expedition from New England excited an outpouring of English patriotic fervour among the victors, but one distinctly tinged with local pride. Nor did the colonists' patriotism extend to unconditional obedience to royal authority: no less than their English cousins, their loyalty was to England's constitutionalism rather than its Crown. The one had sometimes clashed with the other, and might do so again. But as peace returned to the Atlantic world in 1748, their expectation was to continue to reap the bounty of America and practise self-government at the King's command.

[39] Jane T. Merritt, 'Kinship, Community, and Practising Culture: Indians and the Colonial Encounter in Pennsylvania, 1700–1763', unpublished Ph.D. dissertation, University of Washington, 1995, p. 24.

Select Bibliography

BERNARD BAILYN, *The Origins of American Politics* (New York, 1968).

—— and Philip D. Morgan, eds., *Strangers within the Realm: Cultural Margins of the First British Empire* (Chapel Hill, NC, 1991).

PATRICIA U. BONOMI, *Under the Cope of Heaven: Religion, Society, and Politics in Early America* (New York, 1986).

RICHARD L. BUSHMAN, *From Puritan to Yankee: Character and the Social Order in Connecticut, 1690–1765* (Cambridge, Mass., 1967).

—— *The Refinement of America: Persons, Houses, Cities* (New York, 1992).

JACK P. GREENE, *Pursuits of Happiness: The Social Development of Early Modern British Colonies and the Formation of American Culture* (Chapel Hill, NC, 1988).

—— *Negotiated Authorities: Essays in Colonial Political and Constitutional History* (Charlottesville, Va. 1994).

RICHARD R. JOHNSON, *Adjustment to Empire: The New England Colonies, 1675–1715* (New Brunswick, NJ, 1981).

ALLAN KULIKOFF, *Tobacco and Slaves: The Development of Southern Cultures in the Chesapeake, 1680–1800.* (Chapel Hill, NC, 1986).

JOHN J. MCCUSKER and RUSSELL R. MENARD, *The Economy of British America, 1607–1789* (Chapel Hill, NC, 1985).

D. W. Meinig, *The Shaping of America*, Vol. I, *Atlantic America, 1492–1800* (New Haven, 1986).

James Merrell, *The Indians' New World: Catawbas and their Neighbors from European Contact to the Era of Removal* (Chapel Hill, NC, 1989).

Gary B. Nash, *The Urban Crucible: Social Change, Political Consciousness, and the Origins of the American Revolution* (Cambridge, Mass., 1986).

—— *Red, White, and Black: The Peoples of Early North America*, 3rd edn. (Englewood Cliffs, NJ, 1992).

Ian K. Steele, *Warpaths: Invasions of North America* (New York, 1994).

Alan Tully, *Forming American Politics: Ideals, Interests, and Institutions in Colonial New York and Pennsylvania* (Baltimore, 1994).

Peter Wood, *Black Majority: Negroes in Colonial South Carolina from 1670 through the Stono Rebellion* (New York, 1974).

14

The American Colonies in War and Revolution, 1748–1783

JOHN SHY

War seems a transparently clear historical activity. People fighting, or preparing themselves to fight, generate a wealth of evidence, making their actions readily visible to historians. But less clear are the effects—the 'impact'—of war. We assume that war tests and often transforms both structures and consciousness, but it usually does so in conjunction with other contemporaneous forces, and historians of war run the risk of either missing or exaggerating its causative impact, a risk increased by the exciting, dramatic quality of military events, both then and now. People are resilient, and once the fighting has stopped, the lasting effects of war, beyond its memory, are often much less easily seen than was the war itself.[1]

The local impact of the great war of the mid-eighteenth century and the subsequent War of American Independence is complicated by our knowledge that out of these wars came the United States. All too often American historians have tended to view these great struggles through a nationalist prism, unconcerned, perhaps unaware, that Virginia and Massachusetts were acting in a wider context than that officially sanctioned by the formal Declaration of Independence of 1776. But other historians have had difficulty, as is suggested by the anomalous use of 'colonies' for the post-Independence years 1776–83 in the title of this chapter, in finding the right framework for war's American impact during thirty-five crucial years of Imperial history.

The North American colonies of the eighteenth-century British Empire had taken root in a long epoch of warfare—with Spain, the Dutch, and ultimately France. Relations between English colonists and the native peoples were punctuated and, in particular times and places, characterized by warfare of an especially brutal kind. But we can exaggerate the frequency and intensity of colonial American military experience. Most American colonists, most of the time, lived in

---

[1] Jack P. Greene, *Negotiated Authorities: Essays in Colonial Political and Constitutional History* (Charlottesville, Va. 1994), pp. 93–130, is an ingenious attempt to do the opposite—assess the impact of peace—for the eighteenth-century American colonies.

peace, and even in wartime daily life went on more or less untroubled by events on the frontier or at sea.

At the same time the very structure of colonial governments and their Imperial connection had been shaped by war. The provincial 'Governor' was a military functionary, the King's viceroy in distant lands commissioned to command military forces. Elected representative Assemblies, seemingly modelled on the House of Commons, were in fact *ad hoc* creations to secure the vital support, military as well as financial, of numerous and rapidly increasing populations. Adult male colonists, required (with some exceptions) by Crown-approved provincial law to serve in the militia, were led by officers who, even when elected, held their commissions by royal authority.

Recurrent colonial warfare since the late seventeenth century had pushed provincial taxing, borrowing, and spending to levels unimaginable in a more peaceful American world; and with these high levels, government itself, as well as political conflict, took on central importance in colonial American society. Conventional wisdom argues that war enhances central authority, especially executive power. But the financial demands of colonial wars from 1689 to 1748 had, in general, enhanced the power of the elected provincial Assemblies, who had used their power to raise and borrow money and to oversee its expenditure as so many levers to bend British authority to their collective will.[2] Even the most astute and active Governor could not lead his province to war without the support of elected provincial representatives. Hard pressed to finance mobilization, a royal Governor knew that nothing but paper money, issued by authority of the Assembly, although routinely forbidden by his Imperial instructions, would buy vital supplies and pay the indispensable enlistment bounties. The growth of paper currency in the American colonies is a separate economic and political story, but it was closely linked to the exigencies of war and to their constitutional effects.[3]

From about 1740 the scale of North American warfare began to grow, and more Americans, more often, found themselves drawn into the military realm. Even after what seemed the final victory of 1763 against France and Spain, the post-war years were troubled by the effects of the wars just passed, trouble that was a major factor in colonial rebellion and the long war for American independence. Not until the peace of 1783 did war release its grip on a generation of Americans who remembered Governors William Gooch of Virginia and William Shirley of Massachusetts, and who may even have followed the one to disaster at Cartagena in 1740 or the other to victory at Louisbourg in 1745. A younger generation would

---

[2] Leonard W. Labaree, *Royal Government in America: A Study of the British Colonial System Before 1783* (New Haven, 1930), esp. pp. 269–311, and Jack P. Greene, *The Quest for Power: The Lower Houses of Assembly in the Southern Royal Colonies, 1689–1776* (Chapel Hill, NC, 1963), esp. pp. 297–309.

[3] Leslie V. Brock, *The Currency of the American Colonies, 1700–1764* (New York, 1975).

have known few years without war. It may appear obvious that during less than four decades, spanning three major military conflicts, the 'old' thirteen British colonies on the North American mainland had been transformed into the new United States, but exactly how war had affected this transformation deserves careful examination.

Two events of the 1740s marked the new level of direct American involvement in Britain's wars. Governor Gooch had recruited about 3,500 Americans from eleven colonies in 1740 to join the attack on New Spain. That attack had failed; many American soldiers died, and others came home with ruined health, but never before had the mainland colonies come together in such a large military effort. Five years later Governor Shirley mobilized and led a comparable effort: more than 3,000 New England volunteers, with the help of a small British fleet, conquered the great outpost of New France at Louisbourg. The American colonies rejoiced.[4]

Because French armies had won major military victories in the Low Countries, Britain returned Louisbourg to France in 1748, but Parliament also gave Massachusetts £180,000 sterling to reward and reimburse its extraordinary wartime effort, which was used by the provincial government to effect a severely deflationary retirement of paper currency.[5] The Americans recruited by Gooch earlier for the failed expedition in the Caribbean were paid as British soldiers, as were most of the troops led by General James Oglethorpe, Governor of the new colony of Georgia, in an unsuccessful attack on Spanish St Augustine in 1740. New York got little from the war except political trouble in a futile expedition to take the French post at Crown Point on Lake Champlain, but Pennsylvania, with no law requiring militia service, had broken a pacifist tradition in allowing Benjamin Franklin in 1747 to raise a force of armed 'Associators' for the defence of Philadelphia against French and Spanish attack.[6]

Whether Americans generally emerged from 'King George's War' (1739–48) angry at British arrogance and military ineptitude, as some historians have argued, is a very difficult question to answer satisfactorily, but seems doubtful; the elder half-brother of George Washington, who had followed Gooch to the Caribbean, returned to Virginia fatally ill, and yet named his plantation Mount

[4] Douglas E. Leach, *Arms for Empire: A Military History of the British Colonies in North America, 1607–1763* (New York, 1973), chap. 6, and John A. Schutz, *William Shirley: King's Governor of Massachusetts* (Chapel Hill, NC, 1961), chap. 5.

[5] Thomas Hutchinson, *The History of Massachusetts Bay...*, 3 vols. (London, 1768; Cambridge, Mass., 1936), II, pp. 334–37; Lawrence H. Gipson, *The British Empire Before the American Revolution*, 15 vols. (Caldwell, Ida. and New York, 1936–70), X, p. 38.

[6] Stanley N. Katz, *Newcastle's New York: Anglo-American Politics, 1732–1753* (Cambridge, Mass., 1968), pp. 165–85; Esmond Wright, *Franklin of Philadelphia* (Cambridge, Mass., 1986), pp. 77–81.

Vernon in honour of the British admiral often blamed for the failure of the campaign.[7]

At mid-century the peace of 1748 settled none of the issues that had led to the wars just ended. British colonists in North America were pushing beyond the settled areas: north-eastward into Maine, the no-man's land between New England and French Acadia; westward up the Mohawk from the Hudson Valley, and through the Appalachian passes into the upper Ohio valleys; and southward from Georgia against the mission frontier of Spanish Florida. Behind this rising pressure was a rapidly growing population, but encouraging and channelling it were more specific, localized interests. In Massachusetts, with a fertile people and little arable for the rising generation, investors hoped to settle a vast tract of territory in Maine claimed by their company. Pennsylvanians trading with the Indians had pushed their posts as far as the Miami River in the western part of modern Ohio, while a massive stream of immigrants, mostly Germans but many from Ireland, passed through Philadelphia to occupy the last good, cheap lands beyond the Susquehanna, with others turning southward at the Blue Ridge barrier to people the western, 'back' parts of Virginia and the Carolinas. The province of South Carolina, seeking to create a buffer of white settlement between the slave-worked rice plantations of the coastal lowland and the powerful Indian tribes of the backcountry, not only attracted some of these migrants from Pennsylvania to militarized western 'townships' with generous land grants but brought others, many of them Germans, directly through the seaport of Charleston.[8] Two competing Virginia land companies lobbied in London and Williamsburg to secure huge claims to the Ohio country.[9] Seen collectively, all these local phenomena indicated that the peace of 1748 could be no more than a brief truce.

Yet negotiations to prevent or postpone what most sensed would be a great, climactic war for imperial hegemony continued in Paris and London. Undercutting negotiation on both sides were aggressive attitudes and the ever changing situation in North America. French military steps to secure control of their mainland settlements west of British Nova Scotia, and of the Great Lakes basin of the St Lawrence River, were taken in Massachusetts and Virginia, as well as Whitehall, to be clear evidence of a plan to strangle the American colonies.[10] The British establishment in 1749 of a fortified base in Nova Scotia at Halifax, in effect

---

[7] Douglas E. Leach, *Roots of Conflict: British Armed Forces and Colonial Americans, 1677–1763* (Chapel Hill, NC, 1986), pp. 42–75.

[8] Robert L. Meriwether, *The Expansion of South Carolina, 1729–1765* (Kingsport, Tenn., 1940), pp. 17–76.

[9] Thomas P. Abernethy, *Western Lands and the American Revolution* (Charlottesville, Va., 1937), pp. 3–13.

[10] Ian K. Steele, *Warpaths: Invasions of North America* (New York, 1994), pp. 175–77, is a valuable reconsideration of this moment in Imperial history.

answering the threat of Louisbourg to New England's fisheries and territorial ambitions, seemed equally aggressive in Versailles and Quebec.

The explosion triggering a new war came not in Nova Scotia, a focus of negotiation, but in Virginia in 1753–54. There the royal Governor had sent a boyish officer, George Washington, to push a French garrison away from the headwaters of the Ohio River, claimed by both Pennsylvania and Virginia. In a confused woodland encounter, force met force and blood was shed. Young Washington failed, and what would be known as the Seven Years War began, unofficially, in America in 1754.

For once, a British plan was ready. In 1755 New England troops under British command would strike at the French forts around Nova Scotia; other New Englanders would follow Governor Shirley against the French post at Niagara, a threat to the British Indian trade at Oswego, on Lake Ontario. New Yorkers would attack northward through the Champlain corridor toward Montreal; British regulars under a British general would land in Virginia and march to the forks of the Ohio. The Royal Navy would intercept French reinforcements destined for Canada. All this before a declaration of war.

The grand plan of 1755 failed at every point but one. New England volunteers sailing up the Bay of Fundy joined a small force of British troops in overwhelming French Nova Scotian posts, and then in deporting thousands of 'neutral' Francophone settlers from the peninsula. Elsewhere, the Navy missed its prey, the New Yorkers were stopped in a battle at Lake George, and the Niagara expedition ended with a large, crippled force stranded at Oswego. The worst disaster befell the British column marching to the Ohio, which suffered ambush and virtual destruction.

The outcome of 1755 set the pattern for the long American war that ensued. Rather than retell the story of that war, it is more useful to identify elements of the experience that are most relevant to the Empire that emerged victorious. The humiliating defeat of the British regiments in Virginia led to an unprecedented commitment of British forces to North America, and at least tacit acceptance in London of the frequent American plea for the 'extirpation' of New France as the proper strategic objective of the war. But the Virginia defeat had swung the delicately balanced weight of Indian power on to the French side, with devastating effects all along the exposed American frontier.[11]

Anglo-American ineptitude in dealing with Indian peoples had been demonstrated in mid-1754, when New York, ordered by the Board of Trade to co-ordinate Indian policy, convened a meeting at Albany of provincial delegates. Virginia refused to attend, and the other colonies pursued conflicting local interests; the

---

[11] Ibid., pp. 197–99.

chief result of the 'Albany Congress' was a plan for provincial confederation so inappropriate to the crisis that neither the Board of Trade nor any American government gave it serious consideration.[12]

French troops, Canadian militia, and their Indian allies made the next two years, 1756–57, a time of defeat and frustration for Great Britain and her American colonies, even as they were slowly assembling a great military machine. War in Europe, begun in 1756, combined with the Royal Navy to slow French aid to Canada, and a new leader in London, William Pitt, exhorted Americans to make 'strenuous efforts' and promised Parliamentary reimbursement if they did. Virginia could do little but defend its long frontier, while the failure of frontier defence in Pennsylvania brought political turmoil, angry farmers marching against their Quaker leaders in Philadelphia. The main front of the war was therefore northward, where New England and New York faced New France. Pitt's promise persuaded the chief New England colonies, Massachusetts and Connecticut, to mobilize fully, and it eased the political deadlock that had crippled New York.[13] When 1758 brought the first British victories in the taking of Louisbourg and of Fort Duquesne at the forks of the Ohio, the large land and naval forces sent from home were joined by more than 20,000 Americans.

The trend continued in 1759 with massive American contingents joining British forces in the Champlain and Lake Ontario sectors, where Ticonderoga and Niagara fell and Oswego was reoccupied. As the French position crumbled their Indian allies also fell away, and some even assisted the British and the Americans. But the decisive battle was won by British forces almost alone, without significant American or Indian help, at Quebec. When news of the fall of Canada's citadel reached Boston, a day was given over to rejoicing and thanksgiving sermons and prayers.[14]

Americans responded again in large numbers during the next three years, when Canada formally capitulated and the British shifted their military effort to the West Indies, where Martinique, Guadaloupe, and Havana in Cuba fell in turn to British amphibious attack. The war was won decisively not by brilliant strategy or superior tactics, but by overwhelming economic strength, and especially by Pitt's decision to use that strength without reserve in driving the French and their Spanish allies out of eastern North America. One rough calculation is that the

[12] Gipson, *British Empire*, V, pp. 111–66; in Leonard W. Labaree and others, eds., *The Autobiography of Benjamin Franklin* (New Haven, 1964), pp. 209–11.

[13] Harold E. Selesky, *War and Society in Colonial Connecticut* (New Haven, 1990); William Pencak, *War, Politics, and Revolution in Provincial Massachusetts* (Boston, 1981), pp. 149–58; and Patricia U. Bonomi, *A Factious People: Politics and Society in Colonial New York* (New York, 1971), pp. 171–78.

[14] C. P. Stacey, *Quebec, 1759: The Siege and the Battle* (New York, 1959), is an excellent critical account of this legendary campaign.

conquest of Canada cost the British Empire about £4 million over a period when the French budgetary allocation for Canada was less than a tenth of that amount.[15]

In the northern colonies especially, British wartime expenditures had brought sudden prosperity. Although the huge contracts for provisioning were shifted early in the war from American to British firms, American merchants still served the British contractors as agents in New York, Philadelphia, and Boston. American farmers found ready markets in the large armies gathered every spring. American ships were in great demand, and colonial economies north and south rode a wave of paper money, issued by provincial governments to make immediate payment for recruits and their supplies. Early defeats had brought considerable Anglo-American friction and mutual recrimination, and Virginians such as Washington were aggrieved that Pennsylvania's claim to the forks of the Ohio seemed validated by the British choice of the route to Fort Duquesne in 1758, but prosperity and ultimate victory sweetened and repressed the memories of wartime troubles.[16] William Pitt became an American hero.

But two disparate events would give the sweet taste of victory a sour edge. During the final seaborne campaigns in the West Indies British commanders reported to Pitt that American ships were supplying enemy islands targeted for attack; and in 1763 a massive Indian war erupted, from Fort Pitt westward to Detroit and beyond.

Trade with the French and Spanish sugar islands had long been an important but troubled dimension of the colonial American economy. Parliament had responded to pressure from British sugar planters in 1733 to discourage importation of the vast production of 'foreign' sugar, but the so-called Molasses Act went unenforced, and American merchants and shippers continued to balance their transatlantic books with lucrative, if often illicit, ventures in the West Indies. Pitt's anger at reports from his field commanders, and his demand for immediate investigation by the American colonial Governors, suggests how ill-informed most officials in London were about the actual working of the Imperial economy.[17]

They were equally hazy about the Indian population of America. Trouble with the Indians had brought about the abortive provincial congress at Albany in 1754, and had been crucial in the disastrous Ohio campaign in 1755. Fighting the Cherokee of South Carolina in 1759–61 had diverted British forces, and Indian co-operation had been disappointing throughout the war until British victory was assured. To bring some order to Indian affairs after the 1755 débâcle, British 'superintendents' north and south of the Ohio River had been established under

[15] Guy Frégault, *Canada: The War of Conquest* (Toronto, 1969), p. 203.

[16] Fred Anderson, *A People's Army: Massachusetts Soldiers and Society in the Seven Years' War* (Chapel Hill, NC, 1984), emphasizes wartime friction and American alienation, but dwells on the early years.

[17] Gertrude S. Kimball, ed., *The Correspondence of William Pitt*, 2 vols. (London, 1906), II, pp. 320–21.

the loose supervision of the British military Commander-in-Chief for America. But coping with the great northern Indian uprising in 1763–64 with troops weakened by their recent service in the West Indies proved both expensive and difficult. The northern Indian superintendent, Sir William Johnson, effectively saddled the Commander-in-Chief, Sir Jeffery Amherst, but recently a conquering hero, with most of the blame for the outbreak, and officials in London resolved to avoid any such costly surprises in the future.

Directly out of the victorious war came much of what accounts for the conflict between the older mainland colonies and British government in the years immediately after the war, conflict that, amplified by other factors, would lead to Imperial breakdown, civil war, and colonial revolution. Revolution in the American colonies did not originate solely in the prior experience of war, as the ensuing account will make clear, but behaviour in both Great Britain and North America in 1763–75, leading to the revolutionary crisis, was profoundly shaped by the immediately preceding two decades of Imperial warfare. Americans and Britons alike carried attitudes and expectations arising from war into the post-war years, while war itself between 1739 and 1763 had created conditions that rendered many of those thoughts and feelings politically explosive.

Whether or not one accepts the view that revolution is an extraordinary phenomenon, akin to collective madness, with people acting in ways they could barely imagine in the relative calm of normal political and social intercourse, revolution lays a heavy burden on the historian. For decades American settlers and British officials had disagreed, as people do in every political system, about a variety of major and minor points of conflict, but the Imperial system had functioned remarkably well. By 1763 Great Britain and her Empire were admired throughout an Enlightened Europe for their stability, prosperity, and liberty. And yet, within little more than a decade, the Empire broke down in an ugly civil war, triggered by Americans behaving in a frenzy of revolutionary zeal to build anew from the wreckage of the old. How to explain it? Some would say that revolution is not so extraordinary, although its onset is always shocking. The American colonies had been growing rapidly, as well as visibly away from British rule; thoughtful observers knew that separation was inevitable. Equally predictable was British determination to prevent separation, by war if necessary. Again the circle of explanation leads back to war; the prospect as well as the reality of war became the catalysts for revolution. Whichever view one takes of revolution—a collective frenzy, or the continuation of normal politics by other means—the American Revolution challenges the historical imagination.

With vast new territories to defend and govern, from Hudson Bay to the Gulf of Mexico, and over the Appalachians to the Mississippi, an unprecedented military garrison for mainland North America seemed obviously required in 1763. But fifteen regiments of British troops scattered over half a continent would add heavy annual expenses to the gigantic financial burden left by the war, and Americans whose future had been secured by the war might reasonably be expected to contribute to their cost. A new military force might also be used to regulate volatile relations with the Indian occupants of the new territories, policing traders whose sharp methods in the past had provoked Indian retaliation, and controlling the speculators and squatters whose relentless quest for land claimed by the Indians had been an even more serious cause of native disaffection. Whether troops and warships stationed in America might also assist in more effective enforcement of Imperial trade laws, whose flagrant violation by colonial merchants and sea-captains had been so visible in the last years of the war, was less clear, but it was at least an interesting idea.[18] Such was the British mental baggage carried into the post-war period.

Americans, delighted by the dream finally realized of French and Spanish removal, heartened by Britain's wartime generosity, and proud of their own considerable contribution to final victory, looked forward to a golden age in which an enlightened mother country would gently guide the growth of her colonial children. An ever more numerous people, secure in their British liberty, and granted by decades of Imperial precedent a large measure of autonomy, would carry the Empire westward to the glory and profit of all Imperial subjects, British and American. In a word, Americans were never more British than in 1763.

These two differing outlooks were bound to clash, but an inevitable post-war economic recession in America, and a perhaps equally predictable period of political turmoil in Britain, sharpened conflict when it came. Pitt, his talents unsuited to peace, lost power as victory was secured, but lurked dangerously on the flank of successive post-war governments, ready to deploy his charisma for or against, as the mood took him. Americans loved him, and he claimed to love them, although his speeches did not always speak pure affection. In 1763–64, when the government took the first steps to restrict American migration on to lands west of the Appalachian crest, to curb the use of paper money, and to tighten the rules of colonial trade while incidentally raising a revenue that would help defray the new costs of Empire, Pitt did not object, but Americans did, vociferously.

The strong negative response in the colonies after 1763 to what appear to be modest changes in Imperial governance has puzzled historians. The white population of the American colonies was arguably the most gently governed, lightly taxed, least oppressed people in the eighteenth-century Western world. In 1763 its

---

[18] John Shy, *Toward Lexington: The Role of the British Army in the Coming of the American Revolution* (Princeton, 1965), chap. 2, improved by John L. Bullion, '"The Ten Thousand in America": More Light on the Decision on the American Army, 1762–1763', *William and Mary Quarterly* [hereafter *WMQ*], Third Series, XLIII (1986), pp. 646–57.

future looked bright. So why the explosion of discontent that eventually became full-scale revolution?[19]

The best answer lies with those Americans who had been allowed to govern the colonies since their settlement under more or less benign royal supervision: a small minority of families in every colony, from New England to Georgia, often descended from the first settlers of the colony, more affluent, better educated, well known, experienced in governing, and intermarried. This colonial élite had managed their numerous, mobile, fecund, contentious, and increasingly diverse and dispersed constituents not by means of armed force, of which there was virtually none, but by consent and accommodation. Their importance in the political and economic success of the Empire as effective brokers between London, provincial capitals, and the American grass roots can hardly be exaggerated. And yet their role and position were tenuous, not established by statute or royal charter, but based like so much else in the British constitution on long precedent and tacit understanding.[20]

It was this colonial élite that felt itself under direct attack by the new British measures after 1763. In myriad ways, no one of which may be called radically threatening, colonial leaders saw their position being questioned and undermined. The accustomed practice of Imperial rule was eroded by placing Indian affairs (often with the valuable trade) and access to western lands under royal supervision, by establishing a military viceroy in New York with fifteen far-flung regiments of regulars under his command, and by demanding strict enforcement of intricate new parliamentary regulations (twenty bewildering pages in *Statutes at Large*) for colonial trade. But imposing new taxes, however moderate their incidence, to raise a revenue to pay the costs of the new American garrison was truly frightening. Years of precedent had given the elected houses of colonial Assemblies, where so many sons of this élite had learned their role, a function not unlike that of the British House of Commons. Taxation, taking and disposing of property, embodied the essence, on the one hand, of power, and on the other, the porous membrane enclosing liberty. The 'consent' of the taxed on which the legislative right to tax depended was a fiction in Great Britain, but no less so in America. While a much larger proportion of adult white males than in England could take part in choosing their representatives in the colonies, women, non-whites, and all men with little or no property could not vote. And yet, in America as in Britain, the fiction of taxation only by representative consent was effective.

[19] For example, Bernard Bailyn, *The Origins of American Politics* (New York, 1968), pp. 3–13, and Edmund S. Morgan, *The Birth of the Republic, 1763–89*, 3rd edn. (Chicago, 1992), chap. 1.

[20] Leonard W. Labaree, *Conservatism in Early American History* (New York, 1948), remains the best comprehensive sketch of the colonial élite.

Surveying the condition of American society and politics after 1763, the provincial élite had good reason for concern. As Benjamin Franklin had correctly concluded in his famous pamphlet on population, Americans were doubling their numbers every quarter-century, partly through massive migration from Europe and Africa, but mainly through natural increase in a healthy environment.[21] By 1763 almost one person in five was African and enslaved, with most of these in the southern colonies, the economies of which had come to depend on slave-grown staple exports (tobacco from Maryland and Virginia, rice from South Carolina), although the African population was also fairly large in New York and Rhode Island. Heavy immigration from Ireland and south-western Germany had significantly altered the composition of the white majority. Franklin wondered whether the German-speaking 'Palatine Boors' could ever be absorbed by an English culture. Many recent arrivals from Ireland and Germany had moved to the outlying areas of settlement, into New Hampshire; into the Mohawk, upper Schuylkill, and Susquehanna valleys; and into the frontier zones of the southern colonies. Dispersion of population stretched to the limit traditional face-to-face relationships between the élite and the mass of the American people. At the same time, a predominantly Protestant society had undergone since about 1740 waves of religious excitement, upheaval, and division that to some contemporary observers seemed to threaten social order. And then war since 1739 had added its disruptive effects to what already appeared to be ample reason for élite apprehension.

Into this worrisome domestic turbulence new British post-war policies landed like so many grenades. Pitt's wartime measures to reward colonial efforts and to soothe colonial sensibilities wounded by senior British officers had done much to foster, among the American leaders, confidence that government in London understood the difficulty and delicacy of their position, so the steps taken by Pitt's successors in 1763–65, culminating in the Stamp Act, were rude shocks. American leaders protested and, when protest availed nothing, they mobilized mass support and organized direct action.

Even more difficult and contentious questions for historians have arisen from their need to explain American popular response. The real stake in these contested Imperial issues for ordinary American families is not self-evidently clear, and yet their response would be vital to the eventual outcome. Why were colonial leaders so successful in mobilizing popular resistance to new British policies? A few historians have argued that the question is badly posed, because popular American dislike for an intrusive British presence actually pushed leaders further and faster than they

---

[21] Benjamin Franklin, 'Observations Concerning the Increase of Mankind', written in 1751 but published in 1755, in Leonard W. Labaree and others, eds., *The Papers of Benjamin Franklin* (New Haven, 1959–), IV, pp. 225–34.

intended to go; but most concur that the role of leadership was determinative. Then how account for the successful organization of popular energies in a society where all authority was weak, and individualistic behaviour commonplace?

These questions hardly arose for earlier historians, steeped in the legend of national origins. But the professionalization of historiography had by the early decades of the twentieth century formulated two different sets of answers. One was most succinctly set forth in 1924 by the Yale historian Charles M. Andrews: revolution arose from the very Englishness of the Imperial polity.[22] Decentralized, loose-jointed, and guided by the principles of 1688, the Imperial constitution had allowed Americans to persuade themselves that their elective Assemblies were Houses of Commons in miniature, protecting the rights as Englishmen of every New Englander, New Yorker, Virginian, and Carolinian. No effective rebuttal from Britain had lent credibility to these mistaken ideas. So the years of Imperial reform after 1763 inevitably brought confrontation, and Americans, incapable of adapting their ideas to new Imperial realities, rebelled.

Charles Beard, who began to transform American historical consciousness in 1913, offered a different answer.[23] He and his many disciples explained all political behaviour in terms of economic interest. Explaining the American Revolution was as simple as describing the conflicts of economic interest between Great Britain and the American colonies.

Dissatisfaction with both answers was evident before the middle of the twentieth century. Economic explanation had too many logical and evidentiary weaknesses, and a nagging sense of incompleteness clung to what may be called the alternative Whig-Imperial version. Relentlessly, a new answer emerged from the work of Bernard Bailyn at Harvard, his student Gordon Wood, and a growing number of followers.[24] By an imaginative rereading of texts well known for two centuries, they stressed the explanatory force of ideology.

Unlike the pallid constitutional theories emphasized by Andrews, ideology for Bailyn and Wood is a powerful fusion of belief and emotion, a deeply implanted quasi-religious sense of reality pervading colonial America, a belief-system that when challenged, as it was by British measures after 1763, predictably exploded into revolution. This explanation, centered on the twinned though reciprocally antagonistic concepts of liberty and power, has proved highly persuasive, in part at least

[22] Charles M. Andrews, *The Colonial Background of the American Revolution* (New Haven, 1924).

[23] Charles A. Beard, *An Economic Interpretation of the Constitution of the United States* (New York, 1913).

[24] Bernard Bailyn, *The Ideological Origins of the American Revolution* (Cambridge, Mass., 1967), and *The Origins of American Politics* (New York, 1968); Gordon S. Wood, *The Creation of the American Republic, 1776–1787* (Chapel Hill, NC, 1969), and *The Radicalism of the American Revolution* (New York, 1992).

because it readily explains both élite and mass behaviour leading up to 1776, as well as a great deal else about American history afterward.

This digression into historiography is necessary because not all are convinced that ideology answers all the important questions about the American Revolution. A recent major work by a distinguished journalist-historian on the Revolution recasts it as 'a struggle for power', blending the older explanations of Andrews and Beard while giving almost no attention to ideology.[25] To the question of popular mobilization it should be noted that on only three brief occasions was popular response strongly consensual: against the Stamp Act in 1765, against the so-called Coercive or Intolerable Acts in 1774, and during most of the first year of open warfare, 1775–76. For the rest of a twenty-year struggle division, doubt, and apathy were as characteristic as popular enthusiasm or unanimity. That an estimated one out of every four or five white Americans rejected the Revolution should not be forgotten. To the persistent question about popular response, the best answers are still agnostic.

The degree of unanimity in resisting the Stamp Act in 1765 was indeed striking. Riots and popular demonstrations from New England to South Carolina intimidated royal officials and nullified the law before its effective date. Boston and New York were the most violent, and even those who supported resistance were shocked by the spectre of anarchy. Almost every American on record, including many future Loyalists, regarded the Stamp Act as imprudent, and most objected to it as 'unconstitutional'. The consensus against the Stamp Act, which led to an intercolonial 'Congress' and boycott of stamped documents, created a proto-national network that British repeal in 1766 may have vitiated but that subsequent British measures would reactivate and strengthen.

When, in 1767, the Townshend duties imposed a new set of import duties in America, and directed their revenue to support, not the colonial military establishment, but royal officials who in the past had occasionally been pressured by threats from colonial Assemblies to withhold their salaries, the American response was less unified and more hesitant. The Stamp Act had given resistance a tangible target that these new import duties lacked. It took a year and a persuasive campaign, led by the lawyer John Dickinson of Pennsylvania, before many Americans were sure that the Townshend duties, if accepted, posed a genuine threat to their liberty. One of Dickinson's most effective arguments was that the Townshend duties would reduce the colonies to the constitutional status of Ireland. Trade boycotts were organized in 1768–69 within and between the port towns. While the mere threat of boycott had seemed a potent weapon in securing repeal of the Stamp Act in 1765–66, when the effects of post-war recession were still being felt on

---

[25] Theodore Draper, *A Struggle for Power: The American Revolution* (New York, 1996).

both sides of the Atlantic, effective economic pressure against the Townshend duties was far more difficult to create and sustain. Competition and suspicion between the merchants of Boston, New York, and Philadelphia threatened to split the united front, as did sharp differences of interest between northern traders and shippers on the one side, and exporting southern planters on the other.[26]

A British decision in 1770 to repeal all but the duty on tea came just as the American boycott neared collapse, and at the very moment when a violent clash between British soldiers and townspeople took place in Boston, where troops had been sent to curb intimidation of customs officials. This second great crisis of Imperial relations, 1767–70, made clear that neither side comprehended the constitutional logic of the other, and that within the American tactic of using economic pressure lay a dangerous potential for violence.

It seems at the least arguable that Americans generally had not become so imbued since the seventeenth century with a radical ideology that they magnified every new British measure into an apocalyptic threat to liberty. Except for a mob attack in Rhode Island on a British revenue cutter in 1772, trouble seemed to dissipate after 1770. The final explosion of 1774–76 is explicable in terms of initial interests and attitudes, and of the dynamics of the conflict itself, without invoking a putative ideological propellant for American behaviour. What Americans said and did may be as readily grasped by recalling their English identity.

The last crisis followed this lull in Imperial tension. Apparently placated by British concessions in 1770 not unlike those of 1766, many Americans quietly paid the remaining Townshend duty on imported tea, while others drank the cheaper, smuggled variety. The onset of renewed trouble in 1773 had almost nothing to do with the colonies. Granting a one-time rebate to a hard-pressed East India Company of the high domestic tea duty, the government of Lord North in effect sanctioned the dumping of a large quantity of cheap but legal tea on the Imperial market. But North declined to lift the much lower tax on tea collected in America under the one remaining Townshend duty. Americans quickly saw in this curious exception a plot to force the principle of taxation down their throats once more.[27]

Well-honed methods and networks again came into play. While East India Company tea shipments were effectively resisted elsewhere, in Boston Governor Thomas Hutchinson, American-born and as determined as his enemies, resolved to put law to the test. The consequent destruction of about £10,000 of Company tea in Boston harbour triggered a response in Britain that is more fully described in another chapter,[28] but it shocked many in America. The wanton destruction of so

[26] Merrill Jensen, *The Founding of a Nation: A History of the American Revolution, 1763–1776* (New York, 1968), chaps. 10–11.

[27] Benjamin W. Labaree, *The Boston Tea Party* (New York, 1964), pp. 70–73.

[28] See below, pp. 335–37.

much private property seemed an unwarranted revolutionary act. What turned American opinion from criticism to support of Boston's behaviour were the British punitive measures of 1774. These new acts, closing the port of Boston, in effect destroying the livelihood of all for the crimes of an unidentified few, and unilaterally altering the forms of government and justice, were far more distressing than the 'Tea Party' itself. Whatever doubts had existed in American minds for more than a decade about the true motives of British behaviour, they were resolved by new laws that would be branded coercive and intolerable. Any lingering doubts were dispelled by the deployment of a large part of the peacetime British army and navy to Boston, where the former Commander-in-Chief now ruled as Governor.

While cooler heads called for another American 'congress' (as in 1765) of provincial delegates in Philadelphia to concert measures, rather than yield to the demand of radicals for an immediate economic boycott, colonial Assemblies confronted their Governors with gestures of support for Boston. Opposed, prorogued, or dissolved, these representative bodies almost everywhere reconstituted themselves as provincial congresses or conventions, claiming to wield legitimate power in the absence of the executive. Within and between colonies, the degree of unanimity was like that of 1765, but new was the degree of popular involvement and, sometimes, pressure. Mobilizing extra-legislative resistance to the Stamp Act and Townshend duties had exacted a price from the élite, and henceforth it dared not ignore the opinions expressed by private persons or self-constituted groups.

The Continental Congress, meeting in September 1774, quickly adopted the 'Association', a general boycott of trade, and called on local committees to enforce it. The Association, in the tradition of economic pressure against obnoxious British laws and policies, was a long step toward war and revolution. Local committees freely used force and threats of force, a prerogative of government, to achieve compliance with the Association. For those in Britain who had hoped that moderate leaders in the Congress from outside New England would take the first steps toward a settlement of the conflict, news of the Association came as an unpleasant shock. Moreover, because Congress had used language first drafted by a county meeting in Boston, the Association marked a notable step in transforming an Imperial crisis into a popular revolutionary movement.[29]

When the first armed clash took place between British troops and local militia near Boston in April 1775, the other older mainland colonies solidly supported the cause of Massachusetts as the cause of all Americans. Nova Scotia, Quebec, and the Floridas were too isolated or too little developed politically to join the American resistance. The Americans lost the first military battle in April and the second, at

[29] Jack N. Rakove, *The Beginnings of National Politics: An Interpretive History of the Continental Congress* (Baltimore, 1979), pp. 45–49.

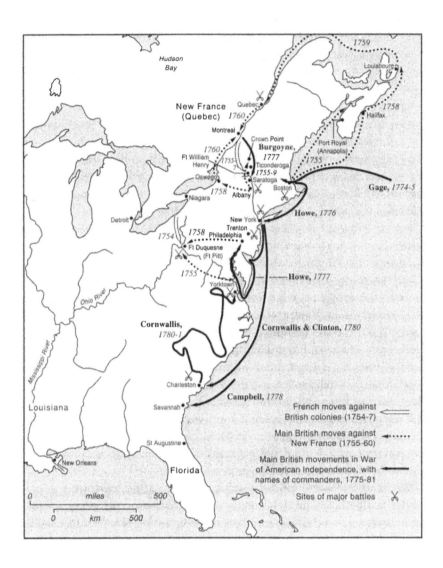

Map 14.1. War in North America, 1754–1783

Bunker Hill, in June, but they exacted a heavy price in British casualties, and blunted the British strategy of isolating and punishing Massachusetts and thereby intimidating the other colonies. The outbreak of war, far from frightening non-New Englanders, rallied support up and down the seaboard. With a small British army penned in on the Boston peninsula by a much larger assemblage of armed militia, a British fleet looking on helplessly, with small contingents of American volunteers on the march from as far away as Virginia and Pennsylvania, the next stage of civil war depended on decisions taken in London.

More than a year of war passed before the colonies declared their independence in July 1776. Just as the logic of resistance had led to war, so war led inexorably towards breaking completely free from Britain; but the process was not simple or easy. New England delegates to Congress, with strong support from Virginians, argued that the colonies had been declared independent by royal action, by the proclamation of August 1775 for suppressing rebellion, and even more so by the King's speech on opening Parliament in October, where he asserted that the war was 'manifestly carried on for the purpose of establishing an independent empire'.[30] And then the Prohibitory Act of December outlawed American ships and trade, unleashing the British Navy and admiralty courts against them.

But other delegates to Congress, especially from New York, Pennsylvania, and South Carolina, resisted and delayed the last step to independence. While the New Englanders and Virginians declared that independence was simply an accomplished fact, more conservative delegates argued that the timing was bad: Congress should secure foreign assistance before, not after, taking the final, irrevocable step; and likewise it should create some kind of governmental structure. Behind these cogent arguments lay the fear of burning bridges, and of popular disorder in colonies already strained by rapid social changes.

In the event, foreign policy and constitution-making were pushed aside by the vocal debate over independence. But the logic of war may have done more than Congressional rhetoric to resolve the issue: demanding that captured Americans must be treated not as criminals but as prisoners of war, invading Canada before the British garrison there could be reinforced, and denying to reluctant Americans any right to remain neutral. All these military measures sanctioned by Congress implied the actions of a sovereign authority.

Reports in early 1776 of British strategy reinforced the movement for independence: after the failure at Boston to isolate and destroy the heart of rebellion, British land and naval forces were clearly massing against New York, the best base from which to conduct a large-scale war of invasion and manoeuvre. In Europe, Britain sought additional troops unsuccessfully from Russia, but eventually hired 18,000 German soldiers from the Hessian states. Rumours of other diplomatic and political moves in London gave the American push for independence its urgency. Real fear existed in Congress and among the more radical American leadership that an attractive British peace move in 1776 might split the unified front of

---

[30] Merrill Jensen, ed., *English Historical Documents: American Colonial Documents to 1776* (New York, 1955), p. 851.

American resistance; in this respect, declaring independence pre-empted the possibility of a negotiated settlement which would imperil New England and Virginia.[31]

The Declaration itself, quickly recorded as unanimous once the conservatives had lost, has been so intensely scrutinized, extolled, and ridiculed that the historical context of both the decision and the document have been obscured. Apart from its reassertion of the right of revolution based on the contractual nature of government, and the equality of natural rights, it offered a questionable history of the causes of the American Revolution. But the decision itself, more than the language of the document, was welcomed by most Americans, energizing and clarifying their mobilization for an escalated war. Other Americans, even some who had supported resistance and subscribed to the Association, could not accept this final step. The latter group, Loyalists who already had been branded by their aroused countrymen as 'Tories', comprised a substantial minority of the American population. While mobilizing the American majority, the Declaration of Independence, more than any other single event of the Revolution, created and motivated American Loyalists.[32]

Joseph Galloway, Franklin's friend and former ally in Pennsylvania, was among the most vocal of Loyalists. He had served in Congress and signed the Association, but after Congress had rejected his plan to create a unified government for the colonies whose powers would be co-ordinate with Parliament, he turned sharply against the leaders of American resistance. Independence, he predicted, would be a disaster, ensuring military defeat and social anarchy. In time, he would turn as bitterly against British leaders who had failed to put down rebellion. Galloway left Congress, and would leave his wife and Pennsylvania estates when British troops left Philadelphia in 1778; he never returned. Not typical of the mass of American Loyalists, Galloway yet shared with almost all of them a belief that Parliament had trampled on American rights, and a pessimism about prospects for the American colonies outside the British Empire.[33]

Rejecting Galloway's plan for reconciliation through confederation, Congress relegated the question of constitutional structure to a committee headed by John Dickinson, Galloway's political rival, but like Galloway an opponent of independence, who soon resigned from Congress. More urgently, it sought help

[31] Henry Strachey to Christopher D'Oyly, New York, 11 Aug. 1776, Strachey Papers, William L. Clements Library. Paul H. Smith and others, eds., *Letters of Delegates to Congress, 1774–1789*, (Washington, 1976–), III–IV, contains much evidence of rumours running in early 1776 to this effect.

[32] William H. Nelson, *The American Tory* (Boston, 1961), remains the best general account, but Paul H. Smith, 'The American Loyalists: Notes on their Organization and Numerical Strength', *WMQ*, Third Series, XXV (1968), pp. 259–77, is an important addition.

[33] Joseph Galloway, *A Candid Examination of the Mutual Claims of Great-Britain and the Colonies* (New York, 1775).

from abroad by despatching America's most famous citizen, Benjamin Franklin, to France.

Military help was desperately needed in the latter part of 1776 as the American war effort very nearly collapsed. The invasion of Canada, at first successful, disintegrated as British reinforcements made Quebec secure and smallpox erupted among the American invaders. The powerful Anglo-German force assembled at New York routed Washington's army in August, and by November had driven its remnants into New Jersey, where they and their commander fled towards Phila-delphia. American civilians in lower New York and across New Jersey, stunned by military defeat, in large numbers sought protection from the victors. By December 'the game', Washington wrote, seemed 'pretty near up'.[34] But William Howe, the British army commander, did not press his advantage to the utmost, and compla-cently spread small garrisons across his front facing the Delaware River. As 1776 ended Washington, reinforced by militia from Pennsylvania, struck back, destroy-ing in succession two of these garrisons, at Trenton and Princeton, then fled for safety to the hills of northern New Jersey. American spirits revived, Washington became a political icon, and what promised to be a short, decisive war became a protracted ordeal of attrition.

Congress, prodded by Washington, after 1776 moved away from a traditional reliance on short-term volunteers from the militia towards a more disciplined, better-trained army enlisted for at least three years. But Congress had quickly stripped John Dickinson's draft 'articles of confederation' of centralized powers to levy taxes, so it could not escape reliance on the traditional mode of war finance: paper money. As it had during earlier wars, paper money worked well for the first few years. Only when the equivalent of more than about £5 million in paper had flooded the American economy would price inflation become an uncontrollable problem, undermining popular support for the war and transforming politics as well.[35]

But politics immediately after the Declaration of Independence quickly took a provincial turn, even as the war went badly. Delegates left Congress to redraw constitutions for their States. Some of them, animated perhaps by the vehement republicanism expressed by Thomas Paine in his widely influential attack on monarchy in the pamphlet *Common Sense*, came home bent on stripping away

---

[34] To Lund Washington, near Trenton, 17 Dec. 1776, in John C. Fitzpatrick, ed., *The Writings of George Washington*, 39 vols. (Washington, 1931–44), IV, p. 347. Don Higginbotham, *The War of American Independence, Military Attitudes, Policies and Practice, 1763–1789* (New York, 1971), is a comprehensive account of the war, but Piers Mackesy, *The War for America, 1775–1783* (London, 1964), provides the wider Imperial context.

[35] E. James Ferguson, *The Power of the Purse: A History of American Public Finance, 1776–1790* (Chapel Hill, NC, 1961), p. 26, where the limiting figure is given as about $25 million, in the monetary unit adopted by Congress.

every vestige of monarchical-aristocratic government, so leaving all power to the people and their elected representatives. In Pennsylvania, where Paine had begun his new career, and where radical leaders had defeated the conservative influence of Galloway and Dickinson, a new constitution centred all power in the elective Assembly and gave the western counties a greatly increased voice, proportional to their population; even the executive was a committee chosen by the legislature. The grandees who ruled Virginia adopted a new constitution even before independence was declared. Like that of Pennsylvania, it gave all power to the Assembly, but it denied a full share of that power to the new western settlements.

Elsewhere, the influence of another viewpoint was apparent. John Adams of Massachusetts had produced a pamphlet, *Thoughts on Government*, to counteract what he saw as the perniciously democratic ideas of Paine, and it circulated in Congress and among the public.[36] The New England States (except New Hampshire) simply retained their colonial charters, purged of royal authority, but other colonies reflected Adams's thinking in their efforts to re-create an American equivalent of mixed government, with bicameral legislature and independent executive and judiciary. Americans, in their long argument with Parliament, had shown an exceptional sensitivity to concentrated power in any form, and Adams's polemic struck a responsive chord. The New York constitution, and later the Massachusetts constitution of 1780, fragmented governmental authority to reduce the chance that liberty might succumb to unchecked power. Less than five years after the war, the new structures in these latter states, and the glaring deficiencies of the Pennsylvania and Virginia constitutions, would influence the drafting of a new federal constitution for the United States.[37]

A complex British military plan for 1777 ended the first phase of the war. An invasion mounted from Canada would capture the critical Champlain–Hudson corridor, cutting New England off from its allies to the southward; and a large-scale move from New York against the rebel capital would force Washington to a decisive battle. Washington's army was again defeated, though not decisively, while the army from Canada foundered in the northern wilderness, trapped in a morass of rebel resistance near Saratoga, New York. British surrender at Saratoga in late 1777 triggered the decisive event of the war: a French alliance in early 1778 with the United States.

With French entry, Britain faced an altogether new war. Defending the West Indies, maritime trade, and Britain herself took precedence over putting down

---

[36] First printed in Philadelphia 1776.

[37] Allan Nevins, *The American States During and After the Revolution, 1775–1789* (New York, 1924), retains its value, but should be supplemented by Willi Paul Adams, *The First American Constitutions: Republican Ideology and the Making of the State Constitutions in the Revolutionary Era* (Chapel Hill, NC, 1980).

American rebellion. Congress, confident that a French alliance ensured victory in some form, dismissed a British offer in 1778 to concede virtually every point at issue in 1775 if independence were rescinded. British strategy, foiled in New England and the middle states for the first three years of war, shifted in 1778 to the South, where thousands of slaves, powerful Indian tribes along the frontier, and a politically divided and more thinly settled white population seemed to offer military opportunities. Active operations in the South and the West Indies could also be co-ordinated, economizing on the use of stretched British forces. British headquarters and a strong garrison remained on and around Manhattan, confronting Washington's main army, posted fifty miles north in the Hudson Highlands. Both Washington and the new British commander, Henry Clinton, believed that he had the other pinned down.

The Franco-American alliance started badly. A combined attack on the British base at Rhode Island in late summer 1778 foundered amidst gale-force winds, an early exit by the French fleet, and major mistakes by the American commander of land forces. A year later, after the British southern campaign had begun with an invasion of Georgia, a combined Franco-American effort to retake the port town at Savannah failed with heavy losses and mutual recrimination. Not until May 1780 did a small French expeditionary force land in Rhode Island, and concerted allied planning for a decisive campaign could begin.

British control of Canada and the Great Lakes had exposed the whole American frontier to attack by Indians, many of whom understandably saw Britain as the lesser evil. Supported by posts at Niagara and Detroit, and often joined by British and Loyalist units, these attacks had devastated settlements in New York and Pennsylvania. While Virginia sent an expedition down the Ohio valley to protect its furthest settlements in modern Kentucky and to seize what it could of modern Indiana, Washington kept Fort Pitt garrisoned as an ineffectual deterrent to enemy raids. In 1779 he directed a large expedition into the lands of the Iroquois Six Nations with the mission of wreaking all possible havoc.

Burning Iroquois villages and laying waste their cultivated fields, the expedition failed to quiet the frontier, but the 1779 campaign destroyed the basis of Iroquois power, leaving it to the Shawnee and other western tribes to contest the post-war American invasion of the Ohio country.[38] The Virginians had failed to smash the Shawnee in a brief war in 1774, but the South Carolinians in 1776 and again in 1780 carried fire and sword to the Cherokee. The estimated 200,000 Indians living in eastern North America would be among the major losers of the American Revolution.[39]

---

[38] Anthony F. C. Wallace, *The Death and Rebirth of the Seneca* (New York, 1969), pp. 134–56.
[39] For a fuller account of the role of Indians in the war, see below, pp. 366–68.

By 1779 supporting the war had become a more critical American problem than fighting it. Congressional paper currency had depreciated to three for one in specie by 1777, but dropped to thirty for one in 1779. Loans negotiated by Franklin and other American emissaries from the French and the Dutch, together with direct subsidies from France, did no more than purchase military supplies in Europe. American resources, men and foodstuffs, were adequate to sustain a war of resistance indefinitely, but logistics were insuperably difficult. With British sea-power controlling the coastal waters, American supply trains were forced to use poor roads crossing the corrugated terrain of the interior, and in the end the military demand for wagons and draft animals simply outran the supply. The costs of transport, perhaps more than any other item, led the rush to national bank-ruptcy, which was conceded by Congress in early 1780.[40]

Congress had no power to tax, and begged the states to shore up Congressional currency by controlling prices and accepting continental paper in lieu of taxes. Reluctant to levy taxes early in the war, and inclined to support the military effort with their own paper issues, most states in 1777 began to tax their citizens more heavily than the colonies had ever done. As Congress lost the ability to pay its army and otherwise support the war, state governments assumed responsibility, more or less, for their own regiments. Administratively chaotic, the shift of effective power from Congress to the states at least kept the war going.[41]

The year 1780 was arguably the low point of the Revolution, worse than 1776. Congress declared bankruptcy. British forces in the South retook Georgia, cap-tured Charleston with a large American garrison, and in August destroyed the southern American field army. Only guerrilla resistance flickered in and around the newly occupied areas, as British officers recruited thousands of southern Loyalists into provincial regiments. Washington, still in the North, was reluctant and slow to detach parts of his army to meet the southern danger, although in October he sent Nathanael Greene, perhaps his ablest lieutenant, to retrieve the situation in the Carolinas. But only weeks before, Washington's best combat leader, Benedict Arnold, had defected to the British. By early 1781, with the unpaid American army wracked by mutinies, the French had laid a secret contingency plan in the event of a total American collapse.[42]

Congressional politics in 1780 were equally grim. With the waning of the power of Congress to make war, the political focus shifted to foreign relations and the strategy of making peace. Bound by the terms of its 1778 alliance to follow the

---

[40] John Shy, 'Logistical Crisis and the American Revolution: A Hypothesis', in John A. Lynn, ed., *Feeding Mars* (Boulder, Colo., 1993), pp. 161–79.

[41] Robert A. Becker, *Revolution, Reform and the Politics of American Taxation* (Baton Rouge, La., 1980).

[42] Charles Royster, *A Revolutionary People at War: The Continental Army and American Character, 1775–1783* (Chapel Hill, NC, 1979), pp. 230–327.

diplomatic lead of France, Congress became embroiled in an explosive mix of personality clashes, Francophobia, and war-induced paranoia. A few delegates suspected that Franklin, their most effective agent in Europe, was a British agent. Others, aroused by increasingly aggressive French involvement in the politics of Congress itself, believed that Versailles would sell out American independence. In 1781, with British warships and transports in Chesapeake Bay, the French minister responded to the American call for naval assistance by suggesting that Congress ratify the long-delayed Articles of Confederation that provided the formal charter for an American national government. Ratification changed little except that Virginia, under British military attack, had placated its neighbours by ceding to Congress its vast western land claims.

Military events later in 1781 resolved the crisis. While Washington insisted on seeking decisive battle in a combined assault by French and American forces on a strongly fortified New York, a French West Indian fleet with troop reinforcements headed for Chesapeake Bay rather than to New York, where Washington had hoped it would go.[43] Meanwhile the British army in the South had exhausted itself chasing Nathanael Greene and American irregulars through the Carolinas and into Virginia, where it took post at Yorktown, expecting as usual to be supported by the Royal Navy. In a remarkable concatenation of improvised strategy, a united French fleet won control of the Chesapeake Capes long enough for a combined Franco-American army, moving swiftly south from New York and Rhode Island, to trap and force the surrender of the British army at Yorktown in September 1781.

The news of Yorktown was a bombshell in British politics and a godsend for American morale. With France still the main threat, a new British government was ready to negotiate a peace with the Americans. The war was effectively over, although armed clashes with Indians and Loyalists would continue beyond the final peace treaty in 1783. Its finances shattered and government a total shambles, the United States simply struggled to survive during the last two years of belligerency, the military pressure mercifully eased.

Peace negotiations in Paris were protracted and tortuous, complicated by a formal cessation of British offensive operations against the Americans while a vigorous and successful war was being waged with France. Franklin, John Adams, and John Jay of New York were the American team, and may have given up more than necessary to secure formal recognition of American independence. Failure to secure legal access to British West Indian trade, and the right to navigate the Mississippi River to the Gulf of Mexico, would return to haunt post-war American politics. But the Shelburne ministry gave the United States far more territory—to

---

[43] John E. Ferling, *The First of Men: A Life of George Washington* (Knoxville, Tenn., 1988), pp. 292–97.

the Mississippi and the southern shore of the Great Lakes—than American soldiers had won on the battlefield, and Shelburne did nothing effective to protect the rights of the American Loyalists.

At the war's end in 1783 the United States confronted the wreckage of war. Governed by a confederation of nominally equal states whose own governments were unevenly responsive to the need for firm direction and the cries of popular distress, victorious Americans faced many of the same problems that a victorious Britain had tried to solve in 1763 and after. No more than Parliament had the American Congress succeeded in establishing a power to tax, but it had the enormous advantage of uncontested title—apart from the Indian inhabitants—to lands beyond the frontier edge of settlement.

Assessing the impact of war is never easy. The death of an estimated 25,000 American soldiers, and the emigration of as many as 100,000 Loyalists, were serious losses, but readily made good in a steadily rising demographic trend.[44] The claimed loss because of wartime disruption of perhaps one in ten of enslaved African-Americans was a major economic blow to southern planters, but a natural rate of increase among the slave population almost equal to that of whites ensured the vitality of American slavery well into the next century. The more direct economic effects of war, on money, property, debt, speculation, taxation, and trade, were fated to be entangled with a post-war economic depression in the complex story of how the United States achieved a stronger central government.

More obviously, the war gave the United States a charismatic national leader whose post-war performance would be crucial in bringing stability to the Revolutionary Republic. David Ramsay, a patriotic admirer of Washington and a contemporary historian, who had seen the murderous struggle of 1780–81 waged in South Carolina, also believed the war had 'not only required, but created talents', bringing together ordinary Americans who 'knew but little of one another, previous to the revolution . . . and the foundation was laid for the establishment of a nation'. But all wars, especially this one, Ramsay thought, injure 'the morals of the people engaged in it'. It could not have been 'carried on without violating private rights, and in its progress, it involved a necessity for breaking promises, and plighted public faith'. Nothing, Ramsay opined, could repair the moral damage done by the war 'till a new generation arises, unpractised in the iniquities of their fathers'.[45]

---

[44] Howard H. Peckham, *The Toll of Independence* (Chicago, 1974), p. 130.

[45] *The History of the American Revolution*, 2 vols. (Philadelphia, 1789), II, 316, 136. The last passage quoted occurs in his discussion of paper money, that 'deluge of legal iniquity'.

Select Bibliography

DAVID AMMERMAN, *In the Common Cause: American Response to the Coercive Acts of 1774* (Charlottesville, Va., 1974).

CHARLES M. ANDREWS, *The Colonial Background of the American Revolution: Four Essays in American Colonial History* (New Haven, 1924).

FRED ANDERSON, *A People's Army: Massachusetts Soldiers and Society in the Seven Years' War* (Chapel Hill, NC, 1984).

BERNARD BAILYN, *The Ideological Origins of the American Revolution* (Cambridge, Mass., 1967).

CARL L. BECKER, *The Declaration of Independence: A Study in the History of Political Ideas* (New York, 1922).

THEODORE DRAPER, *A Struggle for Power: The American Revolution* (New York, 1996).

JOHN E. FERLING, *The First of Men: A Life of George Washington* (Knoxville, Tenn., 1988).

LAWRENCE H. GIPSON, *The British Empire before the American Revolution*, 15 vols., revised edn. (New York, 1958–70).

DON HIGGINBOTHAM, *The War of American Independence: Military Attitudes, Policies and Practice, 1763–1789* (New York, 1971).

MERRILL JENSEN, *The Founding of a Nation: A History of the American Revolution, 1763–1776* (New York, 1968).

BENJAMIN W. LABAREE, *The Boston Tea Party* (New York, 1964).

DOUGLAS E. LEACH, *Arms for Empire: A Military History of the British Colonies in North America, 1607–1763* (New York, 1973).

PIERS MACKESY, *The War for America, 1775–1783* (London, 1964).

PAULINE MAIER, *America Scripture: Making the Declaration of Independence* (New York, 1997).

EDMUND S. and HELEN M. MORGAN, *The Stamp Act Crisis: Prologue to Revolution* (Chapel Hill, NC, 1953).

WILLIAM H. NELSON, *The American Tory* (Oxford, 1961).

CHARLES ROYSTER, *A Revolutionary People at War: The Continental Army and American Character, 1775–1783* (New York, 1979).

JOHN SHY, *A People Numerous and Armed: Reflections on the Military Struggle for American Independence*, revised edn. (Ann Arbor, 1990).

IAN K. STEELE, *Warpaths: Invasions of North America* (New York, 1994).

GORDON S. WOOD, *The Radicalism of the American Revolution* (New York, 1992).

15

Britain and the Revolutionary Crisis, 1763–1791

STEPHEN CONWAY

In 1763 the British Empire in North America had emerged from a triumphant war with spectacular new gains. The whole continent to the east of the Mississippi, from the Gulf of Mexico to Hudson Bay, was under British authority. Yet within twelve years hostilities had broken out between the mother country and thirteen of the old British colonies. These colonies declared themselves independent in 1776 and successfully resisted all attempts to force them into submission over seven years of war. When Britain finally accepted American independence in 1783, all that remained of its North American Empire was Quebec and Nova Scotia.

The loss of the thirteen colonies naturally led many contemporary Britons to attempt to distance themselves from this Imperial catastrophe, and to attribute it to the exceptional perversity and incompetence of those in power at the time. Nineteenth-century historians eagerly took up this theme, and George Grenville, Lord North, and George III have entered popular mythology on both sides of the Atlantic as the British political leaders whose wrong-headedness lost America.

Modern scholarship suggests otherwise. Perversity and incompetence there may well have been, but very few British politicians disagreed significantly with the ideas that lay behind the policies pursued. There was a general consensus on colonial issues between 1763 and the end of 1773, and only a small minority anticipated the consequences that would flow from the measures adopted. A sense of looming disaster—of the likelihood of a bloody civil war within the Empire—did not develop until 1774 or even 1775. British opinion was then plunged into agonized debate, but the government continued to enjoy much public support and was not deflected from launching what it supposed would be limited military operations. Even when full-scale war ensued and ended in failure, there was no fundamental reappraisal of the approach to be followed in what was left of British North America. The broad consensus of the 1760s and early 1770s to all intents and purposes re-emerged. In short, for most of the period under consideration shared assumptions and objectives underpinned the various policies pursued by different governments.

It was generally accepted that the American colonies were essential to Britain—economically, fiscally, and strategically. Transatlantic trade enriched the mother country, boosted government revenues, and helped to provide a ready reserve of trained mariners to serve in the Royal Navy in time of war. The seventeenth-century Navigation Acts, which regulated trade with the colonies, were believed to have secured these advantages for Britain, and they were therefore thought to be 'of the greatest consequence to this country';[1] indeed, they were seen as the vital safeguard of national prosperity and power: even after the final acknowledgement of the independence of the United States, most British politicians thought that the acts, suitably updated, should continue to control the trade and navigation of the remaining British colonies. The importance accorded to the Navigation Acts conditioned the British response to American resistance to Parliament's exercise of authority in other areas; before the War of Independence it was widely feared that *any* weakening of Parliament's position would encourage the colonists to challenge the validity of the Navigation Acts themselves. At the same time there was also considerable, if not always clearly focused, disquiet at what was seen as the growing insubordination of the Americans, together with an associated concern about the increasing difficulty of imposing control and direction from London. And throughout the period the great majority of British politicians believed that ways had to be found to make the colonists shoulder more of the financial burden of Empire.

All of these views had found expression within official circles, and even in Parliament, long before 1763,[2] but the Seven Years War created compelling reasons for British politicians to spend more time thinking about North America, and for such ideas to become common currency. Vast territories had been acquired; the Floridas from the Spanish, Quebec from the French, and the disputed inland wilderness between the Appalachian Mountains and the Mississippi. The defence and development of the Floridas and Quebec became a preoccupation of ministers in London. Quebec, in particular, presented problems. With its 70,000 or so disaffected and potentially mutinous French inhabitants, it could hardly be governed in the same manner as the older British colonies.

The old colonies themselves seemed also to require attention. The war had brought into sharp relief what to many British politicians appeared as undesirable features of the Imperial system. In violation of British commercial regulations, the

---

[1] Charles Yorke, the Attorney-General, 21 Feb. 1766, R. C. Simmons and P. D. G. Thomas, eds., *Proceedings and Debates of the British Parliaments Respecting North America, 1754–1783*, 6 vols. to date (Millward, NY, 1982–), II, p. 283.

[2] Robert W. Tucker and David C. Hendrickson, *The Fall of the First British Empire: Origins of the War of American Independence* (Baltimore, 1982), contend that there was an essential continuity in British policy. Daniel A. Baugh breathes new life into the generally accepted argument that there was a fundamental shift in 1763: 'Maritime Strength and Atlantic Commerce: The Uses of "a Grand Marine Empire"', in Lawrence Stone, ed., *An Imperial State at War: Britain from 1689 to 1815* (London, 1994), pp. 185–223.

Americans had shamelessly traded with the enemy, and some of the colonial legislatures had demonstrated a great reluctance to vote the necessary funds when asked by the Crown to raise local troops for the Imperial war effort. The patchy response of the colonial legislatures, together with the poor performance of those colonial soldiers who were put into the field, convinced the British government of the need to send large numbers of regular troops to the colonies, and persuaded many Britons that they, with very little help from the colonists, had won the war against the French in North America. It was almost axiomatic to most British politicians, therefore, that the colonists owed a great debt of gratitude to the mother country.

But perhaps the major underlying influence on British thinking on America in 1763, and for long after, was the state of the public revenues in Britain itself. The Seven Years War had been expensive, ruinously so in the view of many Britons. The National Debt had risen from £74.6 million at the start of the conflict to £132.6 million at its close. Much of the wartime tax burden had to be retained after the signing of the peace to cover the interest charges and meet the government's other commitments; indeed, a new cider tax was introduced, which provoked a popular outcry, particularly in the apple-growing western counties. Successive administrations were under intense pressure to control public expenditure and find new sources of revenue.

These considerations informed the policies for America adopted from 1763. The laxness that had characterized commercial regulation was to be replaced by a new spirit of thoroughness: existing trade laws were enforced, absentee customs officials were ordered to their posts, and the navy was instructed to act against smugglers. To prevent trouble with the Native Americans, which would inescapably involve the British government in further unwelcome expenditure, a royal proclamation in October 1763 forbade colonial settlement west of a line running along the Appalachians. The Americans were encouraged instead to move north to Quebec and sparsely populated Nova Scotia, or south to the even more sparsely populated Floridas; colonization of these areas by Anglo-Saxon Protestants would make them more defensible. For the foreseeable future, however, the new acquisitions would have to be garrisoned by British regulars, who would also police the frontier. Some 10,000 troops were to be allocated to North America and the Caribbean in the first year of peace, falling to around 7,500 thereafter. To help maintain this army without over-burdening the already hard-pressed British taxpayer, the Americans were to make a contribution by paying taxes levied by the British Parliament. In pursuit of this aim, Parliament passed in 1764 the Revenue or Sugar Act, partly to regulate Imperial trade and partly to raise an American revenue. The Stamp Act of 1765, which imposed a duty on legal documents, newspapers, cards, and dice, was solely and unambiguously intended to raise money in the colonies for the support of the army in America. Parliament's American Mutiny (or Quartering) Act of the same year, by requiring the colonists to supply various items to the troops, also obliged Americans to help meet the costs of the British garrison.

George Grenville, first minister from 1763 to 1765, is usually linked with these measures, not least because of his personal commitment to the Stamp Act.[3] But any temptation to think in terms of a 'Grenville programme' for the colonies should be avoided. The decision to base an army in North America and to make the colonists pay for its upkeep was taken by the King and Grenville's predecessor, the Earl of Bute. And Grenville's forthright views on Parliament's role as an Imperial legislature, complete with taxing powers, were widely shared. As the agent of the Connecticut Assembly reported from London in March 1765, there was hardly an MP willing to dispute 'ye right of Parliament to tax us'.[4] Nearly a year later, when the highly respected former minister William Pitt advanced the proposition that Parliament's sovereignty over the colonies did not extend to taxation, he won little support. After one of the great man's speeches an MP noted: 'I question if there had been a Division whether Mr Pitt would have had 20 voices with him.'[5] We should not be surprised at this near unanimity. Parliament had become an entrenched institution since the Glorious Revolution, meeting every year from 1689. As early as 1720 it had claimed the right to legislate for Ireland, even though Ireland had its own Parliament. By the 1760s nearly all parliamentarians were accustomed to see themselves as members of a legislature that could exercise its authority throughout the Empire, a perception supported by the work of the great legal theorist William Blackstone, the first volume of whose *Commentaries on the Laws of England* was published in 1765.

The argument that the colonists had no MPs at Westminster to defend their interests, put vigorously by the Americans themselves and more tentatively by a handful of MPs, was met with the theory of 'virtual representation'. Government writers maintained that the colonists were represented in the same way as were British non-electors, corporations like the East India Company, and urban centres such as Birmingham and Manchester which sent no members to Parliament: 'none are actually, all are virtually represented', in that there were many members

---

[3] Grenville suggested in 1764 that he would be open to other proposals, but when one was put to him he 'paid little Attention to it, being besotted with his Stamp Scheme, which he rather chose to carry through'. Leonard W. Labaree and others, eds., *The Papers of Benjamin Franklin*, 29 vols. to date (New Haven, 1959–), XIII, p. 449.

[4] 'Fitch Papers', Connecticut Historical Society, *Proceedings*, XVIII (1920), p. 334.

[5] Richard Neville Aldworth's Diary, 4 Feb. 1766, Berkshire Record Office, Aldworth-Neville Papers, D/EN 034/24.

who could speak for interests other than those of their immediate constituents.[6] The number of parliamentary acts specifically relating to towns like Birmingham seemed to prove the point; and we can see that MPs who were confident about their collective ability to cater for supposedly unrepresented interests in Britain had little doubt that they could also legislate for the colonists.[7]

Grenville had fallen from power by the time that news reached Britain of violent American resistance to the Stamp Act. The new ministry was headed by the Marquis of Rockingham, but strongly influenced by the Duke of Cumberland until his death at the end of October 1765. The administration was not committed to the Stamp Act, and Rockingham himself seems initially to have favoured amendment to satisfy the Americans and save the British economy from the consequences of colonial boycotts. It was not until December 1765, when reports of serious disturbances in New York arrived, that he came to the conclusion that amendment was inappropriate because the Act was unenforceable.[8] Even so, persuading all his Cabinet colleagues of the need for outright repeal took time because, as Rockingham remarked, 'the Variety of Opinions of what is right to be done, is no very easy matter to reconcile'.[9] Opposition to repeal was stronger still in Parliament, where Grenville remained a powerful barrier to concessions to the Americans. Many MPs worried about the threat to parliamentary authority—and ultimately to the Navigation Acts—if the Stamp Act were given up. But petitions from manufacturing and trading centres, encouraged by the ministry, and the examination of expert witnesses by the Commons, had an important impact on the waverers. The impression conveyed was that the Act threatened the economic well-being and therefore the social stability of Britain itself. The aged Duke of Newcastle, an enthusiast for repeal, conjured up the image of unemployment bringing on 'Riots, Mobbs, & Insurrections'.[10] Rockingham sugared the pill with a Declaratory Act, based on the Irish Declaratory Act of 1720, which proclaimed Parliament's right to legislate for the colonies 'in all cases whatsoever'.

It would be a mistake to assume that Rockingham's view of Empire was fundamentally different from Grenville's. Rockingham and his supporters had not objected to the introduction of the Stamp Act and they repealed it for reasons of expediency, not because they accepted the constitutional case put forward by the Americans. Whereas Grenville adopted the legalistic approach that

---

[6] Thomas Whately, *The Regulations Lately Made Concerning the Colonies and the Taxes Imposed on them Considered* (London, 1765), pp. 108–09.

[7] See Paul Langford, 'Property and "Virtual Representation" in Eighteenth-Century England', *Historical Journal*, XXXI (1988), pp. 83–115.

[8] John L. Bullion, 'British Ministers and American Resistance to the Stamp Act, October–December 1765', *William and Mary Quarterly*, Third Series, XLIX (1992), pp. 102–05.

[9] Rockingham to Newcastle, 2 Jan. 1766, B[ritish] L[ibrary] Add. MSS 32973, f. 11.

[10] Newcastle to the Archbishop of Canterbury, 2 Feb. 1766 (copy), ibid., f. 343.

Parliament's right to tax the colonies had to be boldly asserted to avoid being lost, Rockingham's spokesmen in the Commons, General Conway and Edmund Burke, said that the right, while 'clear beyond a contradiction',[11] was best not exercised if the consequence was the disruption of a beneficial relationship with the colonies. But the Rockinghams, or at least some of them, were willing to go farther, and exercise the right, if with more discretion than Grenville. A month after the repeal of the Stamp Act, the administration passed its own Plantation Duties Act. This reduced to one penny the duty chargeable on foreign molasses entering the North American colonies for rum production. The Act could, therefore, be said to have fulfilled the wishes of those Americans who had been pressing for such a reduction,[12] and could accordingly be portrayed as an example of the willingness of the Rockinghams to listen to colonial opinion. Grenville, now in opposition, certainly saw the Plantation Duties Act as another concession to the Americans, and attacked the ministry for 'taking off tax after tax'.[13] But pleasing the Americans was not the only, or even the primary, objective of the framers of the legislation. The new penny duty was extended to British West Indian molasses. By treating British and foreign molasses in the same way, the administration abandoned any pretence that it was legislating to regulate trade. The 1766 Act, as William Dowdeswell, the Chancellor of the Exchequer, later conceded, was 'for revenue not for commerce'.[14] And, as one of the clauses made clear, the money was to be used to support the army in America, the expense of which was as much a concern to the Rockinghams as it had been to Grenville.[15]

Rockingham and most of his colleagues left office in July 1766, to be replaced by a ministry led by Pitt, who became the Earl of Chatham. Pitt's speeches during the debates over repeal of the Stamp Act had established his reputation as a friend of America; indeed, he was seen (somewhat unfairly, in view of Rockingham's painstaking work) as the architect of repeal. Conway, a minister under Rockingham with a proven record of sympathy for the colonists, remained in post. The Earl of Shelburne, the Secretary of State with responsibility for America, seemed similarly well disposed. 'The weight ... of this administration', an American agent in London concluded in November, 'will be friendly to the Colonies.'[16]

---

[11] *Proceedings and Debates*, II. p. 143.

[12] See 'Jasper Maudit ... 1762–1765', Massachusetts Historical Society, *Collections*, LXXIV (1918), p. 135.

[13] *Proceedings and Debates*, II. pp. 377–78.

[14] Paul Langford, 'The Rockingham Whigs and America, 1767–1773', in Anne Whiteman, J. S. Bromley, and P. G. M. Dickson, eds., *Statesmen, Scholars and Merchants: Essays in Eighteenth-Century History Presented to Dame Lucy Sutherland* (Oxford, 1973), p. 147.

[15] See, for instance, Conway's comments of 2 May 1766, Clarence E. Carter, ed., *The Correspondence of General Thomas Gage*, 2 vols. (New Haven, 1931–33), II. p. 37.

[16] 'The Pitkin Papers', Connecticut Historical Society, *Collections*, XIX (1929), p. 50.

The Americans were to be disappointed. Chatham soon receded into the background: illness and depression obliged him to hand over leadership to the Duke of Grafton. But it was not Chatham's absence that caused the administration to adopt policies that offended the colonists. Chatham, so far as we can tell, approved the measures of his colleagues. He was not in favour of internal taxation of the colonies by Parliament, on the ground that the colonists were not truly represented in Parliament; hence his criticism of the Stamp Act. But he was a staunch defender of Parliament's legislative authority over America, particularly as regards trade. This aspect of his thinking was less clear to the Americans in 1766 than was his opposition to the Stamp Act; their faith in him as a friend to the colonies was largely misplaced. And his ministers, whatever their initial inclinations, were confronted with a range of colonial problems which could not be ignored. The Massachusetts Assembly had provocatively taken upon itself to indemnify Boston's Stamp Act rioters; the New York Assembly had refused to comply with the billeting clauses of the American Mutiny Act; American defence costs were escalating at an alarming rate.

On 5 August 1766 the Cabinet, with Chatham present, agreed that it was 'the indispensible duty of his Majesty's subjects in America to obey the acts of the legislature of G. Britain'.[17] The Privy Council, in line with well-established practice, disallowed the Massachusetts act of indemnity. Shelburne had hoped that the New York difficulty required no more that 'a little good humour & Firmness to finish'.[18] It soon became clear, however, that the New York Assembly was obdurate. After considering a number of options, including the Draconian suggestion that it be made '*High Treason* to refuse to *obey* or *execute*' any laws of Parliament,[19] he finally settled on a bill to suspend the Assembly until it fulfilled its obligations. Shelburne also explored new sources of revenue in America to relieve the British taxpayer. He favoured using quitrents and payments for future land grants in the colonies, though in March 1767 he saw these as merely supplementary to 'requisitions from the different provinces to be granted annually by their Assemblies according to their respective abilities',[20] a solution that might well have been acceptable to the Americans.

Shelburne's plans for an American fund avoided a return to parliamentary taxation. Charles Townshend, the Chancellor of the Exchequer, was less inhibited. In January 1767 he announced in the Commons that he intended to raise additional revenue in America. It transpired that duties were to be imposed on glass,

[17] PRO 30/8/97, f. 79.

[18] Shelburne to Chatham, [3 Aug. 1766?], PRO 30/8/56, pt. i, f. 61.

[19] Shelburne to Chatham, [8 March 1767?], ibid., f. 89.

[20] 'Reasons for not Diminishing American Expence this Year', 30 March 1767, William L. Clements Library, Shelburne Papers.

lead, paper, paint, and tea imported into the colonies from Britain. Townshend argued that the Americans had rejected internal taxation by Parliament but were prepared to accept external taxation, taxation, that is, of their external trade. He denied the constitutional validity of the distinction, but by using it he was able to claim that he had devised a system of taxation that would satisfy the colonists. To make the new duties more effective an American Board of Customs Commissioners was established at Boston.

Townshend did not intend his duties to help to meet the costs of defending America. They were, rather, to 'lay a foundation for such taxation as might in time save this country of a considerable part of the burthen for the colonies'.[21] His experience as a member of the Board of Trade suggested that the fundamental problem in America was the dependence of royal officials in many of the colonies on salaries paid annually by the local Assemblies. This reliance on the Assemblies naturally made executive and judicial officers responsive to popular pressure and reluctant to offend local interests by rigorously applying instructions from London. The Stamp Act crisis reinforced Townshend's belief that executive authority in America had to be strengthened—not only to make the colonies more amenable to British direction and management, but also to raise any significant revenue in the future. Grenville's mistake, in this view, was to try to tax America without first preparing the ground. Townshend's aim, accordingly, was 'independent Salaries for the civil officers in North America'.[22]

Grafton was later to claim that Townshend acted upon his own initiative, and without proper consultation with this Cabinet colleagues.[23] This may well have been the case in January, but by the time the scheme was formally introduced in May 1767 there had been plenty of opportunity for ministers to raise objections. In fact, even in Parliament Townshend's duties provoked little adverse comment; the Rockingham opposition did not vote against them and it was left to Grenville to offer criticism of the mode of taxation, though not, of course, of the principle. The rest of the ministry's American measures also passed with little difficulty. New York's defiance of parliamentary authority angered the Rockinghams as much as anyone; Charles Yorke and Sir George Savile called for 'strong measures' and Dowdeswell, while disapproving of the suspension of the Assembly, favoured local magistrates enforcing the Mutiny Act and billeting troops in private homes if necessary.[24] The Rockinghams' stance was perhaps partly conditioned by their desire to form a coalition with Grenville and his supporters (at this time even the

---

[21] *Proceedings and Debates*, II. p. 457.

[22] Townshend to Grafton, [25 May 1767], West Suffolk Record Office, Grafton Papers, Ac 423/445.

[23] Sir William Anson, ed., *Autobiography and Political Correspondence of Augustus Henry, Third Duke of Grafton* (London, 1898), pp. 126–27.

[24] *Proceedings and Debates*, II, pp. 467, 471.

Duke of Newcastle was trying to play down the differences between the two parties), but there was also a widely held feeling that the Americans were ungrateful for the repeal of the Stamp Act and needed chastisement. 'The Colonys are growing worse and worse', wrote an independent MP in February 1767, and their conduct 'has soured the minds of people here in general.'[25]

Townshend died in September 1767, and it was left to other ministers to respond to the fresh American crisis that his duties (and the administration's other colonial measures) had provoked. At the end of 1767 the followers of the Duke of Bedford, known for their hard-line attitude towards the colonies, joined the ministry. The departure of Chatham and Shelburne in October 1768 added to the impression that the government was taking on a more authoritarian complexion, as did the Earl of Hillsborough's appointment to the new post of Secretary of State for the Colonies at the beginning of the year. Hillsborough had already served twice as President of the Board of Trade, and he came into office convinced that the colonies required firm handling. When the Massachusetts Assembly circulated other colonial legislatures to co-ordinate resistance to the Townshend Duties, Hillsborough sent out his own counter-circular (21 April 1768) instructing Governors to prevent their Assemblies from replying to Massachusetts. In June he ordered troops and warships to Boston to aid the hard-pressed customs officers.

Hillsborough, like Townshend, was convinced that colonial government had to be reformed if the British were ever to exert effective control. Shortly after taking office he alarmed Connecticut's agent by seeming to suggest that the colony's charter allowed it too much independence.[26] But his chief target was Massachusetts, which ministers increasingly regarded as the nub of colonial disaffection. The charter given to Massachusetts in 1691 had made it something of an anomaly among the royal colonies. As a concession to its old form of government, the 1691 charter had given Massachusetts an elected Council—in all of the other royal colonies the Council was appointed. Governor Bernard's reports revealed that the Council, chosen by the Assembly, was too much influenced by popular opinion and unlikely to support any exercise of executive authority. Hillsborough in 1769 pressed for a revision of the charter to strengthen executive power; most importantly, he wanted the Council to be appointed. At this stage the King, mindful, no doubt, of the unfortunate seventeenth-century Stuart precedents, advised caution: 'altering Charters is at all times an odious measure'.[27] The plan was shelved, but not forgotten.

[25] Historical Manuscripts Commission, *Stopford Sackville MSS*, 2 vols. (London, 1904–10), I, p. 119.
[26] 'The Trumbull Papers', Massachusetts Historical Society, *Collections*, Fifth Series, IX (1885), pp. 253–64.
[27] Sir John Fortescue, ed., *The Correspondence of King George the Third*, 6 vols. (London, 1927–28), II, p. 84.

If Hillsborough shared Townshend's views about the desirability of restructuring colonial government, neither he nor his colleagues were inclined to defend Townshend's revenue-raising scheme. Lord North, the Chancellor of the Exchequer, saw little virtue in most of the duties, and on 1 May 1769 the Cabinet decided to abolish all of them but that on tea. American protests had not converted the ministry. Indeed, long before the Cabinet reached its decision Hillsborough made it clear that colonial denials of Parliament's right to tax were the most significant obstacle to repeal.[28] Nor did American non-importation agreements play a decisive role: British merchants and manufacturers were much less vocal in 1768–70 than they had been in 1765–66, not least because the British economy was more buoyant than at the time of the Stamp Act crisis. Government spokesmen argued that the commercial illogicality of Townshend's scheme was the decisive factor. The duties, except that on tea, penalized British manufacturers by increasing the cost of their products to colonial purchasers. In March 1770 North, who had succeeded Grafton as premier two months earlier, told the Commons that to tax British exports in this way 'was to the greatest degree absurd'.[29] But, as usual, revenue considerations were important. The duties dropped were yielding little or no profit to government; it was surely no coincidence that the only productive duty—the one on tea—was retained.

The formation of North's ministry could be seen as the beginning of the end of the broad consensus on American affairs. George Grenville's death in November 1770 allowed his followers to join North, and their move completed a process of realignment inaugurated with the entry of the Bedfordites into office in 1767. Under North, nearly all those politicians who had supported firm colonial measures were gathered together, while the Opposition groups under Rockingham and Chatham contained those who had displayed a more conciliatory disposition. But this may well be to anticipate the polarization over American policy that was obvious in 1774–75. The early years of North's ministry were not so clear cut. Opposition politicians showed no particular interest in colonial affairs, and certainly did nothing to justify describing them as 'friends of America'. North, for his part, behaved in a manner which makes it difficult to categorize him as a hard-liner. When, in 1772, Rhode Islanders burned the naval cutter the *Gaspée*, which was acting to enforce the Navigation Laws, North might have reacted violently to this affront to British authority. Instead, he sought to defuse a potentially explosive situation by establishing a commission of enquiry, one of the members of which was the elected Governor of Rhode Island. In the event it proved impossible to identify the culprits, and the matter was quietly dropped.

---

[28] 'The Trumbull Papers', p. 296.
[29] *Proceedings and Debates*, III, p. 228.

North, indeed, had much in common with some of his Rockingham and Chathamite predecessors in that he sought to secure an American revenue without provoking the colonists. He used the remaining Townshend tea duty to pay civil officers in some of the colonies from 1772, and in the following year the government decided to revive Shelburne's quitrent and land-sale scheme, but to apply it to the same end.[30] The more well known Tea Act also had an important revenue-raising aspect. True, the act was a response to the financial crisis threatening the East India Company. To help the Company dispose of its large stocks of unsold tea, the ministry proposed to reduce duties on tea coming into Britain that was re-exported to America, and to establish a system of direct sales through nominated agents to reduce the handling costs charged by colonial merchants. But when an Opposition MP suggested that the Company would be as well served by the removal of the remaining Townshend duty on tea, North revealed that an American revenue was definitely in his mind. There were 'political reasons' for keeping the Townshend duty, he told the Commons.[31] North clearly believed that the Tea Act would generate sufficient revenue to implement more rapidly Townshend's scheme for the payment of civil salaries in the colonies.

Hence the government's firm response to the Boston Tea Party, which was seen as the most flagrant instance of colonial resistance to the Act. If the Americans stopped buying East India Company tea, the strategy pursued by successive British governments since 1767 would have to be abandoned. With the stakes so high, North felt that he had no choice but to punish Massachusetts. But the punitive measures passed in 1774—the Coercive Acts—finally destroyed the parliamentary consensus on America. While the Boston Port Act, which closed Boston to overseas trade until it compensated the East India Company for its lost tea, was generally accepted as an appropriate response to the destruction of private property, the other Coercive Acts met with much criticism from the parliamentary Opposition. The Massachusetts Government Act was seen as a violation of charter rights because it radically changed the system of government granted under the 1691 charter. Hillsborough's scheme of 1769 finally found expression in the provisions strengthening the hand of the Governor and reducing the influence of the 'democratic' part of the constitution, notably in the requirement that the Council henceforth be appointed. The Quebec Act, passed in the same session, added to the impression that the government was set on an authoritarian track. In reality the Quebec Act was the product of long-running enquiries into the best form of

[30] D. H. Murdoch, 'Land Policy in the Eighteenth-Century British Empire: The Sale of Crown Lands in the Ceded Islands, 1763–1783', *Historical Journal*, XXVII (1984), pp. 573–74. For a different interpretation, which emphasizes the desire to slow down emigration from Britain, see Bernard Bailyn, *Voyagers to the West: A Passage in the Peopling of America on the Eve of the Revolution* (New York, 1986), pp. 55–56.
[31] *Proceedings and Debates*, III, p. 492.

government for a non-British and non-Protestant people; but, in the context of the Coercive Acts its clauses, particularly those giving the Catholic church a special status and continuing the system of government without an elected Assembly, were taken as clear signs of despotic intent. One Opposition MP drew parallels with the arbitrary principles that lay behind Jacobitism, and said that the Quebec Bill's passage through Parliament on 10 June (the birthday of the Stuart pretender to the throne) was wholly apposite.[32] Outside Parliament, radicals were even more outspoken. Richard Price, a Dissenting minister, wrote that: 'By the government our ministers *endeavour* to establish in *New*-England, and that which they *have* established in . . . Canada, we see what sort of Government they wish for in this country.'[33]

The uniting of the colonies against the Coercive Acts moved the crisis into a new and dangerous phase. Yet efforts were still made at Westminster to avoid a descent into bloodshed. In the House of Lords Chatham suggested that a permanent all-American legislature, something very like the Continental Congress that had emerged to co-ordinate opposition to the British, should exercise the taxing power claimed by Parliament, while Parliament continued to exercise its sovereignty in other areas. Burke, speaking for the Rockingham group in the Commons, called for a return to the *status quo* of 1763: the repeal of legislation offensive to the Americans and, to pay for Imperial defence, a return to the requisition system that had worked so fitfully in the Seven Years War. Neither proposal had much chance of success in the highly charged political atmosphere of early 1775. Indeed, even North's own conciliation plan almost ran aground when his back-bench supporters expressed disquiet at the apparent softening of his line towards the Americans.[34] In fact North's scheme, which offered to suspend parliamentary taxation for so long as the colonial Assemblies raised the required sums for Imperial defence and administration, was unacceptable to the Americans and was probably motivated primarily by a wish to separate the moderate colonies from seemingly irredeemable New England.

North certainly believed that Massachusetts was already in a state of rebellion. The Commander-in-Chief in America, General Gage, who had been appointed Governor of the colony, was sent reinforcements with the aim of restoring legitimate authority. By the beginning of 1775 the vast majority of the British army in North America was concentrated in Boston. In January Lord Dartmouth, Hillsborough's successor as Secretary of State for the Colonies, ordered Gage to put down the rebellion by seizing its leaders. When Gage received these instruc-

---

[32] Ibid., V, p. 169.

[33] D. O. Thomas and Bernard Peach, eds., *The Correspondence of Richard Price*, 3 vols. (Durham, NC, 1983; Cardiff, 1994), I, p. 189. For the Quebec Act see below, pp. 378–80.

[34] *Proceedings and Debates*, V, pp. 446–47.

tions he started to prepare the expedition that was to lead, on 19 April, to the first armed confrontations at Lexington and Concord.

North and his colleagues had long been of the view that military action might be necessary to subdue Massachusetts, but they seriously underestimated the extent of American disaffection. In January North told Dartmouth that Gage's demand for 20,000 troops was unreasonable; it would 'require us to put our army upon a war establishment', he wrote.[35] Not for some months did it dawn on British ministers that they *were* engaged in a war, and not a police operation. While many of them were less than enthusiastic about such an escalation, no one in government circles seems seriously to have doubted that Britain should fight, if necessary, to keep America within the Empire. The thirteen colonies were useful sources of raw materials and re-exports, and in 1772–73 accounted for about one-fifth of all British exports. British prosperity and power, as we have seen, were generally regarded as contingent on their remaining within the commercial and maritime system created by the Navigation Acts. And if the mainland colonies were lost, it was assumed that the West Indies, believed to be at least as valuable, would probably go too, because the sugar islands were so dependent on provisions from North America. There was also a more abstract (or at any rate less obviously materialist) determination to restore legitimate authority, a conviction that rebellion was inherently sinful and had to be crushed. If the Americans were seen to succeed, other potentially mutinous subjects might follow suit. Ireland was known to be discontented, and at least one minister even feared a rebellion in Britain itself.[36]

The government's decision to use force in America was supported by significant sections of public opinion—probably by the majority of the political nation. Scotland was reported to be solidly in favour of coercion, and the officially published *London Gazette* carried page upon page of loyal addresses from all over the kingdom. Anglican clergymen who condemned the 'unnatural Proceeding'[37] in the colonies, and looked forward to the victory of British arms[38] seem to have reflected a widely held view. Even so, a significant number of Britons opposed the war. A few, like the eccentric Anglican Dean of Gloucester, Josiah Tucker, believed that the country would be better off without her colonies. But most critics of the conflict condemned it for very different reasons. The Rockinghamite

---

[35] Staffordshire Record Office, Dartmouth MSS, D(W) 1778/II/1073.

[36] Shute Barrington, *The Political Life of William Wildman, Viscount Barrington* (London, 1814), pp. 163–64.

[37] Memoranda of the vicar, 1 Jan. 1777, Staffordshire Record Office, Hanbury Parish Register, D 1528/1/4.

[38] See, for example, Revd John Butler to the Earl of Onslow, 17, 24 Dec. 1775, Guildford Muniment Room, Surrey Record Office, Onslow MSS, 173/2/1/114–15.

parliamentary Opposition, although it had not significantly differed from the main lines of government policy before 1774, was convinced that the war was wrong because it would inevitably increase the patronage power of the government and could therefore endanger the British constitution; because it would destroy the prosperity of the colonies and would therefore undermine Britain's own economic strength; and because they believed that the Americans could not be compelled to remain within a system that ultimately depended upon their consent. While Rockingham himself was circumspect in his language, accusing the government of pursuing 'Vindictive & Passionate Measures' without regard to the consequences,[39] some of his less cautious colleagues came very close to hoping for the defeat of the British army. The Declaration of Independence placed the Rockinghams in an awkward position: they wished to preserve the Empire, not to applaud its collapse. They saw no point, however, in compelling the Americans to renounce independence and return to their allegiance, and gradually they embraced the policy of recognizing the reality of separation. Even in the armed forces there were some dissident voices, and in 1775 the loyal addresses had to compete with counter-petitions regretting the war and warning of the dangers it posed to British trade.[40] 'The generous & impartial', a Worcestershire Dissenter wrote, 'are I think in favour of the Americans in this country.'[41] Dissenters were in fact prominent amongst the pro-American party, both in Britain and Ireland, and in some areas they seem to have succeeded in impeding the army's efforts to recruit soldiers.[42]

For North's government, however, a more immediate problem was how to recover from an unpromising start to the war (see Map 14.1). After the skirmishes at Lexington and Concord, Gage's army was besieged in Boston. An attempt to clear the Americans from high ground dominating the town (the Battle of Bunker Hill, 17 June 1775) had been successful, but at an enormous cost. The garrison was now in no condition to mount further offensive operations. Over the next few months most of the British posts in upper New York and Canada fell to the rebels. How could the British reverse their fortunes and reclaim the colonies? Even before the first shots were fired, Lord Barrington, the Secretary at War, had argued for a purely naval subjugation of the colonies. Other leading military and political

---

[39] Rockingham to Sir John Griffin Griffin, 22 Oct. 1775, Essex Record Office, Braybrooke MSS, D/DBy C9/17.

[40] See James E. Bradley, *Religion, Revolution and English Radicalism: Nonconformity in Eighteenth-century Politics and Society* (Cambridge, 1990), chaps. 9 and 10.

[41] Samuel Kenrick to James Wodrow, 19 July 1775, Dr Williams's Library, Wodrow–Kenrick Correspondence, MSS, 24.157 (51).

[42] See G. R. Barnes and J. H. Owen, eds., *The Private Papers of John, Earl of Sandwich*, 4 vols. (London, 1932–38), I, p. 340.

figures, who doubted the army's ability to put down the revolt, also suggested that a naval blockade was the best approach.[43]

Yet the government committed itself to a major land war. This was probably partly due to an understandable desire to end the conflict quickly: naval strangulation of American trade would take time, and might therefore provide an opening for the French, who were believed to be waiting for an opportunity to avenge their humiliating defeat in the Seven Years War. Full-scale naval mobilization, moreover, might alarm the French, causing them to enter the war to protect their apparently endangered possessions in the West Indies.[44] Just as importantly, there were the American Loyalists to consider.

Royal Governors, especially in the southern colonies, argued that their provinces contained many 'friends to government' who, with the backing of British regulars, could be mobilized to restore order. The Governor of South Carolina, for example, told Dartmouth in August 1775 of 'several thousand faithful subjects in the back country who are ready to take up arms in defence of the constitution, had they the least support';[45] while the Governor of North Carolina was similarly confident, referring to the need for no more than 'a small force' of British troops to 'lay open the communication with a large body of well affected People who inhabit the interior parts of this Colony'.[46] British ministers, predisposed to view the turmoil in America as the work of a conspiratorial minority, seem to have taken such reports very seriously. Lord George Germain, who replaced the lukewarm Dartmouth at the end of 1775, was convinced that most colonists were loyal at heart, and only required a British military presence to encourage them to rise up and throw off the 'tyranny' of Congress. Indeed, Germain's faith in the potential of the Loyalists, though sorely tested by the disappointments of the years that followed, remained with him to the end of the war.[47]

In 1776 the British devoted considerable manpower resources to trying to crush the rebellion. The main area of operations was New York, where significant local support was expected.[48] General Howe, Gage's successor as Commander-in-Chief, swept aside the American army at the Battle of Long Island (27 August) and British forces occupied New York City, Newport, Rhode Island, and much of New Jersey.

---

[43] See, for example, Lt.-Gen. Edward Harvey to Lt.-Gen. John Irwin, 30 June 1775, W[ar] O[ffice] 3/5, p. 37.

[44] See Daniel A. Baugh, 'The Politics of British Naval Failure, 1775–1777', *American Neptune*, LI (1992), pp. 221–46.

[45] K. G. Davies, ed., *Documents of the American Revolution*, 21 vols. (Shannon, 1972–81), XI, p. 97.

[46] Josiah Martin to Samuel Martin, 9 Sept. 1775, BL Add. MSS, 41361, f. 289.

[47] See, for instance, his letters of 4 April and 2 Aug. 1781 to Clinton, *Documents of the American Revolution*, XX, pp. 99, 206.

[48] See, for instance, Clinton's comments on New York, 7 Aug. 1775, William L. Clements Library, Clinton Papers.

But the rebels could not be compelled to submit; indeed, they successfully counter-attacked at the end of the year, taking the shine off Howe's triumphs by defeating detachments of his army at Trenton and Princeton. In 1777 Howe again bettered the Americans in the field (at Brandywine Creek, 11 September); he even took Philadelphia, the capital of the new United States. But Howe was bitterly disappointed at the limited Loyalist support that was forthcoming,[49] and by campaigning in Pennsylvania he left exposed a British force under General Burgoyne advancing south from Canada into the upper Hudson Valley. On 17 October Burgoyne's army, worn down and outnumbered, was obliged to surrender at Saratoga. The capitulation of a British field army naturally boosted American morale, and more importantly, encouraged the French, who had already been helping the rebels covertly, to accelerate their plans to enter the war. The conflict, as George III and his ministers fully appreciated, was about to take on a different character. A struggle with France (and probably with her ally Spain) was seen as inevitable even before the Franco-American alliance was concluded in February 1778.

In London consideration was even given to the complete withdrawal of British forces from the rebel colonies to concentrate resources for the expected clash with France. Such a course would probably have won the approval of the Rockinghamite Opposition, but it was rejected by ministers as too drastic a response. However, from March 1778 British operations in North America were subordinated to the requirements of the wider conflict. Sir Henry Clinton, the new Commander-in-Chief, was ordered to abandon Philadelphia and to despatch 5,000 of his best troops for 'an immediate attack upon the French possessions in the West Indies'.[50] A further 3,000 soldiers were to be sent to reinforce the Floridas, thought to be under threat from the Spanish. The only offensive operations recommended by Germain were raids on the American coast and another expedition to mobilize the Loyalist support still believed to exist in the southern colonies. In the hope that a settlement with the Americans might be concluded before the Bourbon war started in earnest, North's government even offered the colonists almost all they had demanded in 1775 (though on the understanding that the Americans recognize Parliament's right to regulate trade). The Coercive Acts were repealed and Parliament renounced its right to tax America. A commission headed by the Earl of Carlisle sailed across the Atlantic to negotiate on the basis of these concessions.

The refusal of Congress to treat with Carlisle, and the refusal of the King and his government to acknowledge American independence, meant that the British were

---

[49] *Documents of the American Revolution*, XV, p. 29.
[50] Ibid., p. 73.

obliged to continue the war in the thirteen colonies. They did so in the hope that they might reclaim at least some of the rebel provinces—the southern ones were seen as particularly valuable and complementary to the British possessions in the Caribbean: Germain described Georgia, in particular, 'as an object of much importance in the present state of things, as from thence our islands in the West Indies might draw supplies of provisions and lumber, for the want of which they are now greatly distressed'[51]—but it was recognized that America could no longer be the first call on military and naval resources. For the British, the war in America diminished in importance once the Caribbean, Europe, India, and Africa became arenas of conflict. In February 1778 some 65 per cent of British land forces were deployed in North America; in September 1780 only 29 per cent. As soon as the government learned of the signing of the Franco-American alliance, the Admiralty ordered twenty of the ninety-two British ships in American waters to return home, and another thirteen to go to the West Indies. Although at various times in the next five years the North American squadron was temporarily reinforced, both the Caribbean and home defence took precedence.

The arrival of the French navy off New York in July 1778 underlined the way in which the character of the war had changed. Admiral d'Estaing's fleet failed to deliver the decisive blow that the French government desired, but later the same month he menaced the exposed garrison at Newport. Whereas General Howe had been able to conduct his operations confident in the knowledge that he was supported by a powerful fleet, poor Clinton, by contrast, was constantly worried by the threat posed to his army by the French navy. At the end of 1778, however, he decided to spare 3,000 troops for an attack on Georgia in belated—and distinctly limited—response to Germain's advice to turn his attention to the south. The Georgia expedition was successful; so much so that an experiment was made in restoring civil government, though the argument that this indulgence would 'deprive the rebellious Leaders of their favorite Topic, that G. Britain means only Blood, Conquest & Slavery',[52] failed to convince Clinton, who, fearful of the disruption of military operations, remained implacably opposed to the restoration of civil authority elsewhere. Even in Georgia, the situation turned out to be not as secure as it had appeared. At the end of the summer of 1779 d'Estaing's fleet, moving up from the West Indies, helped the Americans to besiege the British at Savannah. The garrison held out, repelling a Franco-American assault; but Clinton, ever concerned about the French navy, decided to pull back his force at Newport to the main base at New York. This step did little for British morale,

---

[51] Ibid., p. 178.

[52] 'General thoughts on America', n.d., Bedfordshire Record Office, Robinson Papers, Lucas Collection, L 29/216.

but at least it had the virtue of allowing Clinton to assemble a more formidable field army. At the end of 1779, despairing of bringing Washington to a decisive action in the north, Clinton finally decided to commit significant resources to the southern strategy.

At first, all went well. Charleston was captured in May 1780 and South Carolina appeared to be pacified. Clinton returned to New York with part of the army, leaving General Cornwallis in charge. But although Cornwallis was victorious at Camden in August, the backcountry would not be subdued. A vicious civil war between local partisan groups, in which the rebels were gaining the upper hand, threatened to destroy much of the province. Hoping to escape the growing anarchy of South Carolina, and in search of more plentiful and more resolute 'friends to government', Cornwallis decided to move on into neighbouring North Carolina. It had always been the hope of British planners that there would be an advance northwards from South Carolina—but after that colony had been restored to royal control, not before. In 1781 Cornwallis found that although he could beat the rebel army in the field (at Guilford Court House in March), North Carolinians were generally unresponsive to his requests for help. As he pressed on to Virginia to join a force already sent to the Chesapeake by Clinton to disrupt the local economy and to establish a base for the Royal Navy, Cornwallis left behind him a far from pacified south. Indeed, with Cornwallis operating in Virginia by the summer of 1781, the Americans were gradually able to capture nearly every British post in South Carolina. By September the British were confined to Charleston and its immediate environs.

Cornwallis, meantime, had dug in at Yorktown, Virginia, the site he had chosen for a naval base. On the move, destroying military stores, tobacco stocks, and other local property, he was a formidable foe: very few members of the Virginia militia were initially disposed to obstruct him. But stationary, in an entrenched post, Cornwallis presented a tempting target. The French navy, which had already threatened to trap isolated detachments of the British army at Newport and Savannah, was given the chance finally to realize its potential. After an inconclusive action off Chesapeake Bay, the British fleet retreated to New York to refit. The French now enjoyed local naval superiority. Cornwallis was closely besieged by a Franco-American army, and compelled to surrender almost four years to the day after Burgoyne's capitulation at Saratoga.

News of Yorktown reached London on 25 November 1781. 'A general dispondency was the first effect of Lord Cornwallis's surrender', wrote Lord Loughborough, the Lord Chief Justice. 'All the dissatisfied friends of govt.... blame the system of the war... & declare against its continuance.'[53] As an Opposition MP

---

[53] Loughborough to Eden, 13 Dec. 1781, BL Add. MSS, 34418, f. 213.

more pithily put it: 'every Body seems really sick of carrying on ye American War.'[54] North's majority dropped to about twenty. Germain was offered up as a sacrifice, but the Commons still voted on 27 February 1782 to suspend the war in America. North resigned the next month.

The King very reluctantly accepted a new administration headed by Rockingham which was committed to ending the conflict with the Americans. But within the ministry there was no agreement on the way to proceed. Charles James Fox, occupant of the new post of Foreign Secretary, wanted to recognize American independence to enable resources to be concentrated on the struggle with the Bourbons. Shelburne, however, who was made Secretary of State for Home and Colonial Affairs, claimed that negotiations with the Americans came under his jurisdiction, and he was against formal recognition prior to the settlement of a comprehensive peace. The contest between the two ministers was resolved only with Rockingham's death in July 1782. Shelburne was appointed first minister by the King, and Fox resigned.

Benjamin Franklin, one of the American negotiators, encouraged Shelburne to believe that generosity to the United States would be in Britain's interest, as an Anglo-American agreement would make the French and Spanish more inclined to come to terms. Shelburne was not prepared to go so far as to respond to Franklin's suggestion that Britain cede Canada to the United States, but he was willing to give the Americans as much—if not more—than they could reasonably have expected. He certainly had in mind the strengthening of his position in negotiations with the Bourbons, but he seems also to have been influenced by a positive vision of future Anglo-American relations. Strong trading links with the former colonies would help to boost British manufacturing and commerce, and at the same time would prevent the French from building on their wartime trade with the Americans. There was even the possibility that close Anglo-American trading relations would lead to some form of new political connection between Britain and the United States.[55] Agreement was finally reached on 30 November 1782. By the preliminary terms (they were to be provisional until the conclusion of a general peace), the British recognized the independence of the former colonies and pledged to withdraw their troops from the territory of the new nation. The United States was given the lands between the Great Lakes and the Ohio, and fishing rights off Newfoundland. The Americans in return agreed to honour their debts and promised that Congress would recommend to the states a restoration of British and Loyalist property.

[54] William Weddell to his wife, 13 Dec. 1781, Leeds Archives, Ramsden Papers, Rockingham Letters, vol. 2c.

[55] See H. M. Scott, *British Foreign Policy in the Age of the American Revolution* (Oxford, 1990), pp. 326–27.

Shelburne had left office before the definitive treaties were signed. He had hoped to follow up his generosity to the United States in the peace settlement with reciprocal trading arrangements. But a bill to allow the Americans to be given the same commercial privileges as British subjects was introduced into the Commons only in March 1783, just after Shelburne had resigned, and it ran aground in a hostile House. It hardly helped that the bill was proposed by a caretaker administration rather than a secure minister; more important was the opposition of most MPs to what they saw as a threat to the system created by the Navigation Acts. William Eden, an expert in commercial diplomacy, protested that to allow the Americans to carry goods across the Atlantic as they had done before the war would fatally undermine the British mercantile marine and therefore lead to 'the absolute destruction of our navy'.[56] Lord Sheffield's *Observations on the Commerce of the American States*, which put the case for excluding the former colonists from the benefits of the navigation system, had provided Eden with the arguments that he had employed so effectively to defeat Shelburne's American Intercourse Bill. And the views of Sheffield and those who thought like him continued to be immensely influential. During the short lifetime of the Fox–North coalition (April–December 1783), a series of Orders in Council allowed the Americans to trade with the British West Indies only in British ships. One of the authors of the original order, William Knox, who had been an Under-Secretary for the Colonies in North's day, was so convinced of its importance that he wished to have a copy 'engraved on my tombstone, as having saved the navigation of England'.[57] William Pitt, Chatham's son, who became Prime Minister at the end of 1783, was receptive to the idea of freer trade,[58] but even his administration chose to subordinate new economic doctrines to traditional maritime and strategic considerations. In 1786 Pitt's President of the Board of Trade, Lord Hawkesbury, who as Charles Jenkinson had been in the governments of George Grenville and Lord North, carried through Parliament a new Navigation Act that specifically denied the ships of the United States access to trade with Britain or her overseas territories.

The Crown's remaining possessions in North America also required ministerial attention.[59] Thousands of Loyalist refugees fled from the rebel colonies during the conflict, and still more at its conclusion; in all, some 25,000 settled in Nova Scotia and perhaps 20,000 in western Quebec. The growth of Nova Scotia's population presented less of difficulty. New Brunswick was simply established as a separate

---

[56] W. Cobbett, *The Parliamentary History of England...from 1066 to the Year 1803*, 36 vols. (London, 1806–20), XXIII, col. 604, 7 March 1783.

[57] Knox, *Extra-official State Papers*, 2 vols. (London, 1789), II, p. 53.

[58] As were many of the framers of post-war economic policy. See John E. Crowley, *The Privileges of Independence: Neomercantilism and the American Revolution* (Baltimore, 1993), pp. 75–85.

[59] For a fuller treatment of this subject see below, pp. 381–86.

province, complete with its own legislative Assembly, in 1784. The situation in Quebec was more complex. The Quebec Act of 1774 had continued a system of government without an Assembly, and had given a special status to the Catholic Church. The act was denounced by the parliamentary opposition and the Americans as despotic when it was introduced, but it was based on the reality that the vast majority of the population was French in origin and Catholic in religion. The influx of American Loyalists since the passage of the Quebec Act had greatly increased the size of the English-speaking Protestant minority, and added significantly to the pressure to introduce representative institutions. Pitt's administration accepted the need to respond to this pressure, not least because Quebec was costing the British treasury about £100,000 a year. With a national debt that had grown enormously due to the American war—in 1784 it stood at nearly £243 million—Pitt's government was as anxious to free the British taxpayer of some of the burdens of Empire as his predecessors had been since 1763. The Renunciation Act of 1778 ruled out parliamentary taxation of the colonies, so the only alternative was to raise taxes locally through an Assembly. William Grenville, the minister responsible for colonial affairs from 1789, wanted to ensure that any new arrangements avoided the problems that had arisen in the old thirteen colonies—particularly the rise of uncontrollable and powerful Assemblies, and the consequent weakening of executive and Imperial authority. Quebec was to be divided into two provinces, Upper and Lower Canada; the first based on the centres of Anglophone settlement and the second on the old French heartland. Both new provinces were to have an elected Assembly, and a partly hereditary Legislative Council (Canadian versions of the House of Lords). Grenville also sought to give the joint Governor-General and his deputies in each of the provinces significant patronage powers to build up loyal bodies of supporters in the Assemblies.[60] An Anglican bishop had already been appointed to Nova Scotia in 1787, and Grenville, to further his plans for cementing the loyalty of the new provinces, now proposed to establish the Anglican church in Upper Canada. His scheme was altered slightly after consultation with the Governor of Quebec, and further changes were forced by the Opposition as the bill passed through the Commons. All the same, the Canada Act that finally found its way into the statute-book in 1791 embodied the principles that Grenville regarded as vital—patronage powers for the executive, appointed Councils, and the endowment of the Anglican church in Upper Canada.

While Charles Townshend's scheme of 1767 had sought to restore executive power and Imperial authority in the colonies, Grenville's plans of 1789–91 were designed to avoid the need for such remedial measures in the future. In this sense,

---

[60] See Vincent Harlow and Frederick Madden, eds., *British Colonial Developments, 1774–1834: Select Documents* (Oxford, 1953), pp. 197–210.

the British could be said to have learned from the experience of the American Revolution. Yet, seen from a different perspective, what seems striking is not adaptation but continuity. The right of Parliament to tax the colonies had been surrendered, but in its other essentials—in the commitment to the Navigation Acts, in the aim to circumscribe the power of local legislatures and support local executives, and in the desire to oblige the colonies themselves to bear more of the costs of Empire—British thinking had changed remarkably little through nearly three decades of controversy, crisis, and revolutionary upheaval.

Select Bibliography

DANIEL A. BAUGH, 'Maritime Strength and Atlantic Commerce: The Uses of "a Grand Marine Empire"', in Lawrence Stone, ed., *An Imperial State at War: Britain from 1689 to 1815* (London, 1994), pp. 185-223.

JAMES E. BRADLEY, *Popular Politics and the American Revolution in England: Petitions, the Crown and Public Opinion* (Macon, Ga., 1986).

—— *Religion, Revolution and English Radicalism: Nonconformity in Eighteenth-century Politics and Society* (Cambridge, 1990).

JOHN BROOKE, *The Chatham Administration* (London, 1967).

JOHN L. BULLION, *A Great and Necessary Measure: George Grenville and the Genesis of the Stamp Act, 1763–1765* (Columbia, SC, 1982).

—— 'British Ministers and American Resistance to the Stamp Act, October–December 1765', *William and Mary Quarterly*, Third Series, XLIX (1992), pp. 89-107.

STEPHEN CONWAY, *The War of American Independence* (London, 1995).

JOHN DERRY, *English Politics and the American Revolution* (London, 1976).

JACK P. GREENE, *Peripheries and Center: Constitutional Development in the Extended Polities of the British Empire and the United States, 1607–1788* (Athens, Ga., 1987).

IRA D. GRUBER, *The Howe Brothers and the American Revolution* (Chapel Hill, NC, 1972).

PAUL LANGFORD, *The First Rockingham Administration* (Oxford, 1973).

—— 'Property and "Virtual Representation" in Eighteenth-Century England', *Historical Journal*, XXXI (1988), pp. 88-113.

PHILIP LAWSON, *George Grenville; A Political Life* (Oxford, 1984).

PIERS MACKESY, *The War for America* (London, 1964).

FRANK O'GORMAN, *The Rise of Party in England: The Rockingham Whigs, 1760–1782* (London, 1975).

J. R. POLE, *The Gift of Government; Political Responsibility from the English Restoration to the American Revolution* (Athens, Ga., 1983).

P. D. G. THOMAS, *British Politics and the Stamp Act Crisis: The First Phase of the American Revolution, 1763–1767* (Oxford, 1975).

—— *The Townshend Duties Crisis: The Second Phase of the American Revolution, 1767–1773* (Oxford, 1987).

—— *Tea Party to Independence: The Third Phase of the American Revolution, 1773–1776* (Oxford, 1991).

ROBERT W. TUCKER and DAVID C. HENDRICKSON, *The Fall of the First British Empire: Origins of the War of American Independence* (Baltimore, 1982).

16

Native Peoples of North America and the Eighteenth-Century British Empire

DANIEL K. RICHTER

British–American Indian relations during the long eighteenth century defy a single narrative. At best, not one but three discontinuous stories emerge from the continent's many regional and cultural variations. The first—in *medias res* at the time of the Glorious Revolution and stretching into the 1710s—traces an array of regional wars among English and Indians, Indians and Indians, and English and other Europeans. From the 1720s to the 1750s that turbulent story gave way to a tale of stability, as surviving American Indian groups secured fragile places in a global imperial system. From the period of the Seven Years War to 1815 violence again dominated, but violence that threw British agents into common cause with Native Americans struggling against the newly independent United States. This essay will tell each story in turn, but first it will trace some broad parameters that circumscribed all three.[1]

Parameters

Throughout the eighteenth century and across eastern North America, British–Indian relations took place within the boundaries of prior experience, structural features of the Empire, and political characteristics common to most of the region's native peoples. The importance of experience is easily overlooked, yet eighteenth-century colonials, who, as will be seen below, sometimes spoke of the 'modern Indian', knew better. For North America east of the Mississippi was no longer really a 'new world'; in many places cultural interaction stretched back well over a century. Economic relationships had been established, Christian missionaries had become familiar (and sometimes welcome) sights in Indian villages, military alliances had matured, wars had been fought. Epidemics from Europe and Africa had scythed through Native American populations, forcing survivors to

[1] The author thanks Colin Calloway and Sharon Richter for their thoughtful comments on a preliminary draft of this chapter.

regroup in new, polyglot communities. And both Indians and Europeans had developed firm ideas—however prejudiced and stereotypical—about what to expect from one another.

If historical experience defined one set of parameters for inter-cultural relations, four sometimes contradictory characteristics of the British Imperial system delineated another. First, in what has been labelled 'An Empire of Goods', Indians played roles as consumers of manufactured items and producers of raw materials.[2] 'The Original great tye between the Indians and Europeans was Mutual conveniency', South Carolinian John Stuart wrote to the Board of Trade in 1761. 'A modern Indian cannot subsist without Europeans; And would handle a Flint Ax or any other rude utinsil used by his ancestors very awkwardly; So that what was only Conveniency at first is now become Necessity and the Original tye Strengthned.'[3] Among the necessities and conveniencies that tied eighteenth-century Native Americans into the transatlantic commercial world were knives and hatchets, kettles and spoons, woollens and linens, needles and scissors, earrings and glass beads, liquor and tobacco, firearms and gunpowder. The furs and hides that purchased these became in turn raw materials for other goods manufactured in Europe. There, and in the counting houses of merchant middlemen rather than in Native American villages, profits accumulated. An Iroquois spokesman's description of the New York trading post at Oswego captured the lopsided relationship. The post was, he told provincial Governor George Clarke, 'a vast advantage ... because we can get there what we want or desire. But we think Brother, that your people who trade there have the most advantage by it, and that it is as good for them as a Silver mine.'[4]

If an asymmetrical 'Mutual conveniency' defined much of inter-cultural relations, a second characteristic of the eighteenth-century Empire set boundaries of a different sort. In British North America, not the fur trade but capitalist agriculture, whether on family farms or plantations worked by enslaved labourers, was primary, and persistent immigration of agricultural labour was essential to economic prosperity. The result was an inexorable demand for new agricultural land—land that in one way or another had to be expropriated from its aboriginal owners. The agriculturally based, immigration-driven character, then, of the same 'Empire of Goods' in which Indian

---

[2] T. H. Breen, 'An Empire of Goods: The Anglicization of Colonial America, 1690–1776', *Journal of British Studies*, XXV (1986), pp. 467–99; James Axtell, *Beyond 1492: Encounters in Colonial North America* (New York, 1992), pp. 125–51.

[3] Quoted in Kathryn E. Holland Braund, *Deerskins and Duffels: The Creek Indian Trade with Anglo-America, 1685–1815* (Lincoln, Nebr., 1993), pp. 26, 30.

[4] E. B. O'Callaghan and Berthold Fernow, eds., *Documents Relative to the Colonial History of the State of New-York*, 15 vols. (Albany, NY, 1853–87), VI, p. 177.

consumers and producers found a niche tended to make that niche expendable to British colonists.[5]

These two contradictory aspects of the Empire coexisted uneasily with a third, which gave Indian relations reinvigorated importance to government officials, if not to the majority of provincials. On a continent where Imperial Governors lacked political and military resources, Indian alliances were vital to Britain's conflicts with French and Spanish rivals. In wartime, Native American allies might do most of the fighting on Britain's behalf; at the least, it was vital to keep powerful Indian groups neutral. Wartime alliances had to be based on peacetime relationships—preferably ones that brought economic benefits to Britain rather than her rivals. Moreover, through what historian Francis Jennings labels 'the deed game', Indian alliances created a paper trail of treaties by which territorial claims could be traced in European international law.[6]

These multiple strains illuminate a fourth relevant characteristic of the eighteenth-century Empire: the myriad interests that cut across its decentralized provinces. Political authority was not only fragmented among colonies from Nova Scotia to the Carolinas—in each of which Governors charged with Indian diplomacy contested with elected Assemblies guarding the purse-strings—but it dissipated rapidly as it radiated from seaboard capitals to interior frontiers where settlers frequently defied eastern élites. There would never be *one* British policy toward Native Americans, but rather a host of British people pursuing a variety of interests within parameters set by historical experience, Imperial structures, and finally, basic characteristics of Indian political culture.

Much had changed in Native America since the arrival of Europeans. None the less, Indian politics—and thus Indian diplomacy with the British—remained rooted in autonomous village communities composed of largely autonomous kin groups. 'Brethren you know that we have no forcing rules or laws amongst us', a turn-of-the-century Indian spokesman explained.[7] Headmen of particular lineages or clans forged economic connections with individual Euro-American traders, often at cross-purposes to the efforts of other leaders whose commercial alliances stretched in different directions. Similarly, small-scale military raids remained largely under the control of war chiefs who worked outward from their kin groups to recruit allies among Indians and Europeans. Peacemaking, too, grew from the efforts of clan headmen to resolve disputes that might otherwise end in violence. Indian responses to Christian missionaries fit into the same

---

[5] Denys Delâge, *Le Pays renversé: Amérindiens et européens en Amérique du nord-est, 1600–1664* (Montreal, 1985), pp. 246–67.

[6] Francis Jennings, *The Invasion of America: Indians, Colonialism, and the Cant of Conquest* (Chapel Hill, NC, 1975), pp. 105-45.

[7] Treaty minutes, 12 July 1697, New York State Archives, New York Colonial Manuscripts, XLI, f. 93.

decentralized configurations. Clergymen became spiritual links in complex alliances inside and outside the villages where they preached.[8]

These multi-headed patterns imparted a kaleidoscopic quality to Indian relations with Europeans. Diplomacy could not be a matter of technical agreements secretly contrived by a few leaders. To be effective the process must culminate in public, participatory, and consensual rituals involving diverse constituents not only rhetorically but economically, through the exchange of goods; as one early eighteenth-century headman put it, 'the trade and the peace we take to be one thing'.[9] Even after a broadly based agreement had been reached, the potential remained for headmen of relatively small groups to pursue contrary agendas with Britain's imperial rivals. Alliances, therefore, could never be made just once. Instead, they required periodic collective affirmation in ritualized public councils. 'Each Nation is an absolute Republick by its self...', New Yorker Cadwallader Colden warned Imperial officials. 'They have certain Customs which they observe in their Publick Affairs with other Nations... which it is scandalous for any one not to observe.'[10]

Violent Transitions, 1675–1720

But Colden published those words in 1727; they belong to the second of the stories of British–Indian relations during the long eighteenth century. In the four principal regions of British North American colonization, the first narrative centres on inter-cultural violence rather than diplomatic customs carefully observed. The tale begins not in 1689, but in the mid-1670s, with Metacom's (or 'King Philip's') War in New England, Bacon's Rebellion in Virginia, the establishment of Charleston in South Carolina, and the final English conquest of Dutch New Netherland.[11] From the carnage, a new map of Indian populations and inter-cultural relationships with Europeans would ultimately emerge.

---

[8] John Phillip Reid, *A Better Kind of Hatchet: Law, Trade, and Diplomacy in the Cherokee Nation during the Early Years of European Contact* (University Park, Penn., 1976), pp. 4–17; Mary A. Druke, 'Linking Arms: The Structure of Iroquois Intertribal Diplomacy', in Daniel K. Richter and James H. Merrell, eds., *Beyond the Covenant Chain: The Iroquois and Their Neighbors in Indian North America, 1600–1800* (Syracuse, NY, 1987), pp. 29–39; Daniel K. Richter, 'Iroquois versus Iroquois: Jesuit Missions and Christianity in Village Politics, 1642–1684', *Ethnohistory*, XXXII (1985), pp. 1–16.

[9] Minutes of New York Commissioners for Indian Affairs, 20 Sept. 1735, Public Archives of Canada, R.G. 10, vol. 1819, Microfilm reel C-1220.

[10] Cadwallader Colden, *The History of the Five Indian Nations Depending on the Province of New-York in America* (1727, 1747; Ithaca, NY, 1958), p. xx.

[11] On Metacom's War and Bacon's Rebellion, see Vol. I, chaps. by Peter Mancall and Virginia DeJohn Anderson.

In Metacom's War of 1675–76 colonists killed, subjugated, or dispersed most of southern New England's surviving Algonquian-speaking peoples, but only at a heavy cost in English lives, property, and internal political stability. After Massachusetts Bay lost its charter and all of the region's colonies had been folded into James II's Dominion of New England, war with Indian neighbours resumed. Many of the antagonists were refugees from Metacom's War, and most received arms and encouragement from New France. When the Glorious Revolution brought the English colonies into the War of the League of Augsburg, French support became more open and intense. Raids struck New England's northern borders almost constantly until the end of the War of the Spanish Succession in 1713. Efforts by Massachusetts and Connecticut governments to recruit Indian allies to counter the threat met little success.[12]

A similar story applies to the Chesapeake region where, in the mid-1670s, the inter-cultural violence associated with Bacon's Rebellion spared only small pockets of the original Algonquian-speaking population. Virginia leaders subsequently concluded that Governor William Berkeley's refusal to expand aggressively into Indian lands had been a major cause of the political upheaval sparked by his rival, Nathaniel Bacon. 'A Governour of Virginia has to steer between Scylla and Charyoldis, either an Indian or a Civil War...', concluded Alexander Spotswood, who held that post from 1710 to 1722; 'Bacon[']s Rebellion was occasioned purely by the Governour and Council refusing to let the People go out against the Indians who at that time annoyed the Frontiers.'[13] Although the wars of the League of Augsburg and the Spanish Succession had little direct impact on the Chesapeake, the eighteenth century opened with little more hope for a peaceful future there than in New England.

The tale in the Carolinas was even more unrelievedly violent. Shortly after colonization began in the 1660s, English traders encouraged Indian clients to raid their neighbours for slaves, most of whom would be shipped to the West Indies. First inland Westos attacked coastal Cusabos and others; in the early 1680s the Westos' turn came at the hands of Savannahs (Shawnees) still further in the interior; by 1708 the Savannahs were targets of Siouan-speaking piedmont peoples. The War of the Spanish Succession authorized Carolinians' direct participation in slave raids against Indian communities in Spanish Florida; the main force, however, consisted of Yamasees, who had emigrated northward to escape Spanish domination, and of inland Muskogean-speakers the English called 'Creeks'. By 1715 the Franciscan missions that for over a century had stretched between the Gulf and

[12] Richard R. Johnson, 'The Search for a Usable Indian: An Aspect of the Defense of Colonial New England', *Journal of American History* (hereafter *JAH*), LXIV (1977), pp. 623–51.

[13] Alexander Spotswood to Peter Schuyler, 25 Jan. 1720, Pennsylvania State Archives, Pennsylvania Provincial Council Records, Vol. F, pp. 13–21.

Atlantic coasts were destroyed, and thousands of their Timucua, Guale, and Apalachee residents and allies had been killed or enslaved. At the opposite end of Charleston's brutal universe were the Tuscaroras, whose homes included much of present-day North Carolina. In 1711, pushed to the breaking point by slave raids and an influx of Swiss and German immigrants settling on their lands, they killed over 100 North Carolinians. In response, South Carolina co-ordinated joint expeditions with the Yamasees and other Indian allies that, by 1713, burned most of the Tuscaroras' villages, killed perhaps a thousand men, women, and children, enslaved some 700 others, and left the 2,500 or so survivors refugees.[14]

One reason the Yamasees participated in these expeditions was that they themselves were hard-pressed. In debt to Carolina traders who enslaved defaulters, and confined, since 1707, to reserved lands on the Savannah River, they hoped their service would win them some relief. Abuses continued, however, and Yamasees built an alliance with similarly oppressed Creeks and members of smaller Indian groups. Beginning in April 1715, the alliance struck, attacking frontier settlements and killing Carolina traders as far away as the Mississippi Valley. The war's turning point came in early 1716, when Cherokees influenced by massive gifts of trade goods entered decisively on Carolina's side. Those Yamasees who avoided death or enslavement retreated to Florida, while the Creeks removed their villages farther inland. The result for the Carolinas was decidedly mixed. The Yamasee War—this region's equivalent of Metacom's War or Bacon's Rebellion—cleared vast Indian areas for agricultural occupation, but roughly 7 per cent of the province's 6,000 Europeans lost their lives, and their lucrative slave and deerskin trade networks lay in tatters.[15]

The fourth major arena of British North American colonization superficially presented a more peaceful scene than the Carolinas, the Chesapeake, or New England. But the mid-Atlantic region had long been the site of inter-Indian warfare just as violent as that elsewhere. The early victors (if there were any) were the Five Nations of the Iroquois League, the Mohawks, Oneidas, Onondagas, Cayugas, and Senecas. Beginning in the 1630s they had used the advantage in metal weapons and firearms that their trading ties to New Netherland gave them to lay waste much of the region surrounding their homeland and to incorporate the survivors into disease-depleted Iroquois villages. As the English took over New Netherland, however, the Iroquois were on the defensive, having lost their secure trade ties to the Dutch, facing well-armed Indian enemies, and chafing under a

[14] Gary B. Nash, *Red, White, and Black: The Peoples of Early North America*, 3rd edn. (Englewood Cliffs, NJ, 1992), pp. 128–43; David J. Weber, *The Spanish Frontier in North America* (New Haven, 1992), pp. 141–45.

[15] Verner W. Crane, *The Southern Frontier, 1670–1732* (1928; New York, 1981), pp. 108–86.

peace treaty imposed by New France after an invasion of the Mohawk country in 1666.[16]

In this context, the Governor of the Duke of York's conquered province, Sir Edmund Andros, improvised the first centralized Imperial policy toward Native North Americans. That policy stemmed less from an abstract concern for inter-cultural relations than from the Duke's mandate to establish the New York government's authority over the Dutch and English populations, to resolve favourably the province's ambiguous boundaries, and most importantly, to raise revenue. Andros believed, as did many Imperial administrators who followed him, that centralization of the Indian diplomacy of the various colonies could be an excellent means to such ends. Conflicts such as Metacom's War and Bacon's Rebellion (both of which erupted shortly after Andros's arrival in 1674) were, he concluded, only what the English 'must expect and bee lyable to, so long as each petty colony hath or assumes absolute power of peace and warr'.[17]

As colonists and Indians alike surveyed the damage in New England and the Chesapeake, Andros posed as peacemaker. On both fronts, he found Iroquois leaders eager to work with him. At the peak of Metacom's War, the Governor armed a Mohawk Iroquois force that attacked the New England Algonquians' winter encampment and helped to ensure English victory over long-time Native American enemies of the Iroquois. Then, at war's end, Andros invited Indian refugees to resettle under joint New York and Iroquois protection some twenty miles north-east of Albany, a move that happened to expand New York's claims toward both New France and Massachusetts. Meanwhile, he made similar provisions for the Iroquoian-speaking Susquehannocks, who had borne the brunt of the warfare in the Chesapeake. As these people resettled in the Susquehanna watershed of present-day central Pennsylvania and southern New York, they were joined by Algonquian-speaking Shawnees who migrated from a variety of directions, among them the Carolinas. In these varied transactions lay the origins of the English–Indian alliances known as 'the Covenant Chain', in which New York and the Iroquois attempted to broker relationships among, respectively, the region's English colonies and Indian nations.[18]

The Covenant Chain also extended to the north and west. Because one of New York's main sources of revenue was a duty on beaver pelts shipped through Manhattan, Andros was under instructions to recapture Iroquois commerce

---

[16] Daniel K. Richter, *The Ordeal of the Longhouse: The Peoples of the Iroquois League in the Era of European Colonization* (Chapel Hill, NC, 1992), pp. 50–132.

[17] O'Callaghan and Fernow, eds., *Documents Relative to New-York*, III, p. 271.

[18] Francis Jennings, *The Ambiguous Iroquois Empire: The Covenant Chain Confederation of Indian Tribes with English Colonies from Its Beginnings to the Lancaster Treaty of 1744* (New York, 1984), pp. 145–71.

from French competitors, who must not be allowed to 'come on this side the Lake or River Canada to divert the trade'.[19] Working with sympathetic elements in the Dutch community at Albany, Andros thus revitalized the economic links on which Iroquois military victories had formerly been built. With a secure source of weapons, and with peace on their eastern and southern flanks, Iroquois leaders were freed to move aggressively against Native American allies of New France in a contest for hunting territories in the Great Lakes region. By 1684, the Iroquois and New France were again at war.[20]

Five years later, when England entered into the War of the League of Augsburg, the North American conflict melted into the Anglo-French imperial struggle. But New York's divisive internal politics and empty coffers combined with Whitehall's failure to provide meaningful military support to ensure that the Iroquois forces did nearly all the North American fighting against New France and its Native allies. Worse still, because under the terms of the 'deed game' the Crown that could claim diplomatic authority over the Iroquois could also pretend suzerainty over territories they had supposedly conquered in previous inter-Indian wars, the Treaty of Ryswick that brought a truce to Europe placed the Iroquois in an untenable situation: while New York's Governors argued that the Iroquois, as English subjects, were automatically covered by the treaty, French officials insisted on a separate peace. The stalemate continued for over three years, during which Indian allies of the French relentlessly pounded their Iroquois foes.[21]

In 1700 one faction of Iroquois leaders engineered a surrender which, during the next year, others turned into at least a partial victory. In the summer of 1701 at Montreal an Iroquois delegation made peace with New France and over a dozen of its allies. In exchange for a pledge of Iroquois neutrality in future wars between European empires, Governor Louis-Hector de Callière promised to enforce the peace and to guarantee the right of Iroquois to hunt north of the Great Lakes and trade at the French post of Detroit. Callière did not know, however, that another set of Iroquois headmen was simultaneously treating at Albany, where they surprised their New York hosts with a deed conveying the same Great Lakes territories to the English Crown. In giving each empire an equivalent paper claim to the same territory, this 'Grand Settlement of 1701' used the 'deed game' to counter power with power in hopes of preserving Iroquois independence.[22]

[19] O'Callaghan and Fernow, eds., *Documents Relative to New-York*, III, p. 233.

[20] Daniel K. Richter, 'Cultural Brokers and Intercultural Politics: New York–Iroquois Relations, 1664–1701', *JAH*, LXXV (1988), pp. 48–55.

[21] Allen W. Trelease, *Indian Affairs in Colonial New York: The Seventeenth Century* (Ithaca, NY, 1960), pp. 254–363.

[22] Anthony F. C. Wallace, 'Origins of Iroquois Neutrality: The Grand Settlement of 1701', *Pennsylvania History*, XXIV (1957), pp. 223–35.

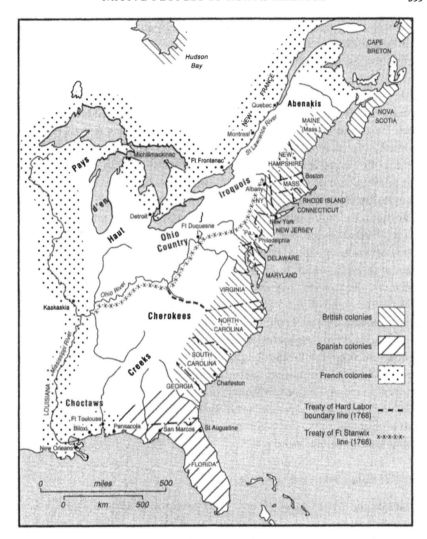

Map 16.1. North America: Indian Peoples and European Colonies in the Mid-Eighteenth Century

Yet the balance-of-power diplomacy harbingered in 1701 remained elusive for the better part of a generation. During the War of the Spanish Succession, French diplomats, traders, and missionaries used increasingly heavy-handed means to force the Iroquois to remain neutral, if not submit to French hegemony. Meantime, the peace that New France pledged to guarantee in the West proved illusive. As a result, in 1709 and 1711, when New Yorkers and New Englanders planned elaborate invasions of New France, hundreds of Iroquois enlisted in the efforts. Neither expedition ever left its staging area, however, and the débâcles helped ensure that, as the War of the Spanish Succession ended, Iroquois relations with both European powers were at their nadirs. Among the irritants, from New York's perspective, was the alacrity with which the Iroquois continued to welcome refugees from wars with other English colonies, most notably between 1,500 and 2,000 Tuscaroras who, after their nation's defeat, migrated northward and were adopted as the Sixth Nation of the Iroquois League. What one Anglican missionary described as the Tuscaroras' 'Implacable hatred against Christians at Carolina' lent political support to those among their new confederates who viewed all Europeans with jaundiced eyes.[23]

By the 1720s those jaundiced eyes looked not only eastward toward New York but southward toward Pennsylvania. Despite William Penn's Quaker insistence that lands be scrupulously purchased from their Indian owners, for Pennsylvania—as for every part of the British North American Empire—the acquisition of ever more territory for a growing European agricultural population was imperative. When Penn died in 1718, grievances were already accumulating among Delawares and Shawnees who had only recently relocated to the Susquehanna watershed under the protection of the Covenant Chain. From the 1720s onward, Pennsylvania's hopes for managing these restive neighbours lay, like New York's for control of the Great Lakes, in the Covenant Chain and the fiction of Iroquois imperial hegemony. In a series of questionable transactions that culminated in the 'Walking Purchase' of upper Delaware River lands in 1737, the Penn family and its agents relied on Iroquois leaders to manage the transfer of territories inhabited by Indian residents unwilling to sell.[24]

Fragile Equilibrium, 1720–1763

Whatever the bitter legacy of such developments, it remains significant that diplomacy in a context of imperial rivalry, rather than violence rooted in economic exploitation and agricultural expansion, had come to dominate intercultural relations in the mid-Atlantic region. The structural characteristics and diplomatic interests of the British colonies found common ground with Indian leaders operating within the decentralized political world of Native America. Some understanding of how, across the continent, this more peaceful story replaced the earlier bloody narrative is conveyed by a look at the map. By the second quarter of the eighteenth century, eastern North America resembled a vast, misshapen imperial doughnut. The Atlantic coast from the Carolinas to Nova

---

[23] Richter, *Ordeal of the Longhouse*, pp. 162–239, quotation from p. 239.

[24] Jennings, *Ambiguous Iroquois Empire*, pp. 301–46.

Scotia was firmly British. The sweeping arc from Cape Breton Island through the St Lawrence Valley was more scantily populated by French *habitants*; that stretching through the portages of the Great Lakes down the Mississippi to New Orleans still more thinly dotted with French forts and trading stations. The military outposts of Spanish Florida completed the squashed circle. Indian country—the doughnut's elongated hole—was dominated by seven clusters of autonomous local communities that acted as more or less coherent political units, while other, smaller, groups clung to the European margins.

Despite vast cultural differences, each of the major clusters shared at least three traits. First, none of them had recognizably existed a hundred years earlier; each was an amalgam of survivors, refugees, and war captives produced by the upheavals that climaxed at the turn of the eighteenth century. People moved frequently among polyglot villages, so much so that one historian has suggested that 'names of communities should often be regarded as "addresses" rather than tribal designations'.[25] Second, each of those addresses enjoyed a geographic location that not only made its residents viable producers for the transatlantic fur and hide trades but also allowed them to deal in two or more competing Euro-American markets. And thus, third, each capitalized on its decentralized, kin-based politics to cultivate connections with rival colonies and so avoid dependence on a single European power. As New York Indian affairs secretary Peter Wraxall observed at mid-century, 'to preserve the Ballance between us and the French is the great ruling Principle of the Modern Indian Politics'.[26]

Most tightly wedged between competing imperial powers, and therefore most tightly constrained in their pursuit of 'the Modern Indian Politics', was a chain of villages stretching from present-day New Brunswick through northern Maine, New Hampshire, and Vermont. Composed of family bands of Penobscots and Kennebecs who spoke the Algonquian Eastern Abenaki language, and Pigwackets, Pennacooks, Cowassucks, Missisquois, Sokokis, and other local groups who spoke Western Abenaki, what the New England colonists frequently referred to as 'Eastern Indians' comprised only the loosest of confederacies. Villages relocated often, and families still more frequently. In peacetime many of these groups welcomed French Jesuit missionaries while trading with New Englanders. Disputes over commerce and land combined with hatreds stretching back to Metacom's War, however, to produce frequent Anglo-Abenaki violence, particularly on the Maine frontier and especially in the episode known variously as 'Dummer's',

[25] Colin G. Calloway, *The American Revolution in Indian Country: Crisis and Diversity in Native American Communities* (Cambridge, 1995), p. xvi.

[26] Peter Wraxall, *An Abridgment of the Indian Affairs Contained in Four Folio Volumes, Transacted in the Colony of New York, from the Year 1678 to the Year 1751*, ed. Charles Howard McIlwain (Cambridge, Mass., 1915), p. 219 n.

'Rale's' or 'Gray Lock's War' in the 1720s. Yet the French colonial government's reluctance to get directly involved in such conflicts reinforced the neutralist imperative of 'the Modern Indian Politics'. Many Abenakis exploited their migratory cultural patterns to pursue what their most careful historian has called a 'strategy of withdrawal, dispersal, and cautious reappearance' to steer between their European neighbours.[27]

A similar lesson in the dangers of 'the Modern Indian Politics' had been learned a generation earlier by the second of the seven population clusters, the Iroquois League. 'If we should Take up the hatchet... The Governor of Canada Would Look down upon us with Indignation, and Set The People round about, who are his Children, upon us, and That would Set all The World on Fire', one headman explained.[28] For Anglophile factions among the Six Nations, the Covenant Chain alliance with the British was real and deep. The 1710 public relations spectacle of the visit to London of four supposed Iroquois 'kings', along with the publication of instalments of Colden's significantly titled *History of the Five Indian Nations Depending on the Province of New-York in America* in 1727 and 1747, made the Iroquois the most well known of Native Americans in Imperial circles. But for most Iroquois leaders, the alliance with their English 'Brothers' and the pretension of suzerainty over a vast empire of Indian Covenant Chain dependents was a carefully cultivated mystique obscuring their countervailing economic and diplomatic ties to New France.[29]

The territories the Iroquois 'deeded' to the English Crown in 1701 witnessed a third variation on 'the Modern Indian Politics'. The Great Lakes area the French called the *pays d'en haut* was what one historian labels 'a world made of fragments', where diverse survivors of wars and epidemics coalesced. Algonquian-speaking Ottawas, Miamis, Illinois, Ojibwas, and Potawatomis interspersed with one another and with Hurons and other Iroquoian-speakers collectively known as 'Wyandots', sometimes in the same villages, more often in discrete towns clustered near such French posts as Detroit and Michilimackinac. Initially they were held together by their common animosity to the Iroquois and their political, economic, and military obligations as 'Children' of their French 'Father'. (In matrilineal societies such as theirs, those terms implied not blind filial obedience but the conditional respect due a powerful dispenser of favours, protection, and advice;

[27] Colin G. Calloway, *The Western Abenakis of Vermont, 1600–1800: War, Migration, and the Survival of an Indian People* (Norman, Okla., 1990), p. 240; Kenneth M. Morrison, *The Embattled Northeast: The Elusive Ideal of Alliance in Abenaki–Euramerican Relations* (Berkeley, 1984).

[28] John Stoddard and others, Journal of Negotiations at Albany, 26 Aug.–28 Sept. 1724, Massachusetts State Archives, Massachusetts Archives Series, XXIX, f. 181.

[29] Richmond P. Bond, *Queen Anne's American Kings* (Oxford, 1952); Dorothy V. Jones, *License for Empire: Colonialism by Treaty in Early America* (Chicago, 1982), pp. 21–35.

had Europeans understood, they would have called the relationship avuncular rather than paternal.) By the 1720s, however, the *pays d'en haut* was bound more by a shared history and by arrangements with their former Iroquois enemies that allowed them to counterbalance French influence with trade at New York's Oswego outpost.[30]

To the south, in what British provincials called the 'Ohio Country', another 'world made of fragments' took shape in the 1720s and 1730s. Entering a region depopulated by wars and epidemics, Shawnees, Delawares, and Iroquois who came to be known as 'Mingoes' (to distinguish them from their confederates who remained in Iroquoia) settled in multi-ethnic villages strategically placed to trade with New France and Virginia as well as with their main suppliers from Pennsylvania. At least three characteristics united the immigrants. First, many were refugees twice removed, having left homes in the Susquehanna watershed to which they or their parents had earlier migrated from elsewhere. Second, determined not to move again, they shared a vigorous distrust of Europeans, particularly the Pennsylvanians whom they blamed for their most recent dispersal. Third, they were almost equally wary of the League Iroquois, whose protection under the Covenant Chain had proved illusory and whose pretensions to diplomatic hegemony they increasingly resented.[31]

Farther southward, three other large, multi-ethnic clusters emerged from the ruins of the Yamasee War to engage in their own variants on 'the Modern Indian Politics'. Cherokees, Creeks, and Choctaws were reconfigurations of populations descended from the great Mississippian chiefdoms whose mounded cities had dominated the region in the sixteenth century. The Cherokees, having sided with the Carolinians against the Yamasees and Creeks, almost immediately retreated from the grip of Charleston to make Virginians their primary trading partners. Their English-versus-English diplomatic balancing act intersected in complex ways with regional and factional divisions among 'Overhill', 'Valley', and 'Lower' towns, with a potential alliance with the French of Louisiana, and with the growth of what were usually described as 'renegade' communities affiliated with Ohio Country villages. The importance of the Cherokees to British Imperial interests was driven home in 1730, when the eccentric Scottish baronet Sir Alexander Cuming travelled from Charleston through Cherokee country and recruited six alleged chiefs for a highly publicized London interview with the Board of Trade.[32]

[30] Richard White, *The Middle Ground: Indians, Empires, and Republics in the Great Lakes Region, 1650–1815* (Cambridge, 1991), pp. 1–185.

[31] Michael N. McConnell, *A Country Between: The Upper Ohio Valley and Its Peoples, 1724–1774* (Lincoln, Nebr., 1992), pp. 6–60.

[32] Marvin T. Smith, 'Aboriginal Population Movements in the Early Historic Period Interior Southeast', in Peter H. Wood, Gregory A. Waselkov, and M. Thomas Hatley, eds., *Powhatan's Mantle: Indians*

As important as the Cherokees were to the south-east's intercultural diplomacy, however, in many respects the Creeks, or Muskogees, were its centrepiece. After the Yamasee War they built a three-way balance-of-power diplomacy on a complex network of internal political factions. In the Lower Creek towns, pro-Spanish leaders drew upon their Yamasee connections to cultivate ties to Florida and to welcome the establishment of Fort San Marcos on Apalachee Bay in 1718. Similarly, factions in the Upper Creek towns had encouraged the French to station a garrison at Fort Toulouse on the Alabama River in 1716. These connections mitigated an economic dependence upon Carolina traders that quickly re-emerged after the Yamasee War, when bovine epidemics in continental Europe created a huge market among English leather-workers for North American deerskins. The Creeks—controlling territories that, due to their own earlier slave-raiding expeditions, were largely emptied of humans but filled with white-tailed deer—were ideally placed to profit from that demand. By mid-century, perhaps a million deerskins a year, half of them harvested by Creeks, moved through Charleston.[33]

Farther westward, in a zone where, as in the *pays d'en haut*, the French were the dominant imperial force, a final cluster centred on the Choctaws of the lower Mississippi Valley. Although they were, on the whole, firm allies and trading partners of their Louisiana French 'Father', diverse allegiances cut across regional divisions among 'Eastern', 'Western', and 'Sixtowns' villages. And, as a bloody assault by pro-English factions on Natchez, Mobile, and other posts in 1747 showed, at least some of these groups maintained ties to more than one imperial power. Louisiana, unable to compete with English traders in either price or quantity of goods, encouraged enmity between Choctaws and the much smaller Chickasaw population to their north, to prevent the former from joining the latter in the Carolinas' commercial network.[34]

While these large multi-ethnic communities prospered in the continental interior, smaller clusters of refugees and survivors regrouped nearer the centres of British occupation, where both economic resources and opportunities for balance-of-power diplomacy were scarcer. Perhaps the most successful of such peoples were the various Siouan-speaking fragments on the Carolina piedmont that became the Catawba nation. Despite a location steadily encapsulated by Anglo-Carolinians, they relied on Charleston's need for a military buffer on the

in the Colonial Southeast (Lincoln, Nebr., 1989), pp. 21–34; Vernon James Knight, Jr., 'The Formation of the Creeks', in Charles Hudson and Carmen Chaves Tesser, eds., *The Forgotten Centuries: Indians and Europeans in the American South, 1521–1704* (Athens, Ga., 1994), pp. 373–92; Crane, *Southern Frontier,* pp. 276–302.

[33] Braund, *Deerskins and Duffels,* pp. 26–80.

[34] Daniel H. Usner, Jr., *Indians, Settlers, and Slaves in a Frontier Exchange Economy: The Lower Mississippi Valley before 1783* (Chapel Hill, NC, 1992), pp. 77–104.

province's borders to preserve their cultural autonomy and, in the words of one early nineteenth-century observer, 'be Indians still'.[35]

On Virginia's frontiers, Tutelo and Saponi tributaries played a similar role from the early 1710s until the 1740s, when they relocated under Iroquois protection to the Susquehanna River watershed in present-day Pennsylvania and New York. There they joined a melange of other Indians from New England as well as points south who, as many Shawnees and Delawares migrated to the Ohio Country, remained amidst powerful British and Iroquois neighbours. Their military strength and the threat of gravitating to the French orbit ensured that most would be British allies rather than subjects, although they lacked the real freedom of manœuvre such larger interior peoples as the Iroquois or Creeks enjoyed.[36]

The same could be said for another set of ethnically mixed refugee communities, except that these tended toward enmity rather than alliance with the British. Located along the St Lawrence River, the Roman Catholic *sauvages domiciliés* of Lorette, Odanak (St François), Kahnawake (Caughnawaga), and Kanesatake (Oka or La Montagne) were the 'French Indians' who haunted the nightmares of readers of the captivity narratives that were an important eighteenth-century New England literary genre. None the less, in peacetime, factions among each of these villages traded with New York or Massachusetts and thus, like the various small communities allied to the British, engaged in a modified form of 'the Modern Indian Politics'.[37]

A final category of eighteenth-century Indians enjoyed no such luxury in their dealings with the British world: those who lived within the borders and under the direct political authority of the colonies. Southern New England, Long Island, and the tidewater Chesapeake in particular were dotted with small Native American communities. Those blessed with out-of-the-way or agriculturally unpromising locales (Martha's Vineyard, eastern Long Island, the Pamunkey and Mattaponi reservations in tidewater Virginia) or those (such as the whalers of Nantucket) who found a niche in the Euro-American economy, survived as Indian communities with considerable control over their lands, their everyday political affairs, and even their Christian churches. Others less isolated from Euro-American land-hunger—the 'praying town' of Natick and the 'Indian district' of Mashpee in Massachusetts, the Pequot and Mohegan reservations of Connecticut, the Narragansett reservation in Rhode Island, the Piscataway tributaries of Maryland, the

---

[35] James H. Merrell, *The Indians' New World: Catawbas and Their Neighbors from European Contact through the Era of Removal* (Chapel Hill, NC, 1989), p. 244.

[36] Peter C. Mancall, *Valley of Opportunity: Economic Culture along the Upper Susquehanna, 1700–1800* (Ithaca, NY, 1991), pp. 27–70; Patrick Frazier, *The Mohicans of Stockbridge* (Lincoln, Nebr., 1992).

[37] Evan Haefeli and Kevin Sweeney, 'Revisiting *The Redeemed Captive*: New Perspectives on the 1704 Attack on Deerfield', *William and Mary Quarterly* (hereafter *WMQ*), Third Series, LII (1995), pp. 3–46.

'Settlement Indians' of South Carolina—gradually lost their lands entirely or clung to small holdings interspersed with those of Euro-Americans. Still others melted into a larger ethnically mixed population of servants and day labourers. Thus, even these Indians carved out a precarious place in the eighteenth-century imperial world.[38]

Already in the late 1730s and 1740s, however, the delicate economic, diplomatic, and political balances of that world were tottering. In every British province the fur and hide trades declined in relative significance, and the demand for agricultural land increased. Immigrants poured into Indian country under only the loosest of supervision by overwhelmed provincial governments. In the southeast the situation was compounded by the establishment of the new colony of Georgia in 1733, which disrupted the equipoise of Carolinian, Spanish, French, Creek, and Choctaw forces. Creeks took to calling Georgians *Ecunnaunuxulgee*, or 'People greedily grasping after the lands of the red people'.[39]

But 'the Modern Indian Politics' faced its most severe challenges in the Ohio Country. New France, finding its geographic pretensions to the region threatened and its Indian trade engrossed by Pennsylvania and Virginia traders, aggressively asserted its claims to the region. In 1749 an expedition commanded by Pierre-Joseph Céloron de Blainville planted lead plates bearing the fleur-de-lis at strategic spots. A string of military posts followed, culminating in Fort Duquesne, erected at modern Pittsburgh in 1754. The disastrously unsuccessful efforts to turn back the French tide by Virginia militia under George Washington in 1754 and by British regulars under Edward Braddock in 1755 were, of course, the first campaigns in the global conflict known in Europe as the Seven Years War and in British America as the French and Indian War.[40]

Long before Braddock had pledged that 'No Savage Should Inherit the Land' and paid for his arrogance with his death, there was little doubt which side Ohio Country Indians would choose.[41] Fortified by French arms from Fort Duquesne,

---

[38] Laura E. Conkey, Ethel Boissevain, and Ives Goddard, 'Indians of Southern New England and Long Island: Late Period', in William C. Sturtevant, gen. ed., *Handbook of North American Indians*, Vol. XV: *Northeast*, ed. Bruce G. Trigger (Washington, 1978), pp. 177–85; Christian F. Feest, 'Virginia Algonquians', ibid., pp. 262–63; Daniel Vickers, 'The First Whalemen of Nantucket', WMQ, Third Series, XL (1983), pp. 560–83; James H. Merrell, 'Cultural Continuity among the Piscataway Indians of Colonial Maryland', ibid., XXXVI (1979), pp. 548–70.

[39] Albright G. Zimmerman, 'The Indian Trade of Colonial Pennsylvania', unpublished Ph. D. dissertation, Delaware, 1966, pp. 463–64; Thomas Elliot Norton, *The Fur Trade in Colonial New York, 1686–1776* (Madison, 1974), pp. 148–50, 221; Michael D. Green, *The Politics of Indian Removal: Creek Government and Society in Crisis* (Lincoln, Nebr., 1982), pp. 17–29 (quotation from p. 26).

[40] W. J. Eccles, *The Canadian Frontier, 1534–1760* (1969; rev. edn., Albuquerque, N. Mex., 1983), pp. 157–85.

[41] Quoted in McConnell, *A Country Between*, p. 119.

Shawnees and Delawares struck back at the Virginians and, especially, the Pennsylvanians, who had forced them out of homes farther east; backcountry cabins burned all along British frontiers. The Anglo-American conquest of Fort Frontenac on Lake Ontario in August 1758, however, cut French supply lines and with them the Ohio Country Indians' ability to make war. In October, at the Treaty of Easton, Pennsylvania yielded its claims to lands west of the Appalachian Mountains to the Iroquois, who in turn pledged through the Covenant Chain to bring the Indian inhabitants of those lands to peace. Ohio Country Delawares accepted the terms of the Easton treaty shortly before French troops abandoned Fort Duquesne to the approaching British forces of John Forbes. These developments were crucial to the British victory over the French that culminated in the fall of Quebec in 1759 and of Montreal in 1760.[42]

Meanwhile, Carolina and Virginia officials had begun the Seven Years War courting Creek and Cherokee allies in an environment where both backcountry whites and anti-English Indian factions were spoiling for a fight. Despite internal quarrels, the Creeks as a whole maintained their neutrality. Some Cherokees, meanwhile, briefly enlisted on Virginia's behalf, but the alliance collapsed amidst mutual accusations of betrayal. In 1759 and 1760 Cherokees won major victories over English forces in Indian country as well as on the Virginia and Carolina frontiers. By 1761, however, British conquests in the north had freed troops to invade Cherokee country and burn some fifteen towns. In December that nation's leaders came to terms.[43] The enormity of the general British triumph over the French and their Indian allies left the Cherokees little choice. When the Peace of Paris of 1763 confirmed the transfer of all Spanish and French claims east of the Mississippi to Britain, the imperial rivalries that, for two generations, had made 'the Modern Indian Politics' possible ceased to exist. Thus the second of the three stories of British–Indian relations came to an abrupt halt.

A Transformed Alliance, 1763–1815

The third narrative briefly threatened to reprise the violent first. In the early 1760s Britain's victory temporarily removed any incentive to acknowledge Native American interests or to observe long-standing rituals of collective diplomacy. 'Our superiority in this war rendered our regard to this people still less, which had always been too little', a contemporary commentator rued. 'Decorums, which are

---

[42] Francis Jennings, *Empire of Fortune: Crowns, Colonies and Tribes in the Seven Years War in America* (New York, 1988), pp. 396–404.

[43] David Corkran, *The Cherokee Frontier: Conflict and Survival, 1740–1762* (Norman, Okla., 1966), pp. 142–272.

as necessary at least in dealing with barbarous as with civilised nations, were neglected.'[44]

Throughout Indian country tempers flared as the British Commander-in-Chief, Jeffrey Amherst, sought to confine inter-cultural trade to army posts, to ban the sale of weapons and ammunition entirely, and to halt the expensive custom of diplomatic gift-giving. In this context, the Delaware religious figure Neolin found receptive audiences in the Ohio Country and the *pays d'en haut* for a nativist message of cultural self-reliance symbolized by a ritual renunciation of European goods. One of Neolin's many disciples was the Ottawa leader Pontiac, who envisioned the expulsion of the British from the Great Lakes region and (along with much of the region's Franco-American and *métis* population) hoped for the restoration of French hegemony. In May 1763 Pontiac initiated what became a six-month siege of the British garrison at Detroit. Almost simultan-eously, but apparently without central direction, other Indian forces attacked posts throughout the north-west; only Niagara, Pittsburgh, and, in the end, Detroit survived. The British regained superiority by late 1763, although fighting continued for two more years. Ironically, the very lack of European trade goods and weapons that Neolin advocated contributed to the Indians' defeat.[45]

After 'Pontiac's War', financial and practical considerations made British officials more conciliatory. The policy shift began with the Royal Proclamation of 1763 which, to the extent it established a boundary between Europeans and natives that followed the Appalachian Mountains, conformed to the principles of the Treaty of Easton and to long-standing aims of Native American leaders. In almost no other way, however, did the Proclamation—to the extent Native Americans understood it—satisfy their demands. On the one hand, the royal government proved powerless to prevent squatters from traversing the line. On the other, whatever guarantees it offered were couched in language that assumed British, rather than Indian, ownership of 'the extensive and valuable acquisitions, in America secured to our Crown by the late definitive treaty of peace'. Indeed, the creation of the new colonies of East and West Florida and Quebec in those territories was the Proclamation's main item of business.[46]

The rethinking of Indian policy in the wake of Pontiac's War in July 1764 produced a short-lived Board of Trade plan to centralize administration in the hands of two regional Superintendents responsible directly to Whitehall and

[44] *The Annual Register, or a View of the History, Politics, and Literature. For the Year 1763,* 2nd edn. (London, 1765), p. 22.

[45] Gregory Evans Dowd, *A Spirited Resistance: The North American Indian Struggle for Unity, 1745–1815* (Baltimore, 1992), pp. 23–36.

[46] The text of the Proclamation is printed in *Annual Register For 1763,* pp. 208–13 (quotation from p. 208).

funded from a tax on furs. The Superintendencies themselves had been created in 1754; William Johnson of New York had held the Northern post since 1756 and John Stuart of South Carolina the Southern since 1762. During the Seven Years War the Superintendents were almost solely responsible for maintaining Britain's few Indian allies. None the less, their efforts were crippled by the patchwork of provincial laws that governed (or rather failed to govern) British–Indian trade, by the independent diplomacy of the provincial Governors, and by the military's control of the Superintendents' budget; thus Amherst had overridden Johnson's objections to the policies that provoked Pontiac's War. The 1764 plan to redress these weaknesses, however, fell victim to the combined pressures of Governors and merchants whose interests it threatened, the inability of Parliament to impose the necessary taxes, and, overwhelmingly, the crisis of Imperial authority in North American provinces that increasingly monopolized the ministry's attention.[47]

Still, by 1768 the Superintendents had gone far towards turning the Anglo-Indian boundary line unilaterally dictated by the Proclamation of 1763 into an agreement satisfactory to Indian leaders. Reviving the traditional 'decorums' of inter-cultural diplomacy, the protracted negotiation of the southern segment of the boundary line began with the 1763 Treaty of Augusta, attended by Stuart, the Governors of Georgia, South and North Carolina, and Virginia, and leaders of the Choctaws, Chickasaws, Catawbas, Creeks, and Cherokees. The most difficult portions of the line concerned the Cherokees, not only because of the recent war but also because of the intense interest of land speculators from Pennsylvania, Virginia, and the Carolinas in Kentucky and Ohio Country territories, where Anglo-American squatters were already building homes. Stuart and Cherokee leaders finally came to terms in the 1768 Treaty of Hard Labor, which ceded lands east of a line that terminated at the intersection of the Kanawha and Ohio Rivers. Significantly, however, the negotiations concluded without participation by Virginia, which claimed Kentucky lands well westward of the Hard Labor line.[48]

Johnson's almost simultaneous manœuvres in the north further muddled Kentucky's status. At the 1768 Treaty of Fort Stanwix (attended by delegations from New York, New Jersey, Pennsylvania, and Virginia) Johnson and the Iroquois leaders with whom he dealt invented an Iroquois claim not only to the Ohio Country but to all of Kentucky as well. In exchange for yielding paper title to these vast territories, the Iroquois received a border with New York and Pennsylvania

[47] Peter Marshall, 'Colonial Protest and Imperial Retrenchment: Indian Policy, 1764–1768', *Journal of American Studies*, V (1971), pp. 1–17; John R. Alden, 'The Albany Congress and the Creation of the Indian Superintendencies', *Mississippi Valley Historical Review*, XXVII (1940), pp. 193–210.

[48] John Richard Alden, *John Stuart and the Southern Colonial Frontier: A Study of Indian Relations, War, Trade, and Land Problems in the Southern Wilderness, 1754–1775* (New York, 1966), pp. 215–39, 262–81.

that protected nearly all of their traditional homelands. A few Ohio Country Delawares and Shawnees were present at Fort Stanwix but were not included in the formal treaty, which the Iroquois signed on their behalf. No representatives of the Cherokees—the most relevant party—were present.[49]

The stage was set, then, for a mad scramble among British interests for control of Kentucky and for a potential renewal of nativist resistance among disfranchised Cherokees and Ohio Country Indians. Matters came to a head in 1774, when agents of the Virginia Governor Lord Dunmore provoked a war between Virginians settled at Pittsburgh and the Shawnees in order to pre-empt the competing claims of Pennsylvanians and the promoters of a proposed new 'Vandalia' colony. At the Treaty of Camp Charlotte, a Shawnee faction was forced to acknowledge Virginia's ownership of Kentucky. The signatories, however, by no means spoke for all Shawnees—much less all Cherokees or Ohio Country Indians—and the death of Sir William Johnson in 1774 threatened to plunge the entire Northern Superintendency into disarray.[50]

Before the implications of these developments became clear, the declaration of United States independence fundamentally changed the diplomatic calculus by reintroducing the balance-of-power potential of 'the Modern Indian Politics'. Paradoxically, however, the British found themselves in the position formerly assumed by the French. At Montreal, in what was now the province of Quebec, the replacement of the French 'Father' by a British one had begun well before 1776. Scottish merchants used their transatlantic connections to drive Franco-American competitors from the market, but for the retail end of their commerce they relied on the same *voyageurs* as had their predecessors. In the garrisons of trading posts in the *pays d'en haut*, red coats merely replaced white, and necessity produced within the army a group of interpreters and agents increasingly skilled in the Native American diplomatic protocols that Amherst had so recently scorned.[51]

The United States, meanwhile, filled the place of the mid-century Indians' British 'Brethren'. As had been the case before Independence, the conflicting economic imperatives of agricultural expansion and peaceful trade rested uneasily with a diplomatic need to play the 'deed game' in a situation where the Congress wrestled with thirteen state governments, private economic interests, and ungovernable backcountry whites for control of relations with the Native American population. Within this strange-yet-familiar diplomatic framework, Indian

[49] Jones, *License for Empire*, pp. 36–119.

[50] Randolph C. Downes, *Council Fires on the Upper Ohio: A Narrative of Indian Affairs in the Upper Ohio Valley until 1795* (Pittsburgh, 1940), pp. 152–78.

[51] W. J. Eccles, *France in America* (New York, 1972), pp. 212–20; Jennifer S. H. Brown, *Strangers in Blood: Fur Trade Company Families in Indian Country* (Vancouver, 1980), pp. 1–50; Colin G. Calloway, *Crown and Calumet: British–Indian Relations, 1783–1815* (Norman, Okla., 1987), pp. 51–76.

leaders attempted to remain neutral, while various factions kept open lines of communication to British and 'Americans' alike. Militants sought to seize the opportunity to ally with the British and regain lost territories; others argued caution on the basis of a generalized distrust of Europeans, the folly of what might prove a self-destructive war, the imperative to keep trading connections intact, or the need to accommodate whomever the eventual victor might be.[52]

As the American War for Independence proceeded, almost no Native American groups managed perfect neutrality, but few unanimously joined the British and still fewer the United States. Along the St Lawrence, the former *sauvages domiciliés*—now called by the British 'the Seven Nations of Canada'—resumed their not-to-be-taken-for-granted role as military buffers. Little such caution was to be found in the Ohio Country, however, with its tradition of nativist pan-Indianism, its recent memories of Fort Stanwix and Dunmore's War, and its ceaseless onslaught of settlers from Virginia and Pennsylvania; anti-United States militants easily prevailed in most, but not all, villages. The frontier war that resulted (or rather continued with hardly a break from 1774 on) entailed ferocious atrocities on both sides and reached its peak in the early 1780s, after fighting between British and US forces had mostly ceased elsewhere.[53]

Meanwhile, the Iroquois were deeply divided between a faction led by the Mohawk Joseph Brant, who sought to fight for the British Crown as he had done in the Seven Years War, a group led by Oneida and Tuscarora Protestants allied to New England missionary Samuel Kirkland, and a majority who hoped to remain aloof from the conflict. The latter position became increasingly untenable, and by 1777 most Senecas and Cayugas had joined Brant's Mohawks as British allies; many Oneidas and Tuscaroras, by contrast, enlisted with the rebels. In 1779 United States armies conducted a scorched-earth campaign through the countries of the Senecas, Cayugas, and the hitherto neutral Onondagas, leaving thousands of refugees to spend the rest of the war encamped at British Niagara. In 1776, 1780, and 1781 similar US expeditions ravaged the Cherokee country, oblivious to that nation's internal controversies over the enlistment of warriors in the British cause. Creeks and Choctaws avoided the destruction suffered by Iroquois and Cherokees, but they too saw their neutrality erode under the twin pressures of United States arrogance and British incentives. Their situations were further complicated by the fact that warriors who enlisted with the British fought against the Spanish allies of the United States who would regain control of Florida at war's end.[54]

[52] White, *Middle Ground*, pp. 315–468.

[53] Calloway, *American Revolution in Indian Country*, pp. 26–46, 129–212; Dowd, *Spirited Resistance*, pp. 47–89.

[54] Barbara Graymont, *The Iroquois in the American Revolution* (Syracuse, NY, 1972), pp. 48–222; Calloway, *American Revolution in Indian Country*, pp. 46–64.

When Britain acknowledged the independence of the United States of America in the Peace of Paris of 1783, the Crown's negotiators ignored the network of Indian alliances built up since 1763. The treaty made no mention whatsoever of Indians and simply transferred to the United States ownership of all territory south of the Great Lakes, east of the Mississippi, and north of the Floridas. Britain's Native American allies reacted with disbelief, as they confronted a victorious republic eager to claim their lands by what it deemed a right of conquest. From the Cherokee country southward, the British abandonment was virtually complete, and only slightly tempered by the reintroduction of a counterbalance to United States power in Spanish Florida. As the Creek leader Alexander McGillivray understated, 'to find ourselves and Country betrayed to our Enemies and divided between the Spaniards and Americans is Cruel and Ungenerous'.[55]

Farther northward, the Treaty of Paris had less immediate impact, as raids and counter-raids scarred Kentucky and the Ohio Country without reference to European diplomacy. At the same time, the continued British military occupation of Detroit and other western posts in defiance of the Paris Treaty prolonged economic support for Indian militants. Moreover, from the Governor of Quebec, Sir Frederick Haldimand, down through the ranks of agents stationed in Indian country, British officers shared the sense of betrayal so prevalent among the Native Americans they had fought beside for nearly a decade, and they worked to mitigate the disaster. In 1784 the Governor granted Britain's refugee Iroquois allies a substantial tract of land on the Grand River in present-day Ontario; ultimately roughly half of the Iroquois population followed Brant to new homes there. From that base, Brant worked with Indian leaders from throughout the Ohio Country and *pays d'en haut* to create a Western Confederacy to carry on the struggle against the United States and defend an Ohio River border with the new republic.[56]

The Quebec government remained officially neutral as the Western Confederacy defeated US armies led by Josiah Harmar in 1790 and Arthur St Clair in 1791. Still, the British agents who participated in the Confederacy's councils and obstructed United States efforts to negotiate a settlement gave every impression that troops would support the Indians in a crisis. In August 1794 the western war reached its climax with General Anthony Wayne's methodical march toward the Confederacy's centres on the Maumee River. Yet when Indian forces who had failed to repulse the invaders at the battle of Fallen Timbers sought refuge at the British post on the Maumee, its commander, fearing he could not resist an attack

---

[55] Quoted in Calloway, *American Revolution in Indian Country*, p. 276.

[56] Calloway, *Crown and Calumet*, pp. 3–18; Isabel Thompson Kelsay, *Joseph Brant, 1743-1807: Man of Two Worlds* (Syracuse, NY, 1984), pp. 320–552.

by Wayne, closed the gates against them. Thus left, as the Delaware leader complained, 'in the lurch', the Confederacy's forces abandoned the field and turned Wayne's relatively minor victory into a major triumph.[57] Over the winter, as word arrived of Jay's Treaty requiring British withdrawal from the western posts, the various nations and factions of the Confederacy—like other abandoned British allies a decade earlier—coped with betrayal as best they could, having, in the words of British Indian agent Alexander McKee, 'lost all hopes of the interference of the government'.[58] The result in the summer of 1795 was the Treaty of Greenville, which yielded most of the present state of Ohio to the United States.

For nearly two decades after the Greenville Treaty the focus of British–Indian relations shifted away from its traditional diplomatic and geographic centres in eastern North America. At the turn of the nineteenth century cut-throat competition among agents of the Hudson Bay, North-West, and several smaller fur companies emphasized commercial expansion north and westward of the Great Lakes toward the Rocky Mountains. The War of 1812, however, briefly retrained British attention south of the Lakes. Facing massive US emigration beyond the long-defunct Greenville Treaty line, Indians throughout the region had been mobilized by a new wave of nativism preached by the Shawnee prophet Tenskwatawa and his brother Tecumseh, who emerged, like Pontiac before him, as the most visible leader of a decentralized political and military movement. Tecumseh of course welcomed British aid, but, well aware of previous betrayals, he directed most of his energies toward the peoples of his home region and toward alliances with like-minded leaders of the Cherokees and Creeks to the southward. In 1813 the ignominious performance of British troops at the Battle of the Thames, in which Tecumseh lost his life, drove home to his followers a now familiar lesson. At the Peace of Ghent in 1814 Britain's Indian allies again were left to make the best terms they could with the United States.[59]

Endings

By 1815, then, the third story of British–Indian relations in eastern North America had come to its bitter conclusion. Like the first two, it was shaped by prior experience, the nature of the Empire, and the culture of Indian politics. Historical precedent thrust the British uneasily into the French role of 'Father' in the

---

[57] Wiley Sword, *President Washington's Indian War: The Struggle for the Old Northwest, 1790–1795* (Norman, Okla., 1985), p. 306.

[58] Dowd, *Spirited Resistance*, p. 113.

[59] Olive Patricia Dickason, *Canada's First Nations: A History of Founding Peoples from Earliest Times* (Norman, Okla., 1992), pp. 184–224; R. David Edmunds, *Tecumseh and the Quest for Indian Leadership* (Boston, 1984).

continent's balance-of-power diplomacy. But in what remained largely an 'Empire of Goods', Indians south of the Great Lakes lost their economic importance as the fur trade shifted elsewhere. Only the diplomacy of the 'deed game' remained as a basis for relations between the British Father and those left behind—and then only during periods of open conflict with the United States. From the 1760s to the 1810s, therefore, Indians increasingly based their struggles for political autonomy less on balance-of-power diplomacy than on the indigenous resources of the religious nativism preached by Neolin and Pontiac, Tenskwatawa and Tecumseh. A tale is told—no less apt because it is apocryphal—that Tecumseh foresaw his own death on the eve of the battle and cast aside his customary British military red coat in favour of traditional Shawnee garb.[60] That story brings the three stories of eighteenth-century Imperial–Indian relations to an appropriate end.

[60] John Sugden, *Tecumseh's Last Stand* (Norman, Okla., 1985), p. 114.

Select Bibliography

JOHN RICHARD ALDEN, *John Stuart and the Southern Colonial Frontier: A Study of Indian Relations, War, Trade, and Land Problems in the Southern Wilderness, 1754–1775* (New York, 1966).

ROBERT S. ALLEN, *His Majesty's Indian Allies: British Indian Policy in the Defence of Canada, 1774–1815* (Toronto, 1992).

KATHRYN E. HOLLAND BRAUND, *Deerskins and Duffels: The Creek Indian Trade with Anglo-America, 1685–1815* (Lincoln, Nebr., 1993).

COLIN G. CALLOWAY, *The American Revolution in Indian Country: Crisis and Diversity in Native American Communities* (Cambridge, 1995).

—— *Crown and Calumet: British–Indian Relations, 1783–1815* (Norman, Okla., 1987).

DAVID CORKRAN, *The Cherokee Frontier: Conflict and Survival, 1740–1762* (Norman, Okla., 1966).

VERNER W. CRANE, *The Southern Frontier, 1670–1732* (1928; New York, 1981).

GREGORY EVANS DOWD, *A Spirited Resistance: The North American Indian Struggle for Unity, 1745–1815* (Baltimore, 1992).

RANDOLPH C. DOWNES, *Council Fires on the Upper Ohio: A Narrative of Indian Affairs in the Upper Ohio Valley until 1795* (Pittsburg, 1940).

WILBUR R. JACOBS, *Diplomacy and Indian Gifts: Anglo-French Rivalry along the Ohio and Northwest Frontiers, 1748–1763* (Stanford, Calif., 1950).

FRANCIS JENNINGS, *The Ambiguous Iroquois Empire: The Covenant Chain Confederation of Indian Tribes with English Colonies from Its Beginnings to the Lancaster Treaty of 1744* (New York, 1984).

—— and others, eds., *The History and Culture of Iroquois Diplomacy: An Interdisciplinary Guide to the Treaties of the Six Nations and their League* (Syracuse, NY, 1985).

DOROTHY V. JONES, *License for Empire: Colonialism by Treaty in Early America* (Chicago, 1982).

MICHAEL N. MCCONNELL, *A Country Between: The Upper Ohio Valley and Its Peoples, 1724–1774* (Lincoln, Nebr., 1992).

KENNETH M. MORRISON, *The Embattled Northeast: The Elusive Ideal of Alliance in Abenaki–Euramerican Relations* (Berkeley, 1984).

THOMAS ELLIOT NORTON, *The Fur Trade in Colonial New York, 1686–1776* (Madison, 1974).

IAN K. STEELE, *Warpaths: Invasions of North America* (New York, 1994).

WILEY SWORD, *President Washington's Indian War: The Struggle for the Old Northwest, 1790–1795* (Norman, Okla., 1985).

RICHARD WHITE, *The Middle Ground: Indians, Empires, and Republics in the Great Lakes Region, 1650–1815* (Cambridge, 1991).

17

British North America, 1760–1815

PETER MARSHALL

In the years between 1760 and 1815 a disparate group of Imperial territories, ultimately to be known as British North America, was acquired by conquest, established through settlement, or exploited for its supplies of fish and furs. For most of this period, the parts were united by no more than their exclusion, or escape, from incorporation into the United States. Distance magnified the contrasting origins of small communities located in widely scattered areas. British victory in the Seven Years War had turned New France into the British Province of Quebec, confirmed the value of the Newfoundland fishery and the Hudson's Bay Company, and opened up prospects of growth for the struggling colony of Nova Scotia. Despite this, any substantial development in the region would long be delayed. The changes that occurred during this half-century, brought about as much by external as by internal influences, would confirm a continued British presence in North America but leave its form in large part undefined.

The territory ceded by France at the Peace of Paris in 1763 extended through barely known tracts of North America. How Imperial control would be established over the settlements stretching along the St Lawrence, the one conquest of sufficient magnitude to require immediate recognition as a colony, presented a daunting problem. No precedent existed for the effective Imperial absorption of a non-British population; there was no possibility that some 70,000 *Canadiens*,[1] whose French law, institutions, and language, together with their Roman Catholicism, rendered them ineligible to enjoy British civil and religious liberty, could be transformed into loyal subjects of the Crown. The problem of Quebec, so quick to emerge, would refuse to depart. Its magnitude was sufficient to dwarf the difficulties posed by the other colonies.

Of these, only Nova Scotia initially qualified for acceptance as a conventional colony, though it hardly provided a striking example. With a population estimated in 1763 at between 8,000 and 9,000 and an economy dependent far more on the stimulus of war than on civil development, Nova Scotia had constituted no more than a minor appendage to the New England colonies from which many of its

---

[1] Francophone colonists. 'English' describes Anglophones, regardless of origin or ancestry.

inhabitants had migrated. After 1763, the government of two adjacent ex-French territories, Île Royale—henceforth Cape Breton—and Île St Jean—to become Prince Edward Island in 1798—would require attention, though their attractions, apart from those offered to some 2,000 French Acadians who had evaded expulsion from Nova Scotia in 1755, were not immediately evident. To the east, Newfoundland presented yet another problem, that of a territory whose colonial existence had constantly been denied, despite the interest of Imperial authorities in it since the earliest days of overseas expansion. By 1760 Newfoundland's unacknowledged permanent population had reached about 8,000. The fiction was still faintly maintained that the island enjoyed only a transitory, summer occupancy by European fishermen, who went home at the end of each fishing season. As long as this was held to be the case, colonial institutions could be

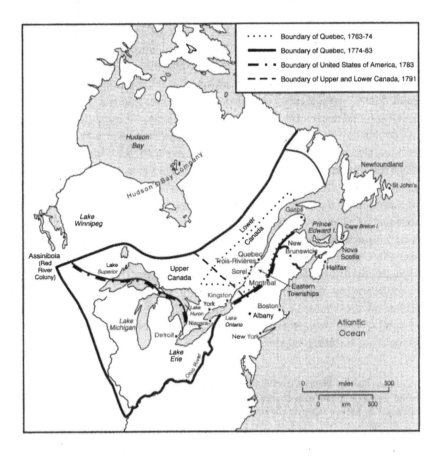

Map 17.1. British North America, 1760–1815

deemed unnecessary and a naval officer left in command. The island was to be considered a warship.

As fish distinguished Newfoundland, so did furs the West. There the Hudson's Bay Company, founded almost a century before in 1669, had established networks of trade without settlement. Its commercial posts west of the Great Lakes were devoted solely to economic activities. There was no clearer proof of the limited extent of the economy of British North America than that its only sought-after staples, the fish of Newfoundland and the furs of the West, required an absence, not a presence, of settlers.[2]

Change would not come quickly. The population of all the territories amounted in 1763 to under 100,000 Old (British) and New (French) subjects. The latter formed a large majority, if we exclude some 200,000 Indians and Inuits spread over the whole area of present-day Canada.[3] Even if additional wealth could be extracted from these remote regions, who would undertake the task?

The acquisition of New France was not a major objective of Imperial ambition at the end of the Seven Years War. Canada was retained to give security to the American colonies on whose behalf the war had been begun, and possibly to ensure British domination of the rich fishing in the St Lawrence Estuary and on the Grand Banks, considered to provide crucial training grounds for seamen. But limited as its value may have been, the return of Quebec in exchange for retaining the rich French West Indian island of Guadeloupe was never politically feasible. Yet 'it was with but grudging and indifferent recognition that Canada was received within the Imperial circle...'. There were no direct commercial benefits to be anticipated, only protection for other, established North American interests. With the exception of the Elder Pitt, ignorance, not Imperial purpose, directed the behaviour of all those involved. Whatever compelled the retention of Canada, 'there is no evidence that any serious thought was given to the general effect of its acquisition either on France or on the American colonies.'[4]

This failure to consider the implications of the treaty, especially in relation to the entire process of establishing a government for the new colony, would soon become all too evident, despite the endeavours of politicians to ignore the problem. Quebec represented more than a new colonial acquisition: it brought into being an enduring Imperial dilemma.

[2] Fernand Ouellet, *Histoire économique et sociale du Québec 1760–1850* (Montréal, 1971). Hilda Neatby, *Quebec: The Revolutionary Age, 1760–1791* (Toronto, 1966); Philip A. Buckner and John G. Reid, eds., *The Atlantic Region to Confederation: A History* (Toronto, 1994); Harold A. Innis, *The Fur Trade in Canada*, rev. edn. (Toronto, 1956).
[3] R. Cole Harris, ed., *Historical Atlas of Canada*, I (Toronto, 1987), Plate 69, Conrad E. Heidenreich.
[4] Ronald Hyam, 'Imperial Interests and the Peace of Paris (1763)', in Ronald Hyam and Ged Martin, *Reappraisals in British Imperial History* (London, 1975), pp. 30, 31, 39.

The peace of February 1763 conveyed to Britain the New World territories of Quebec, the Floridas, and Grenada, four colonies of sufficient size or significance to require their own governments, but without the British inhabitants hitherto thought necessary to sustain an Assembly. What form the new governments would take was therefore unclear. It was, however, a question that could not be indefinitely avoided. The Proclamation of 7 October 1763, the first attempt to confront the issue, provided no more than a temporary administrative response. Unfortunately, it also ventured into basic policy. It stated that George III had:

given express Power and Direction to our Governors of our Said Colonies respectively, that so soon as the state and circumstances of the said Colonies will admit thereof, they shall, with the Advice and Consent of the Members of our Council, summon and call General Assemblies... in such Manner and Form as is used and directed in those Colonies and Provinces in America, which are under our immediate Government...

It was assumed that British immigration would rapidly turn the *Canadiens* into a minority and obliterate their institutions. Their government should therefore be conducted 'as near as may be agreeable to the Laws of England'. Until these arrangements had been made, Governors, with the advice of a Council, would establish courts to try civil and criminal cases, drawing upon English laws. There was no recognition that the government of Quebec would deviate in any fundamental respect from that of other colonies and no indication as to how a convergence would be contrived, if British immigration did not materialize. The assertion in 1766 by the Lord Chancellor, Lord Northington, that 'a very silly proclamation it was' may not have been a considered judgement, but there is little evidence that the Proclamation was shaped by an understanding of the problems it was designed to address.[5]

Only the Lord Chief Justice, Lord Mansfield, was roused to alarm by a report that English law prevailed in Quebec, and then not until December 1764, when he asked: 'Is it possible that we have abolished their laws, and customs, and forms of judicature all at once?—a thing never to be attempted or wished....'[6] If this was undoubtedly wisdom, it was wisdom after the event. For all practical purposes, Quebec in the years leading up to the American Revolution remained a French society under British military occupation. No Assembly was instituted. How this

---

[5] Adam Shortt and Arthur G. Doughty, eds., *Documents Relating to the Constitutional History of Canada, 1759–1791*, 2nd edn., 2 vols. (Ottawa, 1918), I, pp. 163–68; R. A. Humphreys, 'Lord Shelburne and the Proclamation of 1763', *English Historical Review*, XLIX (1934), p. 254. On the background of the Proclamation, see Peter Marshall, 'The Incorporation of Quebec in the British Empire, 1763–1774', in Virginia Bever Platt and David Curtis Skaggs, eds., *Of Mother Country and Plantations* (Bowling Green, Oh., 1971), pp. 43–48.

[6] Mansfield to Grenville, 24 Dec. 1764, in W. J. Smith, ed., *The Grenville Papers*, 4 vols. (London, 1852), II, pp. 476–77.

situation could be reconciled with the theory of an Imperial constitution, based on the rights of Englishmen and representative government, was a question left unanswered.

The northern colonies as a whole after 1763 supplied problems, not profits. Prospects of rapid and spectacular gains from opportunities presented by an unchallenged Imperial hegemony all too rapidly disappeared. As far as the two established colonies, Quebec and Nova Scotia, were concerned, any financial well-being depended, in the absence of other sustaining revenues, upon public expenditures. In consequence, the significance of the military presence, which in the decade after 1763 accounted for over half the garrison in North America, was less political than commercial. If Canadian merchants in 1765 urged as strong a force as possible, their motive was finance, not security.[7]

The expansion of the Empire in northern America failed to pay its way after 1763, not least for lack of constitutional and legal instruments to collect revenue. The end of the war had more than halved Imperial expenditure in Nova Scotia, a decline matched after 1761 by a steady growth in provincial debt. Nova Scotia at least had an Assembly, but this provided a stage on which conflicts about revenue could be played out rather than a means for raising funds to redress imbalances. Lacking an Assembly, the government of Quebec proceeded without agreement as to the legitimacy and ways of collecting a provincial revenue. Similarly, in Newfoundland the Collector of Customs in 1766 found himself without power to impose fees or punish refusals.[8]

If the securing of a public revenue proved elusive, profits from acquisitions of land in Nova Scotia and the Island of St John were seen to offer dramatic opportunities for personal enrichment. Encouraged by the promise in the Proclamation of 1763 of land grants to officers and men who had served in North America, speculators rushed in 1764 to lay claim to estates of up to 20,000 acres. Greed completely outstripped capacity to benefit. Nova Scotia grants, which amounted to over 3,500,000 acres before the boom subsided in 1768, were in great part forfeited in the next decade for failure to comply with the terms of their award. The more than doubling of the colony's population by 1775 to between 17,000 and 18,000 would not seem to have been a consequence of the securing of grants. Genuine growth in immigration could be attributed to a source which

---

[7] Fernand Ouellet, 'The British Army of Occupation in the St Lawrence Valley, 1760–1774 . . .', in Roy A. Prete and A. Hamish Ion, eds., *Armies of Occupation* (Waterloo, Ontario, 1984), p. 48.

[8] Julian Gwyn, 'Economic Fluctuations in Wartime Nova Scotia, 1755–1815', Margaret Conrad, ed., *Making Adjustments: Change and Continuity in Planter Nova Scotia, 1759–1800* (Fredericton, 1991), p. 74; John Bartlet Brebner, *The Neutral Yankees of Nova Scotia* (1937; Toronto, 1969), pp. 130, 191–93; Neatby, *Quebec*, pp. 94–97; K. Matthews, 'A History of the West of England–Newfoundland Fishery', unpublished D.Phil. thesis, Oxford, 1968, pp. 441–53.

owed nothing to dreams of lordships—the migration, particularly from the North Riding of Yorkshire that, beginning in 1772, brought over a thousand rural dwellers to new, but not totally strange surroundings.[9] Although the settlement of the Isle of St John assumed a much more organized aspect under the leadership of the Earl of Egmont, who had an ambitious scheme for settling the whole island in a form of military tenure, this distribution of its territory created a group of absentee landowners. After separation from Nova Scotia and the establishment of a government in 1769, the proprietors were a focus for grievances, even if the settlers' difficulties probably had other causes. A population which by 1775 had only reached about 1,500 was, at best, growing gradually. Expectations had far exceeded achievement, a divergence all too familiar in the early history of new settlements.[10]

The difficulties in developing the Atlantic colonies were, however, overshadowed by the problems of Quebec. The province offered little material advantage beyond the fur trade, while there was no evident solution to the difficulties of incorporating a French Catholic population within the body politic. That the English-speaking Protestant community, composed of a handful of merchants, former military men, and those engaged in supplying the army, remained numerically insignificant may not have silenced their demands for the introduction of English civil and religious liberties, but made them of doubtful relevance. Any transformation of the colony into a society whose political and legal institutions could be regarded as British remained out of the question.

British governments did nothing to implement the pledges of the Proclamation of 1763. In 1764–65 George Grenville had other colonial problems to absorb his attention. Though the Rockingham ministry that succeeded Grenville found time to consider more reports about Quebec during the winter of 1765–66, the difficulty of determining what could be preserved of French institutions and how the necessary changes were to be introduced gave rise to Cabinet disputes. These contributed to the fall of the ministry in July 1766, before anything could be achieved. To make matters worse, Quebec remained without new sources of revenue. The situation did not improve under the Chatham administration that followed, though the Secretary of State, Lord Shelburne, invoked an habitual tactic, a demand for further detail. A report was received in January 1770, after Shelburne had left office, from the Governor, Guy Carleton, but even then the questions of the coexistence of French and English law and the provision of an Assembly remained unresolved. All that seemed certain to Carleton was that 'the Province is in no degree ripe for that Form of Government which generally

---

[9] Brebner, *Neutral Yankees*, p. 79. Bernard Bailyn, *Voyagers to the West: A Passage in the Peopling of America on the Eve of the Revolution* (New York, 1986), pp. 361–429.

[10] J. M. Bumsted, *Land, Settlement and Politics on Eighteenth-Century Prince Edward Island* (Kingston and Montreal, 1987), pp. 13–64.

prevails throughout Your Majesty's other Colonies upon the Continent'.[11] But what other form was to be prescribed?

Carleton returned home on leave in 1771, determined to bring an end to the seemingly interminable deferring of a constitution. Delay continued, however, for another three years. When the Quebec Bill was enacted in July 1774, the parliamentary Opposition denounced its basic elements—that French civil law and English criminal law should be recognized, that Governor and Council should not be accompanied by an Assembly, and that the inhabitants should 'enjoy the free exercise of the Religion of the Church of Rome'—as a triumph of Catholic absolutism over Protestant liberty and of French tyranny over English rights. There were popular demonstrations against the Bill in London. This uproar served the purpose of domestic politics and did not derive from events in Quebec. It was also the case that the outlines of the Act had long been determined. 'On all the important issues', it has been concluded from an account of a Cabinet meeting in June 1771, 'the groundwork for clauses in the future Quebec Act had already been done.'[12] It is the timing, not the content of the legislation that calls for explanation.

The distractions provided by events in the colonies to the south since 1765 had offered convincing excuses for inaction by administrations only too anxious to avoid entanglement in the snares of Quebec. The legislative consequences of the Boston Tea Party in 1773 provided a particular diversion of political energy as the passage of the Coercive Acts consumed parliamentary time after March 1774. When the Acts were passed, the session might have been brought to a close—'it was sometimes thought sharp practice to propose anything serious after the Easter recess'[13]—but the Quebec Bill was, unusually, introduced in the Lords at the beginning of May. This suggests an urgency in complete contrast to the delays that had inhibited previous progress. What had brought about the change?

Popular reaction, a product of London radicalism copied throughout the American colonies, portrayed the Bill as part of the Coercive Acts to punish America. The new Quebec, under authoritarian rule and with its French population conciliated to support the British Crown, would act as the jailer of New England. There is no reason to take this charge seriously, even in the absence of personal and political sources that bear on the making of the Act. What must be taken into account, however, is that the constitutional and legal uncertainty, left unresolved since 1763, was by 1774 being rendered unsustainable by two legal judgements. Canadian historians have paid some attention to Lord Mansfield's judgement in *Campbell* v. *Hall*, a case that originated in Grenada, where a French

[11] Marshall, 'Incorporation of Quebec,' pp. 50–59.

[12] Philip Lawson, *The Imperial Challenge: Quebec and Britain in the Age of the American Revolution* (Kingston and Montreal, 1989), p. 115.

[13] Richard Pares, *King George III and the Politicians* (Oxford, 1953), p. 10 n.

population had also passed in 1763 under British rule, and therefore where an exact applicability to the affairs of Quebec was evident. The Lord Chief Justice determined, in a case that turned on the right of an official to collect duty from a planter, that the King, on the acquisition of a territory, possessed full power to introduce whatever form of government he might prefer, but that any further changes required acts either by the British Parliament or by a colonial Assembly. The government of Quebec had not put into effect the terms of the initial royal Proclamation and a decade of illegality was in consequence open to investigation. Parliament must therefore act urgently to legalize the government of Quebec. This decision in a case that had reached Mansfield prior to the passage of the Quebec Act but on which he had postponed judgement, was not, however, the only danger.

In the previous year the case of *Fabrigas* v. *Mostyn* had seen substantial damages awarded against John Mostyn, the Governor of Minorca, for his illegal expulsion of a local merchant. Mostyn was not an obscure denizen of a distant island: a cousin of Lord Rockingham, he had left Parliament to secure the Governorship, and this suit had attracted considerable attention during the summer of 1773. The Treasury had paid Mostyn's costs, but could not be expected to do so in respect of Quebec, where an abundance of litigious colonials would be all too ready to begin cases. The Governor of Quebec's powers had to be afforded a legal basis by Parliament as soon as possible. These two suits, both attracting widespread attention well before any legislation had been introduced, meant that the organization of government in Quebec was not just a necessity for the colony: it involved nothing less than the survival of the ministry of Lord North. North did not make haste unless it was essential. In this case he must have been informed, almost certainly by Mansfield, that further delay could not be risked.

The need for rapid action may have forced the ministry to reach a decision that in other circumstances would have been still further evaded, but it did not bring an end to the debate, whether in Quebec or in the British Protestant world. The Act extended the province's boundaries west to the Ohio and the Mississippi. This may well have been the best solution available to the problem of western control that had remained unresolved since 1763, but to Americans and to British radicals sympathetic to them, it seemed rather the recourse of a tyrannical ministry to methods that would contain colonial expansion. This objective once discerned, the other details of the Act fell into place: an eastward extension of Quebec to include Labrador and the islands of the St Lawrence; acceptance of the Catholic church and of French civil law; continued denial of an Assembly but appointment of a Council which would include some *Canadiens*, Catholics who would, predictably, refuse to introduce habeas corpus and rejoice at the deprivation of trial by jury for Englishmen. These were all seen as measures to fashion a political instrument designed to put an end to English liberties in the New World. The

North administration's actual intentions, altogether more immediate and prag-matic, were of no account: the opposition, on both sides of the Atlantic, saw clearly the creation of a grand conspiracy to destroy the people's rights—without, it might be added, greatly enlarging those of the *Canadiens*. Many, less disposed to question this aspect of policy, still viewed the lifting of restrictions on Catholics with serious alarm. First, Catholics had been allowed in 1765 to vote and sit in the Assembly in Grenada, the only colony at all comparable with Quebec. Now a more challenging example was offered. When would Ireland follow suit?

In 1775 the Continental Congress, despite the colonists' mistrust of their tradi-tional French enemy, urged the *Canadiens* to join the American cause. It was, however, more realistic to expect support from Nova Scotia, most of whose recent immigrants had arrived from New England, than from a population that had for a century been regarded as the deadly enemy of English America. Friendship was now on offer, but needed to be implemented by the expulsion of the Imperial garrison. Invasion in the autumn of 1775 brought an American occupation of Montreal, and at the close of the year a desperate attack on the city of Quebec saw the death in action of Richard Montgomery, the Irish-born commander of the main force; it was also marked by Benedict Arnold's leading of nearly 1,000 men through 300 miles of virgin, unmapped, northern New England forest, a feat that secured for him an admiration that would be obliterated by his subsequent treachery. More significant than Carleton's holding of Quebec City was the means by which this was achieved—those of the small English-speaking minority that had welcomed the incursion of their fellow colonists had not, as was essential for success, been joined by any significant number of *Canadiens*. Some historians have argued, not very convincingly, that the provisions of the Quebec Act sus-tained the *habitants'* loyalty. It would seem far more likely that the clergy and the Seigneurs, without feeling particularly well-disposed towards the Imperial cause, had even less to expect and more to fear from entry into the new American nation. The first constitution of the United States, the Articles of Confederation, provided for the inclusion of Canada, but the opportunity was never taken up.[14]

That is not to say that the American Revolution made no impression. The necessary deployment of troops in Quebec and the use of Halifax as the reception point of ships and supplies ensured that local economies received a powerful, if not a transforming, stimulus. In Quebec the need for military rations and mater-ials, particularly to maintain Indian relations, meant that the previous dependence on fur exports as the major source of external credit would diminish. A growth in commerce did not placate mercantile opposition: whatever the profits of war,

---

[14] Murray G. Lawson, 'Canada and the Articles of Confederation', *American Historical Review*, LVIII (1952), pp. 39–54.

political hostility to Governor Carleton and to Frederick Haldimand, his successor from 1778 to 1785, constantly erupted. But with the withdrawal of the Americans in the summer of 1776, and General John Burgoyne's ill-fated attempt to effect a division of the rebel colonies, which ended at Saratoga in October 1777, British North America became an essential line of supply rather than a battleground. This brought about an increase of Imperial expenditure in Nova Scotia of 250 per cent over the average for the previous decade. Newfoundland experienced mixed economic fortunes, moving on from a condition in which it could be reported in 1772, as having 'almost become a colony', through the passage in 1775 of an Act, designed—unsuccessfully—to keep fishermen from settlement, into periods of hardship engendered by the disruption of trade with New England and the West Indies. Despite fears of rebellion by the Newfoundland Irish, the New England Nova Scotians, or the *Canadiens* of Quebec, all three colonies appeared to have escaped the ruined venture of the British Empire in North America with remarkably slight damage. The impact of the conflict upon them would only become fully apparent after 1783.[15]

The terms of the Peace of Paris in 1783 contributed much more to the growth of British North America than did the conquest that had been so celebrated twenty years earlier. While 1763 had proved to be an almost literally empty victory, defeat in 1783 generated an influx of settlers on a scale that had long been unavailingly sought, even if the newcomers now came as refugees. Relations between an established population and the new arrivals, both in Quebec and Nova Scotia, proved far from amicable and led to increased tensions between Imperial authority and colonial society. American independence did, nevertheless, provide the stimulus for a belated commitment to developing the remaining colonies. The origins and motives of this new wave of settlement were without British precedent, endowing future generations with a distinctive history.

The end of British rule in the thirteen colonies was accompanied by the departure of a wide range of inhabitants, of whom Loyalists in the strict sense composed but one element. Peace and independence initiated a migration of sufficient magnitude, complexity, and extent to make its numbers hard to estimate. Should a distinction be drawn between a Loyalist and a disbanded soldier? Were blacks and Indians to be included? How late an arrival could a late Loyalist be? What of the many who, either immediately or after some years, would decide that it was preferable to return to the world they had lost than to remain in this new one? Historians have been unable to agree a total: their counts vary between 60,000 and 100,000, of which the most substantial segment threatened after 1782 to

---

[15] On Newfoundland during the war, see C. Grant Head, *Eighteenth Century Newfoundland: A Geographer's Perspective* (Toronto, 1976), pp. 196–202. Matthews, 'Newfoundland Fishery', pp. 455–93.

outnumber the existing population of peninsular Nova Scotia. The arrival of some 15,000 exiles on the St John River brought the establishment of a major settlement and the creation in 1784 of the province of New Brunswick. Some 40,000 came to the Maritimes, mostly from New York, though that city had been for many but a temporary refuge. Into what had previously formed an extension of New England was now introduced an altogether more mixed population of ex-slaves, ex-slave-holders, ex-soldiers, former holders of civil and religious colonial offices, 90 per cent of them American born and mostly of modest social standing. Given the need to establish an existence in virgin territories of limited natural wealth, these characteristics helped rather than harmed their prospects in 'this unfriendly soil'.[16]

Elsewhere, although numbers and talents may have been less, the Loyalist impact was still notable. The Island of St John received a mere 550, including disbanded soldiers, but this provided a sizeable increase to a population said to amount, after twenty years, to no more than 500 families. Although the significance of those who settled in Quebec proved much greater, that did not result from mere numbers: less than 7,000 are estimated to have made their way into the Province, some 500 on the Bay of Chaleurs or Gaspé, a few to Sorel, and the bulk further west. This was not an accidental distribution: Governor Haldimand, at first averse to receiving any Loyalists, refused to permit them to settle among the *Canadiens*, and would not agree to their being placed on lands in what would become the Eastern Townships. His eventual decision to direct them westward was not reached with any enthusiasm. This reluctance seems to have sprung from an inability to be persuaded that American Loyalists could be trusted: not until he was divested of that belief in the course of 1783–84 did he promote their settlement of the future Upper Canada. Some 6,000 were subsequently to be found there, though again uncertainty was present: loyalty vied with land as a motive, and it was always difficult to judge which factor prevailed, the more so with the appearance of 'late loyalists', whose political grounds for migration seemed dubious. The coming of peace had served to enlarge, rather than to reduce, the problems of Imperial rule.[17]

After 1783 there is still little to indicate that the preservation of any part of the Empire in North America seemed inherently important to the London administration. Despite this, hostility with the United States persisted. The War of 1812 can

---

[16] On Nova Scotia Loyalism, see Neil MacKinnon, *This Unfriendly Soil: The Loyalist Experience in Nova Scotia, 1783–1791* (Kingston and Montreal, 1986); James W. St. G. Walker, *The Black Loyalists: The Search for a Promised Land in Nova Scotia and Sierra Leone, 1783–1870* (New York, 1976), pp. 1–93. On New Brunswick Loyalism, see W. S. MacNutt, *New Brunswick: A History: 1784–1867* (Toronto, 1963); Ann Gorman Condon, *The Loyalist Dream for New Brunswick* (Fredericton, 1984).

[17] Changes in Quebec are considered by Graham Richard Swan, 'The Economy and Politics in Quebec, 1774–1791', unpublished D.Phil. thesis, Oxford, 1975.

be seen as the last of the eighteenth-century colonial wars, but one in which former enemies, the British and the *Canadiens*, were now allied in opposition to the inheritors of the former British sphere to the south. The comparative strength of the combatants had not changed and thus, as the weaker side, British North America, like New France in the past, had to rely on whatever assistance it could secure. Accordingly, Indians had not lost their Imperial value. Many Indians had sided with Britain during the war and looked for British protection afterwards.[18] The family of Sir William Johnson of New York, Indian Superintendent until his death in 1774, had remained loyal; so too, more significantly, had many of his officials and Iroquois. With British refusal to surrender the Great Lakes posts yielded in the peace treaty until the Americans had settled their pre-war debts, the Indian Department retained its importance. The United States may have had no coherent and sustained design of acquiring British North America in this period, at the most adopting a position of 'defensive expansionism',[19] but many British North Americans still believed that the ultimate aim was incorporation.

Imperial officials could not have relished a North American posting: military men had to live with a crushing inequality of numbers. It was difficult to determine whether Imperial authority had more to fear from *Canadien* unpredictability or from Loyalist politics. Parliament's 1778 disavowal of its power to tax for revenue in the New World had given rise to financial stasis in Quebec and to constant drama in the Maritimes. This was a part of the Empire in which neither reputations nor fortunes were being made. Prospects of success remained as shrouded as the Newfoundland Banks.

British politicians continued to be as reluctant to legislate for the problems of Quebec in the 1780s as they had been in the first decade of Imperial rule. Pressure for constitutional reform from the Province could be contained: the English-speaking minority might still demand, without much conviction, the introduction of an Assembly, trial by jury, and English commercial law, but numbers and strength told against them; the *Canadiens* kept a closer eye on British intentions than on producing new political proposals of their own, though support for an Assembly was growing on their part.

The Imperial presence became altogether more imposing with the arrival in October 1786 of Guy Carleton, now created Lord Dorchester, once again Governor of Quebec, but also endowed with other titles—Governor of Nova Scotia, of New Brunswick, and Commander-in-Chief in all three provinces and in Newfoundland. He was not made Governor-General, though some moves towards that status seemed likely. With him, as Chief Justice, came William Smith, a figure

---

[18] See above, p. 366–68.

[19] Reginald C. Stuart, *United States Expansionism and British North America, 1775–1871* (Chapel Hill, NC, 1988), pp. 1–76.

prominent in American affairs since his days as a Whig, then Loyalist, in colonial New York, now resuming legal life in the New World. Such reinforcement of the government could not, however, resolve British North America's underlying problems, which remained as much financial as administrative. The Quebec Act had excluded revenue matters and no Assembly existed to fill a deficit greatly increased by financial activities such as those of John Cochrane, son of the Earl of Dundonald, who under the financially oblivious Haldimand had in six months of 1781 drawn bills of credit for £843,000. The extant revenues of the Province did not, and could not, meet its expected costs, let alone these misfortunes. By 1790 it was calculated that the price of retaining Quebec, exclusive of the garrison's pay, amounted to nearly £100,000 a year, a sum that meant the problem could no longer be deferred.[20]

The need for action might be pressing, but there was little incentive for ministers to involve themselves in a part of the Empire that presented more problems than prospects. Thomas Townshend, Lord Sydney, who held the office of Secretary of State from 1783 until 1789, remained neutral on matters of policy: 'no measures affecting the fundamentals of government in the colonies' being taken during his term.[21] As Prime Minister, Pitt did not challenge this indifference, particularly where no obvious benefits could be anticipated or foreseen.

The American Revolution had discredited ambitious Imperial policies. British intentions for North America were now limited to the need to find ways of generating sufficient material wealth while avoiding the example of the thirteen colonies. If economic prospects did not extend beyond the provision of fish and furs, there was still the possibility of aligning the social structure and values of the remaining colonies with the established practices of the mother country. British attempts to do this began in 1784, when the colony of New Brunswick was created out of Nova Scotia.

Of Thomas Carleton, first Governor of New Brunswick and as yet free of an Assembly, it has been said that: 'His principal impulse was to avoid a replica of democratic New England, where popular control was exercised over local affairs.' Townships were to be replaced by parishes. Nova Scotia itself was considered to be too like New England, though even there some improvement was now thought possible. The unprecedented installation of an Anglican bishop brought Charles Inglis, a New York Loyalist determined 'to prevent the importation of American Divinity & American Politics into this Province...', a move which, giving pre-

---

[20] Helen Taft Manning, *British Colonial Government after the American Revolution 1782–1820* (New Haven, 1933), p. 313. The Cochrane affair can be followed in Swan, 'Economy and Politics in Quebec', pp. 165–84, and in A. R. M. Lower, 'Credit and the Constitutional Act', *Canadian Historical Review*, VI (1925), pp. 123–24.

[21] Manning, *British Colonial Government*, p. 33.

eminence to hierarchical over congregational forms of worship, has been credited with ensuring that 'authoritative control from above undermined, and then virtually destroyed, initiative from below'.[22]

A new status was eventually devised for the province of Quebec. Some two years in preparation, the 1791 Constitutional Act would not have reached the statute book without the efforts of William Grenville, Sydney's successor as Secretary of State. Quebec was divided into two separate Provinces with their own governments. The newly settled areas of western Quebec became Upper Canada which, with its English-speaking population, offered an opportunity to create a substantial colony compatible with British ambitions. As J. G. Simcoe, the first Lieutenant-Governor, set out his priorities, he saw it as necessary 'that the utmost Attention should be paid that British Customs, Manners, & Principles in the most trivial as well as serious matters should be promoted & inculcated to obtain their due Ascendancy to assimilate the Colony with the parent state'.[23] In intention, if not in reality, Upper Canada was to become the model North American colony of settlement.

Until the difficulties posed by Quebec, now reduced in extent and entitled Lower Canada, were laid to rest, however, the internal problems of British North America would remain insoluble. The need for revenue demanded the introduction of representative government and gained the province an Assembly of fifty members, of whom the majority could be *Canadien*. Religious tests were not applied and the franchise was not difficult to secure. The danger of democracy was countered by the creation of Executive and Legislative Councils—in which membership was eventually to be hereditary. These were intended to produce a local aristocracy, sustained by the maintenance of the seigneurial system and further supported by the reservation of other grants of land for Anglican clergy. What remained unclear was the ultimate fate envisaged for the *Canadiens* and their institutions. In the debate on the Constitutional Bill, Pitt had been asked 'if it was his intention, by the division of the province, to assimilate the Canadians to the language, the manners, the habits, and above all, to the laws and constitution of Great Britain'. He replied 'that he certainly did mean to do so, though not by force'.[24] In fact, the British presence in North America was not strong enough to bring about such an assimilation of itself, and the outbreak of the great wars in

[22] MacNutt, *New Brunswick*, pp. 55–56; Judith Fingard, *The Anglican Design in Loyalist Nova Scotia, 1783–1816* (London, 1972), pp. 50, 99.

[23] E. A. Cruikshank, ed., *The Correspondence of John Graves Simcoe with Allied Correspondence Relating to the Administration of the Government of Upper Canada*, 5 vols. (Toronto, 1923), I, p. 27.

[24] Peter Marshall, 'North America's Other Eighteenth-Century Constitution', in Thomas J. Barron, Owen Dudley Edwards, and Patricia J. Story, eds., *Constitution and National Identity* (Edinburgh, 1993), p. 106.

Europe after 1793 meant that British governments could not spare the time to legislate or even to acquire the detailed knowledge on which to base further reforms.

The European conflict, relations with the United States, and the internal politics of the colonies dominated the development of British North America between 1791 and 1815. Their effect was to encourage social and economic expansion, but not to bring about unity. British North America remained an Imperial region distinguished by variety. Growth did little to blur its differences.

The population of Lower Canada in 1791 was around 160,000, of whom about 10,000 were English-speakers. Twenty years later it had reached some 275,000, with the Anglophone element, largely American immigrants to the Eastern Townships, increased to above 30,000. Upper Canada's population remained emphatically inferior in numbers, amounting to no more than 35,000 in 1800. Estimates at the time suggest between 75,000 and 80,000 inhabitants in the Atlantic provinces, with an additional 16,000 located on the shores of Newfoundland. That this expansion involved taking in more land rather than concentrating settlement is demonstrated by the fall in the proportion of urban dwellers. Between 1760 and 1800 that of Lower Canada had dropped by half, to some 7 per cent, with 95 per cent of *Canadiens* living in the countryside, engaged in subsistence rather than market activities.[25] Any creation of a distinctively British North America was still being nullified by the numerical domination of an ethnic group that was French rather than British. Given all these difficulties, it is perhaps remarkable that the colonies held together at all.

The role played by North America in the Empire long remained a marginal one. For all the attention given to them, furs and fish did not make essential contributions to the British economy, and certainly did not justify the costs of colonial defence. Only in the later stages of the Napoleonic War did British ministers become aware of the worth of British North America. Until then, spasmodic wheat exports from Quebec and three or four cargoes a year of naval masts from New Brunswick were all that could be set off against the traditional staples. Between 1788 and 1792 Baltic exceeded colonial timber imports into Britain one hundred-fold.[26] For North America the inhibiting factor had not been availability but freight costs and timber quality, considerations that were swept aside with the application of the Napoleonic Continental System. After 1806 and until the outbreak of war in 1812, imports from New Brunswick,

---

[25] Harris, *Historical Atlas*, p. 117.

[26] Arthur R. M. Lower, *Great Britain's Woodyard: British America and the Timber Trade, 1763–1867* (Montreal, 1973), p. 39.

Nova Scotia, and Lower Canada—though these last undoubtedly incorporated sizeable New England supplies—replaced the previously dominant Baltic timber. A new and to-be-cherished resource had been located in colonies no longer associated primarily with the embarrassment of Imperial defeat.[27] What was more, their dormant economic prospects thus received a rude, but not unpleasing awakening.

Napoleon, Jefferson, and Madison did more to stimulate the economic growth of British North America than would any British ministry or its colonial representatives. If the needs of European war gave point to the use of previously disregarded resources, the unresolved antagonisms of the New World, ultimately leading to the War of 1812, supplied the colonies with an economic importance they had hitherto lacked. It has been said of the American embargoes on trade with the British Empire from 1807 that: 'the government of the United States was able to accomplish what no British administration had—namely, the promotion of a serious British North American–West Indian trade'.[28] Deprived of American supplies, the British West Indies had to turn to British North America. War and embargo brought other commercial benefits. Political decisions in Washington on a cessation of trade bore no resemblance to material needs on the border. The colonists found dealing in contraband, whether of British goods across the border into the United States or American exports to Britain, an altogether superior form of commerce. So much so that the war which broke out in 1812 appeared a frivolous challenge to the serious business of evading trade prohibitions. Military or naval campaigns were not conducted in the Maritimes. The cost of interrupting illegal trade with New England would literally have been too great.

Such self-denial was not maintained elsewhere, though both the scale and the significance of the battles won and lost by either side suggest an appendage to the War of American Independence rather than a conflict in its own right. To Britain the war with France until its conclusion in 1814 exerted claims on all save the absolute minimum of military resources. Any prospect of reclaiming the United States for the Empire was out of the question. On the other hand, there seems little reason to believe that annexation appealed to a significant number of Americans, certainly not by means of war. Setting aside the fur trade and the benefits of access to the St Lawrence, 'on the whole, regardless of partisanship or location, few Americans saw the provinces as an asset'.[29] Reluctance to act decisively was

---

[27] Gerald S. Graham, *Sea Power and British North America, 1783–1820* (Cambridge, Mass., 1941), pp. 142–50; Robert Greenhalgh Albion, *Forests and Sea Power: The Timber Problem of the Royal Navy, 1652–1862* (Cambridge, Mass., 1926), pp. 346–49, 356–57, 392–93; Graeme Wynn, *Timber Colony: A Historical Geography of Nineteenth-Century New Brunswick* (Toronto, 1981), pp. 33, 45.

[28] Graham, *Sea Power*, p. 197.

[29] Stuart, *United States Expansionism*, p. 65.

strengthened by an evident lack of encouragement by *Canadiens* or English-Speakers for American ambitions, no matter what hopes or fears of colonial disaffection might circulate. In the east, the war—if a series of awkward military lunges can be so described—was pursued with much less conviction than it was further west, around the Great Lakes, where the established interests of the fur trade and Indian alliances continued to exert their influence on both American expansion and British reactions.

In due course, the War of 1812 would be seen as the foundation on which a Dominion had arisen, an interpretation that owed almost everything to the consequent needs of a would-be Canadian nation situated at a safe distance from the events so celebrated. Whereas both Britain and the United States could also, if it seemed desirable, derive some consolations from the course of the conflict, this was not true of the Indians. The death of Tecumseh, the Shawnee leader, at the Battle of the Thames in 1813, killed after refusing to join the British in their flight or to surrender, offered yet another example of an Indian failure to preserve a balance between opponents, whose understandings, when reached, would not extend to any acceptance or consideration of Indian interests.

What was the condition of British North America in 1815? That the colonies, separately and as a group, had survived and developed was beyond doubt; that the forms and prospects of their future remained uncertain was equally clear.

Newfoundland could now be considered to have ceased to be simply a base for fishermen and to have become a colony, a status that no longer offered an unacceptable challenge to mercantilist principles. So property on land had at last taken its place beside sea-fishery, and politics could enter the island.[30] If Prince Edward Island was still distinguished for the interminable legal and political consequences of its proprietorial origins, Nova Scotia and New Brunswick offered much more familiar examples of colonial polities. They remained dependent on Imperial economic and political imperatives, but maintained a vigorous assertion of local interests whose well-being would rarely be taken for granted. If the Loyalists were fading away, they had left a substantial political bequest: after 1815, for better or worse, the Maritimes could no longer be regarded as a northward extension of New England, though boundary disputes would provide less profit than contraband trade.

Between 1763 and 1815 Quebec (Lower Canada after 1791) remained both the centre of the Imperial presence in North America and its chief problem. Estimates indicate that its population more than doubled between 1790 and 1822,[31] and that

---

[30] A. H. McLintock, *The Establishment of Constitutional Government in Newfoundland, 1783–1832* (London, 1941), p. 105.

[31] F. Murray Greenwood, *Legacies of Fear: Law and Politics in Quebec in the Era of the French Revolution* (Toronto, 1993), p. xiv.

Canadiens constituted a clear majority of the total for all the colonies. In Lower Canada their numbers—well over 300,000—ensured an overwhelming majority in relation to the English-speakers, though this was not reflected in economic and political conditions. Throughout these years *Canadiens* were regarded, and came to consider themselves, as a lesser, subordinate element in a society whose directors, whether Governors, judges, military commanders, or merchants, were intent on Anglicizing the province. As distinctions became more pronounced, the English minority acquired a 'garrison mentality'.[32] That their efforts at Anglicization enjoyed little success was of less significance than *Canadien* perceptions that attempts were being made: specific and tangible instances of English-speakers' dominance could be found in institutions as central as the Councils, the Assembly and the seigneuries, the landholding system of New France extending down the St Lawrence that had been kept in being by the new rulers.

The new constitution introduced in 1792 saw an English majority installed in the Executive and Legislative Councils, and an Assembly elected that contained sixteen English-speakers out of a total of fifty members, a representation that in no way reflected the size of the two communities. If English numbers in the Assembly subsequently declined, this was not true of their penetration of the seigneuries, whose acquisition offered clear proof of a growing and permanent Imperial establishment. By 1791, if surnames are taken as a guide, seigneuries in the government of Montreal had suffered serious English inroads—at least twenty-one out of seventy-seven were in their hands. Trois-Rivières remained decisively *Canadien*, but Quebec's eighty-five seigneuries included at least seventeen English owned. This did not mark the high point: by 1800 about one-third of seigneurial lands had been acquired, and a further twenty seigneuries followed between 1802 and 1812.[33] The process was not confined to these holdings but extended into the Eastern Townships, where predominantly American immigrants were offered tracts on English tenure in communities which, as their name suggests, took their inspiration, if not their form, from further south. Despite the absence of large-scale immigration, the British influence on changes in Lower Canada was becoming increasingly more pronounced.

Recent historians have laid stress on the social and economic sources of *Canadien* political development. There is general agreement that before the passage of the Constitutional Act efforts for reform were led by bourgeois members of both language groups. 'Between 1784 and 1791 political divisions over the constitution and the laws were based primarily on class, not ethnicity',[34] a

---

[32] Ibid., pp. 194–95.
[33] *Historical Atlas*, Plate 51, Louise Dechêne; Fernand Ouellet, *Lower Canada, 1791–1840: Social Change and Nationalism* (Toronto, 1980), p. 61.
[34] Greenwood, *Legacies of Fear*, p. 37.

condition that helps to explain the substantial English-speaking membership of the first Assembly. In the course of the next twenty years, however, such alliances broke down, and a *Canadien* opposition developed that occasioned the 'reign of terror' of Sir James Craig, Governor from 1807 to 1811. Craig precipitated a major crisis that erupted between March 1810 and his departure from the colony in June of the following year.

The Governor's principal target was the physically unimpressive, intellectually ambitious Christian Bédard, 'perhaps the first French-Canadian professional politician'.[35] A comparatively brief but spectacular career in the Assembly had led Bédard, born after the conquest and an admirer of the British constitution, to urge the introduction of ministerial responsibility. The Governor would become no more than the King's representative. Bédard urged this overthrow of executive rule both in political discussion and through his editorship of the recently established *Le Canadien*, the journal of the French party. His arrest in March 1810, shortly after Craig had dissolved the Assembly, marked an unprecedented crisis in politics on the St Lawrence, born not so much of *Canadien* rejection of the Constitutional Act as of a skilful ability to put it to good use.

The introduction of political institutions into Lower Canada had taken place while France was experiencing the tumults of revolution and war. The response of *Canadiens* to these convulsions remained a matter of intermittent British anxiety. Government informers did their best to magnify this concern, but there was little substance to their reports. The Revolution, by its onslaughts on Catholicism, clearly did more to divide than to reunite France and its still-devout former colony. The church in Canada would rather confront English Protestantism than converse with French atheism. Such reactions initially gave support for the British regime from an otherwise unexpected quarter, but a government that was pre-occupied with the much closer and, to many of Loyalist background, more alarming prospects of American hostility did not respond to them. *Canadien* political isolation was thus given powerful justification.

In the way in which they reacted to the American and the French Revolutions, the English-speakers and the *Canadiens* made public the differences between them. While such divisions did little to advance the political ambitions of either community, they helped in the short run to sustain the authority of a government that could secure English support against *Canadien* opposition. This conflict began to assume a form not defined by Bédard, who abandoned politics after his imprisonment, but developed by Joseph Papineau, the founder of a dynasty coterminous with the emergence of nineteenth-century Quebec nationalism.

---

[35] Fernand Ouellet, *Lower Canada*, p. 86.

The hostility of French and English in Lower Canada was only one instance of antagonism within the British North American colonies. The case of Upper Canada showed that there could be disputes even without linguistic differences. Simcoe, the first Lieutenant-Governor, had attempted to establish a new British society there, but by the time of his departure in 1796 his efforts had clearly proved unavailing. The Loyalist settlers could not and would not adopt the institutional features of the mother country; in 1797, for instance, the Chief Justice reckoned that no more than 2 per cent of the population were Anglicans.[36] This was not the only difference, as in increasing measure the colony received Americans whose destination had been determined not by loyalty but rather by land. Population estimates in 1812 vary from 75,000 to 100,000, but agree that a large majority were American immigrants. Outnumbered British office-holders resorted to using the yardstick of loyalty. In Upper Canada Tories such as John Strachan, later to become its bishop, saw civic virtues as deriving from that source: 'proper resignation and obedience to the laws, a due deference and homage for superiors, and for those who are publicly entrusted with the administration of the province.' Recent arrivals from the United States were not distinguished by such behaviour or beliefs. Political dissent, frequently arising from that quarter, was declared sufficient ground for exclusion from the benefits of government of any found wanting in their attachment to a Tory definition of the British constitution.[37] This propagation of British values served to divide rather than unite the society of Upper Canada. If Lower Canada exhibited permanent and exceptional problems, its neighbour did not provide the contrast of a model colony.

Upper Canada by 1815 was no longer the furthest extent of settlement in British North America. Due to the fur trade, what lay beyond to the west was by no means unknown. The Hudson's Bay Company, whose system lay around Lake Winnipeg, was being challenged by the Montreal traders organized, since the winter of 1783–84, into the North West Company. Despite the emptiness of this vast area, the companies still competed for space and trading opportunities.

Competition fostered exploration. Alexander Mackenzie reached the Pacific overland in July 1793, and in the following years routes to the west were developed. At first their use was confined to competing fur trade interests. The next phase of expansion awaited the outcome of the protracted plans emanating from Thomas Douglas, fifth Earl of Selkirk, who had sought since 1803 to establish a Scottish settlement in North America. He had made his way west, abandoning Prince Edward Island for Upper Canada, and by 1806 moving on further to reach Lake

---

[36] Gerald M. Craig, *Upper Canada: The Formative Years, 1784–1841* (Toronto, 1963), p. 55.

[37] Ibid., pp. 47, 52. David Mills, *The Idea of Loyalty in Upper Canada, 1784–1850* (Kingston and Montreal 1988), pp. 18–25.

Winnipeg. In June 1811 Selkirk received from the Hudson's Bay Company title to the colony of Assiniboia, the Red River settlement, whose 116,000 square miles of land cost him ten shillings. Subsequent developments suggested that even that sum had not been a bargain price, but Selkirk's problems marked, however faintly, the beginnings of a process that would extend British North America far beyond the hitherto central feature that had constituted, in the phrase of the historian D. G. Creighton, 'the Commercial Empire of the St Lawrence'.[38]

The achievements of British North America between 1760 and 1815 were real. There had been extensive territorial expansion: settlements had been established, if often by people who had been compelled to leave their old homes rather than by those who had selected their destinations for themselves; governments had coped, no matter how partially and instinctively, with constitutional, political, legal, and religious questions for which no precedents existed. Yet success was acquired at a price: if the land had been claimed, it had still, for the most part, to be occupied and put to use. Historical geographers have judged, that 'British North America ... at the beginning of the nineteenth century was not a premeditated creation, and it was not cohesive, culturally or economically'.[39] By 1815 another war had been survived, but the region's problems still persisted. Whether viewed at Imperial or at colonial level, changes between 1760 and 1815 had been both substantial and indeterminate. British America's existence had been confirmed but its future shape and prospects remained unclear.

In terms of Imperial policy the remaining British possessions in North America had been governed largely by default. Their organization and institutions had been changed only twice by statute: on the first occasion by concealed constitutional necessity, on the second by personal preoccupation with political circumstances that recalled to William Grenville the American problems his father George had sought to resolve between 1763 and 1765. That comparison was less exact than it may have seemed. British North America was still British in 1815 because it remained a group of colonies whose population, resources, and pretensions were no more than modest. If independence depended on material growth, there was no realistic prospect in view of its achievement. Absorption by the United States, out of the question in the aftermath of the War of 1812, was all that might ultimately be imagined.

Revolution, whether expressed in American or French forms, had possessed little relevance or appeal in these years. Both *Canadiens* and English, far from engaging in the creation of new societies, sought rather to preserve remnants of

---

[38] E. E. Rich, *The Fur Trade and the Northwest to 1857* (Toronto, 1968), pp. 186–208; John Morgan Gray, *Lord Selkirk* (London, 1963), pp. 52–66.

[39] Harris, *Historical Atlas*, p. 173.

their *anciens régimes*. The conflict of French and British in North America that had so conspicuously shaped the continent's history throughout the eighteenth century would, therefore, continue indefinitely. Viewed in this light, the conquest of 1760 was not the end but the beginning of both *Canadien* and Canadian history. Its outcome has yet to be determined.

Select Bibliography

ROBERT S. ALLEN, *His Majesty's Indian Allies: British Indian Policy in the Defence of Canada, 1774–1815* (Toronto, 1992).

JOHN BARTLET BREBNER, *The Neutral Yankees of Nova Scotia* (New York, 1937).

PHILIP A. BUCKNER and JOHN G. REID, eds., *The Atlantic Region to Confederation: A History* (Toronto, 1994).

J. M. BUMSTED, *Land, Settlement and Politics on Eighteenth-Century Prince Edward Island* (Kingston and Montreal, 1987).

A. L. BURT, *The Old Province of Quebec* (Toronto, 1933).

COLIN G. CALLOWAY, *Crown and Calumet: British–Indian Relations, 1783–1815* (Norman, Okla., 1987).

ANN GORMAN CONDON, *The Loyalist Dream for New Brunswick* (Fredericton, 1984).

GERALD M. CRAIG, *Upper Canada: The Formative Years, 1784–1841* (Toronto, 1963).

GERALD S. GRAHAM, *Sea Power and British North America, 1783–1820* (Cambridge, Mass., 1941).

F. MURRAY GREENWOOD, *Legacies of Fear: Law and Politics in Quebec in the Era of the French Revolution* (Toronto, 1993).

C. GRANT HEAD, *Eighteenth Century Newfoundland: A Geographer's Perspective* (Toronto, 1976).

PHILIP LAWSON, *The Imperial Challenge: Quebec and Britain in the Age of the American Revolution* (Montreal and Kingston, 1989).

NEIL MacKINNON, *This Unfriendly Soil: The Loyalist Experience in Nova Scotia, 1783–1791* (Kingston and Montreal, 1986).

W. S. MacNUTT, *New Brunswick: A History, 1784–1867* (Toronto, 1963).

HELEN TAFT MANNING, *British Colonial Government after the American Revolution, 1782–1820* (New Haven, 1933).

HILDA NEATBY, *Quebec: The Revolutionary Age, 1760–1791* (Toronto, 1966).

FERNAND OUELLET, *Eléments d'histoire sociale du Bas-Canada* (Montréal, 1972).

—— *Lower Canada, 1791–1840: Social Change and Nationalism* (Toronto, 1980).

E. E. RICH, *The Fur Trade and the Northwest to 1857* (Toronto, 1968).

REGINALD C. STUART, *United States Expansionism and British North America, 1775–1871* (Chapel Hill, NC, 1988).

JEAN-PIERRE WALLOT, *Un Québec qui Bougeait: trame socio-politique au tournant du XIXeme siècle* (Québec, 1973).

18

The Formation of Caribbean Plantation Society, 1689–1748

RICHARD B. SHERIDAN

Compared with the wealth and economic growth generated by the gold and silver mines of the New World in the sixteenth century, the subsequent plantation revolution was a far more dynamic and sustainable force in the development of capitalism in Europe and America.* It was an unprecedented social and economic institution which stemmed from the growing demand of Europeans for a wider range of foodstuffs and raw materials from tropical and semi-tropical regions of open resources. The New World plantation represented the capitalistic exploitation of land with a combination of African labour, European technology and management, Asiatic and American plants, European animal husbandry, and American soil and climate.

After half a century of privateering raids and contraband trade in the Caribbean region, the English established permanent settlements in the Lesser Antilles in the 1620s and 1630s. Companies were organized to colonize unoccupied or sparsely settled territories. Owing largely to the profitability of tobacco-growing, the English established settlements on five islands in the Lesser Antilles: St Christopher [hereafter St Kitts] (1624), Barbados (1627), Nevis (1628), Antigua (1632), and Montserrat (1632). (Map 19.1) Taking the lead was the island of Barbados, which attracted freeholders who engaged in growing tobacco, cotton, indigo and ginger for sale in Europe; and other crops—cassava, plantains, beans, and corn—for their own subsistence. They farmed from about five to thirty acres with the assistance of white indentured servants who laboured for a period of from three to ten years in return for a paid passage and the promise of land when their work contract expired.

---

* The works chiefly relied upon, or given special attention to in this chapter, are: Richard S. Dunn, *Sugar and Slavery: The Rise of the Planter Class in the English West Indies, 1624–1713* (Chapel Hill, NC, 1972); Richard B. Sheridan, *Sugar and Slavery: An Economic History of the British West Indies, 1623–1775* (Barbados, 1974); Richard Pares, *War and Trade in the West Indies, 1739–1763* (Oxford, 1936); Frank W. Pitman, *The Development of the British West Indies, 1700–1763* (New Haven, 1917).

Prior to the nineteenth century, the plantation islands of the Caribbean were the most-valued possessions in the overseas Imperial world. Most valuable by far were the sugar plantations, which ranged from as little as eighty to as much as 2,000 or more acres of land, and from forty to 500 or more slave labourers. The larger plantations were not only subdivided into fields planted with sugar-cane, but also into those growing foodstuffs and forage crops, as well as pastures and woodlands. Sugar plantations were both farms and factories. The reason for this was that ripe canes had to be cut and crushed and the cane-juice boiled within twenty-four to forty-eight hours to prevent fermentation and spoilage. Therefore, it was necessary to locate the sugar mill and other buildings near the fields which grew the cane.

The sugar revolution transformed the economy and society of Barbados during the two decades from 1640 to 1660. In consisted of the following interrelated changes: (1) the transformation of a settler colony combining subsistence farming and small staple production for overseas markets to one of large and labour- and capital-intensive plantations specializing in the growing of sugar-canes and manufacture of crude sugar and rum for external markets; (2) dependence upon outside sources of foodstuffs, building materials, implements and machinery, consumer goods, and shipping, marketing, and financial services; (3) the shift in the labour force from white indentured servants to chattel slaves from Africa; (4) the rise of a wealthy planter governing oligarchy with close socio-economic and political ties with the metropolis; and (5) the emergence of the sugar colonies as major actors in geopolitical and economic rivalry in the affairs of the Atlantic world.

Unlike their counterparts in Barbados, the inhabitants of the English Leeward Islands of St Kitts, Nevis, Antigua, and Montserrat experienced numerous hardships which slowed the transition to sugar production. Nevis was the only island in the group where slave-grown sugar had become the leading staple by the decade of the 1650s. After the early 1670s, however, sugar production was stimulated by increased access to slave labour from Africa. The Royal African Company brought close to 8,000 slaves to the Leeward Islands from 1674 to 1686, and additional numbers were smuggled into the islands by interlopers.[1]

Lord Protector Cromwell's government launched the Western Design which led to the conquest of Jamaica from the Spanish in 1655 and marked an enormous change in the balance of Caribbean power relationships. The third largest island in the region, Jamaica had much more arable land than the other five English sugar islands combined. Moreover, it had easy access to all the Spanish dominions in America with their precious metals, tropical staples, and trade and

---

[1] K. G. Davies, *The Royal African Company* (London, 1957), pp. 145, 310–12, 363.

shipping. Sugar gained a foothold by drawing on experienced planters from the eastern Caribbean. Sir Thomas Modyford arrived on the island in 1664 with some 800 settlers from the eastern Caribbean to fill the dual role of planter and Governor.

By the decade of the 1680s the sugar planters, especially those of Barbados, were feeling the effects of low prices and rising costs of production. The price decline was the result of an increase in supplies of sugar from Brazil and the English and French Caribbean islands relative to consumer demand in European markets. At the same time, costs tended to increase, leading to a cost–price squeeze on planters' profits. Short-run variables which raised costs included storms and hurricanes, drought, fires, accidents, Carib Indian raids, and epidemics, whereas longer-term cost increases resulted from European wars, trade and shipping restrictions, tax and duty increases, and environmental deterioration. Planters complained that the Acts of Trade and Navigation reduced their profits by forcing them to ship their sugar to, and purchase their supplies from, the home market, buy their slaves from the monopolistic African companies, and pay the duties on sugar and other staples. Mitigating circumstances included the lax enforcement of the Navigation Laws and the clandestine trade carried on by the Dutch traders at St Eustatius and Curaçao.[2]

Edward Littleton, the Barbadian sugar planter, told a tale of woe in his pamphlet of 1689, entitled *The Groans of the Plantations*. The immediate grievance of the author was the additional Sugar Duty Act of 1685. The pamphlet also called attention to environmental deterioration and increased hardships imposed upon slaves engaged in sugar production. Many years of constant cropping of cane lands had reduced soil fertility to such an extent that remedial actions were imperative. Terraces were constructed to catch the mould that washed from the cane fields. Slaves carried back the mould collected in gullies in carts or in baskets on their heads; they were said to 'work at it like Ants and Bees'. Vast quantities of dung were accumulated and spread over the cane fields. Littleton wrote that '[s]ome save the Urine of their People (both Whites and Blacks) to increase and enrich their Dung'. The hardships imposed on the slaves began with their capture in Africa and were accentuated on their voyage to the islands and in the period of 'seasoning' or adjustment to plantation life when they got there. For the seasoned slave life was still bleak. A planter who bought a parcel of the best and ablest slaves would, said Littleton, 'lose a full third of them, before they ever come to do him service. When they are season'd and used to the Country, they stand much better, but to how many Mischances are they still subject?' Littleton asserted that 'he that

---

[2] Carl and Roberta Bridenbaugh, *No Peace Beyond the Line: The English in the Caribbean, 1624–90* (London, 1972), pp. 206, 249–62, 307–11, 335–36, 407.

hath but a hundred *Negroes*, should buy eight or ten every year to keep up his stock'.[3]

Except for a peacetime interval of five years, the period from 1689 to 1713 witnessed warfare in Europe and in the American and West Indian colonies. Planters feared protracted war and depredations of the enemy, resulting in the destruction of their plantations and the carrying off of sugar utensils and slaves. War brought military responsibilities to colonial Governors, Councils, Assemblies, and army and navy commanders. Planters were diverted from peacetime occupations to service in militia units. Colonial governments voted money to build and repair fortifications, supply arms and ammunition, to house and maintain British regiments stationed in the islands, and supply vessels and crews to patrol coastal waters in co-operation with warships from the mother country. Largely beyond the control of planter-dominated governments in wartime were enemy depredations on merchant shipping, losses of sugar and rum consigned to British merchants and of plantation supplies normally expected in return. War exacted enormous human costs in loss of lives from disease, starvation, accidents, drownings, and armed conflict.

In the War of the League of Augsburg Jamaica suffered both military and natural disasters. Port Royal, trading centre of the island, was overwhelmed by an earthquake on 7 June 1692. More than 2,000 people lost their lives as the port was half-plunged into the sea. Two years later Jamaica was invaded by a force consisting of some 1,500 men in three warships and twenty-three transports commanded by the French admiral Du Casse. Landing in the easternmost parish, the French marched inland, burning cane fields, destroying over fifty sugar works, and carrying off over 2,000 slaves, 1,200 head of cattle, and 420 horses. During the years from 1691 to 1697 the Jamaican government passed laws to repair the losses of sufferers from the French raid, guard the sea-coasts with two sloops of war, build fortifications, and raise money to discharge debts contracted for wartime expenditures. Shipping losses were enormous despite instructions from the English government to masters of merchant ships 'to put themselves under convoy, or sail in such numbers and fleets, and take such other precautions, as may best prevent their falling into the hands of our enemies'.[4]

Although Jamaica was not invaded in the War of the Spanish Succession, the island was involved in shipping losses, interrupted trade, and defensive military

[3] Edward Littleton, *The Groans of the Plantations* (London, 1689), pp. 1–2, 5–9, 16–17; David Watts, *The West Indies: The Patterns of Development, Culture and Environmental Change Since 1492* (Cambridge, 1987), pp. 395–402.

[4] Clinton V. Black, *History of Jamaica* (London, 1950), pp. 69–71, 74–77; *Journals of the Assembly of Jamaica* [hereinafter *Journals*] (Jamaica, 1811), I, pp. 135, 140, 144–45, 148, 203.

expenditure. There were threats of buccaneering raids from French Saint-Domingue and attacks by squadrons of French warships. Indicative of the import-ance of Jamaica to the Empire was the stationing there of an English regiment of 3,000 trained soldiers under Brigadier General Thomas Handasyd, who was also appointed the island's acting Governor. Handasyd urged the Assembly to raise revenue to support the island's government and defray wartime expenditures. Besides the external threats, white Jamaicans faced internal attacks by the Mar-oons, communities of ex-slaves who had escaped from the plantations and found refuge in rugged interior parts of the island. From 1700 to 1722 hardly a year passed without some conflict between the whites and rebel slaves. Prospects were brighter at the close of the war when Governor Archibald Hamilton wrote that 'the State of the Island is generally much improved of late, with respect to the Seasons; there being a very plentiful Crop of Sugars and Plantation-Provisions in most Parts thereof; which I hope may ease the Inhabitants of those Difficulties they lay under lately through the scarcity of both the one and the other'.[5]

All the islanders in the eastern Caribbean were reduced to a low level of existence in the war years from the shortage of supplies; at the same time they were vulnerable to the enemy because of lack of arms and fortifications. Barbados was less exposed to raids than the Leeward Islands and Jamaica, largely because it was well fortified and to windward of the French islands. Leeward Islanders, on the other hand, suffered from privateers and corsairs based in the neighbouring French islands. In 1706 great damage was inflicted on Nevis by French raiders who carried off 3,187 slaves to Martinique. In July 1712 the corsair Jacques Cassard overran Montserrat and Antigua and carried back to Martinique 1,500 slaves and other valuables. However, by far the heaviest losses fell on the planters and merchants whose wealth was exposed to the hazards of seaborne commerce, where the buccaneers and privateers exacted a colossal toll. St Kitts was the only island to experience a permanent change of sovereignty from wartime activity. In July of 1702 Governor Christopher Codrington sent Lieutenant-Governor Walter Hamilton with some twenty vessels filled with troops from Antigua to St Kitts, and by a show of force compelled the French military commander and his troops to surrender. At the Peace of Utrecht in 1713 the French ceded their half of the island to Britain.[6]

By the end of the seventeenth century the European nations in the West Indies had developed a distinct zone of tropical commodity production that involved the large-scale movement of capital and labour to and from the colonies. In the

[5] Ruth Bourne, *Queen Anne's Navy in the West Indies* (New Haven, 1939), pp. 34–41; *Journals*, I, pp. 207, 226, 229, 255, 366, 372, 401, 409.
[6] Bourne, *Queen Anne's Navy*, pp. 41–57, 189–213.

English West Indies the plantation-based trading system had established permanent connections with the metropolis, Africa, North America, and Spanish America. To John Cary, the influential Bristol merchant, the African trade was 'the best
Traffic the kingdom hath, as it doth occasionally give so vast an Imployment to our
people both by Sea and Land'. Africa supplied the workers 'whereby our Plantations are improved, and 'tis by their Labours such great Quantities of *Sugar,
Tobacco, Cotton, Ginger,* and *Indigo* are raised, which being bulky Commodities
imploy great Numbers of our Ships for their transporting hither, and the greater
number of Ships imploys the greater number of Handecraft Trades at home,
spends more of our Product and Manufactures, and makes more Saylors, who
are maintained by the separate Imploy'. William Wood, who was a merchant in
Jamaica in the early eighteenth century, regarded the trade to Africa 'of the greatest
Value to this Kingdom, if we consider the Number of Ships annually employed in
it, the great *Export* of our *Manufactures* and other Goods to that Coast, and the
Value of the *Product* of our *Plantations* annually sent to *Great Britain*'.[7]

By 1700 sugar was the paramount tropical agricultural commodity entering
Europe from the New World. The English West Indies exported in 1700 about
22,000 tons of sugar to England and Wales, with Barbados supplying approximately half of that amount. From a luxury item in the diet of the English, cane
sugar from the West Indies came to be consumed in growing quantities by the
common people. Thomas Tryon, who was a sugar merchant in London, wrote of
its growing importance. He noted how sugar had the indirect effect of increasing
land values as it was consumed with domestic fruits, grains, and beverages.
Furthermore, sugar had increased the King's customs by occasioning many foreign
commodities to be imported which were unheard of in former days. These
included cocoa, tea, coffee, and fruits. An important reason for the increased
per-capita consumption of sugar in England was the decline in its retail price by
more than half from 1623–32 to 1683–92. While a mass market for sugar emerged
rather tardily, '[f]rom the mid-eighteenth century onward, sugar production in
the imperial economy became more and more important to England's rulers and
ruling class . . . and the masses of English people were now steadily consuming
more of it, and desiring more of it than they could afford'.[8]

Trends in the growth of the white and slave population of the British sugar
colonies from 1700 to 1748 are shown in Table 18.1. What is striking about this data

[7] Peter D. Phillips, 'Incorporation of the Caribbean, 1650–1700', *Review*, I, nos. 5/6 (1986–87), pp. 781–
804; John Cary, *An Essay on the State of England in Relation to its Trade* (Bristol, 1695), p. 131; William
Wood, *A Survey of Trade* (London, 1718), p. 179.

[8] Sidney W. Mintz, *Sweetness and Power: The Place of Sugar in Modern History* (New York, 1985), pp.
44–46; Thomas Tryon, *Tryon's Letters, Domestic and Foreign* (London, 1700), pp. 219–21; Noel Deerr, *The
History of Sugar*, 2 vols. (London, 1949–50), II, p. 528.

TABLE 18.1. *Population of the British West Indies*

	c.1700			c.1748		
	White	Black	Total	White	Black	Total
Barbados	15,400	50,100	65,500	22,500	69,100	91,600
Leeward Islands	8,300	22,200	30,500	8,000	62,800	70,800
Jamaica	7,300	42,000	49,300	10,400	118,100	128,500
Other*	n.d.	n.d.	n.d.	3,000	8,500	11,500
TOTAL	31,000	114,300	145,300	43,900	258,500	302,400

Note: * Virgin Islands, Belize, Cayman Islands, Bahamas.

Sources: David W. Galenson, *Traders, Planters, and Slaves* (Cambridge, 1986), pp. 4–5; Frank W. Pitman, *Development of British West Indies* (New Haven, 1917), pp. 369–83: J. R. Ward, personal communication.

is the small increase in the white population as compared with the black and slave population. The white population increased from 31,000 to 43,900 from 1700 to 1748, or by 12,900, while the blacks, who were almost entirely slaves, increased from 114,300 to 258,500, or by 144,200, during the same period of time. The overall ratio of whites to blacks rose from 1 : 3.7 to 1 : 5.9. While Barbados had a fairly steady ratio of one white to three blacks, the Leeward Islands' ratio increased from 1 : 2.7 in 1700 to 1 : 7.8 in 1748, and that of Jamaica from 1 : 5.8 to 1 : 11.4. In 1748 the slave population of Jamaica was 45.7 per cent of the slave total of the British sugar colonies. However, Jamaica's white population was only 23.7 per cent of the whites in the sugar colonies. From the standpoint of military defence against both external and internal enemies, the most criticial ratio was that between slaves and men able to bear arms. In Barbados this ratio declined from 1 : 6.6 in 1683 to 1 : 12.7 in 1748. The Lieutenant-Governor of Jamaica wrote in 1703: 'Our number of Slaves Augments dayly but to my great grief the Number of white men dayly decrease.' In 1721, when Jamaica had an estimated fighting strength of 3,000, the ratio was one to twenty-six. In 1745 the four major islands in the Leeward group had a total of 2,982 militiamen and 59,522 slaves, or a ratio of one to twenty.[9]

The volume and source of the sugar exported from the British West Indies to England and Wales from 1700 to 1748 are summarized in Table 18.2.

As this data shows, sugar exports nearly doubled from 22,017 tons in 1700 to 41,425 tons in 1748. In 1700 Barbados was the source of nearly half of the exports, followed by the Leeward Islands with one-third, and Jamaica with nearly one-quarter. From 1700 to 1725 the greatest increase came from the Leeward Islands,

[9] Lt.-Gov. Thomas Handasyd to Board of Trade, 5 Oct. 1703, C[olonial] O[ffice] 137/16/G/19; Trevor Burnard, 'A Failed Settler Society: Marriage and Demographic Failure in Early Jamaica', *Journal of Social History*, XXVIII (1994), pp. 63–82.

TABLE 18.2. *Sugar exports from the British West Indies to England and Wales* (tons)

	c.1700	c.1725	c.1748
Barbados	10,099	8,288	6,442
Leeward Islands	7,044	16,784	17,584
Jamaica	4,874	10,249	17,399
TOTAL	22,017	35,321	41,425

Source: Noel Deerr, *The History of Sugar*, 2 vols. (London, 1949–50) I, pp. 193–98.

followed by Jamaica, with the exports from Barbados in decline. Exports from Barbados continued to decline to 1748, whereas those from the Leewards were little changed, while those from Jamaica increased substantially. Of the 41,425 tons exported to England in 1748, Jamaica and the Leewards each accounted for about 40 per cent and Barbados for only one-fifth.

The decline in Barbados's sugar exports is perhaps exaggerated because it ignores qualitative improvements in production. Among the West Indians, the Barbadians were the most advanced in the art of plantership and were regarded as harsh disciplinarians of their slaves. In preparing the land for planting sugar canes, they had made their slaves dig cane holes to check wind and water erosion, protect young cane plants from the trade winds, and concentrate fertilizer. They kept large herds of cattle to provide manure to fertilize their cane lands. They built windmills, which were more efficient than horsemills. Moreover, they improved the quality of their sugar by a process called claying, and distilled the molasses by-product into quality rum for sale in overseas markets. Yet it must be emphasized that these improvements were costly, especially for the slaves, who suffered oppressive toil, received coarse and scanty fare, inferior clothing and housing, and severe discipline. It was not until the late eighteenth century that 'the "material comfort" and humane treatment of slaves became important issues to Barbadian or British West Indian planters'.[10]

Jamaica, which was thirty times the size of Barbados and the Leeward Islands combined, was slow to emerge as the leading sugar island in the British West Indies. In 1700 it produced only one-fifth as much sugar as the other islands; in 1725 two-fifths as much; and in 1748 three-quarters as much. Before 1700 Jamaica's natural resources were underdeveloped owing largely to the attractions of

[10] Jerome S. Handler and Frederick W. Lange, *Plantation Slavery in Barbados: An Archaeological and Historical Investigation* (Cambridge, Mass., 1978), pp. 74–102; Hilary McD. Beckles, *A History of Barbados: From Amerindian Settlement to Nation-State* (Cambridge, 1989), pp. 41–74; Jack P. Greene, 'Changing Identity in the British Caribbean: Barbados as a Case Study', in Nicholas Canny and Anthony Pagden, eds., *Colonial Identity in the Atlantic World, 1500–1800* (Princeton, 1987), pp. 213–66.

buccaneering and the depredations of the Maroons and French privateers. Maroon depredations continued, especially during the internecine struggle from 1729 to 1739. Various reasons advanced for the slow growth included the *Asiento* contract to supply British-traded slaves and manufactures to the Spanish Main; the North American trade to the foreign sugar islands, which tended to raise the prices and limit imports of provisions and building materials; competition from the French and other foreign sugar producers; the cost–price squeeze which depressed the British sugar industry; and the planters' proclivity to engross potentially productive lands far in excess of their needs. The dilemma which confronted the Jamaican plantocracy was that, while a large European population was needed to control the mounting number of slaves and defend the island from internal and external enemies, the plantation economy was tending toward sugar monoculture and taking away the livelihood of smallholders and artisans. Though the sugar estates comprised the greater part of Jamaica's wealth, additional wealth consisted of cattle pens, small staple and provision farms, trading stocks, buildings, and ships. From the British settlement at Belize and trading stations on the Mosquito Coast came logwood, which was transshipped from Jamaica to Europe to be used in dyeing cloth.[11]

Occupying about 5 per cent of the area of the British West Indies, the Leeward Islands by 1748 accounted for 18 per cent of the white population, 24 per cent of the slaves, and 42 per cent of the sugar exports to England and Wales. Antigua, the largest island and seat of government of the Leewards, experienced demographic and economic growth from 1700 to 1748. The white population increased from approximately 2,300 in 1678 to 5,200 in 1724. From this peak it declined to 3,538 in 1745, as the process of amalgamating small farms and plantations into sugar estates gained momentum. As with other sugar islands, ties of kinship and concentration of wealth, status, and power enabled the planter élite to dominate the political and economic life of the colony and acquire substantial influence in the metropolis. The slave population of Antigua experienced almost continuous growth. It was reported in census returns at 2,172 in 1678, 12,943 in 1708, 19,186 in 1720, and 27,892 in 1745. Sugar exports from Antigua to England and Wales increased from 2,639 tons in 1700 to 7,471 in 1725, after which the increase slowed to 8,902 in 1748. By 1751 Antigua was said to be 'improved to the utmost, there being hardly one Acre of Ground, even to the Top of the Mountains, fit for Sugar Canes and other necessary Produce, but what is taken in and cultivated'.[12]

[11] Michael Craton and James Walvin, *A Jamaican Plantation: The History of Worthy Park, 1670–1970* (Toronto, 1970), pp. 51–52, 72–84; Verene A. Shepherd, 'Livestock and Sugar: Aspects of Jamaica's Agricultural Development from the Late Seventeenth to the Early Nineteenth Century', *Historical Journal*, XXXIV (1991), p. 631.

[12] B[ritish] L[ibrary], North MSS, A6, f. 173.

By mid-century the island of St Kitts had come to possess the characteristics of a highly developed sugar colony: dispossession of smallholders, amalgamation of land into large plantations, extensive sugar monoculture, a small landholding plantocracy, and masses of African slaves. The white population of St Kitts declined from 1,897 in 1678 to 1,670 in 1708, rose to 2,800 in 1720, and declined again to 2,377 in 1745. The African slaves, who numbered 1,436 in 1678, increased to 3,258 in 1708, 7,321 in 1720, and 19,174 in 1745. Less than 1,000 tons of sugar were exported from St Kitts annually prior to 1700. Thereafter, owing largely to the addition of the ceded lands taken from the French and the generally fertile soil, the export of sugar rose to 4,437 tons in 1725 and to 8,789 tons in 1748, by which time St Kitts was outproducing Antigua and Barbados. In proportion to its extent, St Kitts was the richest colony in the British Empire by the middle decades of the eighteenth century. Choice cane lands sold for as much as £100 sterling per acre and the island's sugar yielded premium prices in British markets.

Nevis, which is slightly larger than Montserrat, suffered severely from malignant fever in 1689 and 1690 and a French raid in 1706; and, from the standpoint of the white population, never recovered. From a peak of 3,521 white inhabitants in 1678, numbers fell to 1,104 in 1708, increased to 1,343 in 1720, and declined to 857 in 1745. The black population, on the other hand, increased from 3,676 in 1708, to 5,689 in 1720, and 6,511 in 1745. Sugar exports from Nevis to England and Wales in 1700 amounted to 3,094 tons. In 1725 they were 2,969 tons, and by 1748 had declined to 2,011 tons. There may have been, at most, a hundred sugar plantations in 1719, but hardly more than two or three dozen a century later. The Pinney family, which made a great fortune in Nevis and its sister islands, 'added field to field and slave to slave, and in this they were not exceptional'.[13]

Montserrat was the smallest of the British sugar islands. In the seventeenth century the island was almost entirely peopled by Irish. Its inhabitants still speak with a distinct Irish brogue. As a result of wartime raids, endemic and epidemic disease, and the dispossession of smallholders, the white population declined from 2,682 in 1678 to about 1,000 in 1724, then remained stable to 1748. The blacks numbered 992 in 1678; they increased to about 5,000 in 1712 when the French reportedly carried off some 1,200 of them. Scattered census returns show that Montserrat had 4,400 slaves in 1724, 5,855 in 1729, and 5,945 in 1745. Sugar exports from Montserrat to England and Wales increased from 1,486 tons in 1700, to 1,494 in 1725, and 2,473 in 1748. The comprehensive census of Montserrat in 1729 shows that the thirty leading sugar plantations occupied 78.2 per cent of the total land in farms and plantations, and 88.5 per cent of the land planted in cane. The average

[13] Richard Pares, *A West-India Fortune* (London, 1957), pp. 23–25.

sugar plantation in this group had nine Europeans, 115 slaves, 310 acres of land, and two sugar mills.[14]

Much has been written about the West Indians of European extraction and their characteristics and behaviour. To Edmund and William Burke the West Indies opened a fair and ample field to encourage men who had fiery, restless tempers and were willing to undertake the severest labour provided it was rewarded in a short time. They were men who loved risk and hazard. Their schemes were always vast, wrote the Burkes, and they 'put no medium between being great and being undone'. These men brought to the islands the social habits of Englishmen and the goal of establishing landed estates modelled on those of the British gentry. But the expectation of a true gentry life-style was thwarted by an uncertain climate, a hostile disease environment, the threats of slave rebellion and foreign invaders, and the need to combine planting and manufacturing in the production of cane sugar. Azariah Pinney, founder of one of the great sugar fortunes in the island of Nevis, has been described as living in 'a small and close grained society, surrounded by men of another colour, liable to sudden ruin from hurricanes, fires or French invasions, and concentrated on getting rich quick in a trying climate and a strange landscape'. Such men must necessarily have lived on their nerves. Both the founding and subsequent generations of planters tended to seek the best of both worlds, to live extravagantly in the islands and later as absentee proprietors in the mother country. In general, they were acquisitive, quarrelsome, and often ruthless, prone to hard living and heavy drinking, but also men of enterprise and courage. 'Everyone seemed caught up in a race between quick wealth and quick death.' The consequence for the slaves was labour extracted by use of the whip, overwork, poor nutrition, inadequate medical treatment, and, all too often death at an early age. Jack Greene has, however, challenged the image of Barbadian planters as 'extravagant, loose, morally and culturally debased, and riddled with fears of social revolt'. Instead, he contends that the negative identity of white Barbadians had begun to improve by 1740 and, '[i]ncreasingly, between 1740 and 1780, Barbados came to be seen as a settled society whose members, whites and blacks, had come to terms with themselves and their environment with extremely positive results'.[15]

The typical sugar planter was a complex personality. He was at once a landlord, farmer, manufacturer, and merchant. He directed the subordinate whites and slaves in growing the cane, manufacturing the sugar, molasses, and rum, and

---

[14] Riva Berleant-Schiller, 'Free Labor and the Economy in Seventeenth-Century Montserrat', *William and Mary Quarterly*, Third Series, XLVI, (1989), pp. 539–64.

[15] [Edmund and William Burke], *An Account of the European Settlements in America*, 2 vols. (London, 1757), II, p. 106; Pares, *A West-India Fortune*, p. 25: Greene, 'Changing Identity', pp. 226, 264.

conducting the business affairs of his plantation. Although there were common-alities in the characteristics and behaviour of the sugar planters, there was also diversity in their origins and managerial performance. In this period one group of planters came from the professional, administrative, and especially mercantile ranks of West Indian society, while another emerged from subordinate managerial personnel on the plantations. Moreover, minority ethnic groups, chiefly Scots-men, Irishmen, and Sephardic Jews, made notable contributions to the quality of plantation management. Numerous lawyers, doctors, clergymen, merchants, and government officials practised their professions and businesses with a view toward accumulating capital to purchase sugar plantations. Among other professionals, Scottish doctors found a wide field of service and opportunities for personal gain in the sugar colonies. Many of these young men were said to be 'sober, frugal, and civil'; they exhibited managerial skills and accumulated sizeable fortunes.[16]

Barbados was in the vanguard of the British West Indies in the movement toward greater civil rights and political representation within the white commun-ity. The first General Assembly elected by freeholders was convened in 1639. It assumed its lasting form two years later with the right to initiate legislation. A decade later it was established that the government of Barbados should consist of a Governor appointed by the proprietor from England, a Council appointed by the Governor, and an Assembly elected by the freeholders from each parish. The Council and Assembly were regarded by the white settlers as the equivalent of the House of Lords and House of Commons in England. 'Extensive powers of self-government were achieved by the planter élite.' This élite also dominated the vestries which were elected by freeholders in the parishes to oversee the Anglican churches and provide aid to poor white residents. In Jamaica, where the first Assembly was called in 1664, the planters came to regard the main duty of their house of representatives as the protection of their local rights and interests.[17]

To Bryan Edwards, the planter-historian, the 'grand and most plausible' accu-sation against the general conduct of the planters arose 'from the necessity they find themselves under of having an annual recruit of slaves from Africa, to fill up the numbers that perish in the West Indies'. The demographic history of the slave population is discussed in Philip Morgan's chapter which contains an analysis of the 'high rates of natural decrease' among Caribbean slaves. In general, heavy mortality resulted from hard labour, harsh punishment, a low-protein diet, endemic and epidemic disease, and poor sanitation, housing, and clothing. Morgan, however, sees 'a modest birthrate' as the key to 'demographic failure'.

[16] Richard B. Sheridan, *Doctors and Slaves: A Medical and Demographic History of Slavery in the British West Indies, 1680–1834* (Cambridge, 1985), pp. 321–37.

[17] Beckles, *History of Barbados*, pp. 7–12.

Slave women gave birth to few children, among whom there was high infant and child mortality.[18]

Added to the planters' troubles was the difficulty they encountered in controlling their slaves. Slaves responded to harsh day-to-day treatment by individual resistance such as refusing to work, burning cane-fields, breaking tools, wounding and killing livestock, committing suicide, and especially running away. Collective resistance, on the other hand, took the form of conspiracy and revolt. A study of the aborted slave conspiracy in Antigua in 1736 describes the adverse economic conditions and subsistence crises brought on by drought and famine which contributed to increased flight and the conspiracy to gain control of the island. Slaves in the other British sugar islands also resorted to individual and collective acts of resistance and rebellion, especially during the 1720s and 1730s. In Jamaica the Governor, Council, and Assembly sent an address to the King in February 1734, 'to implore your most gracious assistance in our present dangerous and distressed condition'. The slaves were said to be continually deserting their masters in great numbers, and the insolent behaviour of others gave cause to fear a general defection. The defection was particularly feared by the planters in the frontier parishes of the island where the plantations were in close proximity to the Maroons who harboured runaway slaves.[19]

Old and new problems faced the planters in the thirty-five years from 1714 to 1748. As in earlier times, they needed to have access at reasonable prices to African slaves, sugar utensils and machinery, foodstuffs, building materials, and other essentials from abroad; and to adjust the supply of sugar to the metropolitan demand at a price level sufficient to maintain expected profits. Each island colony faced the age-old problem of keeping the slaves at work and preventing absenteeism and insurrection, which entailed having sufficient white men as overseers and militiamen. All of the islands had a problem of land engrossment, that is, large grants of land had been made to numerous proprietors who chose to keep these lands idle or barely used. Among the new problems was heightened international rivalry centred on the *Asiento* contract awarded by Spain to Great Britain; expansion of sugar production in the French colonies, especially Saint-Domingue; growing friction between British sugar planters and North American merchants and traders, leading to the passing of the Molasses Act; the recession in the British sugar industry and trade; clandestine trade and the War of Jenkins' Ear and the

[18] Bryan Edwards, *The History, Civil and Commercial, of the British Colonies in the West Indies*, 2 vols. (Dublin, 1793), II, pp. 134–35 and see below, pp. 467-70.

[19] David Barry Gaspar, *Bondmen and Rebels: A Study of Master–Slave Relations in Antigua* (Baltimore, 1985), pp. 208–10; Michael Craton, *Testing the Chains: Resistance to Slavery in the British West Indies* (Ithaca, NY, 1982), pp. 11–28, 52–57.

War of the Austrian Succession; and the growing problem of absentee proprietor-ship thinning the ranks of resident planters.

Numerous British planters and mercantile writers expressed concern about the growth of the French colonies and the impact of their sugar production upon prices in European markets. Writing to the Board of Trade in 1701, Governor Codrington exclaimed: 'The French begin to tred upon our heels in ye sugar trade; they have better Islands, I assure your Lordships, than wee; and Saint-Domingue will in time be a vast settlement.'[20] In the following decades Saint-Domingue forged ahead of Barbados, Martinique, and Jamaica and by the 1730s was at the beginning of its 'golden age', when it was the most valuable colony in the world. By 1739 it had approximately 350 plantations producing upwards of 40,000 tons of sugar annually, compared with 16,000 for Jamaica. Slave imports increased rapidly and reached unprecedented levels from 1737 to 1743. From approximately 30,000 in 1710, the slave population rose to 117,400 in 1739, at a time when Jamaica had 429 sugar plantations and nearly 100,000 slaves. Compared with British planters who were engaged in a drive towards monoculture in sugar production, French plan-ters produced a much larger proportion of minor staples. In Saint-Domingue more than one-third of the value of the island's exports consisted of indigo, cotton, cocoa, and coffee.[21]

Granting land in large acreages to a substantial number of proprietors, espe-cially in Jamaica, tended to encourage land speculation and check the growth of sugar production. It limited the growth of the white population at a time when slave imports increased in relation to white immigrants. The growing imbalance of the free and slave population enabled the latter to protest against their harsh treatment by running away from their masters and resorting to armed rebellion. William Wood implored the planters of Jamaica to 'lay aside the false and Narrow Notions and Schemes, entertained by too many of *them*; such as *that* the *Produce* of their *Plantations* will sell the *better*, the *fewer* the *Settlements*, which induces them to Engross great Tracts of *Land*'. Efforts to correct the racial imbalance were of long standing, going back to the decades of the 1680s and 1690s. In October 1723 the Assembly of Jamaica passed a bill 'to oblige the several inhabitants of this island to provide themselves with a sufficient number of white people, or pay certain sums of money in case they shall be deficient, and applying the same to several uses'. The failure of this and other Deficiency Laws to maintain a safe ratio of whites to blacks was both cause and effect of the Maroon War which plagued the white community from 1729 to 1739, and gave a check to the extension of sugar

[20] CO 152/4/E./51, f. 106; Malachy Postlethwayt, *Britain's Commercial Interest Explained and Improved*, 2 vols. (London, 1757), I, p. 437.

[21] Robert L. Stein, *The French Slave Trade in the Eighteenth Century* (Madison, 1979), pp. 22-24; Richard B. Sheridan, *Chapters in Caribbean History* (London, 1970), pp. 47-55.

culture. By the treaty of 1739 between the English commissioners and Captain Cudjoe, the Maroon leader, the latter agreed, in return for freedom, limited autonomy, and 1,500 acres of land for his people, to return runaway slaves to their masters for a reward, thus sealing off the interior of the island as a refuge for runaway slaves.[22]

Expansion of the French Caribbean colonies in relation to the British ones led to the former's near take-over of sugar markets in continental Europe, the decline of the British re-export trade, declining sugar prices in Britain and her colonies, and economic recession among British sugar planters and merchants. Moreover, drastic changes occurred in the north–south or 'Yankee–Creole' trade. From the Peace of Utrecht in 1713 the trade of Britain's North American colonies to the French islands assumed large dimensions and attracted almost constant attention by planters and politicians. The products of the North American colonies—fish, flour and bread, horses, lumber, and so on—were in great demand in the French and Dutch West Indies. In exchange, the northern traders returned home with sugar, molasses, cotton, logwood, indigo, currency, and bills of exchange. Molasses was of paramount importance since, unlike the British planters, who distilled their molasses into rum and shipped substantial quantities to British and Irish markets, French planters had no European markets for molasses and rum since the latter was banned in France to protect the brandy distillers. Yankee traders soon learned that they could purchase molasses more cheaply from the French than from the British colonies.

West Indian critics of North American trade with the foreign sugar colonies agreed that the traffic damaged the British sugar planters by depressing the price of West India produce, especially molasses and rum, raising the price of provisions and wood products, and draining currency and bullion from the islands. To discourage the trade, the West Indians circulated pamphlets, petitioned the King and Parliament, and persuaded their parliamentary supporters to introduce bills in the Commons and the Lords. Counter-petitions and pamphlets from the New England and Middle Colonies justified the trade with the French and Dutch colonies on the grounds that the British West Indies offered only a limited market for their products and supplied insufficient quantities of molasses for their rum distilleries. But superior political power was wielded by the West Indians, who were represented in Parliament and Whitehall by absentee planters, agents of the various colonial governments, and commission agents or merchants.

The chief problems which the planters hoped to solve by means of parliamentary legislation were the North American and Irish trade with the foreign sugar

---

[22] Wood, *A Survey of Trade*, p. 172; *Journals*, II, pp. 470, 616, 622; Craton, *Testing the Chains*, pp. 81–96.

colonies and the combinations of London sugar refiners and grocers. The planters understood that these two problems needed to be considered together because the solution of the one would contribute to the other. In other words, if they had a forced market in Ireland and North America, they could channel part of their commodities to these markets and thus force British buyers to pay higher prices for the smaller proportion shipped to the home market. At the same time, the planters hoped to secure legislation that would confine the trade of North America and Ireland to the British sugar colonies so they would be able to purchase plantation supplies more cheaply and have an outlet for part of their plantation produce.

The West India interest gained its first parliamentary victory in 1731, when an act was passed that granted liberty to export rum and other unenumerated commodities directly from the British sugar colonies to Ireland. A more important victory was gained in 1733 when the Molasses Act was passed in the face of strong opposition from the North American colonies. The Act levied near-prohibitive duties on all foreign sugar, molasses, and rum imported into the American colonies. Moreover, it barred French sugar, molasses, and rum from Ireland, and other foreign and British sugar that was imported there had to be shipped from Great Britain in vessels that conformed to the Navigation Acts. Finally, an act of 1739 granted liberty to ship plantation sugar directly to continental European markets. It was designed to give the planters and sugar merchants another weapon with which to harass the sugar buyers of London. The outcome of the above acts of Parliament was mixed. While the North Americans continued to import foreign West Indian sugar products in disregard of the law, the other measures were quite effective in expanding the protected market for West India commodities in the British Isles, and especially Ireland. In addition to Ireland, the planters had acquired a protected market for their commodities when the Act of Union brought Scotland within the scope of the Navigation Acts in 1707.

Planters needed slaves imported from Africa, not only to increase the labour force on existing plantations and settle new ones, but also to replace the slaves who died. In the issue of his *Review* of 10 January 1713, Daniel Defoe explained how the plantation trade of the West Indies was blended and interwoven with the trade to Africa and the North American colonies: '*No African* Trade, *no* Negroes; *no* Negroes, *no* Sugars, Ginger, Indicos, &c.; *no* Sugars, &c., *no* Islands; *no* Islands, *no* Continent; *no* Continent, *no* Trade; that is to say, farewell all your *American* Trade, your *West-India* Trade...' To William Wood the African trade was 'the *Spring* and *Parent* whence the others flow and are dependent', and 'the *Labour of Negroes*' was 'the principal *Foundation* of our *Riches* from the *Plantations*'.[23]

[23] Daniel Defoe, *Review*, 10 Jan. 1713, I, No. 44, p. 89; Wood, *Survey of Trade*, pp. 179-83, 193.

The slave trade from Africa to the British sugar colonies was substantially altered when, in 1713, the *Asiento* or monopoly right to sell slaves to the Spanish American colonies was granted to Britain for thirty years and vested in the South Sea Company. From a trade which had been carried on by the Royal African Company and 'separate' traders and was directed largely to the British-American colonies, there was now a dual system of the South Sea Company's trade to the Spanish colonies and the Royal African Company's trade and that of the 'separate traders' to the British colonies as well as an illicit trade to the Spanish Main. Behind the legal concessions accorded the South Sea Company there were great opportunities for illicit trade, with Jamaica as its centre. Previous to the *Asiento*, the port of Kingston, Jamaica, had a lively trading community and annually employed in the Spanish trade about 1,200 men and 200 sail of sloops which carried slaves and manufactures to the Spanish Main and returned with bullion, coin, and tropical agricultural commodities. The greater part of these independent traders was displaced by the South Sea Company's factors who resided in Kingston and handled the transshipment of slaves and manufactures and Spanish products and currency. William Wood warned of the dangerous consequences of the presence of the South Sea Company in Jamaica, 'by ruining its Trade, and consequently preventing its *encreasing* in People and New Settlements'.[24]

Joining the merchants in complaints against the South Sea Company were the planters, who contended that the greater part of the imported slaves were purchased and resold by the Company's factors to the Spanish, thus narrowing the market and driving up prices charged to local buyers. In order to limit the Company's conduct of the slave trade, the planter-dominated Assembly of Jamaica imposed a heavy duty on the exportation of slaves. This and similar measures drew protests from the Company to the Board of Trade in London, which decreed that from 1727 onwards the Company should be exempted from the duty on slaves who were landed in Jamaica for refreshment only, and also from the differential duties. 'The Asiento', declared Governor Sir Nicholas Lawes in 1717, 'carried all the able, stout, and Young Negroes ... to the Spaniards and Sell none to the planters but old, Sickly, and decrepid, or what are called Refuse...' For choice slaves the planters had to 'give as much or more than the Spaniards, & that in ready money'. Annual import and re-export statistics show that in eight of the twenty years from 1716 to 1735, more slaves were re-exported than retained and sold to the planters of Jamaica. These figures do not necessarily support the planters' case, however, since there is some merit in the South Sea Company's

---

[24] Wood, *Survey of Trade*, p. 285.

contention that, in the absence of the stimulus it gave to the African trade, the planters would have been less well supplied with servile labour.[25]

The War of Jenkins' Ear from 1739 to 1748 has been called the first 'trade war' in British history and the first major European war to be fought expressly for West Indian ends. It followed the breakdown of negotiations over losses suffered by Britain and Spain in carrying out the terms of the *Asiento* Treaty. Spain retaliated against the British smugglers by turning over the enforcement of its trade monopoly to the *Guarda-Costas*, which were fitted out in Spanish or colonial ports and carried commissions from the local Governors to stop illegal trade. It was estimated by authorities in London that 180 British ships were illegally confiscated or pillaged between 1713 and 1731. West Indian merchants took their grievances to King, Parliament, and country. 'It was a sudden and noisy explosion of imperialism,' wrote Richard Pares, 'a good example of the greedy turbulence which foreign observers attributed to the English nation... The interruption of the Spanish trade in general continued throughout the war to be a very important part of the navy's business, especially in the West Indies where some very rich prizes were taken.'[26]

The war between Britain and France, which broke out in 1744, was quite different from that with Spain. Whereas the colonial systems of Britain and Spain produced and exchanged complementary products, that of Britain and France consisted of two sets of sugar colonies that were bitter rivals. War offered Britain the opportunity to cripple French sugar production, since this goal could not be achieved in open competition. Writing to the Duke of Newcastle in 1748, Governor Edward Trelawny of Jamaica warned that 'unless French Hispaniola [Saint-Domingue] is ruined during the war they will, upon a peace, ruin our sugar colonies by the quantity they will make and the low price they afford to sell it at'. Later in the same year Trelawny and Admiral Charles Knowles led a raiding party into Saint-Domingue and captured Fort St Louis, the strongest fort in the colony. Trelawny wrote to the Board of Trade that 'the best policy would probably be not to hold St. Domingue, but rather to desolate all the plantations there'. But by this time the war was near the end and the British forces were withdrawn.[27]

Earlier in the war against France the British had turned to cutting off their trade, and limiting their ability to market their sugar in Europe. The French slave trade was almost completely destroyed. Despite the crises and hardships, the British

---

[25] Lawes to Board of Trade, 11 Nov. 1717, CO 137/O/178; Fuller to Board of Trade, 30 Jan. 1778, CO 137/83/Hh3/4; see below, pp. 458–60.

[26] Peggy K. Liss, *Atlantic Empires: The Network of Trade and Revolution, 1713–1826* (Baltimore, 1983), pp. 10–24; Pares, *War and Trade*, pp. 14–19, 68, 111–14.

[27] Cited in Pares, *War and Trade*, p. 180; and in George Metcalf, *Royal Government and Political Conflict in Jamaica, 1729–1783* (London, 1965), p. 77.

sugar colonies fared much better in wartime than their French rivals. British shipping was better protected and more regular, and freight and insurance rates much lower. On the other hand, North Americans supplied the French islands with provisions under cover of flags of truce, causing considerable suffering for want of such provisions in the British sugar islands. The powerful West India interest used its influence to secure warships to protect the islands and escort convoys which sailed at fairly regular intervals to and from the British colonies. By contrast, the merchants in the major ports of France wrangled among themselves and frustrated the comprehensive convoy plan of the Minister of Marine. The upshot was almost complete breakdown of the French colonial system in the last year of the war: 'her navy was diminished by the loss of two squadrons, and her trade was disorganized and defenceless.'[28]

No important question between Britain and France in the West Indies was settled by the Treaty of Aix-la-Chapelle in 1748. Both nations were strongly opposed to the expansion of sugar production in the region. Therefore, the four disputed islands—Dominica, St Lucia, St Vincent, and Tobago—were declared neutral and both parties agreed to evacuate their settlers from them. In the settlement between Britain and Spain, the South Sea Company received £100,000 sterling and its trading privileges were renewed for four years; however, by a further treaty the *Asiento* and the annual ship were finally surrendered by the South Sea Company in 1750.

Edmund and William Burke said that there were no parts of the world in which great estates were made in so short a time as in the West Indies, whereas Adam Smith asserted that the profits of a sugar plantation in any of the British West Indian colonies were 'generally much greater than those of any other cultivation that is known either in Europe or America'. Smith had in mind the high profits accruing to sugar planters in the period 1749–75, which were considerably greater than those in the 1720s and 1730s. For the inter-war years from 1749 to 1755, J. R. Ward has estimated that the annual rate of profit in British West Indian sugar planting amounted to 10.1 per cent for all of the islands, ranging from 3.4 per cent for Barbados, 10.6 for the Leewards, and 13.0 for Jamaica. Absenteeism in Jamaica had increased to such a point in 1740 that a law was enacted to require the agents and attorneys of absentees and minors to submit annual reports of staple crops and their disposition to the local government. Included among the prominent absentees of the mid-eighteenth-century period were members of the families of Beckford, Long, Codrington, Lascelles, Dawkins, Bayly, Pennant, Fuller, Oliver,

---

[28] Pares, *War and Trade*, pp. 304–25, 392; Pitman *Development of West Indies*, pp. 285–96.

Tudway, Martin, and Drax, who were allied with the landed aristocracy and the commercial bourgeoisie of the seaport towns.[29]

Perhaps the most pressing problem faced by British planters was the low profitability of the sugar industry in the first half of the eighteenth century, especially in the decades of the 1720s and 1730s. The average annual price of colonial muscovado sugar at London declined from 32 shillings per hundred-weight in 1716 to 22s. in 1721, and then recovered to 28s. 4d. in 1724. From 1725 to 1726 prices ranged between 21s. 6d. and 26s. 4d. Then came the devastating drop to 16s. 11¼d. in 1733, the next-to-lowest price during the period from 1674 to 1775. The price of sugar rose to 25s. 8½d. in 1734, and ranged from 18s 9½d. to 32s. ½d. from 1735 to 1740. The Assembly and Council of Jamaica blamed the island's sorry plight on 'the lowness of our produce in Great Britain, the loss of our trade and the heavy taxes we have been under the necessity of raising to defray the expense of the parties fitted out against the rebellious negroes'.[30]

The London grocers and sugar refiners complained that the consistently higher sugar prices in the decades of the 1740s and 1750s resulted from the refusal of Jamaican planters to settle new lands suitable for sugar estates. They were joined by merchants, government officials, and smallholders, who complained that the planters dominated the colonial government and used their influence to secure generous land grants and other favours. The planter-historian Edward Long denied that the planters were restricting sugar production to force up the price, noting that after the Maroon Treaty of 1739 and the passage of several acts of the local government to encourage smallholders, 'settlements began to be formed in those parts where none chose to venture before'. He named ten outlying parishes which 'began to be cleared for plantations'.

It seems evident that around the middle of the century economic conditions began to improve in Jamaica and in other British Caribbean colonies as output increased while prices, sustained by a buoyant demand in the home market, remained at a higher level than in previous decades. Planters, who had endured a long period of low prices, damaging wars, strong French competition, and turbulence among their slaves, entered into the 'silver age' of relative prosperity

[29] [Edmund and William Burke], *European Settlements*, II, p. 104; Adam Smith, *Wealth of Nations* (1776; New York, 1937), p. 366; J. R. Ward, *British West Indian Slavery, 1750–1834: The Process of Amelioration* (Oxford, 1988), pp. 45–51; Eric Williams, *Capitalism and Slavery* (Chapel Hill, NC, 1944), pp. 85–97; Douglas Hall, 'Absentee-Proprietorship in the British West Indies, To About 1850', *The Jamaican Historical Review*, IV (1964), pp. 15–35; Sheridan, *Sugar and Slavery*, pp. 385–88; Keith Mason, 'The World an Absentee Planter and His Slaves Made: Sir William Stapleton and His Nevis Sugar Estate, 1722–1740', *Bulletin of The John Rylands University Library of Manchester*, LXXV (1993), pp. 103–31.

[30] Sheridan, *Sugar and Slavery*, pp. 496–97; *Calendar of State Papers, Colonial Series, America and West Indies, 1734–35* (London, 1953), p. 190.

for much of the second half of the eighteenth century. More and more of them were able to remove from the islands to Great Britain to display their slave-produced wealth and vie with the returning 'nabobs' from the East Indies.[31]

[31] Edward Long, *The History of Jamaica*, 3 vols. (London, 1774), I, pp. 429–35.

Select Bibliography

HILARY McD. BECKLES, *A History of Barbados: From Amerindian Settlement to Nation State* (Cambridge, 1990).

RUTH BOURNE, *Queen Anne's Navy in the West Indies* (New Haven, 1939).

[EDMUND and WILLIAM BURKE], *An Account of the European Settlements in America*, 2 vols. (London, 1757).

JOHN CARY, *An Essay on the State of England in Relation to its Trade* (Bristol, 1695).

MICHAEL CRATON and JAMES WALVIN, *A Jamaican Plantation: The History of Worthy Park, 1670–1970* (Toronto, 1970).

K. G. DAVIES, *The Royal African Company* (London, 1957).

NOEL DEERR, *The History of Sugar*, 2 vols. (London, 1949–50).

RICHARD S. DUNN, *Sugar and Slaves: The Rise of the Planter Class in the English West Indies, 1624–1713* (Chapel Hill, NC, 1972).

BRYAN EDWARDS, *The History, Civil and Commercial, of the British Colonies in the West Indies*, 3 vols. (London, 1793).

JACK P. GREENE, 'Changing Identity in the British Caribbean: Barbados as a Case Study', in Nicholas Canny and Anthony Pagden, eds., *Colonial Identity in the Atlantic World, 1500–1800* (Princeton, 1987), pp. 213–66.

PEGGY K. LISS, *Atlantic Empires: The Network of Trade and Revolution, 1713–1826* (Baltimore, 1983)

EDWARD LITTLETON, *The Groans of the Plantations* (London, 1689).

SIDNEY W. MINTZ, *Sweetness and Power: The Place of Sugar in Modern History* (New York, 1985).

RICHARD PARES, *War and Trade in the West Indies, 1739–1763* (Oxford, 1936).

FRANK WESLEY PITMAN, *The Development of the British West Indies, 1700–1763* (New Haven, 1917).

RICHARD B. SHERIDAN, *Sugar and Slavery: An Economic History of the British West Indies, 1623–1775* (Barbados, 1974).

THOMAS TRYON, *Tryon's Letters, Domestic and Foreign* (London, 1700).

DAVID WATTS, *The West Indies: Patterns of Development, Culture and Environmental Change since 1492* (Cambridge, 1987).

ERIC WILLIAMS, *Capitalism and Slavery* (Chapel Hill, NC, 1944).

WILLIAM WOOD, *A Survey of Trade* (London, 1718).

19

The British West Indies in the Age of Abolition, 1748–1815

J. R. WARD

At the end of the War of the Austrian Succession in 1748 the main British West Indian colonies comprised Barbados, the Leeward Islands (Antigua, St Kitts, Nevis, Montserrat), and Jamaica, all seventeenth-century acquisitions, though St Kitts had not been cleared of its French zone until 1702. There were also minor British outposts on the Bahamas and the Virgin Islands, while a few hundred British settlers defied Spanish territorial claims in the Bay of Honduras (Belize) and in the Mosquito Shore territory (the east coast of modern Nicaragua). As a result of the Seven Years War (1756–63) Britain gained Dominica, St Vincent, Grenada, and Tobago (the 'Ceded Islands'), while the Revolutionary and Napoleonic Wars (1793–1815) brought her Trinidad, St Lucia, and Demerara.[1] Successive agreements with Spain, in 1763, 1783, and 1786, secured the Honduras logwood cutting colony, though the territory remained legally Spanish until 1862, and under a 1786 Convention the British evacuated the Mosquito Shore (see Map 19.1).

The years from 1748 to 1815 thus constitute a new phase of British expansion in the Caribbean, when the region was a main focus of national strategic effort. During this period the West Indies achieved their greatest economic importance within the British Empire. After holding steady at about 10 per cent during the first half of the eighteenth century, their share of British exports and imports rose to about 20 per cent by 1815. Nevertheless, Britain's territorial gains here were modest by comparison with the contemporary advance in India, and they provided a weak basis for future development. Subsequently the British West Indies' relative importance would decline sharply. Their share of British overseas trade fell to 10 per cent in the 1820s and 5 per cent in the 1850s.

The colonies' economic standing was determined above all by their performance as sugar producers. They accounted for about 40 per cent of transatlantic

---

[1] Tobago was held by the French in the periods 1783–93 and 1802–03. The name 'Demerara' is used here to include the adjacent colonies of Berbice and Essequibo, all three of them originally Dutch, and united in 1831 as British Guiana.

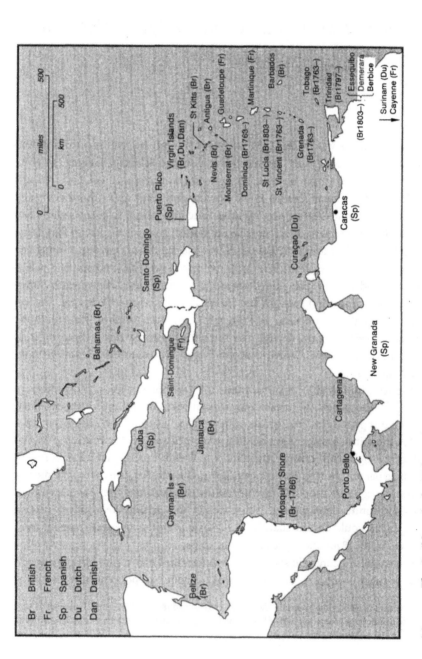

Map 19.1. The Caribbean in the Eighteenth Century

Br   British
Fr   French
Sp   Spanish
Du   Dutch
Dan Danish

Bahamas (Br)

Santo Domingo (Sp)

Puerto Rico (Sp)

Virgin Islands (Br, Du, Dan)

St Kitts (Br)
Antigua (Br)
Nevis (Br)
Guadeloupe (Fr)
Montserrat (Br)
Dominica (Br1763→)
Martinique (Fr)
St Lucia (Br1803→)
St Vincent (Br1763→)
Barbados (Br)
Grenada (Br1763→)
Tobago (Br1763→)
Trinidad (Br1797→)

Curaçao (Du)

Caracas (Sp)

Essequibo
Demerara   (Br1803→)
Berbice

Surinam (Du)
Cayenne (Fr)

Saint-Domingue (Fr)

Cuba (Sp)

Jamaica (Br)

Cayman Is (Br)

Mosquito Shore (Br~1786)

New Granada (Sp)

Cartagena

Porto Bello

Belize (Br)

0   500
miles

0   500
km

sugar consignments to Europe in 1700, 30 per cent in 1748, 60 per cent in 1815, but only 20 per cent in the 1850s, when the lead had been taken by Cuba and Puerto Rico.[2] It is curious that these two islands, both of them still Spanish possessions, achieved such success. The British had long coveted Spanish colonial wealth. Between 1748 and 1815 Spain continued its decline to inconsequence as a European power, while Britain was ascendant, on a number of occasions identifying Cuba and Puerto Rico as possible acquisitions. Yet only Trinidad, the least important of the Spanish West Indies, came under British control. Projects for annexing the main French islands (Saint-Domingue, Martinique, Guadeloupe) also failed.

Many of the forces that cut back the British West Indies' significance in the nineteenth century only came into play after 1815,[3] but the influences prefigured before that date require some discussion here. The British did not take over more territory suitable for low-cost sugar production because of the limits to the military power which they could deploy in the Caribbean, and the diplomatic complications entailed by conquests from European rivals. Therefore much British West Indian investment was concentrated on islands with rather limited natural resources, where many plantations eventually became quite uncompetitive. Development would be restricted further by Parliament's abolition of the national slave trade from Africa in 1807. The colonies depended on slave labour, and abolition caused a long-term decline in the sugar estates' effective work-force, while slave imports to the Spanish West Indies continued on a large scale for another half-century. New metropolitan social forces and moral values persuaded the British to handicap themselves in this way. Economic difficulties stimulated some improvement of West Indian estate agriculture, but innovation was held back by habits of absentee ownership and delegated management among the planter élite, which remained largely transient and expatriate in character. By 1815 the British Caribbean had a quite numerous locally born class of mixed race 'free coloureds'. However, they were still subject to severe discrimination, and could not make up for the deficiencies of the white population in business leadership.

In the early eighteenth century competition from the French West Indies had driven British colonial sugar out of continental Europe and confined it more or less to the protected metropolitan market. The price of sugar fell and British planters complained of economic distress.[4] So for the most part they strongly opposed new Caribbean conquests, which would further depress the sugar trade,

---

[2] Noel Deerr, *The History of Sugar*, 2 vols., (London, 1949–50).
[3] See Vol. III, chap. by Gad Heuman.
[4] See above, p. 413.

raise the cost of imported supplies, and weaken the existing colonies by attracting away settlers. The predominant British view was that military operations in the West Indies should damage or destroy French rivals and foster contraband trade with Spanish colonists, rather than bring more cane land under British rule. Vernon's expedition in 1741 attempted to conquer eastern Cuba, but failed through mismanagement and the inadequacy of the forces put at his disposal.[5] By the time of the Seven Years War circumstances had changed. British naval ascendancy was now so marked that Martinique and Guadeloupe could be captured from France without much difficulty. The fall of Quebec released for Caribbean service several thousand troops, who in 1762 took Havana, Cuba's principal town. Many British West Indian colonists were persuaded that their interests would be best served by subjugating the French islands, which experience had shown to be a serious threat in wartime as privateering bases. Sugar prices had risen considerably since the 1730s. Merchants and refiners complained that the established British islands were apparently unable to meet the growth of national demand, while the planters themselves understood that they now had less to fear from an enlarged supply.

Nevertheless, at the Peace of Paris the British in 1763 took their main winnings in North America. France gave up all claims east of the Mississippi while recovering Martinique and Guadeloupe. Spain gave up East Florida and recovered Havana. In the Caribbean Britain acquired only four small, undeveloped islands. Britain and France had previously agreed to regard three of these (Dominica, St Vincent, Tobago) as neutral, with neither government pressing its claims, though in fact French outnumbered British among the islands' sparse pioneering populations. For security reasons France particularly wanted St Lucia, the fourth neutral island, and to obtain it handed over the marginal colony of Grenada. Within Britain the peace terms were controversial. William Pitt, who had directed British strategy for most of the war, though out of office since 1761, claimed to believe that the country should hold on to most of the conquests, thus permanently weakening France and Spain. A more widely expressed view was that at least Guadeloupe should be kept, perhaps instead of Canada. Guadeloupe, already highly productive, would yield an additional supply of sugar, and an immediate revenue to help defray the costs of the war. An enlarged British Caribbean Empire was required, to discourage the North Americans from bartering their growing surpluses of corn, fish, and lumber for the foreign islands' rum and molasses, in violation of the colonial trade laws. Eliminating the French threat from the north would make the mainland colonists more self-confident and less likely to accept metropolitan authority. So why did the British negotiators prefer Canada?

[5] Richard Pares, *War and Trade in the West Indies, 1739–1763* (Oxford, 1936), pp. 77–85, 92–93.

Some observers claimed that absentee sugar-plantation owners exercised a disproportionate influence as MPs and lobbyists. While colonists in the West Indies might welcome the greater security and the new business opportunities offered by annexations, absentees were safe in England with their fortunes made, and concerned above all to defend monopoly profits by limiting new sugar supplies. In fact the absentees and their merchant friends (the West India 'interest') did not carry enough political weight on their own account to decide a matter of such importance. They were divided among themselves over commercial issues, and had a modest parliamentary representation, with perhaps twenty out of 558 votes in the House of Commons.[6] Their cause enjoyed success only to the extent that it coincided with wider metropolitan interests. British policy was determined above all by war-weariness, by the desire to secure a lasting peace, and by the feeling that as hostilities with France had broken out in North America, the treaty terms should resolve matters by confirming British supremacy there. Diplomatic considerations required the victors to show restraint. If the British insisted on Canada and the Mississippi frontier, then they had to give ground elsewhere. In the West Indies it was reasonable to take the Ceded Islands (but not Guadeloupe) because doing so inflicted little immediate loss on France.[7]

The War of American Independence put the British on the defensive in the West Indies. Between 1778 and 1782 all the Ceded Islands and all the Leewards except Antigua fell to France, though in her exhausted state at the end of the war she could keep only Tobago. During the peace negotiations the British Cabinet agreed, at the instigation of Lord Shelburne and George III, that Spain should be given back Gibraltar in exchange for Puerto Rico, to help restore the overseas Empire after the loss of the thirteen colonies. However, the scheme was abandoned when it caused a public outcry and France withdrew her support for Spain's claim to Gibraltar.[8]

The resumption of hostilities in 1793 gave new opportunities for an expansionist British Caribbean strategy.[9] The French Revolution had provoked political turmoil throughout the French West Indies, and slave insurrection on Saint-Domingue. Royalist planters offered allegiance to the British Crown in return for military intervention. The events of 1778–82 confirmed that sugar islands were highly vulnerable when command of the sea was lost, and that France was still a formidable naval power, largely on the strength of her Caribbean trade. Therefore

---

[6] L. B. Namier, *England in the Age of the American Revolution* (London, 1930), pp. 271–79.

[7] Ronald Hyam and Ged Martin, *Reappraisals in British Imperial History* (London, 1975), pp. 20–43. See above, p. 374.

[8] H. M. Scott, *British Foreign Policy in the Age of the American Revolution* (Oxford, 1990), pp. 332–34.

[9] See above, pp. 186–87.

the British government determined to occupy the French West Indies, certainly for the duration of the war, and permanently if possible.

The expedition sent out in 1793–94 captured Martinique, Guadeloupe, and St Lucia. But the last two of these were soon lost again, while the French retaliated by fomenting revolt in 1795 among Grenada's still numerous francophone settlers and St Vincent's Black Caribs.[10] At the same time rebellion broke out among Jamaica's Maroons, the descendants of slave runaways, recognized by the colonists as free communities under the peace treaty of 1739. New British contingents arrived to help restore order and retrieve the position. They also took Demerara and Trinidad, as the Netherlands and Spain were now allied with France, but in 1797 an attempt against Puerto Rico failed, and the next year the British evacuated their bridgehead on Saint-Domingue. Proposals for the occupation of Cuba came to nothing.

The Caribbean campaigns of the 1790s achieved very little, despite absorbing half Britain's current war expenditures. There was mismanagement and mistiming in the despatch of forces. Troops often arrived during the unhealthiest summer months, aggravating losses from tropical fever. The freeing of the slaves on the French islands, by insurrection and by republican decree, enlarged the opposition forces against which the British had to contend. Military effort was spread over too wide a range of objectives. Hitherto Saint-Domingue, France's richest overseas possession, had seemed impregnable. Now the colony's internal troubles apparently put it within the British grasp, to provide a futile, exhausting diversion. Spain had been spurred by the loss of Havana in 1762 to strengthen defences on both Cuba and Puerto Rico, while Britain could no longer draw strategic support from North America. Finally, France was not effectively challenged during the 1790s on the European continent. Britain had no reliable allies there, partly because of the resentment at her transatlantic preoccupations. These gave the impression that she was concerned above all to monopolize the trade in sugar and coffee, prices for which had risen sharply as a result of the curtailment of exports from Saint-Domingue.[11]

In 1802 Britain felt obliged to return under the Treaty of Amiens all her West Indian conquests except Trinidad, and when war resumed in 1803 the Caribbean was given a much lower priority.[12] The losses of the 1790s had strengthened its reputation as a graveyard for soldiers, deterred army recruitment, and shown how

[10] The Black Caribs were the offspring of unions between escaped slaves and St Vincent's indigenous Amerindians.

[11] Michael Duffy, *Soldiers, Sugar, and Seapower: The British Expeditions to the West Indies and the War Against Revolutionary France* (Oxford, 1987).

[12] Christopher D. Hall, *British Strategy in the Napoleonic War, 1803–15* (Manchester, 1992), pp. 77–79, 95, 109, 184–86.

overseas adventures could undermine European strategy. The scarcities caused by the Saint-Domingue insurrection had stimulated planters elsewhere to increase their output, so now markets were glutted, and further tropical acquisitions would not serve any economic purpose. France was no longer a plausible threat as a colonial or naval power, after the failure of the expedition sent by Napoleon for the reconquest of Saint-Domingue in 1801–02, his sale of Louisiana to the United States in 1803, and the Battle of Trafalgar in 1805. Britain promptly retook the easiest West Indian prizes, but left Martinique and Guadeloupe alone until 1809–10, when they could be dealt with by local forces. Following France's invasion of Spain in 1808 the Governor of Jamaica was ordered to seize Cuba, so that the island would not fall into French hands. These instructions were cancelled as soon as the extent of the anti-French revolt within Spain became clear. The expedition organized for the West Indies went to the Peninsula instead, and no Caribbean projects were allowed that might threaten the British alliance with the Junta of Seville.[13] At the peace negotiations of 1814–15 Britain was concerned above all to maintain the European coalition against France, and not to seem greedy for new colonies. So her only gains were St Lucia (as a naval base), Tobago, and Demerara (where most plantations were already British-owned).[14]

The West Indies' share of British trade increased during the 1748–1815 period partly through their established function as sugar producers. Sugar remained Britain's largest single import from the 1750s, when it overtook foreign linen, until the 1820s, when it was surpassed by raw cotton. The buoyancy of the sugar trade was due above all to the strength of metropolitan demand. British sugar imports, nearly all from the West Indies, doubled between 1700 and 1748 and rose fourfold between 1748 and 1815. The post-1748 acceleration reflected the faster growth of the British population, and the continuing rise in sugar consumption per head, from about four pounds in 1700 to ten pounds in 1748 and twenty pounds in 1800. Then increased import duties halted the upward trend in consumption rates until the 1840s, though sugar sales continued to rise in line with the growth of population. For comparison, French sugar consumption per head averaged only about two pounds in the 1780s.[15] The particular British taste for sugar was a consequence of greater national prosperity, and the changes in diet encouraged by urbanization,

---

[13] William W. Kaufmann, *British Policy and the Independence of Latin America, 1804–1828* (New Haven, 1951), pp. 41–43.

[14] C. K. Webster, *The Foreign Policy of Castlereagh, 1812–1815* (London, 1931), pp. 194–96, 272.

[15] Richard B. Sheridan, *Sugar and Slavery: An Economic History of the British West Indies, 1623–1775* (Barbados, 1974), pp. 20–29, 487–89; B. R. Mitchell and P. Deane, *Abstract of British Historical Statistics* (Cambridge, 1962), pp. 5, 355–56; Robert Louis Stein, *The French Sugar Business in the Eighteenth Century* (Baton Rouge, La., 1988), pp. 163–64.

especially the spread of tea drinking. Apart from the British home market, the sugar re-export trade to continental Europe also enjoyed a modest revival when French competition was eliminated by the Saint-Domingue uprising and the 1793–1815 wars.

The British West Indies' trade was further enlarged through diversification. In the 1750s their exports consisted almost entirely of sugar, rum, and molasses, unlike the French islands where various 'minor staples' (coffee, indigo, cocoa, and cotton) were quite significant. British planters had been led towards monoculture by the strength of demand in the protected national market, where sugar now usually sold at prices some 50 per cent higher than in continental Europe. Heavy import duties restricted British coffee consumption, for the benefit of the East India Company's tea business. Indigo was available from South Carolina and through contraband trade with Spanish Central America. Then from the 1760s the share of British West Indian exports accounted for by commodities other than sugar and rum began to rise, reaching a maximum of about 40 per cent in the Napoleonic War period. French settlers had begun coffee growing on Grenada and Dominica before the islands came into British hands. The crop was developed on a large scale in Jamaica in the 1790s, taking advantage of the shortages caused by the Saint-Domingue rebellion. The conquered foreign colonies, Demerara especially, made a further contribution to the British West Indian coffee trade. Supplies were almost entirely re-exported to the continent until 1808, when a cut in the duty on retained imports established coffee for the first time as an item of British mass consumption. During the 1780s the West Indies briefly became the main source of raw material for the rapidly expanding British cotton industry. Then lower-cost cotton imports from the United States outstripped Caribbean supplies.[16] Between 1748 and 1815 the proportion of British West Indian slaves employed on sugar estates fell from about 70 per cent to 60 per cent, but the tendency to diversify would not be sustained. The British West Indies remained essentially sugar colonies, and continued to feature as such in metropolitan debate on Imperial issues.

In the 1750s and 1760s about 85 per cent of British West Indian exports were consigned to Britain, while nearly all the remainder went to North America in exchange for lumber, grain, flour, and salt fish. The thirteen colonies' rebellion almost completely halted the North American trade, and it was severely restricted after 1782 by the Imperial government's determination to favour Canada and British shipping. From 1793 United States traders were given freer access to the British West Indies, but meanwhile demand for rum and molasses in North

---

[16] Lowell Joseph Ragatz, *Statistics for the Study of British Caribbean Economic History, 1763–1833* (London, 1927).

America had been limited by the growth there of whisky distilling. Also many sugar planters had increased food cultivation on their estates, to reduce dependence on imported supplies. Scottish herrings tended to replace Newfoundland codfish in the slaves' rations. Thus, after 1793 the North Americans recovered only half their pre-1776 share of British West Indian trade.

Imports from the Caribbean to Britain greatly exceeded in value British exports to the West Indies. The difference was covered by the British-controlled supplies of shipping, mercantile services, and African slaves to the sugar islands, by interest charges due to metropolitan creditors, and by estate profits remitted to plantation owners resident in Britain. Between 1748 and 1815 the trade flows became somewhat less unbalanced. Britain's imports from the West Indies increased fivefold, from 21 per cent to 28 per cent of total British imports. Her exports to the West Indies rose tenfold, from 5 per cent to 12 per cent of total exports.[17] The trend resulted partly from larger West Indian purchases of British-supplied goods for local use. Slaves' allowances of imported clothing rose over the period. Sugar planters bought increasingly elaborate processing equipment. The military campaigns of the 1790s further enlarged colonial expenditures. British exports to the Caribbean were also stimulated through the islands' entrepôt function in trade with Spanish America.

British West Indian re-export trade to the Spanish colonies, of considerable importance during the early eighteenth century, was in decline by the 1750s, as Spain began liberalizing her imperial commercial regulations to make foreign contraband less profitable. Further damage was done immediately after the Seven Years War when the British authorities attempted to reassert the principle of exclusive colonial commerce by seizing Spanish ships suspected to be engaged in illicit dealings with British possessions. Britain then tried to retrieve the situation through the Free Port Act of 1766. Four Jamaican ports were declared open to foreign shipping, with the aim of attracting Spanish merchants. Two other free ports were designated on Dominica, as channels for trade with the French islands. At first Spain thwarted the 1766 Act's main purpose by responding with new and more rigorous measures to discourage her colonial subjects from contact with the British. From the 1780s, however, technical progress made British manufactures increasingly competitive. The British government's recognition of industry's growing need for raw materials and market outlets brought a further extension of the free port system in 1787, to Grenada and the Bahamas. Finally, the 1793–1815 wars disrupted Spain's own transatlantic trade as a means of supplying her

[17] Mitchell and Deane, *Abstract of British Historical Statistics*, pp. 310–11. Reference here is to official trade values. Estimates of trade at current market values are rather different, but they indicate the same general patterns: Ralph Davis, *The Industrial Revolution and British Overseas Trade* (Leicester, 1979), pp. 77–117.

colonies with European goods. The occupation of Trinidad gave the British another access point to Caracas and New Granada. The Spanish American independence movements after 1808 effectively eliminated any remaining official restraints on contraband. Towards the end of the Napoleonic period probably about half of Britain's exports to her Caribbean colonies were for shipment onwards to Spanish American customers. In the 1820s the free port trade would decline sharply, as the new Latin American republics became established and foreign merchants could settle there to conduct business directly with Europe.[18]

While the West Indies' commercial importance to Britain increased during most of the 1748–1815 period, West Indian lobbyists' influence over British policy tended to decline, from a high point reached about the middle of the eighteenth century. They did not determine the provisions of the 1763 peace settlement relating to the Caribbean, but on lesser issues had often prevailed. After 1748 they did so less frequently. The West Indians lost favour partly through public resentment at higher sugar prices. Rising profits allowed many more sugar planters to settle in Britain as absentee owners, where they gained a reputation for extravagance and ostentatious wealth, capable of bearing a much heavier tax burden. In 1750 the import duty on muscovado sugar stood at 4s. 10d. per hundredweight (about 15 per cent *ad valorem*). By 1815 the duty had been raised to 30s. per hundredweight (about 50 per cent *ad valorem*).

Politicians were becoming more conscious of colonies' potential value as a strategic asset, and more determined to make them serve the national purpose. Thus, after the Seven Years War commissioners were sent out to sell land in the Ceded Islands at public auction, with the aim of preventing the accumulation of large holdings by well-connected individuals that was believed to have occurred on Jamaica and to be restricting the growth of sugar exports. The 1766 Free Port Act, intended to enlarge British manufacturers' exports and their supply of raw materials, was passed over the objections of West Indian planters, who feared that it would admit foreign-grown produce in competition with their own. The strict line taken after 1783 at the West Indians' expense against North American shipping was intended to benefit the British merchant marine. Such measures assumed that overseas Empire offered the mother country important benefits, which government should try to maximize, overriding special interests where necessary. A more fundamental challenge to the West Indians' political standing came from the thesis elaborated by Adam Smith's *Wealth of Nations* (1776), that artificially promoted colonies and the associated structure of regulated trade diverted resources which might be better employed at home. Some time would elapse before Smith's

[18] Frances Armytage, *The Free Port System in the British West Indies* (London, 1953).

arguments affected the specific detail of commercial policy, but they quickly achieved great intellectual prestige, and by his remarks on the economic disadvantages of slave labour he contributed to a powerful social movement that offered the planters a more immediate threat.

Anti-slavery doctrine was forming and gaining a limited circulation by the 1760s. In 1787 a vigorous public movement was launched for the abolition of the British slave trade from Africa, as the first step towards reforming and eventually eliminating the West Indian slave labour regime. In 1788 Parliament voted to regulate conditions on the slave ships. In 1792 a bill for gradual abolition passed the Commons but was rejected by the Lords. Abolition was finally enacted in 1807, and no significant deliveries of new African slaves reached the British West Indies after 1808. The colonies' effective labour force now began to decline, because of the continuing excess of slave deaths over births, and British plantation exports stagnated, while other American territories increased their slave imports and their share of the European market for tropical produce.

Abolitionist leaders, followed by many British historians, attributed the movement and its eventual success to metropolitan repugnance against an increasingly flagrant moral evil. Details of the inhumane practices associated with slavery and slave trading became more widely known to a public affected by a general growth in philanthropic sentiment. The most celebrated challenge to this 'moral' interpretation of abolitionism was made by Eric Williams's *Capitalism and Slavery*,[19] which argued that while individual campaigners such as William Wilberforce may have been sincere in professing humanitarian concern, their cause only prevailed because it served national economic interests. According to Williams, by the later eighteenth century the British West Indian sugar colonies, their soils exhausted after decades of monoculture, had become hopelessly uncompetitive with the French islands. So initially many British politicians favoured abolition, in the hope that it could be applied generally, to halt the further expansion of the French West Indies by cutting off their labour supply. Britain's new East Indian possessions could then export sugar to Europe. Parliamentary enthusiasm for abolition waned when the destruction of Saint-Domingue improved the British West Indies' fortunes after 1791. However, sugar output from alternative sources grew so rapidly that by 1807 it was thought desirable to abolish the slave trade as a means of limiting over-production. Williams linked abolition, slave emancipation (1833), and the ending of tariff preference for British colonial sugar (1846), as elements in a general strategy for dismantling an archaic structure of protected colonial trade, and allowing the country's dynamic new capitalist industries to deal freely with the world at large.

[19] Eric Williams, *Capitalism and Slavery* (Chapel Hill, NC, 1944).

The 'Williams thesis' has been both widely influential and much criticized. Its detractors have pointed out that when abolitionism first gained ground in the 1780s India did not seem a likely alternative to the West Indies as a source of sugar. The recession of the movement against the slave trade after 1791 is best seen as resulting from the political élite's general reaction against reforming causes in the era of the French Revolution, rather than as an opportunistic response to events on Saint-Domingue. When abolition was finally enacted British West Indian trade stood at record levels. The outlook for the longer-established sugar colonies was perhaps doubtful, but Britain had just gained control over Trinidad and Demerara, where labour was scarce and fertile, under-used land was abundant. Abandoning the slave trade severely limited expansion there.[20]

If abolition did not offer economic advantages, then why was it implemented? Attempts have been made to reaffirm the 'moral' elements in British anti-slavery. Eighteenth-century British empirical philosophy put special emphasis on sympathy and fellow-feeling between individuals as the basis for ethical behaviour. This notion of 'benevolence' was hard to reconcile with slavery. Theologians developed the argument that God revealed his purpose to mankind by stages, so the slave-holding sanctioned in biblical times might no longer be tolerable. Such ideas were common themes of European Enlightenment thought, but they gained the widest currency in Britain through the evangelical movements that affected the established church and the main Dissenting sects.[21] Religious feeling reinforced a strong libertarian consciousness. British people had come to think of themselves as 'freeborn', unlike oppressed continental Europeans, with an instinctive repugnance for slavery and a right to political expression.[22] Together, it is suggested, these influences generated a unique mass mobilization, combined with élite leadership, exerting strong pressure on Parliament through petitioning campaigns. Capitalist industrialization fostered abolitionism not by creating new vested interests that stood to profit directly from the elimination of colonial slavery, but by enlarging the middle class of independent, educated artisans, manufacturers, and traders who were particularly attracted to evangelical religion.[23]

Yet while in Britain abolitionism certainly became a popular cause, to a degree unmatched elsewhere, the fact remains that the decision to end the slave trade was taken by Parliament, where evangelicalism was only a minority sentiment and where practical, strategic considerations were paramount. The widespread enthu-

---

[20] Seymour Drescher, *Econocide: British Slavery in the Era of Abolition* (Pittsburgh, 1977).

[21] Roger Anstey, *The Atlantic Slave Trade and British Abolition* (London, 1975), pp. 91–235.

[22] See above, pp. 226–27.

[23] Seymour Drescher, *Capitalism and Antislavery: British Mobilization in Comparative Perspective* (London, 1986).

siasm for abolition had some influence, but on this issue legislators did not feel themselves to be under irresistible pressure from agitation 'out of doors', as would be the case with electoral reform in 1832, and with slave emancipation in 1833.

The abolitionist cause prevailed in 1807 because moral arguments were reinforced by changing circumstances, which made it seem that Britain could now safely dispense with the slave trade. Until the later eighteenth century the business was considered an unpleasant necessity. The West Indies employed much of the nation's merchant marine, the sugar duties were an important source of public revenue, and the sugar estates required a regular supply of new slaves. By unilaterally renouncing the African slave trade Britain would weaken herself and strengthen her European neighbours to a dangerous degree. From the 1780s these points began to lose their force. The excess of deaths over births among plantation slaves was in decline, holding out the prospect that numbers might be maintained without replenishment from Africa. Many established planters with adequate slave-holdings were reconciled to abolition, privately at least, because it would limit the progress of the more recently acquired colonies. Smith's claim that overseas plantations represented much less secure investments than metropolitan agriculture or industry was confirmed by the British West Indies' difficulties during the War of American Independence, by events on Saint-Domingue, by the Grenada and St Vincent insurrections of 1795–96, and by the early-nineteenth-century fall in commodity prices.[24] The sugar islands' reputation as valuable assets had survived phases of adversity before 1748, resulting from international warfare and French competition, but since then manufacturing's contribution to national wealth and power had become much more obvious. In the 1780s the growth of manufactured exports accelerated remarkably. They were the principal support to the balance of payments during the 1793–1815 war period, when the West Indies' share of Britain's overseas trade was maintained only by the colonies' entrepôt function in the export of British manufactures to Spanish America.

Nevertheless, although the relative importance to Britain of slave-grown Caribbean produce was declining, Williams overstated his case in implying that by the time of abolition the West Indian colonies were regarded as moribund, redundant, and due for liquidation. They still employed, directly or indirectly, half the nation's long-distance shipping. Duties on their produce accounted for an eighth of Exchequer revenue. The credit structures associated with West Indian plantations and trade were a crucial element in the London financial market on which the government floated its war loans.[25] However, the view which prevailed was that,

[24] Patrick Colquhoun, *A Treatise on the Wealth, Power and Resources of the British Empire* (London, 1815), pp. 325–28; 'Essay for Ascertaining the Value of the British Colonies in the West Indies to the Mother Country, 1806', Rhodes House Library, Oxford, MSS West Indies, n. 2.

[25] Duffy, *Soldiers, Sugar, and Seapower*, pp. 21, 385–86.

although established investments had to be maintained, this no longer required the continuation of slave trading. In the 1790s some ministers may have hoped to restore permanently British dominance of the European sugar trade by annexing French colonies,[26] but the Caribbean campaigns' main purpose soon became defensive. There was no strong political impulse to open up new plantation frontiers which would need extra labour from Africa. The British took Trinidad as a base for contraband trade with the Spanish Main, not for growing sugar. Pitt refused to dispose of Crown land on the island, because doing so would stimulate slave imports. Yet at the same time his government subsidized the restocking of St Vincent and Grenada with slaves after the 1795–96 rebellions. Otherwise some leading merchants faced bankruptcy.[27] The occupation of Puerto Rico was attempted to make available a refuge for French planters from Saint-Domingue. The capture of Demerara safeguarded British capital already invested there without official encouragement. The surrender of so many Caribbean gains at the 1802 and 1815 peace settlements provoked no equivalent to the controversy of the early 1760s over Guadeloupe.

The British did not realize that by limiting the development of their own tropical Empire in the Americas they were leaving valuable opportunities to foreign rivals. In 1807 it seemed that Parliament's outlawing of the national slave trade could soon become an effectively international measure. The United States was thought to be on the point of abolishing its own slave trade. Denmark had already done so. Blockade by the Royal Navy had almost annihilated French and Dutch overseas commerce. Portugal was highly susceptible to diplomatic pressure. Spanish American colonists were assumed to be incapable of obtaining slaves in large numbers, except through the services of British or US merchants.[28] No British politician anticipated that Brazil would separate from Portugal and continue the African trade for several decades as an independent state, or that the growth of Cuban slave imports and sugar exports would be so rapid. British abolition was not merely cynical and self-interested, but neither did its authors believe that they were making a significant economic sacrifice.

The accelerated increase of British West Indian plantation exports between 1748 and 1815 was due partly to favourable circumstances: the strong demand for sugar in the still heavily protected home market, the destruction of Saint-Domingue as a

[26] David Geggus, *Slavery, War, and Revolution: The British Occupation of Saint-Domingue, 1793–1798* (Oxford, 1982), pp. 80–87.

[27] S. G. Checkland, 'Two Scottish West Indian Liquidations', *Scottish Journal of Political Economy*, IV (1957), pp. 127–43.

[28] David Eltis, *Economic Growth and the Ending of the Transatlantic Slave Trade* (New York, 1987), pp. 104–07.

commercial rival after 1791, and the opportunities for expansion in the newly acquired colonies. The Ceded Islands, Trinidad, Demerara, and St Lucia, supplied more than a third of Great Britain's sugar imports from the British Caribbean by 1815 (Table 19.1). However, the planters themselves contributed to the growth process by modifying their techniques. On Jamaica much of the post-1748 extension of settlement occurred in the northern parishes, encouraged by the improved security that resulted from the Maroon treaty of 1739. Successful agriculture here involved the sowing of Guinea grass (introduced from Africa) as cattle fodder. With better-fed livestock, the plough could supplement the customary hoe cultivation in the cane fields, and a more abundant supply of manure gave heavier sugar crops. Most of the British colonies benefited from the higher-yielding Pacific and Indian Ocean island cane varieties (such as Otaheite, Bourbon) brought in during the 1790s. More efficient mills were built to crush the juice out of the harvested cane. The adoption of the clarifier speeded up the boiling process that converted the cane juice into exportable sugar.

Agricultural innovation was accompanied by better standards of slave maintenance. In the first half of the eighteenth century slave deaths exceeded births by a wide margin, because of chronic underfeeding and the severe labour associated with sugar cultivation. Regular purchases from Africa were required to enlarge or even maintain slave-holdings. Then planters began to show more concern for encouraging natural reproduction among their slaves, under the influence of the new humanitarian ideas from Europe, and a marked rise during the 1760s in the prices charged for imported Africans. Clothing allowances were increased, doctors engaged, and instructions given that greater care be taken of women in childbirth. When the thirteen colonies' rebellion interrupted access to North American provisions, estates on Barbados and Antigua devoted more land to food crops and less to sugar. Experience showed that the adjustment was profitable. Spending

TABLE 19.1 *Sugar imports from the British West Indies to Great Britain* (tons)

	c.1748*	c.1815†
Barbados	6,442	11,664
Jamaica	17,399	73,849
Leeward Islands	17,584	19,543
Ceded Islands	—	33,716
Trinidad, Demerara, St Lucia	—	26,087
All British West Indies	41,425	164,859

Notes: * Imports to England and Wales; † Average for 1814–16.
Sources : For 1748, see above, p. 401. For 1815, Ragatz, *Statistics for the Study of British Caribbean Economic History*, p. 20.

on purchased supplies declined, the slaves were better fed, while the reduction in
the area under cane was offset by more intensive cultivation and higher sugar
yields per acre. Jamaica relied mainly on food grown by the slaves without any
close supervision on allotments of marginal estate land. The wartime emergencies,
followed by several destructive hurricanes during the 1780s, made masters take
steps to improve the provision ground system. The slaves were given more land,
more time for its cultivation, and encouragement to grow root crops such as yams,
which are less vulnerable to storm damage than plantains, hitherto the customary
staple. After 1787 the onset and the eventual success of the campaign to abolish the
slave trade gave a further impetus to 'amelioration', as planters tried to establish a
self-sustaining labour force. More generous maintenance entailed some incidental
costs, but on balance improved estate efficiency. Less had to be spent on buying
imported Africans. As slaves became better fed, with a greater proportion of them
locally born, they also became from the planters' point of view more useful
workers, less intractable, less likely to be incapacitated by disease, to steal, or to
run away.[29]

These improvements in agricultural methods and slave demography helped to
keep the estates reasonably profitable for most of the period up to 1815, despite the
heavier sugar duties, and the disruptions to the North American trade which
sharply raised the cost of essential supplies.[30] Williams was mistaken in arguing
that as a result of soil exhaustion, technical inertia, and the unfavourable movements of costs and prices, British West Indian plantations had already gone into
terminal decline by the later eighteenth century, with their economic failure
providing a main reason for the abolition of the slave trade. His assumptions
about the estates' fortunes were based on the work of L. J. Ragatz,[31] who derived an
unduly pessimistic impression from the public complaints made by the planters at
particularly difficult moments, for example during the War of American Independence, or in the years 1806–07, when Napoleon's blockade severely limited
sugar and coffee re-exports to continental Europe. The numerous privately kept
estate records that have become accessible since Ragatz's study appeared show
some competence and flexibility in management.

Nevertheless, the adjustments made would not be enough to secure the long-
term viability of the British West India economy as a whole after 1815. First,
substantial technical progress was confined to the sugar plantations. Most
cotton and coffee estates were doomed to extinction by competitors outside

---

[29] J. R. Ward, *British West Indian Slavery, 1750–1834: The Process of Amelioration* (Oxford, 1988), pp.
61–215.

[30] Ibid., pp. 38–50.

[31] Lowell Joseph Ragatz, *The Fall of the Planter Class in the British Caribbean, 1763–1833* (New York,
1928).

the Caribbean who had the benefit of more favourable geography. Secondly, even with sugar, more careful manuring, cultivation, and processing still left output per worker much lower in Barbados, the Leewards, and Jamaica, than on the richer soils of Demerara, Trinidad, some of the Ceded Islands, and Cuba. Finally, apart from Barbados and those marginal colonies where sugar was not grown, British West Indian slave populations failed to achieve natural increase, although the annual rate of natural decrease fell, from about 3 per cent in 1748 to about half a per cent in 1815. Abolitionists noticed the trend and cited it to support their cause. The slave trade, they claimed, was on the way to becoming superfluous, for the older British colonies at least, and if it were stopped completely, would this not give planters the extra incentive needed to make them establish self-reproducing slave populations? The abolitionists hoped that slavery conducted in a humane enough fashion to secure natural increase would soon undergo a peaceful dissolution, of the kind which they believed had ended English serfdom.

Yet when slave imports to the British colonies ceased after 1807, a residual excess of deaths over births persisted, and slave numbers began to decline. The main reason for this demographic failure was that, while better feeding considerably reduced slave mortality, fertility showed little improvement. Birth rates were depressed by irregular, unstable mating habits (associated with endemic venereal disease), and, most of all, by the continuing severity of the sugar estates' labour regime, falling particularly on slave women. Men held nearly all the specialist craft occupations, quite an important employment category because of the need to maintain processing equipment, sugar barrels, and carts for haulage. Women became a large majority in the field gangs that undertook the heavy work of cultivation, cane cutting, and feeding the harvested cane through the mill. Many planters recognized that such tasks limited 'breeding' by causing sterility and miscarriages, but women of child-bearing age were so important a part of the work-force that they could not be given any significant relief without curtailing output to unacceptable levels. Estates on Barbados produced relatively small quantities of high-grade sugar, so here alone among the main British West Indian colonies lighter work-loads made it possible for slave births to exceed deaths.[32]

Contemporaries stigmatized West Indian planters as improvident, lacking in self-discipline, public spirit, or commitment to agriculture. The growth of absentee ownership put most sugar estates under the charge of hired managers, who were said to be often incompetent, negligent, and dishonest.[33] Such criticism was

---

[32] Ward, *British West Indian Slavery*, pp. 119–89.
[33] Ragatz, *Fall of the Planter Class*, pp. 3–14, 55–63.

rather exaggerated. Some dedicated proprietors remained in the colonies. Salaried estate management developed as a profession. New reporting methods allowed absentees to keep a better check on their property. Nevertheless, many plantation owners undoubtedly did live beyond their considerable means, by borrowing on the security of Caribbean property to support lavish personal consumption. Also innovation and expansion entailed heavy investment outlays. Credit was available from British merchants involved in the sugar and slave trades. West Indian development always depended above all on locally generated resources, but in the later eighteenth century external funding became more important, as capital surpluses accumulated within Great Britain, and business techniques for their mobilization were refined. Loan finance supported the rapid settlement of the Ceded Islands after 1763 and the post-1791 boom. These credit-based upswings ended with commercial crises that contributed to the planters' reputation for speculative excess.[34] By 1815 the plantation economy carried a heavy weight of debt, which would be a severe handicap when commodity prices and estate revenues fell in the post-war deflation.

Barbados was an exception on these points. As the first British colony to be developed for sugar growing in the seventeenth century, few estates here were large enough to support the costs of absenteeism. Most planters stayed on the island as resident owners, relatively free of debt, more familiar than the recent immigrants who predominated among the white populations elsewhere with the details of sugar manufacture, and with the peculiarities of local soil and climate. Thus Barbados became through its unusually efficient agriculture the only sugar colony where slave births exceeded deaths, and after 1815 it was the most successful of the longer established British West Indies in holding its own against new, low-cost competitors.

The British West Indies' most striking social feature, the majority of black slaves over whites resulting from the economic preponderance of plantation agriculture, became increasingly marked. Slaves outnumbered whites by about six to one in 1748, and twelve to one in 1815 (Table 19.2), with the largest disproportions occurring by the latter date in the Ceded Islands (20:1) and Demerara (37:1). On Jamaica white and slave numbers grew at roughly the same rate, but many of the whites here were involved with the free port trade to the Spanish colonies. When this business declined after 1815 the white population fell sharply. Estates tended to operate on an ever larger scale, especially when established in the new colonies. More slaves were trained as craftsmen, confining white plantation

---

[34] Jacob M. Price, 'Credit in the Slave Trade and Plantation Economies', in Barbara L. Solow, ed., *Slavery and the Rise of the Atlantic System* (Cambridge, 1991), pp. 293–339.

TABLE 19.2. *Population of the British West Indies* (000s)

	c.1748				c.1815			
	White	Slave	Free coloured	Total	White	Slave	Free coloured	Total
Barbados	22.5	69.0	0.1	91.6	15.5	75.3	3.0	93.8
Leeward Islands	8.0	62.3	(0.5)	70.8	5.3	72.2	6.2	83.7
Jamaica	10.4	116.1	(2.0)	128.5	27.9	339.8	35.0	402.7
Ceded Islands	—	—	—	—	5.2	105.2	10.0	120.4
Trinidad	—	—	—	—	2.5	25.6	7.6	35.7
Demerara	—	—	—	—	2.8	103.8	4.8	111.4
Marginal Colonies*	(3.0)	(8.0)	(0.5)	(11.5)	4.3	21.2	3.8	29.3
All British West Indies	43.9	255.4	(3.1)	302.4	63.5	743.1	70.4	877.0

Notes : The bracketed figures are rough estimates: * Virgin Islands, Belize, Cayman Islands, Bahamas.

Sources : For 1748, F. W. Pitman, *The Development of the British West Indies, 1700–1763* (New Haven, 1917), pp. 369–83; D. W. Cohen and Jack P. Greene, eds., *Neither Slave nor Free; The Freedman of African Descent in the Slave Societies of the New World* (Baltimore, 1976), pp. 194, 218. For 1815, B. W. Higman, *Slave Populations of the British Caribbean, 1807–1834* (Baltimore, 1984), pp. 77, 417.

employees almost entirely to supervisory functions. Official settlement schemes to bring in Europeans as family farmers proved quite ineffective, because of the toll taken by tropical disease, and the fact that sugar occupied so much of the best land. North America was much more attractive to potential migrants of this type. White numbers were limited further by the growth of absentee estate ownership, which affected about a quarter of sugar properties in 1748 and three-quarters in 1815. Planters felt better able to afford absenteeism when the volume and value of their consignments rose. 'First generation' proprietors might remain resident, but their sons were commonly educated in Britain, and reluctant to return to the West Indies. The period's various commercial crises brought many estates into the hands of British-based merchant creditors.

Except for Barbados and some of the newly conquered territories where foreign settlers (French, Spanish, Dutch) were already established, British West Indian whites did not develop integrated, locally rooted societies, comparable with the North American colonies. Most whites were immigrants, hoping to make their fortune and then return home, though only a minority ever did so. White men continued to outnumber white women by at least two to one in Jamaica, and by even wider margins in the Ceded Islands and Demerara. As an extreme case, Tobago's European settlers seem for a time in the 1770s to have been exclusively male. Furthermore, white women in the West Indies each produced on average only half as many surviving children as their counterparts in North America, because of high infant mortality and the frequency with which marriages were interrupted by death.[35]

The main British West Indian and North American colonies shared the same administrative forms: a Governor as the King's agent, some lesser officials, an advisory Council of appointees, and an elected legislative Assembly. The system was introduced to the Ceded Islands after 1763. There were quite narrow limits to the Governor's effective power. He was military Commander-in-Chief, could proclaim martial law, summon and dissolve the Assembly, and veto its measures. But he had no right to initiate legislation, and controlled few official appointments, most of which were determined from Britain. The only important permanent revenue was the $4^1/_2$ per cent export duty payable on exports from Barbados and the Leewards. Otherwise administration depended on taxes granted yearly by Assemblies at discretion, a recurrent cause of friction with the executive arm. British West Indian Assemblies, like those of North America, had since the seventeenth century successfully encroached on the Governor's prerogative by establishing a customary right of detailed supervision over public-works expenditures. Assemblies in the islands, again as on the North American mainland, claimed and jealously defended various privileges analogous to the British Parliament's, for example, the immunity of serving members from arrest for debt.[36]

However, when the more substantive issue of Parliament's right to tax the colonies arose in the 1760s, the West Indians responded cautiously. The Stamp Act provoked rioting on the Leewards. They were especially dependent on imported supplies, and susceptible to North American threats of a boycott against islands which complied with the measure. But in general the planter élite's social ascendancy ensured that good order was maintained. The island Assemblies' public resolutions against the Stamp Act objected to it as inexpedient and impractical, not on grounds of constitutional principle, although more forceful complaints reached ministers through private channels. Most West Indian colonists were conscious above all else of their reliance on British sea-power, and the risks to which libertarian agitation would expose them as a small minority among their slaves. It was out of the question for the West Indies to join the North Americans in revolt.[37]

Nevertheless, the chastening experience of losing the thirteen colonies made ministers more reluctant to challenge representative institutions where they were already firmly entrenched. When Trinidad came under British rule in 1797 the

---

[35] Robert V. Wells, *The Population of the British Colonies in America before 1776: A Survey of Census Data* (Princeton, 1975), pp. 172–258, 269, 272.

[36] George Metcalf, *Royal Government and Political Conflict in Jamaica, 1729–1783* (London, 1965).

[37] Andrew J. O'Shaughnessy, 'The Stamp Act Crisis in the British Caribbean', *William and Mary Quarterly*, Third Series, LII (1994), pp. 203–26; T. R. Clayton, 'Sophistry, Security, and the Socio-

island was not allowed an elected Assembly, because of the problems posed by the numerous Spanish, French, and free coloureds already settled there. A similar line was taken with St Lucia and Demerara. Otherwise, the authoritarian, centralizing tendency that affected later eighteenth-century Imperial policy elsewhere, in India, Canada, and Ireland, reached the West Indies slowly. The strengthening of the islands' fortifications undertaken during the 1780s, and the Caribbean military operations of the 1793–1815 period, were financed principally from London. The locally assessed taxes conceded by West Indian Assemblies still absorbed only about 5 per cent of estate profits. The main fiscal pressure against the West Indies was applied indirectly, by increasing the duties charged on colonial produce landed at British ports.[38]

Apart from the 60 per cent of the slaves attached to sugar plantations by 1815, a further 20 per cent were employed on coffee, cotton, and livestock estates, 10 per cent in other rural activities, and 10 per cent in the towns. Though sugar's relative importance had declined a little, most slaves were still held in large units, organized on a gang labour basis. In 1815 holdings of more than fifty slaves comprised 80 per cent of the slave population. In 1748 about 60 per cent of the slaves were imported Africans; in 1815 the corresponding figure was about 30 per cent.[39] The proportion of locally born (creole) slaves rose because as the original sugar colonies became more fully settled there was less need to enlarge the work-force by purchase, and because of amelioration's effects in reducing mortality.

Creolization brought more-balanced sex ratios (males outnumbered females by two to one in slave cargoes from Africa) and made possible some development of family relationships. By the early nineteenth century about three-quarters of the slaves seem to have lived in family groupings, most frequently children with a single woman whose partner probably belonged to another property. The co-resident slave nuclear family of father, mother, and children, though quite common, remained less characteristic than in North America. Denser island settlement patterns facilitated 'visiting' relationships between partners on different holdings, and West Indian colonists exercised a looser supervision over the slaves' personal lives. Also the single white men who predominated as estate managers and overseers took mistresses from among the younger slave women under their control. Consequently the coloured (mixed race) element grew from about 5 per cent to 10 per cent of the slave population. Coloured slaves were kept somewhat

Political Structure of the American Revolution; Or, Why Jamaica Did Not Rebel', *Historical Journal*, XXIX (1986), pp. 319–44.

[38] D. J. Murray, *The West Indies and the Development of Colonial Government, 1801–1834* (Oxford, 1965), pp. 1–108.

[39] Higman, *Slave Populations*, pp. 68–71, 102–05, 116.

apart from the black majority as a favoured élite, usually exempt from ordinary field labour, the women serving as domestics for the whites, and the men as craft specialists. Miscegenation and the high proportion of non-resident unions were contributory causes of the slaves' unstable mating, and thus of their low fertility.[40]

The failure to keep up slave numbers through natural increase represented the most serious labour management problem during the 1748–1815 period. Amelioration and creolization eased the task of maintaining routine discipline. Slaves still worked reluctantly, under threat of the whip. Only a minority, about 15 per cent of the adults, were given tasks that required special skills. However, the level of motivation and expertise was adequate for the planters' attempts at technical improvement. There is little evidence that slave sabotage held back the adoption of new methods and more elaborate equipment.[41]

Up to 1815 the British West Indies were apparently becoming less liable to collective slave rebellion, despite the growing majority of blacks over whites, and Saint-Domingue's menacing example. Among the older colonies the last major incidents (emergencies provoked by the discovery of suspected conspiracies, rather than actual uprisings) occurred on Barbados in 1692, on the Leeward Islands (Antigua) in 1736, and on Jamaica in 1776. In each of these cases a leading role was attributed to a particular West African ethnic group, 'Koromantis' from the Gold Coast (present-day Ghana). As time passed British traders extended their sources of supply and Koromantis became relatively less numerous among slave imports. General insurrection was precluded by the Africans' more varied origins, and by the growing proportion of creoles, inured from birth to slavery, and possessing a better sense of the white men's military advantages. Slave solidarity was also weakened by the distinctions between blacks and coloureds, and between field labourers and the comparatively privileged (gang drivers, craftsmen, domestics). Planters relied on active assistance from a minority of 'confidential negroes' to maintain routine discipline, catch runaways, and guard growing crops. So long as the master class remained united, order could be maintained without much difficulty. The Saint-Domingue revolt succeeded because of the conflict among the colony's whites generated by the French Revolution. The 1795–96 Grenada rebellion, the one slave uprising in the British Caribbean during the 1748–1815 period which lasted long enough to cause serious economic damage, derived its strength from French instigation and the local leadership provided by resident francophone planters. It was not until after 1815 that the peacetime contraction of military establishments, reports of British anti-slavery agitation, and the focus

[40] Ibid., pp. 147–57, 364–73; Ward, *British West Indian Slavery*, pp. 165–84; see below, pp. 467–70.
[41] J. R. Ward, 'The Amelioration of British West Indian Slavery, 1750–1834: Technical Change and the Plough', *Nieuwe West-Indische Gids*, LXIII (1989), pp. 41–58.

for collective consciousness supplied by the increasingly influential Christian missionaries, provoked the extensive rebellions on Barbados (1816), Demerara (1823), and Jamaica (1831) that led to emancipation.[42]

Between 1748 and 1815 the number of free coloureds in the British West Indies grew from about 3,000 to 70,000, and their share of the total population rose from 1 per cent to 8 per cent. They slightly outnumbered whites by the latter date (Table 19.2). Most of the few slaves who acquired their freedom were the female sexual partners of white men, and the children from such unions. An even smaller number were freed for other special reasons, such as conspicuously 'loyal' service against foreign invaders. By the mid-eighteenth century the persistent deficit of white women in most of the colonies had made concubinage between white men and slave women a tolerated local custom, and the number of manumissions was rising. Furthermore, the free coloureds achieved quite rapid natural increase, the only element in British West Indian society to do so. They were less susceptible than the whites to tropical diseases, they experienced better material conditions than did the slaves, and a large proportion of those manumitted were females and young people.

While individual colonists might sometimes be indulgent towards their own mistresses and children, they were hostile to the multiplication of free coloureds as a social group. It was unthinkable that non-whites should consort with whites on an equal footing. Special laws prevented free coloureds from voting at Assembly elections, from performing jury service, from giving evidence in court, from employment on the estates, and from acquiring considerable amounts of property by inheritance or purchase. With agriculture largely closed to them, most free coloureds congregated in the towns, where they made a living as best they could. It was believed that they inhibited white immigration, harboured runaway slaves, and encouraged theft by dealing in stolen goods. However, the appearance of metropolitan anti-slavery agitation and the emergencies of the 1793–1815 war period brought some relaxation of discriminatory practices. The free coloureds were growing more numerous and assertive; the whites felt more obliged to conciliate them as necessary allies in an increasingly dangerous world. On Jamaica from 1796, for instance, freedmen's evidence was made legally admissible in cases of assault, following the free coloured and black militia companies' exemplary conduct against the rebellious Maroons. In 1813 the colony mitigated further the free coloureds' civil disabilities, and ended the limitations on the amount of property that they might inherit.[43]

[42] Michael Craton, *Testing the Chains: Resistance to Slavery in the British West Indies* (Ithaca, NY, 1982).

[43] Gad J. Heuman, *Between Black and White: Race, Politics, and the Free Coloreds in Jamaica, 1792–1865* (Oxford, 1981), pp. 24–29.

The free coloureds became a conspicuous intermediate element in British West Indian society, but without performing an effective integrating role. They were almost as colour-conscious as the whites. Mixed race people insisted that a degree of European ancestry gave them superiority over the black masses. The easing of the restrictions on landholding came too late for any significant number of free coloureds to become established as sugar planters. They could not remedy one of the estate economy's greatest weaknesses, the shortage of colonial-born resident proprietors, thoroughly familiar with local circumstances, who might have been more capable than the absentees and their managers of adjusting to the harshly competitive trading conditions that lay ahead.

Select Bibliography

EDWARD BRATHWAITE, *The Development of Creole Society in Jamaica, 1770–1820* (Oxford, 1971).

SELWYN H. H. CARRINGTON, *The British West Indies during the American Revolution* (Dordrecht, 1988).

MICHAEL CRATON, *Searching for the Invisible Man: Slaves and Plantation Life in Jamaica* (Cambridge, Mass., 1978).

——— *Testing the Chains: Resistance to Slavery in the British West Indies* (Ithaca, NY, 1982).

SEYMOUR DRESCHER, *Econocide: British Slavery in the Era of Abolition* (Pittsburgh, 1977).

MICHAEL DUFFY, *Soldiers, Sugar and Seapower: The British Expeditions to the West Indies and the War against Revolutionary France* (Oxford, 1987).

ELSA V. GOVEIA, *Slave Society in the British Leeward Islands at the End of the Eighteenth Century* (New Haven, 1965).

DOUGLAS HALL, *In Miserable Slavery: Thomas Thistlewood in Jamaica, 1750–86* (London, 1989).

JEROME S. HANDLER, *The Unappropriated People: Freedmen in the Slave Society of Barbados* (Baltimore, 1974).

B. W. HIGMAN, *Slave Populations of the British Caribbean, 1807–1834* (Baltimore, 1984).

D. J. MURRAY, *The West Indies and the Development of Colonial Government, 1801–1834* (Oxford, 1965).

RICHARD PARES, *War and Trade in the West Indies, 1739–1763* (Oxford, 1936).

——— *A West-India Fortune* (London, 1950).

LOWELL JOSEPH RAGATZ, *The Fall of the Planter Class in the British Caribbean, 1763–1833* (New York, 1928).

RICHARD B. SHERIDAN, *Sugar and Slavery: An Economic History of the British West Indies, 1623–1775* (Barbados, 1974).

——— *Doctors and Slaves: A Medical and Demographic History of Slavery in the British West Indies, 1680–1834* (Cambridge, 1984).

BARBARA L. SOLOW and STANLEY ENGERMAN, eds., *British Capitalism and Caribbean Slavery: The Legacy of Eric Williams* (Cambridge, 1987).

MARY TURNER, *Slaves and Missionaries: The Disintegration of Jamaican Slave Society, 1787–1834* (Urbana, Ill., 1982).

J. R. WARD, *British West Indian Slavery, 1750–1834: The Process of Amelioration* (Oxford, 1988).
ERIC WILLIAMS, *Capitalism and Slavery* (Chapel Hill, NC, 1944).

20

The British Empire and the Atlantic Slave Trade, 1660–1807

DAVID RICHARDSON

English merchants entered the slave trade relatively late, but by 1650 were regular participants in it. Two decades later they had probably become the leading European carriers of slaves, delivering to America each year possibly more slaves than both the Portuguese and Dutch, who had previously dominated the trade. Having established their dominance by 1670, the English remained the major shippers of slaves from Africa to America until 1807, when Parliament outlawed British participation in slave-carrying. Overall, it appears that in the one-and-a-half centuries before 1807 the British shipped as many slaves to America as all other slave-carrying nations put together.[1] In 1660–1807, therefore, the British were the pre-eminent slave traders of the western hemisphere.

The number of slaves shipped by the English before 1660 is, as yet, unknown, but evidence on ships arriving at the African coast suggests that it was probably at least 10,000.[2] Firmer evidence exists on the scale of the British slave trade after the Restoration, although the number of slaves carried in British ships between 1660 and 1807 continues to be debated. Any estimate of the volume of the British slave trade in this period is likely, therefore, to prove controversial. This is true of the data presented in Table 20.1 and Figure 20.1. These are based on the most detailed studies of the magnitude of British slave trafficking available. On balance, they perhaps marginally overstate the level of the trade, especially in 1710–80. The figures in column B of Table 20.1 refer to slaves carried in British-owned ships, while those in column C refer to slaves carried in ships owned in British America. Column D combines columns B and C, thereby providing estimates of slave

---

[1] David Eltis, 'The Transatlantic Slave Trade to the British Americas before 1714: Annual Estimates of Volume, Direction and African Origins', in Robert Paquette and Stanley L. Engerman, eds., *The Lesser Antilles in the Age of European Expansion* (Gainesville, Fla., 1996), pp. 182–205; David Richardson, 'Slave Exports from West and West-Central Africa, 1700–1810: New Estimates of Volume and Distribution', *Journal of African History* (hereafter *JAH*), XXX (1989), p. 11.

[2] Based on Larry Gragg, '"To Procure Negroes": The English Slave Trade to Barbados, 1627–60', *Slavery and Abolition*, XVI (1995), pp. 68–69.

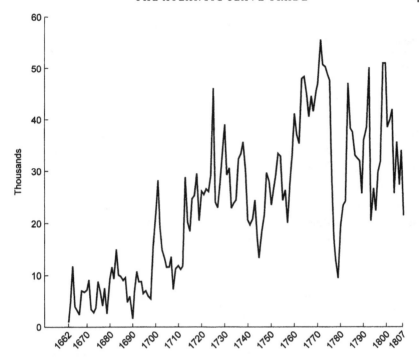

Figure 20.1 Fluctuations in Slave Exports

exports from Africa by all British Empire ships. Column E provides estimates of numbers of slaves arriving in the Americas in the same ships.

From Table 20.1 it appears that ships of the British Empire carried just over 3.4 million slaves from Africa in 1662–1807. This was about a half of all the slaves shipped from Africa to America in this period; most of the remaining slaves were carried in Portuguese, French, and Dutch ships. Of those shipped by the British, 95 per cent were carried by British-owned ships and only 5 per cent by ships owned in the colonies. The British Empire slave trade was, therefore, essentially British-based, though ships from the colonies sometimes made a significant contribution to the trade, notably in the decade before 1776. As a result, British Empire slaving voyages were basically triangular in nature, with ships leaving British ports for Africa and returning to Britain after discharging their African slaves in America. By contrast, Portuguese voyages were mostly bilateral, with ships leaving from, and returning directly to, Brazil with slaves.

Further inspection of Table 20.1 shows that annual shipments of slaves by the British rose about sixfold in the century after 1660, or from 6,700 slaves a year in 1662–70 to over 42,000 a year in the 1760s. Thereafter, annual shipments tended to level out or decline. Nevertheless, shipments of slaves by the British immediately

TABLE 20.1. *Slave exports from Africa and arrivals in America in British and British-Colonial ships, 1662–1807* (nearest 00)

(A)	(B) Exports British ships	(C) Exports Colonial ships	(D) Exports Total	(E) Arrivals Total
1662–70	59,900	—	59,900	47,900
1671–80	71,300	—	71,300	57,000
1681–90	106,800	—	106,800	84,700
1691–1700	91,600	—	91,600	73,300
1700–09	125,600	—	125,600	100,500
1710–19	203,000	5,000	208,000	166,400
1720–29	269,000	7,000	276,000	242,100
1730–39	276,000	20,000	296,000	236,800
1740–49	194,600	14,000	208,600	179,400
1750–59	251,300	22,000	273,300	235,000
1760–69	391,200	33,000	424,200	364,800
1770–79	339,600	23,000	362,600	326,300
1780–89	303,200	3,600	306,800	276,100
1790–99	346,000	3,500	349,500	332,000
1800–07	255,200	100	255,300	242,500
1662–1807	3,284,300	131,200	3,415,500	2,964,800

Notes: (1) The figures for 1662–1709 in column B include both British and colonial ships. (2) Colonial ships in 1710–75 are North American ships, with an allowance of 500 slaves a year for ships from the West Indies. From 1776, colonial refers to West Indian ships alone. (3) There are no figures available for slaves exported in colonial ships in 1780–84. I estimated that exports in these years totalled 1,000 slaves.

Sources: David Eltis, 'The Volume and African Origins of the British Slave Trade before 1714', *Cahiers d'études Africaines*, XXXV (1995), p. 620 (for 1662–1709); David Richardson, 'Slave Exports from West and West-Central Africa, 1700–1810: New Estimates of Volume and Distribution', *JAH*, XXX (1989), pp. 3, 9 (for 1710–85); Stephen D. Behrendt, 'The British Slave Trade, 1785–1807: Volume, Profitability, and Mortality', unpublished Ph.D. dissertation Wisconsin-Madison, 1993, p. 73 (for 1785–1807). Where appropriate, figures on imports into America have been adjusted for slave mortality to derive slave export estimates from Africa.

before abolition in 1807 were still at historically high levels, comfortably exceeding those achieved before 1720 and averaging about 75 per cent of the level achieved at the height of the British Empire slave trade in 1763–93. Moreover, as the French and Dutch slave trades collapsed after 1793, Britain's share of the transatlantic slave trade rose to unprecedented levels in the decade before 1807. British merchants, therefore, remained heavy investors in slaving voyages until 1807, a point emphasized by sceptics of Eric Williams's claim that parliamentary abolition of the slave trade was associated with a decline in the importance of West Indian slavery to the British economy after 1783.[3]

[3] Seymour Drescher, *Econocide: British Slavery in the Era of Abolition* (Pittsburgh, 1977), p. 177. On the Williams thesis, see above, pp. 425–28.

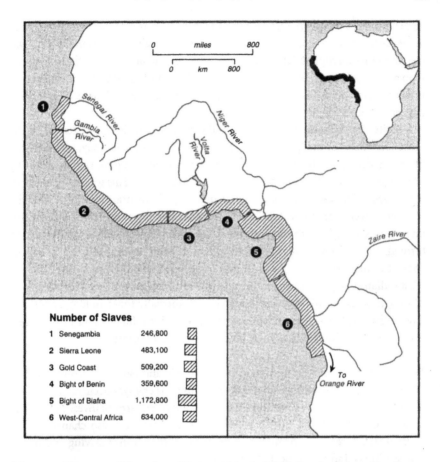

Map 20.1. Shipment of Slaves from Western Africa in British Empire Ships, 1662–1807

Figure 20.1 shows the expansion of the British slave trade in 1660–1807 as far from smooth; annual fluctuations in slave shipments were in fact pronounced. Beneath these fluctuations, however, it is possible to distinguish a number of cycles or phases in British slaving activity up to and beyond the American Revolution. In most cases, the level of slave shipments at the end of each cycle was higher than at the beginning, though the actual peak of activity in the cycle may have been reached before its end. Overall, the growth of the British slave trade was dominated by three major expansionary cycles embracing the years from *c.*1650 to 1683, 1708 to 1725, and 1746 to 1771. Three shorter periods of expansion also occurred in 1690–1701, 1734–38, and 1780–92, but these were less significant than the longer phases in shaping the pattern of growth of British slaving activity between 1660 and 1807. Interspersed with, and in some cases within, these expansionary phases were periods of sharply reduced levels of activity. This was particularly so in 1665–67, 1672–74, 1703–07, 1740–45, and 1776–79 when Britain was at war. Overall, war was the most disruptive factor in the growth of British slaving activity between 1660 and 1807, though problems affecting the West Indies, notably the depression in sugar prices in the 1680s and early 1730s and the financial crisis of 1772, also triggered declines in activity.[4]

Despite the vicissitudes surrounding the trade's growth, the British were the most committed of the transatlantic shippers of slaves in 1660–1807, with declines in shipments caused by war or other events normally being more than offset by prolonged periods of relatively uninterrupted expansion. This was particularly so before 1793. Thereafter, increasingly stringent parliamentary controls over the trade and, even more importantly, war had a dampening effect on levels of British interest in slaving. But British interest in the trade remained comparatively high through to abolition in 1807. Moreover, British merchants continued to supply goods to other slave traders and to deal in slave-produced commodities such as West Indian sugar, American cotton, and West African palm oil well beyond 1807.[5] Although British involvement in the slave trade formally ended in 1807, systems of slavery that exploited African labour remained major influences on British overseas trade and colonial history well into the nineteenth century.

The growth of British slaving activity between 1660 and 1807 was accompanied by major changes in its organization. The most obvious changes occurred in the way in which voyages were financed and managed and in patterns of investment in the trade among British and British colonial ports. There were also changes in the internal structure of the firms that came to dominate British slaving and in the relationship of individual ports to the trade.

In 1660 Charles II granted a one-thousand-year monopoly of English trade to Africa to the Company of Royal Adventurers Trading into Africa, thereby continuing the policy of granting monopoly controls over the African trade to chartered companies that Elizabeth I had initiated in 1588 and that the first two Stuart kings had maintained.[6] Reconstituted in 1663, the Company of Royal Adventurers had its rights over the African trade transferred nine years later to

---

[4] Richard B. Sheridan, *Sugar and Slavery: An Economic History of the British West Indies, 1623–1775* (Barbados, 1974), p. 497; and 'The British Credit Crisis of 1772 and the American Colonies', *Journal of Economic History* (hereafter *JEcH*), XX (1960), pp. 161–86.

[5] David Eltis, 'The British Contribution to the Nineteenth-Century Transatlantic Slave Trade', *Economic History Review* (hereafter *EcHR*), Second Series, XXXII (1979), pp. 211–27; Ralph Davis, *British Overseas Trade and the Industrial Revolution* (Leicester, 1979), p. 39; Martin Lynn, 'The Profitability of the Early Nineteenth Century Palm Oil Trade', *African Economic History*, XX (1992), pp. 77–97.

[6] G. F. Zook, *The Company of Royal Adventurers Trading into Africa* (Lancaster, Penn., 1919), pp. 4, 9; K. G. Davies, *The Royal African Company* (London, 1957), pp. 39–44.

the Royal African Company.[7] Also intended to last for a thousand years, this company's monopoly of the African trade was formally ended in 1698 when Parliament declared the trade open to all merchants in the British Empire on payment to the Royal African Company of a 10 per cent duty on exports to Africa. Fourteen years later this last remnant of Crown control of Britain's trade to Africa came to an end when the Ten Per Cent Act expired. After 1712 the Royal African Company and its successor, the Company of Merchants Trading to Africa (founded in 1750), continued to maintain forts and factories in the Gambia and along the Gold Coast and Slave Coast. In addition, a British naval force in 1758 took St Louis in Senegal from the French, thereby allowing expansion of British trade with the region until 1779 when Senegal again fell to the French. Despite this, responsibility for maintaining Britain's interest in the African trade—described by Davies as 'an essential link in the imperial economy'[8]—lay primarily in the hands of private merchants or 'separate traders' from 1712 onwards. This continued until the slave trade was abolished in 1807.

The transfer of control of the African trade from chartered company to private traders was, however, less dramatic than changes in the laws governing entry into the trade suggest. In many respects the act of 1698 simply confirmed what was already self-evident: namely, that the Royal African Company's monopoly of England's trade to Africa had been broken by 'interlopers'. Interloping was, in fact, common in England's trade to Africa during the seventeenth century.[9] But it is likely that it grew from about 1660 as the demand for slaves in America expanded and the chartered companies, burdened with responsibility for maintaining African forts and with growing debts among credit-hungry planters in America, found it impossible to satisfy this demand. The scale of interloping is naturally difficult to quantify and has been the subject of some debate. However, the most careful investigation of the issue has suggested that, at the peak of the Royal African Company's involvement in the slave trade in 1674–86, perhaps one in four of the slaves reaching English America arrived illegally.[10] Moreover, from the mid-1680s the Royal African Company, like its predecessor, the Royal Adventurers, began licensing others to enter the trade.[11] While the contribution of the chartered companies to the growth of English slave trading after 1660 should not be underestimated, their control of the African trade had plainly been undermined well before it was thrown open in 1698.

[7] Davies, *Royal African Company*, pp. 97–101.

[8] Ibid., p. 349.

[9] John C. Appleby, '"A Business of Much Difficulty": A London Slaving Venture, 1651–1654', *Mariner's Mirror*, LXXXI, (1995), p. 5.

[10] Eltis, 'Slave Trade to British Americas'.

[11] Zook, *Royal Adventurers*, p. 21; Davies, *Royal African Company*, pp. 125–26.

The indications are that most interloping voyages before 1698 were despatched from London and West Indian ports.[12] As the headquarters of the chartered companies and as a major centre of interloping activity, London dominated the English slave trade in the seventeenth century. Despite unrestricted entry after 1698, this pattern continued for some time thereafter, with London merchants financing some 63 per cent of the slaving voyages clearing British and British-colonial ports between 1698 and 1725.[13] By the latter date, however, London's position as Britain's slaving capital was under threat from 'outport' merchants and, as Table 20.2 shows, during the next decade London lost control of the trade to Bristol. But the Avon port's ascendancy in British slaving proved, in turn, to be short-lived as merchants at other ports, notably Liverpool, entered the trade. By mid-century, Liverpool had become the premier British slaving port. And despite a growth of slaving in 1750–75 at other ports such as Lancaster, Whitehaven, and Newport, Rhode Island, as well as a revival in London's interest in the trade after

TABLE 20.2 *Clearances of slave ships from British and British-Colonial Ports, 1699–1807*

	London	Bristol	Liverpool	Newport	Other	Total
1699–1709	545	60	2	1	77	685
1710–19	450	194	75	2	70	791
1720–29	600	332	96	9	70	1,107
1730–39	282	405	231	72	70	1,060
1740–49	81	239	322	46	64	752
1750–59	164	215	521	102	170	1,172
1760–69	335	256	725	152	197	1,665
1770–79	370	153	703	104	89	1,419
1780–89	166	111	646	—	87	1,010
1790–99	173	123	1,011	—	64	1,371
1800–07	185	17	867	—	2	1,071
1699–1807	3,351	2,105	5,199	488	960	12,103

Notes: (1) London clearances in 1710–29 include an allowance for ships which cleared for Cape Verde and Madeira but engaged in slaving (see David Richardson, 'Cape Verde, Madeira and Britain's Trade to Africa, 1698–1740', *Journal of Imperial and Commonwealth History*, XXII (1994), p. 12). (2) Figures in the 'Other' column include an allowance of five ships a year for clearances from colonial ports other than Newport.

Sources: David Richardson, 'The Eighteenth-Century British Slave Trade: Estimates of its Volume and Coastal Distribution in Africa', *Research in Economic History*, XII (1989), pp. 185–95; Jay Coughtry, *The Notorious Triangle: Rhode Island and the African Slave Trade, 1700–1807* (Philadelphia, 1981), pp. 241–61; Behrendt, 'The British Slave Trade', pp. 31–34, 73.

[12] Eltis, 'Slave Trade to British Americas'.
[13] David Richardson, 'The Eighteenth-Century British Slave Trade: Estimates of its Volume and Coastal Distribution in Africa', *Research in Economic History*, XII (1989), pp. 185–87.

1763, Liverpool, as Table 20.2 shows, remained unchallenged as Britain's leading slave port in 1750–1807. Indeed, its hold over the trade intensified as the century wore on, with Liverpool merchants financing 55 per cent of British voyages in 1750–1807 and no less than 75 per cent of those despatched in 1780–1807. Overall, the century after 1698 saw a remarkable shift from the Thames to the Mersey in the location of slaving activity in Britain.

Outside the chartered companies, slaving voyages were financed by partnerships of merchants, tradesmen, and seafarers. Almost invariably, these firms owned both the trade goods exported to Africa and the ship that carried them to the coast. The costs of preparing ships for their voyages naturally varied according to their size. But on the whole, outfitting costs rose from approximately £3,000 at the beginning of the eighteenth century to £8,000 or more by the end.[14] General inflation after 1770 accounted for some of this increase. But the main factors behind it were an increase in the average tonnage of ships employed (and the numbers of slaves they carried) and a rise in the mean price of slaves at the African coast. The former occurred steadily over the century, while the latter occurred mainly from the 1750s.[15] Even at their maximum, financial outlays on slaving voyages were still modest relative to those incurred on voyages to India. But for most outport merchants, slaving voyages represented a sizeable investment. Moreover, the trade was long-winded, with voyages usually taking twelve to eighteen months to complete, and was seen to be fraught with exceptional risks, most graphically highlighted by variations in slave mortality in the notorious middle passage from Africa to America. Not surprisingly, therefore, risk limitation and risk-spreading strategies were an important influence on the organization of the slave trade, particularly outside London. Where pools of potential investors in the trade were limited, as in Lancaster and Rhode Island, merchants tended to employ relatively small ships in the trade.[16] And even when the pool of investors was larger, the funding of slaving voyages often depended on the resources of four to eight or even more partners. What is also clear is that in the major ports the trade tended to be organized around a core of regular and substantial investors who spread their capital across several voyages simultaneously, and at the same time assumed responsibility for managing them on behalf of their 'sleeping

[14] Number of ships sent from the ports of Great Britain by separate traders to Africa 1708–09, C[olonial] O[ffice] 388/12, K53; Account of vessels and amount of their cargo employed in the African slave trade, Liverpool, 3 March 1790, *House of Commons, Accounts and Papers*, XXIX (1790), p. 698.

[15] W. E. Minchinton, 'Characteristics of British Slaving Vessels, 1698–1775', *Journal of Interdisciplinary History*, XX (1989), p. 61; David Richardson, 'Prices of Slaves in West and West-Central Africa: Toward an Annual Series, 1698–1807', *Bulletin of Economic Research*, XLIII (1991), pp. 33–34.

[16] Melinda Elder, *The Slave Trade and the Economic Development of 18th Century Lancaster* (Halifax, 1992), p. 42; Jay Coughtry, *The Notorious Triangle: Rhode Island and the African Slave Trade, 1700–1807* (Philadelphia, 1981), pp. 74–75.

partners'. Furthermore, there are indications that as the century progressed the concentration of control over the slave trade in the hands of the leading investors may have increased at the major slaving ports. Overall, eighteenth-century British slaving activity depended on the resources of a large number of investors brought together by a small body of regular managing-owners.[17]

The reasons for the migration of control of British slaving from London to Liverpool in the eighteenth century are still unclear. One contemporary attributed it to low wage rates in north-west England compared to London, a point perhaps of some significance, given that slave ships were heavily manned.[18] Later commentators have pointed to African demand for textiles and the advantage that Liverpool may have derived from its close proximity to the emerging cotton textile industry of Lancashire.[19] Yet others have suggested that, because of Liverpool's remoteness from the main areas of enemy privateering activity and the problems that London ships faced in clearing the Thames and the English Channel, its merchants were better placed than their southern rivals to sustain their slave trade in wartime.[20]

Such factors may well have contributed to Liverpool's growing dominance of British slaving. But in dwelling on the locational advantages enjoyed by Liverpool, it is possible to overlook the continuing involvement of London merchants in the slave trade and their contribution to Liverpool's success. It is acknowledged, for instance, that despite their eclipse by Liverpool merchants as shippers of slaves, London merchants were vital to the financing of the British slave trade through to 1807, accepting and guaranteeing bills of exchange drawn by slave factors in West Indian and mainland North American ports in favour of Liverpool and other suppliers of slaves.[21] Normally remitted after 1750 by the same ships that delivered slaves, and often having twelve to twenty-four or more months to run to maturity, such bills, when endorsed or accepted by a London house, were apparently used by Liverpool slave traders to settle accounts with their suppliers of trade goods for Africa or, by depositing the bills in a bank, to fund further

---

[17] David Richardson, *The Bristol Slave Traders: A Collective Portrait* (Bristol, 1985), pp. 16–17.

[18] J. Wallace, *A General and Descriptive History of the Ancient and Present State of the Town of Liverpool* (Liverpool, 1795), pp. 232–33.

[19] B. L. Anderson, 'The Lancashire Bill System and its Liverpool Practitioners', in William H. Chaloner and Barrie M. Ratcliffe, eds., *Trade and Transport: Essays in Honour of T. S. Willan* (Manchester, 1977), pp. 59–77.

[20] Kenneth Morgan, *Bristol and the Atlantic Trade in the Eighteenth Century* (Cambridge, 1993), p. 221.

[21] Richard B. Sheridan, 'The Commercial and Financial Organisation of the British Slave Trade, 1750–1807', *EcHR*, Second Series, XI (1958–59), pp. 249–63; Jacob M. Price, 'Credit in the Slave Trade and the Plantation Economies', in Barbara L. Solow, ed., *Slavery and the Rise of the Atlantic System* (Cambridge, 1991), pp. 313–17.

voyages.[22] The reputation of bills drawn on London merchants, therefore, helped to maintain the liquidity of capital invested in slaving. In addition, London merchants were major suppliers of trade goods on credit to outport slave traders. Prominent among such goods were East Indian textiles and cowrie shells.[23] But Londoners also supplied goods such as gunpowder, with merchants in Liverpool and other outports acting as commission agents for suppliers in the capital.[24] The proportion of goods shipped from Liverpool and other outports to Africa that was supplied by London merchants cannot be calculated precisely. East Indian goods alone comprised 28 per cent of the £2.3 million of exports from Liverpool to Africa in 1783–87, while 37 per cent of the £83,000 worth of trade goods shipped to Africa in eighteen voyages of one major Bristol slave trader in 1783–93 came from London.[25] Since most of these were supplied on credit, the bill remittance system was clearly not the only means by which London capital sustained slaving activities from the outports.

None of this can deny the contribution of locational factors to the growth of slave trafficking at ports outside London. It does, however, highlight the complex nature of slaving as a business and underlines the large financial stake of the capital in both the slave system in British America and the traffic in Africans that supported it. Arguably, a division of labour within slave trafficking may have arisen from the 1730s, with outport, especially Liverpool, merchants acting primarily as shippers of slaves and London merchants providing manufactured goods and, above all, financial services to support them. This resulted in a shift of some of the risks of the trade, notably the provision of credit to planters, from the outports to the capital. But it also allowed Londoners to profit from supplying East Indian and other goods to slave traders and from handling the sugar and other goods remitted to Britain to cover bills arising from slave sales. On the basis of voyages accomplished, Liverpool has to be regarded as the most successful slave port of the Atlantic world in the eighteenth century. It is unlikely, however, that the

---

[22] Joseph Caton to James Rogers, Liverpool, 11 Jan. 1790, Chancery Masters' Exhibits, Papers of James Rogers, C[hancery] 107/13.

[23] David Richardson, 'West African Consumption Patterns and their Influence on the Eighteenth-Century English Slave Trade', in Henry A. Gemery and Jan S. Hogendorn, eds., *The Uncommon Market: Essays in the Economic History of the Atlantic Slave Trade* (New York, 1979), p. 307; Jan S. Hogendorn and Marion Johnson, *Shell Money of the Slave Trade* (Cambridge, 1986).

[24] Accounts of gunpowder sales on behalf of Messrs. Taylor Nesfield & Co. of London 1772, Estate of Christopher Hasell, 1771–76, Hasell manuscripts, Dalemain House, Pooley Bridge, Cumbria. I am grateful to Mr Robert Hasell-McCosh for permission to consult his family's papers and to cite material from them.

[25] Sheila Lambert, ed., *House of Commons Sessional Papers of the Eighteenth Century*, 145 vols. (Wilmington, NC, 1975–78), LXVII, pp. 23–28; Masters' Exhibits, Papers of James Rogers, C 107/1–15. It is worth noting that ships trading to Africa from colonial ports mainly carried rum and were thus largely independent of London suppliers of trade goods.

city's slave trade could have reached the extraordinary heights it did after 1750 without London's financial contribution to the development of the slave system within Britain's colonies.

The first major attempt to establish the coastal distribution of slave shipments from Africa was made in 1969 by Philip Curtin.[26] Curtin distinguished seven regions along the Atlantic seaboard of Africa: from north to south these were Senegambia, Sierra Leone, the Windward Coast, the Gold Coast, the Bight of Benin, the Bight of Biafra, and Central Africa (Angola). An eighth slave-supply region was south-east Africa, including Mozambique and Madagascar. Since 1969 further studies of slave exports from Africa have appeared, among them reassessments of the pattern of exports by British and North American carriers. Most of these have adopted Curtin's classification of African regions, though it is now recognized that most of the slaves attributed to the Windward Coast were probably loaded at Sierra Leone. As a result, exports from these two regions have tended to be amalgamated, reducing to six the number of slave-exporting regions along the west coast of Africa.[27] This apart, the regions shown on the accompanying map are those proposed by Curtin. In the case of Central Africa, almost all the slaves exported by the British came from areas north of or bordering the River Zaire, exports from places further south being dominated by the Portuguese.

The latest estimates of British and British-colonial slave shipments in 1662–1807 by African region of departure are presented in Table 20.3. Some caution is necessary in approaching these estimates. In some decades after 1709 the figures derive from accounts covering a few years only. Moreover, these accounts do not cover all the British ports involved in the trade and relate to intended loadings of slaves rather than actual shipments. London and the smaller British slaving ports are under-represented in the figures in Table 20.3 for 1710–79. There are indications that ships from these ports took proportionately more slaves from Sierra Leone and the Gold Coast than Bristol and Liverpool traders.[28] Table 20.3 perhaps understates, therefore, the importance of these two regions as sources of slaves for British traders.

Although it is an imperfect guide, Table 20.3 does, nevertheless, suggest some clear conclusions about the pattern of British slave exports from Africa. First, the slaves shipped to America by the British came overwhelmingly from the Atlantic coast of Africa. Only occasionally, in fact, were slaves taken by the British in any significant numbers from areas beyond the Cape of Good Hope. And even then,

---

[26] Philip D. Curtin, *The Atlantic Slave Trade: A Census* (Madison, 1969).

[27] Adam Jones and Marion Johnson, 'Slaves from the Windward Coast', *JAH*, XXI (1980), pp. 17–34.

[28] Elder, *Lancaster Slave Trade*, p. 57; Stephen D. Behrendt, 'The British Slave Trade, 1785–1807: Volume, Profitability, and Mortality', unpublished Ph.D. dissertation, Wisconsin-Madison, 1993, p. 319.

TABLE 20.3 *Estimated slave exports from Africa in British Empire ships by African region of embarkation, 1662–1807* (nearest 00)

	Sene-gambia	Sierra Leone	Gold Coast	Bight of Benin	Bight of Biafra	West-Central	S. E. Africa
1662–70	1,100	400	8,000	13,700	32,500	4,100	100
1671–80	3,800	1,300	17,500	17,200	22,900	8,300	300
1681–90	8,000	2,700	12,700	40,100	18,200	19,800	5,400
1691–1700	9,800	3,300	17,100	33,400	10,500	17,200	200
1700–09	7,800	2,600	47,100	43,500	15,400	9,300	—
1710–19	30,800	6,900	36,800	20,900	44,800	65,700	2,000
1720–29	41,300	9,300	49,400	28,000	60,000	88,000	—
1730–39	46,700	13,800	55,000	28,700	61,500	90,300	—
1740–49	23,300	11,900	47,900	15,200	75,900	34,200	—
1750–59	23,900	54,600	35,200	18,400	104,100	36,200	—
1760–69	27,400	136,600	43,900	35,600	135,000	45,800	—
1770–79	17,900	111,200	35,500	34,300	151,100	12,200	—
1780–89	600	46,900	27,600	22,700	186,500	22,400	—
1790–99	2,400	42,600	48,200	5,900	142,600	107,600	—
1800–07	2,000	39,000	27,300	2,000	111,800	73,000	—
1662–1807	246,800	483,100	509,200	359,600	1,172,800	634,000	8,000

Notes: (1) The source for the figures before 1710 does not distinguish Senegambian exports from those from Sierra Leone, including them all under 'Upper Guinea'. I have assumed that 75 per cent of exports from Upper Guinea in 1662–1709 came from Senegambia, the rest from Sierra Leone. (2) For slaves carried in ships from the British colonies before 1780 I assumed that these came equally from Senegambia, Sierra Leone, and the Gold Goast (see Richardson, 'Slave Exports', p. 16). Those after 1780 are distributed on the basis of the known British pattern. (3) Because of rounding the totals in this table may differ slightly from those in Table 20.1

Sources: See Table 20.1

the numbers taken were relatively small, accounting for under 5 per cent of the total. By comparison, French shipments of slaves from south-east Africa were at times substantial. Secondly, the six regions along the Atlantic seaboard contributed unequally to British slave exports. Taking 1662 to 1807 as a whole, the Bight of Biafra supplied at least as many slaves to British Empire traders as the next two most important regions—Central Africa and the Gold Coast—combined. Furthermore, these last two regions, in turn, supplied more slaves to the British than the three remaining regions. Overall, over half the slaves exported by British Empire ships in 1662–1807 came from regions east and south of the Bight of Benin and only about a fifth from regions west and north of the Gold Coast. Compared to other traders, relatively few of the slaves shipped by the British came from the Bight of Benin or the so-called 'Slave Coast'. Indeed, as far as British Empire traders were concerned, the Gold Coast—so named because of its association with the gold trade—seems to have been a more important supplier of slaves than its neighbour to the east. Compared to other carriers, the British took far more slaves from the Bight of Biafra and proportionately fewer from the Bight of Benin and Central Africa between 1660 and 1807.[29]

A closer look at Table 20.3 reveals that the contribution of African regions to British slave exports varied substantially through time. Thus, while the Bight of Biafra was the principal source of slaves for the British in the 1660s, the growth of slave shipments during the following two decades was based on regions outside the Bight. Indeed, British exports from the Bight of Biafra slumped in 1670–1700, while exports from the Bight of Benin almost reached their historic peak in the 1680s. Thereafter, shipments of slaves from the Bight of Benin stabilized and later fell away. The next major phase of expansion of British slaving after 1700 thus depended on exports from other regions, notably Central Africa, the Bight of Biafra, the Gold Coast, and Senegambia. During this period, British slave shipments from the last region reached an all-time high, while those from the Gold Coast came close to this. After 1740, however, slave shipments from Senegambia declined more or less permanently, while shipments from the Gold Coast and Central Africa fell appreciably for half a century. Renewed growth of British slave shipments between 1748 and 1776 depended, therefore, almost totally on exports from the Bight of Biafra and Sierra Leone. The latter was perhaps the major single source of slaves for British Empire ships during the 1760s and, together with the Bight of Biafra, may have supplied almost two-thirds of the slaves carried by British and British colonial ships by 1770. Thereafter, however, the popularity of Sierra Leone among British traders declined relatively quickly, as slave shipments from the region fell by over a half between the 1770s and 1780s and remained at this lower level until 1807. As exports from Senegambia and the Bight of Benin also remained depressed at this time, recovery of British slave exports after the War of American Independence depended, therefore, on trade with the Bight of Biafra, the Gold Coast, and Central Africa, with the first region playing the principal role in the 1780s and the last during the 1790s. As a result, by 1807 the two most southerly regions of the Atlantic seaboard accounted together for over 70 per cent of British slave exports from Africa, with most of the others coming from Sierra Leone and the Gold Coast.

The determinants of patterns of British slave exports and changes in regional concentrations of activity are still only vaguely understood. But it is accepted that conditions within Africa had a major impact on regional slave exports. This is illustrated by coastal loading rates of ships which, it appears, were faster at ports in

---

[29] For the coastal origins of slave shipments by other nations see Richardson, 'Slave Exports', pp. 14–17; Johannes Menne Postma, *The Dutch in the Atlantic Slave Trade, 1600–1815* (Cambridge, 1990), p. 121.

the Bight of Biafra and Central Africa than further north.[30] At the same time, the composition of slaves shipped from these two regions differed significantly. Thus, whereas the ratio of male to female slaves shipped from Central Africa was about 70 : 30 during the eighteenth century—a ratio consistent with the preferences of most shippers—at the Bight of Biafra the ratio was nearer 55 : 45.[31] Precise explanations for such regional variations in trade patterns have yet to be found. But they almost certainly lie in the social, demographic, and commercial structures of the societies bordering the Atlantic seaboard of Africa.

While British traders gravitated towards the two regions that offered the fastest loadings of slaves, it is also important to note that they had to compete for slaves with traders of other nations. Given their large share of total slave exports, it is tempting to assume that British traders were highly competitive in most regions of Africa. British traders evidently dominated slave exports from the Bight of Biafra in the eighteenth century, with Bristol and Liverpool traders in particular being especially active in this region. But elsewhere British dominance was much less evident. On the contrary, the French dominated trade with Senegal, while the Portuguese controlled slave shipments from most of the region south of the River Zaire. Furthermore, in other regions British traders were often in retreat in the face of French competition for slaves. Thus, as French slaving expanded British traders seem largely to have withdrawn from the Bight of Benin from the 1720s. And as French trade at the Loango Coast in Central Africa grew, so British trade with this area fell sharply after 1740 and recovered only when the French largely abandoned the slave trade in 1793. Significantly, while the French were increasing slave exports from the Bight of Benin and Central Africa between the 1750s and the 1780s, British Empire traders were opening up trade with Sierra Leone and deepening and extending trade with the Bight of Biafra, particularly the Cameroons.[32] Moreover, at Sierra Leone British traders found themselves under pressure by the 1780s from competition from ex-colonial traders from Rhode Island.[33] Only in the Bight of Biafra, therefore, were the British able to dominate slaving before 1793. Elsewhere in Africa, levels of British slave exports were subject to severe competition from other traders.

---

[30] David Eltis and David Richardson, 'Productivity in the Transatlantic Slave Trade', *Explorations in Economic History*, XXXII (1995), pp. 465–84.

[31] David Eltis and Stanley L. Engerman, 'Fluctuations in Age and Sex Ratios in the Transatlantic Slave Trade, 1663–1864', *EcHR*, Second Series, XLVI (1993), p. 310.

[32] David Richardson, 'Profits in the Liverpool Slave Trade: The Accounts of William Davenport, 1757–1784', in Roger Anstey and P. E. H. Hair, eds., *Liverpool, the African Slave Trade, and Abolition* (Liverpool, 1976), p. 66.

[33] Alison Jones, 'The Rhode Island Slave Trade: A Trading Advantage in Africa', *Slavery and Abolition*, II (1981), pp. 225–44.

The Middle Passage from Africa to America, has properly been 'considered in terms other than economic'.[34] Mortality levels on slave ships varied widely, though for reasons which still escape proper explanation, they were usually higher on ships leaving the Bight of Biafra than other regions along the west coast of Africa. Generally, losses of slaves on British ships roughly halved in the century after the 1680s, but still averaged around 10 per cent on the eve of the 1788 Dolben Act regulating conditions on slaving ships. A further reduction in mortality levels then occurred in 1790–1807.[35] Though they reduced the numbers of slaves carried per ship, the impact on mortality of parliamentary restrictions on carrying-capacities of ships after 1788 remains unclear. Overall, however, the figures given in column E of Table 20.1 suggest that, of the 3.4 million Africans shipped by British Empire traders in 1662–1807, about 450,000 (or 13.2 per cent) died before reaching America. Allowing for losses, slaves delivered to the Americas by British Empire ships rose, as Table 20.1 indicates, from about 5,000 a year in the 1660s to over 36,000 a year a century later. Annual deliveries declined thereafter, but still averaged about 30,000 a year during the quarter-century before 1807. Because of falling mortality levels in the Atlantic crossing, slave deliveries to America tended to rise faster than slave exports from Africa between 1660 and 1807.

The market for slaves in British America grew substantially from the 1640s. This reflected the spread of sugar cultivation throughout the older British West Indies, the adoption of African slave labour by planters in the mainland North American colonies, and British successes in war which brought further American territories under British control. The gains in territory were particularly important during the last half-century of British slaving, when to the established West Indian colonies of Barbados, Jamaica, and the Leeward Islands were added several islands in the Windward Islands group and Trinidad, as well as mainland territories such as Demerara. In addition, war brought temporary British control over various other foreign colonies, including Cuba in 1762–63, Guadeloupe in 1759–63, and Martinique in 1762–63 and again in 1794–1802. As colonies came under British control they were normally targeted immediately by slave traders. Overall, the spread of the slave plantation system and the expansion of the British Caribbean Empire were central to the growth of British slaving between 1660 and 1807. At the same time, the failure of slaves in the islands to sustain their numbers through reproduction created additional demand for slaves, replace-

[34] Davies, *Royal African Company*, p. 292.

[35] Ibid, p. 292; Colin Palmer, *Human Cargoes: The British Slave Trade to Spanish America, 1700–1739* (Urbana, Ill., 1981), pp. 52–54; Roger Anstey, *The Atlantic Slave Trade and British Abolition, 1760–1810* (London, 1975), pp. 414–15.

ment demand for slaves supplementing demands created by expansion of the plantation system.[36]

We do not have detailed breakdowns of the final destinations or even places of first arrival in the Americas of the slaves who survived the Atlantic crossing in British Empire ships. Only before 1713 and after 1784 do we have more or less full information about distributions of slave arrivals. Research in progress promises to produce similar data for the intervening period. But for the moment, the picture of slave arrivals between 1714 and 1784 derives from a mixture of relatively good evidence on slave imports into colonies such as Barbados, Jamaica, South Carolina, and Virginia and rather patchy data for others. Even if data on arrivals in 1714–84 improve, it is still worth noting that available evidence relates primarily to the first place of landing of slaves in British America rather than to their final destination. Most slaves probably worked and lived in the colony where they first disembarked. But at times there developed in some British islands a lively re-export trade in slaves to other colonies, including foreign ones. In addition, British traders sometimes shipped slaves directly to foreign colonies. An examination of slave imports into British America is therefore only the first step in determining the destination of slaves arriving in the Americas in ships of the British Empire.

Expansion of British slaving after 1660, as has been shown, occurred in three major cycles, with peaks of activity in the years around 1683, 1725, and 1770. War caused a sharp fall in the trade in 1776–82, but a strong recovery of slaving activity occurred after 1782. Bolstered by the collapse of French slaving after 1793 and by territorial acquisitions during the wars with France, the trade then continued at historically high levels until 1807. To trace changes in patterns of slave arrivals, we shall begin by examining the distribution of slave imports among Britain's colonies in the decades around 1683, 1725, 1770, and 1800. Determining patterns of slave arrivals in these years permits us then to estimate the numbers of slaves entering the Americas in British Empire ships that went to foreign colonies.

Figures on slave arrivals in British America for the years indicated are given in Table 20.4. The reliability of these figures varies. In particular, estimates of imports into the Leeward Islands and Ceded Islands in 1766–75 are less securely based than other figures. Despite this, Table 20.4 presents a plausible picture of changes in patterns of slave arrivals in British America during the major phases of expansion and recovery in British Empire slaving between the 1680s and 1800s. Thus Barbados, the pioneer British sugar colony, dominated the first phase of expansion, accounting for almost half of the slaves delivered in the 1680s. Most of the remaining arrivals in this period went to Jamaica and the Leeward Islands, though

[36] J. R. Ward, *British West Indian Slavery, 1750–1834: The Process of Amelioration* (Oxford, 1988), pp. 119–89.

TABLE 20.4 *Distribution of slave arrivals among British American colonies, selected periods, 1681–1804* (nearest 00)

	1681–90	1720–29	1766–75	1795–1804
Barbados	39,100	27,000	32,800	17,100
Jamaica	27,700	72,000	76,700	101,100
Leeward Islands	14,100	29,600	45,300	7,100
Chesapeake	3,500	15,000	5,000	—
Carolinas/Georgia	—	9,000	31,800	—
Ceded Islands	—	—	87,500	25,100
Conquered colonies	—	—	—	85,800
Other	300	—	—	5,900
Total				
British America	84,700	152,600	279,100	242,100
All Americas	84,700	242,100	411,300	337,600
Residual	—	89,500	132,200	95,500

Sources: 1681–90: Eltis, 'Slave Trade to British Americas'.

1720–29: CO 33/15–16 (Barbados); CO 137/22, f. 61, CO 137/38, Hh 3–4 (Jamaica); CO 152/15, ff. 332–33, 390–91, CO 152/18, f. 94, CO 152/19, f. 176, CO 318/2, ff. 7–10 (Leeward Islands); Klein, *Middle Passage* [see note 38 below], p. 124 (Virginia); David Richardson, 'The British Slave Trade to Colonial South Carolina', *Slavery and Abolition*, XII (1991), pp. 170–71 (South Carolina).

1766–75: *House of Commons, Accounts and Papers*, XXVI (1789), 646a, part IV, account no. 15; CO 28/32–4, (Barbados); CO 137/38, Hh 3–4 (Jamaica); CO 152/32–3 (Leeward Islands); Klein, *Middle Passage*, p. 124 (Virginia); Richardson, 'Slave Trade to South Carolina' (South Carolina); Elizabeth Donnan, ed., *Documents Illustrative of the History of the Slave Trade to America*, 4 vols. (Washington, 1930–35) IV, pp. 612–25 (Georgia); CO 76/4, f. 45, CO 106/1, CO 318/2, ff. 246, 249, 252; David Richardson, ed., *Bristol, Africa, and the Slave Trade to America*, Vol. 3, *The Years of Decline, 1745–69*, Bristol Record Society Publications, XLII (1991), p. xxix (Ceded Islands).

1795–1804: *House of Lords, Sessional Papers*, VII (1806), p. 201; *House of Commons, Accounts and Papers*, IV (1801–02), 429, XIII (1806), 777 (all colonies); Klein, *Middle Passage*, p. 143 (Jamaica).

sizeable numbers also entered the Chesapeake colonies, thereby facilitating the shift from white indentured to African slave labour in Maryland and Virginia after 1680.[37]

The early dominance of the West Indies over slave arrivals in British America continued beyond the 1680s, but the distribution of slave arrivals among the British islands changed. Thus, between the 1680s and 1720s shipments to Barbados fell while shipments to Jamaica and the Leeward Islands rose significantly. Moreover, within the Leeward Islands group, Antigua and St Kitts replaced Nevis as the principal importers of slaves. At the same time, arrivals of slaves in mainland North America increased as the Chesapeake colonies completed their conversion

[37] Richard N. Bean and Robert P. Thomas, 'The Adoption of Slave Labor in British America', in Gemery and Hogendorn, eds., *Uncommon Market*, p. 378.

to African labour and shipments to South Carolina expanded. As far as British America was concerned, Jamaica, the larger Leewards, and the mainland colonies from the Chesapeake to the south were thus central to the second phase of expansion in slaving in 1708–25.

A glance at Table 20.4 reveals that further shifts in patterns of slave deliveries occurred during the forty years after 1725. On the mainland, shipments of slaves to Virginia peaked during the 1730s and then tailed off as natural reproduction of slaves in the colony reduced the need to import Africans to sustain the plantation labour force.[38] However, imports of slaves into South Carolina continued to grow intermittently until the early 1770s, while Georgia emerged as a significant market for slaves from the 1750s.[39] These changes in slave imports into mainland North America were matched by similar shifts in patterns of imports among the West Indian colonies. Thus, imports into Barbados and Jamaica experienced little growth between the 1720s and 1770, whereas arrivals at Antigua and St Kitts rose by perhaps 50 per cent during the same period. Changes in the older islands were overshadowed, however, by developments in Dominica and Grenada which, along with St Vincent and Tobago, were ceded by France to Britain in 1763. Figures on slave imports into some of the Ceded Islands remain incomplete. But it appears that slave deliveries to Grenada and Dominica increased sharply after 1763 and by the early 1770s perhaps matched deliveries to Jamaica. Overall, the Ceded Islands probably accounted for a third of all the slaves entering the British West Indies in 1766–75. British success in the Seven Years War, therefore, had a radical effect on the geography of slave arrivals in the British West Indies after 1763.

The War of American Independence largely destroyed the British slave trade to mainland North America, though a brief surge of slave deliveries to the former colony of South Carolina took place in 1804–07 when the state legalized imports.[40] This apart, patterns of slave arrivals in British America after 1783 were shaped wholly by developments in the West Indies. In the islands, slave imports recovered strongly at Jamaica and the Ceded Islands from 1783.[41] In Jamaica's case the recovery was sustained until 1807, with imports reaching unprecedented levels in the decade before abolition.[42] But imports into the Ceded Islands fell away sharply after 1793, while arrivals at Barbados and the Leeward Islands remained well below

---

[38] Herbert S. Klein, *The Middle Passage: Comparative Studies of the Atlantic Slave Trade* (Princeton, 1978), p. 124.

[39] Richardson, 'The British Slave Trade to Colonial South Carolina', p. 171.

[40] *Annals of Congress*, 16th Congress, 2nd Session (1820), pp. 72–77; Donnan, ed., *Documents*, IV, pp. 504–22.

[41] *House of Commons, Accounts and Papers*, XXVI (1789), 646a, part IV, account no. 4.

[42] Klein, *Middle Passage*, p. 143; Richard B. Sheridan, 'The Slave Trade to Jamaica, 1702–1808', in Barry W. Higman, ed., *Trade, Government and Society in Caribbean History, 1700–1920* (Kingston, 1983), p. 2.

pre-1776 levels throughout the period from 1783 to 1807.[43] As in the decade before 1776, however, these changes in the distribution of slave deliveries among established British islands were overshadowed after 1793 by the growth of shipments to colonies taken in war. As Table 20.4 shows, these colonies accounted for about a third of the slaves imported into British America in 1795–1804. Particularly important were Demerara, which imported more slaves in the decade before 1807 than the Ceded Islands and Leeward Islands, and Martinique which, in the same period, imported as many as Barbados. As after 1763, therefore, territorial gains in wartime had a major impact on the distribution of slave arrivals in the British West Indies thirty years later.

Table 20.4 suggests that 75 per cent or more of the slaves reaching America in British Empire ships first landed in a British colony. Of these slaves, two-thirds were usually male. Most were aged from 15 to 30 on arrival in America. Irrespective of their age and sex, most were destined to spend the rest of their lives working on plantations in the colony where they first disembarked, producing crops for export to Britain. In many colonies, therefore, a fairly close relationship existed between slave imports and trends in agricultural output and exports.[44] But further inspection of the data reveals that significant proportions of the slaves carried from Africa in British and British-colonial ships were sold outside the British Empire. According to Table 20.4, slave deliveries by British Empire ships to the Americas regularly exceeded imports of slaves into the major British plantation colonies in the eighteenth century by about 40 per cent. Weaknesses in available data mean that the scale of this surplus is possibly exaggerated by Table 20.4. Furthermore, some of the 'surplus' slaves may have gone to non-plantation colonies in British America. This said, there is also firm evidence of British slave deliveries to non-British colonies. Thus, British traders supplied large numbers of slaves direct to Spanish America in the two decades after the signing of the *Asiento* Treaty with Spain in 1713.[45] Thereafter, shipments to the Spanish colonies probably declined for several decades. But British traders were evidently major suppliers of slaves to the French colonies in 1748–91 and, following the relaxation by Spain of restrictions on trade with its colonies from 1789, supplied over 28,000 slaves to Havana before 1807.[46] The number of slaves supplied by British ships directly to all foreign colonies cannot be calculated precisely. But on the evidence presented in Table 20.4, perhaps a quarter—or approximately 675,000—of the slaves

[43] *House of Commons, Accounts and Papers*, XXVI (1789), 646a, part IV, account no. 4; XXV (1792), 766; XLII (1795–96), 849; IV (1801–02), 429; XIII (1806), 777.

[44] Richardson, 'Slave Trade to South Carolina', p. 132.

[45] Palmer, *Human Cargoes*, p. 99.

[46] Curtin, *Census*, p. 219; Robert L. Stein, *The French Slave Trade in the Eighteenth Century* (Madison, 1979), pp. 26, 32; Behrendt, 'British Slave Trade', p. 55.

TABLE 20.5 *Slave imports and exports, Jamaica, 1702–1808*

	Imports	Exports	Exports/Imports (%)
1702–10	30,891	8,526	27.6
1711–20	53,740	24,991	46.5
1721–30	77,689	33,179	42.7
1731–40	73,217	27,148	37.1
1741–50	67,322	15,552	23.1
1751–60	76,183	11,148	14.6
1761–70	71,807	9,889	13.8
1771–80	82,685	11,984	14.9
1781–90	87,113	22,496	25.8
1791–1800	143,825	21,494	14.9
1801–08	66,385	7,880	11.9
1702–1808	830,857	194,287	23.4

Note: The data in this table derive from duties levied on slave imports and exports at Jamaica and probably understate actual movements of slaves into and out of the island. The figures for 1781–90 include an allowance for imports and exports in 1788 based on Klein, *Middle Passage*, p. 143. Sheridan had no data for this year.

Source: Sheridan, 'The Slave Trade to Jamaica, 1702–1808', p. 2.

reaching the Americas in British Empire ships in the eighteenth century were landed in foreign colonies. This calculation excludes shipments to colonies which temporarily came under British control. Overall, it appears that, both in peacetime and wartime, British slave traders were able to meet not only the labour demands of their own colonies but also a part of that of the Spanish and French.

Supplying slaves direct to French and Spanish colonies was not the only way by which slaves exported from Africa in British Empire ships reached non-British markets. A re-export trade in slaves also existed in some British colonies. The re-export of slaves from British islands in the eastern Caribbean, for instance, was common after 1763, accounting at times for more than a quarter of recorded imports at some islands.[47] But exports from these colonies were modest compared with those from Jamaica. Figures relating to Jamaican slave imports and exports are given in Table 20.5. These probably understate actual movements of slaves into and out of the island. However, the evidence suggests that of some 830,000 slaves imported at Jamaica in 1702–1808, no less than 194,000 (or 23 per cent) were later exported. Not all these slaves were sold outside the British Empire. But a report in 1789 suggests that of the 29,600 slaves said to have been exported from the island in

[47] CO 76/4, ff. 45, 49; *House of Commons, Accounts and Papers*, XXVI (646), pp. 50–51, enclosures 11, 12; *House of Lords, Sessional Papers*, VII (1806), p. 202.

1773–87, nearly 25,900 (or 87 per cent) were bound for foreign colonies.[48] Significantly, as Table 20.5 shows, slave exports from Jamaica peaked in 1711–40 and 1781–1800 when conditions favoured shipments to Spanish America. It seems reasonable to assume, therefore, that at least 75 per cent of the slaves leaving Jamaica were intended for foreign markets, with Spanish America being the principal destination.[49] Adding re-exports from the islands to slaves shipped direct to foreign colonies, it appears, then, that of the 2.7 million slaves entering the Americas in British Empire ships in 1700–1807, perhaps 850,000—or nearly one in every three—were ultimately sold to foreign buyers.

Demand for labour in Britain's own colonies was clearly the major factor determining the scale and pattern of slave deliveries by British Empire ships in the Americas between 1660 and 1807. Shifts in patterns of arrivals in the British colonies were largely determined by changes in agricultural output in the major plantation colonies within the Empire and by the entry of new colonies into it. In general, traders evinced a remarkable capacity to adjust slave supplies to changing market opportunities within the Empire. But it is plain that British and British-colonial traders were major suppliers of slaves to colonies of other nations.[50] Apparently, this traffic in slaves outside the British Empire was especially important after 1713. And, while it was never predominant, without it the slave trade of merchants within the British Empire would have been significantly smaller and perhaps less rewarding than it was.

The profits that the British earned from the Atlantic slave trade have been the subject of much debate. The chartered companies of the seventeenth century failed to make the slave trade pay and found it increasingly difficult to raise capital.[51] But the vigour with which they prosecuted the trade suggests that, for private merchants in the following century, slaving was a rather more lucrative activity. Indeed, some merchants evidently grew rich on profits from slaving. Returns naturally varied from voyage to voyage and were largely dependent on loading rates of slaves in Africa, the level of slave mortality in the middle passage, the ability of traders to recover payment for slaves from buyers, and other factors. Overall, however, annual returns from slaving voyages during the last half-century of British slaving averaged about 8–10 per cent.[52] This was a respectable return at

---

[48] Accounts of Negroes imported and exported at Jamaica 1773–87, *House of Commons, Accounts and Papers*, XXIV (1789), 622.

[49] *House of Lords, Sessional Papers*, VII (1806), p. 202.

[50] Curtin, *Census*, p. 219.

[51] Zook, *Royal Adventurers*, p. 19; Davies, *Royal African Company*, pp. 95, 344.

[52] Anstey, *British Slave Trade*, p. 47; Richardson, 'Davenport', p. 76; Behrendt, 'British Slave Trade', p. 108. Cf. Joseph E. Inikori, 'Market Structure and the Profits of the British African Trade in the Late

the time, and seems to have been largely unaffected by parliamentary regulation of the trade in 1788–1807. Ironically, the successful revolt in 1791 by slaves in Saint-Domingue, which destroyed much of French sugar production, may have helped to moderate the impact of parliamentary controls on profits in the British trade by encouraging sugar production and demand for slaves in the British islands in 1792–1807. In Liverpool and London at least, there was little slackening in investment in slaving voyages after 1788.

Some historians have claimed that profits from the slave trade and slavery made a substantial contribution to the financing of the industrial revolution in Britain. In 1944 Eric Williams claimed that slave trade profits fertilized Britain's whole productive system in the eighteenth century.[53] Williams's views echoed claims made by Lorenzo Greene about capital formation in New England.[54] They have, in turn, been echoed by several historians more recently.[55] It is likely, however, that the contribution of profits from the slave trade to capital investment in Britain and New England has been exaggerated. Investment in slaving voyages in Britain probably exceeded £1.5 million a year around 1790 and perhaps yielded £150,000 a year in profits.[56] Assuming £50,000 of this was invested in new enterprises, profits from the slave trade, therefore, probably contributed under 1 per cent of total domestic investment in Britain at this time.[57] Such calculations do not suggest that the slave trade was vital to the financing of early British industrial expansion.

The impact of the slave trade on Britain's economy was not simply confined, however, to its effects on capital investment. Its effects were, arguably, much wider. External trade was a significant and growing sector of Britain's economy in the eighteenth century, and trade with areas outside Europe, notably the American colonies, was the most dynamic component of the external trade sector from 1660 onward.[58] Furthermore, sugar, tobacco, and rice were central to the growth of

Eighteenth Century', *JEcH*, XLI (1981), pp. 745–76; William Darity, jr, 'Profitability of the British Trade in Slaves Once Again', *Explorations*, XXVI (1989), pp. 380–84.

[53] Eric Williams, *Capitalism and Slavery* (1944; London, 1964), p. 105.

[54] L. J. Greene, *The Negro in Colonial New England* (New York, 1942), pp. 68–69.

[55] Ronald Bailey, 'The Slave(ry) Trade and the Development of Capitalism in the United States: The Textile Industry in New England' and William Darity, jr, 'British Industry and the West Indies Plantations', in Joseph E. Inikori and Stanley L. Engerman, eds., *The Atlantic Slave Trade* (Durham, NC, 1992), pp. 205–79.

[56] For investment levels at Liverpool and Bristol at this time, see *House of Commons, Accounts and Papers*, XXIX (1790), 698, p. 500; David Richardson, ed., *Bristol, Africa and the Slave Trade to America*, Vol. IV, *The Final Years, 1770–1807*, Bristol Record Society Publications, XLVII (1996), p. xviii.

[57] C. H. Feinstein, 'Capital Accumulation and the Industrial Revolution', in Roderick Floud and Donald McCloskey, eds., *The Economic History of Britain Since 1700*, 2 vols. (Cambridge, 1981), I, p. 131.

[58] Ralph Davis, 'English Foreign Trade, 1700–1774', in W. E. Minchinton, ed., *The Growth of English Overseas Trade in the Seventeenth and Eighteenth Centuries* (London, 1969), p. 113.

trade within the British Atlantic Empire after 1660 and, in conjunction with British capital, African slave labour was vital to their production. Overall, the number of Africans transported to British America in 1660–1807 exceeded by a factor of probably three to four the number of whites who migrated there, freely or otherwise.[59] The disparity in flows of blacks and whites was, of course, most acute in the case of the West Indies, where blacks comprised about 85 per cent of the population by 1750.[60] But it also appears that arrivals of blacks in mainland North America more than matched those of whites in 1700–75. Despite high rates of natural reproduction of whites on the mainland, a relative 'blackening' of the labour force occurred throughout the plantation economies of British America in the century after 1660.[61] It seems, therefore, that Malachy Postlethwayt's view, expressed in 1745, that Britain's trading Empire in America rested on an African foundation was well based.[62]

While there seems little doubt that enslaved Africans helped, directly and indirectly, to enrich important sections of Britain's mercantile community, assessment of the slave trade's impact on Africa continues to cause controversy. For some, the export of slaves to America was marginal to most of Africa, though it may have had more substantial effects on the population and wealth of societies bordering its Atlantic seaboard.[63] But for others, the Atlantic slave trade is seen to have had devastating consequences for the continent, causing widespread depopulation and economic dislocation and undermining the socio-political fabric of African societies.[64] According to this view, the Atlantic slave trade was tantamount to a 'zero-sum' game, with Europeans and North Americans creaming off the profits of slaving and Africa and Africans assuming the costs associated with it. In short, the slave trade is believed to have caused the 'underdevelopment' of Africa while fertilizing industrialization in Europe and particularly Britain, the leading slave-trading nation.

As data on trends in output and population in pre-colonial Africa are scarce, evaluating such contrasting views of the slave trade's impact on Africa poses major problems. It should be noted, however, that while Europeans controlled the

---

[59] For figures on white migration, see above, pp. 31–32.

[60] See above, Table on p. 433.

[61] Barbara L. Solow, 'Slavery and Colonization', in Solow, ed., *Atlantic System*, p. 27.

[62] Malachy Postlethwayt, *The African Trade, the Great Pillar and Support of the British Plantation Trade in America* (London, 1745).

[63] J. D. Fage, 'African Societies and the Atlantic Slave Trade', *Past and Present*, CXXV (1989), pp. 97–115.

[64] Walter Rodney, 'African Slavery and Other Forms of Social Oppression on the Upper Guinea Coast in the Context of the Atlantic Slave Trade', *JAH*, VII (1966), pp. 431–43; and *How Europe Underdeveloped Africa* (Washington, 1981); Joseph E. Inikori, ed., *Forced Migration: The Impact of the Export Slave Trade on African Societies* (London, 1982), pp. 13–60.

shipping of slaves there is little evidence to suggest that they were able to control slave supply or, except on rare occasions, manipulate prices paid for slaves to their own advantage. On the contrary, control of slave supply remained firmly in the hands of African dealers and merchants, with European traders at the coast being required to negotiate terms of purchase of slaves through local commercial and political élites. Furthermore, even in regions where there were fortified European trading posts, the balance of power in such negotiations seems largely to have rested with slave suppliers. On the whole, the terms of trade—or the amount of goods being given for each slave bought—tended to move heavily in favour of African dealers, at least from the 1750s onwards.[65] In effect, commercial and political élites within West and Central Africa appear to have made large profits from helping to meet the American demand for slave labour.[66]

This is not to deny, of course, that the slave trade caused suffering for many Africans. Those shipped to America as slaves—most in the prime of their life—and those who died during the process of enslavement in Africa and in the middle passage were the most obvious casualties of the traffic. But the impact of the trade on Africa extended beyond its immediate victims. As most slaves were victims of war, slave raiding, and kidnapping, the growing export trade in slaves almost certainly caused increased violence throughout much of West and Central Africa. Moreover, as slave exports mounted and slave prices at the coast rose, the boundaries of slaving and its associated violence tended to extend further inland, intersecting in some cases with the catchment areas for slaves shipped north across the Sahara to the Middle East. At the same time, slaving activities become increasingly entangled with politics and internal warfare, as ruling élites in slave-supply areas sought to use control over the trade to enhance their wealth and power.[67] Overall, therefore, it is almost certain that the impact of the export slave trade on West and Central Africa deepened during the century-and-a-half of British dominance of it, as coastal and inland states in Africa competed for control over slave supply. In this respect, the production of slaves for export to America probably had more harmful effects on the social and political fabric of Africa than trade statistics alone would suggest. Calculating the costs to Africa of the slave trade is almost impossible. But there is little doubt that, as the leading shippers of slaves to America, merchants of the British Empire were major agents in inflicting

[65] Richardson, 'Slave Prices', p. 45; Henry A. Gemery, Jan S. Hogendorn, and Marion Johnson, 'Evidence on English–African Terms of Trade in the Eighteenth Century', *Explorations*, XXVII (1990), pp. 157–78.

[66] John Thornton, *Africa and Africans in the Making of the Atlantic World, 1400–1680* (Cambridge, 1992), p. 125; E. W. Evans and David Richardson, 'Hunting for Rents: The Economics of Slaving in Pre-Colonial Africa', *EcHR*, Second Series, XLVIII (1995), pp. 683–84.

[67] Paul E. Lovejoy, *Transformations in Slavery* (Cambridge, 1983), pp. 78–83.

widespread suffering on the peoples of West and Central Africa in the century-and-a-half after 1660.

Select Bibliography

ROGER ANSTEY, *The Atlantic Slave Trade and British Abolition, 1760–1810* (London, 1975).

JAY COUGHTRY, *The Notorious Triangle: Rhode Island and the African Slave Trade* (Philadelphia, 1981).

PHILIP D. CURTIN, *The Atlantic Slave Trade: A Census* (Madison, 1969).

K. G. DAVIES, *The Royal African Company* (London, 1957).

DAVID ELTIS, 'The Transatlantic Slave Trade to the British Americas before 1714: Annual Estimates of Volume, Direction and African Origins', in Robert Paquette and Stanley L. Engerman, eds., *The Lesser Antilles in the Age of European Expansion* (Gainesville, Fla., 1996).

PAUL E. LOVEJOY, *Transformations in Slavery* (Cambridge, 1983).

COLIN PALMER, *Human Cargoes: The British Slave Trade to Spanish America, 1700–1739* (Chicago, 1981).

DAVID RICHARDSON, ed., *Bristol, Africa and the Eighteenth-Century Slave Trade to America, 1698–1807*, 4 vols., Bristol Record Society Publications (Bristol, 1986–96).

BARBARA L. SOLOW, ed., *Slavery and the Rise of the Atlantic System* (Cambridge, 1991).

ERIC WILLIAMS, *Capitalism and Slavery* (1944; London, 1964).

21

The Black Experience in the British Empire, 1680–1810

PHILIP D. MORGAN

During the 'long' eighteenth century, the black[1] presence in the Empire assumed formidable proportions. Between 1680 and 1810 the Empire's black population rose elevenfold. By the latter date, almost 1 million blacks lived in British territories, in spite of the loss of the 500,000 blacks who in 1776 became residents of the United States (and who in 1810 numbered 1.4 million people). In 1680 blacks in the Empire were largely confined to a few small islands in the Caribbean; a century later blacks were present everywhere along the North American seaboard and formed majorities in county and parish populations from Maryland to East Florida on the mainland and from the Bahamas to Tobago (and in another twenty years, to Trinidad and British Guiana) in the Caribbean. In Britain itself, a small but growing black population emerged not just in London but in provincial seaports and outlying countryside. By 1680 British traders had established secure bases on the African coast, and were already carrying more slaves from Africa than all the other Europeans put together. For as long as they participated in the trade, the British were the major carrier of slaves. From 1680 to 1807 approximately 3 million Africans—over three times the number of Europeans—left their native lands in British ships for the New World. In sheer number of emigrants, British America was actually more black than white, more an extension of Africa than of Europe.[2]

Although most Africans arrived in the British Empire as slaves, their experiences were not uniform. The Caribbean was the heart of their story, for most blacks lived there, but that regional experience varied from an 'old' colony like Barbados to a

---

[1] *Black* is clearly an imprecise word. In most eighteenth-century contexts, it refers to indigenous peoples of Africa and their descendants. It therefore includes most *mulattoes* and *coloureds*, used in the sense of people of mixed European and African origins, many of whom of course looked quite *white*. It also excludes peoples of other continents and their descendants who are often referred to as black, such as East Indians, lascars (Asian seamen), most slaves in the Cape Colony (who were predominantly Madascagan and Asian in origin), and Australian aborigines. In none of these ascriptions, of course, am I assuming that race is an immutable biological fact.

[2] See above, pp. 440–42.

'new' colony like Trinidad, from the 4,411 square miles of Jamaica to the 35 square miles of Anguilla, from a sugar estate to a seaport, from working as a field-hand to serving in a British West India regiment, from a Maroon in the cockpit country of Jamaica to a concubine in the master's great house. In the third quarter of the eighteenth century North America challenged the Caribbean as the central black experience in the Empire. In 1750 50,000 more blacks lived on the islands than on the mainland; on the eve of the American Revolution 30,000 more blacks lived on the mainland than on the islands. In the space of a generation, the black population's centre of gravity had shifted from island to mainland. The North American experience was even more varied than its Caribbean counterpart: the contrast was huge between a New England farm and a Virginia tobacco plantation, between freedom in Nova Scotia and bondage on a South Carolina rice plantation, between Philadelphia and Savannah. Beyond the two heartlands of the black experience in the eighteenth-century British Empire—the Caribbean and North America, each of which had its own centres and peripheries—there were numerous other margins. In eighteenth-century Africa, blacks lived in the forts and factories under British control and increasingly others came under British jurisdiction—in the Crown colony of Senegambia between 1765 and 1783, in Sierra Leone from 1787 onward, and in the Cape Colony from 1795 onward (except for a brief return to Dutch rule between 1803 and 1806). Other marginal areas include Britain, Bermuda, even Australia. Mauritius, which was occupied by Britain in 1810, was marginal only in the sense of location, for it had a large slave population and a functioning plantation system.

To explore the black world in the British Empire, then, is to traverse continents, archipelagos, and an incredible kaleidoscope of experiences. Naturally, the majority—those slaves who lived on Caribbean and North American plantations—will garner most attention. But the many minorities—those who lived in Africa, Britain, or further afield, those who resided in towns and on farms, and those who were free—must also be encompassed. As a way of capturing the normal and the exceptional, this chapter will explore in turn the size and growth of the black population, work patterns, family structures, social relations, cultural development, and political experiences. Many strands and some common threads fashioned the black experience.

A survey of the black population at the beginning, middle, and end of the long eighteenth century highlights the changing distribution of blacks throughout the Empire. In 1680 almost nine out of ten blacks lived in the Caribbean and half resided on the small island of Barbados. By contrast, the black population of Britain's North American colonies was extremely small; the mainland was predominantly white. Seventy years later blacks were much more widely dispersed.

Jamaica had surpassed Barbados as the colony with the largest black population. Most of the Empire's blacks still lived in the Caribbean, but now the region only accounted for just over half of British blacks. What had changed was the enormous increase of blacks in North America, particularly in the Chesapeake. In 1750 four of every ten blacks in the Empire lived on the mainland. Another sixty years later the Caribbean was once again the centre of black life. The loss of the thirteen mainland colonies meant that hardly any British blacks lived in the remaining North American colonies. Within the Caribbean, Jamaica's black population had tripled, but most striking was the enormous increase of blacks in the new sugar colonies. In 1810 one-and-a-half times more blacks lived in the 'new' than in the 'old' West Indian colonies. The other change, although involving smaller numbers, was no less dramatic and even more portentous. In 1810 100,000 blacks lived under British jurisdiction where essentially none had before: either on the African continent—at the two major beach-heads of Sierra Leone and the Cape respectively—or on the western Indian Ocean island of Mauritius. By 1810 a few blacks had even been transported to Australia. The westward thrust of British slavery had now taken an eastward tack (see Table 21.1).

The demographic experience of blacks in the British Empire varied most crucially between those populations that grew by natural increase, that is, by births exceeding deaths, and those that grew only by imports. The great success story was the North American mainland where, by 1720, the annual rate of natural increase of the slave population was greater than the annual increase due to importations. Virginia's black population grew naturally much earlier than South Carolina's, and some northern towns such as Philadelphia contained black populations that failed to reproduce, but overall the mainland slave population from the 1720s onward grew faster from natural increase than contemporary European populations. By contrast, throughout most of the British Caribbean, slave populations registered high rates of natural decrease. Had it not been for the swelling numbers of Africans imported into the region, island populations would have declined. By 1750 the British Caribbean had imported almost 800,000 Africans, but deaths had so far exceeded births that the slave population then stood at less than 300,000. Only slave populations in marginal colonies such as the Bahamas were able to increase naturally during the eighteenth century, although the Barbadian slave population was close to doing the same by the end of the century. The small Maroon population of Jamaica was another exception, as it grew by natural increase after 1750. The small black populations scattered throughout the rest of the Empire exhibited less severe variations of the general Caribbean pattern: the small black population of Britain, living mostly in towns and heavily male in composition, probably failed to grow by natural increase; and the black populations in the castles and later colonies in Africa were also subject to heavy mortality.

TABLE 21.1. *Black population of the British Empire* (000s)

	1680	1750	1810
Caribbean	76	295	824
Old Colonies	55	146	165
Jamaica	20	145	376
New Colonies	—	—	265
Marginal	1	4	18
North America	9	247	11
Chesapeake	4	151	—
Lower South	*	60	—
Mid-Atlantic	2	21	—
New England	*	11	—
Canada	—	—	6
Bermuda	2	4	5
Britain	*	8	10
Africa	*	5	50
Forts, factories	*	5	15
Sierra Leone	—	—	4
Cape Colony	—	—	31
Other			65
Mauritius	—	—	65
Australia	—	—	*
TOTAL	86	555	960

Notes: * = less than 1000. *Old Colonies* = Antigua, Barbados, Montserrat, Nevis, St Kitts, and Virgin Islands. *New Colonies* = Berbice, Demerara, Essequibo, Dominica, Grenada, St Lucia, St Vincent, Tobago, and Trinidad. *Marginal* = Anguilla, Bahamas, Barbuda, Belize, and Cayman Islands. *Chesapeake:* = Maryland and Virginia. *Lower South* = Georgia, North Carolina, and South Carolina.

Mid-Atlantic: = Delaware, New Jersey, New York, and Pennsylvania.

Bermuda is included as part of North America because of geographic proximity, although it had close ties to the Caribbean.

African forts and factories: although technically not part of the Empire because these were rented settlements, not colonies, their black inhabitants and neighbours—the *grumetes*, free labourers, and mulatto traders—were *de facto* participants within the Empire.

Cape Colony: as black, are included Khoisan (15,000), the so-called 'free blacks' (2,000), a guess at the number of African-descended slaves (8,000 of 30,000), another guess at the number of Xhosa that might have been in the colony c.1810 (5,000), and Griqua (2,000). The resulting total is obviously an approximation.

The black population in the Caribbean in 1750 derives from McCusker and Menard and is larger than other estimates, including those in this volume: see chaps. by Richard B. Sheridan and J. R. Ward.

Sources: Stephen J. Braidwood, *Black Poor and White Philanthropists: London's Blacks and the Foundation of the Sierra Leone Settlement, 1786–1791* (Liverpool, 1994), pp. 22–23; Richard Elphick and Hermann Giliomee, eds., *The Shaping of South African Society, 1652–1840* (Middletown, Conn., 1988), pp. 43, 330, 379, 524; B. W. Higman, *Slave Populations of the British Caribbean, 1807–1834* (Baltimore, 1984), p. 77; John J. McCusker and Russell R. Menard, *The Economy of British America, 1607–1789* (Chapel Hill, NC, 1985), pp. 103, 136, 154, 172, 203; Cyril Outerbridge Packwood, *Chained on the Rock: Slavery in Bermuda* (New York, 1975), p. 81; Walter Rodney, *A History of the Upper Guinea Coast, 1545–1800* (Oxford, 1970),

TABLE 20.1 *Continued*

p. 216; James W. St G. Walker, *The Black Loyalists: The Search for a Promised Land in Nova Scotia and Sierra Leone, 1783–1870* (New York, 1976), pp. 32, 40, 128; Robert V. Wells, *The Population of the British Colonies in America before 1776: A Survey of Census Data* (Princeton, 1975), p. 173; Robin W. Winks, *The Blacks in Canada: A History* (New Haven, 1971), pp. 9, 33, 34–35, 37–38, 45; Nigel Worden, 'Diverging Histories: Slavery and its Aftermath in the Cape Colony and Mauritius', *South African Historical Journal*, XXVII (1992), pp. 3–25.

The reasons why the Caribbean was a graveyard for slaves and the mainland a breeding ground are difficult to disentangle. The Caribbean slave population's general inability to grow naturally has usually been attributed to high mortality, not low fertility. In early nineteenth-century Jamaica and Trinidad, for example, slave fertility was not unusually low but slave mortality was exceptionally high. But when the demographic performance of Caribbean slaves is compared to that of their North American counterparts, the critical difference seems to be fertility. Thus, in a comparison of the Jamaican and North American slave population in the early nineteenth century, mortality rates were similar but the fertility of mainland slaves was about 80 per cent higher. In a comparative context, a modest birth rate seems the key to the demographic failure of Caribbean slaves.

A variety of forces shaped these fertility and mortality rates. Perhaps the most important was the work environment. The onerous labour of sugar plantations explains why about half British West Indian slave women never bore a child in the mid-eighteenth century, why those women who did bear children suffered from infertility by their mid-thirties, and why death rates were much lower on all other types of holdings. Wherever slaves were not engaged in sugar production, their chances of living and reproducing were better. Closely related to work demands was the number of Africans and creoles in a population. The higher the labour demand, generally the more Africans were imported. African-born slaves experienced higher age-specific mortality rates and lower fertility rates than creoles born in the colony. Africans lost valuable child-bearing years in their transfer to the New World, often had difficulty in finding mates, may have been reluctant to bear children, and generally breast-fed for quite long periods, which depressed fertility. Also related to the intensity of a sugar economy was nutrition. Slaves engaged in sugar cultivation experienced seasonal hard times when provisions were in short supply. Menarche occurred one to two years later among Caribbean than North American slave women. Deficient in protein and low on fat content, the Caribbean slave diet delayed women's sexual maturity, disrupted menstrual function, and hastened the onset of menopause. Finally, the relative fragility of family life affected fertility. Although a significant minority of the Caribbean slave population did succeed in establishing conjugal ties, the nuclear family was weaker in the sugar islands than among the slaves of North America. Furthermore, white men on the mainland were less likely than in the Caribbean to engage in miscegenation because of the readier availability of white women. The higher the proportion of slave children fathered by whites, the weaker was the nuclear family and the lower the birth rate.[3]

The dominant economic experience of most blacks in the British Empire was work on a sugar plantation. Not until the factory system in Europe was it possible to regiment and discipline workers like the slave gangs on sugar estates, where the working conditions were more severe than for any other crop. In the late seventeenth- and eighteenth-century Caribbean, about 90 per cent of all slaves worked—probably one of the highest labour participation rates anywhere in the world. Children under the age of 6 and a few aged and invalids were the only people exempt from labour. Furthermore, few other regions of the world were more exclusively committed to a single economic activity than was the Caribbean. Some islands were little more than one vast sugar plantation. By the early nineteenth century nine in ten slave workers in Nevis, Montserrat, and Tobago toiled on sugar estates. In general, sugar became more important over time, displacing alternative export crops such as tobacco, indigo, and cotton. To be sure, coffee became an important secondary crop on some British Caribbean islands by the late eighteenth century, but the overall trend in most places (especially when viewed over a 'long' eighteenth century) was not away from, but towards, sugar monoculture. The major exception to this generalization was Britain's largest sugar island, which was always diversified and became somewhat more so over time. In the late eighteenth century the proportion of Jamaica's slaves on sugar estates was about 60 per cent and declining.

Although sugar was the greatest of the slave crops, many Caribbean slaves worked at other activities. A few British Caribbean territories—the so-called marginal colonies—grew no sugar. In Belize most slaves were woodcutters; in the Cayman Islands, Anguilla, and Barbuda, a majority of slaves lived on small diversified agricultural holdings; and on the Bahamas cotton cultivation was important for some decades, and fishing and shipping occupied a significant minority of slaves. Even in a monocultural economy like that of Barbados, about one in ten slaves produced cotton, provisions, ginger, arrowroot, and aloes. Livestock ranching was important on Jamaica, where specialized pens

---

[3] Stanley Engerman and B. W. Higman, 'The Demographic Structure of the Caribbean Slave Societies', *UNESCO General History of the Caribbean*, Vol. III (forthcoming); Robert William Fogel, *Without Consent or Contract: The Rise and Fall of American Slavery* (New York, 1989); Higman, *Slave Populations*; Allan Kulikoff, *Tobacco and Slaves: The Development of Southern Cultures in the Chesapeake, 1680–1800* (Chapel Hill, NC, 1986); and J. R. Ward, *British West Indian Slavery, 1750–1834: The Process of Amelioration* (Oxford, 1988).

emerged. But the major secondary, and in some cases primary, crop at least by the second half of the eighteenth century was coffee, which employed a sizeable number of slaves on Jamaica, Dominica, St Vincent, Grenada, St Lucia, Trinidad, and Demerara-Essequibo, and Berbice. Coffee plantations tended to be more diverse and smaller than sugar estates, provided less occupational diversity, and because of their highland locations were more isolated. The single most important advantage possessed by slaves on coffee, cotton, cocoa, pimento, or provisions plantations was a less arduous work regime than sugar estate slaves.

On the mainland there was never the same concentration on one crop nor quite the same labour participation rate as on the islands. In the early eighteenth century there was a noticeable diversity in slave labour in British North America: in the north most slaves farmed or were domestics; in the Chesapeake most slaves cultivated tobacco, but also tended corn and raised livestock; and in the low-country, they acted as graziers, cut wood, and engaged in a whole array of pioneering activities. By the 1730s tobacco and rice occupied about four out of ten of the mainland's hands, but still the majority were employed in general farming, in domestic service, in crafts, or in other non-farm work. Not until the 1760s did about half of the mainland's slaves grow the three main staples—tobacco, rice, and indigo—but even then wheat farming was occupying the time of more and more slaves in the Chesapeake. As the eighteenth century proceeded, and children and the elderly constituted an ever higher proportion of the mainland slave population, the labour participation rate fell. By the time of the Revolution about 80 per cent of British North America's slaves were active in the labour force.

In other parts of the Empire, where slavery was more marginal than in the plantations of the Caribbean and North America, the work of blacks was far more wide-ranging. In Britain most blacks, even though slaves, occupied a position intermediate between chattel slavery and the domestic service of white servants. Most were household servants, working as pages, valets, footmen, coachmen, cooks, and maids. A significant minority were sailors, some plied a trade or worked as agricultural labourers. A few even gained employment as circus artists, singers, actors, musicians, boxers, prostitutes, as well as bizarre freaks at travelling shows. In late eighteenth-century Canada blacks worked as millwrights, black-smiths, sawyers, caulkers, coopers; a few were printers; others carved gates and fences, drove carriages, and went to sea. In the forts and castles of Africa the *grumetes* or local slaves were often skilled and earned wages, and skilled canoemen and fishermen who were free also worked for the British; in Sierra Leone the black settlers turned to trade to survive; and in the Cape Colony most blacks were either urban domestics, pastoralists, arable farmers, or worked in the burgeoning early nineteenth-century vineyards.

Even on the plantations many slaves escaped field labour because they practised a trade, supervised other slaves, or worked in domestic capacities. In the late seventeenth and early eighteenth centuries slaves gradually replaced whites as skilled workers, as overseers, and as house servants. The extent of the replacement depended on the type of crop, black–white ratio, and size of slave-holding. It was therefore most complete in a heavily black, large plantation, sugar colony like Jamaica and least complete in a predominantly white, small plantation, tobacco colony like Virginia. Mature slave societies generally distributed their employed slaves in the following rough proportions: 70–85 per cent field-hands; 10–20 per cent in skilled, semi-skilled, and supervisorial positions; and about 5–10 per cent in domestic service. These proportions varied considerably from place to place. Sugar plantations, for example, often had twice as many skilled personnel but only half as many domestics as did coffee or cotton plantations. On the mainland, opportunities for skilled work were about one-and-a-half times greater in the low-country than in the Chesapeake. Individuals were allocated jobs according to gender, age, colour, strength, and birthplace. Men dominated skilled trades, and women generally came to dominate field gangs; age determined when children entered the work-force, when they progressed from one gang to another, when field-hands became drivers, and when field-hands were pensioned off as watch-men; slaves of colour were often allocated to domestic work or, in the case of men, to skilled trades; drivers were taller and often stronger than the men and women who laboured in the gangs; creoles were more likely to fill craft slots than Africans, and some African ethnic groups had greater success in avoiding field work than others.

Those slaves in plantation societies who lived in towns and cities also escaped field labour. By the late eighteenth century the percentage of slaves living in urban places ranged from 5 per cent in most North American colonies to 10 per cent in most British Caribbean territories. Unlike most plantation slaves, urban slaves were often outnumbered by whites and freed people, lived on extremely small units, and under the close watch of a resident master who was often female. Within the urban slave population women usually outnumbered men, and coloured slaves were often prominent, as, more surprisingly, were Africans. Most urban slaves worked as domestics, but hawkers, higglers (many of whom were women), and transport workers were far more numerous in town than countryside, and roughly twice as many skilled tradespeople, fishermen, and general labourers lived in urban than in rural settings.

Slaves not only worked for their masters but also for themselves. This ability, however, varied greatly. It was probably most extensive on marginal islands like Barbuda and Great Exuma in the Bahamas, where slaves were virtual peasants, farming extensive provision grounds, owning much livestock, and spending a good deal of time hunting and fishing. Somewhat less advantaged were those slaves who had access to large provision grounds and owned livestock on the larger sugar islands like Jamaica and St Vincent. Even less advantaged were those low-country slaves on the North American mainland who worked by task and had to finish their jobs before being able to raise stock and tend crops on their own grounds. The ability to work for one's self was least extensive on small islands like Antigua and Barbados, in mainland areas like the Chesapeake, or in a diversified farming colony like the Cape, where slaves had little time to themselves and were permitted only garden plots. The impact of the slaves' economy was double-edged. The drawbacks were the lack of time slaves often had to tend their provision grounds, the distance separating slave huts from outlying grounds, the pressures on the aged, infirm, and young slaves, the extra burdens that provision grounds entailed, the greater ill health, lower life expectancy, and lower fertility that usually accompanied provision ground rather than ration systems. The benefits were the variety of the slaves' horticultural repertoires, the material benefits that accrued to slaves from selling and bartering their produce, the increased average size of provision grounds in many places over time, and the firm foundation that independent production gave to the slaves' domestic, religious, and community life.[4]

No longer can it be argued that the family was unthinkable or that the nuclear unit was unknown to most British American slaves. Slavery obviously subjected slaves' familial aspirations to enormous stress, often to breaking point: owners generally recognized only the mother–child tie, bought mostly men who then had difficulty finding wives, separated slave families by sale and transfer, and committed their own sexual assaults on slave women. Yet an emphasis on the instability, promiscuity, casual mating, disorganization, or near anarchy of slave family life is overdrawn. Historians now emphasize the resilience of slave families, the strength of kinship bonds, and the depth of parent–child affection. Nevertheless, it must be admitted that this more positive view of slave family life rests on fragmentary evidence; that much more is known of the structure of slave families than the quality of family relations; and that the information is invariably cross-sectional, providing snapshots of slave families at a point in time, rather than the serial life-cycles of slave families. In short, much is unknown about slave family life, and it is best to emphasize the formidable obstacles facing slaves as they struggled to create and then maintain families.

The possibilities for family life varied enormously over time. Wherever Africans were in the majority, family life was extremely tenuous. In slave populations

---

[4] Ira Berlin and Philip D. Morgan, eds., *Cultivation and Culture: Labor and the Shaping of Slave Life in the Americas* (Charlottesville, Va., 1993).

dominated by Africans, about a half or more lived with friends or other solitaries, not relatives. Nevertheless, Africans often practised a form of 'fictive kinship' particularly toward shipmates, who looked upon each others' children as their own. In early nineteenth-century Trinidad the fortunate Africans who found mates generally found other Africans, but not often from their own ethnic group or even region. Ethnic identity therefore probably dissolved rapidly. When Africans formed families they tended to be nuclear in form. In fact, in early nineteenth-century Trinidad Africans were more likely to be grouped in nuclear families than creoles. Africans probably saw the two-parent family form as the essential building-block of extended or polygamous family types rooted in lineage and locality. As the creole population grew, the larger plantations often became vast kinship networks. The typical slave dwelling comprised a man, woman, and her children, but kinship networks expanded as cross-plantation mating became common, so that many creoles tended to live in mother–children units (with a mate living at a nearby plantation) or in extended units. Family life often centred less on the household or nuclear family than on networks of relationships involving various relatives and spouses.

By the end of the eighteenth century a wide spectrum of family possibilities existed among blacks in North America and the Caribbean. The family, and particularly the nuclear family, was generally stronger among mainland than island slaves. The creolization of the slave population, which occurred earlier in North America than anywhere else, meant that slaves could find partners more readily and have kin around them. It is hard to imagine many slaves in the British Empire matching the experience of one Chesapeake woman who, as early as the 1770s, lived on a quarter surrounded by her five children, nineteen grandchildren, nine great-grandchildren, four children-in-law, and three grandchildren's spouses. She lived enmeshed in one large kinship web. Yet the advantages of mainland slaves should not be exaggerated. Because the presence of slave families generally increased with plantation size, there were likely to be more families on the sugar islands. Furthermore, the prospects of sale and transfer were undoubtedly less on the islands than on the mainland, where a rapidly expanding frontier led to many family disruptions.[5]

In other parts of the Empire the black familial experience was even more varied. In Britain, for example, black men so outnumbered black women that they had to marry white women if they wanted to form families. Many did, as was most graphically displayed when seventy white women, most of them wives to black

[5] Michael Craton and Gail Saunders, *Islanders in the Stream: A History of the Bahamian People*, Vol. I, *From Aboriginal Times to the End of Slavery* (Athens, Ga., 1992), pp. 318–29; B. W. Higman, *Slave Population and Economy in Jamaica, 1807–1834* (Cambridge, 1976), pp. 156–75 and *Slave Populations*, pp. 364–77; Kulikoff, *Tobacco and Slaves*, pp. 352–80; Morgan, *Slave Counterpoint*, chap. 10.

men, accompanied the so-called Black Poor to Sierra Leone in 1787. In the castles and forts dotted along the African coast the shoe was on the other foot, and many white men took black women as their wives. The most complex permutations occurred along the Cape frontier.[6]

The family was the key social institution formed by blacks, but it of course cannot be divorced from the broader social setting. Relations in slave societies can be divided into those social forms that regulated the encounters between the free and the unfree, and those that linked and divided slaves. In the highly polarized world of a slave society, standardized patterns of interaction and carefully defined codes of behaviour arose quickly to govern relations both between whites and blacks and among blacks themselves.

The law was one vital means of institutionalizing interactions between the free and unfree. The British Caribbean territories, with Barbados the prototype, were the first to develop elaborate slave codes; the mainland colonies, with South Carolina taking the lead, began to follow suit in the late seventeenth and more commonly early eighteenth centuries. Police regulations lay at the heart of the slave system. Thus, common features of the black codes were the prohibition and suppression of the unauthorized movement of slaves, the large congregation of slaves, the possession of guns and other weapons, the sounding of horns and drums, and the practice of secret rituals. The punishment for actual or threatened violence against whites was severe. Special slave-trial courts were established in most colonies to provide summary and expeditious 'justice'. Within the Caribbean, Jamaica's penal code was the most savage; South Carolina's was the most severe on the continent. In the late eighteenth and early nineteenth centuries the legislation tended to become a little less terroristic. The murder of a slave by a white man, for example, generally became a crime, but ameliorative legislation was always limited by the sheer fact of planter power.[7]

Furthermore, in all colonies custom was as important as law in shaping the black experience. The way in which slave-owners ruled their slaves varied from person to person, and from society to society, but certain common features held true. One of the most important, a defining characteristic of slavery, was the highly personal mechanisms of coercion; the whip, rather than resort to law, was the

---

[6] Braidwood, *Black Poor and White Philanthropists*, pp. 280–88; Margaret Priestley, *West African Trade and Coast Society: A Family Study* (London, 1969); Elphick and Giliomee, eds., *The Shaping of South African Society*, pp. 201–02, 358–84, 454–60.

[7] Elsa V. Goveia, *The West Indian Slave Laws of the Eighteenth Century* (Kingston, Jamaica, 1970); William M. Wiececk, 'The Statutory Law of Slavery and Race in the Thirteen Mainland Colonies of British America', *William and Mary Quarterly* (hereafter *WMQ*), Third Series, XXXIV (1977), pp. 258–80.

institution's indispensable and ubiquitous instrument. On the plantation or in the household, the master and his delegates used a variety of methods of physical coercion without recourse to, and usually unchecked by, any external authority. Brutality and sadism existed everywhere, but the Caribbean and newly settled areas, where masters felt most isolated and insecure, gained the worst reputations. On the mainland, low-country masters were thought to be more callous than their Chesapeake counterparts. Of other British territories, the Cape Colony was noted for its cruelty, symbolized by the widely used rhinoceros-hide *sjambok*. But the use or threat of force faced blacks everywhere. A black woman in late eighteenth-century Shelburne, Nova Scotia—hardly a place that needed to terrorize blacks—suffered a total of 350 lashes for two acts of petty larceny.[8]

Masters hoped that rewards would offset punishments. Over time, a number of allowances and privileges became entrenched in both custom and even law. Granting slaves half-days or full days to tend their provision plots became commonplace in some societies. Allowing slaves to attend extraordinary social functions such as a neighbourhood funeral became a standard practice. Masters generally allowed slaves time off during the Christian holidays. Christmas, in particular, became a time for permissiveness and even social inversion in some slave societies—a black Saturnalia. Special gratuities became routine: an extra allowance of food here, some tobacco there, a ration of rum for completing the harvest, cash payments for Sunday work. Favours and indulgences were disproportionately allocated: concubines, domestics, drivers, and tradesmen were the primary beneficiaries. Incentives tended to be most elaborate where plantations were large; the privileges of position within a specialized labour force based on rank and seniority generally did not apply to small-scale farms, common in the northern colonies of North America, parts of the Chesapeake, and the Cape colony.[9]

Although masters and slaves were locked into an intimate interdependence, blacks were not just objects of white action but subjects who regulated social relationships among themselves. A crucial distinction was geographical origin. Sometimes Africans from a particular region dominated the forced immigrants into a particular British American colony—in the 1730s three-quarters of slaves imported into South Carolina were from Angola; between 1750 and 1790 Jamaica took a disproportionate share, about 80 per cent, of slaves exported from the Gold Coast. It should be no surprise, therefore, that 'Angolans' were prominent in South Carolina's Stono Revolt of 1739 and 'Koromantis' in Tacky's Rebellion of 1760.

---

[8] Walker, *The Black Loyalists*, p. 56.

[9] Richard Pares, *A West-India Fortune* (London, 1950), pp. 131–2; Robert Dirks, *The Black Saturnalia: Conflict and its Ritual Expression on British West Indian Slave Plantations* (Gainesville, Fla., 1987); Higman, *Slave Populations*, pp. 202–04.

Africans from the same coastal region or of a similar ethnic background sometimes absconded together. Nevertheless, for most of the time ethnic heterogeneity
characterized the provenance of any British American slave population. Africans
from one background had to find ways to communicate and deal with other
Africans. Over time, Africans increasingly ran away with members of other ethnic
groups, and intermarried with one another. An African identity among blacks
emerged from their involuntary and voluntary associations in America.[10]

Creoles and Africans did not always get along. In the early years of almost all
settlements, often extending many decades in most Caribbean territories, the
numerically superior Africans often mocked creoles. But as creoles grew more
populous, the targets of derision tended to shift. Self-confident creoles often
looked down on those directly from Africa, derogatively labelling the newcomers
'Salt-water Negroes' or 'Guineabirds'. Whereas newly enslaved Africans often fled
in groups, creole fugitives usually absconded alone. Creoles sometimes took pity
on or took advantage of Africans. In some Caribbean societies creoles took
Africans into their houses and made them work on their provision grounds.
Where creoles constituted a majority, they set the tone and tenor of slave life
remarkably early. Africans learned the ropes from them. In the Chesapeake, for
example, African newcomers adjusted remarkably quickly to their new surroundings, attributable in large part to their close association with the more numerous
creoles.[11]

The emergence of a creole majority in many ways facilitated cohesiveness
among slaves, but over time gradations of colour, often closely linked to occupational differentiation, divided slave communities. By 1810 coloured slaves comprised about 12 per cent of the slave populations in the older sugar islands like
Barbados, Jamaica, and the Leeward Islands, 10 per cent in the marginal colonies,
and 8 per cent or less in the newer sugar colonies. On the mainland, 8 per cent of
Maryland's slaves in 1755 were listed as mulattoes and, by all accounts, mulattoes
then formed a higher proportion of the black population in the Chesapeake than
in the low-country. Although mainland planters tended to think in terms of just

[10] Peter H. Wood, *Black Majority: Negroes in Colonial South Carolina from 1670 through the Stono Rebellion* (New York, 1974); Orlando Patterson, *The Sociology of Slavery: An Analysis of the Origins, Development and Structure of Negro Slave Society in Jamaica* (Rutherford, NJ, 1969), pp. 113–44; Philip D. Curtin, *The Atlantic Slave Trade: A Census* (Madison, 1969), p. 160; John Thornton, *Africa and Africans in the Making of the Atlantic World, 1400–1680* (Cambridge, 1992); Michael Mullin, *Africa in America: Slave Acculturation and Resistance in the American South and the British Caribbean, 1736–1831* (Urbana, Ill., 1992), pp. 13–74; Sidney W. Mintz and Richard Price, *The Birth of African-American Culture: An Anthropological Perspective* (1976; Boston, 1992).

[11] Edward Brathwaite, *The Development of Creole Society in Jamaica, 1770–1820* (Oxford, 1971), pp. 164–66; Gerald W. Mullin, *Flight and Rebellion: Slave Resistance in Eighteenth-Century Virginia* (New York, 1972), pp. 34–123.

478 PHILIP D. MORGAN

white and black and island planters in terms of white, coloured, and black, slaves of mixed race were often privileged in both regions. To be sure, island planters would almost never work mulattoes in the field, whereas mainland planters often did, but many domestics and skilled slaves in both places were coloured. The Hemings family, who arrived at Thomas Jefferson's Monticello in 1774, serve as a classic example of the privilege that came from mulatto status: they assumed all the primary roles in the household. The most privileged mulatto group in the British Empire were the mixed-race traders—the Caulkers, Clevelands, Tuckers, Rogers, and Brews—who rose to prominence on the African coast. They were the children of white men and their African common-law wives.[12]

Coloured slaves were the most likely of any to be freed, thereby producing the greatest divide among blacks and the slave system's greatest anomaly, a third party in a structure built for two. Freed persons often signalled their freedom by assuming a new name, by changing location, by putting their families on a more secure footing, by creating associations to strengthen community life, by actively buying and selling property, even slaves, and resorting to courts to protect their hard-won gains. But throughout the eighteenth century freed persons were too few to separate themselves markedly from slaves, and many of their closest contacts were still with slaves. In the 1770s free coloureds and blacks were just 2 per cent of the black populations of Jamaica and Virginia, less than 1 per cent of Barbados's and South Carolina's. As the free black population grew the chances for a separate identity expanded, but it was an uneven process. Thus, by 1810 one in four blacks in Belize, one in five in Trinidad, one in ten in Dominica and the Bahamas, one in twelve in Jamaica, one in twenty-eight in British Guiana, and one in thirty-three in Barbados were free. By 1810, then, in Belize and Trinidad a three-tiered caste system had arisen, with free blacks and coloureds playing a buffer role between white masters and black slaves; in Barbados and British Guiana most notably, free blacks and coloureds were still a tiny minority and the society was predominantly two-tiered. There were also gradations among freed persons, with the free coloured identifying most closely with whites and free blacks more oriented toward black slaves.[13]

[12] Higman, *Slave Populations*, pp. 147–57; Winthrop D. Jordan, 'American Chiaroscuro: The Status and Definition of Mulattoes in the British Colonies', *WMQ*, Third Series, XIX (1962), pp. 183–200; Joel Williamson, *New People: Miscegenation and Mulattoes in the United States* (New York, 1980); Lucia C. Stanton, ' "Those Who Labor For My Happiness": Thomas Jefferson and His Slaves', in Peter S. Onuf, ed., *Jeffersonian Legacies* (Charlottesville, Va., 1993), pp. 147–80; Walter Rodney, *A History of the Upper Guinea Coast, 1545–1800* (Oxford, 1970), pp. 200–22; Priestley, *West African Trade.*

[13] Ira Berlin, *Slaves without Masters: The Free Negro in the Antebellum South* (New York, 1974), pp. 3–50; David W. Cohen and Jack P. Greene, eds., *Neither Slave nor Free: The Freedman of African Descent in the Slave Societies of the New World* (Baltimore, 1972); Higman, *Slave Populations*, pp. 76, 107–09; 112; Arnold A. Sio, 'Marginality and Free Colored Identity in Caribbean Slave Society', *Slavery and Abolition,*

Through various forms of social interaction, blacks in the British Empire created cultures and subcultures, the most fundamental building block of which was a language. The array of languages spoken by blacks was enormous. Along the belt of territories that supplied slaves to British America, Africans spoke about 1,000 languages; in late eighteenth-century British Africa blacks employed modes of communication that ranged from the tonal subtleties of Wolof to the implosive consonants or 'clicks' of the Khoisan. In time many African cultural brokers emerged who spoke more than one African language and an English-based creole. In the Cape Colony there were in fact two lingua franca: creolized Portuguese and an evolving form of Dutch, developed in the interaction between settlers, Khoisan, and slaves, which became Afrikaans. Some African languages or forms of them migrated to the New World. In the interior of Jamaica the Trelawny Maroons, while employing English, also held to a form of their Akan language, making use of their own linguistic brokers. In those plantation regions where Africans and blacks were most numerous some Africans for a time would be able to continue speaking their native languages, although they would also more than likely speak a pidgin and, over time, creole languages, perhaps even Standard English. In the towns, among privileged rural slaves, and in societies where Africans and blacks were not numerous, most blacks probably spoke a language undergoing rapid de-creolization, and some no doubt spoke Standard English. Small numbers of slaves spoke predominantly German, as in parts of Pennsylvania; Dutch, as in New York; French, as in Quebec, and the many Caribbean islands captured by the British; and even Gaelic, as in the North Carolina highlands. Without a doubt, blacks were the most linguistically polyglot and proficient of any ethnic group in the British Empire.

In spite of the bewildering variety, the norm was that most blacks in the British Empire spoke a creole language, which derived much of its vocabulary from English, but the phonology and syntax of which owed much to a prior West African creole or pidgin, and beyond that, to various African languages. In other words, Africans grafted a European vocabulary on to West African grammatical structures that had much in common. Although these Atlantic creole languages shared many structural features attributable to the substratum of African languages, they were separate languages. Blacks in the British Empire spoke at least twenty-five identifiable creoles: eighteen English-based (from Bahamian to Krio, from Belizan to Guyanese, from Caymanian to Gullah); two Dutch-based (Berbice and Afrikaans); and four French-based (Lesser Antillean in Dominica and St Lucia, Grenadan, Trinidadian, and Mauritian). Some creoles were profoundly

VIII (1987), pp. 166–82; Gad J. Heuman, *Between Black and White: Race, Politics and the Free Coloreds in Jamaica, 1792–1865* (Westport, Conn., 1981).

influenced by various African languages. Everyday words in Jamaican creole, for example, can be traced to specific African languages, most particularly Twi. Most words in regular use among Gullah speakers in South Carolina derived from Angola, Senegambia, and Sierra Leone, although languages from southern Nigeria and the Gold Coast formed its central syntactic core. On the other hand, on most of the mainland and an island like Barbados where whites were relatively numerous, the African influence on the creole language was much reduced. Moreover, in almost all the mainland territories and on islands such as Barbados and the Caymans, the forces propelling rapid de-creolization were powerful. By the late eighteenth century most slaves in the Chesapeake region—the largest congregation of slaves on the mainland—probably spoke a non-standard English dialect.[14]

In much the same way as a broad spectrum of linguistic forms existed among blacks, a continuous scale of musical expression, ranging in inspiration from Europe to Africa, also unfolded. The variety began in Africa where, for example, peoples of a large section of Dahomey eschewed harmony in their music, while the Ashanti in the neighbouring Gold Coast employed at least two-part and frequently three-and four-part harmony for almost all their music. The variety expanded out of Africa. At one extreme stood George Augustus Polgreen Bridgetower, the virtuoso violinist for whom Beethoven composed the *Kreutzer* Sonata. Brought to England from the European continent by his African father, the 10-year-old gave recitals in the salons of Brighton, Bath, and London. Of lesser renown, but just as popular, were those blacks who became integral members of European military bands. Some black musicians became street players: Billy Waters, for example, a one-legged black ex-navy man, claimed to earn an honest living by the scraping of catgut on London streets. At the other extreme were Africans in the plantation colonies who danced their ethnic dances to their own homeland musical accompaniments—whether banjos, balafos, harps, lutes, gourd rattles, or various kinds of drums. In the Caribbean musical styles were ethnically identifiable, but so-called 'Angolan' and 'Koromanti' music already involved syncretism. Everywhere, blacks invented new music.

Black music developed in ways akin to the formation of creole languages. A basic musical grammar, as it were, with an emphasis on the importance of music and dance in everyday life and the role of rhythm and percussion in musical style, survived the middle passage. Even complex musical instruments made the crossing, although more notable is how slaves adapted traditional instruments, invented new ones, and borrowed Euro-American ones. These adaptations, inven-

---

[14] Mervyn C. Alleyne, *Comparative Afro-American: An Historical-Comparative Study of English-Based Afro-American Dialects of the New World* (Ann Arbor, 1980); John A. Holm, *Pidgins and Creoles*, 2 vols. (Cambridge, 1988).

tions, and borrowings were interpreted and reinterpreted according to deep-level aesthetic principles drawn from different African musical traditions. Blacks retained the inner meanings of traditional modes of behaviour while adopting new outer forms. In musical terms, the key elements of the inner structure were complex rhythms, percussive qualities, syncopation, and antiphonal patterns.[15]

Black religious expression also spanned a large continuum. There were major differences in the ways in which African societies explained evil, in the role allocated to a creator divinity, in the absence or presence of prophetism or spirit possession. Some slaves, particularly from the Upper Guinea coast, were Muslim; some from Kongo had been exposed to Catholicism; in most other places a variety of traditional religions existed. Nevertheless, an extraordinary diversity of religious forms coexisted with certain widely shared basic principles. Most eighteenth-century Africans, for example, drew no neat distinction between the sacred and the profane, shared assumptions about the nature of causality, believed in both a High God and many lesser gods as personifications of the forces of nature and of destiny, thought the dead played an active role in the lives of the living, and saw a close relationship between social conflict and illness or misfortune. In the New World there was enormous variety in black religion: Muslim slaves became particularly noted for the power of their magical charms; in the islands, African-style cults emerged such as Jamaican Myal; some South Carolina slaves may have fled to the Spanish because they were Catholic; and slaves embraced every form of Protestantism.[16]

Perhaps *the* major development that took place in the metaphysics of most slave communities was a shift from the benevolent lesser spirits, the unobservable personal beings so prominent in traditional African cosmologies, to sorcery, the harming of others by secretive means. Because of enforced coexistence with other African groups and because of the serious, everyday problems of dealing with harsh taskmasters, slaves turned to those spirits deemed useful in injuring other people. The most common term for sorcery was *obi* or *obia* or *obeah*, which had multiple African origins, including Efik *ubio* (a charm to cause sickness and death) and Twi *o-bayifo* (sorcerer). The term was current among both North American and Caribbean slaves, although on the mainland 'conjuring' and 'conjurer' were more common. While the boundary between sorcery, folk medicine, and

[15] Dena J. Epstein, *Sinful Tunes and Spirituals: Black Folk Music to the Civil War* (Urbana, Ill., 1977); Kenneth M. Bilby, 'The Caribbean as a Musical Region', in Sidney W. Mintz and Sally Price, eds., *Caribbean Contours* (Baltimore, 1985), pp. 181–218; Richard Cullen Rath, 'African Music in Seventeenth-Century Jamaica: Cultural Transit and Transmission', *WMQ*, Third Series, L (1993), pp. 700–26.

[16] Albert J. Raboteau, *Slave Religion: The 'Invisible Institution' in the Antebellum South* (New York, 1978); Jon Butler, *Awash in a Sea of Faith: Christianizing the American People* (Cambridge, Mass., 1990), pp. 129–63.

divination was porous, the dominant trend was a powerful concentration on those means for injuring people.[17]

The religious world view of early Anglo-American slaves was primarily magical, not Christian. In general, Anglican ministers were not zealous proselytizers of black slaves. The few who were sympathetic to the slaves' needs faced almost insurmountable odds, ranging from the vast extent of many parishes to the institutional weakness of their own church. But the most formidable barriers to the Christianization of blacks was the resistance posed by masters and slaves alike. At any time throughout the eighteenth century there were never more than a few Christian blacks on the Society for the Propagation of the Gospel's own trust estate in Barbados where successive catechists ministered. Even Philip Quaque, born on the Gold Coast in 1741, sent to England, where he was the first African ordained by the Church of England, and returned home in 1766 as a missionary to his own people, had little success over the succeeding half-century when confronted by a deeply entrenched Akan religion. Nevertheless, traditional religious beliefs were not static. Faced with the interpretative challenge of large-scale social change, many blacks in both Africa and America developed a more elaborate and active role for a supreme being, the formerly otiose High God of many traditional cosmologies. When blacks accepted Christianity or Islam, it often owed as much to the evolution of traditional religious beliefs as to the activities of missionaries.[18]

This can help explain how and why blacks infused elements of their traditional religion into Christianity. They did not just accept Christianity wholesale but did so selectively. Nowhere is this better displayed than in beliefs about the role of the dead among the living. For Africans, the funeral was the true climax of life. In Anglo-America many slaves thought death brought a return to Africa. Their common funeral practices included the accompaniment of drumming, dance, and song; feasting and drinking, with liquor and food thrown into the grave; treasured possessions buried with the corpse; broken crockery, upturned bottles, and seashells marking black graves.[19]

Highly expressive funeral practices were not far removed from the typical behaviour of eighteenth-century evangelicals, and it was this form of Christianity that began to appeal to blacks from about mid-century onward. Evangelical

---

[17] Patterson, *Sociology of Slavery*, pp. 182–206; Mullin, *Africa in America*, pp. 175–86; Thornton, *Africa and Africans*, pp. 235–71.

[18] J. Harry Bennett, *Bondsmen and Bishops: Slavery and Apprenticeship on the Codrington Plantations of Barbados, 1710–1838* (Berkeley and Los Angeles, 1958), pp. 75–87; Margaret Priestley, 'Philip Quaque of Cape Coast', in Philip D. Curtin, ed., *Africa Remembered: Narratives by West Africans from the Era of the Slave Trade* (Madison, 1967), pp. 99–139; Robin Horton, 'African Conversion', *Africa*, XLI (1971), pp. 85–108 and 'On the Rationality of African Conversion', ibid., XLV (1975), pp. 219–35 and 373–99.

[19] Brathwaite, *Development of Creole Society*, pp. 216–18; Jerome S. Handler and Frederick W. Lange, *Plantation Slavery in Barbados: An Archaeological and Historical Investigation* (Cambridge, Mass., 1978),

Christianity spread at different rates and in different forms. In South Carolina and Georgia the first inroads were made in the late 1730s by John Wesley and George Whitefield; in Virginia in the 1750s by Presbyterians, and in the 1760s by New Light Baptists; in Jamaica by Moravians in 1754; in Antigua by Moravians in 1756, and by Methodists in the 1760s; and in the Cape by Wesleyan missionaries who joined Moravians from 1798 onward. There were many black evangelicals; by 1776 perhaps a third of Virginia's Baptists were black; by 1790 a quarter of Nova Scotia's Methodists were black; by 1800 28 per cent of the Leewards Islands' 83,000 slaves had been converted by Moravian, Methodist, and Anglican missionaries; and between 1795 and 1815 the intensity of the coverts' zeal among thousands of Khoisan was striking. The evangelical appeal lay in a message of universal salvation through divine grace, an intensity of feeling and physical expressiveness, and a church structure that was quite egalitarian.[20]

Creating a distinctive language, music, and religion—in short, a culture—had political implications, but of profound ambivalence. On the one hand, it was an act of resistance, perhaps the greatest act of resistance accomplished by blacks in the British Empire. By carving out some independence for themselves, by creating something coherent and autonomous from African fragments and European influences, by forcing whites to recognize their humanity, slaves triumphed over their circumstances. They opposed the dehumanization inherent in their status and demonstrated their independent will and volition. On the other hand, their cultural creativity eased the torments of slavery, gave them a reason for living, and made them think long and hard before sacrificing everything in an attempt to overthrow the system. It thereby encouraged accommodation to the established order. This ambivalence is at the heart of the political experiences of blacks in the British Empire.

It is apparent in slave resistance. List all the plots and rebellions in chronological sequence, and slave resistance appears structurally endemic. Recall the bitter fact that the vicious system of Anglo-American slavery lasted for hundreds of years

p. 171–215; Robert Farris Thompson, *Flash of the Spirit: African and Afro-American Art and Philosophy* (New York, 1983).

[20] Harvey H. Jackson, 'Hugh Bryan and the Evangelical Movement in Colonial South Carolina', *WMQ*, Third Series, XLIII (1986), pp. 594–614; Mechal Sobel, *The World They Made Together: Black and White Values in Eighteenth-Century Virginia* (Princeton, 1987), pp. 178–203; Elsa V. Goveia, *Slave Society in the British Leeward Islands at the End of the Eighteenth Century* (New Haven, 1965), pp. 263–310; Mary Turner, *Slaves and Missionaries: The Disintegration of Jamaican Slave Society, 1787–1834* (Urbana, Ill., 1982); Clifton C. Crais, *White Supremacy and Black Resistance in Pre-Industrial South Africa: The Making of the Colonial Order in the Eastern Cape, 1770–1865* (Cambridge, 1992), pp. 82–84, 100–05; G. A. Rawlyk, *The Canada Fire: Radical Evangelicalism in British North America, 1775–1812* (Kingston and Montreal, 1994).

without serious challenge, and its stability seems paramount. No Anglo-American mainland region faced a large-scale slave insurrection in the eighteenth century. No white person was killed in a slave rebellion in the colonial Chesapeake. The most notable incident on the mainland was South Carolina's Stono Revolt in which about sixty slaves killed approximately twenty whites and destroyed much property, but this was small-scale and of short duration. By contrast, the islands were always more brittle, even if (until 1816) Barbadian slaves never mounted a serious slave rebellion. In 1736 Antigua endured a harrowing slave plot in which well over a hundred slaves were put to death or banished. Jamaica experienced many rebellions, none more serious than the island-wide insurrection of 1760 that resulted in the deaths of 90 whites, 400 blacks, and the exile of another 600. Just as slave rebellions varied across space, so they did over time: from events inspired by Africans to events dominated by creoles, from attempts to secure freedom to attempts to overthrow slavery, from acts of rage to forms of industrial action. Slave resistance was also more than collective violence; it encompassed flight, sabotage, and individual murders. But as has been noted, the cook who put ground glass in the master's family food had first to get the job. The slaves who plotted in the market-places had first to produce for the market. There is no simple unilinear gradient from accommodation to resistance.[21]

Even Maroons, the ultimate symbol of rebellion, were forced to accommodate. They emerged almost everywhere: in low-country swamps, on the high seas, on Mountains, as in Dominica and St Vincent, even in the Australian outback in the person of John Caesar, prototypical bushranger. By far the most significant set of Maroons in the Empire established themselves in Jamaica, where at mid-century about 1,000 persons, just under 1 per cent of the slave population, lived under the jurisdiction of two bands. By 1739, when the colonial government of Jamaica recognized their free and separate existence, the Windward Maroons in the eastern mountains and the Leeward Maroons in the western interior had been waging war against whites for more than eighty years. For the most part, the post-treaty Maroons proved effective allies, tracking down slave runaways and rebels, adopting the military hierarchy of the establishment, living in an uneasy symbiosis with their white neighbours, seeking arms, tools, pots, and cloth as well as employment. The white establishment never rested secure, and in 1795 their fears were realized when the Maroons of Trelawny Town engaged in one last two-year war with government troops. When these Maroons finally surrendered, apparently on the

---

[21] Sidney W. Mintz, 'Toward an Afro-American History', *Cahiers d'histoire mondiale*, XIII (1971), p. 321; Edmund S. Morgan, *American Slavery, American Freedom: The Ordeal of Colonial Virginia* (New York, 1975), p. 309; Michael Craton, *Testing the Chains: Resistance to Slavery in the British West Indies* (Ithaca, NY, 1982); David Barry Gaspar, *Bondmen and Rebels: A Study of Master–Slave Relations in Antigua with Implications for Colonial British America* (Baltimore, 1985).

understanding that the government would listen to their grievances, they were transported to Nova Scotia before moving on to Sierra Leone. When they arrived in their new homeland in 1800 their first action was to quell a rebellion by many of Sierra Leone's black settlers, as if to illustrate how rebellion and accommodation went hand in hand.[22]

Blacks were, in fact, found on opposite sides of most political disputes. In the early years of many settlements slaves were often used as soldiers, but as their numbers grew opposition arose to arming them. However, in emergencies—a local rebellion or a foreign invasion—slaves thought to be loyal were periodically placed under arms. Moreover, throughout the century slaves continued to be used as auxiliaries and pioneers; in the islands free blacks became an important part of the militia; during the Revolutionary War the British army raised a black unit, the Carolina Corps; and the Anglo-French War of 1793–1815 made the use of black troops imperative. In 1795 the effectiveness of black troops and the shortage of white manpower led Imperial officials to form black regiments. Eventually twelve black West Indian regiments were raised, and 30,000 black regulars recruited. Their commanders were generally complimentary about their character and conduct. In Africa Britain engaged in its first war against black men (an alliance of Khoikhoi and Xhosa)—the Third Frontier War (1799–1803)—with the assistance of the so-called Hottentot Corps, founded in 1793 by the Dutch, subsequently expanded, strengthened, and ultimately renamed the Cape Regiment.[23]

The eighteenth-century black world was multi-faceted. There was a majority experience—located on plantations—where in many ways slaves suffered a similar fate. They lived short and impoverished lives, worked most of the time, created fragile families, encountered great brutality, spoke creole, developed a distinctive musical style, believed in magic, and generally accommodated themselves to the system of slavery. But this description is a monochrome caricature, not a richly coloured portrait. It fails to do justice to the variations, the subtleties, the many temporal, spatial, and status distinctions in black life. The black experience varied most fundamentally depending on the nature of population growth, the type of employment, the size of the slave-holding unit, the level of material well-being, the quality of family life, encounters with whites, patterns of interaction among

[22] Richard Price, ed., *Maroon Societies: Rebel Slave Communities in the Americas* (1973; Baltimore, 1979); Barbara Klamon Kopytoff, 'The Maroons of Jamaica: An Ethnohistorical Study of Incomplete Politics, 1655–1905' unpublished Ph.D. dissertation, Pennsylvania, 1973; Mavis C. Campbell, *The Maroons of Jamaica, 1655–1796: A History of Resistance, Collaboration, and Betrayal* (South Hadley, Mass., 1988).

[23] Peter M. Voelz, *Slave and Soldier: The Military Impact of Blacks in the Colonial Americas* (New York, 1993); Roger Norman Buckley, *Slaves in Red Coats: The British West India Regiments, 1795–1815* (New Haven, 1979); Elphick and Giliomee, eds., *The Shaping of South African Society*, pp. 35–38, 444–47.

blacks, the extent of cultural autonomy, and the degree of resistance and accom-modation to the system. There was no single black experience in the British Empire. There was, however, a core to the experience: drawing upon some shared principles and passing through the fires of enslavement, blacks everywhere forged a new culture.

Select Bibliography

IRA BERLIN and PHILIP D. MORGAN, eds., *Cultivation and Culture: Labor and the Shaping of Slave Life in the Americas* (Charlottesville, Va., 1993).

MICHAEL CRATON, *Testing the Chains: Resistance to Slavery in the British West Indies* (Ithaca, NY, 1982).

LELAND FERGUSON, *Uncommon Ground: Archaeology and Early African America, 1650–1800* (Washington, 1992).

ROBERT WILLIAM FOGEL, *Without Consent or Contract: The Rise and Fall of American Slavery* (New York, 1989).

DAVID BARRY GASPAR, *Bondmen and Rebels: A Study of Master–Slave Relations in Antigua with Implications for Colonial British America* (Baltimore, 1985).

ELSA V. GOVEIA, *Slave Society in the British Leeward Islands at the End of the Eighteenth Century* (New Haven, 1965).

DOUGLAS HALL, *In Miserable Slavery: Thomas Thistlewood in Jamaica, 1750–86* (London, 1989).

JEROME S. HANDLER and FREDERICK W. LANGE, *Plantation Slavery in Barbados: An Archaeological and Historical Investigation* (Cambridge, Mass., 1978).

B. W. HIGMAN, *Slave Population and Economy in Jamaica, 1807–1834* (New York, 1976).

—— *Slave Populations of the British Caribbean, 1807–1834* (Baltimore, 1984).

KENNETH F. KIPLE, *The Caribbean Slave: A Biological History* (Cambridge, 1984).

ALLAN KULIKOFF, *Tobacco and Slaves: The Development of Southern Cultures in the Chesapeake, 1680–1800* (Chapel Hill, NC, 1986).

SIDNEY W. MINTZ and RICHARD PRICE, *The Birth of African-American Culture: An Anthropological Perspective* (1976; Boston, 1992).

PHILIP D. MORGAN, *Slave Counterpoint: Black Culture in the Eighteenth-Century Chesapeake and Lowcountry* (Chapel Hill, NC, 1996).

MICHAEL MULLIN, *Africa in America: Slave Acculturation and Resistance in the American South and the British Caribbean, 1736–1831* (Urbana, Ill., 1992).

RICHARD B. SHERIDAN, *Doctors and Slaves: A Medical and Demographic History of Slavery in the British West Indies, 1680–1834* (Cambridge, 1985).

MECHAL SOBEL, *The World They Made Together: Black and White Values in Eighteenth-Century Virginia* (Princeton, 1987).

MARY TURNER, *Slaves and Missionaries: The Disintegration of Jamaican Slave Society, 1787–1834* (Urbana, Ill., 1982).

J. R. WARD, *British West Indian Slavery, 1750–1834: The Process of Amelioration* (Oxford, 1988).

PETER H. WOOD, *Black Majority: Negroes in Colonial South Carolina from 1670 Through the Stono Rebellion* (New York, 1974).

22

The British in Asia: Trade to Dominion, 1700–1765

P. J. MARSHALL

At the beginning of the eighteenth century Europe's dealings with Asia, although they had greatly increased in scale, were still set in a pattern that was recognizably one which had endured at least since Roman times. A limited seaborne European presence operated within an Asian world over which, on land, it could exercise little if any control. European purposes in Asia remained essentially commercial. The role of the British was, however, to change fundamentally: beginning in eastern India from mid-century, they were to become conquerors and rulers. By 1765, the closing date for this chapter, a sizeable territorial dominion had been established. From this beginning British power was to engulf the whole of the Indian subcontinent within a hundred years, and in the process the centre of gravity of the whole British Empire would shift from the Atlantic to the Indian Ocean.

Europeans were drawn to Asia in the eighteenth century, as in past centuries, to obtain crops which could not be grown in Europe or manufactured articles whose quality European artisans could not match. Pepper and spices had dominated early trade between Asia and Europe, but during the seventeenth century they were eclipsed by the mass import of textiles, cotton cloth, and raw silk. Indian cotton goods were immensely popular throughout Europe and they had a buoyant re-export market in the Americas and along the West African coast. They fulfilled both the demands of high fashion for dresses and furnishings, and of mass consumption for cheap, washable, lightweight fabrics. In a good year the British imported about 750,000 pieces of Indian calicoes and muslins.[1] Raw silk from Persia, China, and India supplemented Mediterranean sources for European silk weavers. During the eighteenth century Asia became a major supplier of beverages to Europe: Chinese tea and Arabian and Javanese coffee. European gunpowder manufacturers derived much of their saltpetre from India. Even if the scale of the

---

[1] K. N. Chaudhuri, *The Trading World of Asia and the English East India Company, 1660–1760* (Cambridge, 1978), pp. 547–48. This work, and in particular its Statistical Tables, is the basis for the estimates of the volume and the value of the trade throughout this chapter.

trade was not commercially very significant, there was a lively demand by European connoisseurs for exotic Asian items such as Chinese porcelain, lacquer ware, or furniture.

Successful trade with Asia required commercial organization on a large scale. Asian trade was a high-cost operation. The huge distances to be covered round the Cape, with a sailing time that could be six months or more each way, meant that trading capital was tied up for long periods. Large and expensive ships had to be used and elaborate trading agencies had to be maintained permanently in Asian ports to dispose of the cargoes brought out by the ships and to obtain the goods for the return voyage to Europe. High costs and a high level of risk meant that individual voyages or the ventures of small groups were unlikely to succeed. During the seventeenth century trade between Asia and Europe was for the most part in the hands of great East India companies, which raised large sums on a permanent basis, allowing them to spread risk among a corporate body of investors and to pursue long-term commercial strategies. The companies protected their huge outlays by maintaining close links with their parent states, enjoying grants of monopoly over trade with Asia by sea in return for services which included advancing money to the state.

The early-eighteenth-century English East India Company was already set into a pattern that was to last into the nineteenth century. By contemporary standards it was a gigantic organization. Its stock was fixed in 1708 at £3,200,000, subscribed by some 3,000 shareholders, and it borrowed very extensively on bond; £6 million was set as the limit in 1744. It sent twenty to thirty large ships a year to Asia. The value of its annual sales fluctuated between £1,250,000 and £2 million.

At the beginning of each trading cycle orders for goods from different parts of Asia were sent out with the ships that carried such goods as could be sold in Asian markets, mostly woollens and metals. Bullion usually constituted some 80 per cent, and sometimes more, of the value of the outward cargoes. The ships were consigned to the Company's servants stationed in Asian ports. To assemble the cargoes for the return voyage permanent commercial establishments were a necessity. Orders would have to be placed and money laid out long before the ships arrived. A very large number of small producers were involved. Export crops like pepper, tea, or coffee were grown by Asian farmers, and silk was wound, cotton woven, or porcelain baked by Asian artisans in their own homes or in small workshops.

In dealing with a mass of small producers the British Company servants needed the services of Asian merchants and brokers. Where political conditions permitted, Europeans would try to cut out intermediaries and establish direct relations with producers, but even where this was possible, they still needed to employ Asian agents to supervise the cultivators and artisans, and to deal with Asian merchants who purchased imports of European goods or arranged for the exchange of bullion into local currencies. European trade often depended on the credit extended by local merchants or bankers. In short, the Company's servants had to operate within an Asian commercial system.

The Company also had to operate within Asian political systems. Trade on the scale pursued by the East India companies could not be separated from politics. Only at sea or in dealing with small-scale Asian regimes could Europeans hope to impose their own terms. As Portuguese armed ships had demonstrated early in the sixteenth century, Europeans had clear advantages in maritime technology which they could exploit to good effect; European gunned ships were likely to prevail over Asian shipping. Assuming that they had the ships available, Europeans could disrupt Asian trade routes and reduce competition. From their control of the sea, they could also seize bases and small islands. Where valuable crops were concentrated in limited areas, such as the spices of the Moluccas or the cinnamon of Ceylon, they might be brought under European control

Such tactics had been deployed with some success during the seventeenth century by the Dutch. The English, however, had lacked the resources to imitate them and had been on the receiving end of Dutch blockades and prohibitions. As a result, British operations were concentrated on mainland Asia, where the European presence was a microscopic one on the fringes of the great Asian empires. For much of the seventeenth century the Islamic empires, the Ottoman Turks, the Safavids in Persia, and the Mughals in India, maintained their power and in some cases increased the territory under their control. After a great upheaval in mid-century, a new imperial regime in China consolidated its hold and embarked on massive conquests of further territory in the west. Tokugawa supremacy was firmly established in Japan. The military power of these empires seemed formidable by European standards. Large armies were based for the most part on cavalry, but were augmented by infantry and artillery. Weaponry was not significantly different from that of European forces. It would be an extremely expensive as well as a hazardous operation to send European troops by sea to the Indian Ocean or East Asia in numbers that could challenge a major Asian army.

Military intervention seemed to offer few commercial rewards. All Europeans, except for the Dutch, were excluded from Japan and they were tightly controlled in China, but elsewhere European traders were able to accommodate themselves to the great Asian empires without serious difficulty. The stability of the empires for much of the seventeenth century created favourable conditions for trade in general, and Europeans were able to benefit from what seems to have been a period of commercial expansion throughout Asia. Contrary to what most Europeans and many later historians have believed, Asian rulers generally fostered trade, if for no other reason, as a means of increasing the taxable wealth of the areas under their authority. Protection was extended to foreign merchants. Except in China or Japan, Europeans, like other alien merchants, were given certain privileges: they were permitted to live in a 'factory' where they could practise their own religion and exercise a limited jurisdiction over their own employees, and they could compound for customs payments.

At the beginning of the eighteenth century about 90 per cent of the Company's cargoes were obtained from India. In western India the English operated out of the great Mughal port of Surat and from their own settlement granted to the Crown by the Portuguese at Bombay (see Map 23.1). The cargoes consisted mainly of the cotton textiles of the province of Gujarat. Pepper obtained from settlements on the south-west coast was also shipped from Bombay. Madras, held outright on a grant from a local chief, was the major English settlement on the south-east or Coromandel coast. Coromandel textiles were in high demand in Europe early in the eighteenth century. In Bengal, Calcutta, a town largely founded by the English, was growing very rapidly indeed. On the strength of grants from the local ruler, the English had built a fort and exercised authority over the town. Bengal was a rich province, producing silk and cotton cloth for export in great quantities. Early in the eighteenth century it became the major source of British textile exports. From the 1720s shipments through Calcutta usually amounted to at least half of the Indian cargoes. To purchase their textiles, the Company's agents set up factories in several inland weaving centres, accessible from Calcutta along Bengal's river system.

Outside India, small quantities of pepper were bought at Bencoolen in Sumatra, the remnant of what had been a considerable trade conducted by the English in the Indonesian archipelago until the Dutch closed down the English factories. Growing quantities of tea, silk, and chinaware were obtained from China. Tea was to become of great importance and the trade was to be concentrated on the port of Canton, where the Chinese authorities imposed tight regulations. Europeans had no privileges there at all. They were forbidden to reside in the port except during the trading season. They could have no direct dealings with the imperial Chinese government and were to buy and sell only through a guild of licensed Chinese merchants, who were responsible for their strict observance of Chinese law. Customs and other dues were high. For all its rigour, however, what became known as the Canton system still permitted a massive expansion in tea exports during the course of the eighteenth century.

Except when its trade was disrupted by the European wars at the beginning of the eighteenth century, the East India Company was a highly successful commercial organization. The British were pulling ahead of the Dutch East India Company that had enjoyed a dominant position for so long; the value of the British Company's sales exceeded those of the Dutch in the 1720s. The British lead in textiles, the most dynamic element in Asian trade, was clearly established by the beginning of the century.[2] Whereas analysis of the financial position of the Dutch Company suggests that it ceased to operate profitably by the end of the seventeenth century, the British Company only incurred overall losses in two years between 1710 and 1745.[3] By the 1720s a French East India Company was also trading on a considerable scale in Asia. Like the British, the French largely concentrated on Indian trade, establishing their *comptoirs* in the main textile areas; the French headquarters at Pondicherry was, for instance, close to Madras. The volume and the level of profits of French trade was about half that of the British Company in the 1720s, but came close to it in the late 1730s and early 1740s before falling away again.[4]

The history of the British in Asia during the eighteenth century seems to fall into two clearly demarcated phases. A long period of stability ended in mid-century, when the British shifted from apparently peaceful trade to wars and conquests in India. If the contrast between peace in the first half and violence in the later eighteenth century may be somewhat overdrawn, the change in the role of the British was still a spectacular one. It is a transformation that is hard to explain.

It is clearly not the case that Europe was able at this point to assert political or military capacities that were overwhelmingly superior to those of any Asian opponent. British warships had no Asian rivals and, as will be shown, even heavily outnumbered British armies were dauntingly formidable against Asian forces. But the essential technology of warfare, the cannon and the musket, was still the same for both sides, while Indian soldiers provided much of the British manpower. Nor is it easy to find any conscious drive to empire on the British side. British interests in Asia had not changed significantly since the establishment of the Company in the seventeenth century. The British were still in Asia to buy Asian commodities. There had been no major shift in the pattern of the Company's trade in the early eighteenth century, while the quantities of goods which it exported in the middle of the century fluctuated at around the total reached in the 1720s. A commercial

---

[2] Niels Steensgaard, 'The Growth and Composition of the Long-Distance Trade of England and the Dutch Republic before 1750', in James D. Tracy, ed., *The Rise of the Merchant Empires: Long-Distance Trade in the Early Modern World, 1350–1750* (Cambridge, 1990), p. 126.

[3] For the Dutch Company, see F. S. Gaastra, 'The Shifting Balance of Trade of the Dutch East India Company', in Leonard Blussé and F. S. Gaastra, eds., *Companies and Trade: Essays on Overseas Trading Companies during the Ancien Régime* (The Hague, 1981), pp. 62–64; for the British Company, see Chaudhuri, *The Trading World*, pp. 436–52.

[4] Philippe Haudrère *La Compagnie française des Indes au XVIIIe siècle (1719–1795)*, 4 vols. (Paris, 1989), II, pp. 417–36; Catherine Manning, *Fortunes à Faire: The French in Asian Trade, 1719–48* (London, 1996), pp. 35–45.

imperative for territorial empire was not recognized by those who directed the Company's affairs.

Yet fundamental changes took place in the role of the British in India. The year 1744 is the date at which they are conventionally said to have begun. In that year fighting broke out between the British and French at sea. In 1746 hostilities commenced on land in south-eastern India in the territories claimed by the Nawabs of Arcot and later in those of the Nizams of Hyderabad. The British and French fought out their own rivalries in part as allies of contestants for the succession of both the Nawab and the Nizam. War ebbed and flowed across southern India with very little intermission from 1746 until complete British victory brought the fighting to an end in 1761. British victory meant that the territories of the British-backed Nawab of Arcot became a client state of the East India Company.

In 1756 relations between the East India Company and the Nawab of Bengal exploded into violence, when the Company rejected an ultimatum from a new Nawab, Siraj-ud-Daula. The Nawab took the settlement of Calcutta. A British expedition from Madras under Robert Clive recovered it and then turned on the Nawab, defeating him at Plassey in June 1757. Thus Bengal also became effectively a client state with a new Nawab ruling under British protection. Within a few years, however, Bengal had become a province under actual British rule. Successive Nawabs were deposed in 1760 and in 1763, when the deposed Nawab was driven to outright resistance and war. He found allies in northern India in the Mughal Emperor and the Wazir of Oudh. Both he and his allies were defeated at the Battle of Buxar in 1764 and a settlement ensued at the Treaty of Allahabad of 1765 by which the Emperor gave the East India Company the *diwani*, or responsibility for the civil administration of Bengal and the provinces connected with it, while the Wazir of Oudh accepted a British alliance and a British garrison. This settlement gave the British rule over some 20 million people in Bengal together with access to a revenue of about £3 million, and it took British influence nearly up to Delhi.

Only in western India was a British breakout delayed. An expedition from Bombay did, however, establish British control over the port of Surat in 1759.

These cataclysmic events have been variously interpreted. As the brief account of them just given makes clear, by the middle of the eighteenth century the British were dealing not with a unified Mughal empire, but with a number of regional rulers. Western historians have traditionally placed much emphasis on the disintegration of the Mughal empire as having created the conditions of chaos and weakness that made foreign rule in India possible or, in older accounts, that made it necessary. The chain of events that led to the establishment of British rule at a particular point in time is, however, usually given a European first cause. The French and the British companies were drawn into hostilities by the outbreak of wars in Europe in 1744 and 1756. Once embarked on hostilities, the rivals exploited the weaknesses in the Indian political system brought about by the collapse of Mughal power. Bengal was drawn into the vortex of Anglo-French rivalry by the folly of Siraj-ud-Daula in launching his attack on Calcutta in 1756.

The British themselves have long been seen as having done little if anything to create the opportunities from which they were to profit so spectacularly. They are depicted as peaceful traders, living within the confines of their settlements, until Indian disorder and French aggression forced them into action. What earlier generations of historians felt had to be explained about the British was the resourcefulness and vigour with which Robert Clive and his colleagues reacted to situations that were not of their making.

Recent scholarship has begun to revise these interpretations. In the first place, the British presence in India is no longer seen as purely passive until the mid-eighteenth century. The British appear to have been increasingly assertive well before open military and political intervention began. Secondly, the history of eighteenth-century India is undergoing reinterpretation. The proposition that the breakup of the Mughal empire left a void of disorder that the British were eventually obliged to fill is being questioned. On the contrary, some scholars are arguing that British rule was built not on Indian collapse but on the emergence of a new order in eighteenth-century India.

Reassessments of the role of the British in India in the first half of the eighteenth century have arisen primarily from studies of what is called 'private' trade. The Company's own trade might be set into a relatively static pattern, but the trade of the Company was only a part of British activities in Asia; there was a dynamic private sector as well.

The Company's servants' own trade, together with that of a limited number of British people outside the service who resided in the Company's settlements, constituted this private sector. Private British enterprise in the early eighteenth century was chiefly based on the Indian settlements and involved in trading by sea. Since the Portuguese, all Europeans had been concerned not only with procuring cargoes for export but also with profiting from trade from one part of Asia to another. Europeans could earn profits either by shipping their own goods from port to port or through freight paid to them by Asian merchants for having their goods carried on European ships. For most of the seventeenth century the English Company tried to reserve for itself the inter-Asian trade, called the 'country trade' by contemporaries, but from the 1670s the Company largely withdrew, leaving it to private individuals. Madras was the major centre of English country trade around 1700. Ships from the port took Indian textiles to the Persian Gulf and the Red Sea to the west, and to China, the Philippines, mainland South-East Asia, and the

Archipelago to the east. By the 1720s, however, Madras had lost ground to Calcutta. Up to forty private ships a season were being fitted out from Calcutta. The number tailed off somewhat by the 1750s, but a large proportion of the more lucrative parts of India's maritime carrying trade remained in private British hands.[5] The extent to which private individuals participated in India's internal trade is less clearly documented. In Bengal especially, where Company servants were posted at several inland trading centres as well as at Calcutta, there is clear evidence that they did so on a considerable scale. This provoked friction with the Nawab's governments since private British merchants claimed exemption from his customs duties and interfered with trades over which monopolies had been granted.[6]

Private trade extended the links that had been established with Indian commercial communities through the official trade of the Company. Private merchants brought little capital with them from Britain. Their trade therefore depended to a large extent on loans from Indians. A complex pattern of relations developed through which British and Indian traders rendered one another services. Indians characteristically invested funds to be used in European shipping or to be given the additional security of a European name. Wealthy Indian merchants were even willing to become the agents of private Europeans, acting as their *banians* (the term used in Calcutta) or in Madras as their *dubashes*.[7] The growth of private trade thus helped to bind many Indian merchants to the British.

The extent of British trade in relation to the trade conducted by Asian merchants without any European participation is an uncertain and even a contentious subject.[8] The growth of the Company's settlements is, however, a clear indication of the importance of the British in certain regions. Bombay only emerged as the major port of western India towards the end of the eighteenth century, but it had already begun to attract refugees from Surat. Although other ports along the Coromandel Coast were able to hold their own in the early eighteenth century in competition with Madras, more and more Indian merchants moved there to

---

[5] P. J. Marshall, *East Indian Fortunes: The British in Bengal in the Eighteenth Century* (Oxford, 1976), pp. 19–20, 51–75; 'Private British Trade in the Indian Ocean Before 1800', in Ashin Das Gupta and M. N Pearson, eds., *India and the Indian Ocean, 1500 to 1800* (Calcutta, 1987), pp. 279–94.

[6] Marshall, *East Indian Fortunes*, pp. 109–12.

[7] P. J. Marshall, 'Masters and Banians in Eighteenth-Century Calcutta', in Blair B. Kling and M. N. Pearson, eds., *The Age of Partnership: Europeans in Asia before Dominion* (Honolulu, 1979), pp. 203–05; S. Arasaratnam, 'Trade and Political Dominion in South India, 1750–1790: Changing British–Indian Relationships', *Modern Asian Studies*, XIII (1979), pp. 23–26.

[8] Sushil Chaudhury, 'European Trading Companies and Bengal Textile Industry in the First Half of the Eighteenth Century: The Pitfalls of Applying Quantitative Methods', *Modern Asian Studies*, XXVII (1993), pp. 321–40; Om Prakash, 'On Estimating the Employment Implications of European Trade for the Eighteenth-Century Bengal Textile Industry: A Reply', ibid., pp. 341–46.

deal with the British and to enjoy the relative security that they offered.[9] Calcutta, by contrast, totally eclipsed its rivals in Bengal during the first half of the eighteenth century. Its growth was meteoric as Indian merchants, artisans, and labouring people moved into the area under British jurisdiction in huge numbers. Although such estimates are likely to have been grossly inflated, Europeans thought that the city contained more than 100,000 people by the middle of the eighteenth century.[10] Expansion of European settlements on this scale posed obvious problems for Indian rulers. The dissemination of wealth among their subjects through dealings with Europeans was of course welcome, but if that wealth lay beyond the reach of the ruler within what amounted to a foreign enclave, if that enclave was growing very rapidly, and if some of the Europeans within the enclave seemed to be extending the range of their activities, the challenge to the ruler's authority was unmistakable. Calcutta in particular constituted such a challenge to the rulers of Bengal.

Reassessment of the role of the British needs to be seen as part of a much wider reassessment of the history of eighteenth-century India. This reassessment has begun with the Indian economy. The generally accepted view that the prosperity of the seventeenth century under a benign Mughal peace gave way to poverty in the eighteenth century has been questioned. Studies of parts of northern India in particular have indicated that the first half of the eighteenth century was a period of continuing economic expansion, both of agricultural production and of trade.[11] Some historians argue that there is evidence for a buoyant economy in certain areas right through the century.[12]

Established views about the political history of the eighteenth century are also being revised. The facts of Mughal decline and political subdivision are irrefutable, but the conclusion that what then emerged was a general collapse of political authority and a descent into uncontrolled violence and endemic warfare, verging on anarchy, has been questioned.

In some areas, it is argued, Mughal rule was replaced by regional authorities capable of establishing a stable order. Of the areas where the East India Company traded, this was most marked in Bengal. There the Mughal governor freed himself

[9] Sinnappah Arasaratnam, *Merchants, Companies and Commerce on the Coromandel Coast, 1650–1740* (Delhi, 1986), pp. 194–202.

[10] Marshall, *East Indian Fortunes*, pp. 24–25.

[11] Muzaffar Alam, 'Eastern India in the Early Eighteenth-Century "Crisis": Some Evidence from Bihar', *The Indian Economic and Social History Review*, XXVIII (1991), pp. 61–71; Dilbagh Singh, *The State, Landlords and Peasants. Rajasthan in the 18th Century* (Delhi, 1990).

[12] C. A. Bayly, *The New Cambridge History of India*, II. 1, *Indian Society and the Making of the British Empire* (Cambridge, 1988), pp. 32–38.

from all effective central control and founded a dynasty of independent Nawabs, who created an effective autonomous administration. In the south-east the situation was more complex. A large domain was carved out by another Mughal dignitary, the Nizam of Hyderabad. The Nizams' control over what they claimed was, however, often tenuous. Local chieftains maintained much of their autonomy and the dominions of the Nizam were frequently invaded by powers intent on dismembering them.[13] Further south still, along the Coromandel Coast, Mughal rule had hardly been established when the centre relinquished control. Mughal officials were left to impose their authority on unsubdued Hindu Rajas and other chiefs, while defending their gains from outsiders. Those whom the British came to call the Nawabs of Arcot or of the Carnatic had considerable success in stabilizing their rule over the hinterland of Madras, but they remained vulnerable.[14] Conditions at first deteriorated most markedly in western India. In the late seventeenth and early eighteenth century the Marathas succeeded in subverting Mughal rule over large tracts. Trade routes were seriously disrupted and the economy of Gujarat suffered severely, its great port of Surat being a prime victim. From mid-century, however, the Marathas began to establish their own local states, such as those of their titular leader, the Peshwa, or of individual commanders, such as Sindia or Holkar. These rulers maintained stability within their borders, encouraged economic activity, and also checked any attempt at military expansion by the British at Bombay.[15]

Eighteenth-century regional states are said to have acquired certain characteristics. They maintained the outward forms of Mughal rule, while developing techniques that enabled them effectively to extract resources from agriculture and trade. Taxation of the produce of the land was not, as under the Mughals, largely alienated in grants to a military aristocracy in return for contingents of troops, but was directly managed by the agents of the ruler to produce a return in cash. The yield of taxes was anticipated by borrowings from bankers, who were closely involved in the workings of the new states. Cash was used to pay for troops, increasingly armed and trained in the European manner, under the direct authority of the ruler, rather than being the retinue of a Mughal nobleman.

The establishment of viable regional states along these lines in certain parts of India is now often seen as the necessary pre-condition for the rise of British territorial power. British commercial enterprise, particularly that of the private

---

[13] S. Chander, 'From a Pre-Colonial Order to a Princely State: Hyderabad in Transition, c.1748 to 1865', unpublished Ph. D. thesis, Cambridge (1987), pp. 50 ff.

[14] J. F. Richards, 'The Hyderabad Karnatick, 1687–1707, *Modern Asian Studies*, IX (1975), pp. 241–60.

[15] Stewart Gordon, *The New Cambridge History of India*, II. 4, *The Marathas, 1600–1818* (Cambridge, 1993), pp. 185–88.

traders and their Indian allies, could expand within the framework of opportunities offered by local rulers. The needs of these rulers for cash and troops and the ambitions of the British could coincide to enable the British to play a political role as bankers to the state or as military commanders. Political infiltration could later turn to political dominance and eventually to outright rule, as the British took over the administrative structures created for the regional states and made them work for their own purposes, drawing taxation into British coffers and bringing troops into British service. Had eighteenth-century India really been reduced to a wasteland, it is argued, a British Empire in India was hardly conceivable. As it was, British rule was sustained by Indian wealth and built on the foundations laid by the regional rulers.

The implication underlying recent reinterpretations of the rise of the British is that it was a gradual process that can only be understood in the context of the wider changes in eighteenth-century India as a whole, which gave the British their opportunity. The British won power as participants in Indian political struggles. The way in which they exercised their power did not at first mark any sharp break with Indian patterns of rule. As eighteenth-century rulers had done, the British preserved an outward respect for Mughal forms. But also like their predecessors, the British took Indian tax administrators and bankers into partnership. Parts of the Indian economy remained buoyant at least until the end of the eighteenth century, and thus the British were able to raise high yields of taxation and to borrow from indigenous bankers. A new colonial order, involving distinctly British modes of government and a new pattern of economic relations between Britain and India, was a long time in coming.

This reinterpretation of the eighteenth century has been based on the findings of scholars both from South Asia and from the West.[16] It has not, however, won universal acceptance, especially among historians working in India. The relatively favourable verdicts on the eighteenth-century economy and on the capacities of the regional states, the stress on the continuity between the pre-colonial and the early colonial orders, and the assumption that the British rise to power depended on a high level of co-operation with Indian élites have all been rejected.

Insistence on the break in continuity involved in the British take-over is central to all objections to the new historiography of the eighteenth century. The British are seen not as actors in what was essentially an Indian play, but as alien aggressors, seizing power by brute force and using their power to force abrupt changes which

[16] See esp. Muzaffar Alam, *The Crisis of Empire in Mughal North India, Awadh and the Punjab, 1707–48* (Delhi, 1986); Richard B. Barnett, *North India between Empires: Awadh, the Mughals and the British, 1720–1801* (Berkeley, 1980); C. A. Bayly, *Indian Society and the British Empire*, pp. 7–44; David Washbrook, 'Progress and Problems: South Asian Economic and Social History, c.1720–1860', *Modern Asian Studies*, XXII (1988), pp. 57–96.

quickly impoverished the areas brought under their control.[17] Questions of continuity or change in the way in which the British began to rule Indian provinces are the concern of the next chapter.[18] This chapter is concerned with such questions in trying to explain how the British won power. Were they responding to developments in India over which they could exercise little control or were they implementing their own designs for aggrandizement?

Analysis of the role of the British must begin in Britain itself. Had the Directors of the East India Company been able to determine what happened in India, military and political involvement would have been kept to a minimum. The Company certainly wished to protect its trade from what it took to be threats to it by the French. In 1747 it appealed to the national government for warships to be sent to India to prevent its trade from being 'utterly destroyed'.[19] Royal troops were sent as well as naval ships, while the Company increased the supply of recruits for its own troops and permitted its servants at Madras to augment their forces. At intervals thereafter it pleaded for more men and ships from the Crown. The Directors insisted, however, that the forces built up in India were to be used for defensive purposes. They frequently warned their servants against involvement in Indian politics or the acquisition of territory. The reasoning behind such injunctions is clear: the Directors could not envisage commercial advantages that would outweigh the costs of and disruptions from prolonged war. Once what was seen as unprovoked French aggression had been frustrated, the Company's view was that its interests would be best served by preserving the situation in India as it was.

Ministers were in no doubt that Asian trade was a national interest and that the forces of the Crown must support the Company if it was likely to be worsted by the French. The national government did not, however, have any clear policy of its own towards India. Ministers did little more than respond to the Company's pleas for help and adopt the Directors' views about strategy. The admirals and colonels in command of the royal forces sent out to support the Company were told to carry out its instructions. Only towards the end of the Seven Years War did the government begin to formulate strategies of its own for Asian operations. A plan to attack the Spanish at Manila in the Philippines was successfully executed in 1762.

Thus the growth of territorial empire in India was neither planned nor directed from Britain. Ignorance about Indian conditions and slowness of communica-

---

[17] See, for instance, M. Athar Ali. 'Recent Theories of Eighteenth-Century India', *Indian Historical Review*, XIII (1987), pp. 102–10.
[18] See below, pp. 508–29.
[19] Secret Committee to Newcastle, 24 April 1747, C[olonial]O[ffice] 77/18, ff. 32–34.

tions meant that no effective control could be exercised from home. The role of the British in India was determined by men actually in India. It was a classic case of what has been called 'sub-imperialism', that is, of the dominance of local interests over metropolitan ones.

Even if they had little direct influence over developments overseas, authorities in Britain still played a crucial role by providing men in India with sufficient force to act decisively. By the middle of the eighteenth century the British were able to put significant forces into the field in India. Before the 1740s garrisons of a few hundred of the Company's own soldiers were maintained at Madras, Bombay, and Calcutta. During the wars with France royal regiments and increased numbers of recruits for what became the Company's own European regiments were sent out. At the same time the British began to imitate the successor states to the Mughals and to tap their sources for sepoy soldiers, mainly Telugu-speaking people for Madras and north Indian Rajputs and what were called military Brahmins for Bengal. The role of the troops changed from defending the settlements to operating far inland. Numbers remained small: Clive had about, 2,000 sepoys and 900 Europeans at Plassey in 1757, while in 1764, at the very hard-fought Battle of Buxar in northern India, the British had 5,300 sepoys, 850 Europeans, and twenty field pieces. Forces of this size could defeat comparable numbers of French and also win spectacular victories over very much bigger Asian armies. Here the firepower of well-drilled infantry and field artillery together with effective logistical support proved decisive. Indian rulers were rapidly adapting their military structures and tactics to European models, so that within a few years states like Mysore were to press the British very hard indeed, but the initial impact of the new European armies was devastating.[20]

Decisions as to how this force was used were taken by the Governors of the Presidencies with their Councils. The civilian servants of the Company maintained ultimate authority, but military officers, the commanders of the Company's own forces, and royal naval and army officers, were also involved. Neither civilians nor soldiers were much inclined to follow the caution enjoined on them from home.

They became increasingly confident in the efficacy of force. As early as 1751 a free-lance soldier was trying to convince British ministers that the government of Bengal could be overthrown by an expeditionary force of 2,000 Europeans.[21] It became conventional wisdom that 'the Moors are such a despicable cowardly set of people, that there can be no dependence on them, were they opposed by

---

[20] G. J. Bryant, 'The East India Company and its Army, 1600–1778', unpublished Ph.D. thesis, London (1975).
[21] J. Mill to Newcastle, 28 Nov. 1751, CO 77/18, f. 127.

Europeans'.[22] Once the Company had gained control over Bengal, its servants contemplated sending expeditions far into northern India, even up to Delhi.

A robust disdain for the fighting qualities of Indian armies, combined with confidence in own their capacity to manipulate Indian rulers, encouraged the Company's servants to bold and opportunistic use of power. Their objectives were, however, usually limited ones. Indian rulers were to be prevented from exercising any authority in future over the Company's trade or settlements and every opportunity was to be taken for extracting commercial concessions and grants of revenue. Deposing Indian rulers and assuming outright rule over whole provinces were, however, projects that generally remained beyond their calculations. Even Robert Clive was a hesitant empire-builder. He engineered the coup in Bengal that brought a new ruler on to the throne in 1757. Although he raised the possibility of establishing British rule over Bengal in a famous letter to Pitt of January 1759, as the Company's Governor of Bengal from 1757 to 1760 he kept the new Nawab in place. Only on his return to India for a second spell as Governor in 1765, when he knew that the Nawab's government had been completely undermined, did he seriously plan to take 'the whole for the Company'.[23]

Private motives were often mixed with the public purposes which were used to justify resorting to force. The communities in the British settlements had long devoted much of their energies to the pursuit of their private interests. War and upheaval gave them abundant new opportunities. Indians who wished to hire the Company's troops had not only to pay the Company for them but had to reward their officers very handsomely indeed. After Plassey the army and the navy each got some £275,000 to distribute, sums which did not include the huge personal payments made to individual commanders, like Clive.[24] This is the largest and the best-documented case, but every use of the army probably involved private payments. Political changes could also be highly beneficial to the private trade of individuals. This was especially the case in Bengal. There private traders had penetrated inland long before Plassey. With the weakening of the Nawabs after the overthrow of Siraj-ud-Daula, restraints on British participation in Bengal's internal trade were broken through and a boom followed.

Even if their objectives were confined to extracting limited advantages, either for their employers or for themselves, there can be no doubt of the willingness of men in India to exploit to the full every opportunity that seemed to offer itself. Whether opportunities were on offer and how they could be exploited depended,

[22] G. Pocock to Holderness, 13 March 1758, Huntington Library, HM 1000.

[23] G. W. Forrest, *The Life of Lord Clive*, 2 vols. (London, 1918), II, pp. 412–14; Clive to J. Walsh, 4 Jan. 1765, O[riental] and I[ndia] O[ffice] C[ollections], MS EUR D 546/III–VII, ff. 102–03.

[24] Marshall, *East Indian Fortunes*, p. 165.

however, on conditions in India which were largely beyond the control of the British. The conditions which the British encountered at Madras or at Calcutta were very different.

The British at Madras were drawn into outright warfare against the French in a part of India where political authority was fluid, presenting ready opportunities for intervening in rivalries and disputed successions. Although a more assertive British attitude in south India was triggered off by rivalry with the French, it would be misleading to see the wars there simply as an extension of a world-wide Anglo-French rivalry and thus to assume that events in Europe fundamentally changed the course of Indian history. The French retaliated against British seizures of their shipping in Asia from 1744 by attacking and taking Madras in 1746. Peace was concluded in Europe in 1748, but the French had already embarked on ambitious military intervention in the affairs first of the Nawab of Arcot and then of the Nizam of Hyderabad. They did so for Indian rather than for European reasons. Their intervention was not specifically directed against the British, but was a response to offers of concessions in return for troops made by Indian contestants.[25] To the British at Madras, however, the French seemed to 'aim at nothing less than to exclude us from the trade of this coast, and by degrees from that of India'.[26] They therefore offered British support to rival claimants. Above all the British committed themselves to Muhammad Ali as 'their' Nawab of Arcot, who in return made them grants of territory. Nominally as the agents of Indian powers, the British and French fought one another through a period of peace in Europe and into the Seven Years War. The French-sponsored rival to Muhammad Ali was killed in 1752 and two years later Dupleix, the ambitious Governor of Pondicherry, was recalled. With a new French expeditionary force on the Coromandel Coast from 1757, the war intensified. In 1760 the British won a decisive victory at Wandiwash, and Pondicherry surrendered the following year.

The war left the British deeply entangled in the affairs of the Carnatic. Muhammad Ali had survived as Nawab of Arcot and his status as independent ally of the British was recognized in the Peace of Paris of 1763. The Nawab's independence was, however, little more than nominal. He was required to pay off the costs of the war and of a large British army permanently maintained to defend his territory against a French resurgence or against incursions by Indian enemies. To meet his obligations he borrowed very extensively from private British sources. Thus it was in the interest both of the Company and of its servants that the Nawab should be

---

[25] Manning, *Fortunes à faire*, pp. 195–218.
[26] Fort St David to Directors, 12 Feb. 1750, OIOC, H/93, p. 54.

able to increase the area under his effective control and add to the resources at his disposal. Through his borrowings and through other personal favours granted to the British at Madras, the Nawab was able to manipulate his protectors. Within a few years his influence even extended to members of the British House of Commons, who supported his interests in return for favours.[27] British troops helped him to expand the territory under his control in a series of campaigns. Under British protection, a Carnatic state was gradually built up which the Company was formally to annex at the end of the century.

In the south British intervention created a state; in Bengal the Company operated within a state that was already formed. Within a secure framework created by the Nawabs during the first half of the eighteenth century, the Company had increased its purchases of Bengal textiles, private trade had grown, and Calcutta had become a wealthy city. The British presence in Bengal was becoming too intrusive for an ambitious ruler indefinitely to leave unregulated, and it can be argued that from about the 1720s the British and the rulers of Bengal were set on course for a collision that it would be very difficult to avoid.

The collision occurred in 1756, when Siraj-ud-Daula took Calcutta. After the fall of the city an unknown number of prisoners, probably not more than fifty, perished in the Black Hole. Much still remains unclear about the events of 1756 and those that led to the Battle of Plassey in 1757. Siraj-ud-Daula had every reason to view the activities of the British with dislike and apprehension in 1756. There is no evidence that he wished to drive them out of Bengal, but he probably felt, as his predecessors had done, that they should not defy his authority and must contribute more to the needs of the state. The British refused to compromise, and in the loss of Calcutta they paid a very severe penalty for underestimating the seriousness of his intentions and for recklessly ignoring their own weakness.

Calcutta was recovered by Clive's expedition in January 1757. Professing to believe that the Nawab was wholly unreliable and likely to ally with the French, the British soon became aware of an alternative to his rule, which could bring them security and better terms for the Company and spectacular rewards for individuals. The alternative was offered by a group of plotters who wished to see Siraj-ud-Daula deposed in favour of a rival, Mir Jafar. The East India Company's army was to be the instrument of his overthrow. Clive embarked on the venture, taking his army up to Plassey and defeating Siraj-ud-Daula, when the conspirators duly abandoned him.[28]

---

[27] See below, p. 542–43.

[28] For an interpretation of these events which argues for a British plot to provoke instability and change the Nawab, see Sushil Chaudhury, *From Prosperity to Decline: Eighteenth-Century Bengal* (New Delhi, 1995), pp. 306–26.

In the south the British saw no alternative to maintaining Muhammad Ali as the instrument through which resources could be channelled to them. He was therefore able to keep the British at arm's length for some time. In Bengal British supremacy was established over a relatively centralized state, which they eventually felt able to manage for themselves without an Indian ruler. Although Clive intended to maintain Mir Jafar as an autonomous ally of the Company, the rule of the Nawabs was destroyed within eight years as both the Company and private individuals scrambled to appropriate resources which were so readily accessible to them.

The Company was determined to re-establish and expand its Bengal trade after the recovery of Calcutta. Any surplus of Bengal's taxation was therefore to be used for purchasing cargoes of Bengal goods for London or was to be sent to China to buy tea. The first claim on the province's resources was, however, the army that was to protect Bengal and keep in power the new Nawab. To meet these very large demands, the Nawab was required to pledge the taxation of specific areas, which were placed under the Company's control. When Mir Jafar would not make what were regarded as adequate grants, he was deposed in favour of a Nawab who would do so. This still did not meet the Company's needs. It was becoming clear, even before Clive took his decision in 1765 to demand the *diwani,* that only direct control of the whole resources of Bengal would give the Company the funds it required.

Plassey opened up a wide field for individual enterprise. Both Indians and Europeans seized their chances. Company servants joined with the Indian trading partners and agents with whom they had worked in Calcutta. The greatest opportunities after Plassey were in internal trade. As civil servants and army officers moved away from Calcutta, they and their Indian underlings brought profitable local trades under their control. Attempts by Mir Jafar's successor to regulate European trade were resisted, and provoked a war in 1763 that finally destroyed the rule of the Nawabs.[29] There was no real alternative to the direct assumption of British authority over a territory the resources of which had been thoroughly ransacked since Plassey.

By 1765 the East India Company had become outright ruler of limited areas in the south and of the great province of Bengal, which included Bihar. It held the Nawab of Arcot in a tight grip, which gave it effective control over the Carnatic territories of the south-east. It had also taken the Wazir of Oudh under its protection and was maintaining garrisons in his dominions. In short, the East India Company had become an Indian territorial power. How the Company adjusted to its new

---

[29] Marshall, *East Indian Fortunes,* chap. 5.

commitments is the theme of the following chapter, but even by 1765 some of the implications of these great changes were already becoming clear: in particular, the Company was now vitally interested in the levying of taxation, always called 'revenue' in British-Indian historiography, and it could not avoid becoming a player in the complex diplomacy of post-Mughal India.

Indian states were built on the taxation levied from the cultivators of the land; the British Empire in India was built on the same foundations. Whereas the public revenues in British American colonies consisted of grants, usually grudgingly voted by representative Assemblies, or of the limited customs duties actually levied in the colonies, the East India Company inherited a system of taxation which aimed at taking without their consent one-third or even more of the produce of millions of cultivators, and which also laid heavy duties on trade. The finance for the Company's own trade and for its rapidly growing armies depended on maintaining a high level of taxation directly from Bengal and indirectly through the contributions of the Nawab of Arcot. Most collections were made in cash through a complex hierarchy of intermediaries between the peasant and the state. Questions of revenue administration, therefore, involved both setting the level that it was realistic to expect the countryside to pay without causing hardship that would lead to long-term impoverishment, and working out a satisfactory system of intermediaries through whom that assessment could be realized. Much depended on how that issue was resolved. Rights to collect revenue from peasants and to retain a portion of it were a form of property on which the rural élites depended, an area from which revenue was collected constituting a kind of landed estate. In Bengal, for instance, the British received most of their revenue through intermediaries called *zamindars*. In their decisions about the role which *zamindars* would play under their regime, the British were to do much to reshape patterns of land tenure, either strengthening or weakening what seemed to them to be a kind of landed gentry. Authority over revenue also involved presiding over courts in which issues of rights to land and levels of payment were adjusted. The British thus became administrators of Indian law. Control over densely populated Indian territory might offer gratifying prospects of instant wealth to those who had won that control (Clive anticipated an immediate surplus of £1,500,000 from Bengal in 1765),[30] but it quickly sucked them into intricate problems of Indian governance.

To safeguard its hard-won gains in Bengal and the Carnatic, the East India Company had to maintain large armies and enter into diplomatic relations with some of the other regional powers of India. Two of the major states established by former Mughal governors, Oudh and Hyderabad, accepted a degree of British

---

[30] See below, p. 533.

influence. Other states were, however, much less predictable from the British point of view.

The most formidable potential opponents for the Company in northern and western India were the string of Maratha polities, acknowledging a tenuous supremacy to the Peshwa, or chief minister, at Poona. The Maratha confederacy stretched from the southern boundary of Bengal virtually to Delhi and it dominated the west coast of India, hemming in Bombay. In 1761 the Maratha armies suffered a crippling disaster at the hands of the Afghans at the Battle of Panipat in northern India. They were, however, to recover and their rivalry with the British for the succession to Mughal supremacy was not finally resolved until the opening years of the nineteenth century.[31]

In the south the British at Madras also faced a potentially dangerous Indian rival in the state of Mysore, first under Haidar Ali and later under Tipu Sultan. Haidar Ali trained his troops to the standard of the British-Indian army and when he pitted them against the Company's Madras army in 1767 he was able to inflict serious damage on it.

In 1765 no observer, either British or Indian, could have envisaged the possibility of British Imperial supremacy over the Indian subcontinent. What few could have failed to recognize was that the East India Company had become a regional Indian power of some consequence. Outwardly, the British appeared to have become Indian rulers. They had won power through Indian political processes and their rule depended on the yield of Indian taxation levied through Indian administrative systems. The award of Islamic titles to men like Clive suggests that some of the Indian élite hoped that the British might become assimilated into an aristocracy committed to Mughal values.[32]

There certainly was much continuity between early British rule and the Indian regimes they had displaced. Nevertheless, the British were not Indian rulers and Bengal under the Company was not just an Indian regional state: it was a British national possession. Those who ruled it were bound to fulfil British national purposes. However tenuous metropolitan control over them might be, they would not be able to escape that control indefinitely.

The extent of the national interest in India was spelt out in letters from the Directors of the Company to a government minister in 1756. The Directors pointed out that not only was the India trade 'a National Trade', in which 'the Publick is greatly concerned', but that the duties received by the government on Asian goods were four times the shareholders' dividend. The loss of the Company's

---

[31] See below, pp. 511–12.

[32] Abdul Majed Khan, *The Transition in Bengal, 1756–1775: A Study of Saiyid Muhammad Reza Khan* (Cambridge, 1969), pp. xii–xiii.

Indian settlements would mean that a great 'Distress' will 'attend the Nation' and that 'a General Distress upon Public Credit will succeed'.[33]

Threats to the Company's trade at Madras and Calcutta had been beaten off by 1763, but the consequences of victory, as men in India recognized much more quickly than did opinion in Britain, was that the national interest was linked to the security of territorial empire in India as well as to the protection of trade. The profitability of the East India Company's operations now depended on its ability to maintain its control over its provinces. Taxation, collected above all from Bengal, provided the funds for a much larger volume of trade, and it also paid for the army that both protected trade and enforced revenue collection. Military power, revenue extraction, and trade had thus been fused together in a way that was to be characteristic of British India far into the future. Much more was now at risk, and the scale of the damage that failure in India could inflict on Britain had become even greater. If the East India Company became insolvent, it was feared that it would pull down the credit system on which public finance and trade depended. In 1773 it was being said that the loss of India would produce 'a national bankruptcy'.[34]

To guard against such disasters, Britain would be drawn into ever deeper involvement in India. There would be almost no limits to the resources which Britain would be prepared to commit to India. The British-Indian army would be built up to a size that eclipsed all other Indian armies and would enable the British to impose their will on the whole subcontinent. Much as extensions of territory were disliked, new conquests would be reluctantly sanctioned in the cause of safeguarding Britain's stake in India.

The nature of Britain's rule over its Indian provinces would also change, if slowly. Administrative practices inherited from Indian regimes would be dismissed as both inefficient and corrupt. Changing British standards of good governance would become the criteria for reforming the Company's administration.

The interpretation of the British rise to power in this chapter has stressed the importance of developments in eighteenth-century India and has shown the British as responding to these developments and exploiting the opportunities which came their way. They had gained power on Indian terms. The next chapter will, however, deal with the consequences that were to follow, however slowly and uncertainly, from the establishment of a bridgehead in India by a European power

---

[33] Secret Committee to H. Fox, 18 Aug.; 20 Sept. 1756, British Library, Egerton MSS, 3487, ff. 134–35, 143–44.

[34] Huw Bowen, *Revenue and Reform: The Indian Problem in British Politics, 1757–1773* (Cambridge, 1991), p. 22–23.

with political ambitions and military and economic capacities that were undergoing rapid change.

Select Bibliography

MUZZAFAR ALAM, *The Crisis of Empire in Mughal North India, Awadh and the Punjab, 1707–48* (Delhi, 1986).

SINNAPPAH ARASARATNAM, *Merchants, Companies and Commerce on the Coromandel Coast, 1650–1740* (Delhi, 1986).

RICHARD B. BARNETT, *North India between Empires: Awadh, the Mughals and the British, 1720–1801* (Berkeley, 1980).

C. A. BAYLY, *The New Cambridge History of India*, II. 1, *Indian Society and the Making of the British Empire* (Cambridge, 1988).

K. N. CHAUDHURI, *The Trading World of Asia and the English East India Company 1660–1760* (Cambridge, 1978).

SUSHIL CHAUDHURY, *From Prosperity to Decline: Eighteenth-Century Bengal* (New Delhi, 1995).

ASHIN DAS GUPTA and M. N. PEARSON, eds., *India and the Indian Ocean, 1500 to 1800* (Calcutta, 1987).

HENRY DODWELL, *Dupleix and Clive: The Beginning of Empire* (London, 1920).

HOLDEN FURBER, *Rival Empires of Trade in the Orient 1600 to 1800* (Minneapolis, 1976).

PHILIP LAWSON, *The East India Company: A History* (London, 1993).

P. J. MARSHALL, *The New Cambridge History of India*, II. 2, *Bengal: The British Bridgehead, Eastern India, 1740–1828* (Cambridge, 1987).

—— *East Indian Fortunes: The British in Bengal in the Eighteenth Century* (Oxford, 1976).

—— *Trade and Conquest: Studies in the Rise of British Dominance in India* (Aldershot, 1993).

FRANK PERLIN, 'Proto-Industrialisation and Pre-Colonial South Asia', *Past and Present*, XCVIII (1983), pp. 30–95.

EARL H. PRITCHARD, *Anglo-Chinese Relations during the Seventeenth and Eighteenth Centuries* (Urbana, Ill., 1929).

PERCY SPEAR, *Master of Bengal: Clive and his India* (London, 1975).

L. S. SUTHERLAND, *The East India Company in Eighteenth-Century Politics* (Oxford, 1952).

IAN BRUCE WATSON, *Foundation for Empire: English Private Trade in India, 1659–1760* (Delhi, 1980).

23

Indian Society and the Establishment of British Supremacy, 1765–1818

RAJAT KANTA RAY

> This age is not like that which went before it.
> The times have changed, the earth and sky have changed.
> (Mir, 1722–1810)[1]

In 1809 the reformer Raja Ram Mohun Roy, harbinger of modern India, saw the transition from 'the Mogul Government' to the 'British Government' as the passage to a 'milder, more enlightened and more liberal' one.[2] But he belonged to the new generation. In the eyes of the pundit who wrote *The Pleasure of All the Gods* in Sanskrit in or after 1787, the seizure of power by 'the white faced upstarts' was like a recurrence of the age of the demons.[3] What seemed 'Divine Providence' to the intellectuals of the new breed appeared to the learned classes of the older generation to menace caste and the ordered way of life (*varnashrama*), and to spell the destruction of the land of peace (*Dar-ul-Islam*).

The late Mughal poet Sauda (1713–80) was aware of 'living in a special kind of age', when every heart was aflame with grief and every eye brimmed with tears. 'How can I describe the desolation of Delhi? There is no house from which the jackal's cry cannot be heard.' The grief experienced by the Urdu poets at the overthrow of the Mughal ruling class and the sufferings of the people of Hindustan found expression in the thought that fortune was fickle. They groped round for a word to describe the change of fortune and found it in the Arabic and Persian term *inqilab*.[4]

What happened in the eighteenth century was seen by contemporaries as an *inqilab*, an inversion of the existing order in which the high and noble were

---

[1] Khurshidul Islam and Ralph Russell, *Three Mughal Poets, Mir, Sauda, and Mir Hasan* (Delhi, 1991), p. 22.

[2] Ram Mohan Roy to Lord Minto, April (?) 1809, in Dilip Kumar Biswas, ed., *The Correspondence of Raja Rammohan Roy*, I, *1809–1831* (Calcutta, 1992), p. 3.

[3] V. Raghavan, ed., *Sarva-Deva-Vilasa* (Madras, n.d.), pp. 2, 80–81, 90.

[4] Derived from the root verb *qalb* (to invert). Thus Tek Chand Bahar, contemporary lexicographer: '*Inqilab*. To be turned topsy-turvy (*Wazgun shudan*). Used with the words *giriftan, uftadan*, i.e. [for fortune] to be changed totally.' *Bahar-i-Ajam* (AH 1152/AD 1740). Irfan Habib kindly translated the entry.

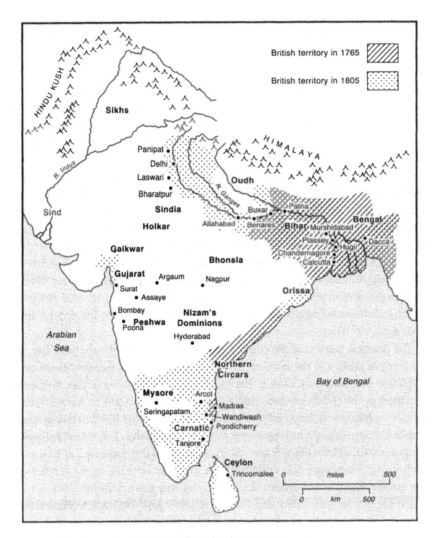

Map 23.1. The Growth of British Territorial Empire in India

overthrown and the lowly rose to the top. 'How can one describe the ups and downs of the world', lamented a Mughal poet. The world around him appeared to have overturned as those who rode elephants formerly now wandered about disconsolately for want of shoes, and those who had once craved for parched grains turned overnight into owners of palaces and elephants. It was a revolution that extended from the political to the social sphere and for better or for worse affected every aspect of life. If Ram Mohun Roy was in no doubt of its positive

benefits for Indian society, the historian Saiyid Ghulam Husain Khan, his grandfather's contemporary and perhaps the first proponent of the doctrine of the Drain
of Wealth from India to Britain, was no less convinced of its negative consequences.

What they were obliged to try and make sense of was a close, ambiguous
encounter between two civilizations. To legitimize its own position in the eyes of
a society rooted so deeply in the Brahmanical and Islamic traditions, and in which
the Mughal Emperor was still recognized to be 'the only legitimate fountain of
either honour or dominion', the East India Company had to fit into the existing
framework of Mughal legitimacy, and to extend patronage to Hinduism and
Islam. Emperor Shah Alam, from whom they derived their authority through
the grant of the Bengal *diwani*, stipulated that the English must govern their new
possessions 'agreeably to the rules of Mahomed and the law of the Empire'.[5]
Warren Hastings, the ruler of British India from 1772 to 1785, for his part felt
that British administration should be conducted 'agreeably to the old constitution
of the Empire'. This was an encounter in which both sides merged into the other. A
meaningful way to enter into India's colonial encounter is to try and relive the
experiences of those who lived through the *inqilab*, and to see the process from
their angle of vision.

The political culture of the country expressed itself through the idea that the
Emperor of Delhi was the Lord of the Universe (*Dillishvaro wa Jagadishvaro wa*).
When the universal dominion of the Mughals passed, the idea of that dominion
persisted in the minds of men, and usurpations were sought to be legitimized
within the framework imposed by that persistent idea. The Marathas had emerged
before the English as the appropriators of the Mughal realm. They readily accepted
Mughal ideals, despite the sedition (*fitva*) upon which they were seen to have built
their power. They were duly endowed with a quarter (*chauth*) of the revenues of
the Mughal empire throughout the country in 1752 and admonished to 'whole-
heartedly execute our orders and punish our enemies'.[6] No such legitimacy was
accorded to Haidar Ali of Mysore who, in Mughal parlance, was 'a rebel and a
usurper',[7] but even in his mosques and from every pulpit of India, prayers were
offered for the reigning sovereign Shah Alam.[8] Notion and reality were both

---

[5] Shah Alam's *farman*, 29 Dec. 1764, in C. U. Aitchison ed., *A Collection of Treaties, Engagements and Sunnuds Relating to India and Neighbouring Countries*, 7 vols. (Calcutta, 1862-65), II, p. 6.

[6] André Wink, *Land and Sovereignty in India, Agrarian Society and Politics under the Eighteenth-Century Maratha Svarajya* (Cambridge, 1986), pp. 40, 102, 133, 144 n.

[7] Proclamation of the Nizam in his capacity as Mughal Viceroy of the Deccan, Aitchison, *Treaties*, V, p. 26.

[8] Mark Wilks, *Historical Sketches of the South of India in an Attempt to Trace the History of Mysoor from the Origin of the Hindoo Government of that State to the Extinction of the Mohammedan Dynasty*, 3 vols. (London, 1810-17), I, p. 173.

graphically illustrated in the formula by which everywhere the town crier drummed the government's orders: 'The universe belongs to God, the [sovereign] realm belongs to the Emperor, [the executive power issuing] the order belongs to... (*khalq-i-khuda, mulk-i-padshah, hukm-i-* ...)'; and here the name of the local potentate—whether the Nawab Wazir of Oudh, the Nizam of Hyderabad, the Peshwa of the Marathas, the Nawab of the Carnatic, or latterly the East India Company in Bengal—would follow.

The two most successful usurpations which acquired legitimacy—Maratha and British—grew within the same framework. Which usurpation would finally gain supremacy was an issue that was not resolved until 1803, when the British captured Delhi and gained permanent control over the person of the Emperor and over the Red Fort. Then the Marathas were shown conclusively to have lost their claim to the supremacy of India. Up to 1803, however, influence over the Emperor, with all its symbolic importance, fluctuated between the Marathas and the East India Company.

After the Battle of Buxar, which had finally guaranteed British control over Bengal in 1764, the British gained temporary possession of the person of the Emperor exiled from Delhi. This prized possession enabled the Company to emerge as a power recognized by the Marathas as a contender for Indian supremacy. Clive, the new Governor of Bengal, established Shah Alam temporarily in the provinces of Cora and Allahabad, and restored Oudh to his defeated Wazir Shuja-ud-Daulah, who became a thankful subsidiary ally. In the vain hope that the British would escort him to the Red Fort, the Emperor bestowed on the Company 'the most important grants ever yet obtained by any European State from the Mogul Court'. British power was thereby placed within the ritualized Mughal framework of gifts, exchanges, and appointments. On condition of paying an annual tribute to the Emperor of Rs.2.6 million (approximately £260,000), the Company obtained, as a free and perpetual gift (*alamgha*), the imperial post of Treasurer (*Diwan*) of Bengal, Bihar, and Orissa. In addition, Clive obtained from Shah Alam a confirmation of the strip of coastal territory called the Northern Circars, till then formally dependent on the Nizam, as a gift (*inam*) for the Company at Madras. Under Imperial sanction, the Nawab of Arcot, in law the Nizam's deputy but in fact the Company's dependant, obtained the Carnatic as an *altamgha* independent of the Nizam, and the Company in turn obtained from the Nawab a confirmation of the *jagir* of land around Madras as its free gift.

In spite of the Emperor's repeated entreaties for help in recovering his capital, the Company's officials adhered to their orders from London, 'Never to engage in a march to Delhi'. The Company appeared to be comfortably ensconced in their new gains in Bengal, in southern India, and at the port of Surat, when the rapid recovery of the Marathas from their great defeat by the Afghans at the Battle of

Panipat in 1761 enabled the officers of the Peshwa, or chief minister of the Marathas, to make an offer to Shah Alam to restore his capital to him. Clive found his arrangements in jeopardy as he discovered the Emperor 'intriguing with those freebooters, & stipulating for their assistance by the grant of territories in the very heart of his Empire'.[9]

Nearly half a century was in fact to elapse before the *fitva* of the Marathas would give way to the sedition of the British within the crumbling Mughal framework. The young Maratha prince Madhav Rao, as he advanced in years, displayed formidable prowess in war. Even Haidar Ali of Mysore, who had given the British at Madras a bloody nose in a war of 1767–68, was made to bite the dust. The weakly garrisoned Presidency of Bombay saw in 'the growing power of the Marathas' a prospect 'much to be lamented'.[10] There were apprehensions even in distant Calcutta when the Peshwa's generals enticed the Emperor out of British care at Allahabad. At length Shah Alam rode into the Red Fort. The Peshwa, already dying of tuberculosis, wrote to his officers in Delhi: 'I quite appreciate the value of a performance which the English desisted from undertaking ... The English if they had been so minded, did certainly possess the strength to place the Emperor on his ancestral throne: but as their power is mainly based on the sea, they declined to go a long way inland without a corresponding advantage. Now, you must remember never to allow the English to make a lodgment at Delhi. If they once obtain a footing, they can never be dislodged ... They have seized strategic points and have formed a ring around the Indian continent, from Calcutta to Surat.'[11]

Although perceptive Indians observed the growth of the British power with apprehension, with good reason they did not as yet see in their corporate and bureaucratic organization a superior strength to their own. One and all believed in Peshwa Madhav Rao's maxim: 'The age-long practice has been that full responsibility is centred in one person, exercising undivided control over all members.' As the Persian chroniclers watched Warren Hastings and his councillor Philip Francis proceed from bad words to duelling with pistols in 1780 over matters of state, while Haidar Ali of Mysore was chasing General Munro of Buxar fame to the very gate of Madras, they saw it as a system in which the man in charge had no full power over his business and must consult and manage with four or five men the English called the Committee; 'and these are perpetually at variance with each other'.[12]

[9] *Fort William–India House Correspondence and other Contemporary Papers Relating Thereto,* 21 vols. (New Delhi, 1958-85), XIV, *Secret and Select Committee, 1752–81,* pp. 15, 162–63, 185.

[10] G. W. Forrest ed., *Selections from Letters, Despatches and Other State Papers Preserved in the Bombay Secretariat, Maratha Series,* (Bombay, 1885), pp. 141, 250.

[11] Govind Sakharam Sardesai, *New History of the Marathas,* 3 vols. (1946–48; New Delhi, 1986), II, p. 515.

[12] Seid Gholam Hossein-Khan, *A Translation of the Seir Mutaqherin or View of Modern Times, being an History of India from the Year 1118 to the Year 1194 of the Hedjrah,* 4 vols. (1789; New Delhi, 1986), III,

Government by committee, or Council, was one of the many legacies of its commercial origins that survived the East India Company's transformation into a ruling power. Orders from Britain came from a Court of Directors responsible to shareholders. In India authority remained divided between autonomous Presidencies—Bengal, Madras, and Bombay—and within the Presidencies, Governors shared their powers with Councils.

The British state moved slowly and uncertainly to remedy the obvious deficiencies of the Company. In 1773 a new office of Governor-General of Bengal was created by act of Parliament and endowed with an ill-defined authority over the other Presidencies.[13] The first holder of this office was Warren Hastings, a man brought up in the Company's service but in no doubt that he was entrusted with great national interests and more than willing to pursue ambitious strategies for the administration of the Company's provinces and in the conduct of war and diplomacy with Indian powers. It was only after Hastings left India in 1785 that the Governor-General was given full power over the other Presidencies and over his Council in Bengal. The new Governors-General, of whom the most notable were Lord Cornwallis from 1786 to 1793 and Lord Wellesley from 1797 to 1805, were mostly drawn from outside the Company, were in effect directly appointed by the national government, and were accountable to ministers rather than to the Court of Directors, their nominal employers.

An administrative and military service much concerned with personal profit was another legacy of the commercial past. The Company's employees had long enjoyed extensive privileges to trade on their own behalf.[14] Conquest greatly enhanced the opportunities for private gain. In the early years of Company rule few British people in India were prepared to forgo such opportunites. For the civil and military officers of the Company it was a question of 'whether it should go into a blackman's pocket or mine'. Warren Hastings's opponents in Council found upon inquiry that 'there is no species of peculation from which the Honourable Governor-General has thought it reasonable to abstain'. Hasting's counter-investigations revealed his opponent Francis, while on a salary of £10,000, yet to be managing to send home remittances touching £45,000. The Governor-General sent his pickings home in the form of diamonds from central Indian mines, carefully sorted in Benares.[15]

---

pp. 127–28, 185–86; G. W. Forrest, ed., *Selections from the Letters, Despatches and Other State Papers preserved in the Foreign Department of the Government of India, 1772–1785*, 3 vols. (Calcutta, 1890), II, p. 665.

[13] See below, pp. 538–40.

[14] See above, pp. 593–95.

[15] *Fort William–India House Correspondence*, XIV, pp. 15, 164; Keith Feiling, *Warren Hastings* (London, 1966), pp. 22, 87, 134, 157; P. J. Marshall, *East India Fortunes: The British in Bengal in the Eighteenth Century* (Oxford, 1976), p. 245.

What struck thoughtful Indian observers of this scene was its novelty. The English, Ghulam Husain Khan saw, had 'a custom of coming for a number of years, and then of going away to pay a visit to their native country, without any one of them showing an inclination to fix himself in this land'; and to this they joined another custom, 'which every one of those emigrants holds to be of Divine obligation, I mean, that of scraping together as much money in this country as they can, and carrying it in immense sums to the kingdom of England'. He recalled a time when these very gentlemen imported gold and silver every year which 'procured an abundant circulation and promoted every one's good'. Observing this revolution of fortunes, he was not surprised that 'these two customs, blended together, should be ever undermining and ruining this country'.[16]

No attempt was made to put a check upon this plunder until the reform of the Company's civil service, which began with the princely salaries introduced after 1786 by Cornwallis with a view to modifying 'the good old principles of Leadenhall Street economy—small salaries and immense perquisites'. The annual drain from India to Britain was calculated by Holden Furber to be around £1,300,000 during the ten years between 1783 and 1793.[17]

The depletion of food and money stocks in the country arising out of the very high level of taxation which the Company enforced on Bengal and the drain of wealth to Britain coincided with a calamitous drought and produced in 1770 a devastating famine which carried away one-third of the population of Bengal. The suffering of the hapless victims was aggravated by the monopolies of rice and other commodities enforced by the Company's senior officers and their Indian associates.[18]

The flow of wealth out of India reduced consumption and employment in the country. As noblemen, soldiers, merchants, and artisans alike fell upon hard days, there were cries of distress. One member of the former Mughal ruling class lamented the fate of 'the remaining stock of the ancient nobility... who in these hard times have not a single resource left under the canopy of the Hindostany heaven'. The precipitous fall of the commanders of Mughal horse threw between 40,000 and 50,000 troopers out of pay in Bengal and Bihar, besides dispersing the 'thousands and thousands of merchants' who followed 'that numerous cavalry'. The even more numerous artisans whom the noblemen had kept 'always busy, sometimes in their own houses', found their patrons no longer capable of sustaining them. Alternative employment was hard to find, for 'as the English are now the

---

[16] *Seir Mutaqherin*, III, p. 194.

[17] Holden Furber, *John Company at Work. A Study of European Expansion in India in the Late Eighteenth Century* (1948, Cambridge, Mass., 1951), p. 309.

[18] Abdul Majed Khan, *The Transition in Bengal, 1756–1775. A Study of Saiyid Muhammad Reza Khan* (Cambridge, 1969), pp. 142–43, 160, 168, 171–77, 217–27, 305.

rulers and masters of the country', and 'because their arts and callings are of no use to the English', they could only thieve or beg. Of the various branches of trade, 'heretofore open to all', none had been left free, in fact they were 'all engrossed' by the Company or its servants. 'Numbers, therefore, have already quitted their homes and countries; and numbers unwilling to leave their abodes, have made a covenant with hunger and distress, and ended their lives in a corner of their cottages.'[19]

Merchants suffered as well as the Mughal nobility and the poor in the areas ruled by the Company. One reinterpretation of eighteenth-century Indian history which has found favour is that post-Mughal society experienced continuous economic development from earlier times. The moneyed groups benefited from the rise of cross-country trade and the monetization of revenue under the successor states. They then put their expanding resources at the disposal of the Company. Far from being predicated on the disruption of the economic organization of Indian society, the paramountcy acquired by the British is seen to be the product of its continuous growth.[20] That, however, is not how contemporaries viewed the matter. For those who suffered, the convulsions of the Mughal empire were accentuated by the grip of the monopolies imposed by the East India Company on ships and commodities all around the peninsula from Surat to Dacca.

To begin with, the pan-Indian economy, linked to the Indian Ocean and built upon the prosperity of the Mughal, Safavid, and Ottoman realms, was disrupted by the simultaneous decline of the three Muslim empires.[21] The catastrophe that overtook the longer-distance exchange of commodities and credit transfers in Mughal India was hardly compensated by the rise of the new economic forces— commercial communities or 'a new gentry' that dealt with the British—which have been identified as 'the foundation of the British colonial regime'. There then followed the abolition of the freedom of trade, both at sea and inland. New monopolies buttressed the Company's 'Investment', that is, the purchase of the cargoes of cotton textiles, silk, indigo, and saltpetre that continued to be shipped to Britain, and the private trade to other parts of Asia of individual British merchants operating on their own behalf.

The English chiefs of Surat imposed a monopoly over shipping to the Middle East, and in Bengal the forcible retirement of 'men of credit and large capital' led to the 'sudden failure of the usual supplies of specie'. A quarter of a century later the

---

[19] *Seir Mutaqherin*, III, pp. 192–93, 202–04.

[20] C. A. Bayly, *New Cambridge History of India*, II. 1, *Indian Society and the Making of the British Empire* (Cambridge, 1988), p. 11; see also above, pp. 495–97.

[21] Ashin Das Gupta, *Indian Merchants and the Decline of Surat, c.1700–1750* (Wiesbaden, 1979).

generation that had known the years before the *diwani* would recall that 'the country had four or five times more current cash than it can pretend to in these days'.[22] The Red Sea and the Persian Gulf no longer 'poured in their treasures' through the ports of Surat and Hugli, and the specie which used to flow into Bengal 'by a thousand channels' now flowed out by the sea.[23] The mechanism behind this reversal was clear to the early British administration too:

The English conquered Bengal and became sovereign of the country, the plunder of the country caused a revolution in the nature of their trade, instead of importing bullion for the purchase of an investment, the investment of India and China was considered as the vehicle of advantageously remitting from Bengal costs and the fortunes of individuals. Bengal supplied bullion, goods, stores and credit to Madras, Bombay, Bencoolen and China and the investment to Britain. The great difficulty of the individuals in Bengal was to remit their fortunes to England. When unable to do this their alternative was to lend money to the Company for the purchase of the Company's India and China investments, the proceeds of which met their bills.[24]

The consequence was an unfamiliar scarcity of coins. The private banker (*sahukar*) and money-changer (*shroff*) sought to relieve it by the increased circulation of the Indian bill of exchange (*hundi*) and the levy of a discount (*anth*) on any trader who insisted on converting his *hundi* into actual coin.[25] But the problem was aggravated by the contraction of agriculture and revenue resources in the areas swept by war, plunder, and famine.

On the eve of the tragic blinding of the Emperor in the Red Fort at Delhi in 1788 by the Rohilla plunderers, the apprehensive Maratha envoy wrote from Shah Alam's court, 'Money is nowhere to be seen'. This was a fact which no ambitious prince could afford to ignore. The Maratha leader, Daulat Rao Sindia, reflected anxiously that 'without money it was impossible to assemble an army or prosecute war'.[26] Whichever power could produce a clear surplus out of its revenue resources, and thereby persuade the *sahukars* and *shroffs* to transfer money to the theatres of war, would be likely to have an edge over its contenders at a time when money was

---

[22] Khan, *Transition*, pp. 171 ff; *Seir Mutaqherin*, IV, p. 21, n. 14.

[23] The Bengal authorities estimated that formerly specie was brought in to the amount of 100 lakhs (Rs. 1 million) whereas it now went out to the amount of 26 lakhs (Rs. 260,000) every year: *Fort William–India House Correspondence*, XIV, pp. 195–96.

[24] 'Historical Review of the External Commerce of Calcutta from 1750 until 1830', Oriental and India Office Collections, MSS, EUR. D. 281, f. 1.

[25] Tapan Raychaudhuri and Irfan Habib, eds., *The Cambridge Economic History of India*, I, *c.1200– c.1750* (Cambridge, 1982), pp. 362–63.

[26] Jadunath Sarkar, *Fall of the Mughal Empire*, 4th edn., 4 vols. (New Delhi, 1985–92), III, p. 254; R. M. Martin, ed., *The Despatches, Minutes and Correspondence of the Marquess Wellesley During his Administration in India*, 5 vols. (1836–37; New Delhi, 1985), IV, pp. 494–97.

tight, and the only means of transferring credit for hungry troops across hostile borders were the *hundis* offered by the private bankers. Such being the situation, every power—with the exception of Tipu Sultan of Mysore, who got rid of his bankers in a rage—depended as a matter of course upon the *hundi* banker's word of honour which held fast to 'a chain that extends everywhere'. The British East India Company was no exception. Its ability to hold its own against its potential Indian rivals depended less on superior European technology and powers of organization than on its ability to mobilize a flow of resources through the good offices of Indian bankers.

The revenue from taxation available to the Great Mughals was assessed at Rs.300 million (or about £30 million) at its greatest extent.[27] The successor regimes had to operate on smaller margins: the East India Company inherited gross revenue resources worth Rs.59 million (nearly £6 million), the Maratha confederacy appropriated around Rs.57 million, and Mysore under Tipu Sultan had Rs.23.7 million.[28] On paper the English and the Marathas were evenly matched, but Maratha finances were too chaotic to yield an assured surplus. As the young Wellington (Arthur Wellesley) found out before the showdown in 1803, 'there is not a Maharatta in the whole country, from the Peshwa down to the lowest horseman, who has a shilling'. The Bengal land tax as fixed in 1793 yielded to the British a steady revenue surplus of Rs.25 million from Bengal at a time when Mahadji Sindia, master of northern India, collected a net sum of Rs.1.2 million from his home base in Malwa.

The assured surplus from the land tax of Bengal led to the growth of a great money market in Calcutta upon which the Company could draw. The decennial loans it floated at 10 per cent fetched it more than Rs.60 million between 1797 and 1803, obtained mostly from European private traders and what were called the agency houses, private British business houses in Calcutta. Bengal was in a position to meet the annual purchase of cargoes for London amounting to Rs.9.1 million from the regular revenue, and to supply Canton with Rs.1.8 million to buy tea, the new Malayan settlement of Penang with Rs.500,000 to meet its operating costs, and Bombay and Madras with Rs.2.5 million each. For additional resources, the money market of Calcutta could be tapped in emergency for seemingly inexhaustible sums. As Madras and Bombay despatched armies in the final war to destroy Tipu Sultan in 1799, Wellesley sent Rs.10 million (£1 million) to the two deficit Presidencies, a sum he raised by loans in Calcutta.[29]

[27] For an explanation of 'revenue' see above, p. 504.

[28] Lakshmi Subramanian, *Indigenous Capital and Imperial Expansion. Bombay, Surat and the West Coast* (New Delhi, 1995), pp. 317 ff; Mohibbul Hasan Khan, *History of Tipu Sultan* (Calcutta, 1951), p. 269.

[29] Amales Tripathi, *Trade and Finance in the Bengal Presidency, 1793–1833* (Calcutta, 1979), pp. 4, 46–47, 72, 80–81; Sarkar, *Fall*, III, p. 241.

With regard to the indigenous system of commercial credit, too, the Company was better placed than the Indian powers by virtue of its reputation as an international capitalist corporation with a developed sense of the importance of paying its debts. It was known, moreover, to have the biggest disposable revenue surplus in the country to offer as collateral for large contract loans obtained from the *sahukaras*. In popular perception, the British did not 'interfere with the wealth of any rich men, bankers, merchants and other people who reside in their cities, but, on the contrary, they are very kind to those who are wealthy'.[30] The rule of the British seemed to the leading *sahukar* of Surat, the house of Arjunjee Nathjee Tarwady, to be synonymous with 'peace and justice'.[31] The Benares bankers, such as the great house of Gopaldas Manohardas, with branches all over India, were the particular allies of the British. They advanced the Company money at relatively low rates of interest and punctually remitted funds to pay British troops wherever they were operating.

The taxes of peasants under the Company's rule and the loans of the Indian bankers enabled the British to wage war against other Indian states. Most wars were fought against the express commands of the Court of Directors in London, who believed that the cost of war would eat into the resources available for trade and cautioned men on the spot 'Never to extend your possessions beyond their previous bounds'. Nevertheless, the Company frequently engaged in war, on a variety of pretexts. In contrast with the spectacular successes gained by Clive and others in the years before 1763, wars during the Warren Hastings period in the 1770s and 1780s rarely produced decisive results. Indian armies had learnt how to meet the Company's forces on more or less equal terms. It was not until the 1790s that the Company's ability to mobilize resources enabled it to put armies into the field on a scale that ultimately overwhelmed Indian rivals. First Mysore and then the Marathas went down to defeat in the great wars under Wellesley.[32]

Events towards the end of Hastings's administration exposed the limits to the Company's military power in the 1770s and 1780s. A round of wars began with the

---

[30] 'Chahar Gulzar Shuja'i' of Hari Charan Das in H. M. Elliot and John Dowson, *The History of India as Told by its Own Historians*, 8 vols. (1867–77; Allahabad, 1964), VIII, p. 229.

[31] The discussion of bankers and politics is based on: Subramanian, *Indigenous Capital*; Lakshmi Subramanian and Rajat Kanta Ray, 'Merchants and Politics: From the Great Mughals to the East India Company', in Dwijendra Tripathi, ed., *Business and Politics in India: A Historical Perspective* (New Delhi, 1991), pp. 37, 50; B. G. Gokhale, *Poona in the Eighteenth Century: An Urban History* (Delhi, 1988); Lakshmi Subramanian, 'Banias and the British: The Role of Indigenous Credit in the Process of Imperial Expansion in Western India in the Second Half of the Eighteenth Century', *Modern Asian Studies*, XXI (1987), pp. 473–510; C. A. Bayly, *Rulers, Townsmen and Bazaars: North Indian Society in the Age of British Expansion, 1780–1870* (Cambridge, 1983); Kumkum Bandyopadhyay, 'Indigenous Trade, Finance and Politics—A Study of Patna and Its Hinterland: 1757 to 1813', unpublished Ph.D. thesis, Calcutta, 1987.

[32] See above, pp. 197–200.

Marathas. Acquisition of the cotton tracts of Gujarat and territories which would furnish a revenue equal to its necessities prompted Bombay, as 'It seemed the very crisis wished for by the Company', to intervene in the commotions at Poona after Peshwa Madhav Rao's death.[33] Eventually there was an Indian confederacy against the British, prompted by the Poona minister Nana Fadnis, who wrote to his old antagonist Haidar Ali of Mysore on 7 February 1780, 'Divide and grab is their main principle ... They are bent upon subjugating the States of Poona, Nagpur, Mysore and Haidarabad one by one, by enlisting the sympathy of one to put down the others. They know best how to destroy Indian cohesion.'[34]

The plan, which did not materialize fully, was to concert operations 'for the expulsion of the English nation from India': the Nizam to recover the Northern Circars, the Marathas of Nagpur to attack Bengal, Poona to operate on the Bombay side, and Haidar Ali to direct his force against Madras. By a series of adroit moves, Warren Hastings detached the Nizam and neutralized the Raja of Nagpur. But the Muslim prince Haidar Ali, accompanied by his son Tipu Sultan, marched to Madras with a view to aiding the Hindu Maratha power of Poona, 'prudently considering', in Tipu's words, 'that although it is declared "Heretics are impure", yet that it was more advisable to afford than refuse his assistance to the infidels belonging to the country (because the supremacy of the English was the source of evil to all God's creatures)'.

There was no political discourse in eighteenth-century India to construe resistance to the foreigners as a national war for the defence of the country. The Mughal Emperor and his Wazir had earlier, at the Battle of Buxar in 1764, cast the struggle in terms of an imperial denunciation of the British as 'naughty and disobedient' rebels who had usurped 'different parts of the Royal dominions'. Tipu later shifted the ground of the struggle to a defence of Islam and Hindustan: 'God is the protector and defender of the land of Hindostan; next to him, this suppliant at the Almighty Throne, does not and will not neglect the defence and service of the people.' All Hindustan, he declared, was overrun by 'infidels' (the Company) and 'polytheists' (the Hindu powers), and he hoped that 'the religion of Islam will obtain exclusive prevalence over the whole country of Hindostan, and that the sinful heretics will with the utmost ease become the prey of the swords of the combatants in the cause of religion'. He took care to specify that he meant 'the treachery, deceit and supremacy of the Christians in the regions of Hindostan'; but he remained somewhat ambiguous with regard to the 'infidels belonging to the country'. As for the Marathas, they had no political vocabulary to express their

---

[33] Representation of W. Taylor on behalf of the Bombay Government to Warren Hastings, 9 Oct. 1775, Forrest, ed., *Selections, Maratha Series*, I, p. 257.

[34] Quoted in Sardesai, *New History*, III. p. 97.

sentiments in terms wider than saving 'the Maratha state' from 'the grasp of foreigners'.[35]

The confederacy of the Indian princes was carried forward on an under-tide of popular anger. Rumours and signals flew far and wide. Throughout the Presidency of Bengal, so it was rumoured in the far off south, 'the English have forcibly taken prisoners, wives and daughters, and carried them off to their own islands and country'. In 1781 Warren Hastings tried to collect money for the war in the peninsula from Raja Chait Singh of Benares. The Raja's retainers forced Hastings to flee into the fort of Chunar, where the British saw 'Chait Singh will pay us our arrears', scrawled on the wall by their own soldiers. A Frenchman living as a Muslim among the Mughal noblemen of Murshidabad in Bengal, seeing that the English had 'alienated all hearts', wrote, 'All hearts! *Can that be true?* . . . yet behold! hardly is this man [Warren Hastings at Benares] supposed killed, than *all, all*, Sir, (It is the very word), *all* think of rising on the English.' All over Benares and the neighbouring dominions of Oudh those hard pressed by taxes to meet the British demands stirred with the idea of driving 'the Fringies out'. And in the Carnatic at this very time the people of the country informed Haidar Ali of every movement of the British troops and helped him storm the fort of Arcot. '[F]rom Ganjam to Cape Comorin', the British officers reported from the Carnatic, 'there was not a native, but proved disaffected to the English . . . so that no intelligence could be had from any of them; or if any at all, it was always a *suggested* one.' As if in concert, rumours of British defeat in the peninsula caused wild excitement in Bengal.[36]

At length the British sued for peace with nothing to show for it; and in no time Mahadji Sindia was back in Delhi (1784), this time on his own, dignified by Shah Alam with the title of Regent (*Wakil-i-Mutlaq*), but unequal, in the event, to the task of protecting his imperial master from being blinded by the Rohilla raiders of Delhi. The *inqilab*, it seemed to the Mughal poet Mir, had completed its course:

> I lived to see the needle draw across the eyes of kings
> The dust beneath whose feet was like collyrium ground with pearls.

Beneath this *inqilab*, another revolution was in motion. This was the introduction of the rule of the law in the English Presidencies, the creation of the modern colonial state inaugurated by Pitt and Dundas, following the India Act of 1784,[37]

---

[35] Rajat Kanta Ray, 'Colonial Penetration and the Initial Resistance: The Mughal Ruling Class, the English East India Company and the Struggle for Bengal, 1756–1800', *Indian Historical Review*, XII (1985–6), p. 53; draft letter of Tipu Sultan to Grand Signor, Constantinople, 10 Feb. 1799, *Wellesley Despatches*, V, pp. 25, 29; Sardesai, *New History*, III, p. 436.

[36] Tipu Sultan to Grand Signor, *Wellesley Despatches*, V, p. 28; Feiling, *Hastings*, p. 266; Haji Mustapha to William Armstrong, 19 May 1790, *Seir Mutaqherin*, IV, pp. 24, 26, 115–16; James Mill, *History of British India*, ed. Horace Hayman Wilson, 5th edn., 10 vols. (London, 1858), IV, pp. 127, 142, 312.

[37] See below, pp. 543–47.

implemented in India after 1786 by the reforming Governor-General Lord Corn-wallis, and the consequent alteration of the balance of power in India between British India and the Indian states.

With the creation by 1793 of Cornwallis's 'government-by-regulations', in Bengal the Company's rule, at least for an élite, ceased to be arbitrary and predatory and became predictable. In what was known as the Permanent Settlement, the taxation assessment on the land of Bengal was fixed for ever, at what was initially a high level, and rights to land were thereby created that could be bought and sold. Money invested in land was permanently secure. Unable to pay the assessment, many old landholders were forced to sell out; those who bought from them were in a sense throwing in their lot with the British. The élite who could use the new legal system were also guaranteed personal security and absolute rights to property through the Company's courts, even against the government itself.

While it was beginning to offer positive inducements to Indians to ally with it, the Company was also putting its own house in order. Pitt's India Act and a subsequent Act of 1786 unified the British state in India under the Governor-General's command. The Governor-General now had clear authority over the other Presidencies and over his own Council. No longer, as the Chief Justice of India had observed, might a whole Presidency be involved in domestic discord with the enemy at the gate and 'the Government-General' a tame spectator of the confusion.

The young Wellington grasped the significance of these developments for the balance of power in India when he saw that the Company's government was now guided by 'all the rules and systems of European policy', whereas the Indian powers, especially the Marathas, hardly knew of such rules and systems, for 'the objects of their policy are always shifting'.[38]

Tipu Sultan, who dimly realized the awesome power of European technology and organization, sought to graft some aspects of it to his state by developing an army with fire-power, government manufacture of armaments, and state management of commercial factories and banking establishments. But Cornwallis hemmed him in by securing the military co-operation of the Nizam and the Marathas in 1792, and Wellesley cut short his experiments in 1799. He had injured the Company's trade by placing an embargo, and had sought an alliance with the French. Tipu was killed when the British took his capital, and the occupation of his territories by the British army brought Arthur Wellesley's forces within striking-distance of Poona, at a critical moment when civil war between Holkar and Sindia paralyzed the internal mechanisms of the Maratha confederacy. Governor-General Lord Wellesley's massive intervention destroyed that confederacy (an abortive

---

[38] *Wellesley Despatches*, V, pp. 182, 335.

attempt to revive it led to the extinction of the Peshwa's state in 1818) and substituted the hegemony of the East India Company for the 'balance of power'.

For Wellesley and that generation, the symbol of this hegemony was possession of the Red Fort and at Delhi its blind Emperor. Wellesley adverted to 'the importance of securing the person and nominal authority of the Mogul against the designs of France, and the encrease of reputation to the British name, which would result from affording an honourable asylum to the person and family of that injured and unfortunate monarch'. But once the Red Fort was in British hands, he saw 'no obligation imposed upon us, to consider the rights and claims of his Majesty Shah Aulum as Emperor of Hindustan'.

The political hegemony of the East India Company visibly transformed the conditions of Indian trade and finance. With more revenues than before—an impressed Persian chronicler who had served in the Imperial treasury at the Red Fort estimated that Lord Wellesley had increased the wealth of the Company's territory from Rs.70 million worth of revenue to Rs.150 million, that is, £15 million[39]—the Company authorities were in a position to clip the wings of the Indian bankers and to break out of the irksome dependence on their *hundis*. These instruments were relegated to inland Indian business, the so-called bazaar, as the Company floated public loans at as low a rate as 6 per cent, and eventually at 5 per cent, on the basis of heightened public confidence.[40]

Part of this confident public was the growing body of non-official Europeans gathered around the houses of agency for the conduct of the private trade. The other part was the emerging Indian public of the Presidency towns, presided over by the landholders and the leaders of the Indian business communities that dealt with the British: Bengali *banians* of Calcutta, the Tamil *dubashes* of Madras, and the Parsee brokers of Bombay, whose function was to act as the intermediaries between the European agency houses and the Indian bazaar.

The favoured agency houses, which had come forward with large loans in the Maratha War, replaced the Company in the commanding heights of India's exchange economy. As the Company's exports of Indian cotton textiles to Europe ceased after the Charter Act of 1813, the agency houses laid out nearly £5 million to develop indigo, cotton, silk, and opium as alternative export items.[41] This fostered a triangular colonial trade between India, China, and Britain, and in the process provided a broader channel for the flow of remittances to England. The compulsory supply of white personnel and services by Britain to India, the shipments of

---

[39] Elliot and Dowson, VIII, p. 439.

[40] John Crawfurd, *A Sketch of the Commercial Resources and Monetary and Mercantile System of British India* (1837), reprinted in K. N. Chaudhuri, ed., *The Economic Development of India under the English East India Company, 1814–58. A Selection of Contemporary Writings* (Cambridge, 1971), pp. 297–98.

[41] Ibid, p. 277.

cotton and opium from India to China, and the exports of tea from China to Britain defined an indirect and less disruptive circuit for the transmission of India's tribute to Britain.

Part of the public subscribing confidently to the Company's loans was the Bengali gentry based on the smaller and exclusive landed properties carved out by the buying and selling of land after the Permanent Settlement of 1793. They had benefited from the ruin of the older generation of revenue-collecting landowners (*zamindars*) and Rajas, whose land was sold when they failed to meet punctually the Company's revenue demand. A numerous body, the gentry multiplied with the complex entitlements to collect rent from the cultivators of the land, which the fixed land tax fostered as it grew less burdensome in real terms. The bigger ones among them, especially those who resided in Calcutta and were connected with the trade and administration of the English, invested largely in the Company's bonds and in the rising urban property market.[42] The link which was in evidence between the Company, the agency houses and the baboos, *banians*, and brokers cut clean across the old links of society. The parvenus and go-betweens were now reckoned more influential than the ruined Mughal noblemen or the fallen old Rajas. The social revolution—an inversion, both perceived and real, of the existing hierarchy—tinged the culture of the age with a profound pessimism, until a generation emerged in Calcutta with a more hopeful outlook.

As the once-prosperous Mughal towns withered away,[43] and while the colonial port cities grew slowly, there sprang into a prominence a brand of late Mughal poetry called the *Shahr-i-Ashob*, or Town in Lament, with *inqilab* at the centre of its theme. The Mughal troopers, lamented the poet Rasikh of Patna, were so afflicted by poverty that they could not command even a toy clay horse. Yet another poet of Patna, Jauhri, saw with shock the cavalry of 'lalas and baboos' (parvenus serving the English) going forth with a tumult through the town. It was a time, the poets complained, when everything had been 'turned upside down', and all were subject to 'the impression of changing fortune'.[44] The flippant art of love, cultivated by cavaliers and courtesans in the decaying Mughal towns, was coloured by the fickleness of fortune:

> I told her the story of my heart: she listened for a while, and said
> 'I have to go. But you can stay; sit there, and go on with your tale.'

---

[42] On the Permanent Settlement and the gentry, see Ratnalekha Ray, *Change in Bengal Agrarian Society c.1760–1850* (New Delhi, 1979); Sirajul Islam, *The Permanent Settlement in Bengal: A Study of Its Operation, 1790–1819* (Dacca, 1979).

[43] Population decline estimates—Dacca: 1800—200,00, 1872—68,595; Murshidabad: 1815—165,000, 1872—46,182; Patna 1811/12—312,000, 1872—158,900 (Irfan Habib, 'Studying a Colonial Economy—Without Perceiving Colonialism', *Modern Asian Studies*, XIX (1985), p. 367).

[44] Kumkum Bandyopadhyay, 'Indigenous Trade, Finance and Politics', pp. 440–49.

The hours spent in the company of the *Saki* might blunt the edge, but would not altogether wipe out the injury done to self-esteem by the humiliating denial of the high offices of the state and the rigid exclusion from the positions of power. A collective racial degradation was implicit in the social revolution that had occurred. 'The greatest men formerly', wrote the Judge and Magistrate of Midnapore in Bengal in response to a query from Wellesley's government, 'were the Musalman rulers, whose places we have taken, and the Hindoo zemindars—These two classes are now ruined and destroyed—The natives mostly looked up to, are our Omlah [subordinate officers] and our domestics: these are courted and respected: they must necessarily be the channel, through which every suitor and every candidate looks up for redress and preferment.'[45]

This was *inqilab*, and of a sort that the Muslim gentry (*ashraf*) of the reduced Mughal towns could not but rage over. The manner in which the men in charge of the affairs of the powerful English households (*mutasaddis*) treated visiting Indian gentlemen of ancient and illustrious families filled Ghulam Husain Khan with indignation at 'a variety of affronts and indignities'. The 'aversion' and 'disdain' which he saw the English evince for the company of the natives, exposed to his view a political hegemony which was at the same time a racial monopoly: 'they are come at last to undervalue the Hindustanees, and to make no account of the natives from the highest to the lowest; and they carry their contempt so far, as to employ none but their own selves in every department and in every article of business, esteeming themselves better than all others put together.'[46]

On this point, Raja Ram Mohun Roy and the new generation of Hindu gentry (*bhadralok*) in Calcutta were at one with Saiyid Ghulam Husain Khan and the older generation of Muslim noblemen (*umara*) of Patna and Murshidabad, however profoundly the Raja would differ from the Saiyid regarding the benevolence of the Mughal and the injustice of the English.[47]

The better classes of the natives of India [so ran an Indian petition to Parliament drafted by Ram Mohun Roy] are placed under the sway of the Honourable East India Company, in a state of political degradation which is absolutely without a parallel in their former history. For even under the Mahomedan conquerors, such of your petitioners as are Hindoos, were not only capable of filling but actually did fill numerous employments of trust, dignity and

---

[45] *The Fifth Report from the Select Committee on the Affairs of the East India Company* (London, 1812), p. 701.

[46] *Seir Mutaqherin*, III, pp. 29, 161–62, 170–71, 190–91.

[47] In Ram Mohun Roy's view, the Muslim rulers had trampled upon the civil and religious rights of the original inhabitants of India for several centuries, until Divine Providence 'stirred up the English nation to break the yoke of those tyrants' and put the natives of India in possession of privileges 'their forefathers never expected to attain, even under Hindu rulers'. For this and subsequent quotations from Ram Mohun Roy, see *Correspondence of Rammohan Roy*, I, pp. 224–25 and *passim*.

emolument, from which under the existing system of the Honourable Company's government, they are absolutely shut out.[48]

The colonial rationale for the disfranchisement of a whole race—'Asiatic
treachery and falsehood' (Wellesley), 'the perverseness and depravity of the natives
of India in general' (John Malcolm)—derived from a particular construction of
the native character which induced the Utilitarian philosopher at India House to
reflect gravely, 'In India there is no moral character'.[49] The proneness of the natives
to 'mendacity and perjury' was for the philosopher James Mill the major obstacle
to ensuring justice through the courts of law. Had he possessed Ram Mohun Roy's
insight into the matter, he would have seen what his more acute Indian contemporary grasped: that it was the existing system of English judges and native
pleaders which promoted the crime of perjury to such an extent as to make it
impossible to distinguish what was true from what was not. The English judges
treated the native pleaders and officers of the court with contempt, while the latter
looked up to the judges as humble dependants of a master rather than independent advocates of the rights of their clients. 'And the whole are so closely leagued
together, that if a complaint is preferred to a higher authority against the judge (he
having the power of promoting or ruining the prospects of Native officers and
pleaders) they are all ready to support him and each other to the defeat of justice,
by false oaths and fabricated documents.'

Indian reactions to the establishment of British hegemony ranged from the
inclination of the doctors of Islamic law (*ulama*) to reject the whole system, to the
design of the English-educated Hindus to turn its internal rules to the advantage of
their countrymen. The essence of the system, as Wellesley explained to the Court
of Directors in 1800, was the rule of the law. He was acquainted with those who
rejected that law and its rule altogether; he hardly yet anticipated those who might
try and turn that law upon its giver.

'The early administration of the Company', wrote the Governor-General to the
Directors, 'succeeded to the despotic power of the native princes,' but experience
of 'the evils attendant on this form of Government' led in due course to a
reconstruction based 'on principles drawn from the British constitution.' Separation of the legislative, executive, and judicial powers of the state provided the basis
of 'the new constitution of the Government of Bengal', wherein it resembled the
British constitution. However, 'it was obviously necessary that the Governor-
General in Council should exercise exclusively the entire legislative authority'.
Wellesley acknowledged the implication of this—'that we excluded our native
subjects from all participation in the legislative authority'—but in his view an

---

[48] Ibid., p. 364.
[49] Mill, *History*, V, p. 408.

effectual security was afforded to them by the proviso that the Governor-General should print and publish every legislative act. 'His executive authority as far as regards the internal government, will be subject to the control of the laws, and the due administration of the laws, will be secured by the courts appointed to administer them being rendered entirely distinct, both from the executive and legislative authority.'[50]

The *ulama* and Muslim gentry were not inclined to accept the English definitions of despotism, law, and liberty. No sooner did Delhi pass under English occupation than the leading Muslim divine of the capital pronounced that Shah Alam, the imperial protector of the Muslims (*Imam-al-Muslimin*), no longer wielded authority in town: 'From here to Calcutta the Christians are in complete control.' Shah Abdul Aziz, therefore, issued a decree (*fatwa*) that India was no longer a land of peace (*Dar-ul-Islam*), but on the contrary a land of war (*dar-ul-harb*), where every Muslim might come under the obligation of holy war (*jihad*). The *Sirat-i-Mustaqim*, a tract which then spelt out the philosophy of the opposition movement, defined a despot as 'a person... who does what he wants without any regard for the *shari'ah* and for custom'. 'It is such people', declared the fundamentalist preacher Shah Ismail Shahid, 'whose government I call despotism and whom I call despots.' The leaders of the movement further declared that it was improper to learn English for the promotion of better relations with Englishmen, or to serve them as clerks (*munshis*), servants, or soldiers.[51]

The movement of fundamentalists' reform coexisted with more liberal attitudes. Before Ram Mohun Roy made his voyage to England in 1831, a series of Muslim visitors from India recorded their admiration of the political and social institutions of the island. Their travelogues aroused a certain amount of curiosity among polite Muslim circles. The Muslim gentry were, however, too secure in their own institutions to show an inclination to innovate. Recognition of the superiority of European technology and organization did not crystallize into a public Indian response to the mentality, intellectual outlook, and sexual ethos of European civilization until the campaign of Ram Mohun Roy of 1815 and the founding of the Hindoo College in 1817 brought forth a new generation in Calcutta.

The Company's press in Calcutta was used initially for printing acts and regulations in the vernacular languages. As the rule of the law set the government firmly into a 'constitutional' framework, the Baptist Mission set up a printing press at Serampore with a more general publishing programme in 1800. In association with Wellesley's Fort William College for training the Company's

---

[50] *Wellesley Despatches*, II, pp. 312–18.
[51] M. Mujeeb, *The Indian Muslims* (London, 1969), pp. 390–98.

civilians, it began publishing printed books in the vernacular languages. Indian-owned printing presses sprang up in Calcutta shortly after: between 1810 and 1820 no less than 15,000 works were printed and sold in the Bengali language.[52] The printing and information revolution introduced, in the words of Ram Mohun Roy, 'free discussion among the natives'. This habit, by inducing them to acquire knowledge, 'served greatly to improve their minds'. In due course, they arranged an enlightened Western education for their sons in the newly founded Hindoo College, existing cheek by jowl with the government-owned Sanskrit College, but a world apart in its curriculum. A fence put up by H. H. Wilson, the British Principal of Sanskrit College, to prevent fisticuffs between his boys and those of Hindoo College set apart the old category of pundits from the new breed of baboos.[53]

This was no *inqilab*, but a revolution of knowledge and sensibilities, behind which lay a social transformation. Tens of thousands of high-caste Bengali Hindus had consolidated their position within the framework of landed property laid down by the Permanent Settlement, and thousands of them had entered the world of service and trade in the now pre-eminent town of Calcutta. The latter were especially keen for their sons to have a liberal English education. The term *bhadralok*, which until 1805 had still implied men of caste and pure birth, shifted subtly in its connotation, so as to imply in 1823 the emerging class of 'Natives of wealth and respectability, as well as the Landholders of consequence', with their position consolidated in the existing framework of property and the rule of the regulations.[54] During the wars that led to the universal acknowledgement of British paramountcy in 1817–18, they offered prayers for the success of the British 'from a deep conviction that under the sway of that nation, their improvement both mental and social, would be promoted, and their lives, religion and property be secured'.

These developments were imperceptible at the turn of the nineteenth century. As late as 1802, Henry Strachey, the prescient Judge and Magistrate of Midnapore, could 'see no tendency whatever to improvement among the natives, except their increasing knowledge of the Regulations, which, in speaking of the progress of political philosophy, is scarcely worth mentioning'. And yet in 1822 Mountstuart Elphinstone noted, from as far afield as Bombay, 'the wonderful improvement of

[52] A. F. Salahhuddin Ahmed, *Social Ideas and Social Change in Bengal, 1818–1835* (1965; Calcutta, 1976), p. 90.

[53] Speech by Raj Narayan Bose at the first reunion of the Hindoo (Presidency) College, 1 Jan. 1875, reprinted as Raj Narayan Bose and Asok Kumar Ray, eds., *Hindu Athaya Presidency Colleger Itivritta* (Calcutta, 1992), p. 27.

[54] Rajiv Lochan Mukhopadhyay, *Maharaj Krishnachandra Rayasya Charitram* (1805; reprint, Calcutta B. S. 1343), p. 33; Bhavani Charan Bandyopadhyay, *Kalikata Kamalalaya* (1823), repr. in Bhavani Charan Bandyopadhyay, *Rasa-Rachana-Samagra* (Calcutta, 1987), pp. 7–10; *Correspondence of Rammohun Roy*, I, p. 211.

the natives that begins to be discernible, in Bengal especially'. The signs were indeed then unmistakable. Ram Mohun Roy took the first public step in the awakening discerned by Elphinstone when in 1815 he assembled the *Atmiya Sabha*, a Western style association for collective discussion and reform, and which issued his tract, in Bengali and English, against *The Practice of Burning Widows Alive* (1818).[55] Suttee, he pronounced, was nothing but murder according to 'the common sense of all nations'. A critical look at his own society convinced him that the Hindus were more superstitious in their religious rites and domestic concerns than other known nations. This was the beginning of a religious and social reform involving the structure of gender relations among the *bhadralok.*

The 'increasing knowledge of the Regulations' produced an advance in political philosophy among the Indians sooner than Henry Strachey had anticipated in 1802. Not seven years elapsed before Ram Mohun Roy, *Diwan* of Collector John Digby, called out Collector Sir Frederick Hamilton of Bhagalpur for the personal indignity of requiring him to come out of his palanquin and perform the *salaam* expected from a baboo. His appeal to the Governor-General, with the admonish- ment that 'the spirit of the British laws could not tolerate an Act of Arbitrary Aggression', led to the Collector being cautioned 'against having any similar altercation with any of the natives in the future'.[56] Ram Mohun Roy and his contemporaries saw that 'the more valuable privileges of the English law, and the rights which it bestows were confined to the ruling class, to Europeans'. Their determination to obtain these rights for themselves initiated the constitutional agitation of the English-educated Indians for the right of self-determination.

News from Europe that the Austrian troops of Prince Metternich had put down the popular revolt in Naples in 1820–21 against the autocratic Bourbon rule brought to Ram Mohun Roy the premonition, 'I would not live to see liberty universally restored to the nations of Europe, and Asiatic nations, especially those that are European colonies, possessed of a greater degree of the same blessing than what they now enjoy'. Nevertheless, he wrote to his friend James Silk Buckingham, the journalist, that he considered the cause of the Neapolitans as his own and their enemies as his enemies. 'Enemies to liberty and friends of despotism have never been and never will be ultimately successful.'[57] The progress of political philosophy and the diffusion of the notions of individual liberty and national self-determina- tion enabled Ram Mohun Roy and his generation to expose the paradox of a

---

[55] S. N. Mukherjee, 'Class, Caste and Politics in Calcutta 1815–38', in Edmund Leach and S. N. Mukherjee, eds., *Elites in South Asia* (Cambridge, 1970), pp. 34–35, 66, 69; Ahmed, *Social Ideas*, p. 130; Edward Thompson and G. T. Garratt, *Rise and Fulfilment of British Rule in India* (1934; Allahabad, 1958), p. 276.

[56] *Correspondence of Rammohan Roy,* I, pp. 5, 11.

[57] Ibid., p. 61.

despotism professedly based on the rule of the law. This was a view that subscribed neither to Wellesley's contention that liberty had replaced despotism nor to Shah Ismail Shahid's judgment that despotism had replaced liberty: embodying both, it reflected the range, ambiguity, and complexity of India's colonial encounter.

Select Bibliography

C. A. BAYLY, *Rulers, Townsmen and Bazaars. North Indian Society in the Age of British Expansion, 1770–1870* (Cambridge, 1983).

HOLDEN FURBER, *John Company at Work. A Study of European Expansion in India in the Eighteenth Century* (1948; Cambridge Mass., 1951).

SEID GHOLAM HOSSEIN KHAN, *A Translation of The Seir Mutaqherin or View of Modern Times: Being an History of India from the Year 1118 to the Year 1194, of the Hedjrah,* 4 vols. (1789; New Delhi, 1986).

P. J. MARSHALL, *East Indian Fortunes. The British in Bengal in the Eighteenth Century* (Oxford, 1976).

JAMES MILL, *History of British India,* ed. Horace Hayman Wilson, 5th edn., 10 vols. (London, 1858).

S. N. MUKHERJEE, 'Class, Caste and Politics in Calcutta, 1815–38', in Edmund Leach and S. N. Mukherjee, eds., *Elites in South Asia* (Cambridge, 1970), pp. 33–78.

PAMELA NIGHTINGALE, *Trade and Empire in Western India, 1784–1806* (Cambridge, 1970).

RAJAT KANTA RAY, 'Colonial Penetration and the Initial Resistance: The Mughal Ruling Class, the English East India Company and the Struggle for Bengal, 1756–1800', *Indian Historical Review,* XII (1985–86), pp. 1–105.

JADUNATH SARKAR, *Fall of the Mughal Empire,* 4th edn., 4 vols. (New Delhi, 1985–92).

LAKSHMI SUBRAMANIAN, *Indigenous Credit and Imperial Expansion. Bombay, Surat and the West Coast* (New Delhi, 1995).

24

British India, 1765–1813: The Metropolitan Context

H.V. BOWEN

During the second half of the eighteenth century the balance of Britain's Imperial interests began to shift from the western hemisphere to the East. As this happened, a form of empire emerged in Asia that was quite unfamiliar to contemporaries who had long placed British imperialism within terms of reference defined by the structures and relationships established in the North Atlantic world. The catalyst for this broadening of the Imperial experience was provided by the dramatic transformation of the East India Company from trader to sovereign during the mid-1760s.[1] In the short term, this development was given an almost unanimous *ex post facto* seal of approval by politicians and commentators in Britain. Over time, however, general ignorance was replaced by a much fuller understanding of what was happening in India, and this gave rise to considerable unease in metropolitan circles about the direction being taken by British activity in South Asia. As a result, the revolution that had entirely recast the Company's position in India served only to foreshadow a much longer revolution in attitudes towards the new Empire of the East.

Before 1780 few observers of Imperial affairs were prepared to argue that India was of more importance to Britain than either North America or the West Indies, but there was nevertheless growing recognition of the different ways in which East Indian affairs bore ever more directly upon the nation's economic and military fortunes. Because of this, successive governments found themselves under increasing pressure to address some of the practical problems associated with the regulation and administration of the East India Company and its territorial possessions. This alone would have served to embed the Indian Empire into the nation's political consciousness, but other factors also contributed. Helping to sustain public interest in Indian affairs throughout much of the period, for example, was the diverting side-show being played out at East India House, where vicious factional infighting created a sense of permanent crisis and upheaval within the Company.[2] At the same time, deep misgivings developed about the conduct of

[1] See above, pp. 501–07.
[2] These aspects of the East Indian problem are examined in L. S. Sutherland's magisterial study, *The East India Company in Eighteenth-Century Politics* (Oxford, 1952).

some of the leading British figures in India. Few observers could avoid being carried along by the extraordinary tide of popular excitement created by attempts to press parliamentary charges related to corruption and the abuse of power against Lord Clive, Warren Hastings, and others. As the founders of the Indian Empire fought to save their reputations and fortunes, reports of their actions touched several raw nerves in British society. Self-righteous metropolitan commentators had little difficulty in identifying the villains of the piece, and abuse was heaped upon 'nabobs' or Company servants who were believed to have returned home to Britain with their pockets stuffed with the ill-gotten gains of service in India.[3]

Several distinct strands were thus evident within the broad patchwork of Indian issues brought before the British public after 1765, and in different ways they each illustrated the fact that the possession of a new territorial Empire represented much more than the uncomplicated extension of metropolitan influence into another sphere of overseas activity. At the very time that American colonists were posing serious challenges to the old Imperial order in the West, British anxieties about some of the negative aspects of imperialism began to manifest themselves in responses to the course being taken by events in the East. In particular, fears began to be expressed about the effect that possession of an Indian Empire based upon conquest might be having upon Britain itself.[4] The forces and influences emanating from the periphery were deemed to be of such peculiar strength that they were held to pose a serious threat to the delicate economic, social, and constitutional balances that existed at the very heart of the Empire. It was thought that misrule, corruption, greed, vice, and arbitrary government would not remain confined to India but might serve to act as corrosive agents and weaken traditional liberties, values, and virtues within metropolitan society. As contemporaries developed a much fuller understanding of some of these unwelcome consequences of what was happening in the East, so they abandoned their initial hesitant and conservative approach to Indian affairs. Indeed, as crisis followed crisis, they became increasingly aware of the need to address the most fundamental question of all; that is, was the East India Company still the most appropriate vehicle for British administrative and commercial activity in India? The answers to this question were eventually to ensure that what began as a limited ministerial incursion into East India Company affairs during the 1760s became the full-scale Crown assumption of responsibility for the Indian Empire by 1813.

---

[3] Philip Lawson and Jim Phillips, ' "Our Execrable Banditti": Perceptions of Nabobs in Mid-Eighteenth-Century Britain', *Albion*, XVI (1984), pp. 225–41.

[4] For the concerns expressed about Britain's new Empire of conquest see P. J. Marshall, 'Empire and Authority in the Later Eighteenth Century', *Journal of Imperial and Commonwealth History*, XV (1987), pp. 105–22.

A number of factors dictated that, in the first instance, political responses to East Indian problems were limited in scope and ambition. First and foremost, at the time it became a territorial power during the mid-1760s, the East India Company operated within a framework determined by its long-standing role as a monopolistic trading organization. But in addition to the exclusive trading privileges that had been bestowed upon it by several royal charters since 1600, the Company also held the right to protect itself, wage war, and govern the small settlements granted to it by various Indian authorities. The Company had thus developed within a commercial environment in which its overseas presence was reinforced by the devolution of considerable local authority from the Crown, and this semi-autonomous position had been strengthened by the failure of successive generations of politicians to monitor British activity in India on a regular basis. Although in theory the sovereignty of the Crown was extended over the Company's possessions, the state had never declared any interest in assuming responsibility for the management of British affairs in India. Ministers knew little about India and they were quite happy to allow the Company's Directors to formulate general guidelines for commercial and administrative policy at the periphery.

These arrangements were deemed appropriate as long as the Company's ambitions were limited to trade for trade's sake. When, however, the Company took effective control of the provinces of Bengal, Bihar, and Orissa in 1765, following Lord Clive's acquisition of the *diwani* from the Mughal Emperor, Shah Alam II, it was acknowledged in some quarters that the relationship between the state and the Company needed to be redefined. As Clive had remarked to William Pitt in 1759 following initial British advances in Bengal: 'So large a sovereignty may possibly be an object too extensive for a mercantile company; and it is to be feared they are not of themselves able, without the nation's assistance, to maintain so wide a dominion.'[5] Many observers shared Clive's fears about the fragility of the British position in India, but few were prepared to endorse his view that a partnership of equals should be created between state and Company. Those with far less knowledge of India than Clive believed that there was no good reason for the state to intervene in affairs that had long been managed with some degree of success by the Company. Years later, Pitt the Younger was to adopt this stance when he contested the long-held view that 'commercial companies could not govern empires'.[6] He argued that this was 'a matter of speculation, which general experience proved to be not true in

---

[5] Clive to Pitt, 7 Jan. 1759, W. S. Taylor and J. H. Pringle, eds., *The Correspondence of William Pitt, Earl of Chatham*, 4 vols. (London, 1838–40), I, pp. 389–90.

[6] W. Cobbett, *The Parliamentary History of England from ... 1066 to 1803*, 36 vols. (London, 1806–20), XXIV, col. 1090.

practice, however universally admitted in theory'. More to the point, as Charles Townshend observed in 1767,[7] the state simply did not have the expertise or resources to tackle formidable administrative problems in such an unfamiliar and little-understood context, and this argument was often rehearsed in ministerial circles over the next thirty years or so.[8]

Initial reluctance to interfere in the affairs of the East India Company was also reinforced by the belief that the newly acquired territorial possessions in India represented a valuable asset which the Company was best placed to exploit in the national interest. By 1770 there was still widespread ignorance about many aspects of Indian society and culture, but informed opinion now recognized that the Company's overseas possessions were no longer distant Imperial outposts that contributed little to the well-being of the mother country. Since 1700 there had been a significant increase in the value of the British import and export trade with Asia,[9] and this was of great benefit to domestic consumers, manufacturers, and Company stockholders. It allowed the political economist Thomas Mortimer to declare in 1772 that the East India trade was now 'one of the chief sources of the power and commercial prosperity of Great Britain'.[10] More importantly, however, the military and political events that had taken place in Bengal during the mid-1760s had provided a golden opportunity to secure financial relief for a hard-pressed national exchequer. Clive's acquisition of large territorial revenues in 1765 transformed perceptions of the Indian Empire and acted as a spur to those who believed that the state had a 'right' to a share of those revenues, not least because the Crown had always been prepared to offer military and naval assistance to the Company in times of need.

In a first flush of ill-informed enthusiasm, it was perhaps understandable that politicians were misled by Clive's exaggerated claim that the Company would be able to secure an annual surplus of £1,500,000 from revenue collection. Yet, long after this level of profit had been shown to be unsustainable, leading figures in the Anglo-Indian world continued to believe that enormous riches could be secured from the Company's possessions in India. As late as 1802, and in the face of almost overwhelming evidence to the contrary, Lord Castlereagh, newly installed as President of the Board of Control, believed that an anticipated revenue surplus of £1,500,000 could be used to ease the Company's burden of debt and provide a

---

[7] Quoted in Sir L. Namier and J. Brooke, *Charles Townshend* (London, 1964), p. 161.

[8] See, for example, the comments made by John Robinson in an undated memorandum written in the late-1770s, B[ritish] L[ibrary] Add. MSS. 38398, f. 107.

[9] Ralph Davis, 'English Foreign Trade, 1700–1774', *Economic History Review* [hereafter *EcHR*] Second Series, XV (1962), pp. 300–03.

[10] T. Mortimer, *The Elements of Commerce, Politics, and Finance in Three Treatises on Those Important Subjects* (1772; London, 1780), p. 131.

donation of £500,000 to the public purse.[11] This type of wild estimate was roundly condemned by those who recognized the Company's shortcomings and, as the Whig MP George Tierney observed towards the end of the period, the reality of the situation was that 'Our Indian prosperity is always in the future tense'.[12]

As well as placing a certain amount of blind faith in the Company as a source of great national profit, many observers of East Indian affairs were united in the strong belief that the most important aspect of the Indian problem was that which centred on finding ways of consolidating the Company's position and maximizing the profits derived from revenue collection. As far as those in London were concerned, it became imperative that the Company dedicate itself to retrenchment and the peaceful cultivation of trade. Further territorial expansion would not only threaten the Company's strategic interests but divert revenue into military expenditure. 'Trade not conquest' became a general maxim. Moreover, because the Company had always managed to secure a reasonable rate of return from its imports of Asian goods, its commercial operations were regarded as the most appropriate mechanism for the transfer of surplus territorial revenues to Britain.

Endless thought was devoted to schemes designed to divert as much revenue as possible into the annual purchase of goods destined for London, and the Chairman of the Company, George Dudley, reminded Clive in 1766 of the need to 'take every measure in your power to put them [the revenues] into a flow of cash'.[13] The development of the Bengal silk industry, increased investment in piece goods, and the dramatic expansion of the China tea trade all represented important responses to this sort of exhortation. Particular attention was focused upon the tea trade because it was recognized that tea was a product much in demand by consumers at home. Funds derived from the Bengal revenues were pumped into Canton, where the Company purchased ever increasing quantities of tea destined for sale in London. At first this strategy proved unsuccessful, serving only to contribute to a deep crisis within the Company's finances during the early 1770s. Thereafter things improved, however, and, following the Commutation Act of 1784 which reduced the import duty on tea from 119 per cent to 12.5 per cent and dealt a heavy blow to smugglers, a restructured tea trade became an area of outstanding commercial success for the Company.[14] Sales of tea, which had averaged 6.8 million pounds a year during the 1770s, soared to 19.7 million pounds a year

[11] C. H. Philips, *The East India Company, 1784–1834* (Manchester, 1940), pp. 125–26.

[12] Quoted in ibid., p. 153. Tierney served as President of the Board of Control in 1806–07.

[13] National Library of Wales, Aberystwyth, Clive MSS, 52, p. 179.

[14] For the tea trade and the Company's financial crisis of 1772 see H. V. Bowen, *Revenue and Reform: The Indian Problem in British Politics, 1757–1773* (Cambridge, 1991), pp. 103–32. For changes in structure and the general importance of the tea trade after 1780 see J. R. Ward, 'The Industrial Revolution and

during the 1790s.[15] Not only did tea, along with cotton cloth, silks, and indigo, help greatly to enhance the position of Asia within the overall profile of the British import trade,[16] but it also played a part in further increasing public awareness of the importance of trading activity in the East.

The commercial initiatives developed during the 1760s all helped to blur the lines between the Company's role as a trading organization and its new function as an agency dedicated to the collection and transfer of revenue. Commercial operations were restructured within a much broader framework of economic considerations, a state of affairs acknowledged by the Bengal Council in 1769 when they observed to the Company's Directors that 'Your trade from hence may be considered more as a channel for conveying your revenues to Britain, than as only a mercantile system'.[17] Edmund Burke was quite correct when he later remarked that in 1765 'a very great Revolution took place in commerce as well as in Dominion'.[18] The nature and consequences of this commercial revolution were such that, in the short term at least, the Company's position was strengthened to quite a considerable degree. As revenue collection and territorial administration were added to commercial activity, it became clear to those in Britain that it would now be extremely difficult, if not impossible, to disentangle the different branches of the Company's operations. Defenders of the Company always made much of this point when responding to government proposals for reform,[19] and even those dedicated to the cause of radical change found that there was no easy solution to this problem. Charles James Fox conceded as much in July 1784, when he told the House of Commons that he had been thwarted in his recent attempt to find a way of 'separating the commerce from the revenue'. He had found that the 'revenue was absolutely necessary to the conducting of the commerce, and that the commerce was essential to the collecting of the revenue'.[20] This meant that any minister who wished to take responsibility for administration and revenue collection away from the Company would also be obliged to assume control of trade.

British Imperialism, 1750–1850', EcHR, Second Series, XLVII (1994), pp. 44–65. For a detailed study of the tea trade during the late eighteenth century see H. C. Mui and L. H. Mui, The Management of Monopoly: A Study of the East India Company's Conduct of its Tea Trade, 1784–1833 (Vancouver, 1984).

[15] Parliamentary Papers (1812–13), VIII, p. 233.

[16] Ralph Davis, The Industrial Revolution and British Overseas Trade (Leicester, 1979), pp. 44–6, 110–17.

[17] N. K. Sinha, ed., Fort William–India House Correspondence and Other Contemporary Papers Relating Thereto (Public Series), Vol. V, 1767–9 (New Delhi, 1949), p. 11.

[18] Reports from Committees of the House of Commons, 1715–1802, 15 vols. (London, 1803–06), VI, p. 54.

[19] See, for example, the reports of speeches made by George Johnstone and Hans Stanley in the House of Commons on 2 June 1773, BL, Egerton MSS, 249, pp. 136–37, 168.

[20] Cobbett, Parliamentary History, XXIV, col. 1128.

Apart from Fox, who believed that the better administration of India demanded that the state take 'the commerce as well as the government',[21] there were few politicians who were prepared to endorse any proposal that might be seen to form part of an assault on the Company's commercial privileges. Ministers always feared the accusation that they were seeking to seize the Company's power and patronage. Furthermore, now that the Company's trade served the important purpose of transferring revenue to Britain, it was difficult to support the anti-monopolist view that the Company did not act in the interests of the nation at large. From the 1760s, any compelling case against the Company would have to be extended beyond simple criticism of commercial practices and demonstrate that the establishment of revised trading arrangements would help to create a reliable channel through which revenue could be remitted to Britain from India. No such case was made before the 1790s and ministers were content to modify existing practices and structures in the hope that the East India Company might prove itself equal to the task with which it had been presented.

If the policy options of several generations of politicians were limited by their inability or unwillingness to see Britain's relationship with India in terms other than those broadly defined by the presence of the East India Company, they were also constrained by the narrow terms of political reference in which East Indian affairs were set during the 1760s. Discussion of the East India Company was seldom taken to represent an opportunity to address issues related to British activity in India; rather, attention was focused on metropolitan aspects of the Company's activities. Throughout the 1760s and 1770s most politicians studiously avoided any detailed consideration of events in India, and debate was instead located in familiar areas associated with chartered rights, high finance, and the informal 'management' of the Company in London.

This circumscribed state of affairs arose from the way in which William Pitt, now Lord Chatham, chose to launch the first ministerial intervention into East Indian affairs during his short-lived administration between 1766 and 1768. Although Chatham established a parliamentary inquiry, he was not concerned with the need to examine the way the Company conducted its activities in India. His aim was to secure a share of the Company's revenues for the state through a formal declaration of the British Crown's 'right' to those revenues. Once such a declaration had been made, the Company would be required to make an annual payment to the Treasury but would be left in place as the representative of British interests in India. This would limit government involvement in overseas affairs, and the Company would be free to proceed with the immediate task of maximizing revenue collection and stimulating trade. Such a policy had much to commend

[21] Ibid., col. 1129.

it to ministers who were seeking to avoid additional Imperial responsibilities, but it was soon revealed to be a most unsatisfactory way of proceeding. Chatham ignored the gathering public unease about the way in which recent events had unfolded in India, and he allowed debate about the Bengal revenues to develop into a controversial issue which inflamed political passions on all sides. Eighteenth-century politicians were always swift to move to the defence of property rights, and Chatham was widely perceived to be launching an attack which had the sole purpose of carrying off the Company's private wealth. This provided the Company, and Chatham's opponents, with firm ground on which to base a vigorous campaign against the government, and throughout the early part of 1767 the minister was embarrassed by dissent from within his Cabinet and close-run divisions in the House of Commons.[22]

Chatham, whose grip on affairs in 1767 was weakened by illness at a time when his ministry needed firm leadership, did eventually secure the financial prize he wanted. After lengthy and acrimonious negotiations, the Company agreed to pay £400,000 a year to the Treasury, and this sum was held to represent the state's share of the Bengal revenues. However, a heavy price was paid. In the short term the whole business dealt a significant blow to Chatham's ministry, but in the longer run several unwelcome East Indian legacies were bequeathed to later administrations. Most important of all, the legal status of the Company's possessions had not been clarified. Numerous assertions of the state's right to the Indian revenues had been made by ministers but these had not been supported in law or statute. Not surprisingly, Chatham's successors were reluctant to reopen such a difficult and contentious issue and they often restricted themselves to simple reassertions of the state's right to the revenues. No one was bold enough to secure a decisive resolution of the problem, and this meant that the East India business continued to be conducted in an atmosphere of confusion and uncertainty surrounding the legal status of British possessions in India.

There is little to suggest that ministers would have broadened the scope of their involvement in East Indian affairs had not various shortcomings in the Company's operations been exposed during the early 1770s. In the first instance, concern centred on the dramatic collapse of the Company's finances in 1772, which threatened the channel that had been established to transfer Bengal revenues to Britain. At the same time, however, persistent criticism of the conduct of Company servants suggested that urgent action was also needed to regulate various aspects of British activity in India. To assist with this process, two committees of inquiry were established in the House of Commons to review the recent history and current state of the Company's affairs. A Select Committee examined the

---

[22] This important episode is examined in Bowen, *Revenue and Reform*, pp. 48–66.

misconduct of leading figures in India, and public attention was captured by what an outraged Horace Walpole described as 'The iniquities of the East India Company and its crew of monsters'.[23] Newspaper readers were brought lurid accounts of crimes and details of corruption on an unimagined scale and, in an atmosphere of feverish excitement, the whole process of inquiry culminated in one of the most dramatic set-piece parliamentary occasions of the century, when Lord Clive survived a ferocious attack on him led by General John Burgoyne.[24] At the same time, however, a small, government-led Secret Committee was busy, well away from the limelight, compiling nine detailed reports on the Company's corporate affairs.[25] This committee did not make any recommendations, but the information contained in its reports helped ministers prepare their case as they endeavoured to establish new ground-rules for the relationship between Crown and Company.

At first Lord North, who had become First Minister in 1770, used formal and informal negotiations to encourage the Company to bring forward reform proposals in return for financial assistance from the state. But when well-organized opposition from within the Company and Parliament made it clear that ministers were unlikely to receive any wide-ranging proposals, North was forced to adopt a much harder line. The type of reform North had in mind became clear during a debate in the Commons on the ministry's Regulating Bill. In responding to Opposition charges that some of the clauses in the Bill, notably that relating to the Crown appointment of judges in a new Supreme Court of Bengal, would give the ministry 'full and absolute power over the possessions of the Company', he stated that 'I have a direct, declared, open purpose of conveying the whole power [and] management of the East India Company directly or indirectly to the Crown'. Company territory, he argued, would be 'better administered by the Crown that is so ill administered by Directors incapable of governing it'.[26]

In the event, in spite of strong words spoken in the heat of debate, the ministry was forced away from the direct management of Company's affairs and, as far as British territory in India was concerned, this meant that general supervision rather than close control became the main feature of state involvement. At first sight, this is rather surprising. North's public stance on the matter had been unequivocal,

---

[23] Walpole to Sir Horace Mann, 4 Nov. 1772, W. S. Lewis, ed., *The Yale Edition of Horace Walpole's Correspondence*, 48 vols. (Oxford, 1939–84), XXIII, p. 441.

[24] Sir George Forrest, *The Life of Lord Clive*, 2 vols. (London, 1918), remains the best biography of Clive. For a modern biography of Clive which contains an account of the proceedings against him, see Mark Bence-Jones, *Clive of India* (London, 1974).

[25] The reports of Select and Secret Committees are to be found in *Reports from Committees of the House of Commons*, III and IV.

[26] BL, Egerton MSS, 249, pp. 84–86.

and the ministry's numerical position in both Houses of Parliament was such that it could have pressed ahead with a much more radical solution to the Indian problem. On closer inspection, however, a simple reason explains why North's settlement eventually proved to be limited in scope and ambition. Neither the question of the state's right to a share of the Bengal revenues nor that of Crown possession of Company territory had been resolved, and this meant that no formal transfer of responsibility from Company to Crown could be contemplated. Again, confusion had reigned on this matter. Ministers had repeatedly asserted Crown rights and, during proceedings related to the conduct of Lord Clive, the House of Commons had resolved that 'all acquisitions made under the influence of a military force or by treaty with foreign princes, do of right belong to the state'.[27] It was widely believed that this expression of parliamentary opinion ensured, in Horace Walpole's words, that 'the sovereignty of three imperial vast provinces [was] transferred from the East India Company'.[28] This, however, did little to clarify the situation. Many legal uncertainties still existed but, more to the point, the Company's financial crisis was now so acute that North was forced to give up hope of the state receiving any of the Company's profits in the immediate future. In effect, this represented a temporary suspension of the Crown's claim to a share of the Bengal revenues, and North used this to wring important concessions from the Company. As far as he was concerned, the whole question of sovereignty would be resolved once and for all when the Company's charter was renewed in 1780.

If this rather tame conclusion to the East India business of 1773 suggests that North had exercised undue caution when dealing with the Indian problem, it must be remembered that many contemporaries believed that he had been bold and innovative. Although his first concern had been to bring financial stability to the Company, he had accepted some degree of responsibility for ensuring that future British conduct in India would be well ordered and held to account. Thus, in addition to the Loan Act (13 Geo. III, c. 64), North's Regulating Act (13 Geo. III, c. 63) incorporated a number of measures designed to effect closer ministerial supervision of Company affairs, both at home and abroad. In a domestic context, successful attempts were made to eliminate abuses within the Company's electoral system and improve continuity in executive decision-making, and both of these reforms facilitated the exertion of ministerial influence over the Company. As far as the Company's position in India was concerned, North sought to separate commercial affairs from those of an administrative and judicial nature. The Governor of Bengal, Warren Hastings, was given authority over all the Company's

---

[27] *Commons Journals*, XXXIV, p. 308.

[28] A. Francis Stuart, ed., *The Last Journals of Horace Walpole during the Reign of George III from 1771 to 1783*, 2 vols. (London, 1910), I, p. 201.

possessions in India, thus becoming Governor-General, and he was supported by four councillors appointed by the Crown and the Company. A Supreme Court was established in Calcutta, where it was presided over by a Chief Justice and three judges appointed by the Crown. All of these high-ranking officials were paid generous salaries in the hope that they would not be drawn into commercial activity, and a number of regulations prohibited Company servants from involvement in private trade or receiving 'presents' from Indians. In order to ensure that all these measures had the desired effect, ministers were to review all incoming Company despatches from India. Critics argued that these measures vested a considerable amount of power and patronage in Crown hands, and many felt that North had dealt a heavy blow to the Company's long-standing rights and privileges. For his part, North believed that much work still needed to be done, and there is no doubt that he saw the Regulating Act as only the first step in the extension of formal government control over the East India Company. George III concurred, if only because he believed that 'new abuses will naturally be now daily coming to light, which in the end Parliament alone can in any degree check'.[29]

In theory, North's measures marked a significant advance towards Crown control over British India, but in practice his system soon ran into unforeseen difficulties. North had seen his settlement as being a short-term measure that would be reviewed in 1780, but the outbreak of war with America in 1775 meant that ministers were unable to devote time and energy to detailed consideration of East Indian affairs. Some thought was given to the management of the Company at home, but the problems related to the Indian Empire were put to one side as the struggle with the American colonies gathered pace. This was unfortunate, because it was at this moment that a number of widely reported episodes heightened public concern about the manner in which British affairs were being conducted in India. As the Select Committee of the House of Commons was to report in 1783, 'during the whole period that elapsed from 1773 to the commencement of 1782, disorders and abuses of every kind multiplied'.[30] Warren Hastings came under fire for his style of government and the ambitious 'schemes of conquest' that informed his actions during the Maratha War (1775–82); scandal surrounded the deposition and subsequent death of the Governor of Madras, Lord Pigot, in 1777; an enormous amount of attention was devoted to the fierce controversy surrounding huge debts owed by the Nawab of Arcot to a number of British creditors; and the outbreak of the Second Mysore War in 1780 seemed to threaten the Company's

---

[29] The King to North, 11 June 1773, Sir John Fortescue, ed., *The Correspondence of George III from 1760 to 1783*, 6 vols. (London, 1927), II, p. 501.

[30] *Reports from Committees of the House of Commons*, VI, p. 53.

position in southern India, not least because it offered the French an opportunity to re-establish their influence in the region.[31]

In different ways, reports of each of these episodes created unease in Britain about the effects that Company policy was having upon the security and good government of British India. Critics condemned the pursuit of an aggressive military strategy, not simply because it was dangerous but because it diverted the Company's attention away from commercial activity. Henry Dundas, the rising Scottish politician who was becoming an expert on India, observed in the House of Commons in April 1782 that, 'As matters stood, military exploits had been followed till commercial advantages were in danger of being lost'.[32] With Warren Hastings in mind, he then reminded the House that no Company servant had the 'right to fancy he was an Alexander, or an Aurengzebe, and prefer frantic military exploits to the improvement of the trade and commerce of the country'. In the economic sphere, Company policies were depicted as an annual plunder that was draining the wealth of Bengal.[33] Specific initiatives, such as the creation of monopolies, were singled out for special criticism, and so helped to fuel human-itarian concern about the lot of the 'unhappy native'. The Company had always professed its desire to protect the happiness and prosperity of the Indian popula-tion, but in the 1770s and 1780s there were few signs that this was being achieved. Instead, extortion, oppression, and poverty were widely believed to represent common experiences for those who lived under the Company's rule, and numer-ous commentators expressed their dismay at actions carried out in the name of Britain in India. For some, such as Edmund Burke, British misrule represented a form of despotism that had destroyed the very fabric of the Indian economy and society.[34] Burke, who in earlier years had applauded the spectacular military and political advances made by Clive in Bengal, now stood forward as the self-appointed guardian of the nation's moral conscience on Indian affairs. He became the principal figure in a relentless campaign waged in Parliament against Warren Hastings, and he secured a spectacular short-term victory in 1787 when, amid great public excitement, the former Governor-General was sent for trial in the House of Lords. Although interest in the impeachment proceedings was soon to diminish, and Hastings's ordeal was to drag on until he was eventually acquitted in 1795,

[31] For the Maratha and Mysore Wars see above, pp. 518–20. The complicated story of the origins of the Nawab of Arcot's debts and his relations with the Company is recounted in detail in J. D. Gurney, 'The Debts of the Nawab of Arcot, 1763–1776', unpublished D.Phil. thesis, Oxford, 1968.

[32] *Parliamentary Register*, VIII (1782), p. 32. Dundas failed in his attempt to have Hastings recalled from India.

[33] See the Select Committee's observations on this in 1783, *Reports from Committees of the House of Commons*, VI, pp. 54–56.

[34] See, for example, Burke's speech on Fox's India Bill reprinted in *The Writings and Speeches of Edmund Burke*, vol. V, P. J. Marshall, ed., *Madras and Bengal 1774–1785*, (Oxford, 1981), pp. 380 451.

Burke's initial success represented yet another manifestation of widespread concern about the unwelcome effects of British rule in the East.[35]

By the beginning of the 1780s other aspects of the British relationship with India were also being reassessed. Thus far, few of the promised material benefits had been realized, and the East India Company was again showing signs of running into serious financial difficulties. George Johnstone, an MP, who was armed with a deep knowledge and understanding of East Indian affairs, even went as far as to question the accepted view of Clive's actions during the 1760s, when he asserted that 'the territories we acquired through him had done a greater injury than a benefit to us'.[36] Such uncertainties did not bode well for a nation already in the process of having to come to terms with the loss of the North American colonies. As Pitt the Younger remarked in 1784, the importance of India 'had increased in proportion to the losses sustained by the dismemberment of other great possessions',[37] and this only increased the pressure on ministers to find a more effective way of exploiting British resources in the East. At the same time, there were plenty of critics who now subscribed to the view that territorial conquest and the suppression of native peoples were damaging Britain itself. The riches of the East were thought to be having a debilitating effect on British virtue and moderation, and it was believed that corrupt practices imported by 'nabobs' from India were infecting the domestic political system and threatening constitutional liberties. In particular, it was feared that resources were being channelled into ambitious political schemes that would exert a corrupting 'East Indian' influence in the House of Commons. Chatham had made this point as early as January 1770, when he warned the House of Lords that 'The riches of Asia have been poured in upon us, and brought with them not only Asiatic luxury, but, I fear, Asiatic principles of government'.[38] He and many others believed that the fabric of the British constitution was being eroded by the way in which 'the importers of foreign gold have forced their way into Parliament, by such a torrent of private corruption, as no private hereditary fortune could resist'. The threat was serious enough when former Company servants were involved, but another dimension was added to the problem in the early 1780s when rumours began to circulate that the Nawab of Arcot was exerting direct influence over six or seven MPs in a campaign designed to secure the support of the House of Commons against

[35] For an account of the proceedings against Hastings see P. J. Marshall, *The Impeachment of Warren Hastings* (Oxford, 1965). See also Geoffrey Carnall and Colin Nicholson, eds., *The Impeachment of Warren Hastings: Papers from a Bicentenary Commemoration* (Edinburgh, 1989).

[36] *Parliamentary Register*, VIII (1782), p. 37 (speech of 9 April 1782).

[37] Cobbett, *Parliamentary History*, XXIV, col. 1086.

[38] *Chatham Correspondence*, III, p. 405.

scheming creditors.[39] For many the danger was clear: if left unchecked, despotism in the East would create despotism in Britain itself.

All of these concerns informed the belief expressed by William Pitt in the mid-1780s that the future of the Indian Empire was now a problem containing several main elements: 'In it were involved the prosperity and strength of this country; the happiness of the natives of those valuable territories in India which belonged to England; and finally the constitution of England itself.'[40] Against this background of changing perceptions, it was clear that North's settlement of 1773 had not gone far enough. A fresh round of inquiry and reform began during the first half of the 1780s, and on this occasion attention was focused on the situation in India itself. In February 1781 a Select Committee of the House of Commons was established to examine the administration of justice in Bengal. The following December, however, the brief of the Committee, the proceedings of which were dominated by Edmund Burke, was extended to a consideration of 'how the British Possessions in the East Indies may be governed with the greatest Security and Advantage to this Country, and by what Means the Happiness of the Natives may be best promoted'.[41] Standing alongside the Select Committee was a Secret Committee of the House of Commons, chaired by Henry Dundas, which had been appointed in April 1781 to enquire into the causes of the Mysore War and the condition of British possessions in southern India. Its terms of reference were also extended in December 1781, when it was ordered to investigate the 'rise, progress, conduct and present state of the Marratta War, and all other hostilities in which the Presidency of Bengal now are, or have been, engaged . . .'[42] Detailed reports from the committees made it quite clear that the government could no longer stand back from direct intervention in the Company's overseas affairs. Indeed, some of the measures implemented by the Directors since 1773 were regarded as a 'total failure', not least because those responsible for implementing Company policy in India had often disobeyed or ignored orders from London.[43] As the full extent of the problem was revealed, few disinterested observers dissented from the King's gloomy view that 'the whole conduct of the Company both at home and abroad must end in destruction if not greatly changed'.[44]

In the wake of the collapse of Lord North's administration in 1782, ministers came and went as the King searched for a stable government. Each short-lived

[39] Jim Phillips, 'Parliament and Southern India, 1781–3: The Secret Committee of Inquiry and the Prosecution of Sir Thomas Rumbold', *Parliamentary History*, VII (1988), p. 84.

[40] Cobbett, *Parliamentary History*, XXIV, col. 1086.

[41] *Commons Journals*, XXXVIII, pp. 599–600.

[42] Ibid., p. 600.

[43] *Reports from Committees of the House of Commons*, VI, pp. 47–48.

[44] The King to Lord North, 5 Aug. 1781, *Correspondence of George III*, V, p. 261.

ministry considered proposals for the better management of British India, but reform of the Company became caught up in the cut-and-thrust of factional politics, and it was not until William Pitt established his ministry during the first half of 1784 that political conditions allowed for the implementation of measures designed to put Crown–Company relations on a new footing. There was broad agreement among politicians about the general form that the redefinition of the Anglo-Indian Imperial connection should take. If there was still a great reluctance to take responsibility for local administration in India out of the Company's hands, it was now deemed to be a matter of some urgency to extend formal state control over the general management of British Indian affairs. Leading politicians had been moving in this direction since 1778, when North's 'man of business' John Robinson had drafted a discussion paper recommending such action,[45] and a start had been made in 1781 when the government had used the opportunity presented by the renewal of the Company's charter to begin the regular scrutiny of the Company's out-letters to India. It did this, however, without creating any specialist administrative machinery for such a task, and ministers were only granted limited powers to revise the contents of Company orders.[46] It was left to Pitt's India Act of 1784, which was based in large part on a bill drafted by Dundas the previous year, to create a Board of Commissioners, comprising six Privy Councillors, charged with the task of reviewing and revising the Company's despatches. The political climate, tactical considerations, and stubborn resistance from the Company ensured that Pitt did not go as far as Charles James Fox and Edmund Burke, who had drafted two bills of a much more radical nature in 1783,[47] would have liked. Nevertheless, the India Act did grant the commissioners, who were soon known as the Board of Control, effective responsibility for the development of policy for all civil, military, and revenue matters in India. The line was drawn, however, at encroachment on to the Company's primary administrative functions, and prevailing commercial and patronage arrangements were left untouched. Pitt argued that the Company's affairs 'were not in a state that called for the revocation of the charter', and he, like many others, still adhered to the belief that the situation in India could be greatly improved through a strengthening of existing arrangements.[48] Ministers contented themselves with increasing the authority of the Governor-General, both within the Supreme Council and over the subordinate presidencies. At the same time, though, restrictions were imposed on the Governor-General and his Council by a clause in the Act which prohibited

[45] BL, Add. MSS, 38398, ff. 108–17.

[46] Under the terms of 21 Geo. III, c. 65 ministers were only permitted to amend the parts of despatches relating to external affairs.

[47] These bills are printed in Cobbett, *Parliamentary History*, XXIV, cols. 62–89.

[48] Ibid., cols. 1087–89 (quotation on 1087).

engagement in any form of offensive warfare. Among a host of minor clauses, the power of Company stockholders to influence decision-making was significantly reduced, and inquiries were launched into several aspects of recent events and mismanagement in India.

Pitt's Act was not without its weaknesses, and contemporary critics complained that it served only to strengthen the power of a delinquent executive in India. More generally, however, the Company's trading and revenue activities remained tightly interwoven and this meant that ministers, despite claims to the contrary, were obliged to involve themselves in matters related to the development of commercial policy. This was resisted by the Company, and relations with the government were soured further by uncertainty over demarcation in the lines of authority between the Board of Control and the Court of Directors. Early tension was caused by a series of disputes over ministerial interference in what many in the Company believed were matters related to internal affairs and patronage.[49] Not only did this mean that the terms of the new relationship had to be clarified in a Regulating Act of 1786 and a Declaratory Act of 1788, but Henry Dundas, who served as the influential first President of the Board of Control between 1784 and 1801, still needed to devote plenty of attention to the maintenance of ministerial influence within the Company's Court of Directors. From the government's point of view, however, the India Act represented a reasonably successful attempt to eradicate some of the failings of the system established by North in 1773. In spite of early difficulties, Crown–Company relations were generally easy and co-operative as they were recast on a more formal basis after 1784. Ministers were now committed to regular and detailed consideration of the development of policy for India. This occurred in the regular meetings of the Board of Control, and the much closer supervision of Indian affairs was symbolized by the presentation of an annual Indian budget to Parliament after 1788. By the 1790s there was broad agreement that the new measures had brought the Company's servants under control, and it was believed that, coupled with military success, they had also promoted stability and prosperity in territories now described as 'national' concerns in India. In 1793 Dundas believed that he was in a position to report to the House of Commons that 'The British possessions compared with the neighbouring states in the peninsula are like a cultivated garden compared with the field of the sluggard'.[50]

Once the government had gained the upper hand in relations between the state and the East India Company, attention could be devoted to a broad range

---

[49] See, for example, Court of Directors to the Board of Control, 2 Nov. 1784, Oriental and India Office Collections, E/2/1, f. 24.
[50] Cobbett, *Parliamentary History*, XXX, col. 602.

of theoretical and practical issues related to the question of the future role to be played by the Company in India. Of course, pragmatic reaction to events on the subcontinent still largely dictated the course taken by political developments, but those in government were now in a much stronger position to develop the Indian Empire along lines demanded by opinion in Britain. This permitted consideration of issues that had once been regarded as beyond discussion, and several long-held assumptions about the Anglo-Indian connection were brought into question between 1784 and 1813. As attempts were made by Dundas to bring the Company's decision-making processes and bureaucratic structures in line with the responsibilities associated with the management of extensive overseas territory, thought was devoted to the question of whether or not the government should consider taking primary administrative functions in India into its own hands. At the same time, the structure and form of the East India trade was re-examined amidst growing concern that the Company was no longer capable of meeting the demands placed upon it by the nation's economic needs.

There can be little doubt that Dundas made a serious attempt to get at the heart of the East Indian problem. While much of his time as President of the Board of Control was taken up with matters of detail, he undertook a thorough review of the arrangements underpinning the British position in India. At times he was inclined to consider taking territorial responsibilities away from the Company,[51] but practical considerations and legal problems always persuaded him that such a decisive move was simply not possible. His attempt to remove the Company's political authority through a declaration of the Crown's sovereignty over all British possession in India came to nothing,[52] and in 1793 he conceded that, as far as claims to the territorial revenues were concerned, there was still 'room for much legal discussion on this subject'.[53] Dundas was also frustrated in his attempts to discover how the Company's commercial and administrative roles could be separated, and he was forced to concur with the opinions of those, such as Lord Cornwallis, the Governor-General from 1786 to 1793, who argued that expediency alone dictated that the Company should be left intact.[54] Thus, when the renewal of the Company's charter was discussed once more in 1793, Dundas put any doubts about the East India Company to one side and declared that he saw no reason why an extensive empire could not be governed by a body of merchants. His conclusion was that in the circumstances it 'is safer to rest on the present system, which

---

[51] See e.g. P. J. Marshall, *Problems of Empire: Britain and India, 1757–1813* (London, 1968), pp. 43–44.

[52] Philips, *East India Company*, p. 49.

[53] Cobbett, *Parliamentary History*, XXX, col. 663.

[54] Philips, *East India Company*, p. 72.

experience has rendered practicable, than to entrust myself to theories, about which ingenious and informed men have not agreed'.[55]

Twenty years later, when the Company's charter was renewed once more, these arguments still held sway in official circles. The exigencies of a wartime situation ensured that little serious discussion was devoted to consideration of the Company's political power and administrative functions, and in 1813 the existing arrangements were extended for another twenty years. Almost as an apologetic afterthought, however, a clause was inserted into the Charter Act (53 Geo. III, c. 155) which asserted the Crown's 'undoubted sovereignty' over all the Company's territories. This declaration carried weight not only because it found expression in statute but because no one could possibly deny that it was an accurate reflection of the political situation in India. By 1813 it was clear that each stage of the Company's advance had seen the reduction of the authority and influence of local rulers, and Mughal sovereignty had long been regarded as little more than a fiction supported only by those who defended the Company's right to the territorial revenues. As far as the British were concerned, the Charter Act simply tied up a legal loose end by adding the *de jure* sovereignty of the Crown to the *de facto* sovereignty that had long been exercised by the Company.

If political events between 1784 and 1813 did little to disturb the Company's administrative and political position in India, the same cannot be said of the legislative arrangements that defined the nature of the British commercial presence on the subcontinent. Men such as Sir William Pulteney, the back-bench MP, who argued in 1801 that 'the character of traders and sovereigns are inconsistent',[56] could have pointed to many administrative shortcomings in the British Indian Empire, but most critics were more concerned about the Company's conspicuous failure to adapt to the new economic conditions that had been created during the 1760s. Attempts to transfer the revenue surplus to Britain had not only been unsuccessful, but they had led to the abandonment of commercial principles as the Company attempted to keep its annual purchase of India and China goods at an artificially high level. Burke's Select Committee had condemned this in no uncertain terms in 1783, stating that the 'Principles and Oeconomy of the Company's Trade' had been 'completely corrupted by turning it into a vehicle for Tribute'.[57] With the Company still struggling to secure a surplus from its revenues, it was now necessary once more to 'fix its commerce upon a commercial basis'. At the same time, with more attention also being focused upon India as an export market, there was a growing feeling beyond London that the Company was not

---

[55] Cobbett, *Parliamentary History*, XXX, col. 666.

[56] Ibid., XXXVI, col. 282.

[57] *Reports from Committees of the House of Commons*, vol. VI, p. 60. For the Company's trade between 1765 and 1813 see Marshall, *Problems of Empire*, pp. 78–101.

serving the needs of those members of the wider manufacturing and merchant community who wished to become involved in the India trade. Statutory obligations had long required the Company to export a certain amount of manufactured goods each year, but this had done little to appease those who demanded direct access to Indian markets.[58] Yet commercial pressure from the outports, even when reinforced by the arguments of political economists and propagandists who depicted the India trade as a 'losing trade',[59] stood little chance of success as long as the Company's commercial operations were regarded as a channel for the flow of revenue from the East. As spiralling civil and military costs in India served to reduce that flow to a trickle, however, those in government became increasingly willing to acknowledge the force of arguments in favour of establishing alternative arrangements for the conduct of British trade with India. By the 1790s responses to pressure from non-Company British merchants in India and manufacturing interests in Britain itself reflected the fact that the Company's commercial privileges were no longer regarded as sacrosanct.

The first breach of the Company's monopoly occurred in 1793. Dundas had long interested himself in schemes designed to boost the Company's trade, and he had also considered plans to effect the transfer of revenue from India in the event of the Company losing its monopoly.[60] He still regarded the Company as a 'most safe vehicle' for the transfer of revenue to Britain, but he was prepared, by way of an experiment, to 'engraft an open trade upon the exclusive privilege of the Company'.[61] Accordingly, under the terms of the Charter Act (33 Geo. III, c. 52) the Company was obliged to provide space on board its ships for the export and import of 3,000 tons of goods a year provided by private individuals. The creation of this 'regulated monopoly' marked a significant concession to commercial pressure but, as Dundas observed, 'in an age of enterprise and improvement, men are unwilling to hear of constraints'.[62] Few in Britain or India were satisfied with the new arrangements, and it soon became clear that the next renewal of the charter would provoke another campaign against the Company's monopoly. This campaign was fought out with ever increasing levels of intensity after the turn of the century and, although rhetoric on all sides drew on familiar arguments that had been deployed in previous debates, it became clear that new battle-lines had been drawn up. It was now widely recognized that there was much more to the

---

[58] For statistical analysis of British exports and re-exports to India during this period see Davis, *The Industrial Revolution*, pp. 88–97, 102–05.

[59] This phrase was used by the anonymous author of the pamphlet *An attempt to Pay Off the National Debt and Other Monopolies With Other Interesting Measures* (London 1767), p. 20.

[60] Philips, *East India Company*, p. 48.

[61] Cobbett, *Parliamentary History*, XXX, cols. 674, 683.

[62] Ibid., col. 661.

issue than the preservation of the 'remittance trade' in the hands of the Company, and this reflected the growing political strength of those who wished to export a greater volume of goods to India. In the short term, the final decision to open the India trade in 1813 was based in part upon the government's wartime need to secure supplies of precious raw materials from India,[63] but the gradual build-up of pressure from the provinces had served to undermine the defences that had long protected the Company's privileged position. For fifty years it had been held that the national interest demanded the preservation of the Company's monopoly. Now, however, it was argued that the nation's interests were best served by open trade rather than tribute, and this reappraisal of the economic connection between Britain and India meant that the Company's commercial privileges could be sacrificed. Although the Charter Act preserved the Company's monopoly of the China trade, British merchants and manufacturers were granted free access to Indian markets.

During the half-century following Clive's assumption of the *diwani* on behalf of the East India Company in 1765, the political, legal, and commercial contours of Britain's Indian Empire were redrawn. This reflected both the transition that had been made from commercial to territorial empire in Asia and, more generally, the exertion of increasing levels of metropolitan authority and control that had taken place across the wider British Empire during the final quarter of the eighteenth century.[64] Yet reform did not belong to any grand Imperial design or project. Rather, it emerged from a series of pragmatic responses to the very serious shortcomings that had become evident within the East India Company at home and abroad. If by the end of the period the Company still remained in place as a powerful administrative and military agency in its own right, the government had assumed direct responsibility for the management and supervision of the territories under British control. Ministers now fully acknowledged their duty to protect a national asset as well as the population living under Company rule. Although effective control of events at the periphery still lay well beyond those in London, the authorities had, through a process of trial and error, created the administrative and legislative machinery that would ensure that the Indian Empire would now carry a much heavier imprint of prevailing metropolitan attitudes, ideas, and wishes.

By 1815 observers of Imperial affairs were stressing the importance of the Empire of the East within an interlinking global network of British commercial and strategic interests. Recent events in the wars against France had highlighted this

---

[63] Anthony Webster, 'The Political Economy of Trade Liberalization: The East India Company Charter Act of 1813', *EcHR*, Second Series, XLIII (1990), pp. 404–19.

[64] On control and authority in the Empire see C. A. Bayly, *Imperial Meridian: The British Empire and the World, 1780–1830* (London, 1989), pp. 100–32.

when a 'swing to the east' in overseas military and naval operations had secured the elimination of French influence in India[65] and the considerable enhancement of British influence, power, and resources.[66] Partly because of this, the metropolitan uncertainties and anxieties about the Indian Empire that had been so evident during the 1770s and 1780s were gradually replaced by a general sense of optimism about the future. Secure in the knowledge that some of the worst aspects of unregulated British rule had been removed, commentators returned once more to consideration of the value of India as an economic prize. Reformed revenue and commercial systems were held to offer the prospect of a broad range of direct and indirect benefits being channelled into metropolitan society.[67] Such was the combined weight of these benefits that most contemporaries would now have offered an unequivocal endorsement of the view that India had now become 'one of the brightest jewels in the British Crown'.

---

[65] See above, pp. 195–203.
[66] See, for example, Patrick Colquhoun, *Treatise on the Wealth, Power, and Resources of the British Empire, in Every Quarter of the World, Including the East Indies*, 2nd edn. (London, 1815), App. p. 43.
[67] Ibid., App. p. 44.

Select Bibliography

PETER AUBER, *An Analysis of the Constitution of the East-India Company* (London, 1826).

G. D. BEARCE, *British Attitudes towards India, 1784–1858* (Oxford, 1961).

H. V. BOWEN, *Revenue and Reform: The Indian Problem in British Politics, 1757–1773* (Cambridge, 1991).

JOHN BRUCE, *Historical View of the Plans for the Government of British India* (London, 1793).

S. V. DESIKA CHAR, ed., *Readings in the Constitutional History of India, 1757–1947* (Oxford, 1983).

PHILIP LAWSON, 'Parliament and the First East India Inquiry, 1767', *Parliamentary History*, I (1982), pp. 99–114.

——and JIM PHILLIPS, '"Our Execrable Banditti": Perceptions of Nabobs in Mid-Eighteenth-Century Britain', *Albion*, XVI (1984), pp. 225–41.

P. J. MARSHALL, *The Impeachment of Warren Hastings* (Oxford, 1965).

—— *Problems of Empire: Britain and India, 1757–1813* (London, 1968).

—— 'Empire and Authority in the Later Eighteenth Century', *Journal of Imperial and Commonwealth History*, XV (1987), pp. 105–17.

——and GLYNDWR WILLIAMS, *The Great Map of Mankind: British Perceptions of the World in the Age of Enlightenment* (London, 1982).

C. H. PHILIPS, *The East India Company, 1784–1834* (Manchester, 1940).

JIM PHILLIPS, 'Parliament and Southern India, 1781–3: The Secret Committee of Inquiry and the Prosecution of Sir Thomas Rumbold', *Parliamentary History*, VII (1988), pp. 81–97.

L. S. SUTHERLAND, *The East India Company in Eighteenth-Century Politics* (Oxford, 1952).

ANTHONY WEBSTER, 'The Political Economy of Trade Liberalization: The East India Company Charter Act of 1813', *Economic History Review*, Second Series, XLIII (1990), pp. 404–19.

25

The Pacific: Exploration and Exploitation

GLYNDWR WILLIAMS

The British arrival in the Pacific in the second half of the eighteenth century was the result of both official and unofficial enterprise. Government was involved, but not consistently; science was represented, notably through the Royal Society; commercial interests became increasingly active; publishers brought out accounts of the voyages; and among individual explorers a naval officer, James Cook, stood supreme. The resources allocated to oceanic exploration were small; but in a region as remote from the main centres of European rivalry as the Pacific they were enough to establish a significant British presence by the end of the century.

European vessels had ventured into the Pacific from the early sixteenth century; but their wanderings were for the most part inconclusive and confusing. The prodigious size of an ocean which covered a third of the globe's surface, imperfect methods of navigation, the ravages of scurvy, and the confines of wind and current presented daunting obstacles to the methodical accumulation of knowledge by Europeans of so distant a region. Knowledge there was, but it was unrecorded, at least in a form recognizable to outsiders. Long before Magellan's ships entered the Pacific in 1520 many of its 25,000 or so islands had been subject to a steady process of exploration, migration, and settlement.[1] Slowly European seamen began to appreciate the achievement of Polynesian navigators, but it took the drawing for Cook in 1769 of a chart by Tupaia from the Society Islands before there was wider recognition of this. The chart showed seventy-four islands scattered across an area of ocean measuring 3,000 miles from east to west, and 1,000 miles from north to south. It was, one of Cook's scientists said, 'a monument of the ingenuity and geographical knowledge of the people in the Society Islands'.[2]

---

[1] See Andrew Sharp, *Ancient Voyagers in the Pacific* (Harmondsworth, 1967) and *Ancient Voyagers in Polynesia* (Auckland, 1963); David Lewis, *We, the Navigators: The Ancient Art of Landfinding in the Pacific*, 2nd edn. (Honolulu, 1994).

[2] Nicholas Thomas and others, eds., *Observations Made during a Voyage round the World* [by Johann Reinhold Forster] (1778; Honolulu, 1996), pp. 310–11; Tupaia's original has disappeared, but Cook's copy of the chart, and the engraved version, have been reproduced many times. See, for example, Andrew David, ed., *The Charts and Coastal Views of Captain Cook's Voyages*, Vol. I, *The Voyage of the Endeavour, 1768–1771* (London, 1988), pp. 130, 132.

By the mid-seventeenth century Europe's process of Pacific exploration had almost halted. To the north Japan had been crudely charted by the Dutch, but the ocean to the north and east remained unexplored. The Pacific coast of Spanish America was known only as far as California, and what lay in the colossal space, 5,000 miles across, between there and the eastern fringes of Asia was a mystery. It might contain ocean or land, a bridge between continents, or the entrance of the North-west Passage. To the south, vessels following the diagonal course of the prevailing winds between Cape Horn and New Guinea, or sailing out of Spanish ports in Peru or Chile, had come across some island groups, but their exact position and extent were often conjectural. In particular, it was not certain whether they were the outliers of a great southern continent—*Terra Australis Incognita*—lying just over the horizon, and perhaps encompassing those stretches of the coasts of New Holland (Australia) and New Zealand revealed by Dutch expeditions.[3]

English seamen had played a minor role in these undertakings. English interest in the Pacific was mainly predatory. Since Drake's circumnavigation of 1577–80, the Pacific had caught the English imagination not as a vast, trackless ocean but as the western rim of Spain's American empire. The 'South Sea' which by the late seventeenth century began to exercise its grip over distant enterprises was confined, in English eyes, to the waters which lapped the shores of Chile, Peru, and Mexico, the hunting grounds of the buccaneers. Exploration was not high among their priorities—'Gold was the bait that tempted a Pack of Merry Boys of us', one of them wrote[4]—but their exploits proved of unending interest to the reading public at home. Prominent among them was William Dampier, an assiduous observer and writer who ventured to New Holland and other areas on the very periphery of Europe's knowledge. His *New Voyage Round the World* of 1697 was reprinted, anthologized, and translated, and in 1699 brought him command of a naval discovery expedition (in itself a rarity). Although this was the year when the long-impending crisis over the Spanish Succession and the future of Spain's overseas empire broke over Europe, there is no evidence that Dampier's voyage represented any serious thrust of national policy. The decision to explore the region around New Holland and New Guinea seems to have been Dampier's rather than the government's, as he responded to an Admiralty request 'to make a proposal of some voyage wherein I might be serviceable to my Nation'.[5] In the

[3] See O. H. K. Spate, *The Pacific Since Magellan*, Vol. I, *The Spanish Lake* (Canberra, 1979), Vol. II, *Monopolists and Freebooters* (London, 1983).

[4] Philip Ayres, *The Voyages and Adventures of Captain Bartholomew Sharp...* (London, 1684), preface. The best study of the English in the South Sea is Peter T. Bradley, *The Lure of Peru: Maritime Intrusion into the South Sea, 1598–1701* (London, 1989), esp. chaps. 5–8.

[5] The main documents about the voyage are printed in John Masefield, ed., *Dampier's Voyages*, 2 vols. (London, 1906), II, pp. 325–30.

event, despite the discovery east of New Guinea of 'New Britain', the voyage was a troubled one which ended in court-martial for Dampier, but as an Admiralty venture of oceanic exploration it was a precedent.

The voyages of Dampier and the privateers such as Woodes Rogers and George Shelvocke who came after him provided more in the way of popular reading-matter than of geographical and mercantile information. After the financial disaster of the 'South Sea Bubble' in 1720 the Pacific dropped out of the reckoning as a sphere of British enterprise for twenty years, though it retained its lure for compilers of the newly fashionable collections of 'Voyages and Travels', and for writers such as Defoe and Swift looking for a safe haven in which to pitch their satires. It was in the final chapter of *Gulliver's Travels* that Swift launched an attack on travel accounts and, more portentously, on the whole process of European overseas discovery. Later in the century such sentiments would be commonplace; in the England of the 1720s they were still novel.

A crew of pirates are driven by a storm they know not whither, at length a boy discovers land from the topmast, they go on shore to rob and plunder; they see an harmless people, are entertained with kindness, they give the country a new name, they take formal possession of it for the King, they set up a rotten plank or a stone for a memorial, they murder two or three dozen of the natives, bring away a couple more by force for a sample, return home, and get their pardon. Here commences a new dominion acquired with a title by *divine right.*[6]

Not until the imminence of war with Spain in 1739 were new Pacific schemes officially considered again. The next year Commodore George Anson's squadron of six ships sailed for Cape Horn and the South Sea on a voyage which left few survivors, but which was saved from total disaster by the capture of the Acapulco treasure galleon off the Philippines. It took thirty-two wagons to carry the silver from Portsmouth to London after Anson's return, and newspaper accounts and individual narratives of the voyage quickly followed. Other publications considered the wider implications of Anson's expedition. The first volume of John Campbell's mammoth collection of voyages and travels advocated the establishment of two Pacific bases, one at Dampier's New Britain, the other on Juan Fernández. Both were well placed, Campbell pointed out, for the exploration and exploitation of the great southern continent. 'It is impossible', argued Campbell, 'to conceive a Country that promises fairer from its Situation, than this of *Terra Australis*...whoever perfectly discovers & settles it will become infallibly possessed of Territories as Rich, as fruitful, & as capable of Improvement, as any that have been hitherto found out, either in the East Indies, or the West.'[7]

---

[6] Jonathan Swift, *Gulliver's Travels* (1726; Harmondsworth, 1967), p. 343.

[7] John Campbell, ed., *Navigantium atque Itinerantium Bibliotheca: or, a Compleat Collection of Voyages and Travels*, 2 vols. (London, 1744–48), I, esp. pp. 65, 325, 328, 331–32, 364–65.

In 1748 the long-awaited official account of Anson's voyage appeared, and was in its fifth edition by the end of the year. It was more than a tale of treasure-seeking on the high seas, though this no doubt was the main reason for its popularity. At another level it was intended to encourage 'the more important purposes of navigation, commerce, and national interest', and with Anson now achieving a dominant position in naval affairs, the opinions expressed in the book were of weightier interest than usual. The Introduction stressed the value of accurate charts, global recordings of magnetic surveys, and proper surveys taken from naval vessels.[8] Despite such exhortations, and the fact that by 1751 Anson was First Lord of the Admiralty, the navy failed to establish any specialist surveying service, or even a hydrographic office on the French model to supervise the publication of charts.

Even so, the proposals for bases in the South Atlantic and South Pacific represented a new turn in British policy, and for a moment appeared to be bearing fruit. Early in 1749, the first year of peace, a naval expedition was prepared for the Falklands, Juan Fernández, and beyond—only to be cancelled after strenuous Spanish protests. The concept of the Pacific as a Spanish lake died hard at Madrid, and the anxiety of the British government not to upset the negotiations in progress on the *Asiento* led it to concede the point—'for the present', and without giving up the 'Right to send out Ships for the discovery of unknown and unsettled Parts of the World'. What Benjamin Keene, Britain's special envoy to the Spanish government, called 'their whimsical notions of exclusive rights in those seas' were to be respected, at least for the time being.[9]

The 'Right to send out Ships' to the Pacific was not to be exercised for another fifteen years, as the approach of global conflict with France turned the attention of the government elsewhere. On the conclusion of peace in 1763 official discovery expeditions were mounted in both Britain and France, with the secrecy of their instructions a sign of continuing rivalry. To some the Pacific, and especially the still-undiscovered southern continent, promised resources of such potential that its exploitation might tip the colonial balance of power. Geographers from the two countries continued to correspond, and British and French explorers would meet and part amicably enough; but beneath the exchanges of mutual compliments national rivalries ran deep and strong.

In 1764 the first discovery expedition of George III's reign, commanded by John Byron, sailed for the Pacific. It was less a precursor of the celebrated voyages to

[8] Glyndwr Williams, ed., *A Voyage Round the World... by George Anson* [by Richard Walter and Benjamin Robins] (1748; London, 1974), pp. 14–18.

[9] The key documents relating to the planned 1749 expedition are in S[tate]P[apers] 94/135, ff. 177–78, 265–72.

come than a throwback to earlier ventures. It was the abortive 1749 expedition writ large, and represented the bringing together of the plans of earlier generations. 'Trade and navigation' were to be the chief beneficiaries; Drake and Dampier were the forerunners; the Falkland Islands and (more tenuously) the North-west Passage were the objectives; of science there was no mention.[10] Byron, on a record-breaking circumnavigation, followed the usual route across the Pacific west-north-west from the Strait of Magellan, and so made no discoveries of note. But while sailing through the northern fringes of the Tuamotu Archipelago in June 1765 he was convinced that there was a land mass not far to the south, probably the great continent,[11] and this was worked into the instructions of the expedition which followed Byron's, that of Captain Samuel Wallis and Captain Philip Carteret. 'There is reason to beleive [sic] that Lands, or Islands of great extent, hitherto unvisited by any European Power may be found in the Southern Hemisphere between Cape Horn and New Zealand, in Latitudes convenient for Navigation, and in Climates adapted to the product of Commodities usefull in Commerce.'[12]

Carteret proved an enterprising commander, and crossed the Pacific farther south than any other explorer had done, so lopping off a slice of the supposed southern continent. Wallis, by contrast, showed little initiative in his track across the Pacific, but his voyage was marked by a chance discovery which had a double significance, for in June 1767 he sighted Tahiti. It was an encounter which was to stamp an imprint both exotic and erotic upon Europe's image of the South Sea, and when a French expedition under Bougainville reached the island the following year reactions were even more effusive. Less publicized was the sighting by the master on Wallis's ship of the tops of mountains sixty miles south of Tahiti, which could only be part of the southern continent.[13] Just as Byron's illusory sense of a land mass to his south had influenced the direction of the Wallis and Carteret expedition, so this imagined sighting two years later was to play its part in the next Pacific voyage, for when Wallis arrived back in May 1768 he found another discovery expedition in preparation.

This, to begin with at least, was different from its predecessors, for its immediate objective was scientific. It was to answer the request of the Royal Society that the Admiralty should send a ship to the South Pacific to observe the Transit of Venus in 1769. As preparations continued, so the novelty of the venture became apparent. To the necessary astronomers were added other civilians—scientists and artists. It

---

[10] For Byron's instructions see Robert E. Gallagher, ed., *Byron's Journal of his Circumnavigation, 1764–1766* (Cambridge, 1964), pp. 3–9.

[11] Ibid., p. 105.

[12] Helen Wallis, ed., *Carteret's Voyage Round the World, 1766–1769*, 2 vols. (Cambridge, 1965), II, p. 302.

[13] Hugh Carrington, ed., *The Discovery of Tahiti* (London, 1948), p. 4.

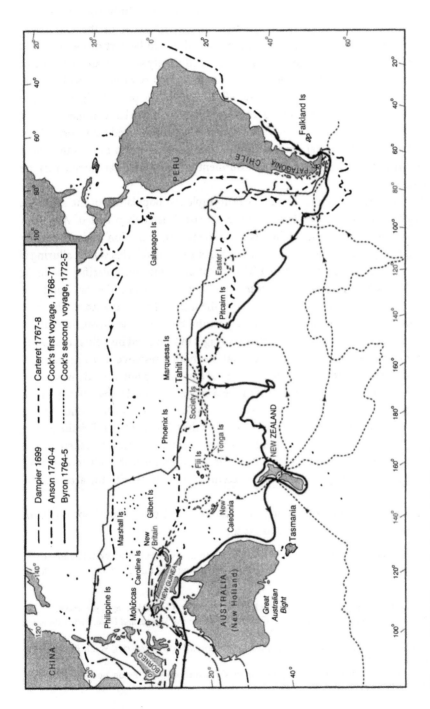

Map 25.1. British Voyages in the South Pacific, 1699–1775

was they, particularly the young and well-connected botanist Joseph Banks, who attracted attention, rather than the unknown commander of the *Endeavour*, Lieutenant James Cook. The expedition seemed not to be part of the sequence of Pacific ventures, for it was not in genesis an Admiralty venture, and had little to do with affairs of state. The change came with the return of Wallis, with official news of the discovery of Tahiti and unofficial news of the possible sighting of the continent nearby. So the second part of Cook's instructions left considerations of science, and returned to the more familiar themes of trade and navigation. After completing astronomical observations at Tahiti Cook was to sail south, where 'there is reason to imagine that a Continent or Land of great extent, may be found'.[14]

For enthusiasts such as Alexander Dalrymple the population of the southern continent might be 50 million or more, its size greater than that of Asia, and 'scraps' from its trade enough 'to maintain the power, dominion, and sovereignty of BRITAIN by employing all its manufactures and ships'.[15] This was an alluring if distant prospect, but to insist that 'Upon that area [the South Pacific] the main drive of national policy was concentrated'[16] is to overstate the case, and the influence of the geographical theorists of the age. Although the Admiralty now saw seaborne exploration as one of its responsibilities, there was no official master-plan of Pacific discovery into which the voyages of Cook and his colleagues neatly fit. More realistically, it can be argued that the modest resources of ships and men committed to Pacific exploration represented a promising but limited investment. If a great southern continent existed, or a navigable North-west Passage, then Britain should make the discovery since it would redound 'to the honor of this Nation as a Maritime Power, to the Dignity of the Crown of Great Britain, and to the advancement of the Trade and Navigation thereof'.[17] If not, then there would be other, perhaps lesser, returns: the training of seamen; the advancement of science; the matching of the nation's recent wartime feats with the accomplishments of peace.

Shortly before the *Endeavour* sailed, the President of the Royal Society, Lord Morton, appealed to Cook and Banks for

the utmost patience and forbearance with respect to the Natives of the several Lands where the Ship may touch . . . To have it still in view that sheding [*sic*] the blood of those people is a

---

[14] J. C. Beaglehole, ed., *The Voyage of the Endeavour, 1768–71* (Cambridge, 1955), p. cclxxxii.

[15] Alexander Dalrymple, *An Historical Collection of the Several Voyages and Discoveries in the South Pacific Ocean*, 2 vols. (London, 1770–71), I, p. xxix.

[16] Vincent T. Harlow, *The Founding of the Second British Empire, 1763–1793*, Vol. I, *Discovery and Revolution* (London, 1952), p. 38.

[17] To repeat the standard wording of explorers' instructions from Byron onwards. This from Gallagher, *Byron's Journal*, p. 3.

crime of the highest nature: They are human creatures, the work of the same omnipotent Author, equally under his care with the most polished European; perhaps being less offensive, more entitled to his favor. They are the natural, and in the strictest sense of the word, the legal possessors of the several Regions they inhabit. No European Nation has a right to occupy any part of their country, or settle among them without their voluntary consent.[18]

Cook's instructions had already advised him that he should obtain 'the Consent of the Natives' before taking possession, but they also reminded him that Wallis had found them 'to be rather treacherous than otherwise'. In general terms Cook was 'to observe the Genius, Temper, Disposition and Number of the Natives'.[19] This latter was easier said than done. Not only was there no fundamental similarity of language and custom among the peoples of the three great divisions of the Pacific—Polynesia, Melanesia, and Micronesia—but in the period before the development of the disciplines of ethnology and anthropology there was no accepted method of classification of human societies. Europeans were entering a region where, after successive migrations, and a seeping of culture influences from one island group to another, societies were organized in a series of overlapping layers—quite baffling to untrained observers. Comprehension was made more difficult by the strained nature of the contact. The Pacific navigators of the period were for the most part moderate and humane, certainly by earlier standards. Even so, the Europeans were intruders, emerging by the score from their great vessel anchored in some island bay, 'men from the sky', appearing and disappearing without warning, often violating sacred sites. An inescapable tension hung over the encounters, sometimes dissipated by individual contacts or trade, but at other times erupting into violence. Though the relationship between Polynesians and Europeans was not the one-sided affair of some portrayals, in the longer term the introduction of venereal disease, alcohol, and firearms brought a depressing train of consequences to the islands—sickness, demoralization, and depopulation.[20]

Cook's first voyage was a sign of things to come. With only one ship, he charted more than 5,000 miles of previously unknown coastline. The twin islands of New Zealand, the east coast of Australia, and Torres Strait at last emerged from the mists of uncertainty. As he reached land uncharted and unvisited by Europeans, so Cook followed his instructions and took possession. That part of his instructions advising him to do this with the consent of the natives was less diligently observed.

---

[18] Beaglehole, *Voyage of the Endeavour*, p. 514.

[19] Ibid., pp. cclxxx, cclxxxiii.

[20] For contrasting interpretations of the contact process, see Alan Moorehead's popular, cataclysmic account, *The Fatal Impact: An Account of the Invasion of the South Pacific, 1767–1840* (London, 1966), and K. R. Howe's more balanced study, *Where the Waves Fall: A New South Sea Islands History From First Settlement to Colonial Rule* (Sydney, 1984).

In January 1770 he claimed possession of Queen Charlotte Sound in New Zealand after a rather inadequate explanation to a small group of Maoris that the posts and flags were being erected 'to shew to any ship that might put into this place that we had been here before'.[21] In August at Cape York Cook annexed the whole of the east coast of Australia from lat. 38°S. on the grounds, as later explained, that it was *terra nullius*, 'no person's land'.[22] As far as the southern continent was concerned, Cook reached lat. 40°S. without sighting land, and noted that the long ocean swell rolling up from the south-east argued against the existence of any land mass in that direction.

On Cook's return the First Lord of the Admiralty, the Earl of Sandwich, took steps to encourage early publication of the journals of the voyage. Banks had argued for this in order to pre-empt French claims, while Cook was emphatic that his and earlier journals should be 'published by Authority to fix the prior right of discovery behond [*sic*] dispute'.[23] The task was entrusted to Dr John Hawkesworth, who fused the individual journals of Cook and Banks into a single narrative to make the *Endeavour* expedition the resounding climax to his three-volume *Voyages* of 1773, which also included the accounts of Byron, Wallis, and Carteret. The hue-and-cry which followed Hawkesworth's editorial methods has obscured the essential point that all the major discovery journals of the reign had been published with official approval and backing. A precedent had been set which would be difficult to reverse.[24]

Cook's second voyage was the logical complement to what had been explored, and left unexplored, on his first. It took place in a context of some diplomatic sensitivity, for both France and Spain had ships out; and there is some evidence that only Sandwich's 'perseverance' prevented cancellation of the expedition.[25] Again there were naturalists (not Banks this time, but Johann Reinhold Forster and his son George), astronomers, and an artist. The novelties of 1768 were becoming standard practice. And, arguably as important as any of the human supernumaries, there were on board for the first time chronometers, one of which was Larcum Kendall's copy of John Harrison's masterpiece, his fourth marine timekeeper. This superb instrument kept accurate time through the buffeting of the long voyage, to show that the problem of determining longitude at sea had at

---

[21] Beaglehole, *Voyage of the Endeavour*, p. 242.

[22] See Alan Frost, 'New South Wales as *Terra Nullius*: The British Denial of Aboriginal Land Rights', *Historical Studies*, XIX (1981), pp. 513–23.

[23] Beaglehole, *Voyage of the Endeavour*, p. 479.

[24] On Hawkesworth and his *Voyages* see John L. Abbott, *John Hawkesworth: Eighteenth-Century Man of Letters* (Madison, 1982), esp. chap. 7.

[25] J. C. Beaglehole, ed., *The Voyage of the Resolution and Adventure, 1772–1775* (Cambridge, 1961), p. 9.

last been overcome. In his three years away Cook disposed of the imagined southern continent, reached closer to the South Pole than any man before him, and touched on a multitude of lands—New Zealand and Tahiti again, and for the first time Easter Island, the Marquesas, Tonga, and the New Hebrides. Almost all had been sighted by earlier expeditions; even in the conventional definition Cook did not 'discover' them for Europe. His contribution was to bring a sense of order to the confusion of the earlier maps and reports, to replace vagueness and uncertainty with a new, pin-point accuracy. There was, he judged, little more to do in the South Pacific: 'The Southern Hemisphere sufficiently explored and a final end put to the searching after a Southern Continent, which has at times ingrossed the attention of some of the Maritime Powers for near two Centuries past and the Geographers of all ages.'[26] On his two voyages he had established the framework of the modern map of the South Pacific: Polynesia and southern Melanesia; New Zealand and New South Wales; Torres Strait and the southern extremities of the great ocean. All this was set out in Cook's splendid account, published in 1777, with some help from Dr John Douglas, *A Voyage Towards the South Pole, and Round the World.*

Cook was never to see his book, for in 1776 he left again for the Pacific on his third and final voyage. This time he was headed for the northern expanses of the ocean in an effort to solve that other long-standing geographical mystery—the existence of a North-west Passage. Once again, the Royal Society was prominent in applying pressure on the Admiralty for the voyage, but Spanish suspicions that there was more to the British swing north than scientific curiosity may have been justified. The year in which war with the American colonies broke out would not appear to be a time when the Admiralty could easily spare for a scientific mission even the three smallish ships it intended to send to the Pacific and (as a support operation) to Baffin Bay. The attempts by the British government to establish a base in the Falklands from 1766 had shown its interest in securing an entrance into the Pacific. It may have been more than a coincidence that the decision to send a naval expedition to look for the North-west Passage was made in the same year (1774) as the enforced abandonment of Port Egmont in the Falklands, one of the conditions for ending the Anglo-Spanish crisis over the islands of 1770–71. The discovery of a northern route to the Pacific might compensate for the loss of control over the longer southern one, and if one were not found then there still might be attractive commercial possibilities in Japan and neighbouring lands.[27]

[26] Ibid., p. 643.
[27] See Howard T. Fry, 'The Commercial Ambitions Behind Captain Cook's Last Voyage', *The New Zealand Journal of History*, VII (1973), pp. 186–91.

In the end Cook found no North-west Passage as he spent the summer of 1778 in hazardous exploration along the broken coastline of North-west America, from Nootka Sound to Bering Strait. In a single season he put the main outline of that coast on the charts, determined the shape of the Alaskan peninsula, and closed the gap between the Spanish coastal probes from the south and those of the Russians from Kamchatka. It was to be his last achievement, for in February 1779 he was killed at Hawaii, the northernmost outlier of Polynesia, unexpectedly encountered by the expedition only the year before. Cook's death at Kealakekua Bay on 14 February 1779 remains a source of fascination and controversy. During the preceding weeks Cook seems to have been regarded by the islanders as the god Lono, bringer of light, peace, and plenty: his escort of priests, the abasement before him of the people, and the protection of the expedition's equipment and stores by the imposition of a *tabu* all indicate this. Some scholars have stressed the series of coincidences which marked the arrival of Cook's ships off Hawaii. It was the time of *makahiki*, the festival of Lono; and the ships with their masts and sails mirrored Lono's iconography. Their slow circuit around Hawaii resembled the annual procession on land in honour of Lono, and their destination was Kealalekua Bay, the site of Lono's temple. Cook continued to conform to sacred tradition by leaving Hawaii as *makahiki* came to an end: the new season was devoted, more ominously, to Ku, the god of war. But when damage to the *Resolution* forced Cook back to the bay a few days later he was out of season, a violator of sacred customs. In the eerie atmosphere of uneasiness which followed, Cook's death at the hands of the islanders was predictable, if not pre-ordained. Not all accept this interpretation. Some scholars insist that Cook's 'deification' is the invention of western, imperialist tradition, and that the initial enthusiasm which greeted him simply represented an attempt to enlist the support of this powerful outsider in inter-island warfare. They explain Cook's death by what they see as his irrational behaviour and uncontrollable outbursts of temper.[28]

News of the killing of Europe's greatest navigator at Kealakekua Bay over-shadowed all other reports from the expedition when it reached England. It brought into sharper focus a conflict of attitudes about the peoples of the Pacific which had developed both among the discovery crews and among the scholars of Europe. To those who had seen the islands, Tahiti and its neighbours seemed at first earthly paradises, but closer acquaintance showed that there was shade as well

---

[28] The episode of Cook's death has served as a launch-pad for scholars interested in the wider implications of Europe's arrival in Polynesia. See Marshall Sahlins, *Islands of History* (Chicago, 1985), esp. chap. 4, and *How 'Natives' Think—About Captain Cook for Example* (Chicago, 1995); Bernard Smith, *Imagining the Pacific: In the Wake of the Cook Voyages* (New Haven, 1992), esp. chap. 10; Gananath Obeyesekere, *The Apotheosis of Captain Cook: European Mythology in the Pacific* (Princeton, 1992).

as light—there was war, infanticide, distinctions of rank and property. The death of Cook, following as it did the massacre of one of his boat crews in New Zealand in 1773, and the killing of the French navigator Marion du Fresne and two dozen of his men not far away a year earlier, together with suspicions of cannibalism among the Maori, were signs to some of an innately treacherous and murderous disposition. Others saw in the islands traces of a golden age, and feared that it was European influences which were corrupting and contaminating. More dispassionate observers were influenced by the fashionable insistence in European philosophical circles on measuring human societies by their capacity and desire for improvement; and they found few Pacific peoples who conformed to western ideals of progress and development.[29]

It was Cook's third voyage, with John Webber as the expedition's artist, which produced the fullest account and illustrations of the Pacific peoples. Scholars who see the lavish official accounts of Cook's voyages as part of a humanizing myth which concealed their rough reality can point to the way in which Webber's set-piece paintings and drawings mostly depicted friendly encounters. Receptions, entertainments, ceremonies, loom large—rather than the clashes which became a depressingly familiar feature of the voyage. This selectivity raises large questions about the value-laden nature of visual representation, and the extent to which the recording of native peoples was a form of cultural appropriation; but to see Cook's artists merely as facilitators of imperialist dominance would be crude and misleading. One of the constraints imposed on ethnographic drawing was that its subjects could not, like some natural history specimen, be pinned to a board. Their co-operation and trust had to be obtained, and the nature of the cultural contact between them and the artist was different from the more fleeting trading or sexual encounters with his shipmates. Yet if the artist represented the soft edge of the contact process, behind him stood the threat of force, of marines, muskets, and great guns. So Webber's celebrated painting of Poedua, daughter of the chief of Raiatea, was probably done during the tense five days that father and daughter were held hostage by Cook.[30]

Although Cook set new standards in the extent and accuracy of his surveys, to see his voyages simply in terms of the accumulation of hydrographical and geographical knowledge would be to miss their broader significance. There was a new methodology, European rather than exclusively English in scope, but shown most clearly in Cook's voyages. His three successive expeditions helped to lift him above other explorers in both official and popular esteem. Bougainville cut a

[29] This paragraph contains a compressed version of the writer's arguments as set out in P. J. Marshall and Glyndwr Williams, *The Great Map of Mankind: British Perceptions of the World in the Age of Enlightenment* (London, 1982), chap. 9.

[30] See Smith, *Imagining the Pacific*, chap. 8.

striking figure among the ranks of Cook's contemporaries, but he never returned to the Pacific after his voyage of 1766–69. His immediate successors, Surville and Marion du Fresne, were lesser figures; while the great French expedition of the late 1780s, that of La Pérouse, vanished without trace. There was a dominance, though by no means a monopoly, of British accounts and charts of the Pacific; and this had come about partly by policy, partly by chance. At the Admiralty Sandwich set the precedent of encouraging prompt and full publication of the discovery journals, whereas other European governments were less committed. In the 1790s Vancouver's record of his voyage to the north-west coast of America was published; the contemporary Spanish surveys of the same region were not. The Spanish expedition of Malaspina (1791–95) was probably the best-equipped of all the eighteenth-century survey ventures, but its findings disappeared into the archives when Malaspina fell from grace after his return to Spain.

So, much was left to Cook, though in many ways he was representative rather than unique in his insistent determination to show things as they were, to dispel myth and illusion by way of empirical observation and prompt publication. The observations made by Cook and his associates played an important role in astronomy, oceanography, meteorology, linguistics, and much else. In the realm of natural history the voyages were among the great collecting expeditions of any era. The amount of material brought back simply could not be assimilated by the older encyclopaedic sciences. Nowhere was this more evident than in the study of the peoples of the Pacific. It was the voyages of Cook and his contemporaries which helped to give birth in the next century to the new disciplines of ethnology and anthropology; for the earnest inquiry by the explorers into the exotic life-styles which confronted them, and their painstaking if uninformed collection of data, brought a new urgency to the need for a more systematic study of humankind.

In more practical ways, too, Cook set new standards. His achievements would not have been possible without healthy crews, and his record here was impressive, especially in the second voyage. There were no recorded deaths from scurvy on any of his voyages, and (except for a disastrous stay at Batavia in 1770, which helped to produce a final mortality rate of 43 per cent on the *Endeavour*) few from natural causes generally. Much research had gone into the causes of scurvy since Anson lost three-quarters of his men on his circumnavigation of 1740–44, notably by James Lind at the Haslar Naval Hospital. He had discovered, or rather rediscovered, the antiscorbutic properties of lemon juice. Paradoxically, Cook's success in keeping his crews alive delayed the acceptance of this remedy for scurvy, for although he used lemon juice he attributed no particular importance to it. What was unusual about Cook was the thoroughness with which he applied a whole range of antiscorbutic measures. Uncertain of the causes of scurvy, Cook combined all suggested remedies. It was, one medical historian has commented, 'a blunderbuss approach to antiscorbutic treatment'.[31]

Even so, as the contributor to a medical journal of the time noted, Cook had 'proved to the world the possibility of carrying a ship's crew through a variety of climates, for the space of near four years, without losing one man by disease; a circumstance which added more to his fame, and is supposed to have given a more useful lesson to maritime nations, than all the discoveries he ever made.'[32] This was but one aspect of the way in which Cook, in Bernard Smith's words, became 'a new kind of hero for a new time'. It is illustrated in Philip Loutherbourg's design for *The Apotheosis of Captain Cook*, published as an engraving in 1794, in which Cook is shown ascending into the clouds after his bloody death at Kealakekua Bay holding in his hand, not a sword, but a sextant. It was an image of the hero particularly appealing to the next century when, to follow Smith's argument further, Cook's achievements were well suited 'to the ideological belief—however distant from the true state of affairs—in a world-wide empire dedicated to the arts of peace (a *Pax Britannica*), not one based upon war'.[33]

If on his three voyages Cook had established the main features of the Pacific, much remained to be done, though rather in the way of detailed surveying than in solving fundamental geographical problems. Dr Douglas, editor of the journals of Cook's third voyage, pointed the way forward to the next stage of Pacific enterprise when he wrote in his Introduction that 'every nation that sends a ship to sea will partake of the benefit [of the published accounts]; but Great Britain herself, whose commerce is boundless, must take the lead in reaping the full advantage of her own discoveries'.[34] By the end of the century there were British settlements in New South Wales; Nootka had taken on a new significance—no longer Cook's watering place on the north-west coast of America but a centre of international dispute; the first missionaries had reached Tahiti, Tonga, and the Marquesas; and everywhere the traders and whalers were beginning to follow the explorers' tracks. With the change from exploration to exploitation came a change of government agency. The Admiralty gave way to departments more closely concerned with trade and colonies. In the 1780s the ministry most involved was the Home Office, whose functions rather incongruously included oversight of Britain's overseas possessions. There was also a change of personalities, for Sandwich resigned in 1782 as the

[31] James Watt, 'Medical Aspects and Consequences of Cook's Voyages', in Robin Fisher and Hugh Johnston, eds., *Captain James Cook and His Times* (Vancouver, 1979), p. 135.

[32] Quoted ibid., p. 129.

[33] Bernard Smith, 'Cook's Posthumous Reputation', in ibid., pp. 168, 175, 177.

[34] James Cook and James King, *A Voyage to the Pacific Ocean...* 3 vols. (London, 1784), I, Introduction [by John Douglas].

American war dragged to its close, and none of his immediate successors showed his commitment to exploration. If there was a single guiding light in the new surge of oceanic endeavour which followed Cook's voyages, it was Joseph Banks. The young naturalist of Cook's first voyage was now one of the most influential men in England: baronet, President of the Royal Society, adviser of Cabinet ministers, patron of the sciences on an international scale. He was an assiduous promoter of enterprises associated with Cook's explorations, and although the new Pacific voyages were more practical and commercial than scientific, Banks seemed to be involved at every turn.[35] It was Banks who, in 1787, was responsible for the despatch of William Bligh to Tahiti to collect breadfruit plants for Britain's West Indian colonies. There, it was hoped, their cultivation would provide cheap food for the slave population. The first attempt at this scheme, characteristic of the global dimension of Banks's projects, was frustrated by the high drama of the mutiny on the *Bounty*.

The South Pacific after Cook was reached simultaneously by settlers and whalers. Cook's favourable report of 1770 on New South Wales (as transmitted by Hawkesworth) was enhanced by Banks's recollection in 1785 that the land at the *Endeavour*'s first landing spot at Botany Bay was 'sufficiently fertile to support a considerable number of Europeans', and that the 'very few' Aborigines there would no doubt 'speedily abandon the Country to the New Comers'.[36] As Evan Nepean, the official most concerned with the settlement, wrote, New South Wales 'appears to be a Country peculiarly adapted for a Settlement, the Lands about it being plentifully supplied with Wood and Water, the Soil rich and fertile, and the Shores well stocked with Shell and other Fish'.[37] This may have been enough to prompt the government to choose Botany Bay as the new site for convicts who previously would have been transported to the American colonies. Less-publicized reasons may also have played a part: the possibility of developing Botany Bay as a base strategically situated on the south or 'blind' side of the Dutch East Indies; the hope of producing naval stores in the form of timber and flax; the necessity of a preventive strike to stifle French moves towards the region.[38] The First Fleet itself, two warships, six transports, three storeships, represented in terms of organization and successful accomplishment of its mission eighteenth-century government at

[35] See H. B. Carter, *Sir Joseph Banks, 1743–1820* (London, 1988) and, more specifically, David Mackay, *In the Wake of Cook: Exploration, Science and Empire, 1780–1801* (London, 1985). See above, pp. 243–44.

[36] H[ome] O[ffice] 7/1 (10 May 1785—no page numbers).

[37] HO 100/18, pp. 369–70.

[38] A long-running debate has taken place among historians on this issue. Some of the main contributions are Ged Martin, ed., *The Founding of Australia* (Sydney, 1978); Alan Frost, *Convicts and Empire: A Naval Question, 1776–1811* (Melbourne, 1980) and *Botany Bay Mirages: Illusions of Australia's Convict Beginnings* (Melbourne, 1994); David Mackay, *A Place of Exile: The European Settlement of New South Wales* (Melbourne, 1985).

its best, rather than (as some historians have maintained) at its worst.[39] The same cannot said of its immediate successors. Despite the poor health of some of the convicts on embarkation, out of 756 adult convicts who sailed from Spithead in the spring of 1787 only thirty-three died on the voyage of more than eight months.

Whalers were among the transports of the First Fleet which arrived at Botany Bay in January 1788, and of subsequent convict fleets. Once released from their transportation duties, they turned to the quest for the great sperm whales of the southern seas, whose oil was more highly valued than that of the 'right' whales of the traditional Greenland fishery. In 1786 an Act for 'The Encouragement of the Southern Whale Fishery' had been passed which marked the beginning of the British fishery in the southern oceans, and of a running tussle with the monopoly rights of the East India Company, whose Directors were fearful that 'the Pacific was the back door to the Indian Ocean and the China Seas and Cook had undone the lock'.[40] Gradually the Company's efforts to limit the whalers' legal areas of operation in the South Seas were beaten down by a combination of government and mercantile pressure, and whalers entered the great ocean both round the Horn and by way of the Cape of Good Hope. By 1790 there were fifty British whalers fitted out for the southern oceans, and within three years this number had almost doubled. A new lure was the fur seal, whose pelt was easily saleable at Canton, and whose southern locations—from South Georgia in the South Atlantic to Dusky Sound in New Zealand—had been identified by Cook on his second voyage.[41]

For the convicts, who, with their guards, were landed at Botany Bay in January 1788, the first years under the command of Governor Arthur Phillip were ones of hardship, sometimes of despair. Nothing was as anticipated. Botany Bay in the heat of midsummer bore little resemblance to the descriptions of May 1770, after the autumn rains had filled the creeks and brought a lush covering of grass. Add also that the bay was shoal water, dangerously exposed to the east, and one can understand why Phillip decided to look for another site. At Port Jackson he found the incomparable harbour where 'a thousand sail of the line may ride in the most perfect security', and moved the settlement to Sydney Cove.[42] If it was a safer anchorage for ships, the mixed community of convicts and their guards seemed little better off. 'Their situation', Phillip wrote after six months, was 'so very

---

[39] On this generally see Roger Knight, 'The First Fleet: Its State and Preparation, 1786–1787', in John Hardy and Alan Frost, eds., *Studies from Terra Australis to Australia* (Canberra, 1989), pp. 121–36.

[40] Vincent T. Harlow, *The Founding of the Second British Empire, 1763–1793*, Vol. II, *New Continents and Changing Values* (London, 1964), p. 305.

[41] See Margaret Steven, *Trade, Tactics and Territory: Britain in the Pacific, 1783–1823* (Melbourne, 1983), chaps. 4, 5.

[42] For more on the first weeks see Frost, *Botany Bay Mirages*, chap. 4; and Glyndwr Williams, 'The First Fleet and After: Expectation and Reality', in Tony Delamothe and Carl Bridge, eds., *Interpreting Australia* (London, 1988), pp. 24–40.

different from what might be expected.' There were huge problems in clearing the ironbarks and redbarks, scurvy had taken a grip, 'the natives are far more numerous than they were supposed to be', and regular food supplies from Britain would be needed for some time to come.[43]

Only with the move inland to the fertile soil of Parramatta and then towards the Hawkesbury river did matters improve, but before that New South Wales had to endure its equivalent of the 'starving time' of earlier North American colonizing ventures. The death of most of the livestock, crop failures, the non-appearance of the promised second expedition in 1789, reduced the settlement to a desperate state. If the worst was over after the arrival of the Second Fleet in mid-1790, there were still hardships and worries to come, but by the time of Phillip's departure at the end of 1792 the future of the young colony seemed assured. There were 2,500 colonists, and settlement had spread on to the Cumberland Plain; 1,200 government acres under crops (and some private farms); sheep, cattle, pigs, and horses. In 1792 officers of the garrison (the New South Wales Corps) were allowed to receive land-grants, and from 1795 free settlers began to arrive in a small trickle. Port Jackson became a calling-place for whalers and sealers, and in other ways too the maritime activities of the little colony were in the early years more striking than its slow expansion on land. Although the barrier of the Blue Mountains hampered interior exploration, seaborne surveys were mounted both from the colony and from Europe. By the early years of the nineteenth century the discovery by George Bass and Matthew Flinders of Bass Strait, and the wider-ranging surveys by Flinders in the *Investigator* and by the French expedition under Nicolas Baudin, had completed the coastal outline of most of the continent. Flinders, in his letters and published *Voyage* of 1814, referred to the continent as 'Australia', and in 1817 Governor Macquarie adopted the title in the hope that it would become 'the Name given to this Country in future'.[44]

Among the problems Phillip left behind was that of relations with the Aborigines. Precisely what was to be the status of the Aborigines in and around the new settlement had never been clear. The instructions given to Phillip were well-meaning but imprecise: 'to open an intercourse with the natives, and to conciliate their affections, enjoining all our subjects to live in amity and kindness with them.'[45] The first contacts seemed peaceable enough, but soon the Aborigines were showing signs of fear and hostility as Phillip's orders to treat them well were ignored by ships' crews and convicts alike. Soon a pattern had emerged of mutual

---

[43] For Phillip's comments in this paragraph see *Historical Records of New South Wales*, I, ii (Sydney, 1892), pp. 122, 123, 153, 155.

[44] See Alan Frost, 'Australia: The Emergence of a Continent', in Glyndwr Williams and Alan Frost, eds., *Terra Australis to Australia* (Melbourne, 1988), pp. 209–38.

[45] *Historical Records of New South Wales*, I, ii, p. 89.

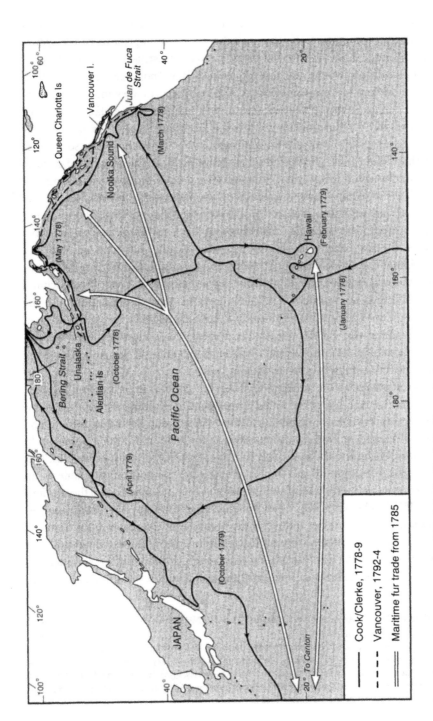

Map 25.2. British Exploration and Trade in the North Pacific, 1778–1800

Queen Charlotte Is

Vancouver I.

Juan de Fuca
Strait

Nootka Sound

(March 1778)

(May 1778)

Bering Strait

Unalaska

Aleutian Is

(October 1778)

Pacific Ocean

(April 1779)

(October 1779)

Hawaii

(February 1779)

(January 1778)

To Canton

JAPAN

Cook/Clerke, 1778-9

Vancouver, 1792-4

Maritime fur trade from 1785

suspicion and occasional violence, intensified when a mysterious outbreak of smallpox in 1789 carried off about half the Aborginal population of the Sydney area. Although by the end of 1790 a certain degree of trust had been restored, one of Phillip's officials pointed out that 'While they [the Aborigines] entertained the idea of our having dispossessed them of their residences, they must always consider us their enemies'.[46] But the matter went further than a clash of material interests, for two incompatible cultures had been thrust against each other. The Aboriginal life-style was based on family groups bonded to the land in so intimate a fashion that their knowledge of its plants, animals, and water allowed them to exist in an environment where strangers would have perished without outside supplies. For all the vaunted superiority of the Europeans, the First Fleet settlers were brought near starvation and death when the follow-up expedition failed to arrive. Aboriginal implements, material possessions, dwellings, were minimal. No greater contrast could exist with the incessant digging, enclosing, and building activities of the newcomers, determined to conquer their environment, and using military discipline and individual ownership as means to that end. The difficulties of understanding experienced by Europeans in their confrontation with the peoples of the Pacific in the eighteenth century reached their most acute form in the encounter with the Aborigines. The ethnocentric attempt of the explorers to find evidence in the Pacific islands of familiar customs and structures ran into a dead end of incomprehension at Sydney Cove.[47]

As the settlement was undergoing its hardest months in early 1790 it was very much in the thoughts of the home government, though in a rather unexpected way. A naval expedition was being prepared which was to call at Port Jackson, and there take on board convicts and members of the New South Wales Corps to help in the establishment of a fur-trading base on the north-west coast of America. This enterprising example of pan-Pacific thinking by the government came as an unexpected crisis with Spain developed over events at Nootka Sound the previous year. It is another reminder of how far-flung was the influence of Cook's voyages, and how much Banks saw himself as the promoter of enterprises connected with those voyages. British ships (from India in the first place) had been among the first to reach the north-west coast after Cook's report of the wealth of sea-otter furs there. In London, Banks was involved in several of these expeditions as he helped

---

[46] David Collins, *An Account of the English Colony in New South Wales* [1798], 2 vols., ed. B. H. Fletcher (Sydney, 1975), I, p. 122.

[47] From an immense and often controversial literature the following might be mentioned: W. E. H. Stanner, *White Man Got No Dreaming* (Canberra, 1979); Keith Willey, *When the Sky Fell Down: The Destruction of the Tribes of the Sydney Region 1788–1850* (Sydney, 1979); Henry Reynolds, *The Other Side of the Frontier: Aboriginal Resistance to the European Invasion of Australia* (Harmondsworth, 1982); Noel Butlin, *Our Original Aggression* (Sydney, 1983).

to shape their instructions and kept in touch with their progress. Although primarily trading ventures, these vessels, often captained by men who had sailed with Cook, also carried out explorations which revived hopes that a navigable strait might be found along the coast. Such a strait, argued Alexander Dalrymple, at this time hydrographer to the East India Company, would make possible a new northern network of trade encompassing North America, China, and Japan.[48] The will-'o-the-wisp of the Japan trade and the potential of the China market also attracted Banks, and like Dalrymple he saw furs from the north-west coast as answering the perennial problem of the East India Company of finding commodities acceptable at Canton to fuel the expanding tea trade.

By the late 1780s there was a great stir of projects centring on the North Pacific. Government was at first not directly involved. The East India Company held trading rights east of the Cape of Good Hope, and it licensed the legal British trading expeditions of these years to the north-west coast. The explorers, maritime and overland, were servants of private companies: the rival fur-trading organizations of the Canadian-based Northwest Company and the London-based Hudson's Bay Company, and the new King George's Sound [Nootka Sound] Company of John Cadman Etches. In Britain, Banks and Dalrymple acted as clearing-houses for the reports of the traders and explorers, and by 1789 were involved in projects for the establishment of a trading base on the north-west coast. This, it was pointed out in familiar language, could also be used to attack Spanish settlements and ships in time of war.[49]

All such plans and projects came to an abrupt halt when, in February 1790, news reached London that a Spanish force (sent north from San Blas to intercept reported Russian vessels) had seized four British trading ships and a shore establishment at Nootka Sound the previous summer. Even before it knew details of what exactly had happened, the response of the Pitt government was clear—and hard. It demanded from Spain the restitution of property, an apology, and in general terms the recognition of the principle of effective occupation. As comparative late-comers to the region, the British set this against the twin Spanish arguments of papal bulls and treaty agreements dating from the late fifteenth century, and prior discovery. The right to trade and establish posts in any area not actually occupied by Europeans was a cardinal feature of British policy in the late eighteenth century, and was used against the Dutch as well as the Spanish. Nootka was a test case, and both British and Spanish governments appeared to be ready to go to war over what, on the face of it, was an insignificant and remote skirmish.

---

[48] See Howard Fry, *Alexander Dalrymple (1737–1808) and the Expansion of British Trade* (London, 1970), chap. 8; Mackay, *In the Wake of Cook*, chaps. 3, 4.

[49] See Mackay, *In the Wake of Cook*, p. 84.

But much was at stake: the fur trade of the north-west coast, and the wider question of territorial rights on that coast and beyond. In April 1789, only a few months before the Nootka incident, two British whalers had been chased off the Patagonian coast by Spanish frigates despite their pleas that it was a 'desert' and unoccupied region where they could water and carry out repairs. As Henry Dundas reminded the House of Commons in one of the Nootka debates, 'We are not contending for a few miles, but a large world'.[50]

In the flurry of fleet mobilization the projected naval expedition to the north-west coast, calling at New South Wales *en route*, was dropped, or at least postponed. The Spanish rearguard action in defence of its traditional rights collapsed, for a France in the grip of revolutionary turmoil was in no position to offer help, and in October 1790 the Nootka Sound Convention was signed. It provided for the restitution of land and buildings seized at Nootka in 1789, for reparations, and for free access and trade to all areas of the coast not occupied by Spain. This would help the fur traders in the north and the whalers in the south. As the government claimed in 1791, 'all British ships...shall have liberty to go round Cape Horn and through the Streights of Magellan to any part of the Western Coast of the Continent of America not occupied by Spain... or to any part of the Pacific Ocean, for the purpose of Trade and Fishery'. [51] If Spanish weakness allowed Britain in 1790 to refute sovereignty based on prior discovery, in the long term it was an even newer arrival in the Pacific, the United States, which was to benefit most. Pitt 'opened the way for other challengers... with even less respect for hoary papal bulls, archaic rites, wooden crosses, and interred bottles testifying to possession'.[52]

With the convention signed, the Pitt government reinstated the expedition to the north-west coast. It was to be commanded by George Vancouver, who had been with Cook on his second and third voyages. He was set two tasks by his instructions of March 1791: to receive restitution of the land at Nootka seized in 1789, and to explore the coast north to latitude 60°N. in search of a waterway through the continent suitable for ocean-going vessels.[53] A year later a matching expedition was being prepared to survey the Pacific coasts of South America with a view to finding a suitable base for the whalers; and this was eventually carried out in 1793–94 by James Colnett in the *Rattler*.[54] On the north-west coast,

---

[50] Quoted in Harlow, *Founding of Second British Empire*, II, p. 464.

[51] Ibid., p. 322.

[52] Warren L. Cook, *Flood Tide of Empire: Spain and the Pacific Northwest, 1543–1819* (New Haven, 1973), p. 249.

[53] See W. Kaye Lamb, ed., *A Voyage of Discovery to the North Pacific Ocean...* [by George Vancouver], 4 vols. (1798; London, 1984), I, pp. 283–86.

[54] See James Colnett, *A Voyage to the South Atlantic and Round Cape Horn into the Pacific Ocean...* (London, 1798).

Vancouver was more at ease with the surveying than the diplomatic part of his mission. His protracted negotiations with the Spanish at Nootka about the details of the restitution provoked an impatient comment from his superiors in London: 'All that We really are anxious about...is the Safety of our National honour which renders a *Restitution* necessary. The *Extent* of that Restitution is not of much moment.'[55] The logical outcome of this attitude was the (Third) Nootka Convention of January 1794, which agreed to a mutual abandonment of Nootka by both Spaniards and British. It was signed as Vancouver was approaching his third season on the coast. His painstaking survey of the tortuous mainland shoreline, much of it repeating work done by Spanish expeditions, was completed in August 1794. He saw his mission, not as an attempt to find the North-west Passage, but as one to prove that it did not exist, at least not in temperate latitudes. In doing so, he saw himself as rescuing Cook's reputation from those theorists such as Dalrymple who had besmirched the great explorer's work on the north-west coast. Vancouver's attitude was characteristic of the practical seamen of his age. From Bougainville to La Pérouse, from Cook to Bligh, they expressed their disdain for the 'theoretical navigators', 'the hypothetical projectors'. In reality, the relationship between explorers and geographers was a complementary one, and the role of the latter in co-ordinating information and stimulating interest in distant regions should not be underestimated.

As was now almost routine, the Admiralty made it clear to Vancouver on his return that it wished the events of the voyage to be made available 'for Publick information', and it paid for the cost of engraving the charts and views in his published account. Significantly, some of these were 'in Mr. Dalrymple's Office'; for in 1795 a Hydrographic Office of the Admiralty had at last been established, with Alexander Dalrymple as the first Hydrographer.[56] After 1815 the Office, increasingly, took over the direction of naval survey expeditions; and a new professionalism replaced the older tradition of individual, and sometimes uncoordinated efforts.

The role of Banks in the surge of British enterprise in the North Pacific after Cook's final voyage varied from encouragement of individuals to direct intervention with the government, from the collecting and distributing of information to the supervision of the scientific side of the voyages. It is a role which is sometimes difficult to assess in precise terms, for much of what Banks accomplished went unrecorded in either state or private papers. For him there was no contradiction between the promotion of the wider objectives of scientific investigation and the

[55] Lamb, *Voyage of Discovery*, I, p. 108.
[56] See Fry, *Dalrymple*, pp. 249 ff.

forthright pursuit of the material objectives of his own country. In 1788 he had put the matter bluntly to a Frenchman: 'I certainly wish that my Country men should make discoveries of all kinds in preference to the inhabitants of other Kingdoms.'[57] In one sense, Banks's role as a co-ordinator of projects of overseas exploration and trade was evidence that, for government, much of this activity was still peripheral. It is perhaps significant that Vancouver's negotiation of what he understood to be the 'cession' of Hawaii to Britain in 1794 was ignored in London, and so faded from sight. Away from the flash-point of Nootka or the much-discussed convict settlement at Botany Bay, most of the new enterprises in the Pacific took place beyond official view or interest.

George Vancouver had seen his Pacific surveys as part of 'that expansive arch, over which the arts and sciences should pass to the furthermost corners of the earth, for the instruction and happiness of the most lowly children of nature ... the untutored parts of the human race'.[58] But the responsibility for this task would not be the government's. It was left to the missionaries to undertake the formidable double task of conversion and protection. In the 1790s the whalers and sealers were using the recently charted Pacific islands for victualling, watering, and refitting; and they paid with firearms and liquor—a lethal combination for many islanders. By the end of the decade the sea-hunters had been joined by traders from Sydney, Europe, and the United States searching for sandalwood, and for dried sea-slugs and birds' nests for the gourmets of China.[59] The missionaries were only slightly slower in arriving—an attempt to send four with Bligh on his second breadfruit voyage to Tahiti in 1791 failed—but the first sermon delivered by Thomas Haweis to the London Missionary Society after its founding in 1795 stressed the opportunities awaiting dedicated workers in the Pacific. 'A new world hath lately opened to our view, call it Island or Continent, that exceeds Europe in size: New Holland; and now become the receptacles of our outcasts of society—New Zealand, and the innumerable islands, which spot the bosom of the Pacific Ocean.'[60] The next year the missionary ship *Duff* left for Tahiti, Tongatapu, and the Marquesas, carrying no fewer than twenty-nine missionaries (and five wives). Within a year of landing on Tahiti the missionaries were involved in local politics, were denouncing infanticide, and had their first confrontation with a trading brig attempting to

---

[57] See Glyndwr Williams, ' "The Common Center of We Discoverers": Sir Joseph Banks, Exploration and Empire in the Late Eighteenth Century', in R. E. R. Banks and others, eds., *Sir Joseph Banks: A Global Perspective* (Kew, 1994), p. 188.

[58] Lamb, *Voyage of Discovery*, I, p. 273.

[59] See I. C. Campbell, *A History of the Pacific Islands* (St Lucia, Queensland, 1990), chaps. 3–5; Howe, *Where the Waves Fall*, pp. 91 ff.

[60] Quoted in Bernard Smith, *European Vision and the South Pacific*, 2nd edn. (New Haven, 1985), p. 144.

exchange firearms for local produce.[61] The pattern had been set for much that was to take place in the islands in the nineteenth century. As the younger Forster had said, though with different and more scholarly considerations in mind: 'What Cook has added to the mass of our knowledge is such that it will strike deep roots and will long have the most decisive influence on the activity of men.'[62]

[61] See C. W. Newbury, ed., *The History of the Tahitian Mission, 1799–1830* (Cambridge, 1961); and, more generally, Niel Gunson, *Messengers of Grace: Evangelical Missionaries in the South Seas, 1797–1860* (Melbourne, 1978).

[62] Quoted in Michael E. Hoare, 'The Forsters and Cook's Second Voyage, 1772–1775', in Walter Veit, ed., *Captain Cook: Image and Impact* (Melbourne, 1972), p. 114.

Select Bibliography

J. C. BEAGLEHOLE, ed., *The Voyage of the Endeavour, 1768–1771* (Cambridge, 1955).

—— *The Voyage of the Resolution and Adventure, 1772–1775* (Cambridge, 1961).

—— *The Voyage of the Resolution and Discovery, 1776–1780* (Cambridge, 1967).

PETER T. BRADLEY, *The Lure of Peru: Maritime Intrusion into the South Sea, 1598–1701* (London, 1989).

ROBIN FISHER and HUGH JOHNSTON, eds., *Captain James Cook and His Times* (Vancouver, 1979).

—— *From Maps to Metaphors: The Pacific World of George Vancouver* (Vancouver, 1993).

HOWARD FRY, *Alexander Dalrymple (1737–1808) and the Expansion of British Trade* (London, 1970).

ROBERT E. GALLAGHER, ed., *Byron's Journals of his Circumnavigation, 1764–1766* (Cambridge, 1964).

VINCENT T. HARLOW, *The Founding of the Second British Empire, 1763–1793*, Vol. I, *Discovery and Revolution* (London, 1952); vol. II, *New Continents and Changing Values* (London, 1964).

K. R. HOWE, *Where the Waves Fall: A New South Sea Islands History From First Settlement to Colonial Rule* (Sydney, 1984).

W. KAYE LAMB, ed., *A Voyage of Discovery to the North Pacific Ocean* [by George Vancouver] (London, 1984).

DAVID MACKAY, *In the Wake of Cook: Exploration, Science and Empire, 1780–1801* (London, 1985).

P. J. MARSHALL and GLYNDWR WILLIAMS, *The Great Map of Mankind: British Perceptions of the World in the Age of Enlightenment* (London, 1982).

GANANATH OBEYESEKERE, *The Apotheosis of Captain Cook: European Mythology in the Pacific* (Princeton, 1992).

BERNARD SMITH, *European Vision and the South Pacific*, 2nd edn. (New Haven, 1985).

—— *Imagining the Pacific: In the Wake of the Cook Voyages* (New Haven, 1992).

O. K. H. SPATE, *Paradise Found and Lost* (Rushcutters Bay, NSW, 1988).

HELEN WALLIS, ed., *Carteret's Voyage Round the World, 1766–1769* (Cambridge, 1965).

GLYNDWR WILLIAMS, ed., *A Voyage round the World . . . by George Anson* [1748] (London, 1974).

—— and ALAN FROST, eds., *Terra Australis to Australia* (Melbourne, 1988).

26

Britain Without America—A Second Empire?

P. J. MARSHALL

Throughout most of the period covered by this volume the British Empire was essentially an Atlantic one. It was held together by the system of commercial regulations embodied in the Navigation Acts. In other respects authority was widely devolved to the local representatives of communities largely of British origin. Metropolitan control was for the most part lightly exerted.[1] The dominant ideology of the Empire, as befitted a largely Anglo-Saxon enterprise, was the freedom of the free-born Englishman.[2] The next volume will describe a nine-teenth-century British Empire that became predominantly an eastern one. Com-mercial regulations were replaced by free trade, while two sharply contrasting patterns of government evolved: white communities were moving from represent-ative government to the full control over their domestic affairs summed up by the term 'responsible government'; non-white populations were subject to govern-ment largely without their consent, supervised from London. To an ideology of liberty, reinterpreted by conflict with the American and French Revolutions, was added pride in the exercise of what was assumed to be a benevolent autocracy over non-European peoples.

These changes constituted a fundamental reordering of the Empire which make it appropriate to talk about a first British Empire giving way to a second one. The timing of change is, however, a contentious matter. The British Empire of the 1830s or 1840s was very different from that of the mid-eighteenth century. But the extent of change by the beginning of the nineteenth century is less clear. Historians have long identified certain developments in the late eighteenth century that under-mined the fundamentals of the old Empire and were to bring about a new one. These were the American Revolution and the industrial revolution. Americans took themselves out of the Empire as millions of Indians were being incorporated into it. The revolt of the thirteen colonies exposed the inadequacies of the existing methods of Imperial governance, while Britain's success in retaining its economic hold on the new United States suggested that the old system of commercial

---

[1] See chap. by Ian K. Steele.
[2] See chap. by Jack P. Greene.

regulation was superfluous to an industrializing economy, whose goods could presumably now gain access to any market on grounds of quality and cheapness alone.

There can be no doubt that the character of the British Empire was changing in the late eighteenth century, or that the loss of America and the rise of British industry exerted considerable influence on these changes. The East was becoming increasingly important, if not as yet at the expense of the West, and there were trends towards more world-wide trade outside the framework of Imperial regulations, more authoritarian forms of government over non-European peoples, and a correspondingly more authoritarian sense of Imperial identity. The pattern of change was, however, a complex one. Responses to the great wars that broke out in 1793 were as important as the challenge of American secession or the needs of industry in bringing about Imperial readjustment. One coherent system did not give way to another. Elements of an old Empire and of a new one coexisted side by side well into the nineteenth century.

The shift in the geographical focus of the British Empire has been neatly encapsulated in the phrase 'the swing to the East'. This expression was coined by Vincent Harlow in the first volume of his *The Founding of the Second British Empire, 1763–1793*, published in 1952. He then wrote of a 'change of outlook on the part of British merchants and politicians', which 'effected a diversion of interest and enterprise from the Western World to the potentialities of Asia and Africa'. He saw this diversion as beginning in about 1763.[3] Even among historians who accept that a major change of direction occurred in the eighteenth century, few endorse Harlow's dating. Other versions have been suggested. For instance, Michael Duffy in this volume postulates a swing to the East beginning in the late 1790s.[4]

Such debates turn on the criteria to be applied. Harlow wrote of 'interest and enterprise'. In crude economic terms, the East did not displace the West at any point in the eighteenth century. Trade statistics show that Asia was a major source of imports, although always a smaller one than the West Indies, throughout the century, but that as a destination for exports it lagged far behind North America, the gap actually widening by the end of the century.[5] 'Interest and enterprise' can, however, be interpreted more widely to include the degree of importance attached to areas by governments as indicated by the despatch of fleets and armies or the

---

[3] Vincent T. Harlow, *The Founding of the Second British Empire, 1763–93*, 2 vols. (London, 1952–64), I. 62.

[4] See above, p. 201.

[5] See above, Table 4.4 on p. 101 and Phyllis Deane and W. A. Cole, *British Economic Growth, 1688–1959*, 2nd edn. (Cambridge, 1969), p. 87.

weight given to them in diplomacy. In so far as it can be assessed, public attention is another indication of priorities.

The loss of the thirteen colonies left the British in the western hemisphere with their colonial possessions in the West Indies, only marginally depleted by French successes in the War of American Independence, together with a remnant of colonies on the mainland that were to form the nucleus of nineteenth-century Canada.

There can be no doubt of the immense importance that the British continued to attach to the West Indies.[6] The output of sugar increased greatly, while sugar remained 'reasonably profitable for most of the period up to 1815'.[7] Huge numbers of troops were deployed in the Caribbean to defend the British colonies by bringing the islands of other powers under British control. Important gains, such as Trinidad and the Dutch Guiana colonies of Demerara, Essequibo, and Berbice, were retained at the end of the war. The decision of Parliament to end the import of slaves into the British West Indies in 1807 might reflect some shift in economic priorities away from the West Indies, but it was not brought about by any calculation that the Caribbean plantations had become disposable assets which could be safely sacrificed.[8]

The campaigns against the slave trade and later against slavery itself receive detailed examination in the next volume.[9] It is, however, important to note that these campaigns did much to focus public opinion on Empire and to change attitudes to it at the end of the eighteenth century. In mid-century, in spite of the presence of considerable numbers of slaves in Britain itself, British people had tended to distance themselves from overseas possessions in the Americas and Asia where British freedom was contaminated by contact with slavery or with despotism.[10] Anti-slavery, however, called for active involvement with the West Indies and with Africa. It was more and more seen as the duty of the British to extend at least a qualified version of freedom to the victims of British misconduct overseas. Opinion was mobilized against the trade on a large scale. 11,000 people, some 20 per cent of the city's population, signed Manchester's first anti-slave trade petition in December 1787. In 1814 750,000 names were put to petitions.[11] For people who signed such petitions, black slaves were no longer outside the pale of concern for

[6] See chaps. by J. R. Ward and Michael Duffy.
[7] See above, p. 430.
[8] See above, p. 427.
[9] See Vol. III, Andrew Porter, 'Trusteeship, Anti-Slavery, and Humanitarianism'.
[10] See above, pp. 225–27.
[11] Seymour Drescher, *Capitalism and Antislavery. British Mobilization in Comparative Perspective* (London, 1986), p. 70; 'Whose Abolition? Popular Pressure and the Ending of the British Slave Trade', *Past and Present*, CXLIII (1994), p. 160.

free-born Englishmen. They had become men and brothers in need of protection. Affording them protection would tighten rather than loosen the ties that held the West Indies within the Empire. If planters would not change their practices in ways that were acceptable to British opinion, reforms must be forced on them by metropolitan authority. The West Indies thus remained in the forefront of British public debate; issues concerning slavery took up far more parliamentary time than any other colonial question.[12]

British governments may have set no high value on those North American colonies that remained British after 1783, but they still recognized an inescapable obligation to keep them within the Empire. The forces of the Crown were deployed to protect Canada from invasion from the United States of America during the War of 1812.[13]

One reason for Britain's determination to maintain territorial possessions in North America was uncertainty about the future of the United States. Although the new United States had received generous terms from Britain at the peace of 1783,[14] the weakness of the new republic quickly became apparent. The union was at first too unstable to conduct effective diplomacy or to follow any coherent economic policy, and it even seemed possible that it would break up. Britain was able fully to recover her markets without making any concessions in return and, although western lands right up to the Mississippi had been handed over to the United States in 1783, it was widely assumed that new settlements would come under the influence of Britain, as British goods reached them either through the St Lawrence or the Gulf of Mexico. The British North American colonies were crucial to hopes for 'a great commercial nexus extending across the Continent to the Pacific and southward into the Middle West'.[15] British agents gave Indian peoples ambiguous support from posts in the North-West that Britain occupied against the treaty of 1783,[16] and plans were formulated for British bases to be established at New Orleans or in the Floridas. With the enacting of the US constitution, Britain had more incentive to take the republic seriously. Ambassadors were exchanged, the Jay Treaty regulating trade was signed in 1794, and Britain seemed to be coming to terms with the westward expansion of the United States. Hopes that Britain might in some sense be able to limit the consequences of the defeat of 1783 and extend her influence on the North American continent

---

[12] D. J. Murray, *The West Indies and the Development of Colonial Government, 1801–34* (Oxford, 1965); Helen Taft Manning, *British Colonial Government after the American Revolution, 1782–1820* (New Haven, 1933), pp. 521–22.

[13] See chap. by Peter Marshall.

[14] See above p. 343.

[15] Harlow, *Second British Empire*, II, p. 725.

[16] See above, p. 368.

beyond her surviving colonies remained alive, however, until the ending of the War of 1812.[17]

By then some British ministers had begun to pursue projects for military action in South or Central America. By the end of the eighteenth century the volume of British trade with Latin America was increasing greatly and the capacity of Spain or Portugal to maintain control over their colonies was in steep decline. Britain helped to engineer a peaceful transfer of authority in Brazil that proved highly beneficial to British commercial interests, but the temptation to speed the collapse of the Spanish empire by military intervention and the seizure of bases was a strong one. Beginning in the 1780s, disaffected Spanish Americans began to appear in London trying to enlist British support for revolutionary projects. From 1798 plans were made for a variety of British expeditions. In 1806–07 the British actually invaded the River Plate, only to be beaten off.[18] In 1808 Britain became the ally and protector of Spain as well as of Portugal. British policy had therefore perforce to shift from predatory raids to attempts to mediate between Spain and her colonists in order to bring about a peaceful transition to independence. While these attempts came to nothing, the ports of the Spanish colonies were generally opened to British trade and British diplomacy was intensely involved in the creation of the new Latin American republics.

As the greatest carriers of slaves, the British were heavily engaged with West Africa throughout the eighteenth century, even if few British people ever went beyond the coast and British political influence was negligible. Rather than reducing British concerns with Africa, attacks on the slave trade led to a deeper involvement. In the 1780s about a dozen British projects were launched for trade or colonization on the West African coast. Behind many of them was a sense of obligation to Africa which grew in tandem with a sense of obligation to the slaves in the West Indies. Opponents of the slave trade believed that Africans must be encouraged to keep their labour at home and to earn profits by selling their own produce to Europeans, rather than selling slaves. Peaceful trade would thus drive out the slave trade. Britain should try to stimulate such developments. An Association for Promoting the Discovery of the Interior Parts of Africa was set up in 1788, among whose purposes was the diversification of Africa's trade. This was one of the motives behind the settling of some black people from Britain at Sierra Leone on the African coast in 1787 and the chartering of a Sierra Leone Company in 1791 to exploit the area. Sierra Leone hardly fulfilled such expectations, but it survived many vicissitudes to become a British colony in 1807.

---

[17] For recent assessments of Anglo-American relations after 1783, see Charles R. Ritcheson, *Aftermath of Revolution; British Policy toward the United States, 1783–1795* (Dallas, 1969); J. Leitch Wright, *Britain and the American Frontier, 1783–1815* (Athens, Ga., 1975).

[18] See above, pp. 192–94.

Freetown in Sierra Leone was the main base from which the Royal Navy launched its first operations to suppress the slave trade of other countries. This was the beginning of a very long commitment.[19]

If there was a swing to the East in the later eighteenth century, there had certainly as yet been no corresponding swing away from the Atlantic. The West Indies remained central to Britain's economy and to the concerns of the huge sections of the British public that supported anti-slavery. Colonies were maintained around the St Lawrence. If further territorial gains in the western hemisphere during the wars from 1793 to 1815 were limited, this was not for lack of trying.[20] In any case, Britain quickly recovered her American markets, which grew spectacularly; by the end of the century the United States was by far the biggest consumer of British exports, while the Spanish and Portuguese empires disintegrated, creating increased opportunities for trade.

If not at the expense of the Atlantic, there was still a massive increase in Britain's involvement in Asia in the later eighteenth century. For Harlow the swing to the East represented a revulsion against territorial rule and colonies of settlement in favour of commercial penetration to gain access to new markets or sources of raw materials. He saw this as taking the British into the Pacific and into South-East Asia, and above all as making China 'the prime object of national policy'.[21] The priorities implied in this formulation, however, elevate what was peripheral in Britain's eastern interests over what was central to them, the possession of a huge territorial empire in India.

For all the public acclaim for Cook's Voyages, Glyndwr Williams sees the British penetration of the Pacific, not as 'the main drive of national policy' but as 'a promising but limited investment'.[22] British expansion in South-East Asia from the end of the eighteenth century is the subject of a chapter in the next volume.[23] Here too objectives were limited. The conquest of territory in India and the increasing commercial importance of China provided the incentive for the British to return to an area from which they had been largely excluded by the Dutch in the seventeenth century. Efforts were made from the 1760s to establish bases on the route from India to China from which Indian goods could be sold to local merchants in return for commodities that would find a market in China. The first of such bases was settled on a permanent footing in 1786 at Penang on the Malay coast. The acquisition of other settlements later gave the British supremacy

---

[19] For attitudes to West Africa see Philip D. Curtin, *The Image of Africa: British Ideas and Action, 1780–1850* (London, 1965).

[20] See above, pp. 186–92.

[21] *The Second British Empire*, I, p. 64.

[22] See above, p. 550.

[23] See Vol. III, chap. by A. J. Stockwell.

over that coast, but this was for long the limit of British territorial ambitions in the region.

Trade with China was certainly important to Britain. It was the source of tea, which had become an item of mass consumption, rivalling sugar as the most valuable import. Some 20 million pounds of Chinese tea were being imported by the 1790s, rising to 25 million pounds in the next decade. Tea was by far the most profitable item in which the East India Company dealt, and the duties levied on it provided the government with 6 or 7 per cent of its total revenue.[24] There was much that was deemed unsatisfactory about the China trade. British access to China was limited to the port of Canton. Conditions there were extremely restrictive: foreigners were forced to deal through a guild of merchants who enjoyed a monopoly, and were at the mercy of a Chinese judicial system that was regarded as at best capricious. Payment for the tea posed problems. If increased purchases of tea were not to lead to a huge outflow of silver, British or Asian commodities had to find a market in China. Projects were therefore devised to gain access to a port, preferably under full British control, through which such goods could be distributed. British ministers hoped that a solution to the problems of the China trade could be found through direct negotiations with the Chinese court. This led to the despatch in 1792 of an embassy under Lord Macartney, who was to ask the Chinese Emperor for a port under British authority or, failing that, for improvements in conditions at Canton. The embassy attracted great interest in Britain but made no obvious progress in China.[25] In retrospect it became clear that the imperial regime was rigidly opposed to any concessions to western barbarians. Even so, an unreformed Canton trade still allowed for huge shipments of tea, balanced by British and Asian imports.

The British stake in India brought about by the grants and conquests between 1765 and 1818[26] completely dwarfed every other British interest in Asia. The East India Company ruled some 40 million people and disposed of a revenue of £18 million raised in taxation, a sum that amounted to around one-third of the peacetime revenue of Britain itself. The Company commanded an army of 180,000 men, and it gave employment with 'liberal incomes' to about 6,000 British people, among whom were 3,000 of its own army officers.[27] India became a source

[24] Hoh-cheung Mui and Lorna H. Mui, *The Management of Monopoly: A Study of the East India Company's Conduct of its Tea Trade, 1784–1833* (Vancouver, 1984).
[25] James L. Hevia, *Cherishing Men from Afar: Qing Guest Ritual and the Macartney Embassy of 1793* (Durham, NC, 1995).
[26] See chap. by Rajat Kanta Ray.
[27] Patrick Colquhoun, *A Treatise on the Wealth, Power and Resources of the British Empire*, 2nd edn. (London, 1815), App., pp. 42–43.

of remunerative employment for socially aspiring British families in a way that was not matched by any other part of the Empire.

India was still imperfectly integrated into the British metropolitan economy by 1815. A new pattern of trade was, however, emerging, speeded up by the ending of the East India Company's commercial monopoly in 1813. Primary products, raw silk and cotton, indigo, and sugar, were replacing cotton cloth as the staple of India's exports to Britain, while India was importing more and more British manufactured goods, textiles above all. Indian commodities both sustained a large part of the China trade and its exports and were the vehicle for the transfer to Britain of up to £5 million a year, consisting of charges that the East India Company was obliged to pay the British state and of private savings being remitted home.[28]

India had thus become a major source of wealth and power to Britain. Assessments of the extent of India's contribution to Britain might vary, but the consequences of the loss of Britain's stake there were deemed to be unthinkable. Britain's system of public and private credit would be at risk.[29] As early as 1773 it was being argued that: 'We cannot now relinquish those possessions without endangering our future freedom and independency as a nation. For were they ever to be taken from us by any European power, it might be the means of throwing too much weight into the scale against us.'[30] India must be defended at almost any cost.

Many British people had also come to see India in terms that went beyond calculations of national interest. Rule in India fulfilled higher purposes. This was a new development. British opinion initially viewed the rise of Empire in India with misgivings. British political virtue seemed to be threatened by the exercise of despotic power.[31] 'Nabobs' were pilloried for their supposed cruelty and avarice. During the 1780s parliamentary attacks on the East India Company, and specifically on Warren Hastings, ran concurrently with the attacks on the slave trade and aroused much the same feelings. Indians were now also coming to be seen as men and brothers needing British protection. The high moral ground in the campaign for Indian reform was taken by Edmund Burke. His version of India as an ancient civilization that must be protected from the barbarism of the East India Company was enunciated above all in the great spectacle of the trial of Warren Hastings between 1788 and 1795.

---

[28] K. N. Chaudhuri, 'Foreign Trade and Balance of Payments (1757–1947)', in Dharma Kumar, ed., *The Cambridge Economic History of India*, II, *c.1757–1970* (Cambridge, 1983), pp. 826–31, 841–48.

[29] See above, p. 506.

[30] *General Remarks on the System of Government in India* ... (London, 1773), p. 12.

[31] See above, pp. 225–26 and pp. 542–43.

Inconclusive as the trial was, the fact that it had occurred at all seems to have been a matter of national pride and to have gone some way to appeasing a sense of guilt about India. 'The humblest subject who was present', a newspaper wrote, 'felt aggrandised in being a member of a community whose laws thus subjected the highest magistrate to their inquisition... and extend the protection of English justice over even the tribes of India.'[32] Well before the end of the trial, the prevailing opinion in Britain seems to have been that protection was now effectively being extended to Indians. British rule in India had become a matter for self-congratulation, not for anxiety and recrimination. Exultation over British victory against Tipu Sultan of Mysore in 1792 was a clear indication of how opinion had changed. William Wilberforce, the scourge of the slave traders, said that the victor, Lord Cornwallis, 'had made the British name loved and revered' in India.[33]

Unlike the opponents of the slave trade, campaigners against Indian abuses did little directly to involve a wider public outside Parliament. The mobilization of opinion on any large scale for a specifically Indian issue came with the missionary movement early in the nineteenth century. By then new British missionary societies were directing their attention to India as well as to the West Indies and Africa. This new missionary movement is dealt with in the next volume,[34] but its ability to induce a wide public to support missions to India must be noted here as an important part of the growing public awareness of Empire in the East. Missionaries began to work in India from 1794. Their right to do so depended, in theory at least, on whether they had permission from the East India Company. Dissenting British Christians did not regard this as satisfactory, and launched a massive campaign for legislation to free missionaries from the Company's control. Their demands were supported by many Anglicans, such as William Wilberforce. Between April and June 1813 some 500,000 people signed nearly 900 petitions.[35]

Contemporaries were not given to listing British possessions overseas in order of priority, still less to pursuing strategies that favoured one area over another. Had they done so, there would probably have been a consensus that at the end of the eighteenth century Jamaica still remained the most valuable of all British colonies, the one whose loss could be least afforded. But there certainly had been a swing to the East in the sense that India had now become a prime concern for British governments, for British commercial interests, for thousands of men and women

[32] *Gazetteer*, 16 Feb. 1788.

[33] P. J. Marshall, ' "Cornwallis Triumphant": War in India and the British Public in the Late Eighteenth Century', in Lawrence Freedman, Paul Hayes, and Robert O'Neill, eds., *War, Strategy, and International Politics: Essays in Honour of Sir Michael Howard* (Oxford, 1992), p. 72.

[34] See Vol. III, Andrew Porter, 'Religion, Missionary Enthusiasm, and Empire, 1783–1914'.

[35] Penelope Carson, 'Soldiers of Christ: Evangelicals and India 1784–1833', unpublished Ph.D. thesis, London, 1988, pp. 282–97.

who hoped to make a career there, and even for a wider public for whom empire in India had become a matter of pride.

Events after 1783 seemed to have vindicated the resounding condemnation of systems of regulating colonial commerce contained in Adam Smith's *Wealth of Nations* of 1776. The immediate recovery of markets in the United States and their subsequent rapid expansion suggested that the exports of British manufacturing industries did not need protection. The fact that Britain continued to act as the first destination for a considerable, if diminished, proportion of America's exports also implied that much colonial produce would come to Britain without compulsion. Contemporaries were well aware of these developments, but they did not lead to any substantial dismantling of the system embodied in the Navigation Acts before the 1820s.

The treatment of the ex-American colonies was the test of whether the system would be modified or not. Were they to be allowed to trade freely within the Empire as before or to be excluded from it as foreigners? The main issue was the conflict between the need to maintain Britain's own merchant marine and to continue the import of food into the West Indies, before 1776 largely provided from America in American ships. To allow what were now foreign ships any part of the carrying trade of the British Empire was, however, seen as a dire threat to the Royal Navy. The seamen who manned these ships would no longer be British and so could no longer be 'pressed' into the Royal Navy in wartime. Britain must therefore build up its own merchant marine, which should be protected from American competition within the Empire. The advocates of naval power prevailed over the West Indies' desire to admit American ships. American shipping was excluded from the West Indies from 1783. In 1786 a new Navigation Act was passed, described as 'a Bill for the increase of Naval Power', which tightened the regulations for determining that every ship that traded within the British Empire was bona fide built and owned in Britain or its colonies. Within a few years rigid British policies began to be modified, both by formal treaty and by making exceptions. Whatever the law might say, American shipping eventually came to dominate the supply of the British West Indies.[36]

In other respects too exceptions were permitted to the Navigation Acts. An Act of 1766 had opened ports in the West Indies to foreign ships, and that principle was further extended and refined by Acts of 1787 and 1805. The existence of foreign settlements ensured that India was never an exclusive sphere for British trade, and

---

[36] On commercial policy towards America, see R. L. Schuyler, *The Fall of the Old Colonial System: A Study in British Free Trade, 1770–1870* (New York, 1945), pp. 80–97; Harlow, *Second British Empire*, II, pp. 254–80.

American ships were later allowed into British Indian ports. Such bending of the principles of the Navigation Acts did not, however, mean the abandonment of a system of commercial regulations that had been in force since the later seventeenth century.

Industrialization did not create a direct challenge to the system of commercial regulation. There is little evidence that manufacturers objected to it. They seem to have valued such protected markets and guaranteed sources of raw materials as the Empire provided. Since the seventeenth century, governments had seen it as their task to enhance the markets and resources of the Empire. Awareness of the needs of new industries gave an added stimulus to such traditional policies. Cotton was the pace-setter of industrialization. Its meteoric rise from the 1780s required huge imports of raw cotton. An important source of supply, Brazil, lay outside British control, but British West Indian production greatly increased with active government encouragement, as did imports through the 'free' ports in the West Indies. During the wars major foreign cotton-producing areas in the West Indies, such as Demerara, were brought into the Empire. Efforts were made to import raw cotton from India. The production within the Empire of dyes for the textile industry was also encouraged. India largely replaced the Carolinas as the source of indigo.[37] Discriminatory duties against the Baltic turned British North America into a major source of timber imports during the Napoleonic War. Efforts to maximize the resources of the Empire extended to transferring crops from one part of it to another.[38]

British governments accepted, however, that their role went beyond developing the resources of the Empire for British industry; British manufacturers had to be helped to expand their markets throughout the world. In the western hemisphere attempts were made to open up new markets by military action. Expeditions were intended 'to occupy strategic points from which to establish commerce with Spanish America—Trinidad, Buenos Aires, New Orleans'.[39] The great accessions of territory were, however, made in the East. Concern for an industrializing economy's need for commodities and customers is difficult to establish as a significant motive for these acquisitions.[40] A recent study has argued that in India, where the most spectacular territorial gains took place, 'annexations were not made with the purpose of serving metropolitan industry', but rather that industrialization provided the resources that made expansion possible.

[37] Harlow, *Second British Empire*, II, pp. 280–93; David Mackay, *In the Wake of Cook: Exploration, Science and Empire, 1780–1801* (London, 1985), chaps. 6 and 7.

[38] Mackay, *Wake of Cook*.

[39] See above, p. 193.

[40] P. J. Marshall and Rudrangshu Mukherjee, 'Early British Imperialism in India', *Past and Present*, CVI (1985), pp. 164–73.

Increased sales of indigo and tea in Britain provided the funds in India for Wellesley's wars.[41]

In spite of efforts to make the Empire serve the needs of a changing British economy, the onset of industrialization, coinciding with the loss of America, was to produce a pattern of overseas trade in which the Empire featured rather less prominently than it had done for most of the eighteenth century. Manufactured goods, above all cotton cloth, dominated the rapid growth of exports from the 1780s. These found their main outlet outside the Empire, in the United States, in Europe, and later in Latin America. Much of Britain's raw cotton came from foreign sources, at first from Brazil and later from the southern United States.

In these circumstances British ministers naturally gave much attention to areas outside the Empire. They were determined that Britain should recover its markets in the United States, they tried to facilitate the access of British goods to Brazil and Spanish America, and they promoted the Macartney embassy to China with its samples of British manufactured goods for the delectation of the Chinese. Increased interest in areas beyond the Empire should not, however, be taken for an aversion to Empire or for systematic policies based on a preference for 'trade' over 'dominion'.[42] Ministers did not believe that Britain's American markets were at risk in the 1780s when they refused to make concessions to American shipping, but their priorities still seem to have been clear: a self-sufficient Imperial trading system must be preserved in the interests of British naval power. The defence of the West Indian colonies was deemed worth sending 35,000 men to the Caribbean in 1795–96, even if 14,000 died in 1796.[43] If ministers in the 1790s and at the turn of the next century really disliked dominion, they were remarkably complaisant about the millions of new subjects who were being brought under British rule in India. British governments wanted both trade and dominion. Industrialization and the loss of America had, however, forced them to look at areas outside Britain's control with a new urgency.

Whatever its effects may or may not have been in other areas, the success of the American Revolution had exposed glaring defects in the way in which the British Empire was governed. Old systems of government had failed comprehensively. From the 1760s the British had embarked on a disastrous course of seeking to enforce sweeping claims to authority, the sovereignty of Parliament over the colonies 'in all cases whatsoever', with a machinery of government totally inadequate for the purpose. The political system at home had proved itself incapable of

---

[41] J. R. Ward, 'The Industrial Revolution and Imperialism, 1750–1850', *Economic History Review*, Second Series, XLVII (1994), pp. 44–65.

[42] See above, pp. 25–26.

[43] See above, p. 190.

devising coherent policies, and the colonial Governors stood no chance of implementing British wishes or even of maintaining order. Effective power had already passed to the Assemblies, and in the crisis that began in 1774 it went from them to the popular movements. If the Empire was to survive, the lesson seemed to be clear: it must radically reform. Logically, it should either abandon its claims to authority or devise proper means to enforce those claims.

The initial response to the débâcle of Imperial government was less than strictly logical in these terms. Much survived unchanged. In some areas the British retreated; in others they tried to reinforce authority.

In the most important of the colonies that remained British after the American Revolution, the West Indian islands, the old system which had failed so disastrously from Britain's point of view remained in operation. Royal Governors continued to depend on elected Assemblies for supply and for consent to legislation. The executive in such colonies remained as weak as it had been in North America before the Revolution.[44]

The most spectacular British retreat occurred even before the recognition of American independence. Parliament gave up its its authority to tax the colonies in 1778. In 1782 it renounced its right to legislate for Ireland. Although the sovereignty of Parliament over the Empire remained unimpaired in all other respects, by the end of the eighteenth century it was generally being used with caution. Where a colonial Assembly existed, Parliament tended to respect its local authority.[45]

Little could be done to reform the old established colonies of the West Indies, but there was scope for new initiatives in what was left of British North America. What was attempted there is the best indication of the lessons derived from the American Revolution. Yet even there, the British government moved slowly and without any strong sense of purpose. There seemed to be general agreement that the thirteen colonies had become ungovernable because of the lack of a social hierarchy capable of exerting leadership over a population without great inequalities, and because of flawed institutions that allowed 'democracy' to dominate colonial government. The Church of England was seen as the natural support for hierarchy and efforts were made to strengthen it in British North America. In 1789 serious attempts began to be made to devise a new constitution for Quebec. Provisions to strengthen executive and therefore Imperial authority were inserted in the Constitutional Act for Canada that finally emerged in 1791.[46] The assumption behind the 1791 Act was that if Canada could be given social and constitutional institutions similar to those of Britain, British authority could be

---

[44] Murray, *The West Indies and Colonial Government*, chap. 2.

[45] Ibid., pp. 1–4; Manning, *British Colonial Government*, pp. 67–74.

[46] See above, pp. 383–86.

maintained and thus the Empire would survive. Many historians have, however, detected as the underlying legacy of the American Revolution an ultimate pessimism about colonies settled by people of British stock. Representative government could not be withheld from such societies, which were inevitably more egalitarian than Britain itself and therefore prone to democracy. Such pressures might be contained for a time by skilful social and political engineering, but this would not last indefinitely.[47]

Societies where the British element was either very small or non-existent posed fewer problems. The British in India vigorously claimed the rights of Englishmen, but they were forced to accept a role as the privileged subjects of an autocracy. A strong executive, based on the personal authority of the Governor-General of Bengal, was created by Acts of 1784 and 1786.[48] During the French Revolutionary and Napoleonic Wars a number of French, Dutch, and Spanish colonies were conquered. Systems of government were devised for them, limiting the representative element to nominated Councils that were to advise the Governors. This model of what came to be called Crown Colony government was applied to the first conquests in the West Indies and later became the standard pattern for new colonies permanently incorporated into the Empire, such as the ex-Spanish Trinidad, the ex-French Mauritius, or the Cape of Good Hope that had been taken from the Dutch. In New South Wales all power was at first vested in the Governor, without even an advisory Council.

Crown Colony government was intended to place colonies under effective metropolitan control. Such a system required an authority in Britain that was capable of exerting that control. For most of the century responsibility for colonial matters had been divided between several departments of state. The lack of coherence and co-ordination in Imperial governance was one of its failings starkly revealed by the American Revolution.[49] Initial reaction to defeat had not been to rationalize the machinery but to get rid of much of it: the third or colonial Secretary of State and the Board of Trade were abolished in 1782. Thereafter new bodies proliferated again. The main responsibility for colonial matters was vested in the office of the Secretary of State for home affairs and was later transferred to the Secretary of State for War in 1801. A distinct colonial department evolved. An Under-Secretary of State with colonial responsibilities was appointed towards the end of the Napoleonic War. Other bodies were also involved in the administration of the Empire. A Board of Control was created to supervise the East India Company in 1784. Commercial questions affecting the Empire were referred to

---

[47] e.g., Manning, *British Colonial Government*, p. 12.
[48] See above, pp. 543–45.
[49] See above, pp. 107–09.

what proved to be a substitute for the old Board of Trade, a Committee of Trade and Plantations, set up in 1784 and reconstructed in 1786.[50]

The American Revolution did not produce a revolution in colonial government. The bureaucracy in Britain remained cumbersome and uncoordinated. Effective supervision of the Empire seems to have depended on the willingness of individual ministers to give time to it among a multitude of other functions. Overseas, fundamental changes had not been introduced in the type of colony that had dominated the eighteenth-century Empire, that is, colonies in which settlers of British origin either predominated or formed the controlling minority. In such colonies there was no retreat from representative government. All that could be done was to try to alter the balance in favour of a more independent executive. Non-white populations had, however, been brought into the Empire by conquest, in India beginning in the 1760s, and in other parts of the world, following the outbreak of war in 1793. Here the British were free to dispense with representative government and did so. The contrast between local self-rule for white societies and autocracy for the rest that marked the nineteenth-century Empire was coming into being. Any sense of a British Imperial identity had now to take account of autocracy as well as freedom.

By the middle of the eighteenth century, 'liberty' had been firmly established as 'the single most important ingredient of an Imperial identity in Britain and the British Empire'.[51] There was, however, no agreed interpretation as to what constituted British liberty. Opposing interpretations gained acceptance on either side of the Atlantic. The revolutionary crisis made it clear how different these interpretations were. After 1783 the British version of liberty, later reinforced by responses to the challenge of the French Revolution, became the prevailing ideology of the white populations of the British Empire.

By the mid-eighteenth century, orthodox British political doctrine stressed that although authority stemmed from the people, it was exercised on their behalf by a legislature in which the powers of King, Lords, and Commons were balanced. Liberty depended on obedience to the authority of this sovereign legislature. As much distinguished scholarship has shown, both doctrine and practice in the colonies often differed from British orthodoxy.[52] The virtues of a balanced constitution were accepted without question by Americans, but liberty was believed to depend not just on obedience to lawful authority; it also involved both participa-

---

[50] D. Murray Young, *The Colonial Office in the Early Nineteenth Century* (London, 1961); Harlow, *Second British Empire*, II, pp. 225–53.

[51] See above, p. 228.

[52] Bernard Bailyn, *The Ideological Origins of the American Revolution* (Cambridge, Mass., 1967) is the classic statement.

tion in that authority through direct representation and the preservation of inalienable rights, even against the legislature. British colonial officials or service officers who knew America reported the existence of 'levelling', 'republican', or 'Oliverian' (that is, Cromwellian) beliefs in the colonies long before the beginnings of overt resistance. The terms in which Americans defied the Stamp Act left no doubt. Their doctrines were said to be 'destructive to all government'.[53] For many people on the British side, the war that ensued was not just fought to preserve the unity of the Empire and the wealth and power accruing to Britain from Empire; it was a war of principle. The principles that the Americans were espousing must be prevented from contaminating Britain and Ireland.[54]

The British case against the American and later against the French Revolution was nearly always argued in terms of liberty. Revolutionary upheaval destroyed true liberty. An ignorant democracy would beat down the other elements of society, property and the rights of individuals would be disregarded, and political instability would end in tyranny. Britain and the British Empire stood for a balanced constitution and respect for law. Some merit was usually accorded to the American constitution, but republicanism was said to lack the enduring stability of the British monarchy. It was the privilege of British communities overseas to approximate as closely as possible to Britain.

The new British Imperial identity, however, depended less on abstract propositions about the nature of liberty than on powerful expressions of an ultimately conservative British nationalism that could be engrafted on to them. It was the patriotic duty of British people to accept their places in a hierarchical society. The King was not simply a hereditary head of the executive; George III in the latter part of his reign was a revered figure, endowed with what were taken to be characteristically British virtues. The British aristocracy were more than the propertied interest in society; they were leaders of their communities and heroes in war.[55] The national religion of Britain was more than a generalized Protestantism, opposed to Popery; it was the Church of England or the Church of Scotland, which inculcated loyalty to the state and to the social hierarchy.

Most of the population of the old thirteen colonies would have felt themselves excluded from such an Imperial identity. Nor did it probably mean much to the mass of the population of the Canadian colonies, even though it was enthusiastically endorsed by articulate Loyalists who had rejected the American Revolution. Conservative values did, however, effectively integrate Scotland and Protestant Ireland into a cohesive Britishness, and they were successfully exported to the

---

[53] Cited in P. J. Marshall, 'Empire and Authority in the later Eighteenth Century', *Journal of Imperial and Commonwealth History*, XV (1987), p. 109.

[54] See above, p. 337.

[55] Linda Colley, *Britons: Forging the Nation, 1707–1837* (London, 1992), chaps. 4 and 5.

British minorities who exercised authority over the non-European British Empire.[56]

The campaigns against the slave trade, the publications of the missionary societies, controversy in the press about India, and a great body of travel writing had made large sections of the British public aware of non-European peoples. For this public, the non-European world was becoming particularly a British responsibility. Huge populations were subject to British rule in India and the West Indies; others had been 'discovered' by the British in the Pacific or were being 'civilized' by British influence on the West African coast. Responsibility implied superiority and inferiority. The late-eighteenth-century view of the world was indeed a strongly hierarchical one. To the ancient European sense of superiority, based on Europe's belief in its unique role as the custodian of the Christian revelation and of the classical tradition of civility against barbarism, was being added newer senses of superiority based on material progress, scientific knowledge, and constitutional government. Europe was sharply distinguished from the 'savages' of the Americas, Africa, and the Pacific, peoples who were dismissed as having made little progress beyond hunting, herding, or basic agriculture. The victories of British arms in India were also demonstrating the gap between Europe and even the 'commercial' societies of Asia, which for all their past achievements, now being revealed by European scholarship, were thought to have atrophied and lost the drive to improvement. By all these criteria, Britain stood pre-eminent in Europe. As Edmund Burke put it, it had been India's fate to be subjugated 'from a learned and enlightened part of Europe, in the most enlightened period of its time' by 'a Nation the most enlightened of the enlightened part of Europe'.[57]

Confidence in British superiority over non-European peoples was deeply entrenched. Superiority was not, however, generally seen as being based on immutable racial difference. A Christian view of the world's history, which assumed a common origin for all humanity in God's creation, was not widely challenged. Differences in the attainments of human societies were attributed to a whole series of environmental and historical causes. Some continued to progress; others had made little progress or had stagnated. In the right circumstances, these differences could be alleviated. It was increasingly seen as the duty of the specially favoured British to create such circumstances, by ending slavery and the slave trade, by propagating Christianity in place of ignorance and idolatry, and in India

---

[56] C. A. Bayly, *Imperial Meridian: The British Empire and the World, 1780–1830* (London, 1989), chaps. 4 and 5.

[57] *The Writings and Speeches of Edmund Burke,* VI, P. J. Marshall, ed., *The Launching of the Hastings Impeachment, 1786–1788,* (Oxford, 1991), p. 315.

by ensuring security of property, and therefore the incentive for economic improvement. The political liberty which the British themselves enjoyed could not be extended to others not ready for it. But the British were now confident that they could exercise autocratic power over others for their benefit, without themselves becoming corrupted by autocracy.[58]

Thus Britain's Imperial identity had been adapted to a much more diverse Empire. Revolution both within the Empire and without had been countered by the affirmation of conservative values of obedience and loyalty, but the British still prided themselves on being a free people, whose freedom was defined by avoiding the excesses of others. This freedom could be exported throughout the Empire. It was the birthright of the white populations, and in a qualified form was Britain's gift to its non-European subjects.

Britain's involvement in the world beyond Europe in the first decade of the nineteenth century was on a much greater scale than it had been early in the eighteenth century. In spite of the loss of the American colonies, many more people lived under British rule, the great majority of them now in Asia. War interrupted British emigration but it was about to resume at a much higher level, which would take people to new destinations, such as Australia, to which convicts were already being despatched. British armed forces had made their presence felt across the world, from the River Plate to the coast of China. British explorers reached out to the furthest shores of the Pacific and into the interior of Africa. British Protestant Christianity was being propagated by new mission societies in Asia, Africa, and the Pacific islands. The volume of British trade with areas outside Europe had grown greatly. More and more imported goods from the tropics were available for British consumers. There was a heightened awareness of a wider world. Government agencies and learned societies recorded observations, collected specimens, and published surveys and maps. The public was regaled with accounts of strange countries and peoples, and its sympathies were enlisted for great causes like the abolition of the slave trade or the support of overseas missions. 'Oriental' motifs were being adopted in literature and the decorative arts.

World-wide expansion on this scale had far outgrown the old Atlantic-based Empire of colonies of British settlement regulated by the Navigation Acts. The old Empire had not, however, been replaced by a new Imperial system. First and second British Empires may be said to have coexisted at the end of the eighteenth century. Dominion in the East, commercial expansion into areas outside the Empire and its regulations, and patterns of governance thought to be fitted to

[58] See above, pp. 425–26.

the needs of peoples recently brought under British rule had been added to the existing structures of Empire.

British interests overseas grew and diversified throughout the eighteenth century, but the pace of change was especially rapid at the end of the century, when the loss of America and the consequences of industrialization played a significant role in creating new patterns of expansion. The success of the American rebellion did not produce a revulsion either against colonies of settlement or attempts to regulate Imperial trade, nor did it trigger off a fundamental reordering of the way in which the Empire was governed, even if it did instill caution, especially in the use of parliamentary authority; but it did place Britain's most important overseas trading partner outside the Empire. In the opinion of most contemporaries, industrialization did not reduce the need for protected markets and guaranteed sources of raw materials within the Empire, but it widened the search for markets and raw materials to take in areas outside the Empire. Thus both the loss of America and the industrial revolution contributed to the 'globalizing' of the British economy during the nineteenth century.[59] Attempts to acquire influence over territories outside the Empire therefore acquired a new urgency.

Such attempts, however, went in tandem with the expansion of the Empire actually under British rule. Expansion changed the character of the Empire as dominion in the East began to play an ever more prominent role, and as huge populations of non-European peoples were incorporated into it. These changes owed much more to success in war than to revolutions in America or in Britain's industrial capacity.

For most of the eighteenth century war had proved to be a generally ineffective instrument of Imperial aggrandizement. Even the spectacular gains of the Seven Years War, which brought a new diversity into the Empire with the incorporation of French societies in North America and the West Indies, were placed in jeopardy in the war for America that followed.[60] Between 1793 and 1815, however, Britain swept the board. Vast numbers of Indians, more French in the West Indies and Mauritius, Dutch in Guiana, at the Cape, and on the Ceylon coast, together with peoples once subordinated to the rule of other Europeans, such as the Khoikhoi of the Cape, were all pulled into the British Imperial net.[61]

The capacity of the British state to wage war was not, however, matched by its capacity to organize an Empire. Authority for Imperial matters within the machinery of government remained subdivided without any overall direction, and Parliament, for all its claims to sovereignty, exercised at best a fitful super-

[59] See Vol. III, chap. by P. J. Cain.
[60] See above, pp. 164–66.
[61] See above, pp. 205–06.

vision. At no point was there any systematic reassessment of the character or purposes of Empire. The force of inertia kept existing structures in being, with new ones being added to them as new problems arose. The Navigation Acts were amended as necessity seemed to require. New systems of government were devised on an *ad hoc* basis for new acquisitions, Canada, India, or the foreign possessions in the Caribbean or the Indian Ocean, which differed from the old norm of colonies with British settlers. It is therefore exceptionally difficult to determine when a first Empire gave way to a second. Contemporaries would probably not even have understood the question. With hindsight, however, it is possible to see that at the end of the eighteenth century what was still recognizably the pattern of an earlier Empire was being engulfed by the scale of the additions being made to it. Old and new Empires were coexisting, but the new was outgrowing the old.

Select Bibliography

C. A. BAYLY, *Imperial Meridian: The British Empire and the World, 1780–1830* (London, 1989).

P. J. CAIN and A. G. HOPKINS, 'Gentlemanly Capitalism and British Expansion Overseas, The Old Colonial System, 1680–1850', *Economic History Review*, Second Series, XXXIX (1986), pp. 501–25.

RALPH DAVIS, *The Industrial Revolution and British Overseas Trade* (Leicester, 1979).

JOHN EHRMAN, *The Younger Pitt*, 3 vols. (London, 1969–96).

VINCENT T. HARLOW, *The Founding of the Second British Empire, 1763–93*, 2 vols. (London, 1952–64).

RONALD HYAM, 'British Imperial Expansion in the late-Eighteenth Century', *Historical Journal*, X (1967), pp. 113–24.

DAVID MACKAY, 'Direction and Purpose in British Imperial Policy, 1783–1801', *Historical Journal*, XVII (1974), pp. 487–501.

—— *In the Wake of Cook: Exploration, Science and Empire, 1780–1801* (London, 1985).

FREDERICK MADDEN with DAVID FIELDHOUSE, eds., *Select Documents on the Constitutional History of the British Empire and Commonwealth*, Vol. III, *Imperial Reconstruction, 1763–1840. The Evolution of Alternative Systems of Colonial Government* (Westport, Conn., 1987).

HELEN TAFT MANNING, *British Colonial Government after the American Revolution, 1783–1820* (New Haven, 1933).

PETER MARSHALL, 'The First and Second British Empires. A Question of Demarcation', *History*, XLIX (1964), pp. 13–23.

D. J. MURRAY, *The West Indies and the Development of Colonial Government, 1801–34* (Oxford, 1965).

R. L. SCHUYLER, *The Fall of the Old Colonial System: A Study in British Free Trade, 1770–1870* (New York, 1945).

J. R. WARD, 'The Industrial Revolution and British Imperialism, 1750–1850', *Economic History Review*, Second Series, XLVII (1994), pp. 44–65.

D. MURRAY YOUNG, *The Colonial Office in the Early Nineteenth Century* (London, 1961).

CHRONOLOGY

Year	Britain and Ireland	North America
1688	Flight of James II	
1689	Accession of William and Mary ('Glorious Revolution')	Glorious Revolution in America: James II's Dominion of New England overthrown
	WAR OF THE LEAGUE OF AUGSBURG ('KING WILLIAM'S WAR')	
1689	War with France	
1690	James II defeated in Ireland by William III at Battle of the Boyne	
1691	Treaty of Limerick ending war in Ireland	Massachusetts new charter establishing royal government
1692		Witch trials at Salem, Massachusetts
1693		Foundation of College of William and Mary, Virginia
1696	Board of Trade created Act strengthening enforcement of Navigation Acts Act prohibiting Irish colonial trade	
1697	Peace of Ryswick	
1698	Molyneux's *Case of Ireland* published Foundation of Society for Promoting Christian Knowledge	
1700		
1701	Foundation of the Society for the Propagation of the Gospel	'Grand Settlement' treaties by Iroquois with English and French
	WAR OF THE SPANISH SUCCESSION ('QUEEN ANNE'S WAR')	
1702	Accession of Queen Anne War with France	
1704	Marlborough's victory at Blenheim Gibraltar captured	*Boston News-Letter* founded

Caribbean and West Africa	Asia and the Pacific	Year
		1688
		1689
		1689
	English settlement at Calcutta established	1690
		1691
Destruction of Port Royal, Jamaica, by earthquake		1692
		1693
		1696
	Dampier's *New Voyage Round the World* published	1697
End of Royal African Company's monopoly: slave trade officially opened to private traders Scottish attempt to found colony at Darien, Panama	New East India Company chartered to rival existing one	1698
Darien colony abandoned		1700
		1701
		1702
		1704

Year	Britain and Ireland	North America
1705	Act to permit export of Irish linen to America	
1707	Union of England and Scotland	
1709		
1710	Four Indian 'Kings' visit London	Capture of Port Royal, Acadia
1711	Creation of South Sea Company	Unsuccessful expedition against Quebec
1713	Treaty of Utrecht: Britain gains Gibraltar and Minorca	Treaty of Utrecht: Britain gains Hudson Bay, Nova Scotia, and Newfoundland
1714	Accession of George I	
1715		Yamasee War of South Carolina against Indians
1717		
1718	Act for Transportation of convicts to America	First wave of Ulster emigration to America
1720	Declaratory Act asserting authority of British Parliament over Ireland South Sea Bubble financial crisis	
1721	Walpole Prime Minister	
1727	Accession of George II	
1729		The Carolinas become separate royal colonies
1730		
1731	Act permitting some direct Irish imports from America	
1732		New colony of Georgia given charter
1733	Political crisis over excise duties	Molasses Act puts duty on non-British molasses Franklin starts *Poor Richard's Almanac*
1736		Wesley minister in Georgia
	WAR OF JENKINS' EAR AND WAR OF THE AUSTRIAN SUCCESSION	
1739	War with Spain	Whitefield's first preaching tour Stono slave rebellion in South Carolina
1740	Thomson's 'Rule Britannia' first performed	

Caribbean and West Africa	Asia and the Pacific	Year
		1705
	Death of Mughal Emperor Aurangzeb	1707
	Two East India Companies unite	1709
		1710
		1711
Treaty of Utrecht: Britain gains all of St Kitts and *Asiento* grant to import slaves into Spanish America		1713
		1714
		1715
	Mughal Emperor gives British customs exemption in Bengal	1717
		1718
		1720
		1721
		1727
		1729
Start of first war against Jamaica Maroons		1730
		1731
		1732
		1733
Slave Plot in Antigua		1736
('KING GEORGE'S WAR')		
Vernon captures Porto Bello Peace settlement with Jamaica Maroons	Nadir Shah of Persia sacks Delhi	1739
	Anson begins voyage of circumnavigation	1740

Year	Britain and Ireland	North America
1741		
1742	Fall of Walpole	
1743		Foundation of American Philosophical Society (refounded 1767)
1744	War with France	
1745	Jacobite rebellion	Capture of Louisbourg by Massachusetts troops
1746	Defeat of Jacobites at Battle of Culloden	
1748	Peace of Aix-la-Chapelle	Louisbourg returned to France
1749		Settlement of Halifax, Nova Scotia
1750		
1754		French establish fort on Ohio Albany conference on projected union of colonies
1755		Braddock defeated trying to take Fort Duquesne 'Neutral' French settlers expelled from Nova Scotia (Acadia)

SEVEN YEARS WAR ('FRENCH AND INDIAN WAR')

Year	Britain and Ireland	North America
1756	War with France Loss of Minorca	
1757	Pitt–Newcastle ministry	French take Fort William Henry
1758		Amherst captures Louisbourg
1759	'Year of Victories': naval victories at Lagos and Quiberon Bay, Garrick's 'Heart of Oak' first performed	Wolfe dies capturing Quebec Anglo-Cherokee War
1760	Accession of George III Opening of Carron iron works	Amherst captures Montreal and New France surrenders
1761	Resignation of Pitt	
1762	Spain enters war	

Caribbean and West Africa	Asia and the Pacific	Year
Vernon fails to take Cartagena		1741
		1742
	Anson takes Manila galleon	1743
	British take French ships: start of hostilities in Asia	1744
		1745
	French capture Madras	1746
	Madras returned to Britain Dupleix starts French intervention in Carnatic	1748
		1749
Company of Merchants takes over administration of African forts	Clive's successful defence of Arcot	1750
		1754
		1755
	Nawab of Bengal captures Calcutta and deaths in Black Hole follow	1756
	Clive recovers Calcutta and defeats Nawab at Battle of Plassey	1757
Capture of St Louis, Senegal, from French		1758
Capture of Guadeloupe from French		1759
Tacky's slave rebellion in Jamaica	Coote defeats French at Battle of Wandiwash	1760
	Capture of French settlement at Pondicherry	1761
Capture of Martinique from French and of Havana, Cuba, from Spanish	Expedition from India takes Manila from Spanish	1762

Year	Britain and Ireland	North America
1763	Peace of Paris Grenville Prime Minister Harrison wins prize for 4th chronometer	Peace of Paris: Britain gains Cape Breton, Floridas, Quebec, trans- Appalachian lands Proclamation fixes limit of settlement Pontiac War with Indians
1764		Sugar Act placing duties on American trade
1765		Stamp Act to tax colonies: riots and boycott of British goods
1766		Declaratory Act asserting authority of the British Parliament over America Repeal of the Stamp Act
1767	Townshend Lord-Lieutenant of Ireland	Townshend Duties on American imports
1768	Wilkes elected MP for Middlesex	Boston riots; British troops sent
1769	Watt's patent for steam engine Arkwright's patent for water frame	
1770	North Prime Minister Hargreaves's patent for spinning jenny	Troops fire on Boston crowd–'massacre' Parliament takes off all duties except on tea
1771	West's *Death of Wolfe* exhibited	
1772	Failure of Ayr Bank and credit crisis	
1773		Boston Tea Party
1774		Coercive ('Intolerable') Acts to punish Boston and Massachusetts Quebec Act includes recognition of Catholicism and French civil law First Continental Congress meets in Philadelphia to organize resistance

WAR OF AMERICAN INDEPENDENCE

Year	Britain and Ireland	North America
1775	Proclamation for Supressing Sedition and Rebellion	Battles of Lexington and Concord outside Boston British take Bunker Hill with severe loss

Caribbean and West Africa	Asia and the Pacific	Year
Peace of Paris: Britain gains 'Ceded' Islands in West Indies and Senegal	War with Mir Kasim, Nawab of Bengal	1763
	British defeat Wazir of Oudh and Mughal Emperor at Battle of Buxar	1764
Riots against Stamp Act in St Kitts and Nevis	Mughal Emperor grants *diwani* of Bengal by Treaty of Allahabad Byron claims Falkland Islands and crosses Pacific	1765
Act creating free ports in West Indies		1766
	Chatham's East India Act Wallis reaches Tahiti	1767
	Start of Cook's first voyage	1768
	Cook charts coasts of New Zealand	1769
	Falkland Islands crisis with Spain: British settlement restored Cook charts east coast of Australia	1770
		1771
Somerset's case: verdict against carrying slaves out of England	Hastings Governor of Bengal Start of Cook's second voyage	1772
	North's Act regulating the East India Company Hawkesworth's *Voyages in the Southern Hemisphere*	1773
		1774
	Start of British war with Marathas in western India	1775

Year	Britain and Ireland	North America
1776	Adam Smith's *Wealth of Nations*	Congress declares American Independence
		British occupy New York and win Battle of Long Island
1777		Burgoyne defeated at Battle of Saratoga
1778	France enters war	
	Irish Protestant Volunteering to extract concessions from Britain	
1779	Spain enters war	
1780	Opening of colonial trade with Ireland	British capture Charleston and begin campaign in South
	Netherlands enter war	
1781		Cornwallis surrenders at Yorktown
1782	Fall of North	
	Act of Irish legislative independence	
1783	Peace of Versailles	Peace of Versailles: Britain recognizes US independence and loses Floridas and western lands
	Pitt Prime Minister	
1784		Loyalist settlement in Canada and creation of new colony of New Brunswick
1785	Bill for free Anglo-Irish trade rejected	
	End of Arkwright's patent	
1786		
1787		US constitution drafted
		Anglican bishop for Nova Scotia
1788		
1789	Outbreak of French Revolution	
	Fall of Bastille	
1790		

Caribbean and West Africa	Asia and Pacific	Year
	Start of Cook's third voyage	1776
	Cook's *A Voyage towards South Pole*	1777
Knight case against slavery in Scotland	Cook charts north-west coast of America	1778
French take Grenada	Death of Cook in Hawaii	1779
	War with Haidar Ali of Mysore: coalition of Indian princes against Britain	1780
French take Tobago		1781
French take St Kitts	House of Commons Select Committee investigates India	1782
Rodney's victory at Battle of the Saintes prevents attack on Jamaica	Peace with Marathas	
Peace of Versailles: Britain loses Tobago and Senegal	Defeat of Fox's India Bills placing India under state control	1783
Order in Council excluding US shipping from West Indies	Pitt's Act regulating India	1784
	Commutation Act reducing tea duty	
	Foundation of Bengal Asiatick Society	
	Peace with Mysore	
	Hastings leaves India	1785
	Cornwallis Gov.-Gen. of Bengal	1786
	First British settlement on Malay coast at Penang	
Settlement, including black Loyalists, at Sierra Leone		1787
Formation of the London Committee for the Abolition of Slave Trade and of Association for the Discovery of Africa	Hastings's trial starts	1788
	First Fleet takes convicts to Botany Bay to establish New South Wales	
First parliamentary motion for the abolition of slave trade	Mutiny on the *Bounty* breadfruit expedition	1789
	War with Tipu Sultan of Mysore	1790
	Crisis with Spain over seizure of fur traders at Nootka Sound	

Year	Britain and Ireland	North America
1791	Foundation of the radical United Irishmen in Belfast	Act providing constitutions for two new Canadian colonies
1792	Baptist Missionary Society founded	

FRENCH REVOLUTIONARY WAR

1793	War with France	
1794		Jay Treaty adjusting territory and trade with US
1795	Foundation of London Missionary Society	
1796		
1797		
1798	Irish rebellion begins: rebels defeated at Vinegar Hill; French invading force surrenders	
1799	Foundation of Church Missionary Society	
1800	Malta occupied	
1801	Irish Act of Union	
1802	Peace of Amiens	

NAPOLEONIC WAR

1803	War with France	
1805	Destruction of French and Spanish fleets at Battle of Trafalgar	
1807		First American embargo on British trade
1808	Start of Peninsular War to eject French from Spain	
1810		Arrest of Bédard, French-Canadian nationalist
1811		Selkirk's Red River grant

Caribbean and West Africa	Asia and Pacific	Year
Outbreak of slave rebellion in French Saint-Domingue	Vancouver leaves for survey of north-west coasts of America	1791
Commons votes for abolition of slave trade	Defeat of Tipu and end of Mysore War	1792
Grey expedition to French West Indies	Macartney's embassy to China East India Co.'s charter renewal	1793
	Carey, Baptist missionary, arrives in Bengal	1794
Abercromby expedition to West Indies War against Maroons in Jamaica Start of Park's first African journey Dutch settlement at Cape of Good Hope occupied	Dutch settlements on Ceylon coast taken	1795
Dutch Guiana occupied		1796
Spanish Trinidad occupied	First London Missionary Society ship to Tahiti	1797
Attempts to conquer Saint-Domingue abandoned and British troops withdrawn	Wellesley Governor-General of Bengal Napoleon's expedition to Egypt	1798
Park's *Travels in the Interior of Africa*	Death of Tipu and conquest of Mysore	1799
		1800
	Carnatic and part of Oudh annexed French defeated in Egypt	1801
Peace of Amiens: Britain gains Trinidad	Peace of Amiens: Britain retains coastal Ceylon	1802
	War with Marathas Victory at Assaye Settlement of Tasmania	1803
	Recall of Wellesley from India	1805
Abolition of slave trade Sierra Leone becomes a Crown Colony		1807
	Rum Rebellion of officers in New South Wales	1808
	French island of Mauritius conquered	1810
	Java occupied and period of British rule under Raffles begins	1811

Year	Britain and Ireland	North America
1812		War of 1812 with US begins
1813		Death of Tecumseh, Indian ally of British
1814		Treaty of Ghent ends war with US
1815	Battle of Waterloo Vienna Settlement: Britain retains Malta, Ionian Islands	

Caribbean and West Africa	Asia and Pacific	Year
		1812
	East India Company Charter Act opens India trade and eases restriction on missionaries' access to India	1813
		1814
Vienna Settlement: Britain retains Tobago, St Lucia, Guiana colonies, and Cape of Good Hope	Vienna Settlement: Britain retains Mauritius, returns Java and other Dutch territory	1815

INDEX

CPSIA information can be obtained
at www.ICGtesting.com
Printed in the USA
BVHW042108130821
614250BV00022B/330

9 780199 246779